Mythology, Chronology, Idolatry

Brill's Studies in Intellectual History

General Editor

Han van Ruler (*Erasmus University Rotterdam*)

Founded by

Arjo Vanderjagt

Editorial Board

C. S. Celenza (*Johns Hopkins University, Baltimore*)
M. L. Colish (*Yale University, New Haven*)
J. I. Israel (*Institute for Advanced Study, Princeton*)
A. Koba (*University of Tokyo*)
M. Mugnai (*Scuola Normale Superiore, Pisa*)
W. Otten (*University of Chicago*)

VOLUME 355

The titles published in this series are listed at *brill.com/bsih*

Mythology, Chronology, Idolatry

Pagan Antiquity and the Biblical Text in the Scholarly World of Guillaume Bonjour (1670–1714)

By

Felix Schlichter

BRILL

LEIDEN | BOSTON

Cover illustration: *Joseph Reading to the Pharaoh*, by Lawrence Alma Tadema. Image in the public domain.

Library of Congress Cataloging-in-Publication Data

Names: Schlichter, Felix, author.
Title: Mythology, chronology, idolatry : pagan antiquity and the biblical text in the scholarly world of Guillaume Bonjour (1670–1714) / by Felix Schlichter.
Description: Leiden : Brill, [2025] | Series: Brill's studies in intellectual history, 0920-8607 ; volume 355 | Includes bibliographical references and index.
Identifiers: LCCN 2024045720 (print) | LCCN 2024045721 (ebook) | ISBN 9789004684959 (hardback) | ISBN 9789004684966 (ebook)
Subjects: LCSH: Bonjour, Guillaume, 1670-1714.
Classification: LCC BX4705.B57635 S35 2025 (print) | LCC BX4705.B57635 (ebook) | DDC 261.2--dc23/eng/20241122
LC record available at https://lccn.loc.gov/2024045720
LC ebook record available at https://lccn.loc.gov/2024045721

Typeface for the Latin, Greek, and Cyrillic scripts: "Brill". See and download: brill.com/brill-typeface.

ISSN 0920-8607
ISBN 978-90-04-68495-9 (hardback)
ISBN 978-90-04-68496-6 (e-book)
DOI 10.1163/9789004684966

Copyright 2025 by Koninklijke Brill BV, Leiden, The Netherlands.
Koninklijke Brill BV incorporates the imprints Brill, Brill Nijhoff, Brill Schöningh, Brill Fink, Brill mentis, Brill Wageningen Academic, Vandenhoeck & Ruprecht, Böhlau and V&R unipress.
All rights reserved. No part of this publication may be reproduced, translated, stored in a retrieval system, or transmitted in any form or by any means, electronic, mechanical, photocopying, recording or otherwise, without prior written permission from the publisher. Requests for re-use and/or translations must be addressed to Koninklijke Brill BV via brill.com or copyright.com.

This book is printed on acid-free paper and produced in a sustainable manner.

To my parents

Contents

Notes XI
Acknowledgements XIII
Abbreviations XVI

Introduction 1

1 **Guillaume Bonjour: His Life and His World** 20
　1　Bonjour in Toulouse 20
　2　Bonjour in Rome 31
　3　Bonjour in the Republic of Letters 56
　4　Bonjour in Montefiascone 69
　5　Bonjour in China – and Beyond 75

PART 1
Mythology

2 **Sacred History and Profane Fables** 89
　1　*Historia sacra* and *historia exotica* in the Seventeenth Century 90
　2　Samuel Bochart and the Biblical Diffusionist Narrative 100
　3　Isaac La Peyrère and the Problematization of Sacred History 113
　4　Pagan Sources for Biblical History: the Case of the Flood 124
　5　Biblical Authority and the Limits of Pagan Evidence 132
　6　Sacred Fables and Profane History 139

3 **The Wisdom of the Egyptians** 143
　1　Egypt, Israel, and the Origins of Human Civilization 143
　2　The Jewish Origins of Egyptian Culture: Serapis 155
　3　The Jewish Origins of Egyptian Culture: Minos, Menes, and Mercury 164
　　3.1　*Minos* 168
　　3.2　*Menes* 169
　　3.3　*Mercury* 172
　4　Sacred History and the Origins of Human Civilization 177
　5　Greek Universal History in a Biblical Context 180

PART 2
Chronology

4 The Chronology of the Septuagint 185
  1 Biblical Chronologies in the Seventeenth Century 185
  2 Chronology and the Septuagint in Bonjour's World 195
  3 Jewish and Pagan Sources in Bonjour's Chronology 201
  4 Bonjour on the Septuagint 206
  5 Biblical Scholarship and the Septuagint in Post-Tridentine Rome 212

5 The Dynasties of Manetho 226
  1 The Antiquity of Egypt 226
  2 Manetho in Early Christian Chronography 233
  3 Manetho after Scaliger 240
  4 Bonjour's Manetho and His Enemies 247
  5 Bonjour on Manetho 254
  6 La Peyrère and the Authority of Manetho 261

PART 3
Idolatry

6 The Gods of the Heathens 271
  1 Antiquarianism and the Study of Pagan Religion 271
  2 Early Modern Histories of Religion 278
  3 Divine Names and Pagan Onomatolatria 288
  4 Pagan Ancestor Worship 294

7 The Religion of China 303
  1 The Problem of China in the Seventeenth Century 303
  2 Chinese Debates in Bonjour's Rome 313
  3 Patristic Apologetics and the History of Idolatry in the Chinese Rites Debate 320
  4 Pagan Animism and the Chinese Names for God 329
  5 Historical Context and Ancient Names for God 336
  6 Bonjour in China: Christian Apologetics at Work 340

Conclusion 347

Bibliography 353
   Manuscript Sources   353
      Rome   353
      Modena   354
      Florence   354
      Montefiascone   354
      Paris   354
      The Hague   355
   Primary Printed Sources   355
   Secondary Printed Sources   376
Index   393

Notes

In general, I have followed the practice of putting my English translation in the main body of the text with the original in the footnotes. I have occasionally deviated from this principle for two reasons. In some cases, I have thought it necessary to cite the original language in the main body of the text in order to highlight a particular word or phrase which is peculiar to the original language. In these cases, I have supplied an English translation in parentheses. In certain other cases, I have left quotes in the original language when I believe their meaning is self-evident, particularly for very short sentences or individual words. All translations are my own unless stated otherwise.

In matters of transcription, I have generally followed the original language and spelling. This means that in quotations from languages such as French, there is a much sparser use of accents than one is accustomed to today. For example, in the seventeenth century, "vérité" is generally written "verité," while "Hébreux" is often written "Hebreux" (as at p. 110, n. 67). In Latin, in order to preserve consistency, I have removed all accents (hence "genealogice" rather than "genealogicé") and ligatures (hence "Aegyptiorum" rather than "Ægyptiorum"). This is not the case for the French, where ligatures (as in "Œuvres") are necessary for spelling French words in a French context. For the transcription of Chinese, I have used common early modern spellings, Bonjour's in particular, rather than modern, more conventional practices of romanization. Hence, I have written *tien* rather than *tian* and *xamti* rather than *shangdi*. In all matters of doubt and in other related issues, I have tried to follow the Chicago Manual of Style as closely as possible.

Given the choice, I have tended to give names in their native rather than Latinized form: hence Baronio rather than Baronius, Huet instead of Huetius, Le Clerc instead of Clericus, Bianchini instead of Blanchinus, and, of course, Bonjour instead of Bonjourius. The only exceptions are those names for which the Latinized form has become the generally accepted version: hence Vossius rather than Vos, Grotius rather than de Groot, and Perizonius rather than Voorbroek. There may be some cases in which scholars might disagree with what I consider a commonly accepted form, such as my preference for Georg Horn over Georgius Hornius. Unfortunately, complete consistency is impossible in this matter and I have aimed for the balance I find most appropriate and readable.

In matters of biblical chronology, I have often referred to the Septuagint chronology on the one hand, and the Masoretic chronology on the other. The former relates to the longer chronology of the Bible currently found in the

Greek Septuagint. The latter is intended to include not only the contemporary Masoretic or Hebrew Bible, but also the Latin Vulgate and the King James Bible. In this sense, "Masoretic" is used as a catch-all term for the shorter biblical chronology. I have refrained from using the term "Hebrew chronology" because it was one of the central contentions of the "supporters" of the Septuagint that the original Hebrew text contained the longer Septuagint chronology. I have also refrained, in certain cases, from using the term "Vulgate chronology," since Protestant chronologists who favoured the Masoretic chronology did not consider the Vulgate authoritative.

In matters of pagan mythology, I have named pagan gods and heroes in both Latin and Greek style depending on the author and context in question.

Acknowledgements

I have been privileged enough to spend an extended and highly enjoyable time conducting research in various scenic locations in Europe in the process of writing this book; the perks, no doubt, of studying a scholar who lived in Rome and corresponded with a great many scholars throughout Italy and France. My thanks, therefore, must go to the Rouse Ball/Eddington Fund of Trinity College, Cambridge, and the Cambridge History Faculty Fieldwork Fund for making these travels possible. I would also like to thank the librarians and archivists of the Vallicelliana, Angelica, and Propaganda Fide archives in Rome, the Biblioteca Nazionale Centrale in Florence, the Bibliothèque Nationale in Paris, and the Royal Library of The Hague for their assistance during this time, and for putting up with my broken French and Italian (I did not try to speak Dutch). I would like to add a special thanks to Anthea Bulloch who provided her kind assistance during my trip to the Italian seminary archives in Montefiascone and allowed me to walk the same halls and examine the same books Bonjour had once done.

Although it was not my immediate intention (nor, I must confess, task), a small section of this work was rewritten while I was an Herzog Ernst Fellow at the Forschungszentrum Gotha in the summer of 2023, and it would be remiss of me not to thank them for offering me (when the future looked a little bleak) my first research position as a postdoc, and by extension the possibility of turning the thesis into a book in the first place. Before this, I spent eight happy years at Trinity College, Cambridge, from my time as an ignorant undergraduate to an ignorant postdoc, and I must thank both the College, the History Faculty, and the University for the years in which they supported my development (so to speak) and my research, and in which they provided for me not only a place of work but also a home. Above all, however, I would like to thank all of those who have taught me in some form or other throughout my long time at Cambridge; I would not be in the position I am now without them. Of these, special thanks must go to Richard Serjeantson, whose kind words and wise advice during my early years helped lay what I consider the platform for all the work which was to come. He is, of course, not responsible should anyone take any major issues with the work to come, or with its proverbial platform (nor indeed are any of the individuals mentioned here, except me).

In preparing this book over many years, sections of it at various stages of completion were read and commented on by a number of people, to whom I will always be grateful for their attention and advice. In particular, I would like to thank Michael Moriarty, who acted as my PhD advisor and read through some very early versions of my work, as well as the members of Scott Mandelbrote's PhD cohort in the years between 2020–2021, who were forced in our bi-weekly meetings to read and discuss some of my most rudimentary and unrefined drafts. Of these, I would like to add special thanks to Derrick Mosley, who allowed me to see what was at that point an unfinished draft of his excellent thesis on John Marsham. I would also like to thank Zachary Case, Alicia Mavor, Gabriel Gendler, Niall Dilucia, Anton Bruder, Santi Wilder, Iona Nicolson, and Emma Cavell, who all kindly provided their assistance with various foreign-language translations or other questions regarding editing in this work, and to add in this context a particular note of thanks to Nathaniel Hess, who provided priceless help in pruning some of my more infelicitous (and occasionally downright incorrect) translations of early modern Latin. I must also thank the two anonymous reviewers at Brill for taking the time to read the work, for their kind comments, and for their helpful individual points of advice, as well as Ivo Romein for helping to shepherd the work through the various stages of revision, proofing, and finalising at Brill. Above all, however, I must thank my two PhD examiners, Felix Waldmann and Noel Malcolm, who read through the work with a level of care and attention which was sometimes lamentably lacking in my own efforts. Their many comments regarding corrections and further improvements for turning the submission into a (more) error-free thesis, and this thesis into a publishable monograph, proved invaluable, and have substantially shaped the transition from dissertation to book.

Writing any lengthy, extended work of research over many years – often in solitude, in unknown foreign locations, and through the occasional worldwide pandemic – comes with its own challenges and I would like to thank all those friends whose encouragement and kindness have made even those many days in which Bonjour tried my patience enjoyable. Special thanks must therefore go to Dan, Matt, Emma, Ben, Zack, Niall, and Alicia for their invaluable companionship during this period. In this, I must also include TCAFC, which, for many years, was, of course, my true home. To Peter and Helene, I say only this: your many flawed opinions have helped me better form my own correct ones.

Of all the individuals associated with this project, particular and special thanks must of course go to my supervisor Scott Mandelbrote, without whom I can say with some certainty I would never have encountered Bonjour, nor therefore have been in a position to foist this scholar onto the academic public. Over the many years, Scott's insight, support, and guidance has been invaluable, and he has helped me see the woods when I would otherwise still be examining the bark of trees.

Lastly, and most importantly, to Mimi, whose support always meant the world; and to my parents, to whom words cannot express my thanks, and to whom I owe everything.

To Bonjour, I bid au revoir.

Abbreviations

Libraries and Collections

AGA	Archivio Generale Agostiniano, Rome
ASPF	Archivio Storico Propaganda Fide, Rome
SOCP	Scritture Originali delle Congregazioni Particolari, ASPF
BAR	Biblioteca Angelica, Rome
BEM	Biblioteca Estense, Modena
BNCF	Biblioteca Nazionale Centrale, Florence
BNF	Bibliothèque Nationale de France, Paris
NAF	Nouvelles Acquisitions Françaises, BNF
NAL	Nouvelles Acquisitions Latines, BNF
BVR	Biblioteca Vallicelliana, Rome
KW	Koninklijke Bibliotheek, The Hague

Bonjour's Major Works

Mercurius — Guillaume Bonjour. "Mercurius aegyptiorum Josephus patriarcha genealogice, chronologice, historice, geographice et hieroglyphice demonstratus ex sacris paginis et exoticis veterum monumentis ex quibus innumerae fabulae historicae veritati restituntur, variis Aegyptiorum illustratis vocibus." BAR, ms.lat.1.

Antiquitas — Guillaume Bonjour. "Dissertatio I. De temporibus ab Adamo ad Christum elapsis, secundum canones ex scriptura excerptos." In Guillaume Bonjour, "Antiquitas Temporum novis plerumque observationibus illustrata ex sacra paginis et exoticae historiae monumentis Chaldaicis, Phoenicis, Aegyptiacis, Sinensibus, & Hebraicae veritati consonantibus." BAR, ms.lat.49.

De dynastiis — Guillaume Bonjour. "Dissertatio Secunda. De dynastiis Aegyptiorum." In Guillaume Bonjour, "Antiquitas Temporum novis plerumque observationibus illustrata ex sacra paginis et exoticae historiae monumentis Chaldaicis, Phoenicis, Aegyptiacis, Sinensibus, & Hebraicae veritati consonantibus." BAR, ms.lat.49.

Aegyptiaca — Guillaume Bonjour. "Aegyptiaca Manethonis Sebennytae summi Aegyptiorum sacerdotis et scribae sub Ptolemaeo Philadelpho." BAR, ms.lat.49.

De nomine	Guillaume Bonjour. *Dissertatio de nomine patriarchae Josephi a pharaone imposito, in defensionem Vulgatae editionis, et patrum qui Josephum in Serapide adumbratum tradiderunt. Appendix altera de tempore Serapiorum ac Passionis S. Marci Evangelistae.* Rome: Francesco de Rubeis and Francesco Maria Acsamitek à Kronenfeld, 1696.
Coptica	Guillaume Bonjour. *In monumenta coptica seu aegyptiaca bibliothecae Vaticanae brevis exercitatio.* Rome: Francesco de Rubeis and Francesco Maria Acsamitek à Kronenfeld, 1699.
Triduanda	Guillaume Bonjour. *Triduanda de canone librorum sacrorum concertatio.* Montefiascone: Ex typographia Seminarii, 1704.
Selectae	Guillaume Bonjour. *Selectae in sacram scripturam dissertationes.* Montefiascone: Ex typographia Seminarii, 1705.

Other Collections

LAA	Gottfried Wilhelm Leibniz. *Sämtliche Schriften und Briefe*. Edited by the Academy of Sciences of Berlin. Series I–VIII. Darmstadt, Leipzig, and Berlin: Akademie Verlag, 1923–. Cited by series, volume, and page. The first series, denoted as I, pertains to the "Allgemeiner, politischer und historischer Briefwechsel"; the second series, denoted as II, pertains to the "Philosophischer Briefwechsel."
PG	Jacques Paul Migne, ed. *Patrologia Graeca.* 162 vols. Paris: Imprimerie Catholique, 1857–1886.
PL	Jacques Paul Migne, ed. *Patrologia Latina.* 217 vols. Paris: Imprimerie Catholique, 1844–1864.
FGrH	Felix Jacoby, ed. *Die Fragmente der griechischen Historiker.* 3 vols. Berlin and Leiden: Weidmann and Brill, 1923–1958.

Introduction

On Christmas day 1714, the Augustinian friar Guillaume Bonjour passed away in the Chinese province of Yunnan, a few kilometres north-east of what is now the China-Myanmar border.[1] If the European Republic of Letters had lost a once promising scholar, it did not know it yet. News from the Far East was not only slow, but often garbled.[2] More apparent, however, was that Bonjour had departed the learned Republic before he departed the mortal realm. His career bears the unmistakable signs of slipping into obscurity while still ongoing. As early as 1706, his failure to publish the works he had promised and which were still expected of him had seen his early promise flicker and wane. By the spring months of 1708, when Bonjour and his five companions stood on the chilly docks of London waiting to board a ship for the Far East, he was leaving behind not only Europe but also a learned community which, in truth, was already beginning to leave him behind. His premature death served only to heighten rather than precipitate this neglect.

It had not always been this way. When Bonjour arrived in Rome in the autumn of 1695 with the promise of the mentorship of the great Augustinian scholar Enrico Noris (1631–1704) and armed with a letter of introduction to the eccentric librarian Antonio Magliabechi (1633–1714), bibliophile and correspondent to Europe's scholarly elite, he was entering a learned world seemingly ripe for his estimable scholarly talents and extravagant scholarly ambitions. The origins of pagan religion, the chronology of the biblical text, the history of the ancient Near East, the arcane language of the Egyptians – these were issues which plagued and united scholars across national and confessional

---

1 Jean-Baptiste Du Halde, *Description géographique, historique, chronologique, politique, et physique de l'Empire de la Chine et de la Tartarie Chinoise* (The Hague: Henri Scheurleer, 1736), 1:xliii. Ugo Baldini, "Guillaume Bonjour (1670–1714): Chronologist, Linguist and 'Casual Scientist,'" in *Europe and China: Science and the Arts in the 17th and 18th Centuries*, ed. Luis Saravia (Singapore: World Scientific, 2013), 279, gives the town as "Menglian," the area known today as the Menglian Dai, Lahu, and Va Autonomous County, but Mario Cams, *Companions in Geography. East-West Collaboration in the Mapping of Qing China (c. 1685–1735)* (Leiden and Boston: Brill, 2017), 130, gives it as Mengding.
2 An illustrative example is the reaction of Gisbert Cuper, who believed Bonjour had been killed in a (fictional) massacre of Christian missionaries on the orders of the Chinese Kangxi Emperor in February 1714. See Gisbert Cuper to Jean-Paul Bignon, 23 February 1714 and 10 July 1714 in *Lettres de critique de littérature, d'histoire, &c. écrites à divers savans de l'Europe, par feu Monsieur Gisbert Cuper*, ed. Justin De Beyer (Amsterdam: J. Wetstein, 1743), 326, 331, and the relevant notes in KW 72 H 20.

boundaries, and, for a short time, it appeared that here was a scholar who might help solve them.

Initially, Bonjour worked on these problems with some success. Indeed, during his first years in Rome, the extent of Bonjour's industry was matched only by the growth of his reputation. In the Angelica and Vatican libraries in Rome, he studied ancient texts and composed weighty tomes on Greek mythology, Egyptian history, Jewish chronology, Roman religion, and Coptic grammar; in the learned communities of Paris and Amsterdam, the ducal libraries of Hanover and Modena, and the antiquarian provinces of Dijon and Deventer, scholars sought and traded information regarding the development of these projects and the nature of their findings. When in 1699 the young German philosopher Johann Franz Buddeus (1667–1729) reviewed Bonjour's survey of Coptic monuments in the Vatican library for the *Acta eruditorum*, the foremost journal of European erudition, he proclaimed that a new *doctissimus* author had been revealed to the learned world.[3] Yet this learned world was ultimately to be disappointed. While erudite, the material Bonjour was able to publish never amounted to more than "a sample of the larger works that he promises," as the great Genevan numismatist and diplomat Ezekiel Spanheim (1629–1710) noted in 1697.[4] Eventually, there arose the suspicion that these larger works would not appear. In 1699, the Ethiopic scholar Hiob Ludolf (1624–1704) wrote to Gottfried Wilhelm Leibniz (1646–1716) that Bonjour "repeats nothing regarding his great promises."[5] The comment encapsulates some of the disappointment – and even disillusion – which scholas came to feel. Unable to fund the costly printing of his works, and unable to convince the printers of the Roman Propaganda fide of their missionary utility, Bonjour was forced to lay aside the projects with which he had hoped to make his name and fulfil his reputation. A year was spent rearranging the Greek and Latin manuscripts of the Biblioteca Angelica, the Roman library in which he conducted much of his research; two more were spent on a learned yet futile and eventually aborted attempt, instituted by Clement XI (r. 1700–1721), to further perfect the Gregorian calendar. As the years progressed, many of the scholarly luminaries who had once mentored his projects, patronized his learning, and eulogised his abilities themselves died, and others who remained turned their attention

---

3 Johann Franz Buddeus, "In monumenta Coptica seu Aegyptiaca," *Acta eruditorum* (1699): 233.
4 Ezekiel Spanheim to Claude Nicaise, 25 June 1697, in Émile du Boys, ed., *Les correspondants de l'abbé Nicaise I. Un diplomate érudit du XVII siècle: Ézéchiel Spanheim lettres inédites (1681–1701)* (Paris: Alphonse Picard, 1889), 53–54: "un échantillon de plus grands ouvrages qu'il promet."
5 Hiob Ludolf to Gottfried Wilhelm Leibniz, 17 June 1699, in LAA, I, 17:284: "qui de magnis suis promissis nihil repetit."

to scholars who would not only promise but also publish. By the time of Bonjour's departure from Rome in October 1707, only one scholar remained in Bonjour's Republic who despaired at the imminent departure of a once vaunted prodigy. For the last ten years, the Dutch burgomaster, scholar, and enthusiastic antiquarian Gisbert Cuper (1644–1716) had nursed a correspondence with Bonjour shaped by their shared love of learning and for matters obscure, ancient, and arcane. The date at which the Romans had closed the temple of Janus; the poems of the fifth-century Christian gentleman Paulinus of Nola; a mysterious inscription from an ancient Chinese mirror; antique coins imported from Cadiz; the etymology of the Egyptian god Osiris; the lifespans of the postdiluvian patriarchs; the ancient cult of the Greek god Pan; an elephant skeleton discovered in Thuringia; the ten Hebrew names for God; the definite article in the Coptic language; the minor gods of ancient Aleppo; imperial inscriptions in classical Rome; the Syriac ascetic saint Simeon Stylites; the era of the Seleucids – these were the subjects which guided an epistolary exchange which was both learned and playful, crammed with recondite erudition and classical quips from Ausonius to Horace.[6] "All right all right, I yield to the power of your learning," wrote Cuper to Bonjour in 1700; "You, William remain obstinately silent like a mute inhabitant of the Spartan Amyclae, or as if the Egyptian Sigalion sealed your lips," he jested when his Augustinian friend did not reply quickly enough a few years later.[7] And yet, this erudition was also mixed with something else, something rarer: genuine human tenderness. Cuper, it seemed, cared greatly for this far-off Augustinian scholar, who began their correspondence as a learned contact and ended it as a cherished friend. In December 1707, returning from a visit to the suburb of Hof tot Oxen, Cuper found a wearied Bonjour, en route from Rome to London, resting in his attic

---

6   Bonjour's letters to Cuper, 17 in total, are in KW 72 H 20. Unfortunately they are unpaginated. Most of Cuper's letters to Bonjour (21 in total), are in BAR, ms.lat.395; copies of 3 further letters not in BAR can be found in KW 72 H 20. Cuper's letters in BAR have been published in Léon-Gabriel Pélissier, ed., "Lettres inédites de Gisbert Cuper à P. Daniel Huet (1683–1716) et à divers correspondants," *Mémoires de l'Académie nationale des sciences, arts et belles-lettres de Caen* (Caen: Henri Delesques, 1902–1905). The page numbers, which are not sequential, are as follows: 1902: 259–297, 1903: 41–103, 1904: 299–361 (104–165), 1905: 1–145 (166–309).

7   Gisbert Cuper to Guillaume Bonjour, 7 February 1700, BAR, ms.lat.395, fols. 20r–21v and in Pélissier, "Lettres inédites de Gisbert Cuper," (1905): 82 (246): "Jamjam efficaci do manus scientiae," citing Horace, *Epodi* 17.1; Gisbert Cuper to Guillaume Bonjour, 24 July 1702, BAR, ms.lat.395, fols. 24r–25v and reprinted in Pélissier, "Lettres inédites de Gisbert Cuper," (1905): 95 (259): "tu velut Oebaliis habites taciturnus Amyclis/Aut tua Sigalion Aegyptius oscula signet/Obnixum Wilhelme taces," citing Ausonius (*Epistulae* 29.26–28). Ausonius' original reads Paulinus rather than William, unsurprisingly. Cuper enjoyed this classical "joke" so much he also used it in his letters to Benedetto Bacchini and Pierre-Daniel Huet.

in Deventer.[8] For two days the two scholars drank chocolate in Cuper's library, discussing the etymologies of Manetho and the ancient rites of Heliopolis. Six years later, the memory of Bonjour's erudition and friendship remained a cherished memory in the aged Dutchman's mind. "There is," he wrote to the French royal librarian Jean-Paul Bignon (1662–1743) in February 1714,

> a first-rate scholar here who believes that the Egyptian language is the original language of mankind, and an Englishman who a few years ago wrote in a little book that it was Chinese. I wish with all my heart that Bonjour was here: he understood perfectly Egyptian and Chinese, as I learned from his letters, his books, and also his conversation, having had the honour of hosting him here for a few days before, *jussu Superiorum*, he undertook his journey to China.[9]

By all measures, Bonjour had a remarkable and successful life. Born in Toulouse in 1670, his scholarly and missionary career took him from the banks of the Garonne to those of the Tiber and the Yangtze, in the course of which he gained the confidence of two popes and, eventually, the Kangxi Emperor (r. 1661–1722). In many ways a typical example of that particular breed of early modern *polyhistor*, his works spanned such diverse fields as chronology, lexicography, philology, numismatics, ecclesiastical history, astronomy, linguistics, mythography, and theology, and treated such diverse subjects as the pharaohs of ancient Egypt, the Translation of St. Augustine's bones, Clavius' correction of the Gregorian calendar, the pseudo-Isidorian decretals, ancient paschal cycles,

---

8 See the unpaginated manuscript fragments in KW 72 H 20: "Eram 20. Decembris die profectus in villam, cui nomen in veteribus scriptis Latinis, Chastres vocant, *Curia Oxensis*, *Den Hof tot Oxen*, ut inspicerem operarios; postero die invisi Comites de Flodrof, et eadem vespera, brevissimo totius anni die Daventriam redii. Continuo mihi nuntiatur in cenaculo Gallum esse, qui adferebat literas, et qui reditum meum expectabat summo cum desiderio. Eum nobilissima herba Thea se refocillantem in ultimis aedibus meis in conspitio filiarum mearum adeo; continuo surgit, me amplectitur dicitque: Ecce habes, Domine, Guielmum Fabri; ego continuo laetabar immensum, testabarque nihil mihi acceptius evenire posse, quam recipere virum tam eruditum aedibus meis."

9 Gisbert Cuper to Jean-Paul Bignon, 23 February 1714, in Beyer, *Lettres de critique*, 326: "Il y a un Sçavant du premier ordre, qui croit que la Langue Egyptienne est la Langue originaire du Genre humain, & un Anglois s'est déclaré il y a quelques années dans un petit Livre pour la Chinoise, comme j'ai appris par ses Lettres, par ses Livres, & même par sa conversation, ayant eu l'honneur de le loger chez moi pendant quelques jours, avant qu'il entreprît, *jussu Superiorum*, le Voyage de la Chine." The Englishman in question is almost certainly the architect and amateur scholar John Webb (1611–1672), who argued in his *Historical essay* of 1669 that Chinese was the primitive language of mankind.

Coptic manuscripts, Antiochene medals, Chaldean etymologies, and Chinese Confucianism. Many of these dissertations are not only representative of the particular methodology of late seventeenth-century scholars but are also testament to the prevalence of those central religious issues which plagued scholars working in a time that the French historian Paul Hazard, in his epochal 1935 history of the period, once described as a "crisis" of the European mind.[10] Indeed, Bonjour's manner of tackling these issues remained deeply indebted to an authoritative and orthodox, if by his time slightly outdated and in later years oft-lampooned, approach to sacred and biblical history which was primarily geared towards defending such long-standing notions as the historical authority of the Bible, the chronology of the Vulgate, and the primacy of Moses and the Jews through the seemingly tenuous citation of non-biblical, profane evidence. That Bonjour was briefly mocked in the fourth edition of Thémiseul de Saint-Hyacinthe's notorious satire *Le chef d'oeuvre d'un inconnu* (1716) for working out the specific date for biblical Creation from an allusion in Virgil's *Georgics* (2.336–342) gives some indication of the type of orthodox tradition he worked in.[11] As we shall see, in defending these orthodox assumptions, Bonjour oft had recourse to scholarly practices which have encountered derision even from able, serious, and influential twentieth-century historians, not to mind eighteenth-century French libertines. Yet there can be no doubt that, however apparently abstruse some of Bonjour's theories and identifications, however symptomatic and typical he was of a certain type of late seventeenth-century orthodox scholar, he was not merely one of the bottle but also an innovative and original scholar of exceptional diligence and intelligence.

There is no better example of this fact than Bonjour's scholarship on Coptic, the ancient demotic language of Egypt and the liturgical language of the Coptic church. For centuries the language had remained virtually unknown to western Europeans, a matter not necessarily improved when that learned, esoteric, bombastic, and controversial Jesuit Athanasius Kircher (1602–1680) published the first grammar on the language – the *Prodromus coptus* – in 1636. While the recent work of Daniel Stolzenberg has highlighted that Kircher – who encountered so much ridicule and disdain in the eighteenth and nineteenth centuries – was not merely an Indian summer of outdated and esoteric *prisca theologia* but was also indebted to the new antiquarian and scholarly techniques then shaping the Republic of Letters, there can be little doubt

---

10 Paul Hazard, *La crise de la conscience européenne (1680–1715)* (Paris: Boivin, 1935).
11 Thémiseul de Saint-Hyacinthe, *Le chef d'oeuvre d'un inconnu. Poëme heureusement découvert & mis au jour, avec des Remarques savantes & recherchées* (The Hague: Pierre Husson, 1716), 42.

that his linguistic skills were far from perfect.[12] According to Louis Picques (1637–1699), himself a noted scholar of Coptic, librarian of the Mazarine in Paris, and a future correspondent of Bonjour, Kircher knew only German and a little Latin.[13] Even if this is somewhat harsh, it is clear that Kircher did not have an adequate understanding of Coptic or even Arabic, the necessary preliminary language for Coptic study. When, therefore, Bonjour first began to turn his attention to Coptic in around 1697, he was working in a language almost completely unknown to Europeans of which the only previous treatment contained gross and basic mistakes.[14] And yet, within two years of intense work, Bonjour had produced a grammar of the language which remained unsurpassed until the nineteenth century.[15] It is a scholarly achievement which should rank among the greatest of his generation.

The time Bonjour spent in China has meant that his name occasionally appears in histories of the Chinese missions, if somewhat peripherally. It is also in this context that he appears as the protagonist of a 2013 article by Ugo Baldini, to my mind the first English-language study of Bonjour to date.[16] Although I shall hope to sufficiently expand – and, in certain cases, amend – Baldini's biography, it is an important and highly competent survey of a scholar who not only no one knew but barely anyone had heard of.[17] Despite this, Bonjour's most prominent and to a certain extent only legacy for posterity

12   Daniel Stolzenberg, *Egyptian Oedipus: Athanasius Kircher and the Secrets of Antiquity* (Chicago: Chicago University Press, 2013).
13   Alastair Hamilton, *The Copts and the West, 1439–1822: The European Discovery of the Egyptian Church* (Oxford: Oxford University Press, 2006), 215.
14   For the relationship between Kircher and Bonjour's work see Sydney Aufrère and Nathalie Bosson, "*De Copticae Guillelmi Bonjourni grammaticae criticis contra Athanasium Kircherum*. La naissance de la critique de *l'Opera Kicheriana Coptica*," *Études Coptes* 8 (2003): 5–18.
15   As remarked by Hamilton, *The Copts and the West*, 232.
16   Baldini, "Guillaume Bonjour."
17   Pre-existing if somewhat cursory biographies include: Louis Ellies Du Pin, *Bibliothèque des auteurs ecclesiastiques du dix-septie'me siecle, 11. Suite de la Ve partie: des auteurs vivans* (Paris: André Pralard, 1708), 84–87; Louis Moréri, *Nouveau supplément au grand dictionnaire historique, généalogique, géographique, &c.* (Paris: Jacques Vincent, J. B. Coignard & A. Boudet, P. G. Le Mercier, J. Desaint & C. H. Saillant, and Jean-Thomas Herissant, 1749), 1:148–149; Jean Raynal, *Histoire de la ville de Toulouse. …* (Toulouse: Jean-François Forest, 1759), 393–394; François Xavier de Feller, *Dictionnaire historique ou histoire abrégée des hommes qui se sont fait un nom par le génie, les talens, les vertus, les erreurs, depuis le commencement du monde jusqu'à nos jours* (Liège: F. Lemarié, 1797), 2:290; Gaetano Moroni, *Dizionario di erudizione storico-ecclesiastica da S. Pietro …* (Venice: Tipografia Emiliana, 1840–1861), 6:26. Cf. Eelcko Ypma, "Les auteurs augustins français: Liste de leurs noms et de leurs ouvrages," *Augustiniana* 18 (1968): 222–224.

concerns his work on Coptic. This was a process which began while he was still alive. In 1701, he was visited by the Jansenist and Oriental scholar Eusèbe Renaudot (1646–1720), who had come to Rome as a companion of Louis Antoine, Cardinal de Noailles (1651–1729), for the papal conclave which elected Giovanni Francesco Albani (1649–1721) Pope Clement XI, and who stayed there for a further year, tasked with opposing the Jesuits and their protector, the Cardinal de Bouillon (1643–1715), in a number of ecclesiastical disputes.[18] As a young man, Renaudot had spent much time studying at the Oratory and under the noted Orientalist Barthélemy d'Herbelot (1625–1695) in Paris and had reputedly come to master up to seventeen different languages, including Coptic; since the 1670s, he made use of these formidable skills by studiously collecting material on the ancient Eastern Churches for additional volumes of the *Perpetuité de la foy*, Antoine Arnauld and Pierre Nicole's famous Jansenist work which documented the antiquity of the doctrine of the Real Presence of Christ in the Eucharist against the arguments of the Protestant minister Jean Claude (1619–1687).[19] Whilst in Rome, Renaudot not only read Bonjour's Coptic grammar and discussed it with Clement XI – to whom Renaudot dedicated the additional volumes of the *Perpetuité* when they began appearing in 1711 – but also wrote an approbation of the grammar in which he testified that it was *accuratissimus* and worthy of publication.[20] Although this never came about, Renaudot's visit helped keep alive knowledge of Bonjour's Coptic abilities and the manuscripts stashed away in the Biblioteca Angelica. In his *Liturgiarum orientalium collectio* of 1715, Renaudot described Bonjour as a *vir doctissimus*, "who out of a few books, studied the Coptic language on his own, and composed an accurate grammar far better than others produced either in Latin or Arabic."[21] In the following years, Bonjour's Coptic works were continually referenced by some of the most important scholars in the discipline.[22] With the

---

18   See Antoine Villien, *L'abbé Eusèbe Renaudot: Essai sur la Vie et sur son Œuvre liturgique* (Paris: Victor Lecoffre, 1904), 111–117; and Pierre-François Burger, "L'abbé Renaudot en Italie (1700–1701)," in *Dix-huitième siècle* 22 (1990): 243–253.

19   Cornel Zwierlein, "Orient contra China: Eusèbe Renaudot's Vision of World History (ca. 1700)," *Journal of the History of Ideas* 81 (2020): 26, esp. n. 10.

20   Eusèbe Renaudot, "Encomio dell'Elementa linguae copticae," BAR, ms.lat.475, fols. 351r–352v; and "Copie du certificat envoyé au P. Bonjour, Augustin, à Rome, pour l'approbation de la Grammaire Copte, suivant le témoignage que j'en rendis au Pape le dernier Aoust 1701," BNF, NAF 7483, fol. 282r–v.

21   Eusèbe Renaudot, *Liturgiarum orientalium collectio* (Paris: Jean-Baptiste Coignard, 1715), 1:cxii: "qui ex paucis libris, proprio marte linguam Copticam edidicit, illiusque accuratam, & aliis quae vel Arabice vel Latine prodierant praestantiorem Grammaticam composuit."

22   A list of the Coptic manuscripts can be seen at Ignazio Guidi, *Catalogo dei codici Orientali di alcune Biblioteche d'Italia* (Florence: Tipografia dei successori le Monnier, 1878), 77–81.

exception of the German-born Oxford scholar David Wilkins (1685–1745), who published the first Coptic New Testament in 1716 and who consulted Bonjour's manuscripts in Rome while Bonjour was still in China, they were generally met with praise.[23] Mathurin Veyssière La Croze (1661–1739), an erstwhile French Benedictine who converted to Protestantism and settled as Prussian royal librarian in Berlin, was informed of the existence of Bonjour's *In monumenta Coptica* by Cuper and read it enthusiastically, while the Augustinian Orientalist Agostino Antonio Giorgi (1711–1797) later revisited Bonjour's manuscripts and attacked Wilkins vehemently for his superficial judgement.[24] "Father Bonjour appeared destined to arrange this truth in the highest degree of evidence. He was an Augustinian from Toulouse, who was discriminating and learned. Called to Rome by Cardinal Noris, he published several works, among others some observations on the Coptic manuscripts preserved in the Vatican. He made great progress in the language of these manuscripts; an irregular language, bristling with difficulties and composed of many dialects, whose character must be disentangled," wrote Jean-Jacques Barthélemy (1716–1795), a French linguist who came to decipher both the Palmyrene and the Phoenician alphabets, in 1768.[25] Had it not been for a curious twist of fate, Bonjour's grammar may even have had a direct influence on later Coptic studies. In the mid-eighteenth century, the Italian cardinal and prefect of the Propaganda fide, Giuseppe Spinelli

[23] David Wilkins, "Dissertatio de lingua Coptica," in *Dissertationes ex occasione sylloges orationum dominicarum scriptae ad Joannem Chamberlaynium*, ed. John Chamberlayne (Amsterdam: William and David Goereus, 1715), 92–93; David Wilkins, *Novum Testamentum Aegyptium vulgo Copticum ex MSS. Bodlejanis descripsit, cum Vaticanis et Parisiensibus contulit et in Latinum sermonem convertit* (Oxford: Ex Theatro Sheldoniano, 1716), iii: "Post eum [Thomas Marshall, 1621–1685] Doctissimus *Bonjourius* Italiam instituto suo, *Evangelia Coptica* cum versione Arabica & Latina imprimendi, implevit; ac cum ipsius absentis MSS. Codices paucissimis paterent, benigno Papae *Clementis* XI jussu (qui me crebris alloquiis suis eruditione plenis dignatus est, ac quam comiter pro innata sua erga advenas humanitate excepit) mihi in Collegio S. Augustini Romae aperiebantur, ubi priorum quorundam capitum S. Matthaei initium Copto-Arabicum inveni, nec quosnam progressus in hac lingua fecerit exinde dijudicare potui."

[24] Mathurin Veyssière La Croze to Gisbert Cuper, 28 January 1710, KW 72 H 18, n. 40 (see also Cuper's letter in Beyer, *Lettres de critiques*); Agostino Antonio Giorgi, *Fragmentum evangelii S. Iohannis Graeco-Copto-Thebaicum ...* (Rome: Antonio Fulgoni, 1789), iv–v.

[25] Jean-Jacques Barthélemy, "Réflexions générales sur les rapports des langues Égyptienne, Phénicienne & Grecque," *Mémoires de littérature, tirés de l'Académie royale des inscriptions et belles-lettres* 32 (1768): 214–215: "Le P. Bonjour paroissoit destiné à mettre cette vérité dans le plus haut degré d'évidence. C'étoit un Augustin de Toulouse, qui avoit de la critique & de l'érudition. Appelé à Rome par le cardinal Noris, il y publia quelques ouvrages, & entre autres des observations sur les manuscrits cophtes conservés au Vatican. Il avoit fait de très-grand progrès dans la langue de ces manuscrits; langue irrégulière, hérissée de difficultés, & composée de plusieurs dialectes, dont il faut démêler le caractère."

INTRODUCTION 9

(1694–1763), tasked the Orientalist Raphael Tuki (1701–1787), a Copt from Girga in Egypt who converted to Catholicism in 1719, with editing and publishing Bonjour's Coptic grammar. As provocative, argumentative, and opinionated as he was intelligent, Tuki chose to ignore Spinelli's orders and instead decided to compose and publish his own grammar (how much Tuki took from Bonjour is still a matter of debate).[26] And yet, Bonjour's reputation lived on even among some of the most illustrious scholars of ancient Egypt and its mysterious languages. Fifty years after Tuki, his work was still being read and praised by none other than Jean-François Champollion (1790–1832); in the 1808 *Recherches critiques et historiques sur la langue et la littérature de l'Égypte*, one of the first histories of Coptic scholarship by the French Orientalist Étienne Quatremère (1782–1857), who also owned a copy of Bonjour's biblical dissertations, Bonjour appears as a somewhat mysterious yet nevertheless important early scholar of the language.[27] When the great Ernest Renan (1823–1892) toured the libraries of Italy in the mid-nineteenth century, he still felt it apt to comment on the young Augustinian's abilities. "I also leafed with interest through the collection of the works of Guillaume Bonjour, an Augustinian monk born in Toulouse and one of the first people to occupy himself with the Coptic language," he wrote to the Minister of Education and Public Worship, Félix Esquirou de Parieu (1815–1893), in February 1850. "His grammar, his dictionary, and his dissertations attest to laudable efforts at the least, and deserve a mention in the history of scholarship on Oriental languages."[28]

---

26   Hamilton, *The Copts and the West*, 95ff., 101, 232; Tommaso Valperga di Caluso, *Literaturae copticae rudimentum* (Parma: Ex Regio Typographo, 1783), 27–28; Giorgi, *Fragmentum*, vi–vii; Barthélemy, "Réflexions," 215; Étienne Quatremère, *Recherches critiques et historiques sur la langue et la littérature de l'Égypte* (Paris: Imprimerie Impériale, 1808), 92. Cf. Sydney Aufrère and Nathalie Bosson, "Le Père Guillaume Bonjour (1670–1714). Un orientaliste méconnu porté sur l'étude du copte et le déchiffrement de l'égyptien," *Orientalia* 67 (1998): 498, who claim that Tuki took much material from Bonjour. Cf. Raphael Tuki, *Rudimenta linguae Coptae sive Aegyptiacae* (Rome: Sacra congregatio de Propaganda fide, 1778).

27   Jean-François Champollion, *L'Égypte sous les pharaons, ou recherches sur la géographie, la religion, la langue, les écritures et l'histoire de l'Égypte avant l'invasion de Cambyse* (Paris: Bure frères, 1814), 1:16–17; Alain Faure, *Champollion: le savant dechiffré* (Paris: Fayard, 2004), 136; Quatremère, *Recherches*, 67–70. A copy of Bonjour's *Selectae in sacram scripturam* with Quatremère's bookplate can be found in the Bayerische Staatsbibliothek, 4 Exeg. 94d.

28   Ernest Renan to Félix Esquirou de Parieu, 15 Februrary 1850, in Ernest Renan, *Correspondance générale*, ed. Maurice Gasnier and Jean Balcou (Paris: Honoré Champion Éditeur, 2008), 3:197: "J'ai aussi feuilleté avec intérêt la collection des travaux de Guillaume Bonjour, moine augustin, né à Toulouse, un des premiers qui se soient occupés de la langue

It is within the context of Bonjour's work on Coptic that he has also been rediscovered more recently, a rediscovery which has led to the first modern efforts to try and lift the veil of obscurity which still shrouds this scholar *méconnu*. The chief vanguards in this rediscovery are Sydney Aufrère and Nathalie Bosson, who first began publishing articles on Bonjour's work on Coptic in 1998 and who are responsible for editing and publishing a magnificent, long-awaited edition of Bonjour's Coptic grammar in 2005, more than three hundred years after the same work had been lauded by Clement XI, approved by Renaudot, and spurned by the Propaganda fide.[29] Since then, Bonjour's work on Coptic has been further elucidated by Alastair Hamilton, who published an excellent history of Western interest in the Coptic church and the Coptic language in 2006.[30] Given that Aufrère and Bosson are themselves prominent Egyptologists, and Alastair Hamilton ranks among the foremost living authorities on early modern Oriental scholarship, we have never been better placed to understand Bonjour's remarkable aptitude for the Coptic language, nor better informed of his importance within the history of western Coptic scholarship. It is due to the work of these three scholars that both the life and the scholarship of this unknown Augustinian was first revealed, or perhaps re-revealed, to contemporary historians.

The present volume does not intend to discuss Bonjour's scholarship on the Coptic language or his place within Coptic scholarship further. Such a project is not possible for someone without the necessary understanding of Coptic or Arabic and, thanks to the work of Aufrère, Bosson, and Hamilton, it is no longer necessary. What I aim to present here is a broader look both at Bonjour's scholarship more generally and the scholarly world which shaped this scholarship. Above all, I hope that this monograph can accomplish three things.

My first aim is to sketch, somewhat more fully, a picture of Bonjour's life, his institutional and religious context, and his scholarly interests. This, in essence, is a matter of expanding and bringing to light new biographical information which has not yet been covered in studies that have, quite understandably,

---

copte. Sa grammaire, son dictionnaire, ses dissertations attestent au moins de louable efforts, et mériteront une mention dans l'histoire de l'étude des langues orientales."

[29] Sydney Aufrère and Nathalie Bosson, "Le Père Guillaume Bonjour (1670–1714)"; "*De Copticae Guillelmi Bonjourni*"; "Remarques au sujet du *Lexikon Aegyptio-Latinum* F. Guillelmi Bonjour Tolosani Augustiniani," *Études Coptes* 9 (2005): 17–31; *Guillaume Bonjour Elementa Linguae Copticae. Grammaire inédite du XVIIe Siècle* (Geneva: Patrick Cramer, 2005).

[30] Hamilton, *The Copts and the West*; Bonjour is also discussed in Alastair Hamilton, "From East to West: Jansenists, Orientalists and the Eucharistic Controversy," in *Essays on Literary Imagination, the Canon and the Christian Middle Ages for Burcht Pranger*, ed. Willemien Otten, Arjo Vanderjagt, and Hent De Vries (Leiden: Brill, 2010), 83–100.

focussed on a specific part of Bonjour's scholarship. As Hamilton noted in his review of Aufrère and Bosson's 2005 work, Bonjour continues to retain an element of mystery despite the recent revival of scholarly interest.[31] It is my hope that this work can at least partially uncover that which remains mysterious.

My second aim is to contextualize Bonjour's work on Coptic within his broader scholarly and religious interests. The current focus on Bonjour as primarily a scholar of Coptic is an indication of our own somewhat rigid sense of academic disciplines rather than Bonjour's. While it understandable that we see Bonjour's Coptic grammar as perhaps his greatest scholarly achievement, it is less likely that Bonjour would have seen it this way. Ultimately, composing a grammar was not an end in itself but a means to an end. In his memoirs, the French scholar Pierre-Daniel Huet (1630–1721), whom we shall meet several times in the course of this study, described languages not as objects of learning themselves but rather "the keys by which the doors of learning are opened."[32] It appears that Bonjour saw the matter in much the same way. Above all, Bonjour was interested in the way biblical knowledge had been preserved among ancient pagan nations, an enterprise for which the ancient Egyptian language proved a crucial tool. In March 1698, a month after he had begun working on a trilingual Arabic-Coptic-Latin Pentateuch, he wrote to Antonio Magliabechi in Florence that his work on Coptic was intended "principally for those who are searching for various monuments of holy scripture in profane writers."[33] For Bonjour, the Egyptian language held the key to understanding the antiquities of Egypt, and the antiquities of Egypt held the key for elucidating, confirming, and defending biblical history. It is for this reason that Bonjour composed an extensive treatise on Egyptian chronology which he initially planned to print alongside his never completed Coptic-Arabic-Latin Bible and, later, alongside his never published Coptic grammar. "Meanwhile, since the ancient language of the Egyptians is greatly useful to me, I am now devoted to disentangling every aspect of this. The insights that are born from the explication of the

---

[31] Alastair Hamilton, "Guillaume Bonjour *Elementa linguae copticae*," *Church History and Religious Culture* 87 (2007): 125–127.

[32] Pierre-Daniel Huet, *Memoirs of the Life of Peter Daniel Huet, Bishop of Avranches: written by himself; and translated from the original Latin with copious Notes, Biographical and Critical*, ed. John Aikin (London: Longman, Hurst, Rees, Orme, and Cadell and Davies, 1810), 1:223; translated from Pierre-Daniel Huet, *Commentarius de rebus ad eum pertinentibus* (Amsterdam: Henri du Sauzet, 1718), 156: "Linguis sic tanquam clavibus reserantur fores doctrinae."

[33] Guillaume Bonjour to Antonio Magliabechi, 1 March 1698, BNCF, *Fondo Magliabechiano* VIII, cod. 317, fol. 25v: "quelli principalmente che vanno cercando nei scrittori profani diversi monumenti della scrittura sacra."

Egyptian antiquities are excellent," he wrote to Cuper in February 1698.[34] In March, he followed this with a similarly indicative statement, noting of his study of Coptic biblical manuscripts that "nothing more extraordinary could happen to me for clearly elucidating the dynasties of Egypt, where sacred history in particular has a connection with the Egyptian."[35] Indeed, from the manner in which Bonjour described his work both in his letters and within the works themselves, there appears one overriding theme which informed Bonjour's scholarship on Egypt: his attempt to synchronize the ancient history of the Jews with those of contemporary, neighbouring nations and in so doing produce a single, unified, harmonious historical system which would ultimately uphold the authority of the biblical history and by extension the truth of the Christian religion.[36] It is my intention to explore how this interest both shaped Bonjour's particular approach to Egypt and to sacred history, as well as the extent to which this interest was shaped – and shared – by Bonjour's contemporaries throughout the learned, pan-European, Republic.

This, in turn, leads me to my third and broadest aim: to use a study of Bonjour – and not only Bonjour but also those influences who shaped his work, those learned contemporaries with whom he shared his work, and those readers who read his work: in short, the scholarly world Bonjour inhabited – in order to say something more general about the development of orthodox religious scholarship, and the use of non-biblical, profane history within this orthodox scholarship, in the last decades of the seventeenth and the first decades of the eighteenth century. Traditionally, historians have earmarked these years as the key period in which the traditional authority of the Bible underwent a profound and lasting change. Particularly influential remains Paul Hazard's famous *La crise de la conscience européenne*, in which Hazard argued that it was between the years 1680 and 1715 that the European scholarly community witnessed an intellectual and religious crisis during which long-standing orthodox assumptions were torn asunder and from which a secular, rational,

---

34   Guillaume Bonjour to Gisbert Cuper, 8 February 1698, KW 72 H 20: "Quia interim mihi maxime necessaria est vetus lingua Aegyptiorum, totus in hac extricanda nunc incumbo. Egregia sunt quae in enodationem antiquitatum Aegyptiacarum inde enascuntur lumina."
35   Guillaume Bonjour to Gisbert Cuper, 22 March 1698, KW 72 H 20: "Quod interim spectat pentateuchum Aegyptio-Arabicum, ita modum loquendi veterum Aegyptiorum affectat; ut nihil insignius contingere mihi potuerit ad dynastias Aegyptiorum plane illustrandas, ubi praesertim historia sacra nexum habet cum Aegyptiaca." The manuscript is unpaginated.
36   "Exoticae antiquitatis monumentas conferens cum sacris paginis," as he wrote to Cuper on the 31 August 1697, KW 72 H 20.

and critical Enlightenment spirit emerged.[37] According to Hazard, this change affected the way scholars studied both the Bible as a text and the history of which the Bible narrated. Increasingly, scholars came to view biblical history not as universal history but as a specifically Jewish history; the biblical text as a human product and therefore subject to human corruption; and the religion of the ancient Israelites as primitive and uncivilized. In Hazard's narrative, the principal agents of this change were radicals and freethinkers, such as Thomas Hobbes (1588–1679), Benedict Spinoza (1632–1677), or the English deists, who rationalised and secularised the study of the biblical history and the ancient Jewish religion.[38] Moreover, Hazard made the study of pagan antiquity an important part of this development. According to Hazard, new chronological and ethnographic information, whether rediscovered in classical antiquity or recently discovered among non-European civilizations, contradicted the biblical framework for universal history and thereby came to undermine the special, privileged status of the ancient Hebrew Bible.[39]

Recent scholarship has made a number of important revisions to Hazard's narrative. Above all, scholars have highlighted that many heterodox ideas used to undermine biblical authority and institutional religion had their origins in earlier Christian scholarship which was first developed with the intention of *defending* orthodox principles. Hans-Joachim Kraus and Nicholas Hardy, for example, have highlighted that late seventeenth-century biblical text criticism, which questioned the history and reliability of the biblical text, had its origins in the confessional scholarship of such figures as Jean Morin (1591–1659) and Louis Cappel (1585–1658), who believed that *Kritik*, or *eruditio*, could help reveal, rather than undermine, the Word of God.[40] In a similar vein, Peter Miller and Dmitri Levitin have shown how the historicization and

---

37   Hazard, *La crise de la conscience européenne (1680–1715)*. A number of English translations exist. I have consulted the first, Paul Hazard, *The European Mind: The Critical Years, 1680–1715*, trans. J. Lewis May (New Haven: Yale University Press, 1953), but have diverged from it in certain places.

38   This narrative has particularly influenced the work of Margaret C. Jacob and Jonathan Israel: see Margaret C. Jacob, *The Radical Enlightenment: Pantheists, Freemasons and Republicans* (London and Boston: George Allen and Unwin, 1981); Jonathan Israel, *Radical Enlightenment: Philosophy and the Making of Modernity, 1650–1750* (Oxford: Oxford University Press, 2001), and Jonathan Israel, *Enlightenment Contested: Philosophy, Modernity, and the Emancipation of Man, 1670–1752* (Oxford: Oxford University Press, 2006).

39   Hazard, *The European Mind*, 40–48.

40   Hans-Joachim Kraus, *Geschichte der historisch-kritischen Erforschung des Alten Testaments* (Neukirchen-Vluyn: Neukirchener Verlag, 1982); Nicholas Hardy, *Criticism and Confession: The Bible in the Seventeenth-Century Republic of Letters* (Oxford: Oxford University Press, 2017).

contextualisation of biblical study first began within early seventeenth-century orthodox scholarship.[41] These new insights have their origin in a historiographical as well as merely a temporal or intellectual shift. In particular, such revisionism has become a defining hallmark of the growing body of work known as "the history of scholarship," a field of historical study which has reconfigured not only which texts we study but also the way in which we understand intellectual change. By placing more emphasis on both the immediate contexts in which certain works were produced and, more importantly, the historical sources the author in question utilized, we have shifted our perception as to which texts can truly be said to have helped bring about the seismic religious and intellectual changes so brilliantly and poetically described by Hazard. Through a focus on "scholarship," historians have begun to realise that works which were seen as radical did not have to be written by radical scholars; and that scholars who were later vaunted for their radical theories borrowed much from the very scholars whom they branded as learned but sterile pedants.

There are questions – at least in my mind – about whether this approach has gone too far. To claim that the contextualisation and relativisation of ancient religion in the work of John Toland (1670–1722) or Viscount Bolingbroke (1678–1751) was not original is not to say that it was not radical; to claim that certain works were written with great piety and with "orthodox" goals in mind does little to quell the possible radical influence they may have had. Even if heterodox scholars merely twisted or inverted the findings of "orthodox" scholars, we should not fail to recognise that this "twist" was in itself both radical and original. Whereas orthodox scholars advanced their narratives in order to defend the authority of the Bible, heterodox scholars did so with the explicit aim of striking at institutional religion. Even if eighteenth-century *philosophes* plundered the scholarly advancements of their *érudit* predecessors, they were still the first to self-consciously and publicly conceptualise these advancements as challenges to, rather than evidence for, commonly-held religious beliefs. It is important to recognise that the manner in which a certain interpretation or historical argument was mobilised is as important as the origins of the interpretation or the historical argument itself. And yet, there can be no doubt that the new approaches fostered through the burgeoning "history of scholarship" tradition have fundamentally enriched and improved

---

41 Peter Miller, "The 'Antiquarianization' of Biblical Scholarship and the London Polyglot Bible (1653–57)," *Journal of the History of Ideas* 62 (2001): 463–482; Dmitri Levitin, "From Sacred History to the History of Religion: Paganism, Judaism, and Christianity in European Historiography from Reformation to 'Enlightenment'," *The Historical Journal* 55 (2012): 1117–1160.

our understanding of early modern religious and intellectual history, and the manner in which influential and ultimately seismic changes within this discipline came about. Above all, historians have placed a renewed focus on the originality, impact, and importance of orthodox religious scholarship in breaking down long-standing orthodox religious doctrines and assumptions. As Sarah Mortimer and John Robertson have put it, scholarly debates in which scholars vied for orthodoxy eventually paved the way for heterodoxy: by seeking to confirm their orthodoxy by applying new text-critical, historical, and philological techniques to the study of biblical history and the biblical text, these scholars gradually began to wear away at pre-established norms and dogmas and supplied heterodox scholars with the necessary tools for challenging biblical authority and institutional religion directly.[42] Consequently, the binary opposition of orthodoxy and heterodoxy – in which heterodoxy is portrayed as a conscious rebellion against its polar opposite, orthodoxy – has been reconfigured. On the one hand, orthodox scholarship once considered sterile or slavishly pedantic is now considered diverse, fruitful, and, ultimately, influential.[43] It was from the orthodox centre, to borrow a famous phrase of Noel Malcolm's, rather than from the heterodox fringes of scholarship that the most profound changes in early modern biblical criticism, chronology, and sacred historiography emerged.[44] On the other hand, orthodox scholarship on biblical history and the biblical text is now thought to have shaped later attacks on biblical authority. The relationship is akin to that of a Trojan horse, or, in the words of Miller, a ticking time-bomb.[45] Once scholars subjected the biblical text to serious text criticism, they quickly came to recognise the instability of the text itself; and once scholars believed that an understanding of the languages, history, and culture of the Near East could help them better

---

[42] Sarah Mortimer and John Robertson, "Nature, Revelation, History: Intellectual Consequences of Religious Heterodoxy c.1600–1750," in *The Intellectual Consequences of Religious Heterodoxy 1600–1750*, ed. Sarah Mortimer and John Robertson (Leiden and Boston: Brill, 2012), 1–46, especially 12–13.

[43] See generally Jean-Louis Quantin and Christopher Ligota, "Introduction," in *History of Scholarship: A Selection of Papers from the Seminar on the History of Scholarship Held Annually at the Warburg Institute*, ed. Chistopher Ligota and Jean-Louis Quantin (Oxford: Oxford University Press, 2006), 1–38; and Dmitri Levitin, *Ancient Wisdom in the Age of the New Science: Histories of Philosophy in England, c. 1640–1700* (Cambridge: Cambridge University Press, 2015), 1–4.

[44] Noel Malcolm, "Hobbes, Ezra and the Bible: The History of a Subversive Idea," in Noel Malcolm, *Aspects of Hobbes* (Oxford: Oxford University Press, 2002), 430; and re-used by Levitin, "From Sacred History to the History of Religion," 1135.

[45] Peter Miller, "Taking Paganism Seriously: Anthropology and Antiquarianism in Early Seventeenth-Century Histories of Religion," *Archiv für Religionsgeschichte* 3 (2001): 200.

understand the ancient Jewish religion, they tacitly admitted that this Jewish religion was the product of a specific historical period and a specific historical context. To borrow another image once used to describe Erasmus' relationship to Luther, it was from an orthodox egg that heterodox critiques later hatched. This basic notion has allowed recent scholars to save the reputation of their cherished *érudits* from that famous and influential damnation of the *philosophe* d'Alembert.[46]

It is within this tradition that I also want to study Bonjour's contributions – my own cherished *érudit*, so to speak. In many ways, Bonjour's scholarly approach encapsulates the complicated relationship between criticism (*Kritik*, or *eruditio*) on the one hand, and religious orthodoxy, or Christian apologetics, on the other. Bonjour himself was a "critical" scholar, in the seventeenth-century sense of the word. He believed in the proper application of text-critical and historical scholarship to ancient evidence, whether sacred or profane, and yet did not, as later scholars would do, suppose that this critical approach might weaken the biblical edifice he was defending. For Bonjour, not only were the tools of erudition to be wielded in defence of Christian orthodoxy but their correct application to the relevant texts would necessarily support said orthodoxy. This meant that Bonjour trod the fine, if in the seventeenth century also much-trodden, line between historical criticism and Christian apologetic. Throughout his scholarly life, he never deviated from the basic orthodox principles of the Catholic Church, such as the authority of Jerome's Vulgate, Mosaic authorship of the Pentateuch, Hebraic primacy, or the universal authority of the chronology of the Bible. Like many of his contemporaries, he believed that historical scholarship in particular was the best method for proving the authority of scripture and the truth of the Christian religion. As a result, he believed that the development, refinement, and improvement of historical scholarship would further and even more convincingly confirm what he already knew to be true from reading scripture, the Fathers, and the decisions of the Church and its Councils. Yet this also meant that the manner in which Bonjour defended long-standing orthodox principles changed as historical and critical scholarship developed. In this sense, Bonjour is within Noel Malcolm's orthodox centre – or perhaps more accurately, one of the orthodox

---

46   Jean le Rond d'Alembert, "Discours préliminaire" in *Encyclopédie ou dictionnaire raisonné des sciences des arts et de métiers par une société de gens de lettres*, ed. Jean le Rond d'Alembert and Denis Diderot (Paris: Briasson, David, Le Bret, Durand, 1751–1765) 1:i–xlv and d'Alembert, "Erudition," in *Encyclopédie*, 5:914–918. Cf. J. G. A. Pocock, *Barbarism and Religion* (Cambridge: Cambridge University Press, 1999–2015), 1:169, and Anton M. Matytsin, "Enlightenment and Erudition: Writing Cultural History at the Académie des inscriptions," *Modern Intellectual History* 19 (2022): 323–348.

centres – from which emerged those profound changes to early modern biblical scholarship. As we shall see, this is particularly the case if we consider Bonjour's many historical treatments of pagan antiquity. In seeking to defend the authority of the Bible, Bonjour rarely referenced either its divine provenance or its prophetic quality. Instead, he sought to defend biblical authority by supposing that, if the historical information in the Bible was genuine, then it would conform to and uphold the basic rules of historical scholarship. It is a fine line between studying the Bible as a historical text and supposing that it is *merely* a historical text. Consequently, Bonjour's exposition of sacred history and his defence of biblical authority already holds within it the implicit contextualisation, historicization, and relativisation of biblical history which later heterodox scholars would seize upon explicitly.

It is clear that Bonjour was not alone in this practice and that he was not a scholar who necessarily furthered this development. He was, however, representative of a broader scholarly development which profoundly affected the intellectual and religious history of western European historiography and theology. Consequently, what I principally understand by Bonjour's "world" are those scholars whom he read and corresponded with who were grappling with the same problems as Bonjour. Ultimately, the question of Egyptian antiquity, the original chronology of the Bible, or the true nature of the Chinese religion were not issues particular to Bonjour. As I hope to show further in this work, they troubled a range of scholars of different national, theological, and confessional identities, and were often considered problematic for the Christian religion in general. This also led scholars to formulate intellectual responses which transcended confessional and national boundaries. One of the main reasons I want to focus not merely on Bonjour but also on his world is due to my contention that changes in the scholarly conceptualisation of pagan history and religion were not particular to individual scholars but symptomatic of a broader, general, and more long-lasting development which affected a whole generation of scholars and an entire genre of scholarship.

The present study has been split into four sections, the last three of which are further subdivided into two chapters. The first section-cum-chapter will deal primarily with Bonjour's life as a scholar and his immediate institutional and cultural context. Above all, it is intended to provide new information on Bonjour (and his context) which is hitherto unknown. Since it is primarily biographical, it will serve as a propaedeutic to the three following sections, which will examine Bonjour's works from an intellectual and scholarly perspective.

These following three sections encompass Bonjour's work on mythology, chronology, and idolatry respectively. To a certain extent this division is arbitrary. As we shall see, ancient myths were important historical evidence for writing a universal chronology, just as they were vital sources for understanding the origins of pagan idolatry, and hence the history of religion. It is, however, necessary to provide some structure to the work, and I believe the present division is most in line with Bonjour's own interests and the development of his scholarship. In the first section, I will concentrate primarily on those texts in which Bonjour explicitly discussed pagan myths and attempted to use these myths to elucidate and confirm particulars within sacred history. Here, I shall primarily focus on his first unpublished work (the *Mercurius aegyptiorum*), the various preliminary dissertations he wrote in preparation of this work, his first published *opuscula* (the *De nomine patriarchae Josephi*), and the collection of apologetic and biblical dissertations he published when serving as professor of theology in Montefiascone. In the second section, I will concentrate primarily on Bonjour's biblical criticism and chronology, with a special focus on Bonjour's attitude towards various competing biblical texts as well as his interest in ancient Egyptian chronology. This section will primarily focus on Bonjour's unpublished *Antiquitas temporum*, a lengthy exposition of both the biblical chronology of the Vulgate and the infamous dynasties of Manetho. It will hope to show how, by the late seventeenth century, an increasing number of Christian chronologists made pagan, in particular Egyptian, chronology an essential piece of evidence when it came to establishing the true chronology of the biblical text. In the final section, I will examine Bonjour's work on ancient pagan idolatry – which is to say, the manner in which primitive ancient nations first diverged from the true religion, and the corresponding question of what the true nature of paganism was and how it related to the Christian religion – before going on to show how Bonjour mobilised this work within the context of the Chinese Rites debate. In doing so, I hope to show both how scholarship on ancient paganism informed scholarly conceptualisations of Chinese religion and how the comparison of pagan, Chinese, and Jewish idolatry led even "orthodox" scholars like Bonjour to increasingly view religion as an anthropological rather than merely theological entity, dependent as much on cultural context and linguistic expression as on the Christian dichotomy between true and false religion.

In each section, I will examine a specific aspect of Bonjour's scholarly interests and output and highlight how they reflect broader intellectual, religious, and scholarly changes in the late seventeenth century. In this sense, my work hopes to not merely reveal the scholarly contributions of a previously neglected figure but also those important influences, issues, and controversies which shaped the intellectual, scholarly, and apologetic context in which he produced them. Bonjour himself was neither a cause of nor a contributor to the decline of biblical authority; yet I will hope to show how his works were part of a more general scholarly development which helped make this decline possible. In the course of this, I hope also to fulfil the basic motivation for writing history which is as old as Herodotus: to elucidate the life of an erudite, important, yet forgotten scholar so that "the memory of the past may not be blotted out from among men by time" (1.1).[47]

---

[47] Translation from Herodotus, *The Persian Wars*, trans A. D. Godley (Cambridge MA: Harvard University Press, 1926).

CHAPTER 1

Guillaume Bonjour: His Life and His World

1 Bonjour in Toulouse

Bonjour was born in Toulouse in 1670, either in the last days of February or on 1 March.[1] His mother's maiden name was almost certainly "Fabri," which Aufrère and Bosson have suggested was a meridional version of Fèvre. Bonjour later took on the surname Fabri, sometimes francized as "Favre" or "Fabre," in a generally unsuccessful attempt to hide his Augustinian missionary identity when travelling through northern Europe to find passage to the Far East.[2] His father, meanwhile, may have been of Italian origin "and was called by many Buongiorno": so Bonjour told Cuper when the two met in Deventer.[3] The Augustinian Basile Rasseguier (1659–1734), a close friend of Bonjour's who followed him from Toulouse to Rome in 1696 and who was later responsible for cataloguing Bonjour's manuscripts in the Biblioteca Angelica, described Bonjour's parents simply as "civils et pieux."[4] Of the rest of Bonjour's background or family we know next to nothing, save for the fact that he was in some way related to the French official Jacques de Clary.[5] A *conseiller au*

---

1 There is some debate as to this date. Sydney Aufrère and Nathalie Bosson claim that he was born on 26 or 27 of February, cf. "Introduction," *Elementa Linguae Copticae*, xl. In this they are followed by Baldini, "Guillaume Bonjour," 242. However, their evidence is a colophon at BAR, ms.or.67, 245, which states that on 23 March Bonjour is 29 years and 23 days old. The colophon can be viewed in Georg Zoëga, *Catalogus codicum Copticorum manu scriptorum qui in Museo Borgiano* (Rome: Congregationis de Propaganda fide, 1810), 3. The date of 1 March would also agree with a contemporary biography by Giacinto Gimma: *Elogj Academici della Società di deglie Spensierati di Rossano Parte II* (Napoli: Carlo Troise, 1703), 344.
2 Aufrère and Bosson, "Introduction," *Elementa Linguae Copticae*, xl–xli; Baldini, "Guillaume Bonjour," 242, n. 1.
3 KW 72 H 20: "addebatque patrem originem Italum esse, dictosque majores Buon Giorno." Aufrère and Bosson claim that the name Bonjour originates from the Puy de Dôme: "Introduction," xl. Initially I considered Bonjour's statement an admission that his father *was* of Italian origin; but the context of the admission might also imply that Bonjour invented the Italian origin of his father in the context of acquiring Roman citizenship for his mission to China. See the relevant discussion of Bonjour's journey to China in chapter 7.
4 On Rasseguier: "Regestum Antonii Pacini III, 1695–1696," AGA, DD135, 300; "Index Manuscriptorum; a P. Basilio Rasseguier patria Tholosano, in hac Bibliotheca per 30. ferme annos substituto et die 14. Martii anni 1734," BAR, ms.lat.1078; Aufrère and Bosson, "Introduction," xl, xliv–xlv.
5 I have not been able to identify dates or any more specific biographical information on this Jacques de Clary.

parlement first in Toulouse and later in Paris, Jacques belonged to the noble family of Clary, or "Claris," which originated from the small hill-top town of Cordes-sur-Ciel some seventy kilometres northeast of Toulouse.[6] In a letter to Magliabechi from July 1697, Bonjour called him "Giacomo, Baron de Clari ... mio amico singulare ed ancora cugino," my singular friend and also cousin.[7]

In the seventeenth century Toulouse was something akin to a hotbed of Jansenism, in particular during the archbishopric of Charles de Montchal (1589–1651) and after the founding of the devotional Institut des filles d'enfance de Jésus-Christ by Madame de Mondonville (1624–1703) and Gabriel de Ciron (1619–1675) in 1661/2.[8] In Bonjour's life, Jansenism, or at least Jansenist sympathies, remained a constant background presence, as we shall see, although it is doubtful whether they had much direct influence on his work. In any case, as Robert Schneider notes, by the 1680s Jansenism in Toulouse was in sharp decline and in 1686 the Institut was forcibly disbanded.[9] Yet Toulouse remained a thriving municipal city in which religion, scholarship, and art routinely intersected. In the Dominican Church of the Jacobins was situated the head of Thomas Aquinas, the finest altar John Locke (1632–1704) had ever seen; for more than thirty years the city had been the home of Pierre Fermat (1607–1665); and in the year of Bonjour's birth, Pierre Bayle (1647–1706), then a good Roman Catholic, was studying at the local Jesuit college.[10] Moreover, Toulouse was home to one of the oldest and most prestigious French universities, at which each of the four mendicant Orders held a chair in theology, and home also to one of the oldest literary institutions in the Christian West, the *Jeux Floraux*, a lyric poetry festival which was recognized as a royal academy in 1694. Bonjour, however, was not educated by the Jesuits as so many of his contemporaries were, nor did he study at Toulouse's great university. Instead, at the age of fifteen, he joined the Order of Hermits of Saint Augustine (OESA).

Although there were different communities calling themselves Augustinians and living under the Rule, or *Regula*, of Augustine in the early thirteenth century, the formal union of these disparate elements occurred only with the

---

6   Louis de la Roque, *Armorial de la noblesse de Languedoc. Generalité de Toulouse* (Toulouse and Paris: Delboy Fils, E. Dentu and Aug. Aubry, 1863), 1:194–195.

7   Guillaume Bonjour to Antonio Magliabechi, 13 July 1697 and 14 September 1697, BNCF, *Fondo Magliabechiano* VIII, cod. 317, fols. 16r, 18r.

8   Sandra La Rocca, "L'institut des Filles de l'Enfance: le Port-Royal toulousain?" in *Toulouse, une métropole méridionale: Vingt siècles de vie urbaine*, ed. Bernadette Suau, Jean-Pierre Almaric, and Jean-Marc Olivier (Toulouse: Presses universitaires du Midi, 2009), 613–623.

9   Robert A. Schneider, *Public Life in Toulouse, 1463–1789: From Municipal Republic to Cosmopolitan City* (Ithaca NY: Cornell University Press, 1989), 191–219.

10 John Lough, ed., *Locke's Travels in France 1675–1679. As related in his Journals, Correspondence and other papers* (Cambridge: Cambridge University Press, 1953), 139.

papal bull *Licet Ecclesiae* of April 1256.[11] As a mendicant Order, the Augustinian hermits were, as a collective, not allowed to possess property, but they were allowed what were known as *bona immobilia* and held what could be termed fairly moderate opinions on such questions as poverty, fasting, and discipline.[12] The primary guide for monastic life remained the *Regula*, which was supplemented by an official constitution. Even in the seventeenth century, this constitution remained largely the same as that promulgated at Ratisbon in 1290 and amended by Thomas of Strasburg (d. 1357) in the mid-fourteenth century; the last minor changes to the constitution came in a redraft of 1686, after which it remained unchanged for the following two hundred years. Both the daily life and the structure of the Order were regulated according to this constitution, from the educational system to the colour and length of the habits to the recital of matins, mass, and vespers. Although the frequency of these recitals was dependent on the number of religious at a convent, Bonjour spent his life at two of the largest convents the Augustinians possessed and it is highly likely that he practiced these recitals daily. For the erudite religious, pious scholarship was matched by daily piety.

Different religious had different reasons for joining different Orders. Not all these reasons should always be taken at face value. The Augustinian Order in particular prided itself for its close relationship with its eponymous "founder" and a common theme which emerges from Augustinians of this period is their particular veneration for the writings of Augustine. This was prominently so in the case of perhaps the greatest Augustinian scholar of the seventeenth century, Enrico Noris, who first studied with the Jesuits in Rimini before joining the Augustinian Order after supposedly falling in love with the Church Fathers and above all Augustine, whom he read twice.[13] Whether this is wholly true is debatable. Léon-Gabriel Pélissier, the French historian who published a number of Noris (and Bonjour's) letters at the turn of the twentieth century, pointed to Noris' love for fine wine, gelato, an ample salary, and other material comforts

---

11 See David Gutierrez and John Gavigan, *The History of the Order of St. Augustine* (Villanova: Augustinian Press, 1971–), 1; Max Heimbucher, *Die Orden und Kongregationen der katholischen Kirche* (Paderborn: Ferdinand Schöningh, 1933–34), 539–571; and for a contemporary history Luigi Torelli, *Secoli Agostiniani overo Historia generale del Sagro Ordine Eremitano del Gran Dottore di Santa Chiesa S. Aurelio Agostino vescovo d'Hippona* (Bologna: Giacomo Monti, 1659–1686).

12 See also Harold Samuel Stone, *St. Augustine's Bones: A Microhistory* (Amherst and Boston: University of Massachusetts Press, 2002), 38–39.

13 Pietro and Girolamo Ballerini, "Henrici Norisii Cardinalis vita," in *Henrici Norisii Veronensis Augustiniani Opera Omnia*, ed. Pietro and Girolamo Ballerini (Verona: Typographia Tumarmaniana, 1728–1732), 4:xiii–xlii; Michael Klaus Wernicke, *Kardinal Enrico Noris und seine Verteidigung Augustins* (Würzburg: Augustinus-Verlag, 1973), 11.

as evidence that Noris joined the Order because it gave him the freedom and security to pursue his scholarly ambitions rather than on account of any particular religious zeal.[14] According to Pélissier (who appears to have delighted in his discovery), Noris was tantamount to an "épicurien," who mocked, if amicably, the austere piety of many of his *confrères*. Although Michael Klaus Wernicke, Noris' (Augustinian) biographer, is certainly right to point out that Noris demonstrated a very sincere love for Augustine throughout his life – and throughout the many polemical battles his notorious defence of Augustine engendered – it is clear that, particularly in Italy, religious Orders offered a convenient pathway for individuals who wanted to devote their life to scholarship.[15] This was, perhaps, especially so in the case of the Augustinians, for whom scholarship ranked above both missions and pastoral care as the chief merit of the Order.[16] Indeed, throughout the sixteenth and seventeenth centuries, the Augustinian Order still produced a number of distinguished if not necessarily exalted scholars, such as the humanist Giles of Viterbo (1472–1532), the theologian Girolamo Seripando (1493–1563), the Veronese antiquarian and historian Onofrio Panvinio (1529–1568), the biblical scholar and poet Luis de Léon (1527–1591), the Louvain-based Church historian Christian Lupus (1612–1681), and the French ecclesiastical geographer Augustin Lubin (1624–1695). Noris' scholarship itself was quite clearly shaped by the example of Panvinio, a fellow Veronese and a leading authority on Roman chronology, as well as the advice of Lupus, whom Noris served as a quasi-assistant while Lupus was in Rome to defend himself from charges of Jansenism between 1655 and 1660.[17] As for Bonjour, it is clear not only from his life-long commitment to scholarship but also the speed with which his education progressed while in Toulouse that the Augustinian commitment to learning proved a significant draw to the Order.[18] In addition, we should note two things that might further explain Bonjour's commitment to the monastic life: firstly, that throughout his life Bonjour was continually praised by his contemporaries for his piety; and secondly, that within seventeenth-century Toulouse the Augustinian Order, and its convent, took a prominent place within the scholarly and religious life of the city.[19]

---

14   Léon-Gabriel Pélissier, ed., "Le cardinal Henri de Noris et sa correspondance," in *Studi e documenti di storia e diritto* (Rome: Tipografia Vaticana, 1890), 11:27–32. Cf. Aufrère and Bosson, "Introduction," xliv.
15   Wernicke, *Kardinal Enrico Noris*, 11.
16   Heimbucher, *Die Orden*, 554.
17   See Lucien Ceyssens, "Chrétien Lupus: sa période janséniste," *Augustiniana* 16 (1965): 264–312.
18   Cf. Baldini, "Guillaume Bonjour," 243–246.
19   Pierre Salies, *Les Augustins, origine, construction et vie du grand couvent toulousain au Moyen âge, XIIIe–XVIe siècles* (Toulouse: Architra, 1979).

Toulouse-Aquitaine was one of four Augustinian provinces in France and contained the largest monastery in the country outside of Paris – today it is a museum of fine arts. Initially established in 1310, it had been almost entirely destroyed in a fire which engulfed most of the city in 1463 before being rebuilt and expanded over the following two centuries.[20] At its peak in around 1500 – shortly before the influence of the Order's black sheep Luther helped lead a mass exodus of religious across Europe – the convent contained some 200 friars; by the late seventeenth century it contained less than 60 and perhaps as few as 31.[21] Nevertheless, the convent still maintained a reputation for learning and was large enough to offer the *studium generalis*, or *maius*, which offered education in all faculties of the arts as well as theology, rather than the more limited *studium provincialis*, or *minus*, which pertained merely to the propaedeutic study of logic.[22] Since we know that Bonjour was a *lector* in early 1693 and professor of theology before his departure in 1695, he likely entered the novitiate at the age of fifteen: it was also following the novitiate that he likely took on, as was customary, the name of "Guillaume," in possible reference to either the famous fourteenth-century Augustinian theologian and mystic William of Toulouse or, further back, to the religious community of Williamites who joined the Augustinian Order in the union of 1256.[23]

During the following years, Bonjour would have completed the traditional *studium*, which included one year of grammar and logic and three years of philosophy and some elementary theology, before being allowed to pass on to the advanced study of theology which was reserved only for exceptional students.[24] At that time, the dominant theologians in the curriculum remained Aquinas and then Augustine (with a specific focus on Augustine's writings

---

20 See Raynal, *Histoire*, 425; Jules Chalande, "Histoire des rues de Toulouse: 229. – Le couvent des Augustins (Rue du Musée)," *Mémoires de l'Académie des sciences, inscriptions et belles-lettres de Toulouse*, series 11, 9 (1921): 142–148; Henri Rachou, "Le couvent des Augustins," *Congrès archéologique de France. XCII^e session tenue a Toulouse en 1929 par la Société Française d'Archéologie* (Paris: Picard and Ste Génle d'Imprimerie, 1930), 120–133; and Augustin Lubin, *Orbis Augustinianus sive conventuum ordinis eremitarum sancti Augustini chorographica & topographica descriptio* (Paris: Giles Alliot, 1672), 11, 57.

21 See the different estimations in Gutierrez and Gavigan, *The History of the Order*, 1, part 2: 61, and 2:107; Aufrère and Bosson, "Introduction," xli; Baldini, "Guillaume Bonjour," 243, n. 9.

22 *Constitutiones Ordinis F. F. Eremitarum Sancti Augustini Recognitae, & in ampliorem formam ac ordinem redactae* (Rome: Haeredum Corbelletti, 1686), 397–398. Augustinians at smaller convents were expected either to move to a larger convent or attend one of the major French universities.

23 Aufrère and Bosson, "Introduction," xli.

24 *Constitutiones Ordinis*, 406–411; Aufrère and Bosson, "Introduction," xl–xliii; Baldini, "Guillaume Bonjour," 243–246.

concerning Grace, predestination, and "disputationibus iis annexis"), as well as the work of the late thirteenth- and early fourteenth-century Augustinian theologian Giles of Rome (Egidio Colonna, c.1243–1316), who was confirmed as the official theologian of the Order at the general chapters of 1465 and 1491. To this was added a healthy sprinkling of other Augustinian theologians, in particular the work of Gregory of Rimini (1300–1358), who also lectured on what remained one of the central propaedeutic texts in theological education, Peter of Lombard's *Sentences* (mid-twelfth century).[25] Before Bonjour's arrival one of the most celebrated teachers at the convent was Fulgence Lafosse (c.1640–c.1684), who is mentioned in Bonjour's *Mercurius* and who published his *Theologia secundum genium S. P. Augustini* in Toulouse in 1672 but who moved to Bordeaux in 1683.[26] Instead, it appears that Bonjour's primary teacher – "il maèstro principale che hò havuto nella relligione [sic] di S. Agostino," as Bonjour wrote to Magliabechi – was a certain Bernard Lapeyre. Of Lapeyre we know very little. According to Bonjour, he was a *nipote* of the Augustinian theologian Jean Dupuy, or Johannes Puteanus (d. 1623), the erstwhile royal professor at Toulouse whose major work, a three-volume commentary on Aquinas's *Summa*, appeared posthumously in 1627.[27] Yet it appears that Lapeyre was, at that time, an Augustinian theologian of some standing: provincial of Toulouse, an acquaintance of Noris (whom he later visited in Italy), and, by the 1690s, the *Docteur Regent* and holder of the Augustinian chair in theology at the University of Toulouse.[28] We do not know, however, of any publications, and he is missing even from Augustinian histories of the Order and its learned representatives.

---

25 *Constitutiones Ordinis*, 399–401; Gutierrez and Gavigan, *The History of the Order*, 4:230; cf. Domenico Antonio Gandolfo, *Dissertatio historica de ducentis celeberrimis Augustinianis scriptoribus ex illis, qui obierunt post magnam unionem Ordinis Eremitici usque ad finem Tridentini Concilii* (Rome: Giovanni Francesco Buagni, 1704), 20.

26 Aufrère and Bosson, "Introduction," xlii; Baldini, "Guillaume Bonjour," 244–245. Cf. Léon Renwart, "Fulgence Lafosse O.E.S.A.: Représentant méconnu de l'école augustienne," *Augustiniana* 42 (1992): 173–206.

27 Guillaume Bonjour to Antonio Magliabechi, 30 May 1699, 6 June 1699, and 18 May 1705, BNCF, *Fondo Magliabechiano* VIII, cod. 317, fols. 46r, 48r, 95r. On Puteanus see Torelli, *Secoli Agostiniani*, 8:534; Johann Felix Ossinger, *Bibliotheca Augustiniana historica, critica, et chronologica* (Ingoldstadt and Augsburg: Joannis Francisci Xaverii Craetz, 1768), 723–724; and Gutierrez and Gavigan, *The History of the Order*, 2:161.

28 "Regestum Antonii Pacini II, 1694–1695," AGA, DD134, 330; and see the approbation of Pierre Alabert, *Traité du sacrement de mariage avec les plus belles décisions prises du droit canonique & civil* (Toulouse: J. J. Boude, 1699). At the University of Toulouse each of the four mendicant orders held a chair in theology: see L. W. B. Brockliss, *French Higher Education in the Seventeenth and Eighteenth Centuries* (Oxford: Clarendon Press, 1987), 33.

It was during his formative years in Toulouse that Bonjour already began to shape his own scholarly proclivities. In later years, he spoke of this development to Cuper, who noted:

> Guillaume also recalled that as a young man he was truly dedicated to poetry, but abandoned that study, when he noticed that it was occupied around exquisite words and ways of speaking, and that it accordingly contained nothing solid, and he recalled that, from then on, so greatly wearied by poetry and also by philosophy and scholastic theology, to which he had also given his diligent effort, he devoted himself to sacred scripture itself, and to the Greek, Hebrew, Syriac, Arabic, and Coptic languages, and to the customs and ritual of ancient times, both those which in the west and in the east were in use among the Greeks and Romans. And so many observations hence arose by themselves; and he composed a book on the dynasties of the Egyptians, which he left in manuscript in the hands of the most reverend Adeodato Nuzzi.[29]

Although these interests diverged somewhat from the traditional Augustinian *studium*, they were not uncommon for scholars of the Order. Indeed, throughout the period, an increasing number of prominent Augustinians were turning their attention away from scholastic or speculative theology and towards topics related to antiquarianism, geography, and, above all, ecclesiastical history.[30] In the sixteenth century these interests were primarily exemplified by Onofrio Panvinio, who became that century's great authority on the Roman *Fasti*, the list of Roman consuls which formed the chronological bedrock for ancient Roman and therefore also early Christian history. In the seventeenth century, this tradition was partly represented by Lupus, who published an important, seven-volume study of various ancient Church councils between 1665 and

---

29   KW 72 H 20: "Referebat etiam Guielmus sese juvenem valde poeticae deditum fuisse, sed studium illud abjecisse, cum animadverteret, versari circa voces et exquisitos loquendi modos, et ita nihil solidi continere, atque inde pertaesum poëticam, et etiam philosophiam atque adeo Theologiam scholasticam, cui etiam diligentem operam dederat, sese contulisse ad ipsam sacram scripturam, linguasque Graecam, Hebraeam, Syram, Arabicam et Coptam vel Aegyptiam, veterumque temporum mores, ritum, tam qui in oriente quam occidente apud Graecos n. et Romanos, in usu fuerunt. Atque ipsi natas esse tot observationes; et composuisse librum de Dynastiis Aegyptiorum quem mss reliquit inter manus Reverendissimi viri Adeodati Nuzzi."

30   See Francis Roth, "Augustinian Historians of the xviith Century," *Augustiniana* 6 (1956): 635–658. Roth calls the seventeenth century "a golden era of Augustinian historiography" (635).

1682, and by Lubin, who was appointed royal geographer by Louis XIV. By far the most celebrated scholar in this regard however was Noris, who once wrote to Magliabechi that his passion for ecclesiastical history was so great that as a young man he had continued his clandestine research at night after his superiors had ordered him to direct his attention elsewhere.[31] In particular, Noris' work exemplified a committed interest in both recondite antiquarianism and positive theology, drawing out chronological and cultural information on the ancient world through his study of obscure texts and ancient coins while also grounding his theological arguments on a detailed, contextual, and critical study of early Church history. Having first made his name with the learned if controversial *Historia pelagiana* in 1673, in which he traced the origins of Pelagianism back to Origen and accused the Jesuits of being heirs of semi-Pelagianism, Noris spent the following twenty years as professor of ecclesiastical history and sacred scripture in Florence and Pisa, during which he published authoritative antiquarian studies on a Pisan cenotaph dedicated to the adopted sons of Augustus, Gaius and Lucius, and on the hitherto unknown chronological epochs of the ancient Syrians.[32] By 1692, he had firmly established himself as one of the leading lights of European scholarship – the French antiquarian Claude Nicaise (1623–1701) called him "like the dictator of the Republic of Letters" – and in the same year he was appointed *custos* of the Vatican library following the death of the Flemish historian Emmanuel Schelstrate (1649–1692).[33] It seems clear that Noris' stock was as high among the Augustinians in Toulouse as it was among the Catholic hierarchy in Rome: an oration celebrating Noris by Lapeyre – the "Distichi in laudem Eminentissimi Cardinalis De Noris" – can be found among Bonjour's papers, while Thomas Bouges (1667–1741), Bonjour's *confrère* and companion in his earliest chronological studies in Toulouse, serenaded Noris in a poem he submitted to the *Jeux Floraux*.[34] It therefore appears that Bonjour – partly due to the reputation

31 See Enrico Noris to Antonio Magliabechi, [undated], BNCF, *Fondo Magliabechiano* VIII, cod. 294, fol. 257r; and Wernicke, *Kardinal Enrico Noris*, 15–16.
32 Enrico Noris, *Historia Pelagiana & dissertatio de synodo v. oecumenica* (Padua: Pietro Maria Frambotti, 1673); Enrico Noris, *Cenotaphia pisana Caii et Lucii Caesarum dissertationibus illustrata* (Venice: Paulo Balleoni, 1681); and Enrico Noris, *Annus et epochae syromacedonum in vetustis urbium Syriae nummis praesertim Mediceis expositae* (Leipzig: Thomas Fritsch, 1696) (first edition Florence, 1689).
33 Claude Nicaise to Guillaume Bonjour, 10 October 1697, BAR, ms.lat.395, fols. 151r–152v, reprinted in Léon-Gabriel Pélissier, ed., "Lettres inédites de Claude Nicaise a Huet et a G. Bonjour tirées des bibliothèques italiennes (1679–1701)," *Bulletin d'histoire & d'archéologie religieuses du diocèse de Dijon* 7 (Dijon: Damongeot et Cle, 1889), 193.
34 Bernard Lapeyre, "Distichia in laudem Eminentissimi Cardinalis de Noris," BAR, ms.lat.635, fol. 112r; Thomas Bouges, "Sonnet a la louange," BAR, ms.lat.635, fol. 122r.

and example of Noris – did not face the same strictures which once bedevilled a young Noris' researches in ancient history. It is noticeable that Bonjour described *il mio maestro* Lapeyre as not only "very learned in philosophy, and without an equal in theology whether scholastic, polemical, or moral" but also as "delighting even more in the study of medals."[35] Bonjour's early scholarship was shaped by this same interest.[36] When Bonjour, alongside his companion Bouges, first reached out to Noris in late 1692, their discussion centred on the chronology of Christ and the genealogy of the Herods, with a particular focus on a recently discovered medal which purported to date the beginning of the reign of Herod Antipas, Herod the Great's successor in Galilee.[37]

It was also through this numismatic interest that Bonjour first came into contact with scholars outside of the Augustinian community. Of particular importance was his early acquaintance with Jean-Pierre Rigord (1656–1727), a naval officer based in Marseille who had studied at the Oratory in Paris but later abandoned Saint-Sulpice and the religious life in favour of an administrative career which allowed him to indulge in his passion for numismatics.[38] By the late 1680s Rigord had become part of a distinguished network of antiquarian and numismatic scholars which included Raffaello Fabretti (1620–1700) in Rome, Nicolas Toinard (1628–1706), Jean Foy-Vaillant (1632–1706), André Morell (1646–1703), and Ezekiel Spanheim in Paris, Antoine Pagi (1624–1699) in Aix, Gisbert Cuper in The Hague, and the *bête noire* Jean Hardouin (1646–1729), who was then engaged in an acrimonious numismatic dispute with Noris.[39] Around the same time, he also came into direct contact with Noris and helped facilitate the path of Noris' works into France through his acquaintance with a Florentine merchant in Marseille called Bartoli. As part of his administrative duties Rigord

---

35   Guillaume Bonjour to Antonio Magliabechi, 30 May 1699, BNCF, *Fondo Magliabechiano* VIII, cod. 317, fol. 46r: "Lui è dottissimo nella philosophia, non ha pari nella Theologia tanto scholastica che polemica e morale. E benche avanzato nell'eta, faversi per excellenza. Si diletta di piu nello studio delle medaglie."

36   See on numismatism and antiquarianism more generally Arnaldo Momigliano, "Ancient History and the Antiquarian," *Journal of the Warburg and Courtauld Institutes* 13 (1950): 285–315.

37   Enrico Noris to Guillaume Bonjour and Thomas Bouges, 2 September 1692, BAR, ms.lat.395, fols. 240r–241r.

38   Émile Perrier, "Jean-Pierre Rigord," in *Les bibliophiles et les collectionneurs provençaux anciens et modernes* (Marseille: Barthelet, 1897), 451–459.

39   See the relevant letters in Enrico Noris, "Lettera del Card. Noris," in Enrico Noris, *Istoria delle investiture delle dignità ecclesiastiche scritta dal Padre Noris* (Mantua: Alberto Tumarmani, 1741) and Léon-Gabriel Pélissier, ed., "Lettres de l'abbé Nicaise au cardinal Noris (1686–1701)," *Le bibliographe moderne courrier international des archives et des bibliothèques* 7 (Paris: 38, Rue Gay-Lussac, 1903), 176–214.

often undertook journeys through the regions of Guyenne, Gascony, Béarn, and Languedoc, and in 1693 he visited the convent of the Augustinians where, as he wrote to Nicolas Toinard, he met Bonjour and Bouges already working on a complex, expansive chronological system for ancient history.[40] What is more, it was Rigord who had initially acquired the aforementioned, much-debated coin depicting Herod Antipas which became the subject of Bonjour and Noris' correspondence and it was he who published the first learned dissertation on the subject in 1689.[41] In his letter to Bonjour of September 1692, Noris therefore advised Bonjour to get in touch with Rigord – "qui Tolosae pluribus est notus" – personally.[42] In the following months, the two became friends. At one point, Bonjour even visited Rigord's antiquarian cabinet in Marseille, where he inspected a coin depicting a beardless Osiris with a mysterious inscription. This coin had previously been discussed by Rigord and his antiquarian friend, the Nîmes-based lawyer François Graverol (1636–1694), and Bonjour later used it as a key piece of evidence in his *Mercurius aegyptiorum* and *De nomine patriarchae*.[43] It also appears that it was Rigord who introduced Bonjour to one of his closest friends, the French official and equally enthusiastic antiquarian Michel (or "Le Grand") Bégon (1638–1710), who a few years before had been responsible for obtaining for Rigord the post of commissioner of the navy in Marseille. At some point in late 1694 or early 1695, Bonjour stayed for a week at Bégon's house in Rochefort, where he inspected Bégon's collection of Egyptian antiquities. In an episode somewhat illustrative of Bonjour's early scholarly interests, Bonjour examined there an Egyptian tomb from which, according to Bégon, he proceeded to draw out the entire compendium of Egyptian mythology in a manner reminiscent of the extravagant, esoteric interpretations of

---

40   Jean-Pierre Rigord to Nicolas Toinard, 10 May 1693, BNF, NAF 563, fol. 194v. Cf. Jean-Pierre Rigord, "Article CLXXVIII; Lettre de M. Rigord Commissaire de la Marine aux Auteurs des Memoirs de Trévoux sur un Livre qui a pour titre *Monumenta Coptica*," *Journal de Trévoux* (1703): 1878–1879.

41   Jean-Pierre Rigord, *Dissertation historique sur une médaille d'Hérodes Antipas* (Marseille: Jean Anisson, 1689); Enrico Noris, "Epistola ad P. Ant. Pagium," in *Annus et epochae syromacedonum*, 62–80; Emmanuel Schelstrate, *Antiquitas ecclesiae, dissertationibus, monimentis ac notis illustrata* (Rome: Propaganda fide, 1692), 1:27–34. For an overview of the later discussion on this contentious coin, see Louis Jobert, *La science des médailles nouvelle édition*, ed. Joseph de Bimard de La Bastie (Paris: De Bure, 1739), 2:443–444.

42   Enrico Noris to Guillaume Bonjour and Thomas Bouges, 2 September 1692, BAR, ms.lat.395, fol. 241r.

43   François Graverol and Jean-Pierre Rigord, *Dissertation de Monsieur Graverol avocat de Nismes à Monsieur Rigord de Marseille, sur l'explication d'une médaille grecque qui porte le nom du dieu Pan* (Marseille: Jean Anisson, 1689); *Mercurius*, fol. 37r–v; *De nomine*, 9–11. See Guillaume Bonjour to Gisbert Cuper, 10 February 1698, KW 72 H 20.

Athanasius Kircher.[44] Despite Bégon's somewhat lukewarm evaluation of Bonjour's ambitious interpretation, both he and Rigord remained friends and key contacts for Bonjour throughout his time in Rome, informing French scholars of Bonjour's projects, sending Bonjour new material from their *cabinets*, and helping distribute Bonjour's works to booksellers in France, including the famous bookshop of the royal printer Jean Anisson (1642–1721) in Paris.[45]

Meanwhile, in Toulouse, Bonjour was hard at work. From a mixture of ancient coins and texts in not only Latin and Greek but also in Hebrew, Arabic, and Syriac, he was investigating those secrets of Egyptian antiquity which he had partially observed on Bégon's tomb. As we have already noted in the introduction, Bonjour's interest in ancient Egypt stemmed from its particular connection with the sacred history of the Bible. The work he produced, the *Mercurius aegyptiorum Josephus patriarcha*, made this connection explicit: through the tangled thicket of pagan mythology, those corrupted fragments of profane *fabula*, Bonjour spied the original sacred history of the biblical patriarch Joseph. In Toulouse, Rigord watched his scholarship advance

---

44   Michel Bégon to Esprit Cabart de Villermont, 31 January 1700, in "Lettres de Michel Bégon," *Archives historiques de la Saintonge et de l'Aunis*, ed. Louis Delavaud and Charles Dangibeaud (Paris and Saintes: A. Picard and Delavaud, 1930), 48:10–11: "J'ay eu icy, il y a cinq ou six ans, pendant sept ou huit jours, le P. Bonjour, dont je fis à peu près le mesme jugement que celuy que vous me mandez en avoir esté fait par Mr Piques, auquel je crois avoir dit que dans l'explication qu'il avoit faite de mon tombeau Egyptien il en avoit parlé à l'avanture, comme le P. Kirker a fait des obélisques de Rome. Cependant cet homme estant très jeune et s'apliquant, comme il fait, aux langues orientales qui ne sont point la magie noire, il n'y a pas lieu de douter qu'il n'y fasse un gran progrèz, et qu'il se sçache aujourd'huy, ce qu'il ne sçavoit pas lorsqu'il n'a pû répondre aux questions de Mr Piques." See also Michel Bégon to Claude Nicaise, 24 February 1697, BNF, Français 9361, fol. 88v; Michel Bégon to Claude Nicaise, 5 May 1699, BNF, Français 9360, fols. 344r–345v. Only one letter by Bégon to Bonjour remains in BAR, Michel Bégon to Guillaume Bonjour, 30 December 1696, ms.lat.395, BAR, fol. 205r. This letter was mis-identified by Baldini, "Guillaume Bonjour," 285, as being from Rigord. Other letters either do not survive or are held in private collections: a letter by Bonjour addressed to Bégon was recently sold among a collection of Bégon's correspondence by the auction house Aguttes after the liquidation of Aristophil in 2018 (lot no. 79, BÉGON MICHEL (1637–1710) INTENDANT DE LA MARINE, ÉRUDIT ET COLLECTIONNEUR, L.A.S., 1688–1712). Bégon's letter to Bonjour in BAR is reprinted in Exupère Caillemer, ed., *Lettres de divers savants à l'abbé Nicaise publiées pour l'academie des sciences, belles-lettres et arts de Lyon* (Lyon: Association Typographique, 1885), 187.

45   See Jean-Pierre Rigord to Guillaume Bonjour, 18 January 1700, BAR, ms.lat.395, BAR, fol. 206r; and Honoré Rigord to Guillaume Bonjour, 15 September 1699, BAR, ms.lat.395, fol. 194r. Pierre-Daniel Huet was just one of the many scholars who procured copies of Bonjour's books from Anisson.

with interest and wrote of its development to Magliabechi in Florence.[46] In August 1694, Bonjour's manuscript was first submitted for inspection to the rector of Toulouse-Aquitaine province Guillaume Abraham and the prior of the Augustinian convent Fulgence Courbiat.[47] It seems that Bonjour was asked to revise his manuscript further, although no reasons are given. Then, on 22 March 1695, he was given permission to travel to Rome.[48] There seem to be two distinct reasons for this decision: firstly, because it would allow Bonjour to revise his manuscript further under the guidance of Noris; secondly, because it was suggested that Bonjour might find it easier to locate the Oriental type-face necessary for printing the Hebrew, Syriac, and Arabic characters which he had come to include in the *Mercurius*. In addition, it seems that Noris welcomed the opportunity to work alongside this talented young scholar and personally facilitated his transfer. With that, the die was cast: in the autumn of 1695, Bonjour set off for Rome.[49]

2   Bonjour in Rome

In Rome one had to be careful that one didn't trip over the many antiquities scattered around the banks of the Tiber. According to what was almost certainly an apocryphal story, an Italian gentleman called Malatesta Strinati (1642–1720) spent almost 60 hours underground after falling into a crevasse in the Mausoleum of Cecilia before he was able to clamber to safety.[50] Though the greatest age of the city had long passed, Rome remained an extraordinary melting pot of Renaissance art, pagan relics, popular superstition, noble patronage, scientific experiments, archaeological excavations, and valuable antiquities. There one could visit, in the Palazzo Borghese, a room filled with Titian; in the Pantheon, supported by columns taken from the temple of Isis,

---

46 Jean-Pierre Rigord to Antonio Magliabechi, 4 September 1695, BNCF, *Fondo Magliabechiano* VIII, cod. 341, fols. 28secondo(r)–29r [the numbering is faulty for this manuscript, and the number 28 duplicated].
47 "Regestum Antonii Pacini II, 1694–1695," AGA, DD134, 170.
48 "Regestum Antonii Pacini II, 1694–1695," AGA, DD134, 349.
49 As stated in Jean-Pierre Rigord to Antonio Magliabechi, 4 September 1695 (as above) and Guillaume Bonjour to Antonio Magliabechi, 22 September 1696, BNCF, *Fondo Magliabechiano* VIII, cod. 317, fol. 3r–v.
50 As told in Maximilien Misson, *A new voyage to Italy. With curious observations on several other countries; as, Germany; Switzerland; Savoy; Geneva; Flanders; and Holland. Together with useful instructions for those who shall travel thither* (London: R. Bonwicke, Ja. Tonson, W. Freemen, Tim. Goodwin, J. Walthoe, M. Wotton, S. Manship, B. Tooker, J. Nicholson, R. Parker, and R. Smith, 1714), 2:158.

the tomb of Raphael; in the prison of the Castello Sant'Angelo, the medic and heterodox theologian Giuseppe Francesco Borri (1627–1695), still conducting his various alchemical experiments; in the vast Roman crypts, the bodies of what legend held were Christian saints and martyrs; in the Basilica di San Giovanni in Laterano, the Ark of the Covenant, the rods of Moses and Aaron, and the foreskin of Christ; and, outside that same Basilica, a great Egyptian obelisk, laying bear "to the Eyes of the Publick the Secrets of their *Divinity*, *Astrology*, *Metaphysick*, *Magick*, and all the other Sciences that were cultivated by the *Egyptians*."[51] The Huguenot Maximilien Misson (1650–1722), author of this description and traveller to Rome in the 1690s, mocked many of these displays of Catholic ostentation. Like Luther before him, he noted the almost infinite number of courtesans and the similarities between the Rome of the ancient heathens and that of the present Catholic hierarchy.[52] He scoffed at the myth of Peter in Rome and embraced the myth of Pope Joan.[53] Yet even he could not help marvel at the splendour of Rome's antiquity and its art:

> The first and general Prospect of *Rome* does not present any surprizing Beauties to the Beholder, especially if he has already seen several other large and fine Cities: but the longer he stays in it, far the more the Discoveries of Things doth he make, that deserve to be consider'd. You meet frequently with some Remainders of its ancient Grandour, that that haughty Mistress of the Universe was wont to enrich herself with. The best Spoils of her conquer'd Provinces; *Porphyries*, *Granites*, and the finest oriental *Marble*; were more common there than Bricks, or Stones that were dug out of her own Quarries. The Statues of *Rome* have been call'd a *Great Nation*; and we may add not unfitly, that the *Colosses* were the Giants. This proud City was adorn'd with Temples, Palaces, Theatres, *Naumachias*, Triumphal Arches, Baths, Cirques, Hippodromes, Columns, Fountains, Aqueducts, Obelisks, *Mausolaeums*, and other magnificent Structures; but now all these Things may be truly said to be bury'd in their own Ruins, tho' these Ruins, as dismal as they are, seem still to retain something more or less of their ancient Splendor.[54]

---

51   As reported by Misson, *A new voyage to Italy*. See on the Palazzo Borghese, 2:9; 2:69–70; on the Pantheon, 2:9–11; on Borri, 2:31; on the crypts, 2:161; on the Basilica di San Giovanni di Laterano, 2:148; and for the quote on the Egyptian pillar, 2:105.
52   Misson, *A new voyage to Italy*, 2:215.
53   Misson, *A new voyage to Italy*, 2:79–80 and 2:122ff.
54   Misson, *A new voyage to Italy*, 2:4–5.

As Arnaldo Momigliano has pointed out, in seventeenth-century Italy scholarship remained the product of individual initiatives and personal contacts rather than the result of systematic instruction and collective projects.[55] Certainly there was no scholarly community close to rivalling the Bollandists of Antwerp, the Maurists of Paris, or even the Jansenists of Port-Royal. Yet Rome remained the epicentre of the Catholic ecclesiastical hierarchy and its various religious Orders, and as a result it still contained a diverse religious and scholarly community in constant flux. It was in this world of antiquarian and ecclesiastical scholarship that Bonjour moved. At the French Minim monastery of Trinità dei Monti on the Pincian hill, the future location of the greatest edition of Newton produced in eighteenth-century Italy, he befriended the French ecclesiastical historian François de la Porte, "mio amico singolarissimo," then writing a history of his home region of Narbonne;[56] at the Jesuit Collegio Romano, which, in the words of the great Maurist scholar Bernard de Montfaucon (1655–1741) "surpasses all the Monasteries in *Rome* in Magnitude, and magnificent Structure," he presented the Jesuit procurator general with copies of his books and befriended the Bollandist scholar Conrad Janninck (1650–1723), then in Rome to defend Daniel Papebroch (1628–1714) from the attacks of the Carmelites;[57] at the house of the Benedictine Maurists, he met the procurator general Claude Estiennot (1639–1699) and his successor Guillaume Laparre (1666–1741), who wrote of Bonjour's work to their illustrious colleagues at Saint-Germain-des-Près;[58] and in the Dominican monastery of Santa Maria sopra Minerva, where rested the tomb of Thomas Cajetan (1469–1534), he discussed Chinese antiquities with the Toulousian theologian Antonin Massoulié

---

55   Arnaldo Momigliano, "Gli studi classici di Scipione Maffei," in Arnaldo Momigliano, *Secondo contributo alla storia degli studi classici* (Rome: Edizioni di Storia e Letteratura, 1960), 255–256.

56   Guillaume Bonjour to Antonio Magliabechi, 23 June 1702, BNCF, *Fondo Magliabechiano* VIII, cod. 317, fol. 63r. He is also mentioned by Bernard de Montfaucon, *Diarium Italicum sive monumentorum veterum, bibliothecarum, musaeorum, & c.* (Paris: Jean Anisson, 1702), 229. I have not managed to establish any dates for La Porte.

57   Montfaucon, *Diarium Italicum*, 245. Translation from Bernard de Montfaucon, *The Travels of the Learned Father Montfaucon from Paris thro' Italy*, trans. John Henley (London: D. L. for E. Curll, E. Sanger, R. Gosling, W. Lewis, 1712), 238; see Conrad Janninck to Guillaume Bonjour, 5 May 1702, BAR, ms.lat.395, fol. 109r-v and Guillaume Bonjour to Antonio Magliabechi, 28 March 1699, BNCF, *Fondo Magliabechiano* VIII, cod. 317, fol. 42r.

58   Claude Estiennot to Jean Mabillon, 16 June 1699, Émile Gigas "Lettres des Bénédictines de la Congrégation de St. Maur 1652–1700," *Lettres inédites de divers savants de la fin du XVIIme et de commencement du XVIIIme siècle*, ed. Émile Gigas (Copenhagen: G.E.C. GAD, 1892), 2, part 1:247. Cf. Montfaucon, *Diarium Italicum*, 103.

(1632–1706), "one of the ablest Men in Divinity and Ecclesiastical Discipline" and assistant to their procurator general, Antonin Cloche (1628–1720).[59]

Moreover, even if Rome was lagging behind the cutting-edge patristic and text-critical scholarship of France and the Netherlands, it remained a place of pilgrimage for scholars throughout Europe. Whether the antiquarian cabinets of Livio Odescalchi (1652–1713) or Raffaello Fabretti (according to Montfaucon, "the greatest Antiquary of Rome"), the libraries of Girolamo Casanata (1620–1700), Pietro Ottoboni (1667–1740), and Giuseppe Renato Imperiali (1651–1737), or the edifice of the Propaganda fide, "furnish'd with printed Books almost in all Languages" so that young missionaries were prepared to "go into all the world, and preach the gospel to every creature," Rome remained a city unrivalled for its cultural and scholarly heritage, universally cherished for the number of its ancient treasures, the diversity of its antiquarian collections, and the riches of its numerous libraries.[60] And there was nothing in Europe to compare with the Vatican library, which, as Montfaucon noted, "far surpasses all others in the World in Extent and Magnificence."[61] Decorated with the paintings of Michelangelo, Raphael, Pinturicchio, Daniele da Volterra, and, to the Huguenot Misson's displeasure, Giorgio Vasari's triptych depicting the murder of Coligny, the library had been significantly expanded in the seventeenth century by the acquisition of the Heidelberg *Bibliotheca Palatina* (spoils of the Thirty Years War gifted to Pope Gregory XV by Maximilian I of Bavaria), the library of the Duke of Urbino, and the manuscripts of Queen Christina of Sweden.[62] By the late seventeenth century, it contained up to 25,000 manuscripts, including the famous Codex Vaticanus of the Greek Septuagint Bible, the love letters of Henry VIII to Anne Boleyn, and a handwritten German Bible, supposedly by Luther, which was inscribed with a derogatory poem and which the library's Catholic custodians could not refrain from showing to their Protestant

---

59   Antonin Massoulié to Guillaume Bonjour, 28 March 1705, BAR, ms.lat.395, fols. 61r–63v. The quote is from Montfaucon, *The Travels*, 283–4, a translation of Montfaucon, *Diarium Italicum*, 246: "ingenio vir aliisque animi dotibus praestans, & P. Massoulier Assistens, ut vocant, in primis fertur qui Theologiam disciplinasque Ecclesiasticas profitentur."

60   Misson, *A new voyage to Italy*, 2:20–28; 2:108; Montfaucon, *Diarium Italicum*, 273, 276–8. See also Jacques-François Deseine, *Rome moderne, première ville de l'Europe, avec tout ses magnificences et ses delices* (Leiden, Pierre vander Aa, 1713), 4:1080–1084. Bonjour met Deseine while the French traveller was in Rome: Guillaume Bonjour to Claude Nicaise, 21 July 1699 in Caillemer, *Lettres de divers savants à l'abbé Nicaise*, 101. The quote on the Propaganda fide is from Montfaucon, *The Travels*, 263, i.e., Montfaucon, *Diarium Italicum*, 230.

61   Montfaucon, *The Travels*, 324, i.e., Montfaucon, *Diarium Italicum*, 276: "Bibliotheca Vaticana aedificii amplitudine & magnificentia omnes quotquot in orbe sunt, longe multumque superat."

62   Misson, *A new voyage to Italy*, 2:19.

visitors – not to mention numerous Bibles in obscure foreign tongues and all manner of valuable ancient manuscripts concerning classic poetics, patristic apologetics, Byzantine chronologies, or Jewish histories.[63] Both learned and popular travellers like Montfaucon and Misson made the Vatican library the central object of their Italian peregrinations, and it became for Bonjour a frequently visited treasure trove of ancient manuscripts some thirty minutes' walk from the Augustinian convent where he lived.

It was in this Rome of famous libraries and visiting scholars that Bonjour quickly emerged as a figure of some standing. In many of their contemporary travel accounts he is mentioned. Thus when Montfaucon arrived in Rome in September 1698, he met Bonjour in the Angelica and remarked that he was "vir doctus Copticaeque linguae scientissimus," a learned man very knowledgeable in the Coptic language.[64] Throughout Montfaucon's time in Rome, Bonjour showed him a number of Egyptian and Coptic artefacts and transcribed the Coptic manuscripts which Montfaucon had brought with him from Venice.[65] In his *Palaeographia Graeca* (1708), Montfaucon recalled how Bonjour had obtained for him an inscription of the epitaph of Sempronius Nicocrates which Montfaucon believed Fabretti had transcribed incorrectly.[66] It was also Montfaucon who facilitated the correspondence between Bonjour and the French Orientalist Louis Picques in Paris.[67] But it was not only French Catholic travellers who enriched scholarly exchange in the city. In his first years in Rome, Bonjour frequently accompanied visiting scholars from Protestant Europe who were searching in Rome for hidden manuscript treasures. When the young Swedish botanist Olof Celsius (1670–1756) arrived in Rome in 1698, Bonjour

---

63   Cf. Misson, *A new voyage to Italy*, 2:28: "O Gott durch deine gute/Bescher uns kleider und hute/Auch mentelmund rocke/Fette kalber und bocke/Ochsen, schafe, und rinder/ Viele weiber, wenig kinder/Slechte speis und trank/Machem einen tag jahr lang." Misson noted the poem depicts Luther "pour un débauche."

64   Montfaucon, *The Travels*, 288; Montfaucon, *Diarium Italicum*, 249.

65   Cf. Montfaucon, *Diarium Italicum*, 69. The Coptic manuscript Montfaucon purchased contained the Pentateuch, the book of Daniel, the twelve minor prophets, and the entire New Testament.

66   Bernard de Montfaucon, *Palaeographia graeca, sive de ortu et progressu literarum graecarum* (Paris: Louis Guerin, Jean Boudot, Carol Robustel, 1708), 169–171, 313; Bernard de Montfaucon, *L'antiquité expliquée et représentée en figures: supplément II, le culte des grecs, des romains, des égyptiens, et des gaulois* (Paris: Jean-Geoffroy Nyon, Etienne Ganeau, Nicolas Gosselin, and Pierre Francois Giffart, 1724), 197–198. Montfaucon later wrote to Bonjour from Paris: Bernard de Montfaucon to Guillaume Bonjour, [undated, c.1702], BAR, ms.lat.395, fol. 119r. Cf. Aufrère and Bosson, "Le Père Guillaume Bonjour (1670–1714)."

67   See the letters in Gigas, *Lettres inédites de divers savants*, 2, part 1:247.

took him on a tour of the Vatican library, showed him the much-maligned copy of Luther's Bible, and gently suggested converting to Catholicism.[68] It was in the same year that Bonjour accompanied the young Danish scholar Frederik Rostgaard (1671–1745) and his Dutch companion Joannes Kool (1672–c.1708) in the Vatican library as they searched for letters of the fourth-century Sophist Libanius and geographical manuscripts of Arrian.[69] By then Bonjour, in Rome for just three years, had already begun to amass something of a reputation, despite having published, up to that point, just two small *opuscula*. In 1699, this was noted explicitly by a more unlikely visitor to Rome, a young Henry St. John, the future 1st Viscount Bolingbroke, who passed through the eternal city while on his grand tour of France, Switzerland, and Italy. Writing to the former Tory statesman William Trumbull (1639–1716), Bolingbroke noted,

> I have seen at Rome a French Augustinian monk who is extremely famous; the last book he put out is called *In Monumenta Coptica Bibliothecae Vaticanae brevis exercitatione et in fine digressio de LXX hebdomadibus Danielis revocatis ad novos calculos*. I met him in the Vatican and remember he told me he was about many things, among the rest an Egyptian grammar, to which he designs to join some other works concerning the Alexandrian church. Besides this Magliabechi sends me word he is going to publish *Il Pentateucho Coptico-Arabico con Prolegomenis*. His name is Father Bonjour.[70]

Bonjour's entry to both the Italian scholarly community in Rome and the transalpine Republic of Letters was largely facilitated by Magliabechi, whom Bonjour visited in Florence while on his way to Rome in late 1695.[71] Magliabechi

---

68   Enni Lundström, ed., *Olof Celsius d. ä:s Diarium öfver sin resa; Italien åren 1697 och 1698* (Gothenburg: Eranos Förlag, 1909), 34–6. He is also mentioned in a number of Magliabechi's letters, among them his correspondence with Bonjour.

69   Guillaume Bonjour to Antonio Magliabechi, 13 December 1698, BNCF, *Fondo Magliabechiano* VIII, cod. 317, fol. 36r, Guillaume Bonjour to Gisbert Cuper, 30 May 1699, KW 72 H 20, and Fredrick Rostgaard to Étienne Baluze, 10 March 1699, BNF, Baluze 354, fols. 115r–116r. On Kool in Italy see also Koen Scholten and Asker Pelgrom, "Scholarly Identity and Memory on a Grand Tour: The Travels of the Joannes Kool and his Travel Journal (1698–1699) to Italy," *Lias* 46 (2019): 93–136.

70   Henry St. John, Viscount Bolingbroke to William Trumbull, 19 June 1699, *Report on the Manuscripts of the Marquess of Downshire* (London: His Majesty's Stationery Office, 1924), 1, part 2: 792.

71   Rigord had been in correspondence with Magliabechi since 1687: BNCF, *Fondo Magliabechiano* VIII, cod. 341. Magliabechi reported of the visit several times in his letters to Cuper: 20 June 1696, 3 June 1697, 24 March 1699, KW 72 D 10, fols. 116v, 123v, 142r.

himself was a strange and idiosyncratic character. Eccentric, slovenly, intransigent, and curmudgeonly, holed up in a house on the Via della Scala crammed with books and surviving on a diet of salami and eggs, a "Glutton of Literature" who devoured books like basking sharks devour plankton, Noris called him βιβλιοθήκην περιπατοῦσαν, a walking library.[72] To some it was a fault that he devoured books rather than digesting them. When Celsius met Magliabechi in Florence, he commented that Magliabechi's knowledge consisted more of "cognitio librorum et auctorum," knowledge of books and authors, than true erudition.[73] In turn Bolingbroke, who was expecting to find a man considered the "most learned of this age," found instead "an old, vain, senseless pedant, a great discoverer of books without any method or judgement to digest what he reads, a kind of Bethlem character, one that is always busy proposing to himself any end."[74] Yet despite these faults Magliabechi was an extraordinarily well-connected scholarly figure whose vast library and network of contacts made him an indispensable source for literary information and one of the few outstanding Italian figures in the European Republic of Letters.[75] When scholars had literary queries, they directed them at Magliabechi. It was Magliabechi to whom Bonjour turned when he wanted to know if Theon of Smyrna, author of a manuscript he had discovered in the Angelica, was different from the Theon of Alexandria who wrote commentaries on Porphyry's mathematics; and it was Magliabechi to whom the great Italian historian Ludovico Antonio Muratori (1672–1750) turned when, engaged in an argument with a pompous Frenchman, he wanted to know whether Charles V was said to have spoken Italian to men and French to women or vice-versa.[76] Similarly, it was because of Magliabechi's peregrinations through Florentine libraries in the company

---

72 Noris' epithet is reported in Guillaume Bonjour to Antonio Magliabechi, 22 September 1696, BNCF, *Fondo Magliabechiano* VIII, cod. 317, fol. 3r–v. On Magliabechi see Isaac Disraeli, *Curiosities of Literature* (London: Routledge, Warne, and Routledge, New York, 1863), 1:394–397; and Michael C. Carhart, *Leibniz Discovers Asia: Social Networking in the Republic of Letters* (Baltimore: John Hopkins University Press, 2019), 50–51.
73 Lundström, *Olof Celsius*, 19.
74 Henry St. John, Viscount Bolingbroke to William Trumbull, 19 June 1699, in *Report on the Manuscripts of the Marquess of Downshire*, 1, part 2: 791.
75 As noted by Arnaldo Momigliano, "Mabillon's Italian Disciples," in Arnaldo Momigliano, *Essays in Ancient and Modern Historiography* (Oxford: Basil Blackwell, 1977), 280–1, and Françoise Waquet, *Le modèle français et l'Italie savante (1660–1750): conscience de soi et perception de l'autre dans la République des Lettres* (Rome: École Française de Rome, 1989), 399.
76 Guillaume Bonjour to Antonio Magliabechi, 14 September 1697, BNCF, *Fondo Magliabechiano* VIII, cod. 317, fol. 18r–v; and Ludovico Antonio Muratori to Antonio Magliabechi, 10 December 1701, BNCF, *Fondo Magliabechiano* VIII, cod. 1239, fol. 148r.

of the Rouen bibliophile Emery Bigot (1626–1689) that such precious manuscripts as a disputed letter from John Chrysostom to the monk Caesarius (which supposedly opposed the Catholic doctrine of transubstantiation) were first discovered, and it was through his ability as a scholarly mediator – an epistolary octopus with tentacles all over erudite Europe – that a manuscript of the Roman *Fasti* preserved in *The Chronograph of 354* could make it from a library in Vienna to Noris' desk in Florence.[77] It was also Magliabechi – with whom Bonjour maintained a lengthy correspondence and even friendship despite the Florentine's idiosyncrasies – who brokered contact between Bonjour and a number of notable Italian and transalpine scholars, who notified these scholars of Bonjour's current projects and impending publications, and who sent Bonjour's works to be reviewed by learned journals in northern Europe.[78] Indeed, many of Italy's greatest scholarly luminaries first learnt of Bonjour through Magliabechi. It was through Magliabechi, for example, that Bonjour first came to the attention of Benedetto Bacchini (1651–1721), the great ecclesiastical historian and long-time librarian at Modena. Bacchini met Bonjour in Rome in February 1697 while travelling around Italian archives on the hunt for medieval manuscripts and went on to review Bonjour's first work, the *De nomine patriarchae Josephi*, in glowing terms in his *Giornale*.[79] It was also through Magliabechi that Bonjour first came into contact with Ludovico Antonio Muratori, then librarian at the Ambrosiana in Milan. Muratori himself had been working on an edition of the poems of the late fourth- and early fifth-century Roman-governor-turned-Christian-saint Paulinus of Nola, which

---

77 Cf. Leonard E. Doucette, *Emery Bigot: Seventeenth-Century French Humanist* (Toronto: University of Toronto Press, 1970); Noris, "Dissertationes tres," in *Annus et epochae syromacedonum*, 28; and on the manuscript itself, Alden A. Mosshammer, *The Easter Computus and the Origins of the Christian Era* (Oxford: Oxford University Press, 2008) and Johannes Divjak and Wolfgang Wischmeyer, ed., *Das Kalenderhandbuch von 354. Der Chronograph des Filocalus* (Vienna: Holzhausen, 2014). The manuscript had initially been transcribed by the Bollandist Conrad Janninck, who later came to Rome where he befriended Magliabechi and Bonjour personally.

78 See for example Antonio Magliabechi to Otto Mencke, 5 March and 4 September 1696, BNCF, *Targioni Tozzetti* 82, 20, 22. This led to the reviews "Dissertatio de Nomine Patriarchae Josephi," *Acta Eruditorum* (1697): 6–10, and "In Monumenta Coptica seu Aegyptiaca," *Acta Eruditorum* (1699): 232–236. Reviews in the *Acta Eruditorum* were anonymous but can be discovered through the work of A. H. Laeven and L. J. M. Laeven-Aretz, *The authors and reviewers of the Acta Eruditorum 1682–1735* (Molenhoek: Electronic Publication, 2014).

79 See Guillaume Bonjour to Antonio Magliabechi, 22 December 1696 and 3 February 1697, BNCF, *Fondo Magliabechiano* VIII, cod. 317, fols. 9r, 10r; Benedetto Bacchini to Antonio Magliabechi, 13 September 1697 and 5 October 1697, BNCF, *Fondo Magliabechiano* VIII, cod. 1242, fols. 457r, 466r; Benedetto Bacchini, "Dissertatio de nomine patriarchae Joseph ...," *Giornale de' Letterati dell'anno 1696* (1697): 239–245.

he had recently discovered in manuscript in the library. Two of these poems contained references to the fact that the patriarch Joseph might be identified with the Egyptian god Serapis, an identification which Bonjour himself had discussed in his *De nomine patriarchae Josephi*. It was for this reason that, in 1696, Magliabechi suggested that Muratori might want to get in touch with this learned Augustinian directly. This initial exchange paved the way for a decade of amicable correspondence and even friendship: while Muratori dedicated one of the dissertations in his *Anecdota Latina* (1697) to Bonjour, Bonjour soon got into the habit of sending a copy of each of his published works to Muratori, a practice which lasted until his departure for China in 1707.[80] It is somewhat indicative that, as Bruno Neveu has pointed out, Muratori – later to become the pre-eminent Italian historian of the first half of the eighteenth century and a towering figure in Italian intellectual history – appears to have much admired the scholarship of Bonjour, who was two years his senior.[81]

Throughout his time in Rome, Bonjour's home remained the Augustinian headquarters. The convent itself had originally been built in 1459 just around the corner from what would later become the Piazza Navona and had initially been served by the ancient church of San Trifone on the corner between the Via dei Portoghesi and the Via della Scrofa.[82] Over time, this church was replaced by the Basilica Sant'Agostino, which was completed in the late fifteenth century. By the late seventeenth century, the convent and basilica had become part of a tripartite block of buildings all owned by the Augustinians, alongside the Biblioteca Angelica in which Bonjour spent his working life in Rome and which still houses Bonjour's manuscripts today.[83] Originally constructed through the amalgamation of two libraries, that of the convent itself and the private library, consisting of up to 20,000 volumes, of the printer and humanist Angelo Rocca (1545–1620), it became one of the world's first public libraries in

---

80 Ludovico Antonio Muratori, ed., *Anecdota, quae ex Ambrosianae bibliothecae codicibus nunc primum eruit* ... (Milan: Gioseffo Pandolfi Malatesta, 1697). See further Ludovico Antonio Muratori to Antonio Magliabechi, 22 August 1696, BNCF, *Fondo Magliabechiano* VIII, cod. 1239, fol. 24r ("Mi sono scordato il nome di quel valoroso Padre che ha composta la dissertazione sopra il Dio Serapide, che altro non ascondea che il Patriarca Gioseffo. Il dice ancora il mio San Paolino, e perciò vorrei citare il detto Signore"); Ludovico Antonio Muratori to Guillaume Bonjour, 15 January and 1 June 1697, in Matteo Campori, ed., *Epistolario di L. A. Muratori* (Modena: Società Tipografica Modenese, 1901), 2:204–205, 249–250; and Gisbert Cuper to Antonio Magliabechi, 3 November 1696, BNCF, *Fondo Magliabechiano* VIII, cod. 261, fol. 37r–v.
81 Bruno Neveu, *Érudition et religion aux XVIIe et XVIIIe siècles* (Paris: Albin Michel, 1994), 112.
82 Lubin, *Orbis Augustinianus*, 6; Deseine, *Rome moderne*, 1:52.
83 Cf. Elisabetta Sciarra, "Breve storia del fondo manoscritto della Biblioteca Angelica," *La Bibliofilía* 111 (2009): 251–282, especially p. 263.

the early seventeenth century and was renamed Angelica after Rocca's death. In the course of the century, it was significantly augmented with the private library of the Vatican librarian Lukas Holste (1596–1661) and was lauded by the Italian antiquarian Lorenzo Pignoria (1571–1631) as being "so full with the best books that it is almost a miracle" – a comment which, when he visited the library more than half a century later, the great Maurist scholar Jean Mabillon (1632–1707) still concurred with.[84] Not, of course, that this opinion was always shared. When Montfaucon visited some fifteen years later he called it "indifferently furnish'd," and, as we shall see, the library proved as much a bane to Bonjour's scholarship as it did a haven.[85]

When Bonjour first arrived in Rome in the autumn of 1695, he initially planned to work on editing and revising the *Mercurius* – today MS 1 in the Angelica – under the guidance of Noris. Almost immediately his plans were stymied by a development of great boon to the Augustinians and great detriment to Bonjour's scholarly career: on 12 December 1695, and to the horror of the Jesuits, Noris was elected cardinal, the first Augustinian since Gregorio Petrocchini (1535–1612) in 1589.[86] The promotion marked the final stage of Noris' decidedly reluctant entry into the Catholic ecclesiastical elite.[87] Although his best scholarly years lay behind him, his reputation had never been greater. In the Republic of Letters, he was widely cherished as an excellent historian, a brilliant chronologist, and a skilled numismatist. In Catholic Italy, he had emerged as the figurehead of that particular Italian theological tradition of Augustinianism – *Augustinianismo rigido* – which was later adopted by Domenico Passionei (1682–1761) and Giusto Fontanini (1666–1736) and then developed further by the early eighteenth-century Augustinian theologians Fulgenzio Bellelli (1675–1742) and Giovanni Lorenzo Berti (1696–1766).[88]

It is worth dwelling briefly on Noris' Augustinianism. Above all, Noris believed, as Jean-Louis Quantin wrote of late seventeenth-century Augustinianism more generally, that Augustine's later anti-Pelagian writings were "the

---

84   Lorenzo Pignoria, *Symbolarum epistolicarum liber primus* (Padua: Donati Pasquardi, 1629), 39: "Bibliothecam tuam Angelicam Vir Reverendissime ego multis nominibus suspicio. Tum quia Libris referta est optimis ad miraculum usque"; Jean Mabillon and Michel Germain, *Museum Italicum seu Collectio veterum scriptorum ex bibliothecis Italicis* (Paris: Edmund Martin, Jean Boudot, Etienne Martin, 1687), 93: "aitque refertam esse libris *ad miraculum optimis.*"

85   Montfaucon, *The Travels*, 288.

86   Wernicke, *Kardinal Enrico Noris*, 83.

87   Cf. Wernicke, *Kardinal Enrico Noris*, 58.

88   See Arturo Carlo Jemolo, *Il Giansenismo in Italia prima della rivoluzione* (Bari: Gius. Laterza & Figli, 1928); Pietro Stella, *Il Giansenismo in Italia* (Rome: Edizioni di Storia e Letteratura, 2006).

final expression of the faith of the church on grace and predestination," and sought to mobilise his prodigious skills as a historian to prove that this was the case.[89] In his most famous and controversial work, the *Historia pelagiana* of 1673, he tried to show that not only the heresy of Pelagianism but also semi-Pelagianism – an attempt by various, predominantly French, theologians of the fifth and sixth centuries to find a compromise between Augustine and Pelagius' views on free will, grace, and predestination – had been roundly and decisively condemned by the early Church. For Noris, the history of the ancient Church, and early Church councils in particular, provided the basis for outlining what was orthodox and what was heterodox in Christian theology (and in seventeenth-century Catholic theology in particular). A particular, and particularly illustrative, flashpoint was the Second Council of Constantinople in 553, which Noris sought to prove had wholly and unambiguously rejected the (proto-)Pelagian teachings of Origen. For Noris, proving that the Council had anathematised Origen was identical to proving that Origen's teaching was heretical; the historical authority of the Church was the sole judge and arbitrator of Christian orthodoxy and, as a result, historical scholarship could uncover the true meaning and significance of the very decisions which defined this orthodoxy.

In all this, Noris' perpetual target and enemy were the Jesuits, whom Noris accused of reviving condemned semi-Pelagianism. To these Jesuits, meanwhile, Noris was a Jansenist, pure and simple, and certainly there were similarities in the manner in which Noris sought to draw a more rigid Augustinian theology from a historical study of Augustine and the ancient origins of, and disputes concerning, Pelagianism, as Cornelius Jansen (1585–1638) had famously done in his much-disputed *Augustinus* (1640).[90] Moreover, Noris shared what remained perhaps the single unifying characteristic of all the varying forms of French Jansenism, namely, a hostility to the Jesuit Order in general and to their moral probabilism and casuistry in particular. In the third part of his *Historia pelagiana*, the *Vindicae Augustinianae*, he took explicit aim at three Jesuits, Jean Adam (1608–1684), François Annat (1590–1670), and Jean Martinon (1586–1662), while his interpretation of various important historical events, from the arguments of John Maxentius' sixth-century Scythian monks to the anathemas of the Second Council of Constantinople in 553 or

---

89 Jean-Louis Quantin, "Reason and Reasonableness in French Ecclesiastical Scholarship," *The Huntington Library Quarterly* 74 (2011): 404, n. 17.
90 See illustratively Wernicke, *Kardinal Enrico Noris*, 117; and John L. Heilbron, "Francesco Bianchini, Historian. In Memory of Amos Funkenstein," in *Thinking Impossibilities: The Intellectual Legacy of Amos Funkenstein*, ed. Robert S. Westman and David Biale (Toronto: University of Toronto Press, 2008), 230.

the condemnation of the Saxon theologian Gottschalk in the mid-ninth century, were expressly directed against the contrary interpretations of a variety of Jesuit historians, be it Pierre Halloix (1571–1656), Louis Maimbourg (1610–1686), Jean Garnier (1612–1681), or Jean Hardouin. It is not surprising that certain (largely mysterious and as yet unidentified) French Jansenists sought to publish an edition of Noris' *Historia pelagiana* in France through the mediation of Noris' close friend, the Cistercian cardinal Giovanni Bona (1609–1674), although this project eventually came to nothing.[91]

There were, however, also important differences between Noris' Augustinianism and French Jansenism. Firstly, we should note that the strict doctrinal definition of "Jansenist" pertained merely to those theologians who continued to uphold the five propositions taken from Jansen's *Augustinus* that Pope Innocent X (r. 1644–1655) had condemned as heretical in 1653, a condemnation which Noris (alongside certain French Jansenists who claimed that the propositions were a misinterpretation of Jansen's work) supported. Yet there were also other, more notable differences. For one thing, Noris did not share the strong Gallican tendencies which pervaded the theology of Port-Royal; for another, he and his followers made no attempt to change religious practice or alter church discipline. Indeed, Noris himself claimed that he had only (briefly) read Jansen's *Augustinus* after composing his own *Historia*.[92] "Cosi oggi va il mondo, e chi non è molinista, è eretico," so goes the world today, who is not a molinist is a heretic, Bona once wrote to Noris as controversy first engulfed Noris' *Historia* in 1673.[93] Yet it should also be noted that Noris always maintained the support of the papal hierarchy; even when his *Historia* was posthumously included on the Spanish Index in 1747, it was swiftly removed by Pope Benedict XIV (r. 1740–1758) in 1758.[94] Undoubtedly the crowning moment of this support, however, was Noris' election as cardinal – a decision which led to a new slew of unsuccessful attack pamphlets against his theology and his character by Jesuit polemicists. Noris' Augustinianism, unlike French Jansenism, was compatible with and even supported by the papal hierarchy.

As we shall see, Bonjour took on a number of Noris' key notions. In particular, he shared Noris' central belief that history rather than philosophy was

---

91 Wernicke, *Kardinal Enrico Noris*, 27; and see the letters between Bona and Noris in Giovanni Bona, *Joannis Bona ... Epistolae selectae*, ed. Roberto Sala (Turin: Ex typographia regia, 1755), 298–306.
92 Enrico Noris to Claude Nicaise, 27 September 1690, in "Lettera del Card. Noris," in *Istoria delle investiture*, cols. 350–1.
93 Giovanni Bona to Enrico Noris, 17 March 1674, in *Joannis Bona ... Epistolae selectae*, 304–305; as also cited in Stella, *Il Giansenismo in Italia*, 1:62.
94 Wernicke, *Kardinal Enrico Noris*, 115.

the handmaiden of theology and that it was the study of history that could separate truth from falsehood in matters of faith and doctrine, although he abstained from the positive theology and the theological controversies which marked Noris' career. For Bonjour, however, Noris' election to cardinal presented a more immediately practical problem. Given his new duties, Noris was simply too busy to provide the mentorship he had promised Bonjour. To Magliabechi, Noris wrote that he no longer had time to write nor money to print, the latter of which was being spent on the upkeep of a new carriage that Noris repeatedly and pointedly rode past the Jesuit college.[95] Almost immediately after arriving in Rome, Bonjour wrote to Magliabechi that Noris, while pleased with his *Mercurius*, had no time to read it through properly.[96] Added to this was the difficulty of finding (and financing) a printer with the requisite Arabic and Hebrew typeface, which proved more difficult in Rome than first expected. Eventually, these issues led Bonjour to lay aside the larger *Mercurius* in favour of printing what he described to Magliabechi as "clever abortions of a less practical work."[97] This was the *De nomine patriarchae Josephi*, a dissertation essentially lifted from the tenth chapter of the *Mercurius* in which Bonjour analysed the name by which the Egyptian pharaoh had called the patriarch Joseph at Genesis 41:45. To this short study Bonjour also appended two chronological dissertations, the first treating the lifespan of the Greek astronomer Geminus, the second the correct date for the passion of St. Mark. Ratified by the prior general of the Augustinians Antonio Pacini (r. 1693–1699) in June 1696, Bonjour was in a position to send a copy of this work to Magliabechi later that month. By the following year, the work had been reviewed in France, Germany, Holland, and Italy, and its recondite learning had won admirers from across the transalpine Republic.[98]

As is clear from the structure and especially the appendix of the *Mercurius* – which will be the subject of chapter 3 – chronology, and the chronology of Egypt in particular, was already among Bonjour's primary interests in Toulouse. In Rome, surrounded by authentic Egyptian monuments, Bonjour planned to develop this initial interest through a detailed study that harmonized Egyptian history with the chronology of the Bible. This project appears to have gripped

---

95   Enrico Noris to Antonio Magliabechi, 21 June, 28 June 1692, and 4 September 1694, BNCF, *Fondo Magliabechiano* VIII, cod. 294, fols. 187r, 188v, 202v.
96   Guillaume Bonjour to Antonio Magliabechi, 15 November 1695, BNCF, *Fondo Magliabechiano* VIII, cod. 317, fol. 1r.
97   Guillaume Bonjour to Antonio Magliabechi, 22 December 1696, BNCF, *Fondo Magliabechiano* VIII, cod. 317, fol. 9r: "un aborti d'ingegno poco prattico."
98   In addition to the reviews in the *Acta eruditorum* and the *Giornale* (op. cit.) the work was also reviewed in the *Journal de sçavans* (1697): 109–111.

Bonjour almost immediately upon his arrival in the eternal city. As early as January 1696, Magliabechi was writing to Jean Mabillon that Bonjour was printing a work entitled "Dynastiae aegyptiorum novis observationibus et calculis illustratae in defensionem editiones Vugatae [sic] seu Hebraicae veritatis vindicias a Graecis codicibus."[99] Among Bonjour's papers we can also find an approbation by Pacini for an introductory work on ancient pagan history, the *Characteres chronologicos*, which is dated to July 1696.[100] It appears that between July 1696 and the spring of 1697, Bonjour spent his time working on what would later become his most extensive chronological work, the *Antiquitas temporum*.[101] This work – an extensive survey of both ancient biblical and Egyptian history – was examined by Noris, who judged it satisfactory, and by Pope Innocent XII (r. 1691–1700), who (according to Michel Bégon) was pleased with it.[102] It seems, however, that the same problems which bedevilled the *Mercurius* also thwarted Bonjour's attempt to print the *Antiquitas temporum*. To Cuper and Magliabechi, Bonjour wrote of his increasing frustration regarding the difficulties he faced when it came to printing the work and, by November of 1697, he had once again decided to lay the work aside and turn his attention to a new project. As late as 1699, the manuscript of the *Antiquitas temporum* lay "ready to print," but no printer had been found.[103] Ultimately, only small excerpts of Bonjour's work on the chronology of the Flood, on the Septuagint, and on the corpus of Flavius Josephus were eventually published in a collection of dissertations, the *Selectae in sacram scripturam*, in 1705.

The abandonment of Bonjour's *Antiquitas temporum*, his major work on chronology and the subject of chapters four and five, leads us to the last of Bonjour's great unpublished projects: his work on Coptic. As Aufrère and Bosson have noted, Bonjour does not seem to have known any Coptic until late 1697 at the earliest.[104] His *Mercurius* does not contain any Coptic, nor do any of the notes or preliminary dissertations on the identity of Mercury which

---

99   Antonio Magliabechi to Jean Mabillon, 3 January 1696, in Gigas, *Lettres inédites*, 2, part 1: 241.
100 BAR, ms.lat.635, fol. 27r.
101 "Regestum Antonii Pacini IV, 1696–1697," AGA, DD136, 352; Guillaume Bonjour to Gisbert Cuper, 26 May 1697, KW 72 H 20.
102 Michel Bégon to Claude Nicaise, 21 May 1697, BNF, NAF 4368, fol. 142r–v. This letter, like many others sent to Nicaise, is reprinted in Caillemer, *Lettres de divers savants à l'abbé Nicaise*, 187, and François Fossier, ed., *L'abbé Claude Nicaise facteur du Parnasse* (Paris: L'Harmattan, 2019) 574. The latter is possibly the worst edited book in academic history. As we have noted above, Bonjour was likely in direct contact with Bégon, but their letters have either been lost or dispersed.
103 As reported by Bernard de Montfaucon to Nicolas Clément, 3 February 1699, in Gigas, *Lettres inédites de divers savants*, 2: part 1: 298.
104 Aufrère and Bosson, "Introduction," xlvi–xlvii.

remain among Bonjour's manuscripts. Instead, the first Coptic word we find in Bonjour's works comes from the last page of his *De nomine* and is taken directly from Kircher's *Prodromus coptus*.[105] It seems that Bonjour began to dedicate himself more extensively to Coptic after the completion of his *Antiquitas temporum* in the autumn of 1697. In November, he wrote to Magliabechi that he had begun to study Arabic seriously, a crucial tool for learning Coptic, and in February of the following year he enquired whether Magliabechi had access to a treatise on the Egyptian language by the French Orientalist Claude Saumaise (1588–1653).[106]

Bonjour's decision to turn to Coptic throws open a prickly question in Bonjour's life, namely, his own connection to Jansenism – or, at the very least, that peculiar form of Roman "Jansenism," or *Augustinianismo rigido*, which had Noris as a figurehead. In the seventeenth and eighteenth centuries, there was often a strong link between Catholic research in Eastern Churches and Jansenist affinities, particularly on matters concerning transubstantiation. Alastair Hamilton has gone as far as to say that anyone who worked on the Copts between 1660 and 1710 mentioned the Eucharist, and the career of Eusèbe Renaudot is a case in point.[107] Nor is Bonjour exempt from this tendency. Noticeably, his *In monumenta coptica*, a small survey of Coptic manuscripts in the Vatican library first published in 1699, begins with a *confessio* of St. Basil (330–379) that ostensibly evidences Basil's belief in the doctrine of transubstantiation. In his notes, Bonjour commented that Basil's *confessio* refuted the heresy of Wycliffe as recently revived by Calvin, and in their letters, both Honoré Rigord (Jean-Pierre's brother) and Montfaucon noted the

---

105 *De nomine*, 56, citing Athanasius Kircher, *Prodromus coptus sive aegyptiacus* (Rome: Typis S. Cong. de propaganda fide, 1636), 127.

106 Guillaume Bonjour to Antonio Magliabechi, 23 November 1697 and 3 February 1698, BNCF, *Fondo Magliabechiano* VIII, cod. 317, fols. 23r, 24v. The works of Saumaise which Bonjour read are Claude Saumaise, "Epistola De Cruce," in Thomas Bartolin, ed., *De latere Christi aperto dissertatio accedunt Cl. Salmasii & aliorum, De cruce epistolae* (Leiden: Johannes Maire, 1646), 213–528; Claude Saumaise, *De annis climacteris et antiqua astrologia diatribe* (Leiden: Officina Elzevir, 1648); and Claude Saumaise, *Epistolarum liber primus* (Leiden: Adriani Wyngaerden, 1656), as recorded in Bonjour's notes at BAR, ms.lat.631, fols. 156v, 161r–161bis.

107 Hamilton, *The Copts and the West*, 154, and Hamilton, "From East to West." Bonjour is cited in this context by Renaudot: Antoine Arnauld, Pierre Nicole, and Eusèbe Renaudot, *La perpetuité de la foy de l'eglise catholique sur les sacrements* (Paris: Jean-Baptiste Coignard, 1713), 5:689: "Qu'ils disent tout ce qu'ils voudront contre Abraham Echellensis, & les autres qui ont escrit à Rome, qui se réduisent neantmoins depuis prés de soixante ans à Fauste Nairon, & à un petit ouvrage du P. Bonjour Augustin François, tres-sçavant, & encore plus recommandable par sa pieté & par sa modestie, ces reproches sont presentement inutiles."

importance of this evidence.¹⁰⁸ "There is enough to convince the Huguenots of the ancient profession of the Copts, on which they are in error," wrote Honoré to Bonjour in September 1699.¹⁰⁹ Yet this is also the only explicit reference to transubstantiation in Bonjour's Coptic work, and it is shaped as much by the material he found as the doctrine he wished to defend. Certainly, it does not appear that an interest in the Eucharist shaped the rest of Bonjour's interest in Coptic or ancient Egypt more generally.¹¹⁰

Instead, I believe it is more profitable to see Bonjour's interest in Coptic as a development of his biblical chronology and, in particular, his interest in the history of ancient Egypt. Moreover, we should note that the primary reason for Bonjour's turn to Coptic was a commission from his ecclesiastical superiors. At some time between February and March 1698, Bonjour received through the mediation of Noris and Noris' close friend Girolamo Casanata – the future dedicatee of both Bonjour's Coptic Bible and his Coptic grammar – a request from the prefect of the Vatican library Lorenzo Zaccagni (1652–1712) to begin work on an edition and a Latin translation of a Coptic-Arabic Pentateuch found in manuscript in the Vatican library.¹¹¹ Ever the enterprising scholar, Bonjour took on this task with enthusiasm, believing not only that a study of the Coptic Pentateuch would allow him to further penetrate the question of the ancient connection between sacred and Egyptian antiquities, but also that this new biblical edition would allow him to publish an edition of the Coptic-Arabic Psalter and his work on the dynasties of ancient Egypt as an appendix. Bonjour worked on this Bible for the next six months. It was also during this period that, unable to work in the Vatican throughout June due to a fever, he began work on

---

108   *Coptica*, 2–3: "Toto fere saeculo tempus illud antevertit suscitatam a Wiclefo Berengarianam haeresim, multis post annis redivivam in Calviniana, contra veritatm corporis & sanguinis Christi Domini in sacratissimo Eucharistiae sacramento, pro qua potissimum militat praefata *Confessio* in hunc modum."

109   Honoré Rigord to Guillaume Bonjour, 15 September 1699, BAR, ms.lat.395, fol. 194r: "Il y a de quoy convaincre les Huguenots par la profession anciennes de Coptes quoy qu'ils soint dans l'erreur"; Bernard de Montfaucon to Nicolas Clément, 3 February 1699, in Gigas, *Lettres inédites de divers savants*, 2: part 1: 297: "Il [Bonjour] donne d'abord une confession de foy en cette langue, où les Cophtes confessent les deux natures en J.C. sans aucune confusion. La présence réelle de J.C. en l'eucharistie s'y trouve aussi en termes formels."

110   Even some Protestants believed that the early Greek church believed in transubstantiation: see Mathurin Veyssière La Croze to Gisbert Cuper, 14 August 1709, KW 72 H 19, n. 26. Cuper's reply, 1 September 1709, is in KW 72 H 19, nn. 27–28 and reprinted in Beyer, *Lettres de critique*, 37–41.

111   Guillaume Bonjour to Antonio Magliabechi, 1 March 1698, BNCF, *Fondo Magliabechiano* VIII, cod. 317, fol. 25r–v; also Guillaume Bonjour to Gisbert Cuper, 22 March 1698, KW 72 H 20.

his famous Coptic grammar. Notwithstanding his poorly condition, his work ethic remained undiminished. "I cannot express what effort it costs me to put everything in order," he wrote to Magliabechi.[112] By October of that year, he had decided to publish his dynasties and a dissertation on the Alexandrian church alongside the grammar rather than the Bible, with the former not only approaching completion but also receiving official approval by Pacini.[113] By February 1699 at the latest, the work was ready to print – a fact which suggests that Bonjour had learnt an otherwise unknown language and written a grammar on it within a year and a half.[114] As we know, the Coptic grammar, the *Elementa linguae copticae*, eventually shared the fate of Bonjour's *Mercurius* and his *Antiquitas temporum*. According to Montfaucon, who watched over Bonjour's Coptic work with interest, the *Elementa* was initially mooted to be published by the Propaganda fide press once Giulio Ambrogio Lucenti's supplement to Ferdinando Ughelli's *Italia sacra* (1643–1662) had been published.[115] If this is true, then it is indicative that Lucenti's supplement was only published five years later, in 1704, and not by the Propaganda fide but by the printer Angelo Bernabò. As late as 1702 Clement XI, to whom the grammar had been re-dedicated following the death of Casanata, voiced his hope that the work would soon be published in line with Renaudot's authoritative recommendation. By then, however, it seems that even Bonjour had lost some of his earlier optimism. "I see that this very tumultuous time is not very favourable for following the intentions of this most holy pastor," he wrote to Magliabechi.[116] In this he was, of course, correct.

What, then, lay at the heart of Bonjour's inability to publish those works for which he was beginning to accumulate renown in France, Germany, and the Netherlands? Partly the answer must stem from the scholarly interests

---

112 Guillaume Bonjour to Antonio Magliabechi, 28 June 1698, BNCF, *Fondo Magliabechiano* VIII, cod. 317, fol. 28r: "Non posso esprimerli con quanta fatiga l'ho mesa in ordine." See also Ludovico Antonio Muratori to Antonio Magliabechi, 14 May 1698, BNCF, *Fondo Magliabechiano* VIII, cod. 1239, fols. 75v–76r.

113 "Regestum Antonii Pacini VI, 1698–1699," AGA, DD138, 184. Cf. Bernard de Montfaucon to Louis Picques, 23 September 1698, in Gigas, *Lettres inédites de divers savants*, 2, part 1: 292 and Francesco Bianchini to Antonio Magliabechi, 14 November 1698, BNCF, *Fondo Magliabechiano* VIII, cod. 298, fol. IV.

114 Guillaume Bonjour to Claude Nicaise, 10 February 1699, BNF, Français 9361, fol. 133r, reprinted in Fossier, *L'abbé Claude Nicaise*, 629–630.

115 Bernard de Montfaucon to Nicolas Clément, 3 February 1699, in Gigas, *Lettres inédites de divers savants*, 297–298.

116 Guillaume Bonjour to Antonio Magliabechi, 4 February 1702, BNCF, *Fondo Magliabechiano* VIII, cod. 317, fol. 56v: "Ma vedo che questo tempo turbatissimo non e molto favorevole a secondare le intenzioni di quel santissimo pastore."

which dominated Italy at the time, as well as the pitiful state of Italian printing and even "learning" more generally. As has been pointed out in landmark articles by Eric Cochrane and Arnaldo Momigliano, historical studies in late seventeenth-century Italy had begun to turn away from classical and especially Greek scholarship and towards archaeology, the Etruscans and Pelasgians, and, above all, the municipal history of medieval Italy.[117] Bacchini, as Momigliano has pointed out, learnt from Mabillon to put "ecclesiastical history and the Middle Ages before pagan antiquities and modern Italian literature."[118] Montfaucon, who journeyed through Italy some fifteen years after his Maurist colleague Mabillon, was unable to have the same regenerative influence on scholarship and by 1700 Greek learning in particular found itself at a low ebb. As a result, prominent scholars, among them Bacchini and Muratori and in future years Giusto Fontanini, Apostolo Zeno (1668–1750), and Scipione Maffei (1675–1755), looked towards France and the text-critical methodology of the Maurists as their scholarly models but sought thereby to revive specifically Italian scholarship and knowledge of Italian history.[119] Particularly in Rome, scholars were bibliophiles, antiquarians, collectors, ecclesiastical historians, archaeologists, numismatists – even, as in the case of Francesco Bianchini (1662–1729) or the Celestine monk Celestino Galiani (1681–1753), astronomers and natural philosophers who conducted experiments with optics in the Quirinal palace and read their Newton studiously.[120] Yet text criticism, Greek patristics, biblical chronology, and, above all, Oriental languages appeared far away from the chief interests of the scholarly world which Bonjour inhabited. Illustratively, Bonjour himself appears to have quickly realised the incompatibility of his own interests with those of the Roman scholarly world and the printing presses in particular. As early as November 1695, he noted to Magliabechi that he would be unable to publish the *Mercurius* in Rome because it was too expensive, but that he hoped to return to France where he would be able to do

117   Eric Cochrane, "The Settecento Medievalists," *The Journal of the History of Ideas* 19 (1958): 35–61; Momigliano, "Mabillon's Italian Disciples."
118   Momigliano, "Mabillon's Italian Disciples," 284.
119   See also Waquet, *Le modèle français et l'Italie savante*.
120   See Valentin Kockel and Brigitte Sölch, ed., *Francesco Bianchini (1662–1729) und die europäische gelehrte Welt um 1700* (Berlin: Akademie Verlag, 2005); Luca Ciancio and Gian Paolo Romagnani, ed., *Unità del sapere, molteplicità dei saperi: Francesco Bianchini (1662–1729) tra natura, storia e religione* (Verona: QuiEdit, 2010); Brendan Dooley, *Science, Politics and Society in Eighteenth-Century Italy: The Giornal de' Letterati d'Italia and its World* (New York and London: Garland Press, 2018) and John L. Heilbron, *The incomparable Monsignor: Francesco Bianchini's world of science, history and court intrigue* (Oxford: Oxford University Press, 2022).

so free of charge.[121] As the years passed, this sort of comment became an ever more increasing refrain. In May of 1697, Bonjour wrote to Cuper of his desire to leave Italy soon for either Germany or Belgium, and in August Magliabechi noted to Cuper that only the pleas – and promises – of Noris were keeping Bonjour from quitting Rome.[122] A major source of chagrin was undoubtedly the lack of funds, which prevented Bonjour from printing his major (and more costly) works, and which determined the format of Bonjour's first two published works, the *De nomine* of 1696 and the *In monumenta coptica* of 1699. Both works were published at the house of Francesco Maria Acsamitek, son of the noted printer Zaccaria Domenico Acsamitek (d. 1691) who had come to Rome from Bohemia and who worked at the press of the Propaganda fide (and also helped print Kircher's *Oedipus aegyptiacus*). And yet, neither work was more than a pamphlet in length; the *In monumenta coptica* did not even feature a dedication or preface due to a shortage of funds.[123] Small surprise, then, that Bonjour quickly became disillusioned with the platform that the Roman scholarly world was able to provide for his interests. "The condition of a writer," Bonjour wrote to Claude Nicaise in 1697, "is so miserable in this country so incurious about these sorts of matters that nothing can be printed here except at one's own expense."[124] In this, Bonjour's stance never changed. "Certainly if I could free myself from this country," he wrote to Magliabechi in 1702, when Clement XI had made more unfulfilled noises regarding the publication of the Coptic grammar, "I would do it as soon as possible."[125]

To a great extent, Bonjour's remarks concerning both the state of Italian scholarship and the state of Italian printing were echoed by his contemporaries.

---

121 Guillaume Bonjour to Antonio Magliabechi, 15 November 1695, BNCF, *Fondo Magliabechiano* VIII, cod. 317, fol. 1r.

122 Guillaume Bonjour to Gisbert Cuper, 26 May 1697, KW 72 H 20; Guillaume Bonjour to Antonio Magliabechi, 3 February 1698, BNCF, *Fondo Magliabechiano* VIII, cod. 317, fol. 24r.

123 As noted by Bonjour to Antonio Magliabechi, 7 March 1699, BNCF, *Fondo Magliabechiano* VIII, cod. 317, fol. 37r. On Acsamitek see (briefly) Alberto Tinto, "Giovanni Giacomo Komarek tipografo a Roma nei secoli XVII–XVIII ed I suoi campionari di caratteri," *La Bibliofilía* 75 (1973): 194; and Moroni, *Dizionario*, 14:239. Acsamitek was also responsible for publishing Noris' *Historica dissertatio de uno ex trinitate carne pasto* in 1695.

124 Guillaume Bonjour to Claude Nicaise, 9 July 1697, in KW 72 D 2, fol. 127v and BAR, ms.lat.635, fol. 68v, and also quoted in Claude Nicaise to Pierre-Daniel Huet, 1 August 1697, in Pélissier, "Lettres inédites de Claude Nicaise," 148: "la condition d'un écrivain est si misérable dans ce paÿs peu curieux de ces sortes de matières qu'on n'y peut rien imprimer qu'à ses propres despens."

125 Guillaume Bonjour to Antonio Magliabechi, 22 April 1702, BNCF, *Fondo Magliabechiano* VIII, cod. 317, fol. 61r: "certamente se potessi liberarmi di questo paëse, l'ho farei quanto prima."

It is noticeable that Francesco Bianchini, to take one illustrious example, was able to publish his 1697 *Istoria universale* – which will be discussed in more detail in chapter 2 – due to the patronage of Pietro Ottoboni, but that between 1698 and 1723 he was able to publish just a single new work, his *De kalendario et cyclo Caesari* of 1703. For much of the seventeenth century the zenith of Italian printing was Venice and, after *c*.1670, Padua, where Cardinal Gregorio Barbarigo (1625–1697) – a friend of Leibniz and reader of Kepler who narrowly missed out on becoming pope – founded a printing press which became renowned for its printing of Greek.[126] Yet even these traditional centres were suffering, a decline exacerbated by the effects of the Nine Years War in the early 1690s. Particularly suggestive of this dispiriting state of affairs is the case of Muratori. In 1697 and 1698, Muratori had published the first and second volumes of his *Anecdota latina*, both in Milan; in 1699, however, he found the proposed publication of the first volume of his *Anecdota graeca* and the third volume of the *Latina* increasingly stymied. Frequently he complained of the high prices and tardiness of the printers at Padua.[127] "In Italy, it is difficult; outside of Italy very inconvenient; and in Milan, impossible," he wrote of the printing process to Magliabechi in 1699.[128] It is somewhat indicative that the first volume of the *Graeca* did not appear until 1709, and the third volume of the *Latina* not until 1713. Moreover, Muratori shared Bonjour's pessimism regarding the status of learning in Italy. "In truth," he wrote to Magliabechi in 1697, "I cannot complain enough about the poverty or ignorance of our books."[129] Two years later, his comment was echoed by the ever-acerbic Bolingbroke, who surmised that "knowledge is at present in Italy drawn down to so low an ebb and serves so little to the advancement of a man that there is scarce any-one who aims at it."[130] More illuminating still is what Muratori had to say about Oriental learning. For a long time, Bonjour had exhorted Muratori to apply himself to Greek, to Hebrew, and to Arabic. These exhortations fell upon deaf ears, and yet

---

126 See John L. Heilbron, *The Sun in the Church* (Cambridge MA: Harvard University Press, 1999), 185.

127 Ludovico Antonio Muratori to Antonio Magliabechi, 26 December 1696, BNCF, *Fondo Magliabechiano* VIII, cod. 1239, fol. 28r-v.

128 Ludovico Antonio Muratori to Antonio Magliabechi, 11 February 1699, BNCF, *Fondo Magliabechiano* VIII, cod. 1239, fol. 100r-v: "Son però molto imbrogliato nel determinarmi, ove si possa stampar questa mia povera fatica. In Italia è difficile; fuori d'Italia è molto incommodo, ed in Milano impossibile."

129 Ludovico Antonio Muratori to Antonio Magliabechi, 12 June 1697, BNCF, *Fondo Magliabechiano* VIII, cod. 1239, fol. 34r: "per verita io non so abbastanza dolermi della povertà, o ignoranza de' nostri librari."

130 Henry St. John, Viscount Bolingbroke to William Trumbull, 19 June 1699, in *Report on the Manuscripts of the Marquess of Downshire* 1:791.

Muratori was perspicacious enough to realise that his disinterest in these sorts of matters were as much a reflection of his environment as they were of his personal inclination. "You say, I handle the Egyptian, Arabic, and Syro-Arabic manuscripts in order to promote the majesty of the Holy Books. Clearly an honourable plan, but one that would strike the reader with a holy terror," wrote Muratori to Bonjour in 1698. "Those barbarian characters, and the exotic sense of those languages, are so far removed from the mindset of the Italians, as Egypt and both Arabias are from us. What you will just about be able to obtain from us will be a certain mute veneration, which even the ignorant owe to the most precious works."[131]

The other restriction on Bonjour's scholarship, or perhaps more accurately, Bonjour's mobility as a scholar, was the Augustinian Order itself. Unlike Francesco Bianchini, who was employed as librarian for Pietro Ottoboni; unlike Giusto Fontanini, who came to Rome in 1697 after being offered the position of librarian to the avid bibliophile Giuseppe Renato Imperiali and whose house became a noted meeting place for the cultural elite of Rome; unlike Giovanni Pastrizio (born Ivan Paštrić, 1636–1708), the Croatian-born Oriental scholar and long-time correspondent of Bonjour who served as professor of Hebrew at the Collegio Urbano; unlike even Noris, who spent twenty years as professor of sacred scripture under the protection of the Grand Duke of Tuscany Cosimo III de' Medici (1642–1723), Bonjour had – at least until 1704 – no income or occupation outside of the Augustinian Order. Although his status as a hermit allowed him to pursue a scholarly career with some security, it did not necessarily allow him to choose the objects of his scholarly labours. Nor did Bonjour's position allow him to finance the printing of works considered either unnecessary or, more commonly, simply too expensive. We should remember that even Noris spent more than half a year's salary seeing his 1681 *Cenotaphia pisana* through the press, and more than a year's salary for his *Annus et epochae syromacedonum* in 1689.[132] Furthermore, it was the Order which put Bonjour to work on certain tasks which prevented him from pursuing his own research further. In May 1697, for example, he noted to Cuper that he was currently being detained

---

131 Ludovico Antonio Muratori to Guillaume Bonjour, 4 June 1698, BAR, ms.lat.49, fol. 374r–v and reprinted in Campori, *Epistolario di L. A. Muratori*, 1:322: "Aegyptiacos, inquis, arabicos et syro-arabicos codices verso ut Sacrorum Bibliorum majestatem promoveam. Egregrium sane consilium, sed quod lectorem sacro quodam terrore corripiat. Barbari illi characteres, atque exoticus linguarum illarum sensus tam longe ab Italorum ingeniis abest, quam sunt a nobis Aegyptus, ac utraque Arabia. Quod a nobis impetrare vix poteris, muta quaedam veneratio erit, quam vel ignari pretiosissimis operibus debent." Cf. Hamilton, *The Copts and the West*, 229–230.
132 Wernicke, *Kardinal Enrico Noris*, 45, 56.

in the Angelica by some recently discovered manuscripts which needed to be catalogued.[133] The organization of the library and the education of young Augustinians at the convent next door remained an ever-present obstacle to continuing his own work. "I really do not know how I should do my treatise on the ecclesiastical cycles, being obliged to give up any desire to study in order to put our library in order. And this is something which takes some time. On the other hand, any small period of quiet is used for the studies of others, rather than one's own," he wrote to Magliabechi in April 1702.[134] Even when Bonjour was left to do his own work, the focus of this work could be directed, or redirected, by his superiors. Thus, in September 1696, he was asked to write a dissertation on the history of the Augustinian Order and the Translation of Augustine's bones from northern Africa to Pavia following the discovery of what were rumoured to be the bones of Augustine in the Cathedral of San Pietro in Ciel d'Oro in Pavia in October 1695 – a discovery which elicited a long-running debate about their authenticity and which detained Pacini in Pavia for four months.[135] Unsurprisingly, it is the only work of Bonjour's to have been published by the Augustinian Order itself, having (belatedly) appeared in the 1902 and 1903 editions of the *Analecta Augustiniana*.[136]

The most important redirection in Bonjour's early career, however, came in 1701, when he was selected as part of the congregation for calendar reform established by Clement XI following his election as pontiff in November of the previous year. For much of the preceding century, the superiority of the Gregorian over the Julian calendar had been a distinct source of pride for Catholics. Indeed, during the 1690s, a number of leading Protestant scholars, including Leibniz, were pushing for the adoption of the calendar in their countries.[137]

---

133   Guillaume Bonjour to Gisbert Cuper, 26 May 1697, KW 72 H 20.
134   Guillaume Bonjour to Antonio Magliabechi, 22 April 1702, BNCF, *Fondo Magliabechiano* VIII, cod. 317, fol. 61r: "Non so veramente come ho da fare per il mio trattato de cyclis ecclesiasticis, vendendomi obligato a renunciare a qualsi voglia studio per mettere in ordine la nostra libreria. E una cosa che vuole durare un pezzo. D'altra parte un minimo tempo di quiete a da servire alli studii degl' altri, piu tosto che alli proprii."
135   See Antonio Magliabechi to Otto Mencke, 4 September 1696, BNCF, *Targioni Tozzetti* 82, n. 22. Cf. Guillaume Bonjour, "De loco obitus s. Augustini. De sepultura et translatione ejusdem. Prima et secunda. De Augustinianorum in Gallia continua successione," BAR, ms.lat.629, fols. 1r–36v; Stone, *St. Augustine's Bones*.
136   *Analecta Augustiana* 2 (1902): 487–492. Cited in Gutierrez and Gavigan, *The History of the Order*, 1, part 1: 6; Benedict Hackett, "San Pietro in Ciel d'oro Pavia," in *Augustine in Iconography*, ed. Joseph C. Schnaubelt and Fredrick Van Fleteren (New York: Peter Lang, 1999), 213, n. 6, and 214, n. 11; Stone, *St. Augustine's Bones*, 56.
137   See G. W. Leibniz to Claude Nicaise, 12 July and 11 October 1694, in Victor Cousin, ed., *Fragments philosophiques* (Paris: Ladrange, 1838), 2:251–252. The calendar had already

Not content, however, with resting on their calendrical laurels, Clement XI's congregation was designed to perfect the calendar further. The Italian Giovanni Domenico Cassini (1625–1712), undoubtedly the leading astronomer of the late seventeenth century and royal astronomer to Louis XIV, had recently discovered that Christopher Clavius (1538–1612), the German Jesuit in charge of implementing the Gregorian calendar in 1582, had made a minor error regarding the "moons in century dates not also leap years," and Clement XI's congregation was intended to correct this minor but irksome mistake.[138] Officially founded on 14 September 1701, the congregation was headed by Noris, featured Bianchini as secretary, and included a number of prominent mathematicians from the Sapienza university, such as Giordano Vitale (1633–1711) and Domenico Quartaironi (1651–1736), as well as the Vatican librarian Zaccagni.[139] For Bonjour, the calendar was not a new interest. As Noris had taught in his *Annus et epochae syromacedonum*, knowledge of ancient calendars was crucial for understanding ancient history, and as early as February 1697 Bonjour had been discussing – and correcting – Tommaso Santagostini's *Novissima epatta lunisolare* in the presence of Bacchini.[140] Indeed, Bonjour's membership in the congregation, which was scaled down in 1702 and abandoned in 1703 (the differences in calculation being so minimal as to render them pointless), proved productive. During this period, he published two works: the 1701 *Calendarium romanum* – which outlined a historical calendar composed of a four-year cycle repeated 432 times, which Bonjour christened the *periodus Norisiana* in honour of his mentor – and an introduction to the Church *computus* in 1702. In addition, it was during this time that he established contact with some of the most notable astronomers of his day, including Bianchini, Eustachio Manfredi (1674–1739), Filippo della Torre (1657–1717), and Cassini himself, who reviewed Bonjour's *Calendarium* for the *Journal de savants*.[141]

---

been adopted in some Protestant kingdoms, notably Prussia, as early as the early seventeenth century.

138 Quote from Heilbron, *The Sun in the Church*, 42; see also ibid, p. 145; as well as John L. Heilbron, "Bianchini as an Astronomer," in Kockel and Sölch, *Francesco Bianchini*, 68–69.

139 Ossinger, *Bibliotheca Augustiniana*, 140–141; Aufrère and Bosson, "Introduction," lxxi; and Cesare Bigliotti, "Vita del Giordano da Bitonto," in *Le vite degli arcadi illustri, scritte da diversi autori*, ed. Giovanni Maria Crescenzi (Rome: Antonio de Rossi, 1714), 3:184–185.

140 Benedetto Bacchini to Antonio Magliabechi, 17 April 1697, BNCF, *Fondo Magliabechiano* VIII, cod. 1242, fols. 453r–v.

141 Giovanni Domenico Cassini, "Article XIII; Remarques de M. Cassini sur le Calendrier du P. Bonjour," *Journal de Trévoux* (1702): 148–158; Giovanni Domenico Cassini to Guillaume Bonjour, 4 September 1702, BAR ms.lat.395, fols. 111r–112v; Guillaume Bonjour to Francesco Bianchini, 15 March and 22 October 1704, BVR, U15, fols. 253r–255r, 250r; Francesco Bianchini to Filippo della Torre, 21 July 1703, 5 April 1704, BVR, S 83, fols. 494v, 503r; Eustachio

Bonjour's own work on the calendar was more historical than it was explicitly astronomical. In particular, he was concerned with bringing the contemporary ecclesiastical calendar back to its original state, which is to say, the state it was in even before it was (supposedly) authorized at the Council of Nicaea in 325.[142] In doing so, he often cited the words of Nicolas of Cusa (1401–1464), the German astronomer and philosopher who had worked on calendar reform during the Council of Basel in 1436: "if one wants to undertake a complete and successful restoration of the calendar, one can do no better than to bring the calendar back to that true state in which it was found according to the rules of the ancients, and as transmitted to us by the holy councils."[143] It is apparent that even in matters concerning the calendar, Bonjour approached the question not through mathematics or astronomy, but through patristic scholarship and in light of ancient Church tradition. For Bonjour, establishing the correct ecclesiastical calendar meant applying historical and philological tools to ancient patristic texts so as to work out the true calendar in the time of the primitive Church. Of particular importance were the works of the ante-Nicene paschal chronologists Theophilus I of Alexandria, Anatolius of Laodicea, Cyrill of Alexandria, Origen, and ps.-Cyprian, on whose *De pascha computus* Bonjour

---

Manfredi, *Epistola ad virum clarissimum Dominicum Quartaironium qua anonymi assertiones XVI pro reformatione calendarii* (Venice: Antonio Bortoli, 1705), 40, and Francesco Bianchini, *Solutio problematis paschalis* (Rome: Typis Rev. Cam. Apost., 1703), xxxii, 14, 16. Bonjour's cycle was based on the one in Enrico Noris, "Dissertatio de Paschali Latinorum Cyclo Annorum LXXXIV," in Enrico Noris, *Diagramma cycli civilis et ecclesiastici annorum LXXXIV in sex tessaradecaeteridas distributi* (Florence: Typographia Sereniss. Magni Ducis, 1691). The 84-year cycle, which Noris discovered in the *Fasti Consulares*, would have to be repeated 23 times to cover the *periodus Norisiana* of 1932 years.

142 Bonjour defined the Gregorian and the Clementine reform as intended to "conformandosi all' institutione del Concilio di Nicea e de I santi Padri che l'havevano preceduto": in "Dell'uso del Calendario e de i cicli lunisolari nella chiesa," BAR, ms.lat.629, fol. 169v.

143 Cited in Guillaume Bonjour, "De difficultatibus epactarum calendarii Gregoriani," BAR, ms.lat.629, fol. 154v; Guillaume Bonjour, "Enodatio dubiorum de kalendario Gregoriano, sacrae Congregationi super hoc negotio institutae, humiliter exhibita, a F. Guillelmo Bonjour Tolosano, ordinis Eremitarum S.P.N. Augustini," BAR, ms.lat.629, fol. 172r; Guillaume Bonjour, "In calendarium Gregorianum oratio prima," BAR, ms.lat.630, fol. 12v. On Cusa see C. Philipp E. Nothaft, "Strategic Skepticism: A reappraisal of Nicholas of Cusa's Calendar Reform Treatise," in *Le Temps des Astronomes; L'astronomie et le décompte du temps de Pieirre d'Ailly à Newton*, ed. Éduoard Mehl and Nicolas Roudet (Paris: Les Belles Lettres, 2017), 65–102; and Nicholas of Cusa, *Die Kalenderverbesserung: De correctione kalendarii*, ed. Viktor Stegemann (Heidelberg: F. H. Kerle Verlag, 1955). The citation can be found on p. 68: "Unde si plena et perfecta reformatio kalendarii fieri debet, nihil melius inveniri posse, quam reducere Calendarium usque ad eum statum, quod regulae antiquorum in sacris conciliis tradita, redeant ad veritatem, quanto levius, et facilius, et verius hoc fieri poteri."

made several lengthy philological observations based on the 1682 critical edition of John Wallis (1616–1703).[144] From these works, Bonjour tried to establish what he called a "regula sanctorum patrum," a patristic consensus regarding the calendar of the ante-Nicene church which could inform and help construct a correct ecclesiastical calendar in Bonjour's own day. And yet, despite certain commonalities, it is still clear that the work marked a major divergence from his earlier work on sacred history and the antiquities of Egypt. It is noticeable that, in February 1701, just as Bonjour was beginning work for the calendrical congregation, he wrote to Magliabechi that he was now engaged "in other studies of greater concern."[145] Meanwhile, in April of that year, Nicaise remarked that Bonjour "has bid farewell to Egypt and its antiquities."[146] This news evoked disappointment in Nicaise, but anger in Cuper. In October 1701, having not received a letter from Bonjour in a year and having been informed by Nicaise that Bonjour had stopped working on Egypt, he wrote to Magliabechi of his resentment that Bonjour had been prevented from continuing his work on biblical criticism and Egyptian chronology:

> I, indeed, am angry with those teachers, nor can I understand how it could have come into their mind that the explanation of the ancient and sacred rites and the investigation of the versions of the Old and New Testament were not worthy of monks; both areas Bonjour adorned so beautifully, having published a dissertation on the name of Joseph and a sample of Coptic translation; I say again, I am angry with the stern, and, to speak frankly, overly pious men, all the more so because they deprive me of the pleasure, which I was singularly accustomed to derive from the letters of a learned man.[147]

---

144 See "De pascha computus," BAR, ms.lat.629, fols. 135r–155v; "Observationes in computum paschalem tributum S. Cypriano," BAR, ms.lat.629, fols. 196r–198r; "Nota super computum Cypriani de Paschate," BAR, ms.lat.630, 70r–71v.

145 Guillaume Bonjour to Antonio Magliabechi, 20 February 1701, BNCF, *Fondo Magliabechiano* VIII, cod. 317, fol. 54r: "in altri studii di maggiore premura."

146 Claude Nicaise to Enrico Noris, 10 April 1701, BAR, ms.lat.49, fols. 369r–370r, reprinted in Pélissier, "Lettres de l'abbé Nicaise au Cardinal Noris (1686–1701)," 213: "se validixisse Aegypto et antiquitatibus illius."

147 Gisbert Cuper to Antonio Magliabechi, 26 October 1701, BNCF, *Fondo Magliabechiano* VIII, cod. 261, fol. 68v: "Ego quidem magistris illis irascor, nec capere possum, quomodo in mentem ipsis venire potuerit, monachos non decere illustrationem antiquorum sacrorumque rituum, et investigationem versionum Veteris et Novis Testamenti; quam utramque provinciam Bonjourius tam pulchre exornavit, edita dissertatione de nomine Iosephi, et specimene interpretationis Copticae; iterum dico irascor austeris, et, ut sic

By the following spring, his anger had yet to abate: "I am greatly grieved that I no longer receive any more letters from the very learned Bonjour, and I am angry with those scrupulous and crude superiors; for I was truly taken by reading them, from which I derived exceptional and singular fruit," he informed the helpless Magliabechi.[148]

3 Bonjour in the Republic of Letters

Cuper's anger goes some way to outlining the disjunct that existed between Bonjour's own scholarly projects, those expected of him across the Alps, and those demanded of him in Rome. Bonjour himself was very much a child of the Republic, born at a time when extensive networks of correspondence and scholarly exchange already united scholars between Rome, London, Paris, Amsterdam, Hanover, and a myriad of other libraries, universities, academies, seminaries, and monasteries. Yet it was also a time in which knowledge of a scholar could abound before any scholarship had been produced. It is one of the noteworthy disparities in Bonjour's life that his reputation was greatest when his published output was lowest. It appears that, for many scholars across the Alps, imagining what Bonjour might be able to achieve seemed more tantalising than the achievements themselves.[149]

The conduits of this flow of information were Rigord, Bégon, and, above all, Magliabechi. It was due to Magliabechi that scholars like Celsius and Rostgaard sought out Bonjour when they visited Rome and that Bonjour's works were sent to Otto Mencke (1644–1707) in Leipzig to be reviewed in the *Acta eruditorum*.

---

loquar, nimium piis hominibus, idque eo magis, quia me defraudant voluptate, quam ex viri docti epistolis singularem capere solebam."

[148] Gisbert Cuper to Antonio Magliabechi, 26 April 1702, BNCF, *Fondo Magliabechiano* VIII, cod. 261, fol. 71r–v: "Doleo vehementer me nullas amplius literas accipere ab eruditissimo Bonjourio; et irascor scrupulosis illis atque asperis superioribus; capiebar enim valde earum lectione, et singularis inde eximiusque fructus ad me rediebat, et, quod me summopere exhilarabat, edocebar Eminentiss. Norisium mei subinde meminisse." Both letters are reprinted in Antonio Magliabechi, *Clarorum Belgarum ad Ant. Magliabechium nonnullosque alios epistolae* (Florence: Ex typographia Magni Ducis, 1745), 1:81–85.

[149] See more generally the work by Herbert Jaumann, ed., *Die europäische Gelehrtenrepublik im Zeitalter des Konfessionalismus: The European Republic of Letters in the Age of Confessionalism* (Wiesbaden: Harrassowitz Verlag, 2001); Noel Malcolm, "Private and Public Knowledge: Kircher, Esotericism, and the Republic of Letters," in *Athanasius Kircher: The Last Man Who Knew Everything*, ed. Paula Findlen (New York: Routledge, 2004), 297–308; and Anthony Grafton, "A Sketch Map of a Lost Continent: The Republic of Letters," in *Republic of the Letters: A Journal for the Study of Knowledge, Politics and the Arts* 1 (2009).

It was likewise through Magliabechi that notices of Bonjour first appeared in Bacchini's *Giornale* and the *Biblioteca volante* of Giovanni Cinelli Calvoli (1626–1706).[150] Yet Magliabechi himself could only pass information from Italy to the Republic; he could not further spread knowledge of Bonjour in transalpine Europe. Instead, this task fell primarily to two distinctive and somewhat eclectic scholars of the Republic of Letters, who took an early and sustained interest in Bonjour's work and who informed their many correspondents of its progress: the Dijon-based antiquarian Claude Nicaise and, of course, the Deventer official Gisbert Cuper.

Claude Nicaise is representative of a curious sort of late seventeenth-century scholar who enjoyed some standing in the Republic of Letters based on the extent and breadth of his correspondence rather than the quality or proficiency of his scholarly output. In the nineteenth century, Léon-Gabriel Pélissier called him "neither learned nor a scholar," but "un homme mediocre."[151] Certainly it is true that Nicaise was essentially a middleman who encouraged and united diverse scholars in an epistolary network which spread across western Europe but did not produce, nor perhaps was capable of producing, much scholarship himself. Yet Nicaise still performed an important and in some senses invaluable role within the Republic: his vast network was crucial in facilitating and enabling scholarly exchange across national and confessional boundaries. Particularly important were Nicaise's extensive contacts in Italy. Nicaise had himself visited Rome in 1655, where he was ordained and met Queen Christina; he later made a second voyage in 1665–1666, and he counted such important cultural figures as Giovanni Bona, Giovanni Francesco Albani (the future Pope Clement XI), Gregorio Barbarigo, Athanasius Kircher, Lukas Holste, Francesco Barberini (1597–1679), Leo Allatius (c.1586–1669), Giovanni Bellori (1613–1696), and Nicolas Poussin (1594–1665) among his friends and correspondents.[152] Of all the many scholarly disciplines, Nicaise's chosen field was antiquarianism, more specifically numismatics, and Nicaise spent many years establishing, maintaining, and augmenting his friendship with leading numismatists across Europe, including Noris in Rome. Particularly indicative of his passion for this subject – which flowered in and has since become indelibly associated with the late seventeenth century – is his 1691 *Les sirenes*, a dissertation on whether the mythological sirens could be biologically classified as birds or fish (let it never be said that antiquarians failed to tackle the most

---

150 Giovanni Cinelli Calvoli, *Biblioteca volante di Gio Cinelli Calvoli* (Venice: Giambattista Albrizzi q. Girolamo, 1734), 1:184–186.
151 Pélissier, "Lettres inédites de Claude Nicaise," 11.
152 Caillemer, *Lettres de divers savants à l'abbé Nicaise*, 8–13.

pressing questions of the day), which he began with a eulogy on the Parisian numismatic scene then at its flowering zenith.[153]

It was on account of this interest in antiquity – especially recondite pagan antiquity – that Nicaise also took an interest in the scholarly fortunes of a young French Augustinian working in Rome. Nicaise had first heard of Bonjour through Bégon, who, in February 1697, wrote to Nicaise of "a young man very skilled in matters of antiquity," a student of Noris, and the recent author of a work entitled *De nomine patriarchae Josephi*, "the prelude of a larger work" on Egyptian antiquity.[154] In July 1697 Nicaise contacted Bonjour directly, asking him if he would be kind enough to send him three copies of his "preliminary dissertations," namely the *De nomine patriarchae*, which Nicaise intended to pass on to Ezekiel Spanheim, Pierre-Daniel Huet, and Gisbert Cuper, the "plus savant triumvirate de sçavans de l'Europe."[155] This initial exchange paved the way for sustained correspondence. To a significant extent, Bonjour replaced the correspondence Noris was now unable to maintain with transalpine scholars due to his new ecclesiastical duties. Indeed, having a well-connected contact in Rome appeared particularly useful to Nicaise in the years around 1699, when Nicaise eagerly if unsuccessfully sought news about the ongoing examination of François Fénelon's *Maximes des saints* (1697), which Nicaise detested.[156] "Everything that is being debated is only conjecture," wrote Bonjour to Nicaise in February of 1699, "since the cardinals keep the matter so secret that no-one can penetrate it."[157] In addition, Bonjour was already in contact with Nicaise's primary conduit in Rome, the representative of the Cistercian Order Étienne Prinstet (1651–1727), a Jansenist sympathiser who in 1713 called the Bull *Unigenitus* "a thing from hell" and who was forced to leave

---

153 Claude Nicaise, *Les sirenes, ou Discours sur leur forme et figure* (Paris: Jean Anisson, 1691).
154 Michel Bégon to Claude Nicaise, 24 February 1697, BNF, Français 9361, fol. 88v, reprinted in Fossier, *L'abbé Claude Nicaise*, 567: "jeune homme tres versé dans l'antiquité"; "le prelude d'un grand ouvrage."
155 Claude Nicaise to Guillaume Bonjour, 9 July 1697, BAR, ms.lat.395, fols. 148r–150v and reprinted in Pélissier, "Lettres inédites de Claude Nicaise," 189–190. Quote from the following letter, Claude Nicaise to Guillaume Bonjour, 10 October 1697, BAR, ms.lat.395, fols. 151r–152v and Pélissier, "Lettres inédites de Claude Nicaise," 192.
156 Eg. Claude Nicaise to Guillaume Bonjour, 10 January 1699, BAR, ms.lat.395, fols. 160r–161r, reprinted in Pélissier, "Lettres inédites de Claude Nicaise," 201–202: "le quiétisme ruine les belles-lettres."
157 Guillaume Bonjour to Claude Nicaise, 10 February 1699, BNF, Français 9361, fol. 132r–v; reprinted in Fossier, *L'abbé Claude Nicaise*, 629–630: "Tout ce qu'on en debite ne sont que des conjectures car les Cardinaux tiennent la chose si secrete, qu'on ne scauroit la penetrer."

Rome when Clement XI called for him to be interrogated.[158] It was to Prinstet that Bonjour passed on the three requested copies of his *De nomine* and it was Prinstet who later helped transport four copies of Bonjour's *In monumenta coptica* to Cîteaux when he returned there for the general chapter.[159]

Above all, however, Nicaise celebrated Bonjour's interest in ancient Egypt. "I hope," he wrote to Bonjour in October 1697, "that you will develop all the secrets of the philosophy of the Egyptians."[160] These hopes led him to contact a number of illustrious scholars in his epistolary network whom he believed receptive to Bonjour's interest in arcane Egyptian wisdom and mythology. In March 1697, Nicaise passed Bégon's letter concerning Bonjour to Pierre-Daniel Huet, author of the *Demonstratio evangelica* (see chapters 2 and 3), and by August 1698 Huet had obtained the copy of Bonjour's *De nomine* which Nicaise had left for him with Jean Anisson.[161] Yet Huet was just one of the many "illustres personnages de la République des lettres," as Nicaise described them to Bonjour, whom Nicaise notified of this *jeune Augustin*.[162] In 1697, for example, Nicaise told Ezekiel Spanheim that Bonjour was to Egyptian scholarship what Johann Georg Graevius (1632–1703) was to the Romans, Jakob Gronovius (1645–1716) to the Greeks, and Jacobus Perizonius (1651–1715) to the Babylonians, and offered to procure for Spanheim a copy of Bonjour's *De nomine*.[163] In 1698, Nicaise also discussed Bonjour with Graevius himself, who was eagerly awaiting delivery of Bonjour's *De nomine* and who was under the mistaken belief that Bonjour's

---

158   Claude Nicaise to Guillaume Bonjour, 9 July 1697, BAR, ms.lat.395, fol. 148r–v and in Pélissier, "Lettres inédites de Claude Nicaise," 189, in which Nicaise calls Prinstet "le procureur général de l'ordre de Cisteaux." On Prinstet and his comment on *Unigenitus*, see Patrick Arabeyre, "Étienne Prinstet, Illustrateur du Grand Atlas de Cîteaux," *Mémories de la commission des antiquités de la Côte-d'Or* 38 (1997–1999): 241–267 ("une pièce sortie de l'enfer").

159   Guillaume Bonjour to Claude Nicaise, 12 May 1699, BNF, Français 9361, fols. 130r–131r, reprinted in Fossier, *L'abbé Claude Nicaise*, 642; and Claude Nicaise to Guillaume Bonjour, 5 June 1699, BAR, ms.lat.395, fols. 167r–168r and Pélissier, "Lettres inédites de Claude Nicaise," 205–206.

160   Claude Nicaise to Guillaume Bonjour, 10 October 1697, BAR, ms.lat.395, fols. 151r–152v, and in Pélissier, "Lettres inédites de Claude Nicaise," 193: "developpez tous les secrets de la philosophie des Egyptiens."

161   Pierre-Daniel Huet to Claude Nicaise, 19 April 1697, BNF, Français 9359, fol. 108r; Claude Nicaise to Pierre-Daniel Huet, 14 September 1698, in Pélissier, "Lettres inédites de Claude Nicaise," 158.

162   Claude Nicaise to Guillaume Bonjour, 9 July 1697, BAR, ms.lat.395, fols. 148r–150v, and in Pélissier, "Lettres inédites de Claude Nicaise," 189–190.

163   Claude Nicaise to Ezekiel Spanheim, 25 July 1697, in Feller, *Otium Hanoveranum*, 101.

"Dissertationem de Epochis Aegyptiacis" had already been printed.[164] In the same year, Nicaise also mentioned Bonjour's Egyptian projects to Perizonius and Johan de Witt (1662–1701), son of the homonymous, publicly-decapitated Dutch politician and himself a noted antiquarian who had spent time in Italy.[165] Ultimately, it was Nicaise who passed copies of Bonjour's *De nomine* to Cuper, Graevius, Huet, and Perizonius, and, in 1699, copies of the *In monumenta coptica* to Huet, Hiob Ludolf, G. W. Leibniz, and the Cistercian chronologist Paul Pezron (1639–1706).[166]

If Nicaise was one of the primary figures who helped facilitate the exchange between French and Italian scholars in the late seventeenth century, then it was Gisbert Cuper who took on a similar if not even more important role for the Netherlands. As Jetze Touber has pointed out, Italo-Dutch correspondence – for geographical as well as confessional reasons – was far less developed during this period and essentially hinged on two hubs, Magliabechi in Florence and Cuper in The Hague and Deventer.[167] Cuper had been in touch with Magliabechi since at least the 1670s and was one of the few scholars of the period to recognise and cherish the historical and antiquarian scholarship coming out of Italy. In the following years, he established correspondence not only with the leading members of the present generation of Italian learning, such as Noris, Bacchini, and Fabretti, but also with the most promising prospects of the next,

---

164 Johann Georg Graevius to Claude Nicaise, 31 March 1698, BNF, NAF 4368, fol. 60v; reprinted in Caillemer, *Lettres de divers savants à l'abbé Nicaise*, 176, and Fossier, *L'abbé Claude Nicaise*, 603–605. For Graevius' mistake, see Johann Georg Graevius to Antonio Magliabechi, 24 September 1696, in Magliabechi, *Clarorum Belgarum*, 1:315.

165 Johann de Witt to Claude Nicaise, 8 May 1698, BNF, NAF 4368, fol. 110v; reprinted in Caillemer, *Lettres de divers savants à l'abbé Nicaise*, 94, and Fossier, *L'abbé Claude Nicaise*, 610: "je ne me souviens pas d'avoir jamais entendu parler de lui. Est-il François de nation?"; Perizonius' reply is cited in Claude Nicaise's letter to Guillaume Bonjour, 10 June 1698, BAR, ms.lat.395, fols. 156r–157r and in Pélissier, "Lettres inédites de Claude Nicaise," 198.

166 As recorded by Nicaise to Guillaume Bonjour, 10 June 1698, BAR, ms.lat.395, fols. 156r–157r and in Pélissier, "Lettres inédites de Claude Nicaise," 198–199; and Claude Nicaise to Guillaume Bonjour, 6 August 1699, BAR, ms.lat.395, fol. 164r, and Pélissier, "Lettres inédites de Claude Nicaise," 203.

167 Jetze Touber, "Religious Interests and Scholarly Exchange in the Early Enlightenment Republic of Letters: Italian and Dutch Scholars, 1675–1715," in *Rivista di storia della Chiesa in Italia* 68 (2014): 411–436; and Jetze Touber, "'I am happy that Italy fosters such exquisite minds'; Gisbert Cuper (1644–1716) and intellectual life on the Italian peninsula," *Incontri. Rivista europea di studi italiani* 30 (2015): 91–106. See generally Bianca Chen, "Digging for Antiquities with Diplomats: Gisbert Cuper (1644–1716) and his Social Capital," *Republic of Letters: A Journal for the Study of Knowledge, Politics, and the Arts* 1 (2009): 1–18; and Bianca Chen, "Gisbert Cuper as a Servant of Two Republics," in *Double Agents: Cultural and Political Brokerage in Early Modern Europe*, ed. Marika Keblusek and Badeloch Vera Noldus (Leiden: Brill, 2011), 71–94.

such as Muratori, Fontanini, and Bianchini.[168] Indeed Cuper, a former student of Johann Friedrich Gronovius (1611–1671) and a learned scholar of pagan iconography and religion in his own right, was not only a facilitator of scholarly exchange but an enterprising figure who discovered – and prided himself on discovering – young scholarly talent in places many of his contemporaries ignored or avoided.

The first notice of Bonjour came to Cuper from one of Magliabechi's regular dispatches concerning scholarly and literary news from the Italian peninsula. There is also here, wrote Magliabechi in late 1696, "a young man just twenty-five years old, very learned in sacred and profane scholarship and skilled in Oriental languages and literature, which he has combined with a great modesty."[169] Not only did Cuper press Magliabechi for further information on this scholar – who appeared to possess all those qualities which would make him a fitting heir to Noris – but early the next year he was also contacted by Nicaise, who wrote of "a young Augustinian from Toulouse called Father Bonjour, who is very learned in antiquity."[170] Always one to be proactive, by the summer of 1697 Cuper was writing to Bonjour directly, a correspondence which would last more than ten years and would continue until Bonjour reached the Cape of Good Hope in the Autumn of 1710.

Of all the many diverse, erudite subjects which populated Cuper and Bonjour's correspondence, perhaps their primary shared interest was the question of pagan worship, ritual, cults, and religion more generally, particularly in connection with epigraphic or numismatic evidence. One of the chief objects of their early correspondence concerned a coin inscribed ΘΕΟΥ ΠΑΝΟC, which Bonjour had inspected in Rigord's cabinet in Marseille and later discussed in his *De nomine*.[171] Moreover, Cuper often included Bonjour in what had become a coterie of scholars whom he consulted on matters concerning numismatics, pagan religion, and Oriental languages. In 1702, he asked Bonjour to give his opinion on an inscription excavated at Aleppo dedicated to either one, or two, or even three unknown gods, "Jupiter Madbachus and Selamanes." Bonjour's reply was eventually included in a supplement to Pierre Jurieu's *Histoire des dogmes et des cultes* (1705), alongside contributions by a veritable smorgasbord

---

168   See the relevant letters in The Hague, KW 72.
169   Antonio Magliabechi to Gisbert Cuper, 20 June 1696, KW 72 D 10, fol. 116v: "giovani di solamente venticinque anni, e versatissimo nell' erudizzione Sacra é Profana, perito nelle Lingue Orientali e alla letteratura, hà congiunta una somma modestia."
170   Claude Nicaise to Gisbert Cuper, 8 April 1697, KW 72 D 2, fol. 111v: "un jeune Augustin nommé P. Bonjour Tholosain [*sic?*] qui est beaucoup versé dans l'Antiquité."
171   Gisbert Cuper to Guillaume Bonjour, 30 May 1698, BAR, ms.lat.395, fols. 6r–9v, and in Pélissier, "Lettres inédites de Gisbert Cuper," (1905): 62 (226).

of Cuper's chosen experts (see chapter 6).[172] A few years later, when Cuper's close friend Nicolaes Witsen (1641–1717) obtained a mysterious Chinese mirror from Siberia, it was to Bonjour that Cuper sent a copy of the inscription to interpret. Similarly, when in 1705 Cuper believed that a Palmyrene inscription in Rome had been inaccurately reproduced in the collections of Jan Gruter (1603) and Jacob Spon (1685), it was Bonjour whom he turned to (this request was later passed on to Bianchini, who eventually discovered the inscription in 1709).[173] And it was also Cuper who extolled Bonjour continuously to his many illustrious friends in the Republic of Letters. To Antonio Magliabechi he described Bonjour as "a man of the highest erudition"; to the great Orientalist Antoine Galland (1646–1715) as "my great friend"; and to Nicaise as possessing "a truly profound and extensive knowledge."[174] Bonjour is "a religious between thirty and forty years old, highly skilled in Oriental languages, in the Fathers, and in all that concerns *belles-lettres*," he wrote to Pierre Jurieu (1637–1713) in 1704.[175] As we have noted, as late as 1714, Cuper was still writing to Jean-Paul Bignon that Bonjour was "a scholar of the first rank."[176] Ultimately, it was due to Cuper that Bonjour's work became known and accessible to scholars such as Mathurin Veyssière La Croze even after Bonjour's departure for China and his subsequent demise.

172 The original reply is Guillaume Bonjour to Gisbert Cuper, 6 January 1703, KW 72 H 20; Gisbert Cuper and Pierre Jurieu, ed., *Supplément a l'histoire critique des dogmes et des cultes, & etc. ou dissertation par lettres de Monsieur Cuper* (Amsterdam: François l'Honoré, 1705).

173 Gisbert Cuper to Guillaume Bonjour, 22 August 1705, BAR, ms.lat.395, fols. 48r–49v, and in Pélissier, "Lettres inédites de Gisbert Cuper," (1905): 129–131, 293–295; Gisbert Cuper to Giusto Fontanini, 20 February 1708, BVR, T43, fols. 49r–50v; Francesco Bianchini to Gisbert Cuper, [1708], BVR, T43, fols. 51r–52v; Gisbert Cuper to Francesco Bianchini, 1 June and 13 July 1709, BVR, T43, fols. 57r–60v, 62r–67r. The letter was reprinted in Francesco Bianchini, *Opuscula varia* (Rome: Giovanni Lorenzo Barbiellini, 1754), 1:51–76. On the importance of the inscription see Jetze Touber, "Tracing the Human Past: The Art of Writing Between Human Ingenuity and Divine Agency in Early Modern World History," in *Enlightened Religion: From Confessional Churches to Polite Piety in the Dutch Republic*, ed. Joke Spaans and Jetze Touber (Leiden and Boston: Brill, 2019), 60–103.

174 Gisbert Cuper to Antonio Magliabechi, 23 April 1704, KW 72 D 12, fol. 51r; Gisbert Cuper to Antoine Galland, 18 November 1710, in Beyer, *Lettres de critique*, 254; Gisbert Cuper to Claude Nicaise, 7 October 1697, BNF, Français 9359, fols. 423r–v, reprinted in Fossier, *L'abbé Claude Nicaise*, 585–586.

175 Gisbert Cuper to Pierre Jurieu, 7 June 1704, in Beyer, *Lettres de critique*, 467: "un Religieux d'entre trente et quarante ans, très versé dans les langues Orientales, dans les Pères, & dans tout ce qui regarde les Belles Lettres."

176 Gisbert Cuper to Jean-Paul Bignon, 23 February and 10 July 1714, in Beyer, *Lettres de critique*, 326, 330: "un sçavant du premier ordre."

Whatever the case in Rome, Bonjour's talents and interests came at a fortuitous time in the broader (and, perhaps, more broad-minded) transalpine scholarly community. As Anthony Grafton has noted, in the years around 1700 there existed several issues which were of particular concern throughout the learned Republic: Newton's physics, Locke's politics, the mythology of ancient Greece, and the chronology of ancient Egypt.[177] Although Bonjour worked extensively on both of these last two issues, his reputation in the Republic was almost entirely founded on his work on Egypt. This nascent field of proto-Egyptology was undoubtedly critical, not least because of its connection to sacred history and, consequently, the ramifications it had for biblical authority. Sure, wrote Nicaise to Bonjour in July 1697, Gronovius and Graevius were celebrated as the greatest living authorities on Greek and Roman antiquity respectively, yet "your works, my reverend father, will take precedence over those and I hope that we will see there Moses instructed in all the science of Egypt surpassing all the beauties of Athens and Rome."[178] And yet, for such an important subject, it clearly lacked learned authorities. When Johann de Witt learned that Bonjour was working on Egyptian antiquity, he replied that "he is therefore unique in this science."[179] Meanwhile Huet, writing to Nicaise, considered Egyptian antiquity "one of the largest fields of study, which not everyone is permitted to traverse."[180] The problem, according to Huet, was that the study of Egypt required a number of scholarly tools few scholars possessed, namely, an extensive knowledge of Oriental languages, sacred and profane antiquity, and the necessary Arabic historians. This difficulty was only heightened by the perceived failure of the two previous scholars to tackle ancient Egypt, the German Jesuit Athanasius Kircher, who published a number of bombastic,

---

177 Anthony Grafton, *What was History? The art of history in early modern Europe* (Cambridge: Cambridge University Press, 2007), 1.
178 Claude Nicaise to Guillaume Bonjour, 9 July 1697, BAR, ms.lat.395, fols. 148r–150v and Pélissier, "Lettres inédites de Claude Nicaise," 190: "les votres, mon révérend père, primeront sur celles-là, et j'espère que nous y verrons Moyse instruit de toute la science d'Egypte surpassant toutes les beautés d'Athène et de Rome."
179 Johann de Witt to Claude Nicaise, 8 May 1698, BNF, NAF 4368, fol. 110v; reprinted in Caillemer, *Lettres de divers savants à l'abbé Nicaise*, 94, and Fossier, *L'abbé Claude Nicaise*, 610: "il est donc l'unique en cette science."
180 Pierre-Daniel Huet to Claude Nicaise: letter not in Fossier, but a copy is cited by Claude Nicaise to Gisbert Cuper, undated [1697], KW 72 D 2, fol. 128r; and by Claude Nicaise to Guillaume Bonjour, 10 October 1697, BAR, ms.lat.395, fols. 151r–152v, as also in Pélissier, "Lettres inédites de Claude Nicaise," 192–193: "... les antiquités Egyptiennes; c'est un des plus vastes champs de la littérature et où il n'est pas permis à tout le monde de s'engager. Il faut pour cela un grand usage des langues orientales, des antiquités sacrées et profanes, et des historiens arabes."

idiosyncratic, and elaborate studies of Egypt in the mid-seventeenth century, and the English chancery clerk and amateur scholar John Marsham (1602–1685), whose *Chronicus canon*, a controversial chronological study of ancient Egypt, first appeared in 1672.[181] As Huet continued:

> Father Kircher was mistaken in the principle he applied to Egyptian languages in the *Prodromus coptus*; he treated so many things that it was inevitable that he was often mistaken; his knowledge of languages was not exact, nor was he well versed in the learning of the ancients. Mr. Marsham was without comparison more so; but he knew little of the languages of the East; in a word, I do not know of a man alive today with a knowledge so profound and extensive that this project should not frighten him.[182]

In the Republic of Letters, Huet's mistrust of Kircher was largely replicated. As we have seen, Louis Picques thought Kircher barely knew Latin, while Mathurin Veyssière La Croze called him the greatest imposter and boldest liar the Republic of Letters had ever produced.[183] The Ethiopic scholar Hiob Ludolf, who learned of Bonjour's projects through Nicaise, was less damning but no more complimentary. "That man [Kircher]," he wrote to Bonjour in 1700, "was not as solidly imbued with a knowledge of oriental languages as he himself assumed; as can be observed throughout his works."[184] In particular,

---

181   My thanks go to Derrick Mosley who allowed me to see an early unpublished draft of his own PhD thesis on John Marsham.

182   Claude Nicaise to Gisbert Cuper, undated [1697], KW 72 D 2, fol. 128r; Claude Nicaise to Guillaume Bonjour, 10 October 1697, BAR, ms.lat.395, fols. 151r–152v; Pélissier, "Lettres inédites de Claude Nicaise," 192–193: "Le P. Kircher s'est trompé dans le principe, dans son *Prodromus Coptus* touchant la langue égyptienne. Il embrassoit tant de choses qu'il estoit inévitable qu'il se trompait souvent. Il n'estoit pas exact dans la connaissance des langues et il estoit peu versé dans la lecture des anciens. M. Marsham l'étoit sans comparaison davantage, mais il avoit peu d'usage des langues d'Orient. En un mot, je ne connois point d'homme vivant d'un sçavoir si profond et si étendu que ce dessein ne doive effrayer." See for a similar judgement Huet, *Memoirs*, 1:224.

183   Mathurin Veyssière La Croze to Gisbert Cuper, 16 January 1713, KW 72 H 19, n. 24: "le plus grand imposteur & les plus hardi menteur que la Republique des Lettres ait jamais produit." See further on La Croze, Martin Mulsow, *Die drei Ringe: Toleranz und clandestine Gelehrsamkeit bei Mathurin Veyssière La Croze (1661–1739)* (Berlin and New York: Max Niemeyer Verlag, 2001).

184   Hiob Ludolf to Guillaume Bonjour, 13 April 1700, in *Iobi Ludolfi et Godofredi Guilielmi Leibnitii commercium epistolicum*, ed. Augustus Benedictus Michaelis (Göttingen: Victorinus Bossigelius, 1755), 214–217: "ille enim ea peritia linguarum exoticarum, quam prae se tulit, solide imbutus non fuit: quod in eius scriptis passim observare est."

Ludolf, was critical of Kircher's suggestion that Greek had derived from Coptic. The basic upshot of their criticisms, however, was the same: Huet, Ludolf, and Cuper all hoped that Bonjour's knowledge of Egyptian would help rectify the errors of Kircher.[185]

It was for this reason that Bonjour appeared, for at least a short time, to fill a gap in the scholarly market. Yet if scholars knew that Bonjour was working on Egypt, they did not always know on precisely which aspect. Consequently, their expectations often clashed with Bonjour's interests. In a 1698 letter to Bonjour, Nicaise highlighted Bonjour's ability to discover the recondite wisdom of the Egyptians, above all their music, in a manner not dissimilar to Kircher, whom Nicaise described to Bonjour as "nostre bon amy."[186] Yet it is noticeable that Bonjour never mentioned Egyptian music once. With Louis Picques, who received copies of Bonjour's work through Rigord and who corresponded with Bonjour through Montfaucon, the discussion primarily concerned Coptic grammar.[187] Not all their conversations were equally productive, and occasionally the two scholars got their wires crossed. Picques was particularly piqued when Bonjour asked him whether he knew the Coptic conjugations. "Of what use, I ask you, is this question? he who has a whole grammar ready-made!" wrote Picques to Montfaucon in 1699.[188] Moreover, Picques disagreed with Bonjour's interpretation of the Egyptian name which the pharaoh had given Joseph.[189] Yet Picques was also highly complimentary of Bonjour's general aims, in particular his desire to publish a Coptic Bible, which Picques thought "would render a great service to the Church."[190] In a letter to Isaac Jacquelot (1647–1708), he even christened Bonjour "ce Titan Gascon."[191]

Of a somewhat different opinion was Gottfried Wilhelm Leibniz. As Michael Carhart has recently shown, linguistic enquiries and the reconstruction of the

---

185   Cf. Gisbert Cuper to Claude Nicaise, 7 October 1697, BNF, Français 9359, fols. 423r–v; reprinted in Fossier, *L'abbé Claude Nicaise*, 585–586.
186   Claude Nicaise to Guillaume Bonjour, 15 August 1698, BAR, ms.lat.395, fol. 155r, and in Pélissier, "Lettres inédites de Claude Nicaise," 197.
187   In Gigas, *Lettres inédites*, 2. On Picques see Francis Richard, "Un érudit à la recherche de textes religieux venus d'Orient, le docteur Louis Picques (1637–1699)," in *Les pères de l'Église au XVIIe siècle*, ed. E. Bury and B. Meunier (Paris: Les Éditions du Cerf, 1993), 253–277.
188   Louis Picques to Bernard de Montfaucon, 30 March 1699, in Gigas, *Lettres inédites*, 2:311: "A quel usage, je vous prie, cette question? luy qui a une grammaire toutte [sic] preste!"
189   See Hamilton, *The Copts and the West*, 226.
190   Louis Picques to Bernard de Montfaucon, 30 March 1699, in Gigas, *Lettres inédites*, 2:311: "rendra un grand service à l'église."
191   Louis Picques to Isaac Jacquelot, 11 October 1697, in Charles Étienne Jordan, ed., *Histoire de la vie et des ouvrages de Mr. La Croze* (Amsterdam: François Changuion, 1741), 295.

historical relationship between languages were of primary interest to Leibniz in this period.[192] Leibniz had even been persuaded by the recent work of Andreas Acoluthus (1654–1704) that Coptic had descended from Armenian.[193] The search for linguistic answers led him to treasure scholars particularly versed in esoteric languages. To Nicaise, who first informed Leibniz of Bonjour's projects, he wrote that he hoped that Bonjour could do for Egyptian what he considered Samuel Bochart (1599–1667) to have done for Phoenician and Phrygian (*phoenicia passim et phyrgia*), William Camden (1551–1623) and Jacobus Pontanus (1571–1639) for Gallic (*gallica*), and Thomas Reinesius (1587–1667) for Punic (*punica*).[194] Furthermore, Leibniz believed that scholars with particular skills had a duty to aid their fellow scholars in the Republic of Letters. Once, in 1693, he had pressed Nicaise to convince Noris to stay in Rome rather than return to Florence because he believed Noris "can aid scholars and be of service to the public."[195] Throughout 1697 and 1698 he frequently repeated his desire, through Nicaise, for Bonjour to produce what he called a "recueil *vocabulorum Aegyptiorum apud veteres repertorum*," a word-list of ancient Egyptian terms which he found in ancient authors, particularly in Plutarch's *De Iside et Osiride*. This, Leibniz argued, was a project which would make use of Bonjour's specialist linguistic skill for a broader scholarly audience.[196] Bonjour's reticence in this matter – and, more pertinently, Bonjour's frequently stated desire to use his Egyptian learning to both synchronise pagan mythology with biblical history and support the chronology of the Vulgate over that of the Septuagint – made Leibniz uneasy. To Nicaise he wrote that Bonjour's aims were "so flat and devoid of realities," and to Spanheim he noted that perhaps Bonjour "had boasted a little too much" of his abilities.[197] Similarly sceptical was Leibniz's friend and frequent correspondent Hiob Ludolf, who cherished the Septuagint text which Bonjour was seeking to undermine (see chapter four). In later years the two scholars even took to ironically calling Bonjour "Agathemerus," a Greek

---

192 Carhart, *Leibniz Discovers Asia*.
193 Hamilton, *The Copts and the West*, 221; G. W. Leibniz to Johann Georg Graevius, October 1702, in LAA, I, 21:105.
194 G. W. Leibniz to Claude Nicaise, 30 April 1697, and 27 December 1697, LAA, II, 3:303, 3:407.
195 G. W. Leibniz to Claude Nicaise, 25 May 1693, in Caillemer, *Lettres de divers savants à l'abbé Nicaise*, 33: "peut obliger les sçavans et rendre service au public."
196 G. W. Leibniz to Claude Nicaise, 30 April 1697, and 27 December 1697, LAA, II, 3:303, 3:407. Nicaise transmitted the request to Bonjour on 8 February 1698, BAR, ms.lat.395, fols. 151r–152v, reprinted in Pélissier, "Lettres inédites de Claude Nicaise," 197. See also Claude Nicaise to G. W. Leibniz, 27 February 1698, LAA, II, 3:414.
197 G. W. Leibniz to Claude Nicaise, 16 August 1699, LAA, II, 3:589: "si seche et vuide de realités"; G. W. Leibniz to Ezekiel Spanheim, 20 February 1699, LAA, I, 16:602: "s'etoit un peu trop vanté."

geographer of the third century AD and an in-joke I have yet to unravel.[198] It should be noted, however, that Leibniz's disappointment with Bonjour's Egyptian scholarship did not necessarily suggest a low estimation of Bonjour's scholarly abilities. Indeed, it was precisely because Bonjour was talented that Leibniz considered his talent wasted. Moreover, Leibniz continued to remain appreciative of Bonjour's scholarly abilities after Bonjour's departure from Rome. Discussing the recent events in China in 1712, and apparently unaware that Bonjour himself was en route there, he wrote to Mathurin Veyssière La Croze that:

> I believe that the *Pope* would have done better to send to *China* a man like *Father Bonjour*, than a man like *the Cardinal Tournon*. He would have had less authority, but he could have reported back with more knowledge of the matter. To tell the truth, I have always found the behaviour of this Cardinal more suitable for a *Visionary Saint*, than for a man whose zeal is regulated *by science*.[199]

Perhaps the final scholar we should mention when considering Bonjour's transalpine reputation is the Genevan-born biblical critic, journalist, and theologian Jean Le Clerc (1657–1736), who spent most of his working life in Amsterdam. In the following chapters, we shall have recourse to both Le Clerc's stance on ancient pagan mythology and his approach to biblical text criticism, much of which was directed against the scholarly tradition of *historia sacra* which Bonjour incorporated and built on in his work. Yet despite these broader conceptual differences, Bonjour and Le Clerc shared interests in the same scholarly subjects. Le Clerc himself had been a long-term correspondent of Cuper and first heard of Bonjour when Cuper told him of the various antiquarian letters he was planning to print as a supplement to Jurieu's *Histoire critique des dogmes et des cultes*, a supplement Le Clerc later came to cite in his somewhat belated 1705 review of John Selden's *De diis syris* (first published in

---

198 See Hiob Ludolf to G. W. Leibniz, 27 June 1702, LAA, I, 21:357: "Literas Agathemeri ('Ἀγαθήμερου Bonjour), quarum in prioribus mentionem facis ...".

199 G. W. Leibniz to Mathurin Veyssière La Croze, July 1712, in Jordan, *Histoire de la vie et des ouvrages de Mr. La Croze*, 174: "je crois que *le Pape* auroit mieux fait d'envoyer à *la Chine* un homme comme le *Pere Bonjour*, qu'un homme comme *le Cardinal de Tournon*. Il auroit eu moins d'autorité, mais il auroit pu faire des rapports, avec plus de connoissance de cause. Car pour dire la vérité, j'ai toujours trouvé le procédé de ce *Cardinal*, plus convenable à un *Saint Visionnaire*, qu'à un homme dont le zèle est reglé par *la Science*"; cf. Louis Dutens, *Gothofredi Guillelmi Leibnitii opera omnia* (Geneva: Fratres de Tournes, 1768), 5:503–504.

1617).[200] Reading this review in Rome, Bonjour was particularly interested in Le Clerc's discussion of the etymology of Osiris, which Le Clerc, in opposition to Selden, had traced back to the Egyptian *os* (many) and *iri* (eye) and therefore given as πολυόφθαλμον, many-eyed, as once suggested by Plutarch (*De Iside et Osiride* 355A) and Diodorus (1.11.2).[201] Bonjour himself had discussed the etymology in similar terms in his *De nomine* and, in 1707, Cuper passed Bonjour's contribution on to Le Clerc at the Augustinian's request.[202] When Bonjour was in Amsterdam in January 1708, on his path from Cuper's house in Deventer to The Hague and thence to London, he even visited Le Clerc and demonstrated what Le Clerc later described as an enviable skill in Coptic.[203] What is more, the visit seems to have awakened Le Clerc's interest in Bonjour's scholarship. In the 1708 volume of his *Bibliothèque choisie*, Le Clerc wrote a lengthy review of three of Bonjour's works, the *Calendarium romanum*, the *In monumenta coptica*, and the *Selectae in sacram scripturam*, the collection of biblical dissertations which Bonjour wrote while professor of theology in Montefiascone. Although not unanimously positive about some of Bonjour's decisions, most notably his attempt to synchronize pagan mythology with sacred history, Le Clerc nevertheless described Bonjour as an erudite and sophisticated scholar.[204] In 1709, he also managed to read Bonjour's *De nomine*, after Cuper had procured for him a copy.[205] In subsequent years, Le Clerc still retained an interest in and a fondness for Bonjour's work. As late as 1717, apparently unaware of Bonjour's demise, Le Clerc noted in a review of David Wilkins's Coptic Pentateuch that he hoped Bonjour would publish his Coptic grammar upon his return from the Far East.[206] Three years later, he was still referencing Bonjour's proposed emendations to Josephus in his discussion of the recently published *Flavii Josephi opera omnia* by the English classicist John Hudson (1662–1719).[207]

200 Gisbert Cuper to Jean Le Clerc, 24 October 1704, in Jean Le Clerc, *Epistolario*, ed. Mario Sina and Maria Grazia Zaccone-Sina (Florence: L. S. Olschki, 1987–1997), 2:479.
201 Jean Le Clerc, "Article II: remarques sur le livre de *Jean Selden* intitulé *des Dieux des Syriens*," in *Bibliothèque choisie: pour servir de suite à la Bibliothèque universelle* 7 (1705): 131–132.
202 *De nomine*, 9; Guillaume Bonjour to Gisbert Cuper, 3 May 1706, KW 72 H 20; Gisbert Cuper to Jean Le Clerc, 10 January 1707, in Le Clerc, *Epistolario*, 3:52–53.
203 Jean Le Clerc to Gisbert Cuper, 18 December 1707, in Le Clerc, *Epistolario*, 3:117–119.
204 Jean Le Clerc, "Article IV," *Bibliothèque choisie: pour servir de suite à la Bibliothèque universelle* 15 (1708): 187–246.
205 Gisbert Cuper to Jean Le Clerc, 1 January 1709, in Le Clerc, *Epistolario*, 3:123–124.
206 Jean Le Clerc, "Article V: Novum Testamentum Aegyptium, vulgo Copticum," *Bibliothèque ancienne et moderne: pour servir de suite aux Bibliothèques universelle et choisie* 7 (1717): 199.
207 Jean Le Clerc, "Flavii Josephi Opera," *Bibliothèque ancienne et moderne; pour servir de suite aux Bibliothèques universelle et choisie* 14 (1720): 267.

4 Bonjour in Montefiascone

It can sometimes be difficult to determine the exact level of influence Noris had over Bonjour's studies. Although Noris was an exceptional numismatist, ecclesiastical historian, and chronologist he did not share Bonjour's interest in biblical criticism, Egyptian antiquity, or Oriental languages such as Syriac, Arabic, or Coptic. Noris' chronological and antiquarian works largely concerned early Church history: the reigns of the emperors, the genealogy of the Herods, Pelagianism, the Donatists, the condemnation of Origen at the Second Council of Constantinople, and the Investiture crisis. These were matters of ecclesiastical rather than recondite history. In 1697, he described Bonjour to Nicaise as "totus ... antiquarius," a complete antiquarian. "He inquires into the obsolete and with marvellous erudition examines ancient names according to the idioms of various peoples so that he shakes off a certain astonishment, even laughter; led by his genius, his mind troubles itself with matters so greatly remote from the memory of men," he continued, a passage which expresses both his admiration of Bonjour's learning and a certain distance or even lack of familiarity with Bonjour's chosen subjects.[208] Yet, it should be noted, Bonjour's life as a scholar was also determined by Noris. It was Noris who read and approved Bonjour's chronological works and undoubtedly his influence which saw Bonjour come to the attention of Pope Clement XI and join the congregation for the reform of the calendar. As we have seen, Bonjour's interest in the Church *computus* and the paschal cycles of the ante-Nicene Fathers was shaped by Noris. Like Noris, it seems that Bonjour was committed to a form of positive theology determined by the study of ecclesiastical history, rather than scholastic theology or metaphysical philosophy. Above all, Bonjour shared Noris' assumption that historical scholarship held the key to correctly understanding an ancient Church tradition which separated orthodoxy from heresy. It also appears that, in both Rome specifically and the Republic of Letters more generally, scholars saw Bonjour as Noris' student and possible successor. In August 1703, Clement XI was reported to have spared Bonjour from the missions to the Far East because "he was a great subject who could do more good here than in the missions, and that if God takes Cardinal Noris, currently ill with dropsy, from us, then it is said he is the man to succeed him, because of

---

208 As cited by Claude Nicaise to Pierre-Daniel Huet, 1 August 1697, in Pélissier, "Lettres inédites de Claude Nicaise," 148: "Is sane juvenis totus est antiquarius; obsoleta inquirit ac miro studio vetusta nomina juxta diversarum gentium idiomata inspicit ut quemdam stuporem, imo etiam risum excutiat; eo genio ductus ingenium vexat in rebus ab hominum memoria remotissimis etc. etc. ...". Noris' letter is dated 2 July 1697.

his great learning accompanied by a rare humility."[209] By late 1703, Noris was severely ill, and he died in March the following year. As a result, Bonjour was forced to look for a new patron.

This patron turned out to be Marc-Antonio Barbarigo (1640–1706), a distant relative of the same Gregorio Barbarigo who had founded the printing press in Padua. Marc-Antonio had initially served as bishop of Corfu until 1686 when a diplomatic incident incurred the wrath of the future Doge of Venice Francesco Morosini (1619–1694). Forced to return to Rome, he was rewarded there by being made cardinal and bishop of Montefiascone and Corneto.[210] Montefiascone itself was a small hill-top town some one hundred kilometres north of Rome and fifteen kilometres from Viterbo overlooking lake Bolsena, particularly famous for its legendary white wine. "The little Mountain is very agreeable," wrote Misson on his Italian journey, "and the Country fruitful every where in the Neighbourhood: and the Wines above all seem'd so delicious to a certain Doctor whom we saw there, as well as to the Abbot *d'Est Est Est*, that he cannot believe that *Monte-Fiascone* signifies any Thing but *Monte de Fiascone*, (Flagons, or large Bottles)."[211] Alongside wine, however, the little town also offered religious education. A seminary with an adjoining library had initially been established there by Cardinal Paluzzo Paluzzi Altieri degli Albertoni (1623–1698) in 1667, and when Barbarigo became bishop in 1687 he restored the seminary, augmented the library, and established at considerable cost a printing press complete with both Hebrew and Syriac type-faces in a manner clearly influenced by the example of his more illustrious relative.[212] The seminary itself employed five professors of theology and philosophy, four masters

---

209   Nicolas Charmot, "Biographie et lettres du P. Nicolas Charmot," BNF, Français 25060, 2455: "c'estoit un grand sujez qui pouvoit faire ici plus de bien que dans les missions et que si dieu disposoit du Cardinal Noris (malade une hydropisie ententé) c'est dit un homme a lui succeder [ver]ité cause de sa grande science accompagnée d'une rare humilité cela n'est il pas vray."

210   Cf. Gian Franco Torcellan, "Barbarigo, Marco Antonio," *Dizionario Biografico degli Italiani* 6 (1964).

211   Misson, *A new voyage to Italy*, 2:235.

212   Cf. Giancarlo Breccola, "La tipografia del seminario di Montefiascone," *Quaderno della Rivista del Consorzio per la gestione delle biblioteche comunale degli Ardenti e provinciale Anselmo Anselmi di Viterbo* 25 (1997); Giancarlo Breccola, "La biblioteca del seminario Barbarigo di Montefiascone: problemi di conservazione, ipotesi di valorizzazione," in *Le biblioteche dei seminari delle antiche diocesi di Viterbo, di Tuscania, di Montefiascone, di Acquapendente, di Bagnoregio, e del Seminario regionale della Quercia: problem di conservazione, ipotesi di valorizzazione*, ed. Luciano Osbat (Viterbo: Cedido, 2009), 18–30; Dennis E. Rhodes, "Note sui primi libri stampati a Montefiascone," *La Bibliofilía* 76 (1974): 139–142; Dennis E. Rhodes, "Primo libro stampato a Montefiascone?" *La Bibliofilía* 77 (1975): 253–254.

of rhetoric and grammar, and one teacher of Latin and Greek; its students were primarily composed of young members of the clergy as well as some lay boarders, often but not exclusively from noble families.[213] In a letter to Magliabechi, Bonjour described it as constituted "nel modo che si costuma in Francia," and estimated that it comprised about 150 people in total.[214] Among the first professors to teach there was the Irish priest Michael Moore (1639–1726), a former provost of Trinity College Dublin, Censor of the Index in Rome, and later Rector of the University of Paris, who was professor of Greek between 1696 and 1701. Another was the French Orientalist Jean Bouget (1692?–1775), originally from Saumur, whose *Brevis exercitatio ad studium linguae Hebraicae* (1706) Bonjour approved for use by the theology students in 1705.[215] In later years a notable student was Giuseppe Bianchini (1704–1764), nephew of Francesco, who boarded there between 1720 and 1725 and who went on to become a noted Orientalist and biblical scholar in his own right.[216] We might note here that Bonjour himself was responsible for approving Francesco Bianchini's 1703 *De kalendario et cyclo Caesaris* for use in the seminary in 1704.[217]

We know Bonjour had been in touch with Barbarigo as early as February 1698, when, in one of his outbursts against the deplorable state of Italian printing, Bonjour remarked to Magliabechi that he had had an invitation from Barbarigo to print some of his works in Montefiascone, "where his Eminency has constructed a most beautiful printing press."[218] This invitation also led Bonjour to temporarily shelve his plan to return to France. It must be said, however, that Barbarigo's initial invitation came as a surprise to Bonjour, who had yet to meet "quel gran protettore delle lettere" himself. In the following years, Bonjour and Barbarigo began establishing closer ties. Having first visited Montefiascone at Barbarigo's request in early 1698, Bonjour returned in 1702 to teach the *computus* and to print his *Tractatus de computo ecclesiastico* at the

---

213 Antonio Patrizi, *Storia del seminario di Montefiascone* (Montefiascone: Sistema Biblioteca "Lago di Bolsena," 1990), 29ff., 144–146.
214 Guillaume Bonjour to Antonio Magliabechi, 26 January 1704, BNCF, *Fondo Magliabechiano* VIII, cod. 317, fol. 73r.
215 Jean Bouget, *Brevis exercitatio ad studium linguae hebraicae* (Montefiascone: Ex typographia Seminarii, 1706). See the copy in the Montefiascone seminary library; I have not found a copy elsewhere.
216 In addition to Patrizi see the somewhat dated Josepho Sartinio, *Vitae illustrium professorum seminarii et collegii Faliscodunensis* (Montefiascone: Typis Seminarii et Collegii, 1844). The few sources on Bouget date his birth to 1692, but this would make him just 14 when he published his first work on Hebrew.
217 Guillaume Bonjour to Francesco Bianchini, 22 October 1704, BVR, U15, fol. 259r.
218 Guillaume Bonjour to Antonio Magliabechi, 3 February 1698, BNCF, *Fondo Magliabechiano* VIII, cod. 317, fol. 24r: "dove la sua Eminenza a fatto fare una stamperia belissima [sic]."

seminary press.[219] In a 1703 letter to Barbarigo, the only letter of their correspondence known to survive, Bonjour outlined the necessity of his studies for combatting "Hebrews and Heretics, who currently busy themselves much with holy scripture."[220] During this time, Barbarigo retained his initial enthusiasm for the learned and by now widely-respected Bonjour. In 1702, he wrote to the director of the seminary, Alessandro Mazzinelli (1671–1741), that he admired Bonjour's humility, his learning, and, in particular, his abilities in Greek and Hebrew.[221] Indeed, it appears from both the Oriental type-face of the printing press and the publication of such works as Bouget's introduction to Hebrew that Barbarigo particularly encouraged the study of languages. In the following years, he frequently lobbied Pope Clement XI to release Bonjour from his duties in Rome so he could take up a teaching post in Montefiascone. Finally, in January 1704, with Noris on his deathbed, Bonjour wrote to Magliabechi that he had been appointed as professor of *sacra scrittura* at the seminary.[222]

In Montefiascone, Bonjour attempted to implement the same values which informed his scholarship in Rome. In particular, he focussed on teaching theology and the Bible through the means of ancient history, Oriental languages, patristic apologetics, biblical chronology, and even the knowledge of ancient calendars. Somewhat suggestive of his interests and methods are the two works he saw through the seminary press in 1704 and 1705 respectively, the *Triduanda de canone librorum sacrorum concertatio* and the *Selectae in sacram scripturam dissertationes*. Although compiled and printed on the orders of Barbarigo, the works were intended to convey the type of material Bonjour was teaching his students.[223] Composed of various dissertations often structured as dialogues between interlocutors at the seminary, the works tackled such concerns as the composition of the biblical canon, the chronology of the Vulgate, the true antiquity of Moses, and the primacy of the Hebrews through recourse to the study of Greek and Near Eastern chronology, pagan mythology, biblical manuscripts, and even the textual history of the *corpus* of Flavius

---

219   Guillaume Bonjour to Antonio Magliabechi, 2 October and 7 October 1702, BNCF, *Fondo Magliabechiano* VIII, cod. 317, fols. 65r, 70r.
220   Guillaume Bonjour to Marc-Antonio Barbarigo, 18 August 1703, BAR, ms.lat.395, fol. 3r: "li quali oggidi s'affatigano molto nelle sacre scritture."
221   Marc-Antonio Barbarigo to Alessandro Mazzinelli, 28 January 1702, Montefiascone Seminary Archives, Press 4, Shelf D, 23.
222   Guillaume Bonjour to Antonio Magliabechi, 26 January 1704, BNCF, *Fondo Magliabechiano* VIII, cod. 317, fol. 73r.; Patrizi, *Storia del seminario*, 162; see also Guillaume Bonjour to Gisbert Cuper, 26 January 1704, KW 72 H 20; and Francesco Bianchini, "Vita del Cardinal Enrico Noris," in *Le vite degli arcadi illustri*, 1:214.
223   Guillaume Bonjour to Ludovico Antonio Muratori, 5 July 1705, BEM, *Archivio Muratori*, MS 84.16 [unpaginated].

Josephus. Similarly indicative of Bonjour's teaching methods is a lesser-known, three-volume series of biblical exercises which he prepared explicitly and exclusively for use at the seminary. Each of these volumes contained a number of supposed contradictions within the Bible which the students were asked to solve or explain. Thus the first of these volumes discussed contradictions in the Gospels, such as the fact that the Evangelist Mark (1:2) claimed that the quote "ecce ergo mitto Angelum meum ante faciem tuam, qui praeparabit viam tuam" came from the prophet Isaiah when it actually comes from Malachi 3:1; the second volume contradictions in Genesis, as when God makes light at Genesis 1:3, but only divides it from darkness at Genesis 1:4, or the question as to why the wives of Esau are different in Genesis 26:34 and Genesis 36:2–3; and the third volume contradictions in Exodus, including the notable issue as to whether the 430-year period referred to the years the Israelites spent in Egypt (Exodus 12:40) or the time between God's covenant with Abraham in Canaan and Moses receiving the Decalogue on Mount Sinai (Galatians 3:16–17).[224] None of these dissertations seem to have been intended for use outside of Montefiascone. They do, however, give us an indication of the type of teaching Bonjour was offering in Montefiascone. It seems clear that, for Bonjour, teaching "holy scripture" meant defending its authority against a range of possible opponents: contemporary freethinkers who denied the authority and authenticity of the Books of Moses; heretics (Protestants) who denied that Peter had journeyed to Rome where he was established as "prince of all the Apostles and rector of the universal Church"; "Gentiles" who claimed that the chronology of Jesus in Matthew 1:1–17 contradicted the Old Testament; and "Greeks" who celebrated Easter on the wrong day.[225] Above all, it shows how Bonjour took on what he had learnt from Noris, whom he called the "prince of the theologians of our time, whose cardinal purple ecclesiastical history celebrates all over the world": namely, that it was the study of sacred and ecclesiastical history which was the handmaiden of theology and which was necessary for establishing the truth of Church tradition.[226]

---

[224] Guillaume Bonjour, *Quaestiones evangelicae proponendae in Academia Divinarum literarum et solvendae à theologis seminarii Montis-Falisci* (Montefiascone: Ex typographia Seminarii, 1705); Guillaume Bonjour, *Academica exercitatio in scripturam sacram et ritus ecclesiasticos* (Montefiascone: Ex typographia Seminarii, 1705); and Guillaume Bonjour, *Academica exercitatio in scripturam sacram et ritus ecclesiasticos* (Montefiascone: Ex typographia Seminarii, 1706). The only copies I have found are in the Montefiascone seminary archives.

[225] As noted in the "Propositiones disputandae," in Bonjour, *Quaestiones evangelicae*.

[226] Guillaume Bonjour, "Brevis ad theologos praelectio. De necessitate studiorum Historiae ecclesaisticae," BAR, ms.lat.630, fols. 200v–202r: "princeps theologorum nostri temporis Em. Cardinalis Norisius, cujus purpuram orbe toto celebrat historia ecclesiastica." See

During Bonjour's years in Montefiascone he maintained a lively and erudite correspondence with Cuper in Holland, Muratori in Modena, Magliabechi in Florence and with his many friends in Rome, such as Bianchini and Pastrizio and to a lesser extent Fontanini and Massoulié. In October 1704, Bonjour visited Orvieto, while in 1705 he spent a few weeks in Rome for the Augustinian general chapter.[227] He was also visited in Montefiascone by the Bishop of Rosalie Artus de Lionne (1655–1713), who was in Rome on account of the Chinese Rites and who was accompanied by Arcadio Huang (1679–1716), a young Chinese man who was later to achieve fame in Paris, and who was plagiarised there by Étienne Fourmont (1683–1745).[228] Apart, however, from the opportunity afforded to him by the printing press, Bonjour's stay in Montefiascone does not appear to have been especially fruitful. Since much of Bonjour's time was spent teaching, and the rest seeing his works through the press, he found it difficult to continue with his research. A more pressing issue was the paucity of the seminary library, particularly when compared to the abundance in the Angelica or the bounty of the Vatican: according to a 1695 inventory which has recently been examined by Giancarlo Breccola, the library consisted of just 110 folio books and a further 193 volumes in quarto or octavo.[229] Even Barbarigo's attempts to procure more works for Bonjour and his success in obtaining for Bonjour permission to read banned books (Bonjour cited both Hobbes' *Leviathan* and Walton's polyglot in his 1705 *Selectae*) proved insufficient.[230] "The lack of many books makes my ignorance grow every day, and prevents me from giving adequate answers to the questions asked," Bonjour wrote to Magliabechi in May 1706.[231] When Marc-Antonio Barbarigo died

---

further fol. 199r: "Cum theologia scholastica non excitatis e flexionum et circuitionum metaphysicarum rivulis inflata atque anhelata vaporibus, sed exploratis, sed statis ratisque, sed validissimis et sacrae scripturae et sacrorum canonum et sanctorum patrum longe nervosius instituta, munita, obfirmata praesidiis sequestres et confirmatores ecclesiastica antiquitatis omnino postulet; jam intelligitis, Auditores religiosissimi, quid praeloqui vos manet ad studium historiae ecclesiasticae excitandos."

227   Guillaume Bonjour to Antonio Magliabechi, 1 October 1704, BNCF, *Fondo Magliabechiano* VIII, cod. 317, fol. 84r. Also mentioned in Gisbert Cuper to Guillaume Bonjour, 22 August 1705, BAR, ms.lat.395, fols. 48r–49v, and in Pélissier, "Lettres inédites de Gisbert Cuper," (1905): 130 (294).

228   Guillaume Bonjour to Antonio Magliabechi, 21 December 1704, BNCF, *Fondo Magliabechiano* VIII, cod. 317, fol. 104r. See for more on this chapter 7.

229   Breccola, "La Biblioteca del seminario Barbarigo di Montefiascone," 19. A different number is given by Patrizi, *Storia del seminario*.

230   Marc-Antonio Barbarigo to Alessandro Mazzinelli, 28 January 1702 and 10 January 1706, Montefiascone Seminary Archives, Press 4, Shelf D, 24, 147; Baldini, "Guillaume Bonjour," 250, n. 33.

231   Guillaume Bonjour to Antonio Magliabechi, 31 May 1706, BNCF, *Fondo Magliabechiano* VIII, cod. 317, fol. 112r: "La mancanza de' molti libri fà crescere ogni giorno la mia

soon after, the matter appeared decided. In 1705 Adeodato Nuzzi (1658–1720), one of Noris' longest and closest friends, had been elected prior general of the Augustinian Hermits. It appears that Nuzzi – who was later in charge of organising Bonjour's posthumous manuscripts alongside Basile Rasseguier – was more receptive to Bonjour's particular scholarly interests.[232] Following Barbarigo's death on 26 May 1706, Nuzzi officially recalled Bonjour to Rome, where he resumed work on many of the Coptic manuscripts which had lain neglected since 1701.

5   Bonjour in China – and Beyond

When Bernard de Montfaucon first met Bonjour in the winter of 1698–99, he was impressed but also somewhat alarmed by the industry and ambition of this young Augustinian. "Father Bonjour is a tireless worker: he has also copied the whole Bible and translated these two versions into Latin on the basis of the promise made to him to have them printed, but I do not know whether he will complete this," he wrote to the librarian Nicolas Clément (1647–1712) in Paris. "This task is so great that apparently his patrons will no longer be alive when he has achieved it."[233] What Montfaucon prophesized eventually came to pass. Not only did Noris and Barbarigo soon die, but so too did Casanata and Nicaise. As Bonjour wrote to Magliabechi a few days after Barbarigo's death, "behold, here is the second cardinal protector I have lost during my time in Italy. But as I placed my hope in the Lord, and since I have no other desire than to study for His glory and in the service of religion, then even if I were capable of it, I will not lose heart."[234]

---

ignoranza, e m'impedisce dare risposte adeguate a' quesiti fatti." See also Guillaume Bonjour to Antonio Magliabechi, 27 October 1704, BNCF, *Fondo Magliabechiano* VIII, cod. 317, fol. 86r: "Non ho qui la multiplicità de' libri che havevo in Roma, e cosi non posso scrivere tutto quello che desiderarei."

232   Nuzzi later corresponded with Cuper regarding Bonjour's manuscripts: Gisbert Cuper to Adeodato Nuzzi, 18 February 1708, 1 June 1709 and 25 August 1709, and Adeodato Nuzzi to Gisbert Cuper, 5 May 1708, are in KW 72 G 23; Cuper's letters are reprinted in J. A. F. Orbaan and G. J. Hoogewerff, ed., *Bescheiden in Italië omtrent nederlandsche kunstenaars en geleerden* (The Hague: Martinus Nijhoff, 1911–1917), vol. 3.

233   Bernard de Montfaucon to Nicolas Clément, 3 February 1699, in Gigas, *Lettres inédites*, 2:298: "Le P. Bonjour est d'un travail infatigable: il a copié de même toute la bible et tourner en latin ces 2 versions sur la promesse qu'on luy avoit faire de les faires imprimer, mais je ne scais s'il achevera. Ce travail est si long qu'apparement ses patrons ne seront plus en vie quand il l'aura achevé."

234   Guillaume Bonjour to Antonio Magliabechi, 31 May 1706, BNCF, *Fondo Magliabechiano* VIII, cod. 317, fol. 113r: "ed ecco il secondo protettore porporato che io hò perso dal tempo

Somewhat curiously, the second half of 1706 and the first half of 1707, the year Bonjour spent in Rome before setting off for China, marks a lacuna in Bonjour's scholarly correspondence. Indeed, there exists no correspondence between Bonjour and Cuper from May 1706, when Bonjour was still in Montefiascone, to December 1707, when Bonjour wrote to Cuper from Dusseldorf. Similarly, the last known letter Bonjour wrote to Muratori also dates from May 1706, and the last letter to Magliabechi from June of that year. It seems, however, that during this period Bonjour returned predominantly to his work on Coptic biblical manuscripts. Above all, he appears to have been working on a Coptic-Arabic Psalter, collating a manuscript from the Camaldolese convent of Sant' Antonio Abate on the Esquiline hill with a manuscript originally owned by Nicolas-Claude Fabri de Peiresc (1580–1637) which had been stolen by pirates and reached the Barberini library in Rome via the Knights of Malta.[235] As is well known, this task was soon interrupted by Bonjour's somewhat remarkable decision to abandon Rome for the Chinese missions.

The initial impetus for Bonjour's mission was the question of the notorious Chinese Rites, the long-standing debate in the Catholic Church as to whether the Rites dedicated to Confucius and the Chinese ancestors were merely civil and political, as the Jesuits argued, or religious and therefore idolatrous (a debate I will cover in detail in chapter 7). More specifically, Bonjour's mission was a direct consequence of the 1702 decision to send Charles-Thomas Maillard de Tournon (1668–1710) to the Far East as papal legate *a latere* in order to inspect the evangelising methods of the Jesuits. Tournon himself was a native of Turin and had long had connections with the Roman cultural world. He was, for example, a member of the Italian literary academy, the Arcadia, which counted Noris, Bianchini, and Clement XI among its members.[236] His interest in pastoral poetry, however, did not translate into an ability as a missionary mediator. Initially tasked with observing missionary practices and

che sono in Italia. Ma come ho meso le mie speranza nel signore, e che non ho altro desiderio di studiare che per la sua gloria ed il servizio della religione, se pure ne fossi capace, non perdo animo."

[235] See "Psalterium Copto-Arabicum," BAR, ms.lat.45; Hamilton, *The Copts and the West*, 254; Guidi, *Catalogo*, 77–79; Agostino Antonio Giorgi, *De miraculis Sancti Coluthi et reliquiis actorum Sancti Panesniu martyrum thebaica fragmenta duo alterum auctius alterum nunc primum* (Rome: Antonio Fulgoni, 1793), 37. On Peiresc and his world see Peter N. Miller, *Peiresc's Orient: Antiquarianism as Cultural History in the Seventeenth Century* (Surrey: Ashgate, 2012).

[236] See Antonin Massoulié to Antonio Magliabechi, 29 April 1702, BNCF, *Fondo Magliabechiano* VIII, cod. 364, fols. 37r, 38v; Ludwig Freiherr von Pastor, *The History of the Popes from the Close of the Middle Ages*, trans. Ernest Graf (London: Kegan Paul, Trench, Trubner & co., 1940), 33:412–413.

preserving harmony among the missions, Tournon instead provoked outrage with his swift condemnation of Jesuit accommodationism – a bull in a China shop, so to speak. During a six-month layover in Pondicherry in 1704, he declared the Malabar Rites then being practiced by Indian neophytes idolatrous and threatened to excommunicate several prominent Jesuits who refused to submit to his authority. Upon his arrival in China, he had several disastrous meetings with the Kangxi Emperor in which he attempted to explain why Chinese Confucianism was idolatrous. In February 1707, Tournon published a decree, the so-called *decreto nanchinese*, which threatened excommunication for any missionary who refused to submit to the papal decision of 1704 that had first banned the rites. This led to the retributive arrest of Tournon by the Chinese imperial authorities and his exile to Macao, where he was imprisoned under the supervision of the Portuguese Jesuits.[237]

By 1707, then, both the rapidly deteriorating relations between the papal representatives and the Chinese authorities as well as the deplorable state of the missions more generally appeared to render a new mission under the direct jurisdiction of the Propaganda fide necessary.[238] From China and Macao, Tournon frequently wrote of the need for new, non-Jesuit, missionaries who would prove loyal to his cause.[239] One such letter addressed to Nuzzi can still be seen in the Biblioteca Angelica.[240] Over the following months Cardinal Giuseppe Sacripanti (1642–1727), secretary of the Propaganda fide, wrote letters to different Italian seminaries, including to Barbarigo in Montefiascone, appealing for young volunteers to come to Rome and be prepared for missionary work at the Collegio Urbano.[241] The main impetus for Bonjour's mission, however, was provided by a letter from the Kangxi Emperor which arrived in Rome in July 1707, requesting the pope to send him three musicians, three

---

237 Pastor, *The History of the Popes*, 33:432–446; Claudia von Collani, "Charles Maigrot's Role in the Chinese Rites Controversy" in *The Chinese Rites Controversy: Its History and Meaning*, ed. D. E. Mungello (Sankt Augustin: Institut Monumenta Serica and San Francisco: The Ricci Institute for Chinese Western Cultural History, 1994), 149–183.

238 See for example "Congregazione Particolari sopra l'Indie Orientali," 25 September 1710, ASPF, *Acta CP* 2, fol. 158r–v: "lo stato deplorabile di queste Missioni del bisogno urgentissimo di qualche provvedimento."

239 For example, "Congregazione Particolari sopra l'Indie Orientali," 26 September 1706, ASPF, *Acta CP* 2, fol. 85r; "Congregazione Particolari sopra l'Indie Orientali," 30 December 1706, ASPF, *Acta CP* 2, fol. 99v.

240 Charles Thomas Maillard de Tournon to Adeodato Nuzzi, 5 May 1706, BAR, ms.lat.891, fol. 53r.

241 Marc-Antonio Barbarigo to Cardinal Giuseppe Sacripanti, 13 February 1706, ASPF, SC *Missioni* 1, fol. 499r. The plea by Sacripanti can be found in the same volume, fols. 487r–488r. See also Baldini, "Guillaume Bonjour," 256.

surgeons, and three mathematicians. On 1 August it was decided to make Tournon cardinal and to send to China the requested missionaries along with the cardinal's hat for Tournon.[242] For this mission Bonjour was selected as resident mathematician.

Bonjour and his companions met Clement XI in their new roles as missionaries for the first time on 26 August 1707. Alongside Bonjour, the mission included Onorato Funari, a forty-year-old priest from Fondi; Gioseppe Cerù, a member of the Clerics Regular Minor from Lucca; Domenico Perrone, originally from Naples, who was a cleric regular of the Santa Maria in Campitelli church in Rome; Gennaro Amodei, who had come from Naples and had spent two years preparing for the missions at the Collegio Urbano; Matteo Ripa (1682–1746), later to become a (somewhat mediocre) painter, who had accompanied Amodei from Naples and whose diary remains the best source on this mission; and, finally, a secular surgeon, Giacomo Guarmani, who was originally from Bologna but who was practicing in a local Roman hospital.[243] The special congregation for missions to the East ratified their mission on 25 September. Provisions were made for their financial and travel arrangements, with the missionaries given permission to practice confession and administer the sacraments amongst each other. They were also given passports and letters of recommendation by the generals of the Augustinian, Dominican, Franciscan, Discalced Carmelite, and Jesuit Orders. Particular attention was paid to Bonjour. As the "mathematician," he was given several mathematical books to take to China, including Christoph Scheiner's *Pantographice, seu ars delineandi* (1631), and a pantograph, which Bonjour would proceed to lose en route in London.[244] More interestingly, Bonjour was given Roman citizenship to mask the fact that he was an Augustinian monk and it was for this reason that he changed his name from Guillaume Bonjour to Guglielmo Fabri.[245] After a final meeting with the pope on 8 October, in which the missionaries were blessed by Clement XI, the party set off from Rome on the thirteenth.

---

242 "Biographie et lettres du P. Nicolas Charmot," BNF, Français 25060, 2466.
243 See Matteo Ripa, *Storia della fondazione della congregazione e del collegio de' Cinesi* (Napoli: Manfredi, 1832). I do not have dates for Bonjour's companions other than Ripa, as can be seen.
244 "Scritture Originali delle Cong:ni Parti.ri dell'Indie Orientali e China del 1707 e 1708 e 1709," ASPF, SOCP 24; Ripa, *Storia*, 1:60–61.
245 "Scritture Originali delle Cong:ni Parti.ri dell'Indie Orientali e China del 1707 e 1708 e 1709," ASPF, SOCP 24, fols. 13r, 28r, 37r. Bonjour signed his letters back to Rome with the name "Guillaume Fabri" from then on. See Guillaume Fabri [Bonjour] to Adeodato Nuzzi, in BAR ms.lat.891, fols. 87r–104v; Baldini, "Guillaume Bonjour," 260; Giambattista Cotta, *Dio, sonetti, ed inni di F. Gio Battista Cotta, colle annotazioni dello stesso* (Venice: Tommaso Bettinelli, 1745), 375.

The many twists and turns by which Bonjour and his companions reached China is in itself an entertaining and sometimes farcical adventure. The first part of their journey took the missionaries north, through the Dolomites, Austria, and Germany, until they reached the Netherlands. In the northern Italian town of Brixen, or Bressanone, Funari was struck down by apoplexy while celebrating mass in the church of the Capuchin Fathers and was forced to return to Rome.[246] As the most senior member of the expedition Bonjour subsequently took care of the cardinal's hat. In Augsburg, meanwhile, Ripa recorded his first sighting of a priest's wife.[247] In the Netherlands, Bonjour took advantage of a few days' pause to visit Cuper in Deventer and Jean Le Clerc in Amsterdam. Meanwhile, in Rotterdam, Ripa, surrounded by Protestants, noted the "debauchery of these heretics" as two young ladies sat down at their dining table "and began with shameless freedom to play and joke around with us."[248] Despite donning secular clothes to hide their purpose, the motley group were easily uncovered as missionaries in The Hague and then again in London, and relied on the goodwill of their discoverers to avoid arrest.[249] More misfortune struck in London, where they were forced to hide below deck for several months after Queen Anne ordered the arrest of Catholic ecclesiasts due to James Stuart's aborted attempt to land at the Firth of Forth in March 1708.[250] Eventually, the companions managed, by hook or by crook, to obtain passage on an East India Company ship, the *Donegal*, which set sail for the East Indies in June 1708 and reached open sea on 4 July. On board, the group chose Saint Joseph as their patron saint and abandoned keeping Lent when it proved detrimental to their physical (if not their spiritual) health.[251] Bonjour even found time to write a dissertation against the Chinese Rites, primarily based on Aquinas' definition of "religious rites" in the *Summa*, which he sent back to Rome.[252] By late July, their ship had passed the equator, and on 6 September they reached the Cape of Good Hope. Because Bonjour had a letter of recommendation from Nicolaes Witsen, Cuper's friend who was also

---

246 Ripa, *Storia*, 1:69–70.
247 Ripa, *Storia*, 1:71.
248 Ripa, *Storia*, 1:80–81: "In questa Città cominciammo a sperimentare la dissolutezza di quegli Eretici; dapoichè appena seduti a tavola per cenare la sera, si posero al nostro fianco due giovanette, che con isfrontata libertà principiarono a trastullare, e scherzare con noi, del che non sì tosto ci rendemmo accorti, che senza far motto alcuno, abbassati i nostri cappelli avanti agli occhi, senza curarle, attendemmo a cenare ...".
249 Ripa, *Storia*, 1:82, 89.
250 Ripa, *Storia*, 1:92.
251 Ripa, *Storia*, 1:98.
252 Guillaume Bonjour, "De ritibus sinicis opusculum R. P. Bonjour Augustiniani quod composuit in navi dum pergeret ad Indias ex Beneplacito Clementis XI. Pont. Max.," BAR, ms.lat.49, fols. 359r–362v.

the former Director of the Dutch East India Company, he alone was allowed to dine with the government officials and ship captains at the table of the local governor Louis van Assenburgh (c.1657–1711).[253] By February 1709, the *Donegal* had reached Calcutta and in July of that year the companions disembarked at Manilla.[254] There, they met Giovanni Battista Sidoti (1667–1715), an Italian missionary who was later arrested in Japan which he had tried to enter illegally while optimistically disguised as a samurai, and the Lazarist Teodorico Pedrini (1671–1746), who had disguised himself as a ship's captain in order to sail to Macao.[255] On Pedrini's precarious vessel – it was only divine providence, noted Ripa, which saved the boat from capsizing – the group reached Macao in January 1710, where they met Tournon and presented him with the cardinal's hat. By now, however, Tournon's long stay in prison, the dispiriting state of the Chinese missions, and his increasing paranoia had together contributed to Tournon's steadily declining health, and he died in June.[256]

Fortunately for Bonjour, Tournon had informed the Kangxi Emperor of their arrival before his demise, in a letter in which he described Ripa as a painter, Pedrini as a musician, and Bonjour as a mathematician. In July 1710 these three missionaries were called to Canton (Guangzhou) so they could learn Chinese, and in November they submitted a plea for an audience with the Kangxi Emperor through the medium of two Jesuits living there, the Portuguese João Francisco Cardoso (or "Corderò," 1677–1723) and the German Franz Thillisch ("Tilis Boemo," 1670–1716).[257] On 27 November, Bonjour, Ripa, and Pedrini were ordered to leave Canton for Beijing, which they reached on 6 February. A few days later, alongside the Jesuit interpreters Kilian Stumpf (1655–1720) and Pierre Jartoux (1669–1720), they had their first meeting with the Kangxi Emperor, who asked them questions about music, painting, and mathematics. It was a meeting both uncomfortable and hilarious. Quizzed about his subject of expertise, Bonjour admitted that he knew no algebra, had lost the pantograph in London, and was unable to answer the Emperor's mathematical questions. The only book he could present to the emperor was Philippe de la Hire's *Traité du mouvement des eaux et des autres corps fluids*

---

253 Gisbert Cuper to Adeodato Nuzzi, 1 June 1709, in Hoogewerff, *Bescheiden en Italië*, 3:80; Guillaume Fabri [Bonjour] to Adeodato Nuzzi, 13 September 1708, BAR, ms.lat.891, fol. 90r; Ripa, *Storia*, 1:134.
254 Guillaume Fabri [Bonjour] to Adeodato Nuzzi, 18 February and 4 July 1709, BAR, ms.lat.891, fols. 93r–v, 97r.
255 Ripa, *Storia*, 1:293–294.
256 Baldini, "Guillaume Bonjour," 261–263; Ripa, *Storia*, 1:296–297.
257 Guillaume Bonjour to Adeodato Nuzzi, 13 November 1710, BAR, ms.lat.891, fol. 103r; Ripa, *Storia*, 1:350; Baldini, "Guillaume Bonjour," 263–265.

(1686).²⁵⁸ Subsequent meetings did not go much better. When Bonjour was asked by the emperor to give him two numbers, one of which is two-thirds of the other and both of which total to make 25, Bonjour replied that the answer was 8 and 16.²⁵⁹

Despite his mathematical failures – as also recorded by Cardoso in the archives of the Propaganda fide – Bonjour and his companions were able to reside at the imperial court for the following months, where he went by the Chinese name "Shan Yaozhan."²⁶⁰ In mid-July, he was assigned to the great Jesuit cartographic project then seeking to map China, the project which would keep him occupied in China throughout his remaining years. In 1711 and 1712, Bonjour and his companions Jartoux and Xavier Ehrenbert Fridelli (1673–1743) traversed the central and western parts of Mongolia, the north-eastern part of Xinjiang, and northern Gansu; in 1713 he was sent to map Sichuan, Yunnan, Guizhou, and Hunan provinces. On the banks of the river Kherlen, he was said to have held conversations with Buddhist lamas on religion and world geography. Yet Bonjour was never able to make something of the knowledge he acquired in this new land. In December 1714, he and his travelling companion fell ill in the small border town of Mengding or Menglian, presumably of malaria or perhaps of food-poisoning. He died shortly after, on Christmas day; his body was transported the many miles back to Beijing where it was given a funeral ceremony which mixed Christian with Chinese elements. Baldini, in his article on Bonjour, has noted the unseemly dispute which emerged among competing missionaries regarding the ownership of Bonjour's "spoils."²⁶¹ Perhaps we should add just one more coda to Bonjour's stay – and spoils – in China: among the scant possessions Bonjour brought with him, one discovered just recently

---

258 Teodorico Pedrini to the Special Congregation of the Propaganda fide, 7 February and 4 March 1711, ASPF, SOCP 26, fols. 293v–294r. The meeting is also descriped by Ripa, *Storia*, 1:370–374; and in Matteo Ripa to the Sacred Congregation of the Propaganda fide, 3 June 1711, ASPF, SOCP 26, fols. 311r–314v.

259 Teodorico Pedrini to the Special Congregation of the Propaganda fide, 2 June 1711, ASPF, SOCP 26, fol. 301r.

260 See ASPF, SOCP 26, fol. 33r: "et il P. Guglielmo Fabbri Agostiniano co'l nome di Perito de calcoli astronomici, e non di quello di Matematico, della qual scienza *egli non è intelligente* [*si dice non esser egli intelligere*]; e si è qualificato in matematico, et ad una interrogazione dell' Imperatore non seppe rispondere e da quello scrivo il Sigr. Abbe Cordero." Cf. Cams, *Companions in Geography*, 137, n. 338.

261 See on this Baldini, "Guillaume Bonjour," 266–280, and on the *spolia*, 280–282. Baldini's account is much more extensive than my own. In addition, see Cams, *Companions in Geography*, 126–130, and Matteo Ripa, *Giornale (1705–1724): Testo critico, note e appendice documentaria di Michele Fatica*, ed. Michele Fatica (Napoli: Istituto Universitario Orientale di Napoli, 1996), 2:1–92.

was the great Renaissance handbook of pagan mythography, Natale Conti's *Mythologiae* (1588 edition), inscribed with the mark of "Bonjour-Fabri."[262] Whether in Toulouse, or Rome, or Beijing, Bonjour kept the secrets of pagan antiquity close to hand as he travelled the world.

With the exception of his work on Coptic, which was consulted even in manuscript, Bonjour's posthumous reputation – and citations of his work – were limited to the few small *opuscula* he was able to publish. It is for this reason that scholars cited Bonjour on specific, minor points regarding Coptic grammar, pagan cults, Oriental languages, or biblical chronology, rather than in reference to his more over-arching theories concerning the relationship between biblical history, Egyptian chronology, and Greek mythology which we shall subsequently explore. It is within these specific contexts, for example, that the Maurist editor of Jerome, Jean Martianay (1647–1717), cited Bonjour's supposition that Jerome knew Egyptian; that the Dutch Hebraist Campegius Vitringa (1659–1722) criticised Bonjour's comments on the Coptic article ϕⲓ; that the Dominican theologian Ignace-Hyacinthe-Amat de Graveson (1670–1733) discussed Bonjour's identification of Serapis and Joseph; that the Bollandist Jean-Baptiste du Sollier (1669–1740) referenced Bonjour in his treatise on the patriarchs of Alexandria; and that Pierre Henri Larcher (1726–1812), the popular French translator of Herodotus, made reference to Bonjour's dating of the astronomer Geminus.[263] As is clear, these references often pertained to individual points of erudition, rather than grand scholarly projects or theories. And it is also clear that many scholars had only learnt of Bonjour's work through some form of personal contact. It was for this reason, to name a few specific examples, that Bonjour's works came to be discussed, if briefly, by Jacobus Perizonius, Thomas Bouges, Eusèbe Renaudot, Francesco Bianchini,

---

262 Noël Golvers, "Reading Classical Latin Authors in the Jesuit Mission in China: Seventeenth to Eighteenth Centuries," in *Receptions of Greek and Roman Antiquity in East Asia*, ed. Almut-Barbara Renger and Xin Fan (Brill: Leiden and Boston, 2018), 58.

263 Jean Martianay, *Sancto Hieronymi operum* (Paris: Jean Anisson, 1699), 2:339–340; Campegius Vitringa, *Observationum sacrarum libri septem* (Amsterdam: Fredericus Horreus, 1727), 1:67–69; Jean-Baptiste du Sollier, *Tractatus historico-chronologicus de patriarchis Alexandrinis* (Antwerp: Peter Jacobs, 1708), 1:6–7; Ignace-Hyacinthe Amat de Graveson, *Historia ecclesiastica Veteris Testamenti* (Rome: Hieronymus Maynard, 1727), 1:115–119; Pierre Henri Larcher, ed., *Histoire d'Hérodote traduite du Grec* (Paris: Musier & Nyon, 1786), 2:155–156. See also in a similar vein Eybo Hoppe, *Dissertatio academica de philosophia Josephi pro-regis Aegypti* (Helmstedt: Georg Wolfgang Hamm, 1706) and Christian Reineccius, *Illustre dominatori Aegyptii Josephi nomen …* (Weißenfels: Literis G. A. Legii, Aul. August. Typogr., 1725). Although promisingly entitled, neither pamphlet engages extensively with Bonjour's *De nomine*.

and Johann Albert Fabricius (1668–1736).[264] Personal contact remained crucial for spreading knowledge of works which were often difficult to acquire. When the German biblical scholars Gottfried Kohlreif (1676–1750) and Johann Gottlob Carpzov (1679–1767) referenced Bonjour's proposed emendations to a passage in Josephus' *Antiquitates judaicae* in the 1730s, they did so not because they had read the *Selectae in sacram scripturam* but because the emendation had been mentioned by Le Clerc in his 1720 review of John Hudson's *Opera omnia*.[265] Perhaps the only exception to this trend is the work of the Augustinian Orientalist Agostino Antonio Giorgi, a friend of Casanova and later prior general of the Augustinians who also worked in the Biblioteca Angelica in Rome.[266] Not only did Giorgi defend Bonjour's Coptic work publicly, but in his monumental 1761 monograph on Tibet, which linked Buddhism to Manicheanism, he made frequent use of Bonjour's unpublished manuscripts on ancient Egypt.[267] Indeed, it was due to Giorgi's *Alphabetum tibetanum* that, in 1764, the French archaeologist Gabriel Fabricy (c.1725–1800) went on to reference Bonjour's contentious claim that the most ancient pharaoh was Necherophes, a contemporary of Abraham.[268] The importance – and immediate context – of this claim will be the subject of chapters three and five. There, we can hopefully give some of Bonjour's great scholarly labours the attention they deserve.

---

264   See Jacobus Perizonius, *Aegyptiorum originum et temporum antiquissimorum investigatio* (Leiden: Johannes van der Linden, 1711), 400–401; Thomas Bouges, *Dissertation historique et polemique sur les soixante-dix semaines du prophète Daniel* (Toulouse: G. Robert, 1702), 86–87, 182–183; Renaudot, *Liturgiarum orientalium collectio*, 1:342; Bianchini, *Solutio problematis paschalis*, xxxii, 14, 16; Johann Albert Fabricius, ed., *Procli philosophi platonici vita, scriptore Marino Neapolitano* (Hamburg: Gottfried Liebezeit, 1700), 72. For Fabricius see Johann Albert Fabricius to G. W. Leibniz, 28 September and 20 October 1697, and G. W. Leibniz to Johann Albert Fabricius, 15 October 1697, LAA, I, 14:509, 574–575, 621; and for Perizonius, Claude Nicaise to Guillaume Bonjour, 10 June 1698, BAR, ms.lat.395, fols. 156r–157r and in Pélissier, "Lettres inédites de Claude Nicaise," 198.

265   Gottfried Kohlreif, *Chronologia sacra a mundo condito* (Hamburg: Theodor Christoph Felginer, 1724), 152; Johann Gottlieb Carpzov, *Critica sacra Veteris Testamenti* (Leipzig: Johann Christian Martin, 1748), 957; citing Le Clerc, "Flavii Josephi Opera," *Bibliothèque ancienne et moderne*, 267.

266   See Trent Pomplun, "Agostino Antonio Giorgi, OESA (1711–1797): Between Augustinianism and the History of Religions," *History of Religions* 59 (2020): 193–221.

267   Agostino Antonio Giorgi, *Alphabetum Tibetanum missionum apostolicarum* (Rome: Propaganda fide, 1762).

268   Gabriel Fabricy, *Recherches sur l'époque de l'équitation et de l'usage des chars équestres chez les anciens* (Marseille and Rome: Jean Mossy and Pierre Durand, 1764), 1:40.

Perhaps we should end by remarking something on Bonjour the person, as well as Bonjour the scholar. The only known portrait of his can still be found in Montefiascone: it depicts a serious young man, with an oval face, a high forehead, round eyes, thick lips, a cleft chin, and a quite remarkably large nose.[269] His personality is somewhat harder to picture. Many of his letters – particularly to transalpine correspondents whom he had never met – are deliberately learned, as was customary for the Republic at the time. Only to Magliabechi did Bonjour appear happy to also express his hopes, his fears, his disappointments, and his frustrations. From these letters however, and from the testimonies of those who knew him, certain commonalities emerge: he was deeply pious, he was extremely talented, he was generous, he was humble and modest, he was hard-working to the point of exhaustion, he was so ambitious that his ambitions overwhelmed him, he was beholden to his duty but not above complaining, he loved passionately the antiquities he studied, he longed to see northern Europe, and although he had no love for the religion of the heretics he made little distinction between his Protestant and Catholic friends. It is, perhaps, particularly the last point which we should note: a propensity for friendship and for inspiring affection, even across confessions. In Cuper, he evoked a form of tenderness which is quite remarkable; and in Rome, he made himself a reputation which, if built on his scholarly ability, was maintained through friendship. He was known not only to haughty scholars but to eclectic figures such as Calvoli and Giacinto Gimma (1668–1735) – who included him in his fictional learned society of Rossano – and he maintained an extensive and impressively cordial relationship with the ever-prickly Magliabechi.[270] When dawn broke on Olof Celsius' planned departure from Rome, it was Bonjour who accompanied the young Swede to the city gates and presented him with copies of his published works, for which he was still remembered as "mihique olim Romae amicus, & benevolus, Guillelmus Bonjour" half a century later.[271] Perhaps particularly noteworthy is Bonjour's friendship with the Italian poet and fellow Augustinian Giovanni Battista, or Giambattista, Cotta (1668–1738). In Cotta's 1722 collection of poetry, entitled *Dio, sonetti, ed inni*, Bonjour appears not only as a learned source but also in Cotta's poem "Il Mare" as "il tolosan Guglielmo." More noticeable still is that the volume ends with a *breve episodio*

---

269 Reproduced in Patrizi, *Storia del seminario*.
270 On Gimma see Harold Samuel Stone, *Vico's Cultural History: The Production and Transmission of Ideas in Naples 1685–1750* (Leiden: E. J. Brill, 1997).
271 Lündstrom, *Olof Celsius d. ä:s Diarium öfver sin resa*, 69; Olof Celsius, *Hierobotanicon, sive de plantis sacrae scripturae* (Amsterdam: J. Wettstein, 1748), 278.

which gives us perhaps the longest, although still very brief, published biography of Bonjour by a known acquaintance.[272] At the end of the account, there is also a poem on Bonjour written by the Neapolitan lawyer Biagio d'Avitabile Maioli (c.1670–c.1745).[273]

> Del gran GUILIELMO i decantati allori
> Va al nuovo mondo a pubblicare, o Fama,
> Vanne colà, dove erudita brama
> A' popoli stranieri accende i cori
>
> Dì, che da la sua penna il volo implori,
> Dì, che degli astri interpetre è si chiama,
> Dì, che le laudi sue Pallade acclama,
> Dì, che sudano i torchj a darli onori.
>
> Il fiato impetra, e i vigorosi accenti
> Dal' suo spirto, che puo su dotte scene
> Parlar stupori, e palesar portenti.
>
> E del Garonna, dì, presso a le arene
> Rinovate per lui veggon le genti
> L'antica Roma, e la superba Atene.
>
> [Of great Guillaume, the praised laurels,
> Go to a new world to publish, oh Fame,
> Go thither, where learned yearnings
> Ignite the hearts of foreign peoples
>
> Say, that from your pen the flight is implored,
> Say, that the interpreter of the stars is called,
> Say, that the praises acclaim her Pallas,
> Say, that the press strives to give them honours

---

272 Cotta, *Dio, sonetti, ed inni*, 58–60, 326, 359–363, 374–377.
273 Cotta, *Dio, sonetti, ed inni*, 376–377. The sonnet was first published in Gimma, *Elogj*, 2:357, but also appears in a slightly different version in Biagio d'Avitabile Maioli, *Rime di poeti illustri viventi parte prima* (Faenza: Girolamo Maranti, 1723), 94. I have followed Gimma's version. I have, however, corrected "interpetre" to "interprete."

> The breath procures, and the vigorous accents
> From his spirit, which can on erudite stages,
> Speak wonders, and reveal portents
>
> And of the Garonne, say, close to the arena,
> Renewed by him the people see,
> Ancient Rome, and proud Athens.]

A slightly bizarre epitaph to an unfulfilled career.

PART 1
Mythology

CHAPTER 2

Sacred History and Profane Fables

Throughout his scholarly life, Bonjour's many historical and biblical projects were shaped by one fundamental principle: "exoticae antiquitatis monumenta conferens cum sacris paginis," joining together monuments of heathen antiquity with holy scripture.[1] This stance informed not only the mythographic projects he first developed in Toulouse but also the Egyptian chronology he studied in Rome and the apologetic dissertations he later published in Montefiascone. In 1694, he began his *Mercurius* by stating that the historical events preserved in the ancient writings of the Gentiles – *ex scriptis ethnicorum* – pertained to the same events recorded more faithfully in holy scripture; in 1705, he still noted that certain biblical events were preserved "ex historia tam Sacra quam Barbarica," as much in sacred as in profane history.[2] It was this notion which led him to derive pagan myths from biblical history, to find in Greek poetry fragments of God's Creation, and to bend ancient Egyptian chronologies so that they could fit within and support the chronological framework of the Bible. It was for this reason that he, and his contemporaries, identified Noah with Saturn, Moses with Mercury, Joseph with Serapis, Adam with Prometheus, and Joshua with Hercules.

This particular approach to pagan antiquity was widely mocked and pilloried in the eighteenth century and is still met with confusion and even derision by certain historians today.[3] Above all, it has been contrasted negatively to the progressive, rational, and intellectually sophisticated scholarship of such writers as Bernard de Fontenelle (1657–1757), Pierre Bayle, or the English deists, who, in the early eighteenth century, divested the study of pagan myth from the study of biblical history and first subjected it to "psychological" or "philosophical" analysis.[4] It should be noted, however, that the scholarly tradition which

---

1 Guillaume Bonjour to Gisbert Cuper, 31 August 1697, KW 72 H 20. Cuper would describe Bonjour's work in the same way to Adeodato Nuzzi as "sacram Historiam cum profana consentire": Hoogewerff, *Bescheiden*, 3:94.
2 *Mercurius*, fol. 2v: "Unde cum sacris divinisque paginis optimo eorum exemplo me totum tradedem, plura etiam, quae vel ipsos fugerant, ex scriptis Ethnicorum cum iis contuli, ac eodem pertinere expertus sum"; *Selectae*, D.II.19, 53.
3 As most recently in Jed Z. Buchwald and Mordechai Feingold, *Newton and the Origin of Civilization* (Princeton: Princeton University Press, 2013).
4 In particular Frank Manuel, *Isaac Newton: Historian* (Cambridge: Cambridge University Press, 1963) and Frank Manuel, *The Eighteenth Century Confronts the Gods* (New York: Atheneum, 1967).

Bonjour followed when synchronizing pagan antiquity and biblical history was, at its time, not only popular but also authoritative and widely respected. Moreover, it is clear that Bonjour followed this tradition because he considered it not only a convenient apologetic tool but also a legitimate form of historical interpretation. Certainly, Bonjour believed that the practice of harmonizing sacred with profane history would, by definition, help confirm the truth of biblical history and by extension the Christian religion, but he also believed that the practice was in accordance with sound principles of historical criticism and methodology – in short, he believed that it was able to substantiate the truth of the biblical record precisely *because* it was historically accurate (or at least probable) rather than merely religiously or doctrinally expedient. Throughout the many centuries of biblical scholarship and Christian apologetics there had existed a multitude of ways of defending the authority of the Bible, and it is important to note, and understand, why Bonjour and his contemporaries chose to do so in their own, highly distinctive, way. Since this method forms the bedrock of Bonjour's many projects – and those of his major influences and contemporaries – it remains the key to understanding not only his scholarship but that of his age. This chapter will therefore seek to introduce some of the more general, underlying historical assumptions which informed Bonjour's historical, biblical, and mythographic work, and in so doing provide a potted history of a scholarly tradition which both dominated the late seventeenth century and contributed to that period's future neglect.

1 *Historia sacra* and *historia exotica* in the Seventeenth Century

This notion of "harmonizing," "uniting," or "concording" information which was, as Bonjour stated so frequently, "as much in profane as in sacred history" (which is to say, in both pagan, usually Hellenistic, as well as Judaeo-Christian, usually biblical, sources) rested on understanding two dichotomies. Firstly, we have the distinction between *sacra* and *profana*, the sacred and the profane; secondly, we have the distinction between *historia* and *fabula*, history and myth. Let us start, then, by going back to the beginnings. In principle, the term *historia sacra* could, as historians such as Eric Cochrane and Simon Ditchfield have pointed out, refer in a general sense to the history of the Church up to and including the history of the sixteenth and seventeenth centuries.[5] Since the

---

5 Eric Cochrane, *Historians and Historiography in the Italian Renaissance* (Chicago and London: The University of Chicago Press, 1981), 445–478; Simon Ditchfield, "What was Sacred History? (Mostly Roman) Catholic Uses of the Christian Past after Trent," in *Sacred History:*

opposite of *sacra* was *profana*, it notionally included any form of history which was guided by divine providence and therefore included such disciplines as hagiography and ecclesiastical history. Francesco Bianchini, in the preface of his *Istoria universale*, defined *historia sacra* (or as he named it, *istoria ecclesiastica*) as a history which "guides us to a much greater wisdom through means and through examples which mostly surpass nature," whereas profane history related merely to "the facts, and the events of men, directed purely by natural cognition, and simply established through human relations."[6] In Bonjour's scholarship – and, consequently, throughout this work – *historia sacra* was often understood in a somewhat more specific sense: as the study of the biblical history of the Old Testament, before the foundation of the Christian Church and the subsequent development of ecclesiastical history which documented the history of the Church as an institution.[7] In this sense, the disciplines most closely related to *historia sacra* were not ecclesiastical history or hagiography but rather any study of the history of the biblical patriarchs and the Jewish nation in the historical period covered by the Old Testament. This included, for example, the discipline of *geographia sacra*, which Zur Shalev has defined as the field of study concerned with the reconstruction of the biblical landscape by turning the sacred text into a map.[8] It also included the study of the origins and nature of ancient idolatry, an area of particular scholarly interest from the early seventeenth century onwards. As we shall see in the last section of this work, for many seventeenth-century scholars of *historia sacra* the deviation of ancient nations from the original monotheism of Noah and the subsequent development of idolatrous cults was crucial for understanding postdiluvian biblical history.

Uses of the Christian Past in the Renaissance World, ed. Katherine van Liere, Simon Ditchfield, and Howard Louthon (Oxford: Oxford University Press, 2012), 72–98.

6   Francesco Bianchini, *La istoria universale, provata con monumenti, e figurata con simboli de gli antichi* (Rome: Antonio de Rossi, 1697), 12–13: "La prima ad un termine di natural cognizione per esempj, e per mezi humani conduce. L'altra à sapienza molto maggiore ne guida per mezi, e per esempj, che per lo più trapassano la natura ... Quel tutto, che da noi si propone à trattare nella presente Opera si è l'*Istoria profana*. In questo termine d'*Istoria profana* si rinchiudono *i fatti, e gli avvenimenti de gli uomini, diretti da cognizione puramente naturale, e pruovati con relazioni semplicemente umane*. Non è già che vogliamo tacere tutti que' fatti, di che parlano l'istorie divine: le quali nel rappresentare un'azione nascondono ancora un mistero."

7   See Arnaldo Momigliano, "The Origins of Ecclesiastical History" in *The Classical Foundations of Modern Historiography* (Berkeley and LA: University of California Press, 1990), 132–156.

8   Zur Shalev, *Sacred Words and Worlds: Geography, Religion and Scholarship, 1550–1700* (Leiden: Brill, 2012).

Notionally, *historia sacra* was still defined by its opposition to profane history, which was often given the name of *historia exotica*, or *profana*, or even *barbarica*. When in 1613 Jacques Cappel (1570–1624), theologian and Hebrew professor at Sedan, published his universal chronology, he called it *Historia sacra et exotica ab Adamo usque ad Augustum* to highlight the fact that his historical timeline included events from both biblical and pagan history interchangeably.[9] Hence if the entry for *annus mundi* 2423, 1577 BC, marked the birth of Moses, then the following entry, *annus mundi* 2425, 1575 BC, marked Hercules' victory over the half-giant son of Neptune, Antaeus.[10] The tendency to describe works of ancient, primordial history as being both "sacra" and "exotica" remained omnipresent throughout the following century. Ostensibly, there was a clear way of demarcating between the two categories: while the former dealt with the history of the chosen Jewish people who had access to divine revelation and whose history was recorded in the divinely inspired, and therefore authoritative, Hebrew Bible, the latter concerned Gentile nations who had access merely to natural reason, fallible memory, and poorly preserved historical records, whose histories were products of barbarous ignorance and subject to malicious corruption.

In reality, as Cappel's chronology shows, the line between the two was more blurred. The Old Testament and, more specifically, the Pentateuch written with divine aid by *sacer historiographus* Moses, contained two, interlaced histories. Firstly, the Pentateuch contained a primordial, universal history within which was contained the histories of all peoples who had ever lived, what Adalbert Klempt has called "a complete handbook of universal history." This universal history was largely – although not exclusively – contained in Genesis 1–11. Secondly, the Pentateuch contained a specific providential history of God's chosen people, the Jews.[11] In both cases, there were clear connections with profane, non-sacred history. On the one hand, the Bible spoke of universal events which affected not only the Jews but all peoples, such as the Flood or the repopulation of the earth by Noah's descendants.[12] It therefore made sense to assume that some memory of these events might still be preserved among Gentile nations. On the other hand, the Bible made constant references

---

9   Jacques Cappel, *Historia sacra et exotica ab Adamo usque ad Augustum* (Sedan: Jean Iannon, 1613).
10 Cappel, *Historia sacra*, 76.
11 Adalbert Klempt, *Die Säkularisierung der universalhistorischen Auffassung: zum Wandel des Geschichtsdenkens im 16. und 17. Jahrhundert* (Göttingen: Musterschmidt Verlag, 1960), 91: "ein lückenloses Handbuch der Universalhistorie."
12 One such event which was not contained in Genesis 1–11 was the Egyptian famine, which Bonjour argued was universal.

to contemporaneous Gentile nations with whom the biblical patriarchs and the ancient Jewish nation had interacted. Scholars knew, for example, from the twelfth chapter of Genesis that an Egyptian kingdom with a pharaoh at its head must have existed since at least the time of Abraham. Consequently, it was natural enough to assume that even corrupted Egyptian records preserved some knowledge of an ancient Chaldean traveller whose brief visit to the Egyptian kingdom had brought with it plagues and pestilence.

Yet there was another reason as to why profane history could be of apologetic use. If the book of Genesis provided a basic framework for universal history and an outline for the ancient history of the biblical patriarchs, it did not provide all the historical data. Famously, the Egyptian pharaoh whom Abraham met was unnamed. It was due to the existence of these lacunae that profane history proved as much a supplement as it did an alternative to sacred history. As William Adler has pointed out, it was the profane history of Egypt which allowed the Fathers of the early Church – seeking to combat the damaging pagan accusation that Christianity was a recent invention – to identify Abraham's pharaoh and in so doing establish to the Greeks that Moses was as old as their most ancient king Inachus. It was for this reason that, in the first centuries of the Church, Christian chronographers were given a latitude towards using pagan sources which was not extended to other disciplines.[13] To a great extent, this practice continued and even increased in the seventeenth century. With the exception of a few isolated figures such as the French Calvinist Mathieu Béroalde (1520–1576) or the English theologian and Hebraist Hugh Broughton (1549–1612), historians accepted the necessity of using ancient, non-biblical, and non-sacred sources within their studies of *historia sacra* and the study of ancient, primordial history.[14] What was, of course, a matter of often fierce debate was both the extent and the type of pagan sources which could, or should, be used.

But what were these pagan sources – the *historia exotica* – which could offer historical information able to supplement the sacred authority of the Bible? Ultimately, the Bible itself was considered authoritative not merely because it was divinely revealed but also because it was first, an original historical document composed long before idolatrous nations had constructed their own

13   William Adler, *Time Immemorial: Archaic History and its Sources in Christian Chronography from Julius Africanus to George Syncellus* (Washington DC: Dumbarton Oaks, 1989); and William Adler, "Moses, the Exodus, and Comparative Chronology," in *Scripture and Traditions: Essays on Early Judaism and Christianity in Honor of Carl R. Holladay*, ed. Patrick Gray and Gail R. O'Day (Leiden and Boston: Brill, 2008), 47–65.
14   Mathieu Béroalde, *Chronicum, scripturae sacrae authoritate constitutum* (Geneva: Antoine Chuppin, 1575); Hugh Broughton, *A Concent of Scripture* (London: William White, 1588).

histories based on deficient memory and fallible human reason. "Id esse verum quodcunque primum, id esse adulterum quodcunque posterius," what is first is true, what is posterior is false – so wrote the Church Father Tertullian in his riposte to the heretical Monarchian Praxeas in the third century, a dictum cited programmatically at the beginning of Samuel Bochart's great, influential work on sacred history, the *Geographia sacra* of 1646 (which we shall come to shortly).[15] Hence, however valuable *historia exotica* might be, it must necessarily be less authoritative, less reliable, and more recent than the basic framework for ancient history, which remained the Jewish Old Testament.

Ironically, the basic understanding of the relationship between *historia sacra* and *historia profana* or *exotica* was largely taken from the ancient Greeks; in particular, from the Greek conceptualisation of recondite human history. Essentially, the Greeks themselves had openly supposed that they possessed no accurate historical information on – which is to say, actual *histories* of – the earliest period of human existence, and early modern scholars often cited their words to this effect. Hence, in his history of ancient Egypt, John Marsham cited Diodorus' assertion that no list of official magistrates existed before the first Olympiad in the early eighth century, as well as Josephus' statement that the first Greek historical documents were Dracon's seventh-century laws on homicide.[16] It was in the same vein that the Huguenot theologian Pierre Jurieu supposed that the first truly "historical" event in Greek historiography was Cyrus' reign in Persia, which began in the late sixth century.[17] "Indeed, as to the events of the period just preceding this, and those of a still earlier date, it was impossible to get clear information on account of lapse of time," wrote Thucydides at the beginning of his history of the fifth-century Peloponnesian war (1.1.2), a statement still cited in the early modern period by such important historians as Bochart, the English apologist and later Bishop of Worcester Edward Stillingfleet (1635–1699), and the great Italian "philosopher of history"

---

15 Bochart, *Geographia sacra*, 1; and cited to similar effect in René-Joseph de Tournemine, "Addition pour les mémoires de Novembre & Décembre; Seconde partie du projet d'un ouvrage sur l'origine des fables," *Journal de Trévoux* 5 (1702), 2–3: "la verité est toûjours plus ancienne que le mensonge." See further Alphonse Dupront, *Pierre-Daniel Huet et l'exégèse comparatiste au XVIIe siècle* (Geneva: Libraire Droz, 2014), 61–62.

16 John Marsham, *Canon chronicus Aegyptiacus, Ebraicus, Graecus, et disquisitiones* (London: Thomas Roycroft and William Wells & Robert Scott, 1672), 14–15, citing Josephus, *Contra Apionem*, 1.20–22, and Diodorus, 16.7.5.

17 Pierre Jurieu, *Histoire critique des dogmes et des cultes, bons & mauvais, qui ont été dans l'Église depuis Adam, jusqu'à Jésus-Christ, ou l'on trouve l'origine de toutes les idolâtries de l'ancien paganisme, expliquées par rapport à celle des Juifs* (Amsterdam: François l'Honoré, 1704), 182.

Giambattista Vico (1668–1744).[18] Naturally enough, these statements were placed in stark contrast to the reliability and authority of *sacer historiographus* Moses, who wrote long before the Greeks of events largely unknown to Greek historians. "Holy scripture is the only rule for all of ancient history, and the touchstone from which we can know the Truth," wrote the French scholar of ancient history Étienne Fourmont around the beginning of the eighteenth century, while also pointing out that "the Greeks ... completely ignored the history of the earliest times and of distant countries."[19] For what other reason had Juvenal mocked the lies "that Greece dares tell as history" (10.174), and Quintilian remarked that "Greek historical narratives often display an almost poetic licence" (2.4)?[20]

Although this supposition was useful for confirming the superiority of biblical history, it was of little use for those scholars who sought to supplement their biblical histories with pagan evidence. If the Greeks admitted to having no histories for recondite periods of human existence, from where else might one gather historical information? Once again, the answer was provided by the Greeks: ancient myths.

As Jean Seznec has shown in his famous *La survivance des dieux antiques*, classical antiquity had provided a number of ways of interpreting pagan myths in a manner which remained formative for Christian scholars of the early Church, the Middle Ages, and the Renaissance. In particular, Seznec noted three distinctive mythographic traditions: a physical tradition, which interpreted the gods as planets or forces of nature, and which turned mythical tales into vast cosmogonies; a philosophical tradition, which supposed that myths were intended as moral fables or as encoded wisdom; and a historical tradition, which considered myths corrupted and embellished narratives of real

---

18 Bochart, *Geographia sacra*, "ad lectorem praefatio," sig. †iiir; Edward Stillingfleet, *Origines sacrae, or A Rational Account of the Grounds of the Christian Faith* (London: Henry Mortlock, 1662), 66; Giambattista Vico, *The First New Science*, ed. Leon Pompa (Cambridge: Cambridge University Press, 2002), 29. Translation from Thucydides, *History of the Peloponnesian War*, ed. Charles Forster Smith (Cambridge MA: Harvard University Press, 1928), 1:3.
19 BNF, NAF 8944, fol. 279r–v: "L'Ecriture S.te est l'unique regle de toute l'ancienne histoire, et la pierre de touche avec laquelle nous pouvons connoitre la Verité" and "Les Grecs ... ont ignorés entierement l'histoire des preimers tems et des païs eloignes."
20 Cited by Fourmont, BNF, NAF 8944, fol. 279v. Translation adapted from Juvenal and Persius, *Juvenal and Persius*, ed. Susanna Morton Braund (Cambridge MA: Harvard University Press, 2004), 381: "Quidquid Graecia mendax audet in historiis" and Quintilian, *The Orator's Education*, ed. Donald A. Russell (Cambridge MA: Harvard University Press, 2001), 1:289: "Graecis historiis plerumque poeticae similis est licentia."

historical events.[21] Christian mythographers came to recognise these various hermeneutic traditions, or "senses," explicitly, in a manner not unlike the biblical *quadriga*.[22] In one of the first post-classical handbooks of pagan mythology, the *Genealogia deorum gentilium*, Giovanni Boccaccio (1313–1375), citing Macrobius' *Somnium Scipionis* (1.2.17–18), noted four senses (*polisenus*) of myth, the historical or literal, the allegorical, the moral, and the anagogical; in 1738, the French mythographer Antoine Banier (1673–1741) was still advancing a similar quadripartite division in his monumental, three-volume compendium of pagan mythology.[23] It is clear, however, that the seventeenth century was dominated by the historical interpretation of myth, and that scholars believed that a detailed critical and etymological study of pagan myths would uncover an original historical core.[24] In his 1635 *Mare clausum*, the British jurist and antiquarian John Selden (1584–1654) noted that mythology was nothing but "manifest historical truth ... though wrap't up in the mysteries of Heathen Priests and Poets"; half a century later, a prominent critic of Selden's mythography, Jean Le Clerc, similarly supposed that "it is not simple fictions or facts invented for pleasure which were the origin of the fables which we read today in the Greek authors; but true Histories that have been excessively embellished, or rather obscured by ridiculous circumstances."[25] The culmination of this tradition is

---

21   Jean Seznec, *La survivance des dieux antiques. Essai sur le rôle de la tradition mythologique dans l'Humanisme et dans l'art de la Renaissance* (London: The Warburg Institute, 1940). I have also used the following English translation: Jean Seznec, *The Survival of the Pagan Gods: The Mythological Tradition and Its Place in Renaissance Humanism and Art*, trans. Barbara F. Sessions (New York: Pantheon Books, 1953). See also for a brief introduction Marcel Detienne, "Mythology," in *The Classical Tradition*, ed. Anthony Grafton, Glenn W. Most and Salvatore Settis (Cambridge MA and London: The Belknap of Harvard University Press, 2010), 614–617.

22   The *quadriga* were the so-called four senses of scripture, as first defined by the late fourth- and early fifth-century theologian John Cassian: the literal (historical), the allegorical, the moral (tropological), and the anagogical. They were famously defined in the rhyme by Augustine of Dacia (d. 1285): "littera gesta docet, quid credas allegoria, moralis quid agas, quo tendas analogia."

23   Giovanni Boccaccio, *Genealogy of the Pagan Gods*, ed. Jon Solomon (Cambridge MA: Harvard University Press, 2011), 51; Antoine Banier, *La mythologie et les fables expliquées par l'histoire* (Paris: Briasson, 1738), 1:28. Cf. Louis de Jaucourt, "Mythologie," in *Encyclopédie, ou Dictionnaire raisonné des sciences, des arts et des métiers*, ed. Denis Diderot and Jean le Rond d'Alembert (Neufchâtel: Samuel Faulche, 1765), 924–926.

24   See statements to this effect in Seznec, *The Survival of the Pagan Gods*, 321–322, and Don Cameron Allen, *Mysteriously Meant: The Rediscovery of Pagan Symbolism and Allegorical Interpretation in the Renaissance* (Baltimore and London: The John Hopkins Press, 1970), 247ff., 303.

25   John Selden, *Mare Clausum, seu de dominio maris* (London: William Stansby, 1635), 33: "Sed involutam Poetarum & Theologorum gentium mysteriis historicam veritatem e

often regarded as Banier's *Mythologie et la fable expliquées par l'histoire* (1738), in which Banier sought "to bring to light this Treasure of History, that lies hidden under the Disguise of Fable."[26] Yet it is clear that Banier did not think his approach unusual but rather typical for his time. As Banier noted:

> The Learned of this Age, from a persuasion that the History of the Period after the Deluge lies hidden under the ingenious Mask of Fable, have set themselves to take off the mysterious Mask which concealed the Truths that were under them from Persons of less Discernment. There are times which favour certain Opinions, and this of the Truth of Fables has so far prevailed, that from henceforth we must either frankly give up all Pretensions to make tolerable Sense of them, or reduce them to History.[27]

More important still was the historical period which seventeenth-century scholars believed the veil of myth obscured. In short, the information which scholars gleaned from myth was thought to pertain specifically to historical events which preceded the advent of Greek history (and historiography). The underlying principle for this assumption was the division of history first advanced by the first-century Roman antiquarian and polymath Marcus Terentius Varro, whom Augustine had once called "vir doctissimus et gravissimae auctoritatis" (*De civitate dei* 4.1). According to Varro, history was divided into three ages: the unknown (ἄδηλον) period which preceded the flood of Ogyges; the mythical (μυθικόν) period which separated the flood from the first Olympiad in 776 BC;

---

vetustissimis historicis exhibemus," with translation from John Selden, *Mare Clausum: the Right and Dominion of the Sea in Two Books*, trans J. H. Gent (London: Andrew Kembe and Edward Thomas, 1663), 47; Jean Le Clerc, "Temporum Mythicorum Historia per Generationes digesta, in qua quid in antiquis fabulis latent Historica aperitur," *Bibliothèque universelle et historique* 1 (1686): 262: "ce ne sont pas de simples fictions, ou des faits inventez à plaisir, qui ont été l'origine des fables que nous lisons aujourd'hui dans les Auteurs Grecs; mais de veritables Histoires qu'on a trop embellies, ou plutôt obscurcies de circonstances ridicules."

26 Banier, *La mythologie et les fables expliquées*, 1:ii–iii: "C'est ce fond d'Histoire caché sous l'enveloppe de la Fable, qui fut le principal objet de mes recherches." Translation from Antoine Banier, *The Mythology and Fables of the Ancients, Explain'd from History* (London: A. Miller, 1739), vi.

27 Banier, *La mythologie et les fables expliquées*, 1:vii–viii: "Aujourd'hui les Sçavans, persuadés que les Fables cachent sous d'ingenieuses enveloppes l'Histoire des temps qui suivirent le Deluge, se sont appliqués à lever le voile mysterieux qui deroboit à des yeux peu clair voyants les verités qu'elles renferment. Il est des temps favorables à certaines opinions, & celle de la verité des Fables a tellement pris le dessus, qu'il faut desormais renoncer de bonne grace à y trouver aucun sens raisonnable, ou les rapporter à l'Histoire." Translation adapted from Banier, *The Mythology and Fables of the Ancients*, 1:x.

and the historical (ἱστορικόν) period which began with the first Olympiad.[28] Not only did this division confirm that the Greeks had no proper historical information, which is to say, actual *histories* of the period, before, at the very earliest, the first Olympiad, but it convinced scholars that myths still told of a distinct period in human history, one which Francesco Bianchini called "tempus quod Varroni Mythicum dicti qui populis a se prognatis dedere nomina in Africa, Asia et Europa ex Diodori Apollodori."[29] As Peter Bietenholz has noted, Varro's division, which notionally divided myth from history, actually coupled them together. With Varro, myths and the mythical age became an integral part of the universal span of history.[30] In this sense, myth was a distorted form of knowledge which preceded the practice of preserving historical records and the development of historical study but still told of historical events. Moreover, Varro's division supported the popular notion that the first "historians" and theologians among the Gentiles were poets.[31] In his 1606 *Thesaurus temporum*, Joseph Scaliger (1540–1609) – one of the key figures in first comparing sacred history with ancient pagan testimonies – cited Varro and supposed that before Herodotus "memory of primitive things was extant either in ancient monuments or among the poets, or even in common songs"; almost ninety years

---

28 As preserved in Censorinus, *De die natali* 21.1–2. "Et si origo mundi in hominum notitiam venisset, inde exordium sumeremus; nunc vero id intervallum temporis tractabo, quod historicon Varro appellat. Hic enim tria discrimina temporum esse tradit: primum ab hominum principio ad cataclysmum priorem, quod propter ignorantiam vocatur adelon, secundum a cataclysmo priore ad olympiadem primam, quod, quia multa in eo fabulosa referuntur, mythicon nominatur, tertium a prima olympiade ad nos, quod dicitur historicon, quia res in eo gestae veris historiis continetur. Primum tempus, sive habuit initium, seu semper fuit, certe quot annorum sit, non potest conprehendi. Secundum non plane quidem scitur, sed tamen ad mille circiter et sescentos annos esse creditur: a priore scilicet cataclysmo, quem dicunt et Ogygii, ad Inachi regnum annos circiter CCCC computarunt, hinc ad excidium Troiae annos DCCC, hinc ad olympiadem primam paulo plus CCCC; quos solos, quamvis mythici temporis postremos, tamen quia a memoria scriptorum proximos, quidam certius definire voluerunt." Text from Censorinus, *Censorini de die natali liber*, ed. Ivan Cholodniak (St. Petersburg: Russian Imperial Academy of Sciences, 1889).

29 BVR, S 81, fols. 1r, 123v; see also Bianchini, *La istoria universale*, 19, where Bianchini divides the ages of the world into *prima, incerta, mitica o favolosa*, and *istorica*.

30 Peter G. Bietenholz, *Historia and Fabula: Myths and Legends in Historical Thought from Antiquity to the Modern Age* (Leiden: E. J. Brill, 1994), 37–38.

31 See for example Stillingfleet, *Origines sacrae*, 57–60; and also Jean Le Clerc, *Ars critica* (Amsterdam: G. Gallet, 1697), 1:218: "Poetae, qui antiquissimas Graecorum opiniones compectuntur." See further on this Gianfranco Cantelli, "Mito e storia in J. Leclerc, Tournemine e Fontenelle," *Rivista critica di storia della filosofia* 27 (1972): 269–286, 385–400; Arnaldo Momigliano, "Perizonius, Niebuhr and the Character of Early Roman Tradition," in *Essays in Ancient and Modern Historiography*, 231–232.

later, the French Oratorian Louis Thomassin (1619–1695), who synchronized pagan myths with Christian doctrine in a manner which would have repulsed Scaliger, still supposed that "neither as Poets, nor as Theologians, nor as Philosophers, did the Poets render this illustrious testimony to the truth: but as Historians. For we have shown in the same place that all these qualities were united in the person of the ancient Poets."[32] This notion not only legitimised the popular scholarly practice of hunting for historical nuggets in the swamp of Greek mythology, but also the equally popular practice of citing works of Greek and Roman poetry as key sources for a history which preceded Homer, let alone Ovid or Virgil, by many thousands of years.

It is precisely this notion that should make us rethink the manner in which seventeenth-century scholars conceptualised the meaning of *fabula*, particularly when used to help verify, supplement, and explicate biblical *historia*. Certainly it is true that the term *fabula* was continually used to describe pagan lies, which is to say, pagan testimonies which openly (and even deliberately) conflicted with biblical testimony. It was precisely in this context that Jean Martianay, who spent much time defending the authority of Jerome's Vulgate, once stated that the antiquities of Egypt "ont toûjours passé pour fabuleuses," since they contradicted the Vulgate Bible.[33] For Martianay, the opposite of *fabula* was not so much *historia*, but *veritas*. Yet this understanding of *fabula* was not necessarily shared by all of Martianay's contemporaries. For Bonjour and other scholars who synchronized biblical history with pagan myths, profane *fabula* still conveyed historical information: *fabula* was opposed to *historia* not because one was genuinely true and the other wholly false, but because one contained authoritative, stable, firm and certain historical information, the other corrupted historical fragments obscured by the ravages of time and embellished by the fancies of the poets – Selden's "manifest Historical Truth …

---

32 Joseph Scaliger, "Iosephi Scaligeri Iulii Caesaris Filii Animadversiones in Chronologica Eusebii," in *Thesaurus temporum. Eusebii Pamphili Caesareae Palaestinae Episcopi* (Leiden: Thomas Basson, 1606), 4: "vel in veteribus monimentis vel apud Poetas, vel etiam in vulgaribus carminibus extabat priscarum rerum memoria"; Louis Thomassin, *La méthode d'étudier et d'enseigner chrétiennement et solidement les historiens profanes par rapport à la religion Chrétienne, & aux écritures* (Paris: Louis Rolland, 1693), 1:4: "que ce n'est ny comme Poëtes, ny comme Theologiens, ny comme Philosophes, que les Poëtes ont rendu cet illustre témoignage à la verité; mais comme Historiens. Car nous avons montré au mesme endroit, que toutes ces qualitez estoient reünies dans la personne des anciens Poëtes." Anthony Grafton calls this passage "his [Scaliger's] favourite fragment of Varro": see Anthony Grafton, *Joseph Scaliger: A Study in the History of Classical Scholarship* (Oxford: Clarendon Press, 1983–1993), 2:716.

33 Jean Martianay, *Défense du texte hébreu et de la chronologie de la Vulgate contre le livre de L'antiquité des tems rétablie* (Paris: L. Roulland, 1689), 432.

wrap't up in the mysteries of Heathen Priests and Poets." As Plutarch had once written in the *De Iside et Osiride*, his major work on Egyptian mythology, ancient myths, though they contained "loose fictions and frivolous fabrications" also contained "narrations of certain puzzling events and experiences":

> Just as the rainbow, according to the account of the mathematicians, is a reflection of the sun, and owes its many hues to the withdrawal of our gaze from the sun and our fixing it on the cloud, so the somewhat fanciful accounts here set down are but reflections of some true tale which turns back our thoughts to other matters [358F–359A].[34]

It was precisely these fables, and this approach to ancient fables, which first evoked excitement in Bonjour while in Toulouse. Indeed, they became the explicit subject of his first major scholarly project, the *Mercurius*. As Rigord wrote to Magliabechi in September 1695, "he [Bonjour] has carefully examined the fables of the ancients and through the darkness in which they are shrouded unravelled the historical truth."[35]

2 Samuel Bochart and the Biblical Diffusionist Narrative

If the historical interpretation of myth gave scholars the basic tools for writing the primordial history of the world, then it was another historical narrative which allowed them to identify this primordial history with the biblical record of Moses: the narrative of biblical diffusionism, the process by which biblical knowledge had been transmitted to the various Gentile nations of the ancient world. The fundamental question which prompted the development of this theory was, what was the history which lay underneath Banier's "Mask of Fable"? – and, if it was indeed biblical, how was it possible that pagan poets had gained knowledge of biblical events? To a certain extent, the basic answer to this question had already been provided by the Church Fathers, who remained – and it is important to stress this fact – the accepted, explicit, authorities for evaluating ancient pagan wisdom and placing it within

---

[34] Translation from Plutarch, "Isis and Osiris," in *Moralia*, trans. Frank Cole Babbitt (Cambridge MA: Harvard University Press, 1936), 5:50–51.

[35] Jean-Pierre Rigord to Antonio Magliabechi, 4 September 1695, BNCF, *Fondo Magliabechiano* VIII, cod. 341, fol. 28secondo(v): "il a examiné avec attention les fables des anciens et au travers de l'obscurité dont elles sont enveloppées il a demelé la verité historique."

a Judaeo-Christian framework for universal history, even in the seventeenth century. To combat their pagan opponents who considered Christianity a recent invention, the Church Fathers attempted to show that the most laudable tenets of Greek philosophy and culture were themselves derivative.[36] In particular, the Fathers exploited the common Greek *topos* that Greek wisdom had its origins in the ancient Near East and Egypt, where Greek philosophers from Plato to Pythagoras had journeyed to receive their education, in order to suggest that the real origin of this wisdom was Jewish. In the seventeenth century, many scholars remained indebted to this so-called "Eusebian" tradition.[37] In line with Fathers like Eusebius, scholars supposed that pagan cults were a corrupted deviation from Noachic monotheism and that biblical truths had passed from Israel to Egypt and thenceforth to Greece. Furthermore, what Dmitri Levitin has dubbed the "patristic paradigm" – the notion that the pagans had either derived or stolen the key principles of their theology, cosmology, and philosophy from Christianity – remained central to defending the primacy and thereby superiority of the Christian religion.[38] Apologetic authors such as Hugo Grotius (15830–1645) or Theophilus Gale (1628–1678) continued to suppose that Christian ideas, such as the Trinity or the immortality of the soul, were confirmed by pagan theology. Gale's opening statement in his *The Court of Gentiles* (1669/72), that "the choisest Contemplations of *Gentile Philosophie*, were but some corrupt Derivations, or at best but broken Traditions, originally traduced from the *Sacred Scriptures*, and *Jewish Church*" is, by and large, a suitable way to describe the "patristic paradigm" as outlined by Levitin.[39]

Yet scholars of the seventeenth century also took this patristic paradigm in new and influential directions. Above all, there are two differences of major importance. The first is that seventeenth-century scholars chose to not only identify certain aspects of pagan wisdom with Christian doctrine but also to

---

36 Adler, *Time Immemorial*; Arnaldo Momigliano, "Pagan and Christian Historiography in the Fourth Century A.D.," in *Essays in Ancient and Modern Historiography*, 107–126; Arthur J. Droge, *Homer or Moses? Early Christian Interpretations of the History of Culture* (Tübingen: J. C. B. Mohr, 1989).

37 On which see Richard Serjeantson, "David Hume's *Natural History of Religion* (1757) and the End of Modern Eusebianism," in *The Intellectual Consequences of Religious Heterodoxy 1600–1750*, ed. Sarah Mortimer and John Robertson (Leiden and Boston: Brill, 2012), 270.

38 Dmitri Levitin, "What was the Comparative History of Religions in 17th-Century Europe (and Beyond)? Pagan Monotheism/Pagan Animism, from T'ien to Tylor," in *Regimes of Comparatism: Frameworks of Comparison in History, Religion and Anthropology*, ed. Renaud Gagné, Simon Goldhill, and Geoffrey Lloyd (Leiden and Boston: Brill, 2018), 52–57.

39 Theophilus Gale, *The Court of the Gentiles: or A Discourse touching the Original of Human Literature, both Philologie and Philosophie, from the Scripture & Jewish Church* (Oxford: H. Hall, 1672), "advertissements," 1: sig. *4v.

identify the historical information derived from pagan myths with the historical record of the Bible. Ultimately, the majority of the Church Fathers – and, for that matter, the Renaissance syncretists of the fifteenth and sixteenth centuries – still supposed that pagan myth primarily concerned ancient *pagan* history and the origins of the idolatrous heathen gods, rather than the lives of the biblical patriarchs. In his hugely influential *Institutiones divinae*, the late third- and early fourth-century Church Father Lactantius had supposed, largely on the evidence of Euhemerus' *Iera Anagraphē* (Secret History), that pagan kings such as Jupiter had been divinized on account of the beneficence they had bestowed upon their grateful subjects (1.11–15).[40] In the Euhemerist literature of the early Middle Ages, this notion remained formative. In a famous passage from his seventh-century *Etymologiae*, Isidore of Seville stated explicitly, citing Lactantius, that "those who the pagans assert are gods are revealed to have once been humans, and after their death they began to be worshipped among their people because of the life and merit of each of them" (8.11.1).[41] Yet as the work of Lactantius and Isidore shows, the mortal origins of pagan gods always lay with gentile kings and warriors, not with the biblical patriarchs. The Fathers demarcated a clear distinction between pagan myths which recalled primordial *pagan* history, and the true *divine* history of the Bible. In the seventeenth century, this relationship fundamentally changed, as scholars increasingly came to the conclusion that the original history hidden underneath the veil of pagan mythology was not profane but biblical. It was during this period that identifications between pagan gods such as Saturn and biblical patriarchs such as Noah or Abraham became *de rigueur* and a celebrated classicist and

---

40 See Lactantius, *Divine Institutes*, ed. Anthony Bowen and Peter Garnsey (Liverpool: Liverpool University Press, 2003), 92: "That makes it clear that they were men; it is also clear why they began to be called gods. If there were no kings before Saturn or Uranus, because of the lack of population – life was rustic, and people lived without rulers – then no doubt that was time when people began to honour a particular king and all his family with special adoration and new distinctions, to the point of actually calling them gods, either for their remarkable good qualities (an opinion which would be honestly held by people still rough and simple) or, as tends to be the case, in deference to their actual power, or because of their welcome promotion of civilisation. Since those kings were highly regarded by the people whose lives they had civilised, at their deaths a great yearning ensued for them. Hence the statues of them that people put up, so that by gazing at the likeness they could find some consolation; taking it a bit further, out of their affection they began to cultivate a memory of the dead, partly to show their gratitude to men who had served them well and partly to spur their successors to a desire to be good rulers themselves."

41 Translation from Isidore of Seville, *The Etymologies of Isidore of Seville*, trans. Stephen A. Barney, W. J. Lewis, J. A. Beach, and Oliver Berghof (Cambridge: Cambridge University Press, 2006).

philologist such as Pierre-Daniel Huet, one-time tutor to the Dauphin, could come to identify (almost) the entire canon of pagan deities with Moses. As Huet pointed out in his *Demonstratio evangelica*, all those ancient men whom the pagans worshipped as learned, divine, or illustrious – and whom *both* pagan and patristic Euhemerists considered to be the origins of pagan gods and heroes – were, in fact, "nothing else than imitations copied from the original of Moses."[42]

The origin of this new approach can be dated to around the beginning of the seventeenth century, largely due to the influence of one of the most celebrated scholars of the period, Joseph Scaliger. Son of the noted Italian natural philosopher Julius Caesar Scaliger (1484–1558), then living in France, Joseph Scaliger converted to Calvinism as a young man and went on to establish his scholarly reputation with a series of acclaimed classical editions which demonstrated his formidable text-critical abilities. In 1593, following the retirement of Justus Lipsius (1547–1606), he moved to Leiden, the city and university where he reached the pinnacle of his reputation and with which he remains indelibly associated. His first major chronological success, however, came while still in France: in 1583, he published the first edition of his monumental and influential *De emendatione temporum*, one of if not the most important early modern study of ancient chronology. It was in this work that Scaliger made the decision to use the testimony of the ancient Chaldean historian Berosus, alongside other ancient pagan authors, such as Megasthenes, to help construct a history of the Near East from the eighth to the fifth century without impinging, at least in his eyes, on the biblical record.[43] Although the credibility of both Berosus and Megasthenes had been damaged by the notorious forgeries of Annius of Viterbo (1437–1502), Scaliger believed that the fragments preserved by Josephus and Eusebius were genuine. As Anthony Grafton has noted, this suggestion proved to be one of the most contentious features of the first edition of Scaliger's work and led to the frequent and often mischievous accusation that Scaliger privileged lying pagans over sacred oracles. Scaliger, never one to take even gentle criticism lying down, responded by publishing, as an appendix

---

42 Pierre-Daniel Huet, *Demonstratio evangelica* (Amsterdam: Janssonio-Waesbergios, & Hendrick & Theodore Boom, 1680), 67: "Nam quae se expugnari non patietur pertinacia, siquidem ostendero quidquid apud antiquissimas gentes, & ingenii ac doctrinae laude imprimis florentes, divinum, praestans, illustre, & valde vetustum habitum est, Deos puta, Diisque prognatos Heroas, conditores etiam urbium, ac legumlatores, nihil aliud fuisse quam expressas ad Mosis exemplar imagines." See in this context my earlier work: Felix Schlichter, "Euhemerus and Euhemerism in the Seventeenth and Eighteenth Centuries," *Journal of the History of Ideas* 84 (2023): 653–683.

43 Grafton, *Joseph Scaliger*, 2:424.

to the second edition of his *De emendatione temporum* (1598), a collection of ancient texts entitled "Veterum Graecorum fragmenta selecta." Here, Scaliger concentrated on sources from ancient nations known to have had some ancient interaction with the Jews, such as the Chaldeans and Phoenicians. From these sources Scaliger believed, as he stated in the suffix of the title, that "several very obscure places of sacred chronology and the biblical books are elucidated."[44]

One pertinent and indicative example of just such a source is the history of the ancient Phoenician writer Sanchuniathon, which was translated into Greek in the first century AD by the obscure Phoenician historian Philo of Byblos, but was only partially preserved in Eusebius' *Praeparatio evangelica*.[45] In his so-called *Phoenician History*, Sanchuniathon presented a narrative in which the earliest stages of Phoenician history mixed cosmological with mythological elements. When studying Philo's surviving translation, Scaliger remarked on a number of passages in which Sanchuniathon had appeared to borrow from Mosaic scripture, particularly concerning certain divine etymologies or mythological narratives. For example, Scaliger argued that the two Mosaic Hebrew expressions *tohu* (תהו) and *bohu* (בהו), which Moses had used to describe the shapelessness and emptiness of the world at Genesis 1:2, could be identified with the mythological Phoenician wind Baau (Βάαυ) – which along with Kolpia was responsible for engendering the first mortals Protogonos and Aïon – as well as the Phoenician god Τάαυτος. He also supposed that Sanchuniathon's story of Kronos offering his "only-begotten" son Iehud as a sacrifice to his father Uranus was derived from the biblical story of Abraham and Isaac.[46] While it is true that these identifications were limited – Scaliger did not suppose, as later scholars would do, that the tangled mythological thicket of Kronos myths were all corrupted Abrahamic remnants – his scholarship did open the door for future scholars. Most importantly, Scaliger – who initially faced opprobrium for his extensive use of pagan sources – taught future scholars that certain, "very obscure" biblical passages could be "elucidated" with pagan evidence. This idea was to prove significant in shaping sacred history and biblical chronology in the following century. Certainly, by the end of seventeenth century, scholars in both disciplines explicitly acknowledged Scaliger's authority and implicitly adopted his methods, even if they almost certainly took them in directions which Scaliger would have strongly disapproved of.

---

44 Grafton, *Joseph Scaliger*, 2:424–34; Joseph Scaliger, "Veterum Graecorum fragmenta selecta," in *Opus de emendatione temporum* (Leiden: Officina Plantiniana, 1598): "quibus loci aliquot obscurissimi Chronologiae sacrae & bibliorum illustrantur."
45 See Albert I. Baumgarten, *The Phoenician History of Philo of Byblos. A Commentary* (Leiden: E. J. Brill, 1981).
46 Scaliger, "Veterum Graecorum fragmenta selecta," xxv, xliii–xliiii.

The second pivotal development was the emergence, growth, and eventual acceptance of the short-lived yet highly influential narrative of biblical diffusionism, which allowed scholars to explain how biblical knowledge had come to be transmitted throughout the ancient world, including to nations which had not had any ostensible ancient commerce with the Jews. Once again, some of the kernels of this notion can be found in the second edition of Scaliger's *De emendatione temporum*. In examining the manner in which "native" heathen writers retained, in their records, corrupted narratives of biblical events, Scaliger suggested that the origins of the Phoenician gods lay in the false interpretation or the corrupted knowledge of Hebrew scripture.[47] Importantly, this single notion later became the founding principle of John Selden's *De diis syris*, in which Selden traced the origins of the idolatrous gods of Greco-Roman polytheism back to the biblical idols of the Old Testament.[48] According to Selden, biblical knowledge had been transmitted from the once isolated Hebrew nation to the nascent Greeks through the mediation of the ancient Phoenicians.[49] Consequently Selden was able to connect *historia sacra*, the sacred history of the Jewish people in the biblical Near East, with the pagan myths of the Greco-Roman Mediterranean West.

The key work in this regard, however – a monument to a scholarly tradition which formed the basis of Bonjour's major projects – was the *Geographia sacra* of the Huguenot scholar Samuel Bochart. An erstwhile student of the great Arabist Thomas Erpenius (1584–1624), Bochart spent most of his working life in Caen, where he devoted his life to biblical scholarship and learning an immense number of Oriental languages; Pierre Bayle later called him "one of the most learned men in the world."[50] The *Geographia sacra*, first published in two parts in 1646, was the fruit of many years of research and became perhaps the most cited, and certainly most respected, work on *historia sacra* of the seventeenth century.[51]

In the *Geographia sacra*, Bochart expanded, systematized, and amplified what was once an ancient *topos*, as recently revived by Selden: that Greek learning had Egyptian or ancient Near Eastern origins and may have been transmitted westwards by the sea-faring Phoenicians.[52] In the first part of his work, he

---

[47] Scaliger, "Veterum Graecorum fragmenta selecta," xxv; "videmus igitur, quomodo Phoenices Deos suos ex vetustis Hebraeorum libris mutuati, falso sint interpretati."
[48] G. J. Toomer, *John Selden: A Life in Scholarship* (Oxford: Oxford University Press, 2009), 1:212.
[49] See John Selden, *De diis syris* (London: William Stansby, 1617).
[50] Pierre Bayle, *Dictionnaire historique et critique* (Rotterdam: Reinier Leers, 1715), 1:633: "un des plus savans hommes du monde."
[51] See generally Shalev, *Sacred Words and Worlds*, 141–203.
[52] For example, Herodotus, *Histories* 2.48–9, 2.123.3; Diodorus, 1.69.4, 1.69.2, 1.97.7; Plato, *Timaeus* 21E–25D; Plutarch, *De Iside et Osiride* 254E–F; and in particular Josephus, *Contra*

outlined how all the peoples of the ancient world could be traced back to the descendants of Noah as recorded in the genealogical table at Genesis 10. In the second part, he detailed how the Phoenicians, whom he identified with the original inhabitants of Canaan before their expulsion by Joshua and whom he considered the ancient mercantile and sea-faring nation *par excellence*, had, by establishing colonies throughout the Mediterranean world, spread knowledge of Hebrew scripture to pagan nations otherwise thought to have had no ancient interaction with the Jews. In his later *Hierozoicon* (1663), Bochart described the work in the following terms:

> Some years ago we dealt with the first inhabitants of the earth, whose origins were submerged in deep darkness and obscured by remote antiquity, and we tried to extricate them, chiefly from the writings of Moses, who in one chapter of Genesis has things that are more numerous and certain on this subject than all surviving monuments of the Greeks and Romans. We joined to these the ancient navigations of the Phoenicians, who, several centuries before Jason and the Argonauts, began to spread themselves throughout the entire Mediterranean, and to disseminate [their] colonies in many parts of Europe, Asia, and Africa.[53]

For Bochart, the rise of ancient, Near Eastern, and, by extension, human civilization could therefore be traced back to the various peregrinations of Noah's direct descendants. As Zur Shalev has noted, the ultimate source for these peregrinations was the Bible, specifically Genesis 10, which told a history of the origins of human civilization not extant elsewhere.[54] In this sense, Bochart presumed that the Hebrew Bible was both the authoritative and only surviving complete account of universal, primordial, history. Yet he also supposed that the records of certain ancient pagan nations retained corrupted knowledge of both the primordial Flood and the origins of human civilization.

Apionem 1.63. Cf. Erik Iversen, *The Myth of Egypt and its Hieroglyphs in European Tradition* (Princeton NJ: Princeton University Press, 1993), 8ff., and Droge, *Homer or Moses?*

53 Samuel Bochart, *Hierozoicon sive Bipartitum opus de animalibus sacrae scripturae* (London: Thomas Roycroft, 1663), "praefatio ad lectorem," sig. a1r: "ante aliquot annos egimus de primis terrarum incolis, quorum origines in profundis tenebris mersas, & longa vetustate obsitas eruere conati sumus, partim ex Mosis scriptis, qui in uno capite Geneseos de hoc argumento plura habet & certiora quam quotquot Graecorum supersunt aut Romanorum monumenta. His antiquas Phoenicum navigationes subjunximus, qui aliquot annorum centuriis ante Jasonem & Argonautas, per totum mare Mediterraneum coeperunt se diffundere, & in multis Europae, Asiae & Africae locis colonias disseminare."

54 Shalev, *Sacred Words and Worlds*, 178–180.

Consequently, the corrupted fragments of pagan *fabula* still told of the same events as recorded in faithful biblical *historia*.

Bochart's synchronism between the sacred and the profane was based on historical rather than philosophical or theological parallels. Moreover, his synchronism was *selective*. He rejected, for example, the notion that the pagans worshipped Moses as a god, a supposition first found in the late third- and early second-century BC work of the Jewish Hellenist Artapanus and popularised many hundred years later by the Dutch classicists Daniel Heinsius (1580–1655) and Gerardus Vossius (1577–1649), who identified Moses with Bacchus/Dionysus. According to Bochart, it was unlikely that the Egyptians, who openly despised the Israelites, would have accorded the rank of divinity to one of their number.[55] Despite supposing that the commercial and colonial activities of the Phoenicians were responsible for spreading knowledge of sacred history westwards, he was also keen to point out specific historical examples of this cultural transmission. He supposed, for example, that the Phoenician hero Cadmus, whom the pagans credited with bringing the alphabet to Greece, had been expelled from Canaan, the original native land of the Phoenicians, by Moses' successor Joshua.[56] Particularly important was his use of Sanchuniathon, whom Bochart considered more ancient than the Trojan war. As we have already noted, Sanchuniathon's work had first been studied by Scaliger. In later years, he was also cited by Gerardus Vossius and Hugo Grotius, who sought to highlight that Phoenician theology contained a number of similarities with the Mosaic account of Creation.[57] While Bochart

---

55 Bochart, *Geographia sacra*, 485: "Non tamen inde collegerim cum viro magno Mosem esse Phoenicum & Aegyptiorum Bacchum. Neque enim verissimile est virum tam multis nominibus utrisque odiosum pro Deo benefico potuisse ab illis coli. Tantum puto fabulatores ad Mosis historiam sic allusisse, quomodo in Sileni fabula ad prophetiam de Silo. Et vero non Mosis solius, sed & aliorum historiae latent in Bacchi mythologicis." In response Huet cited Petronius's dictum that "primus in orbe deos decit timor" (Statius, *Thebaid* 3.661) to suggest that the Egyptians made Moses a god not out of love but out of fear. He also pointed to Exodus 7:1, in which God tells Moses that he has been appointed God over the Pharaoh: Huet, *Demonstratio evangelica*, 127.

56 Bochart, *Geographia sacra*, 486: "Ita tamen ut ex historia Mosis petantur multo plura, quia cum primum Phoenices Cadmo duce in Graeciam appulerunt, recens erat adhuc memoria rerum a Mose gestarum. Cadmus enim sub Iosua vixit, & eorum dux fuit qui ut imminenti exitio se proriperent, mari se commiserunt alias terras inquisituri." See on this further Paul Pezron, *Origine des Lettres*, BNF, Latin 17397, 4–20, who uses the testimonies of Critias (fr. B 2 West) in Athenaeus *Deiphnosophistae* (1.28c), Lucan (*Pharsalia* 3.220–224), Herodotus (5.58–60), and Pliny (5.12 and 7.56 (7.192)) to evidence the Phoenician origins of Greek letters.

57 Hugo Grotius, *Sensus librorum sex, quos pro veritate religionis Christianae* (Leiden: Johannes Maire, 1627), 24, 27; Hugo Grotius, *De veritate religionis Christianae* (Paris:

also made reference to these similarities, the novelty of his approach rested on the manner in which he studied Sanchuniathon as an historic individual. Most importantly, Bochart noted two avenues of transmission which explained how a Phoenician historian had become a reader of Moses.[58] The first was the so-called "arcanae Ammoneorum literae," the sacred writings of the Ammoneans (Ἀμμυνέων/Ἀμμυνέοί), which, according to Philo of Byblos, was one of Sanchuniathon's major sources. According to Bochart, the word "Ammoneans" came from the Hebrew *hammanim* (חמנים) which both the Septuagint (Ezechiel 6:4, 6:6) and Jerome (2 Chronicles 14:5) had translated as "temples." Consequently, Bochart suggested that the writings of which Philo spoke were not those of the unknown "Ammonean" people but were instead secret temple records ("literae in sacris receptae"), more specifically, the secret writings found in the temples of the Jews.[59] The second notable source was the mysterious Hierombalus, an ancient priest of "Ieuo" (ΙΕΥΩ) whom Porphyry had denoted as Sanchuniathon's chief source and whom Scaliger and later Grotius considered a priest of YHWH. Here, Bochart broke new ground by identifying this mysterious Hierombalus with the Hebrew judge Gideon. In the Bible Gideon was also called "Ierubbaal" (Judges 7:1, 8:35), and on this basis Bochart made the comparatively simple deduction that Philo's Ἱερομβάλος was a (poor) transliteration of the Hebrew ירובעל. Bochart strengthened this identification by highlighting, firstly, that after Gideon's death the Israelites fell once again into the idolatrous worship of "Baalberith" (Judges 8:33); and secondly, that this city "Berith" was the same as Sanchuniathon's hometown of "Berytus." As a result, Bochart was able to provide definitive historical evidence for ancient commerce between the Jews and Sanchuniathon's Phoenicians around the time of Gideon, and explain how Sanchuniathon may have procured information from Hebrew scripture.[60]

It was on the basis of these specific instances of historical transmission, or biblical diffusion, that Bochart came to identify certain pagan myths with biblical narratives. Indeed, Bochart began his work with perhaps the most famous identification between sacred and profane history in the seventeenth century. On the first page of the *Geographia sacra*, Bochart argued that Noah could be identified with Saturn and Noah's three children Ham, Sem, and Japhet with

---

Sébastien Cramoisy, 1640), 239, 305, 319–320, 324; Gerardus Vossius, *De theologia gentili et physiologia Christiana; sive de origine ac progressu idololatriae* (Amsterdam: Johannes and Cornelius Blaeu, 1641), 142–3, 163–4, 206.

58 Bochart, *Geographia sacra*, 782–790, 855–864.
59 Bochart, *Geographia sacra*, 857.
60 Bochart, *Geographia sacra*, 858–859. Bochart also explained that the designation of Gideon as a priest by Sanchuniathon was an unfortunate pagan misinterpretation.

Saturn's three children Jupiter Ammon, Pluto, and Neptune respectively.[61] A number of earlier scholars, such as Jean Lemaire de Belges (1473–1525), Wolfgang Lazius (1514–1565), and the celebrated Hebraist Guillaume Postel (1510–1581) had already suggested that understanding the history of Noah and his immediate descendants was pivotal for understanding the origins and development of human civilization.[62] By supposing, however, that the division of the different parts of the world to Noah's successors was reflected in the pagan myth of Saturn's division of the world to his three children, Bochart also suggested that not only Moses but also certain pagans had knowledge of this central development in human history. Despite the obvious corruptions in the pagan mythological narrative, Bochart explicitly supposed that the Mosaic "historia de Noa & tribus filiis accurate confertur cum fabula de Saturno & Saturni tribus liberis" – that the *history* of Noah connected accurately with the *fable* of Saturn.[63] Bochart's formulation is indicative of how scholars of this period came to blur the distinction between *historia sacra* and *historia exotica*. Certainly, Bochart was still aware that one narrative was biblical *historia* and the other pagan *fabula*, and therefore that one was far superior to the other. Yet Bochart still suggested that *both* pagan myth *and* biblical history told the same narrative of the origins of civilization. In the following chapters, Bochart continued to explore the many ways in which the pagan myths surrounding Saturn and his children conformed to the biblical account. In doing so, he highlighted how *historia sacra* was still preserved in *historia exotica*.

Bochart's *Geographia sacra* marked a new stage in the study of sacred history. Although not explicitly apologetic, his narrative of biblical diffusionism through Phoenician navigation and Sanchuniathon's discovery of biblical source material provided a historical basis on which future scholars could build all manner of synchronic, apologetic fantasies. Perhaps the most obvious – and

---

61 See for example Matthias Prideaux, *An Easy and Compendious Introduction for Reading All Sorts of Histories: Contrived in a More Facile Way Then Heretofore Hath Been Published, Out of the Papers of Mathias Prideaux* (Oxford: Leonard Lichfield, 1648), 5; Gale, *The Court of the Gentiles*, 2:9; Huet, *Demonstratio evangelica*, 220; Bonjour, *Selectae*, 97ff. See also Don Cameron Allen, *The Legend of Noah: Renaissance Rationalism in Arts, Science, and Letters* (Urbana: University of Illinois Press, 1949), 80.

62 See Allen, *The Legend of Noah*, 115–117; Paul Alphandery, "L'évhémérisme et les débuts de l'histoire des religions au moyen-âge," *Revues de l'histoire des religions* 109 (1934): 8; Seznec, *The Survival of the Pagan Gods*, 24; Claudine Poulouin, *Le temps des origines et les temps reculés de Pascal à l'Encyclopédie* (Paris: Honoré Champion, 1999), 36–37; Umberto Eco, *The Search for the Perfect Language*, trans. James Fentress (London: Fontana Press, 1997), 73–116.

63 Bochart, *Geographia sacra*, 1. Vossius (*De theologia gentili*, 118) had already made this parallel, but not as extensively as Bochart.

famous – student of Bochart was Pierre-Daniel Huet, who earned both admiration and ridicule for arguing that (almost) all pagan gods were distorted reflections of Moses. "While I compared this inexhaustible store of sacred and profane erudition with my scanty and inconsiderable stock, it was a real pain to the eyes," Huet later wrote in his memoirs. "I thus resigned myself to an entire intimacy with Bochart, and the whole train of my studies depended upon his advice."[64] Although Bochart and Huet would later have a prominent falling out over a passage in Huet's edition of Origen, the manner in which Bochart conceptualised *historia sacra* remained formative for Huet's *Demonstratio evangelica*, in which he called Bochart "vir doctrinae singularis," a man of singular learning.[65] Indeed, the parallels were so stark that what I have called influence a number of seventeenth-century contemporaries called plagiarism.[66] But it is worth noting that Bochart's influence extended far and wide, from the nonconformist and somewhat eccentric Calvinist Theophilus Gale, a committed proponent of Reformed covenant theology who met Bochart in Caen and who must rank surely as one of Bochart's crudest imitators, to the French Oratorian Louis Thomassin and the bellicose Huguenot Pierre Jurieu, both of whom held to Bochart's central notion of historical transmission.[67] In the words of Han

---

64 Huet, *Memoirs*, 1:36–38.
65 Huet, *Demonstratio evangelica*, 127. See for Huet's influences, and his relationship with Bochart, Dupront, *Pierre-Daniel Huet et l'exégèse comparatiste*, 95–110, as well as April G. Shelford, *Transforming the Republic of Letters: Pierre-Daniel Huet and European Intellectual Life, 1650–1720* (Rochester: Rochester University Press, 2007), 27–28; and also Guy Stroumsa, "Noah's sons and the religious conquest of the earth: Samuel Bochart and his followers," in *Sintflut und Gedächtnis: Erinnern und Vergessen des Ursprungs*, ed. Martin Mulsow and Jan Assmann (Munich: Wilhelm Fink, 2006), 314.
66 See Pierre-Daniel Huet to Claude Nicaise, 21 October 1698, BNF, Français 9359, fol. 101v, and in comparison Mathurin Veyssière La Croze to Gisbert Cuper, 22 May 1714, KW 72 H 19, n. 5: "Je suis fâché que ce savant Evêque n'ait pas plus respecté la mémoire de Mr. Bochart, à qui il doit la meilleure partie de sa reputation & même de son savoir. Feu Mr. Baillet m'a dit à Paris l'an 1694 que le Traitté du Paradis Terrestre de Mr. Huet étoit un ouvrage de Mr. Bochart que cet Evêque s'étoit approprié. Mr. Baillet ajoutoit qu'il en avoit des preuves positives, & qu'il les avoit inserées dans son Traitté Manuscrit des Plagiaires."
67 See Gale, *The Court of the Gentiles*, 1:23: "if those ancient Monuments of the *Phoenicians* were yet extant we should thence receive a great light, both as to *sacred*, and *profane Historie*; and that great *hiatus*, or gap, betwixt *Moses* and the *Grecians*, would be filled up," citing Bochart, *Geographia sacra*, sig. ++v. Gale's references to numerous "oral conferences" with Bochart span both the first and second part of his work. On Gale see Levitin, *Ancient Wisdom*, 146–153. For Thomassin see Louis Thomassin, *La methode d'étudier et d'enseigner chrétiennement & solidement les lettres* (Paris: François Huguet, 1681) 1: sig. e5v: "Et que bien que les Gentiles ne se convertissent pas entierement, ils recevoient toûjours des Hebreux quelque nouvelle augmentation de lumieres, & purifioient de plus en plus la Religion & la Fable, que les Italiens & les Grecs emprunterent des Pheniciens,

Vermeulen, "the acceptance of Bochart's views was so complete that Johann David Michaelis, the Göttingen Orientalist, quipped a century later, 'Previous authors on the origins of peoples believed they were founding themselves on the ancient Hebrew Moses, whereas, in fact, they based themselves on the new French Bochart.'"[68] It is illustrative that later French mythographers, such as Antoine Banier and Nicolas Fréret (1688–1749), continued to respect Bochart as a leading scholar of antiquity even after they had helped bring to an end that particular mythographic tradition which Bochart had been so central in developing and which he continued to embody.[69]

In Toulouse, Bonjour was a child of Bochart and Huet, the two contemporary scholars whom Bonjour referenced explicitly in the preface of his *Mercurius* and whom he continued to cite throughout his work.[70] On the one hand, these two scholars informed the basic scholarly principles which allowed Bonjour to offer a synthesis of pagan myth with *historia sacra* based upon the traditional diffusionist assumption that knowledge of biblical history had passed from Israel to Egypt to Greece via the travels of the Phoenicians.[71] If it was from Bochart that Bonjour took this more general notion of transmission, then it was from Huet that he took the idea of analysing pagan gods through historical and etymological scholarship which would allow him to reduce myriad myths to the history of one particular patriarch. On the other hand, many of Bonjour's individual identifications were also taken from Bochart and Huet's work. In the opening pages of his *Mercurius*, for example, he cited a lengthy passage from the *Geographia sacra* in which Bochart had identified the mysterious messianic character of Genesis 49.10, Shiloh, with the Greek god Silenus.[72] As we shall see in due course, much of his work on such mythological figures as Mercury, Menes, and Minos was deeply influenced by the sources cited and the interpretations proffered by Huet.

---

des Egyptiens, des Chaldéens, & des Assyriens, parmy lesquels des Hebreux avoient long-temps conservé"; for Jurieu see *Histoire critique des dogmes et des cultes*.

68   Han F. Vermeulen, *Before Boas. The Genesis of Ethnography and Ethnology in the German Enlightenment* (Lincoln and London: University of Nebraska Press, 2015), 73.

69   Banier, *La mythologie*, 1:iii; Fréret, "Manuscrit Original sur la Geographie Sacrée de Sam. Bochart," BNF, NAF 10925.

70   *Mercurius*, fol. 2v.

71   *Mercurius*, fol. 4v, citing Herodotus, 2.50.1 ("Σχεδὸν δὲ καὶ πάντων τὰ οὐνόματα τῶν θεῶν ἐξ Αἰγύπτου ἐλήλυθε ἐς τὴν Ἑλλάδα") and Josephus, *Contra Apionem*, 1.63 ("Phoenices ergo propter negociationem ad Graecorum provinciam navigantes, repente sunt agniti, & per illos Aegyptij, & omnes a quibus ad Graecos onera devehebant, immensa maria proscindentes").

72   *Mercurius*, fols. 10v–11r; Bochart, *Geographia Sacra*, 482.

Bonjour's debt to this tradition informed essentially all his major scholarly, historical work. In the apologetic dissertations which he composed for the theological students of the Montefiascone seminary in around 1705, his defence of the Christian religion continued to rely on common, historical parallels between the biblical record and ancient pagan sources, as once suggested by Bochart and Huet, amongst others. He cited, for example, not once but twice the famous testimony of the second-century Platonist Numenius, later repeated by Clement of Alexandria (*Stromata* 1.22), that Plato was nothing but an Attic-speaking Moses, "Moses Atticissans."[73] In a similar vein he suggested that Homer had encountered Hebrew scripture when in Egypt and had adapted his description of Achilles' shield in the *Iliad* (18.478ff.) to the Mosaic account of Creation, a parallel first voiced in ps.-Justin Martyr's *Cohortatio ad Graecos* (28).[74] Indeed, for Bonjour, the entirety of pagan cosmography was derived from and mirrored "what divine Moses says about Creation itself in Genesis."[75] In subsequent pages, he presented a cornucopia of pagan evidence in which each aspect of the Mosaic Creation narrative was preserved: hence the testimonies of Thales and Hesiod confirmed that night preceded day; those of Varro and Plutarch that darkness preceded light; those of Euripides and Apollonius of Rhodes that matter was created "ex nihilo"; those of Martial, Propertius, and Horace that man was made from mud. It was also for this reason that Adam is Saturn, and also Prometheus, and that even the Garden of Eden could be gleaned in the Garden of Alcinous.[76] The same could be said not only for pagan cosmology, but even for pagan "ideas." When defending Mosaic primacy, Bonjour outlined how the simple notion that God, but not man, could predict the future was made clear not only in Isaiah 44:7 or Ecclesiastes 8:7 but also in Statius (*Thebaid* 3.562–563), Horace (*Epodi* 3.29) Juvenal (*Saturae* 6.556) and Pacuvius (*apud* Aulus Gellius, 14.1.33): "ex sacra tam barbarica."[77]

---

73 *Triduanda*, T.I.33, 11; and *Selectae*, D.III.di.I.40, 152–153.
74 "Observationes Criticae," BAR, ms.lat.629, fol. 208r–v.
75 *Selectae*, 144: "quod in ipso Genesis exordio ait divinus Moyses."
76 *Selectae*, 144–152. For Bonjour's sources see Hesiod, *Theogony*, 116, 123–124; Thales in Diogenes Laertius 1.36; Varro in Aulus Gellius, 3.2.4–5; Plutarch, *De Iside et Osiride* 355F; Euripides, *Menalippe* 488 [cf. Euripides, *Fragments: Aegus-Meleager*, ed. Christopher Collard and Martin Cropp (Cambridge MA: Harvard University Press, 2008), 583]; Apollonius Rhodius, *Argonautica* 1.496–501; Martial, 10.39; Propertius, 3.5.7; Horace, *Carmina* 1.16.13–14; Ovid, *Metamorphoses* 1.5–88. On Adam see *Selectae*, 150–152, and consequently Apollodorus, 1.7.1; Apollonius Rhodius, *Argonautica* 4.676; Archelaus in Diogenes Laërtius, 2.4.17; Pausanias, 10.4.4; Homer, *Iliad* 18.478ff; Homer, *Odyssey* 7.324; Hesiod, *Theogony* 644. These are just some of the many illustrative examples; those who peruse them will see that the similarity between the sacred and pagan text is often only very slight.
77 *Triduanda*, T.I.26, 8–9.

Underpinning these comparisons remained Bochart's notion of Hebraic transmission. Unsurprisingly, the four ancient pagan nations which Bonjour cited when it came to preserving the Mosaic Creation narrative in their myths were Egypt, Phoenicia, Greece, and Rome, and it is similarly unsurprising that Bonjour not only used Sanchuniathon as his chief source for Phoenician theology but also cited both Bochart's conjecture regarding the writings of the Ammoneans and the identity of Hierombalus-Gideon to substantiate his historical link to Hebrew scripture.[78] Nor is it surprising that Bonjour's contemporaries such as Cuper squarely associated him with this tradition and identified him as an heir of Bochart. When Bacchini read Bonjour's *De nomine patriarchae Josephi*, in which Bonjour used examples of pagan mythology to substantiate his translation of "Zaphnath paaneah" (Genesis 41:45) as "salvatorem mundi," he described Bonjour's goal as being:

> to find in holy scripture with the guidance of languages and the most recondite erudition, the foundation of the Theology, and Mythology of the Gentiles, an undertaking attempted by the very famous ancients Clement of Alexandria, Justin, Eusebius, and others, and these days by Bochart, and writers from a similar sphere.[79]

Of similar inclination was Muratori, Bonjour's friend and admirer. When he read Bonjour's *Selectae* in 1705, his enthusiasm was unbounded; to Bonjour he wrote earnestly, if somewhat excessively, "Oh what erudition! Oh what wonderful things you have your dialogists say! I seem to be reading a Bochart, a Huet, a Vossius, or similar great men."[80]

3 Isaac La Peyrère and the Problematization of Sacred History

The notion of biblical diffusionism was the reason Bonjour and his contemporaries considered it a legitimate historical practice to identify pagan myths with narratives of sacred history. Yet a question remains: in the words of the French

---

78 *Selectae*, D.II.87 and D.III.di.I.3–6, 118, 144; *Triduanda* T.II.28, 24.
79 Bacchini, *Giornale*, 239–245, quote from 239: "di trovare nelle Sacre Scritture con la guida delle lingue, e dell'eruditione più recondita il fondamento della Teologia, e Mitologia de' Gentili, impresa tentata da' celeberrimi antichi Clemente Alessandrino, Justino, Eusebio, & altri, e modernamente dal Boccarto, e da' Scrittori di simile sfera."
80 Ludovico Antonio Muratori to Guillaume Bonjour, 21 October 1705, BAR, ms.lat.395, fol. 131r: "Oh quanta erudizione! Oh che belle cose fa ella dire a que' suoi Dialoghisti! Mi par di leggere un Bocharto, un Huet, un Vossio, e simili valentuomini," reprinted in Campori, *Epistolario di L. A. Muratori*, 2:536.

historian Alphonse Dupront, precisely *why* did comparative mythology – and biblical diffusionism – become such a popular method for defending the truth of the Christian religion and the authority of *historia sacra* in the late seventeenth century? and why did Bonjour, though enamoured with the erudite, authoritative, and widely-respected examples of Bochart and Huet, consider it useful or even necessary to synchronize pagan myth and biblical history in the manner in which he did?[81]

Recent historians have advanced a number of possible explanations. According to Seznec, the study of pagan mythology was primarily influenced by the concomitant study of the Hebrew language and biblical scholarship. In particular, Seznec notes how the notion of Hebraic primacy and the supposition that the Hebrew language was, as Bochart defined it, the *matrix linguarum*, led scholars to further pursue their search for the Hebraic origins of pagan culture.[82] Other scholars, meanwhile, have pointed to the influence of particular individuals whose scholarly methodology and text criticism pushed the boundaries of *historia sacra*. According to Anthony Grafton, it was Joseph Scaliger who first supposed that scholars must use non-biblical sources alongside the biblical record in their writing of ancient history. Meanwhile, other historians have highlighted how John Selden and his "antiquarianisation" of biblical scholarship convinced scholars that understanding the origins of the Greco-Roman gods would allow for a more complete understanding of the biblical world of the ancient Near East.[83]

Perhaps the most cited contributing factor to this reconceptualisation of sacred history, however, was the changing relationship between sacred and profane history, or, more accurately, between sacred and profane historical data. The seventeenth century in particular was marked by the discovery of new "profane" data, whether rediscovered in classical antiquity or newly discovered by missionaries in the Americas and the Far East. This new data provided something of a challenge to seventeenth-century scholars; for, rather than necessarily confirming or supplementing the key tenets of *historia sacra*, it often appeared to contradict what scholars knew to be true from perusing the history of Moses. Perhaps most representative of this new data, as Paolo Rossi has pointed out, were the rediscovered histories of Egypt and Chaldea

---

[81] Dupront, *Pierre-Daniel Huet et l'exégèse comparatiste*, 123.
[82] Seznec, *The Survival of the Pagan Gods*, 250; Bochart, *Geographia sacra*, 57ff.
[83] On Selden's importance see in particular Miller, "Taking Paganism Seriously"; Martin Mulsow, "John Selden's De Diis Syris: Idolatriekritik und vergleichende Religionsgeschichte im 17. Jahrhundert," *Archiv für Religionsgeschichte* 3 (2001): 1–24; and Guy Stroumsa, "John Spencer and the Roots of Idolatry," *History of Religions* 41 (2001): 1–23.

and the newly-discovered history of China.[84] All three nations provided scholars with new, seemingly reliable, historical sources which overtly contradicted the chronology of the Bible, whether by extending beyond the Hebrew date for Creation or by suggesting the existence of pagan kings before the biblical Flood. As a result, they offered a new and pressing challenge to scholars who wanted to defend the authority of the Bible on historical grounds. As we shall see in chapter five, Manetho's dynasties in particular were of critical importance in Bonjour's biblical chronology.

However, as Anthony Grafton has pointed out, pagan sources alone could not upset the biblical applecart.[85] Despite the discovery of new profane data, many of the problems which seventeenth-century scholars faced had already existed in the time of the Church Fathers. Even Augustine, confronted in the fifth century with the vagaries and vastness of Egyptian history, had once taught Christian scholars to simply reject pagan *fabula* which contradicted sacred *historia*.[86] While it therefore behoved scholars to highlight how pagan sources confirmed sacred history, it also behoved them to demonstrate how pagan sources which contradicted this history were fallacious. Since *historia exotica* or *profana* was built on uncertain *fabula* rather than certain *historia*, not all or even much of its information could be considered genuine. Ultimately, identifying Moses with Bacchus did not mean that one need believe that Moses had once journeyed to Argos where he induced women to devour the flesh of their infants, as Apollodorus taught of Bacchus.[87] Just because Huet had proven that Apollo, Pan, Priapus, or Aesculapius, were phantoms of Moses should not mean that one should begin worshipping them as law-giving Jewish prophets, as the French Dominican Noël Alexandre (1639–1724) pointed out in 1700.[88] By selecting from pagan myths those narratives which supported biblical history and rejecting those which did not, scholars made sure that ancient pagan sources remained subservient to the authority of Bible. The same thing was

---

84   Paolo Rossi, *The Dark Abyss of Time: The History of the Earth & The History of Nations from Hooke to Vico* (Chicago & London: The University of Chicago Press, 1984); this triumvirate featured prominently in Isaac Vossius, *Dissertatio de vera aetate mundi; qua ostenditur natale mundi tempus annis minimum 1440 vulgarem aeram anticipare* (The Hague: Adriaan Vlacq, 1659), xxix–xlviii.

85   Anthony Grafton, "The Chronology of the Flood," in *Sintflut und Gedächtnis: Erinnern und Vergessen des Ursprungs*, ed. Martin Mulsow and Jan Assmann (Munich: Wilhelm Fink, 2006), 69.

86   *De civitate dei* 18.40.

87   Apollodorus, *Bibliotheca* 3.5.2–3.

88   Noël Alexandre, *Conformité des cérémonies chinoises avec l'idolâtrie grecque et romaine pour servir de confirmation à l'Apologie des Dominicains missionnaires de la Chine* (Cologne: Heritiers de Corneille d'Egmond, 1700), 65–66.

true for historical and chronological as it was for mythological information. To suppose that the histories of Egypt and China could lead scholars to question or even abandon the historical authority of the Bible would only make sense if scholars considered them of comparable status and reliability to the biblical narrative. It was for this reason that, for many centuries, the status of the Pentateuch as the only complete, universal, and authoritative account for ancient and primordial history remained largely unchallenged.

Yet it is also true that, at some point in the seventeenth century, this relationship changed, at least subtly. In particular, orthodox scholars increasingly came to incorporate notionally contradictory pagan sources into their accounts of sacred history, rather than simply dismiss them as fabulous. It is a feature that we shall investigate further in chapter five, on Bonjour's treatment of Manetho's dynasties of Egypt. It is my contention that this development could not merely have been in reaction to general developments in methodology and foreign travel – the former of which must have also developed in response to something, the latter of which could offer data, but no framework for interpreting this data – but must also be considered as a response to certain, specific challenges to traditional conceptualisations of *historia sacra*. Indeed, it was precisely in the seventeenth century that certain individuals – "heretics," as they were branded by their orthodox counterparts – began to use such pagan sources to undermine long-standing assumptions concerning the nature of sacred history. The challenge these individuals provided also changed the manner in which orthodox scholars viewed pagan mythology and pagan antiquity more generally.

For the Church Fathers, paganism, and therefore pagan mythology, was the direct enemy. They cited pagan testimony so as to convince their pagan opponents that Christianity was prior and superior. As Christopher Ligota has pointed out, in the seventeenth century, paganism was not the enemy but a potential ally.[89] The heretics whom Huet and Bonjour had earmarked as their enemies – "those who currently devote great labour to holy scripture," as Bonjour wrote to Marc-Antonio Barbarigo in 1703 – did not want to replace Christianity with paganism.[90] Instead, they cited pagan evidence in order to better understand the true nature of biblical history, albeit a version of biblical history unpalatable to orthodox scholars because, as the English

---

[89] Christopher Ligota, "Der apologetische Rahmen der Mythendeutung im Frankreich des 17. Jahrhunderts (P. D. Huet)," in *Mythographie der frühen Neuzeit: Ihre Anwendung in den Künsten*, ed. Walther Killy (Wiesbaden: Otto Harrassowitz, 1984), 150.

[90] Guillaume Bonjour to Marc-Antonio Barbarigo, 18 August 1703, BAR, ms.lat.395, fol. 3r: "li quali oggidi s'affatigano molto nelle sacre scritture."

jurist Matthew Hale (1609–1676) pointed out, it was considered "contrary to the Authority and Infallibility of the Sacred Scriptures"[91] Consequently, the evidence of pagan mythology was no longer the counterpart to biblical history but rather the battleground upon which the orthodox and the heterodox fought for their respective conceptualisations of the *nature* of sacred history. The integration of pagan myth and sacred history was not only intended as a general defence of the truth of the Christian religion but also as a specific response to the way certain heterodox scholars were using pagan sources to discredit the accepted, universal nature of biblical history.

By the time Bonjour began to study sacred history, orthodox scholars were faced with what was, by then, a notorious heretical triumvirate: Thomas Hobbes and his *Leviathan* (1651), Isaac La Peyrère and his *Praeadamitae* (1655), and Benedict Spinoza and his *Tractatus theologico-politicus* (1670). In the apologetic dissertations in his *Selectae*, Bonjour named these three authors explicitly, since they "negant tamen antiquissimum genuinumque esse Pentateuchum Mosaicum."[92] Although the citation of Hobbes in particular is suggestive – the mention of Hobbes would make Bonjour perhaps the first scholar in Rome to cite Hobbes outside of the members of the Congregation of the Index – this reference is evidence not that Bonjour read Hobbes but rather that he was a close reader of Huet, who had cited the same triumvirate in his *Demonstratio evangelica*.[93] Of these three figures, however, one stands out in importance: while Bonjour did not mention Hobbes and Spinoza again, La Peyrère and his infamous *Praeadamitae* remained a constant presence and an explicit opponent throughout both Bonjour's published dissertations and unpublished manuscripts.

In his *Praeadamitae*, Isaac La Peyrère (1596–1676), a Calvinist theologian of possible Marrano descent from Bordeaux who served as secretary to the Prince of Condé, argued that Adam was not the first man but the first Jew, and therefore that men, and many men at that, had existed before Adam.[94] Consequently, he

---

91 Matthew Hale, *The Primitive Origination of Mankind, Considered and Examined According to The Light of Nature* (London: William Godbid, 1677), 185.
92 *Triduanda*, T.I.15, 6: "auctor tractatus Theologico-Politici, Auctor systematis Praeadamitarum, & Thomas Hobbius Anglus in suo Leviathane."
93 Huet, *Demonstratio evangelica*, 254–255. This triumvirate soon became notorious: see Malcolm, "Hobbes, Ezra, and the Bible," 387–389. I thank Felix Waldmann for pointing out the significance of Bonjour's citation of Hobbes.
94 The most recent study of La Peyrère is by Richard H. Popkin: *Isaac La Peyrère (1596–1676): His Life, Work and Influence* (Leiden: Brill, 1987), while there is also an important essay by Anthony Grafton: "Isaac La Peyrère and the Old Testament," in *Defenders of the Text: The Traditions of Scholarship in the Age of Science, 1450–1800* (Cambridge MA: Harvard

supposed that the Mosaic Pentateuch was not, as previously believed, a complete account of universal history but rather a specific account relating only to the history of the divinely elected Jewish people. La Peyrère's theory was not, strictly speaking, an original invention. The Swiss physician and alchemist Theophrastus von Hohenheim (1493–1541), better known as Paracelsus, and the English playwright Christopher Marlowe (1564–1593) have been suspected of advancing similar notions.[95] In his 1584 *Spaccio de la bestia trionfante*, the Italian Neoplatonic scholar Giordano Bruno (1548–1600) had claimed that only "certi magri glosatori" believed that the world was 6,000 years old.[96] Bruno was subsequently tried for heresy and burnt at the stake in the Campo de' Fiori in Rome.[97] Moreover, the constant refrain of seventeenth-century scholars to "pre-Adamites," in the plural, suggests that they considered pre-Adamitism an underground movement, rather than necessarily the work of one eclectic scholar. "It is claimed," wrote Pierre Jurieu in 1704, "that this man [La Peyrère] made himself the leader of a sect, to which we give the name of Pre-Adamites, and he made a System of Theology in order to immortalise his name and his memory."[98] Indeed, rumours of the pre-Adamite theory and pre-Adamite manuscripts had been circulating at least a decade before the publication of La Peyrère's *Praeadamitae*. Hugo Grotius' *De origine gentium Americanarum*

University Press, 1994), 204–213. A dated if entertaining treatment of La Peyrère can also be found in Philalethes, "Peyrerius, and Theological Criticism," *The Anthropological Review* 2 (1864): 116–121. My own reading of La Peyrère is based on the 1655 edition, but it is worth noting the recent publication of a new critical edition: Isaac La Peyrère, *Praeadamitae-Systema theologicum (1655)*, ed. Herbert Jaumann, Reimund B. Sdzuj, and Franziska Borkert, 2 vols (Stuttgart-Bad Cannstatt: Frommann-Holzboog, 2019). For the impact of La Peyrère's theory in the nineteenth century see Giuliano Gliozzi, *Adamo e il nuovo mondo: la nascita dell'antropologia come ideologia coloniale: dalle genealogie bibliche alle teorie razziali (1500–1700)* (Florence: La nuova Italia, 1977).

95 Popkin, *Isaac La Peyrère*, 26–41.
96 Giordano Bruno, *Spaccio de la bestia trionfante, proposto da Gioue* (Paris: 1584), 230; cf. Anthony Grafton, "Kircher's Chronology," in *Athanasius Kircher: The Last Man Who Knew Everything*, ed. Paula Findlen (New York: Routledge, 2004), 172; and Grafton, "The Chronology of the Flood," 67–68.
97 See Anthony Grafton, "Tradition and Technique in Historical Chronology," in *Ancient History and the Antiquarian: Essays in Memory of Arnaldo Momigliano*, ed. H. H. Crawford and C. R. Ligota (London: The Warburg Institute, 1995), 15.
98 Jurieu, *Histoire critique des dogmes et des cultes*, 176: "On prétend que cet homme s'est fait le chef d'une secte, à laquelle on donne le nom de Pre-Adamites, il a fait un Systeme de Theologie pour immortaliser son nom & sa memoire." In the preface (sig. *4r) Jurieu compared the pre-Adamites to the heretical gnostic sects of the early Church, such as the Valentinians and the Marcionites. See 175–181.

dissertatio (1643) was itself an early refutation of La Peyrère.[99] Nevertheless, it was La Peyrère's *Praeadamitae* which soon became the most notorious expression of the pre-Adamite theory in the late seventeenth century.

La Peyrère's theory allowed him to propose what he considered an elegant solution to a problem of biblical exegesis which was said to have troubled him since childhood: the question of where Seth's wife had come from.[100] It also allowed him to re-establish a clear division between the progeny of the Gentiles and that of the divinely elected Jewish people.[101] Dmitri Levitin has argued that, while fascinating, La Peyrère's influence was limited and his followers few.[102] This is true as long as we define by "influence" only those scholars who consciously embraced La Peyrère's theory. Certainly, many of the claims La Peyrère advanced in his *Praeadamitae* could appear abstruse and even laughable to scholars of the late seventeenth century. "The book of the *Pre-Adamites* ... is a pitiful work," wrote the Jesuit scholar and journalist René-Joseph de Tournemine (1661–1739) in 1703. "An Author who wants to prove through Saint Paul that Adam is not the first man, and who wants us to accept as certain what the Egyptians feigned of the reign of the Sun and that of Sirius, is not a very dangerous Author."[103] In another sense, however, La Peyrère's impact was critical. In the immediate years following the publication of the *Praeadamitae*, there emerged no less than seventeen refutations of La Peyrère's theory.[104] In 1656, La Peyrère was forced to recant his views and he subsequently converted to Catholicism. Despite this, numerous scholars, particularly scholars of *historia sacra*, biblical chronology, and pagan antiquity,

---

99   Eric Jorink, "'Horrible and Blasphemous': Isaac La Peyrère, Isaac Vossius and the Emergence of Radical Biblical Criticism in the Dutch Republic" in *Nature and Scripture in the Abrahamic Religions: Up to 1700*, ed. Jitse M. van der Meer and Scott Mandelbrote (Brill: Leiden, 2008), 437.

100 Jorink, "Horrible and Blasphemous," 433.

101 La Peyrère, *Systema theologicum, ex praeadamitarum hypothesi*, 49–116, particularly 49: "Gentiles non oriundos esse ex stirpe & prosapia Iudaeorum; imo genere diversos, dignoscere erit, ex illis quae de Electione Iudaeorum & Gentium dicemus."

102 Levitin, "From Sacred History to the History of Religion," 1128; Levitin, *Ancient Wisdom*, 10.

103 René-Joseph de Tournemine, "Article CXXXXI: Réponse du P. de Tournemine à la Dissertation precedente," *Journal de Trévoux* 7 (1703): 1423–1424: "Le livre *des Préadamites*, que vous paroissez n'avoir pas vû, puisque vous redoutez un autre La Peyrere, est un pitoyable ouvrage. Son titre seul a fait du bruit. Dès qu'on l'a lû il est tombé. Un Auteur qui veut prouver par Saint Paul qu'Adam n'est pas le premier homme, & qu'il veut nous faire recevoir comme certain ce que les Egyptiens ont feint du regne du Soleil & de celui de la canicule, n'est pas un Auteur fort dangereux." Tournemine's mention of Sirius, or the 'Dog-Star', refers to the famous 'Sothic cycle' of the ancient Egyptians.

104 As noted by Rossi, *The Dark Abyss of Time*, 137.

continued to reference and refute La Peyrère's theory well into the early eighteenth century. Something in La Peyrère's heretical scheme clearly grated, and scholars were constantly at pains to prove that La Peyrère's system was as fallacious as it was bizarre.

In book three of his *Systema theologicum, ex praeadamitarum hypothesi*, La Peyrère supposed that the histories of the ancient Chaldeans and Egyptians proved that men had existed long before Adam.[105] His citations, as Anthony Grafton has shown, were not particularly learned, and his chronological information was dated.[106] He was unaware, for example, of Scaliger's rediscovery of Manetho's Egyptian dynasties in 1602. Yet the manner in which he conceptualised the relationship between sacred and profane history was pivotal. At no point did La Peyrère suggest that the historical and chronological facts in the Bible were wrong, unlike the pagans whom Augustine had been refuting. He did, however, suggest that these facts referred not to the history of the world but merely to the history of the Jews. The 1656-year timespan which separated Adam from the Flood was not the period of time between the Creation of the world and a universal Deluge, but between the establishment of the Jewish nation and a sizeable but ultimately local flood in the biblical Near East. In this sense, La Peyrère used pagan chronology not so much to attack the accuracy of the Bible but to reconceptualise what biblical history was fundamentally *about*.[107] According to La Peyrère, pagan evidence helped clarify the *true* meaning of Genesis. By making biblical history relevant merely to Jewish history and pagan history the only relevant source for universal history, La Peyrère could resolve the apparent contradictions between sacred and profane history without asserting that one or the other must be mistaken. As La Peyrère outlined,

> To say, that the first men were created before *Adam*, doth neither derogate from Christianity, nor with the history of *Genesis*: nay, that it gives light to both. And that it every way agrees with the monuments and histories of Nations.[108]

---

105   Isaac La Peyrère, *Praeadamitae sive exercitatio* (Leiden: Daniel Elzevir, 1655), 29; Isaac La Peyrère, *Systema theologicum, ex praeadamitarum hypothesi* (Leiden: Daniel Elzevir, 1655), 116–160.
106   Grafton, "Isaac La Peyrère and the Old Testament."
107   As pointed out by Popkin, *Isaac La Peyrère*, 2–3.
108   La Peyrère, *Praeadamitae sive Exercitatio*, 25: "Statuere primos homines creatos ante Adamum, neque officere doctrinae Christianae, neque historiae Geneseos: imo utramque elucidare. Congruere omnino cum historiis & monumentis Gentium." English translation from Isaac La Peyrère, *Men before Adam, or A Discourse upon the twelfth, thirteenth and*

For La Peyrère declaring biblical history specific merely to the Jewish people did not impinge upon biblical authority. His contemporaries did not agree. As Matthew Hale wrote in his *The Primitive Origination of Mankind*, first published posthumously in 1677,

> If there were no other fault in this Author, there is this one that renders him inexcusable; In that he in all places of his Book pretends to own and maintain the Truth and Sacred Authority of the *Mosaical* History, and seems to maintain some of his Tenets by Scriptural Suffrage, and yet substitutes such Assertions as any Man, and much more the Ingenious Author himself could not, cannot choose but see, that if they were true would necessarily not only weaken but overthrow the Authority and Infallibility of the Sacred Scriptures.[109]

It was for this reason that La Peyrère's work posed a new problem for the Christian understanding of the relationship between *historia sacra* on the one hand and *historia exotica* on the other. In previous centuries, scholars such as Béroalde or Broughton had rejected pagan testimony because it was irreparably corrupt. Consequently, they supposed that *only* biblical history could offer verifiable information on ancient history. Early modern scholars, particularly after Scaliger, rejected this approach on historiographical and methodological grounds. Despite the universally accepted superiority of biblical over pagan evidence, it was a mistake to suppose that the latter could not offer *some* information relevant to ancient history, even if this information had been subject to later corruptions and interpolations. La Peyrère, however, inverted this relationship. Since the Bible pertained merely to the divinely elected Jewish people, it could offer *no* information on the many centuries of ancient history which preceded the birth of Adam. Instead, any universal history must rely on Gentile sources. In this sense La Peyrère, by undermining the authority of *historia sacra*, heralded the authority of *historia exotica*. Once upon a time, Augustine had told his readers to dismiss pagan evidence because it did not conform to the biblical narrative. La Peyrère's pre-Adamite hypothesis explained *why* pagan sources featured so few similarities – but also why these sources could still be considered historically accurate, authoritative, and verifiable despite this very fact. In doing so, La Peyrère divorced *historia sacra* from *historia exotica*, and by extension biblical history from pagan mythology.

---

fourteenth Verses of the Fifth Chapter of the Epistle of the Apostle Paul to the Romans. By which are prov'd That the first Men were created before Adam (1656), 18.

109 Hale, *The Primitive Origination of Mankind*, 185. Cf. Popkin, *Isaac La Peyrère*, 52.

After La Peyrère, as Paolo Rossi has pointed out, scholars intent on preserving the historical authority of the Bible were left with essentially two options. On the one hand, they could dismiss pagan chronology and history as pagan lies, invented by pagans to flatter their own nationalistic vanity or discredit the Christian religion they so openly resented. On the other hand, they could attempt to synchronize these histories with the chronology of the Bible by altering, emending, or reinterpreting the relevant pagan sources, and thereby prove to La Peyrère that his separation of *historia exotica* from *historia sacra* was incorrect. Both responses, though practiced by orthodox scholars, also contained the seeds of heterodoxy: the former because it could lead scholars to argue that the Jewish Bible was itself a product of nationalistic vanity and Jewish *fabula*, the latter because it appeared to give too much weight to non-biblical sources within the writing of ancient universal history.[110]

Bonjour was much preoccupied with La Peyrère and his work which, it is worth noting here, was censured by the Bishop of Namur and banned in Paris but was never officially listed on the Roman Index.[111] Unlike the case of Spinoza and Hobbes, Bonjour's work features detailed refutations not only of La Peyrère's general theory but also his specific claims regarding original sin, his exegetical work on the first chapters of Genesis, and his interpretation of Romans 5:12–14.[112] Yet it is clear that Bonjour thought the most problematic aspect of La Peyrère's work was the manner in which he conceptualised the relationship between biblical history and pagan antiquity. "I do not think that the controversy regarding men created before Adam, so strenuously debated in the present dispute against the most impious fabulist Isaac La Peyrère, can be brought to a conclusion, Most Eminent Prince, if we do not briefly challenge those monuments of the Gentiles, out of which the most foolish author concluded that the Gentiles, in contrast to the Jews, traced their diverse origins long before Adam," wrote Bonjour in one of his manuscript dissertations (the intended addressee is unknown).[113] Bonjour's chief concern, as is apparent

---

110 Rossi, *The Dark Abyss of Time*, 152.
111 Cf. Heinrich Reusch, *Der Index der verbotenen Bücher. Ein Beitrag zur Kirchen- und Literaturgeschichte* (Bonn: Max Cohen & Sohn, 1885), 2:131.
112 See for example "Conclusio priors dialogi. Vanissimum est systema Praeadamitarum et plane contrarium divinis scripturis ..." BAR, ms.lat.630, fols. 213r–224v; "Dialogus I. De vanissimo Praeadamitarum systemate," BAR, ms.lat.630, fols. 248r–253v. See also the illustrative comments at BAR, ms.lat.49, fol. 180r, and *Selectae*, D.II.44–45, 86–87.
113 BAR, ms.lat.630, fol. 212r: "Controversiam de hominibus ante Adamum conditis strenuissime agitatam in praesenti concertatione adversus impiissimum fabulatorem Isaacum Peyrerium, ad exitum adducendam non puto, Princeps Eminentissime, nisi breviter oppugnemus illa Gentilium monumenta, ex quibus auctor nugacissimus confecit Gentiles genere diversos a Judaeis originem longe ante Adamum suam traxisse."

from the aforementioned quote, was the manner in which La Peyrère's theory weaponised Bonjour's beloved pagan antiquities against sacred history. Moreover, he was concerned that the threat posed by La Peyrère had led some of his contemporaries to turn against *historia profana*. Even if scholars were not convinced by La Peyrère's theory, it is noticeable that a number of La Peyrère's immediate opponents chose the former of the two options outlined by Rossi and thought it more convenient to brand potentially dangerous ancient profane sources as mendacious pagan lies, rather than proving how they might be integrated with sacred history. It is no coincidence that the first scholar to call into doubt the historical testimony of Sanchuniathon, Bochart's cherished Phoenician historian, was a Lutheran historian called Johann Heinrich Ursinus (1608–1667) who had been one of the first scholars to refute La Peyrère in 1656. In 1661, Ursinus published his *De Zoroastre Bactriano, Hermete Trismegisto, Sanchoniathone Phoenicio* in which he discredited any ancient pagan philosophical tradition which existed independently of biblical revelation and Hebrew scripture with the explicit intention of refuting La Peyrère and his heretical predecessor Giordano Bruno.[114] Consequently, Ursinus argued that not only Sanchuniathon but also Zoroaster, Hermes Trismegistus, and the primordial columns of Seth were spurious products of a diabolical anti-Christian fraud. The approach of scholars like Ursinus highlights the fact that the true (or at least, important) difference of opinion within seventeenth-century *historia sacra* lay not between La Peyrère and his opponents, but between different opponents of La Peyrère who profoundly disagreed on the best way of refuting him. Consequently, Bonjour sought to refute La Peyrère not merely by proving to La Peyrère that ancient pagan texts were important historical sources which could be harmonized with the biblical record but also by proving this fact to many of his orthodox contemporaries. For Bonjour, pagan antiquities remained a key source for writing the primordial history of the world and consequently defending the truth of the Christian religion, and he strongly objected to scholars who denied this fact. In doing so, however, he also came to synchronize pagan and biblical sources in a manner and to an extent which many of his own contemporaries and correspondents considered unsuitable.

---

114   Johann Heinrich Ursinus, *Novus Prometheus Praeadamitarum* (Frankfurt: Christian Hersmdorf, 1656); Johann Heinrich Ursinus, *De Zoroastre Bactriano, Hermete Trismegisto, Sanchoniathone Phoenicio* (Nuremberg: Michael Endtner, 1661). On Ursinus see Michael Stausberg, *Faszination Zarathustra. Zoroaster und die Europäische Religionsgeschichte der Frühen Neuzeit* (Berlin and New York: Walter de Gruyter, 1998), 626–634, and Helmut Zedelmaier, "Der Ursprung der Schrift als Problem der frühen Neuzeit," in *Philologie und Erkenntnis. Beiträge zu Begriff und Problem frühneuzeitlicher 'Philologie'*, ed. Ralph Häfner (Tübingen: Max Niemeyer Verlag, 2001), 207–223.

I want to end this chapter with a case-study which demonstrates this tendency explicitly: Bonjour's work on the biblical Flood. In his *Praeadamitae*, La Peyrère explicitly rejected the existence of a universal Flood as related in the book of Genesis. In turn, Bonjour sought to write a history of the Flood which relied on sources from both sacred and profane history. In doing so, he also used pagan myths to elucidate historical particulars on which Moses had remained silent and made little explicit differentiation between information derived from sacred *vis-à-vis* pagan sources. This practice highlights both the manner in which La Peyrère had problematized the relationship between *historia sacra* and *historia exotica* as well as the manner in which certain responses to La Peyrère came to blur the distinction between these two *historiae* more than was generally considered customary, or even appropriate.

4 Pagan Sources for Biblical History: the Case of the Flood

The question of the origins and nature of Noah's Flood had occupied Christian scholars since the first centuries of the Church. How large was the ark? What material was it made from? Where had all the water come from? How many animals were there in the ark in total? As Don Cameron Allen has shown, these questions elicited interesting, often eclectic, and occasionally very humorous responses.[115] Rarely, however, had scholars linked these questions to the broader question as to whether the Flood had really existed. For over a thousand years, the universality of the biblical Flood remained largely unquestioned – and why should it not? Christian scholars knew it was universal because Moses had said so:

> And the flood grew forty days upon the earth: and the waters increased, and lifted up the ark on high from the earth. For they overflowed exceedingly; and filled all on the face of the earth: moreover the ark fleeted upon the earth; and all the high mountains under the whole heaven were covered. Fifteen cubits higher was the water above the mountains, which it covered. And all flesh was consumed that moved upon the earth, of fowl, of cattle, of beasts, and of all creepers, that creep upon the earth: all men, and all things, wherein there is breath of life upon the earth, died.[116]

---

115 Allen, *The Legend of Noah*.
116 Genesis 7:17–23. This translation, with spelling adapted, is from the Douay-Rheims Bible, first published in 1582: *The Holie Bible Faithfully Translated into English out of the*

Nor did Church Fathers such as Augustine think it necessary to supplement the biblical account of the Flood with non-biblical testimony. To suppose that Xisurthrus, the ancient Babylonian king in whose reign Berosus had placed a universal flood, was the Chaldean version of Noah was dangerously close to suggesting that Noah was merely a Jewish version of Xisurthrus.[117] As we have highlighted above, pagan myths concerning the creation of the world and the first centuries of human existence were rival narratives to the biblical account the Fathers considered authoritative. The Fathers, intent on proving the inherent superiority of the biblical account and its fundamentally different nature to pagan *fabula*, sought to separate the divinely inspired Noachic narrative from the native myths of idolatrous, ignorant, and boastful pagans.

According to Allen, seventeenth-century diluvian scholarship was shaped by the "rationalisation" of biblical scholarship: the attempt to explain biblical history through reason. As the study of natural philosophy developed, scholars became increasingly interested in applying their scientific knowledge to an analysis of the Flood.[118] Some of them, such as the English theologians Thomas Burnet (1635–1715) and William Whiston (1667–1752), advanced new-fangled cosmographical explanations for how such a large amount of water might have covered the earth.[119] Others, such as Bianchini, believed that the existence of a primordial deluge could be demonstrated by examining the sediment unearthed during excavations of Mount Vesuvius.[120] When the German scholar Wilhelm Ernst Tentzel (1659–1707) discovered an elephant skeleton buried in Thuringia, it led Cuper to suppose in his epistolary exchange with Bonjour

---

        authentical Latin, diligently conferred with the Hebrew, Greek, & other Editions in divers languages (Douai: John Cousturier, 1635), 1:24–5.

[117] As also pointed out by Allen, *The Legend of Noah*, 74.

[118] See in contrast to Jean Le Clerc's rather dismissive judgement the passages in Allen, *The Legend of Noah*, 88.

[119] Thomas Burnet, *Telluris theoria sacra. Originem & mutationes generales, quas aut jam subiit, aut olim subiturus est, complectens* (London: G. Kettilby, 1681); William Whiston, *A New Theory of the Earth From its Original, to the Consummation of All Things, Where the Creation of the World in Six Days, the Universal Deluge, And the General Conflagration, As laid down in the Holy Scriptures, Are Shewn to be perfectly agreeable to Reason and Philosophy* (London: Benjamin Tooke, 1696).

[120] See Nicoletta Morello, "Steno, the fossils, the rocks, and the calendar of the Earth," in *The Origins of Geology in Italy*, ed. Gian Battista Vai and W. G. E. Caldwell (Boulder: Geological Society of America, 2006), 81–93; and Nicoletta Morello, "Tra diluvio e vulcani: Le concezioni geologiche di Francesco Bianchini e del suo tempo," in *Unità del sapere, molteplicità dei saperi: Francesco Bianchini (1662–1729) tra natura, storia e religione*, ed. Luca Ciancio and Gian Paolo Romagnani (Verona: QuiEdit, 2010), 185–206.

that the bones had been washed up during the Flood.[121] Yet the most popular tradition of diluvian scholarship rested upon finding evidence of flood narratives among various Gentile and non-European peoples, a *consensus gentium*, so to speak. An early statement to this effect came in Hugo Grotius' *De veritate religionis Christianae*. In the first edition (1627) Grotius had supposed that the Flood was a memory common to all peoples. However, the testimony Grotius cited in his defence remained that of ancient Near Eastern or Greek writers.[122] By the third edition (1633) he had supplemented this account with the evidence of such far-flung places as Cuba, Nicaragua, Mexico, and Peru.[123] In the course of the seventeenth century, the number and variety of these collateral diluvian testimonies increased. The English scholars Edward Stillingfleet and John Webb (1611–1672) pointed to the flood narratives of China, while Bianchini cited those of the Japanese and the native Americans.[124] "However, Heathen writers also agree in many places with Moses. Consequently, we shall repeat what we have said above, that the fame of a Flood in which, with a few survivors, the remaining men died, is spread among all peoples," wrote Bochart in the preface to his *Geographia sacra*.[125]

Partly, this tendency highlights the pressing need for scholars to fit newly-discovered nations, particularly those of the Americas and the Far East, into the commonly accepted Judaeo-Christian narrative for universal history. Even

---

121 See Wilhelm Ernst Tentzel, *Epistola de sceleto elephantino Tonnae nuper effosso* (Gotha: Litteris Reyherianis, 1696), and then Gisbert Cuper to Guillaume Bonjour, 11 July 1699, in Pélissier, "Lettres inédites de Gisbert Cuper," (1905): 81 (245), and the reply from Guillaume Bonjour to Gisbert Cuper, 30 May 1699, KW 72 H 20.

122 Grotius, *Sensus librorum sex*, 26–27.

123 The citation of the flood narratives of the Americas was not included in the first edition of Paris (1627, see p. 27) or the second edition of Leiden (1629, see p. 32), but was first included in the third edition: Hugo Grotius, *De veritate religionis Christianae* (Leiden: Johannes Maire, 1633), 47: "Sed & in Americae partibus Cuba, Mechoacana, Nicaraga diluvii, animalium servatorum, quin & corvi & columbae servatam memoriam" ("but in several parts of *America*, as *Cuba, Mechoacana, Nicaraga*, is preserved the Memory of the Deluge, the saving alive of Animals, especially the Raven and Dove"). English translation is from Hugo Grotius, *The Truth of the Christian Religion in Six Books*, ed. Jean Le Clerc, trans. John Clarke (London: John and Paul Knapton, 1743), 51. See also Jan Paul Heering, "Hugo Grotius' *De Veritate Religionis Christianae*," in *Hugo Grotius Theologian: Essays in Honour of G. H. M. Posthumus Meyjes*, ed. Henk J. M. Nellen and Edwin Rabbie (Leiden: E. J. Brill, 1994), 41–52, and Allen, *The Legend of Noah*, 86, 92.

124 For Stillingfleet and Webb see Allen, *The Legend of Noah*, 93–94; and Bianchini, *La istoria universale*, 186–201.

125 Bochart, *Geographia sacra*, "praefatio," sig. i3r-v: "Sed & Ethnici scriptores in multis Mosi concinunt. Ut rem repetamus paulo altius, diluvij fama quo paucis superstitibus reliqui homines perierint apud omnes gentes increbuit."

more important, however, was the fact that, almost a millennium and a half after the Greek philosopher Celsus had suggested that the biblical Flood was just one in an ancient cycle of floods and conflagrations (Origen, *Contra Celsum* 4.11), certain scholars had once again begun to question the universality of the biblical Flood, and were citing non-biblical testimony concerning the Flood, as well as the history of the newly-discovered nations in the Americas and the Far East, in order to undermine this universality.

No text of the seventeenth century questioned traditional assumptions about the nature of the biblical Flood as radically as La Peyrère's *Praeadamitae*. That is not to say that La Peyrère himself was particularly concerned with the Flood. Yet the manner in which he reconceptualised the relationship between universal history and the biblical text had profound ramifications for his understanding of the nature of the Flood. Apart from Creation itself, the Flood was the only biblical event which was supposed to have covered the whole world and consequently affected all peoples. In his *Praeadamitae*, La Peyrère had suggested that Gentile nations had remained unaffected by the events narrated in the Bible and that God had set apart a special land for the Jewish people, distinct from those of contemporaneous pagan nations. Consequently, he argued that the Flood was not universal but local to Palestine and had destroyed not all the peoples of the world but merely the Jews.[126]

There were two corollaries to this notion. Firstly, La Peyrère supposed that pagan evidence opposed the notion of a universal biblical Flood. According to La Peyrère, the different floods of Gentile mythology were not corrupted retellings of a single primordial Flood but evidence for the existence of many other ancient floods, some of which preceded, others of which succeeded the Jewish Flood.[127] Secondly, La Peyrère's localisation, or de-universalisation, of the biblical Flood reinforced the notion that biblical history could not be considered a reliable source of universal history. All the historical material preserved in the Pentateuch was relevant merely to ancient Palestine.

By the late seventeenth century, discussions surrounding the chronology, nature, and existence of the Flood were shaped by the agenda set by La Peyrère. Moreover, it appears that, in the specific case of the Flood, La Peyrère's conclusions did enjoy some acceptance. In 1659, the Dutch scholar Isaac Vossius (1618–1689), in agreement with his most notorious and forthright critic Georg Horn (1620–1670), rejected La Peyrère's argument that the Flood had not affected all peoples and supposed that all nations had retained

---

126 La Peyrère, *Systema theologicum, ex praeadamitarum hypothesi*, 203ff.
127 La Peyrère, *Systema theologicum, ex praeadamitarum hypothesi*, 146.

some memory of it.[128] He did, however, mischievously suggest that the Flood was not geographically universal. According to Vossius, the short timespan between Creation and the Flood did not allow for the population of the entire earth. Consequently, he suggested that the Flood covered only the regions of Palestine and specific neighbouring countries in which the world's population was still assembled.[129] In later years, Vossius' more palatable reconceptualisation of the traditional Flood narrative found a groundswell of sympathy. In his *Origines sacrae* (1662), Edward Stillingfleet endorsed Vossius' view and by 1693 Jean Le Clerc was writing of two prevailing opinions about the Flood, one which considered the Flood universal and another which considered it "particular."[130]

Bonjour wrote a number of unpublished dissertations intent on defending the conventional depiction of the Flood, each of which was constructed as a riposte to La Peyrère. When he came to treat the Flood in his 1705 *Selectae*, his work was explicitly situated in the same context, and his dissertation began with the important statement that:

> Isaac La Peyrère, the author of the pernicious Pre-Adamite system, dared to deny the universality of the Noachic Flood. This most impious storyteller was seized by this delusion, with the result that he stated that the various nations, originating with the most ancient progeny of the world, had their origin before Adam and had advancement in the time of the Noachic Flood.[131]

As is to be expected, Bonjour's response consisted in turning La Peyrère's new distinction between *historia sacra* and *historia profana* on its head. For La Peyrère, *historia exotica* was the source of the true history of the ancient world and the emergence of human civilization and therefore had nothing in common with *historia sacra*. For Bonjour, the existence of a single universal Flood

---

128 Vossius, *De vera aetate mundi*, liii: "Nullum itaque relinquitur dubium, quin unum tantum fuerit diluvium, idque universale, cujus apud omnes pene gentes exstat memoria."
129 Vossius, *De vera aetate mundi*, liv.
130 Stillingfleet, *Origines sacrae*, 539–540; Jean Le Clerc, *Genesis sive Mosis prophetae liber primus* (Tübingen: Johann Georg Cotta, 1693); Jean Le Clerc, "Dissertation v: Concerning the Flood," in *Twelve Dissertations out of Monsieur Le Clerk's Genesis*, trans. Thomas Brown (London: R. Baldwin, 1696), 152–169.
131 *Selectae*, D.II.43, 86: "Pestiferi Praeadamitarum systematis auctor Isaacus Peyrerius ausus est negare universalitatem diluvii Noetici. Hoc captus est errore fabulator impiissimus, ut statueret ortas stirpe antiquissimâ varias orbis nationes originem ante Adamum & progressionem tempore diluvii Noetici habuisse."

could be derived "ex historia tam Sacra quam Barbarica."[132] This informed his approach to the Flood in three ways.

Firstly, Bonjour supposed that because the Flood was universal, knowledge of it could be discovered in the primordial myths of all peoples. In the Biblioteca Angelica he copied out reports from Christian travellers who had discussed flood myths among indigenous populations. One indicative example is a letter in the 1701 edition of the *Journal de Trévoux* by the French traveller Jean Marshal. According to Marshal, Brahmin tradition told of how water had once covered the entire surface of the earth except for one mountaintop, on which seven women, one man, and two animals of every species had survived the deluge. A footnote inserted by the editor of the *Journal* noted the significance of this story explicitly: "*Voilà*, another fable in which one can clearly see the truth of the Flood."[133] In his *Selectae*, Bonjour offered similar proofs for the universality of the Flood, which could be substantiated by "antiquitates & Graecorum in Europa, & Aegyptiorum in Africa, & Chaldaeorum in Asia, & Sinarum in finibus Orientis."[134]

Secondly, Bonjour was intent on proving that not just one or two but all the mythological flood narratives of the Greeks had derived from the biblical original. This allowed him to prove not only that the biblical Deluge was universal but also that the history of the biblical Deluge was the origin of all subsequent flood narratives. Much of Bonjour's historical information was taken from Bochart's *Geographia sacra*. For example, he followed Bochart's etymology for Ogyges – from the Hebrew "Hog-hug," since "the cosmographic Hebrew word Hog was used in scripture for the cycle of the heaven, the earth and the sea" – in order to align him with Noah.[135] Like Bochart and Francesco

---

132   *Selectae*, D.II.19, 53.
133   Jean Marshal, "Extrait d'une lettre de Mr. Jean Marshal écrite des Indes Orientales au Sieur Coga, contenant une relation de la religion, des rites, notions, coutumes, & mœurs des prêtres payens, appellez communément Brachmanes," in *Journal de Trévoux* 1 (1701): 185–188: "Voilà encore une Fable au travers de laquelle on voit assez clairement la verité du Deluge"; BAR, ms.lat.634, fol. 46v. The same narrative is recounted in Jean Marshal, "Account of the Religion, Rites, Notions, Customs, Manners of the Indian Priests, called Bramins," in *The Philosophical Transactions of the Royal Society of London* 4 (1809): 537.
134   *Selectae*, D.II.47, 89.
135   *Selectae*, D.II.16, 52–53: "Doctissimus Bochart lib. 1. De Phoenicum Coloniis, cap. 36. videns Hebraicum verbum *Hog* in scriptura cosmographicum, de circuitu coeli, terrae & maris usurpari, docet inde natam vocem Ὠγηνοῦ, quae in Lexico Heyschii exponitur Ὠκεανός *Oceanus*, mare illud vastissimum, quod terram circumquaque cingit." See also BAR, ms.lat.1, fol. 87r–v. The reference is to Bochart, *Geographia sacra*, 709: "Hanc doctissimi Vossij observationem ideo maxime probo, quia *og* in Scriptura video verbum esse cosmographicum."

Bianchini, Bonjour considered Lucian's description of Deucalion's flood the most accurate pagan flood myth, given that, in the *De dea syria* (2), Lucian had, unlike many of his pagan counterparts, explicitly supposed that Deucalion's flood was universal.[136] However, Bonjour also sought to synthesize a number of seemingly contradictory pagan testimonies with the biblical account. An indicative case is his use of the third-century Latin grammarian Solinus. In his *Polyhistor*, Solinus had supposed that the flood of Ogyges lasted for nine months (11.18), which Bonjour used to verify the (identical) length of the biblical Flood. However, Solinus had also placed 600 years between the floods of Ogyges and Deucalion, both of which Bonjour supposed were pagan corruptions of the biblical Deluge. Rather than dismiss this facet of Solinus' testimony, Bonjour sought to correct it so that it might further concur with the testimony of the Bible. Moses had recorded that Noah was 600 years old when the Flood began (Genesis 7:6); Bonjour therefore supposed that Solinus had mistakenly assumed a 600-year gap between the flood of Ogyges (which was Noah's Flood), and the flood of Deucalion (which was also Noah's Flood) when, in actual fact, the historical account only supposed that Ogyges (who was Noah) was 600 years old when it occurred – in what was, for Bonjour, a typical pagan miscomprehension of biblical particulars.[137] In doing so, Bonjour also went further than many of his contemporaries and predecessors. According to Bonjour, there did not exist a single pagan flood narrative independent of the biblical original.

Thirdly, Bonjour supposed that pagan flood narratives were not only corollary evidence for the existence of a primordial and universal biblical Flood but that they were also historical evidence in themselves. Once again, we see how the apologetic necessity of defending the authority of holy scripture informed historical and mythographic scholarship. In the *Selectae*, Bonjour not only wanted to prove that the Flood had occurred but he also wanted to write a complete history of the Flood. Given that the Flood was a real event, it must have a specific day on which it began, a specific calendar which Moses had used to chart its progression, and a specific location where Noah's ship was marooned when the Flood ended. For Bonjour, the Flood began on 3 June 2290 BC – equivalent to the 17th day of the Egyptian month Athyr or the

---

[136] Bochart, *Geographia sacra*, "praefatio," sig. i3v; Bonjour, *Selectae*, D.II.17, 53; See for example Lucian, *The Syrian Goddess*, trans. Herbert A. Strong and John Garstang (London: Constable & Company, 1913), 50–51.

[137] *Selectae*, D.II.17, 53.

15th day of the Chaldean month Desius – lasted 187 days, and ended when Noah's ark came to rest on Mount Ararat.[138]

Yet Bonjour's desire to write a *complete* history of the Flood also required something he did not have: historical evidence. Although the account of *sacer historiographus* Moses provided many historical details it did not, as Bonjour himself admitted, provide all. Rather, however, than leaving certain parts of the Flood narrative unknown, Bonjour mobilised his supposition that pagan myth was a corrupted version of biblical history to his defence. Let us take one particularly emblematic example. According to Moses, Noah had released a raven from the ark forty days after the first mountains became visible on the horizon, a raven which was not to return until "siccarentur aquae super terram," till the waters were dried up from the earth (Genesis 8:7). A short time later, Noah also released a dove – which, seeing the earth still covered in water, shortly thereafter returned to the ark. This was the essential narrative which Bonjour sourced from the Mosaic Pentateuch. And yet, Moses had not recorded *all* the historical information. On what day, or how many days after the raven, had the dove been released? In this case, as Bonjour himself openly conceded, "non exprimit scriptura," scripture does not pronounce [this].[139] This meant that Bonjour was forced to rely on non-biblical testimony. Through Solinus and Plutarch (*De sollertia animalium* 13, 968F), he could prove that Noah (in Solinus "Ogyges," in Plutarch "Deucalion") had indeed released a dove.[140] The date itself he confirmed not through biblical testimony but through Chaldean mythology. According to a fable recounted by the Greek historian Abydenus (*c*.200 BC) and preserved in Eusebius' *Praeparatio evangelica* (9.12), the ancient Chaldean king Xisurthrus had survived a large flood in an ark which he had built on the orders of the god Kronos. In the seventeenth century, scholars routinely considered Xisurthrus a pagan corruption of Noah.[141] More importantly, Abydenus stated that Xisurthrus had released some birds – which Bonjour interpreted as the dove – from his ark three days after the rain had ceased (*Praeparatio evangelica* 9.12). Bonjour used this testimony to fill in the blanks left to him by scripture.[142] What Abydenus said of Xisurthrus must therefore be true of Noah: from the testimony of Abydenus, Bonjour could work out the time at which Noah had let the dove fly for the first time.

---

138 *Selectae*, 57–85.
139 *Selectae*, D.II.20, 54.
140 *Selectae*, D.II.20, 54.
141 See Allen, *The Legend of Noah*, 74.
142 *Selectae*, D.II.20, 54.

5 Biblical Authority and the Limits of Pagan Evidence

On the surface, there is much that is conventional in Bonjour's work on the biblical Flood. His decision to date the Flood according to the Egyptian and Chaldean calendars was part of a long-standing scholarly tradition which, as C. P. E. Nothaft has shown, supposed that the chronology of the Flood was the oldest evidence for the state of the Mosaic calendar.[143] According to Bonjour, Moses used the ancient Egyptian calendar of 365 days which, until the invention of the Julian *bissextiles*, was made up of 12 months of 30 days and one *epagomena*, an intercalary month.[144] Moreover, Bonjour's use of Egyptian calendrical information, principally sourced from Plutarch's *De Iside et Osiride*, was indebted to a well-established and long-standing notion that the Egyptian calendar had been influenced by the original calendar of Noah. Nor was Bonjour's decision to supplement the chronology of the Bible with pagan mythological information unusual. Ultimately, Grotius had suggested as early as 1627 that Abydenus was a particularly amenable pagan source for confirming the truth of the biblical Flood in general and Noah's dove in particular, alongside Berosus and Plutarch.[145] And yet, Bonjour's scholarship also shows how the relationship between pagan myth and biblical history, which is to say between *historia sacra* and *historia exotica*, was beginning to change. Notionally, Bonjour used pagan evidence because it could confirm the information he had obtained from scripture. In this sense, pagan myth was simply a corrupted retelling of biblical history. Yet the way Bonjour used Abydenus also suggests a slightly different relationship. According to Bonjour, Abydenus preserved knowledge of biblical history which was not recorded in the Bible. This leads us to a basic question: where had Abydenus taken his knowledge from? As far as I can tell, there are only two possible options. On the one hand, Abydenus' myth might be a corrupted mythological account which derived from an earlier draft of scripture, a draft which was more complete than the Vulgate version Bonjour had at his disposal. This, however, would suggest that Bonjour agreed with certain more controversial contemporaries, notably the Oratorian biblical critic Richard Simon (1638–1712), who supposed that the surviving editions of scripture were a heavily altered and redacted version

---

143 C. Philipp E. Nothaft, "Noah's Calendar: The Chronology of the Flood Narrative and the History of Astronomy in Sixteenth- and Seventeenth-Century Scholarship," *Journal of the Warburg and Courtauld Institutes* 74 (2011): 191–211.

144 *Selectae*, D.II.27, 58. A "bissextile" was an quadrennial intercalary day required to make a leap year. An "epagomena" was a period of five days added on to the end of a 360-day year composed of 12 months of 30 days. See Mosshammer, *The Easter Computus*, 36–37.

145 Grotius, *Sensus librorum sex*, 26–27.

of a much more extensive original text. On the other hand, Bonjour's use of Abydenus might suggest that although the sacred history recorded by Moses was authoritative, it was not complete – which is to say, that certain details of sacred, universal, history were preserved in pagan, non-biblical, mythological sources but not in the biblical history of Moses. Yet this would suggest that non-biblical evidence, rather than merely confirming *historia sacra*, was itself a valuable source for writing an ancient history which was only partially preserved in the biblical account.

I do not think that Bonjour would have accepted either of these two implications. Ultimately, Bonjour's use of pagan mythology remained determined by his broader aim of using pagan mythology to buttress a sacred history which he already knew to be universal and authoritative. As we shall see towards the end of chapter seven, Bonjour believed his duty as an apologist was to mobilise pagan sources so as to uphold the biblical narrative, and it is clear that his work on the Flood follows this criteria. Yet I do believe that his use of pagan myth highlights the manner in which La Peyrère's conceptualisation of the relationship (or lack thereof) between *historia sacra* and *historia exotica* challenged and changed the way scholars used pagan myth within their work on sacred history. Bonjour's dissertation on the Flood sought not only to confirm that the Flood was universal, but also that pagan mythology could help scholars construct a detailed history of the biblical Flood itself. As a result, the difference between the *fabula* of *historia exotica* and the *historia* of *historia sacra* was narrowing and the boundary between the two becoming increasingly hazy.

In this, too, Bonjour found himself part of that predominantly French tradition which Bochart had helped inaugurate and which Huet's *Demonstratio evangelica* later exemplified. By comparing pagan myths and biblical history in the manner in which he did, Bonjour accorded a far greater importance to non-biblical, pagan, evidence in the writing of the history of the patriarchs than many of his contemporaries. It was precisely this facet which was frequently remarked upon in the somewhat mixed reaction that Huet's *Demonstratio evangelica* first received following its initial publication in 1679. On the one hand, it must be said, the work was a success. It was welcomed in Rome and by the 1730s had gone through eight editions. As the nineteenth-century historian Mark Pattison remarked, the *Demonstratio* became the standard work for any scholar who sought to buttress their exposition of sacred history with pagan testimony.[146] In his *Selecta historiae ecclesiasticae* of 1689, the Dominican theologian Noël Alexandre, when arguing that pagan myth was corrupted sacred

---

146 Mark Pattison, "Review of Christian Bartholomés *Huet Evêque d'Avranches*; *ou les Scepticisme Théologique*," in *Quarterly Review* 97 (1855): 313.

history, credited Huet, alongside Bochart and Gerardus Vossius, for developing this insight.[147] On the other hand, however, certain individuals, including one of the authors of the approbation, the great French theologian Jacques-Bénigne Bossuet (1627–1704), were more sceptical of Huet's *Demonstratio evangelica*, and it was opposed by a number of prominent theologians in the Sorbonne.[148] The source of much of this disapproval was not so much directed at the fact that Huet had synchronized pagan myth and biblical history but rather the extent to which he had done so. In a 1702 address to the *Académie royale des inscriptions et belles-lettres*, Eusèbe Renaudot, while praising Huet's learning and pious aims, also supposed that these identifications may have furnished *libertins* with ammunition.[149] As Martin Mulsow has pointed out, Huet's methods were particularly opposed by Jansenist scholars in the circle of the Port-Royal theologian Antoine Arnauld (1612–1694), who thought that Huet, in comparing pagan myth with biblical history, had gone too far in dissolving the special status of Christian religion. According to Mulsow, many of Arnauld's fears were later realised.[150] In the first half of the eighteenth century, some of Huet's parallels between pagan myth and biblical history were inverted by deists and freethinkers who, rather than supposing that all pagan deities and lawgivers had derived from Moses, supposed that Moses was simply another mythic legislator who had emphasised his special access to divine revelation as a coercive political tool. In a 1709 review of John Toland's *A Treatise of the Origins of the Jews*, a supplement to Toland's *Adeisidaemon* (1709), the reviewer supposed that Toland's entire premise, the comparison of Moses with a number of other pagan lawgivers such as Minos, the Spartan legislator Lycurgus, and the minor Greek deity Zalmoxis, was an inversion of Huet's reading of Strabo. In the *Demonstratio evangelica*, Huet had celebrated Strabo for the "Candid and Honourable Account he gives of *Moses* in particular, and in general of the *Jewish* Nation." For Huet, Minos, whom Strabo had praised as an exceptional lawgiver (10.8), was comparable with Moses in the sense that those feats which Strabo credited Minos for were in actual fact corrupted recollections of Moses' legislative achievements.[151] Toland, however, supposed that Minos and Moses

---

147 Noël Alexandre, *Selecta historiae ecclesiasticae Veteris Testamenti* (Paris: Antoine Dezalier, 1689), 2:232–244.
148 Dupront, *Pierre-Daniel Huet et l'exégèse comparatiste*, 10–13.
149 Dupront, *Pierre-Daniel Huet et l'exégèse comparatiste*, 150–151.
150 Martin Mulsow, "The Seventeenth Century Confronts the Gods," in *Knowledge and Profanation: Transgressing the Boundaries of Religion in Premodern Scholarship*, ed. Martin Mulsow and Asaph Ben-Tov (Leiden: Brill, 2019), 159–196. On this see also Rossi, *The Dark Abyss of Time*, 157.
151 Huet, *Demonstratio evangelica*, 166–171.

were equivalent and comparable examples of ancient mythic legislators and highlighted, in contrast to Huet, the extent to which Strabo's account differed from the account in the Pentateuch.[152]

There is, perhaps, a similar tendency in Bonjour's work. In 1697, Bonjour had stated that:

> Just as the Jews derive their Jewish antiquities from the origin of the world, so do the Chaldeans their Chaldean antiquities, and the Egyptians their Egyptian ones.[153]

In his following *Selectae in sacram scripturam*, Bonjour then compared the many creation narratives of the Egyptians, Phoenicians, Greeks, and Romans with that of the Jews. In later years, however, a scholar such as Bolingbroke had to do very little in order to recast this supposition in a fundamentally heterodox light:

> The Chaldeans may be coupled, on this occasion, with the Persians, as the Phoenicians and the Israelites with the Egyptians. They were all distinct nations; they had all their distinct religions and traditions; but they agree in one, the beginning of the world, how many different fictions soever they might relate concerning the time and manner of this beginning.[154]

As Colin Kidd has emphasised, defenders and subverters of Christianity often used the same repertoire of methods, but with a twist or inversion to suit their particular purpose.[155] In Huet's case, the identification between Moses and various pagan gods, while notionally championing Hebraic primacy, also brought divine history and pagan myth closer together. Huet's supposition that similarities between biblical history on the one hand and pagan mythology on the other evidenced the primacy and truth of the former rested on his ability to prove that the former was chronologically prior.

---

152 [anon.] "Adeisidaemon, *sive* Titius [sic] Livius *à superstitione vindicatus*, &c. Or, a Vindication of Titius [sic] Livius *from the Charge of Superstition* (1709)," *The History of the Works of the Learned. Or An Impartial Account of Books Lately Printed in all Parts of Europe* 11 (1709): 377.
153 BAR, ms.lat.49, fol. 134r: "sicut Judaei Judaicas antiquitates ab origine mundi repetunt, Chaldaïcas Chaldaei; ita Aegyptii Aegyptiacas."
154 Henry St. John, Viscount Bolingbroke, "The Substance of Some Letters written originally in French about the year 1720 to M. de Pouilly," in *The Works of Lord Henry St. John Bolingbroke* (Philadelphia: Carey and Hart, 1841), 2:480.
155 Colin Kidd, *The World of Mr. Casaubon: Britain's Wars of Mythography, 1700–1810* (Cambridge: Cambridge University Press, 2016), 47–48.

In this sense, we should also note that Bonjour's particular approach to pagan mythology, though still part of a prominent tradition, also came at a time when this tradition was beginning to flicker and wane. When in 1681 the Anglo-Irish chronologist, theologian, and later non-conformist Henry Dodwell (1641–1711) launched a second, major attack on the authenticity of Sanchuniathon, it was illustrative that he did so by questioning the general utility of explaining historical passages of the Old Testament through ancient heathen authors.[156] In later years, this was a criticism which scholars such as Jean Le Clerc, Anthonie van Dale (1638–1708), Louis Ellies Dupin (1657–1719), and Jacques Basnage (1653–1723) all directed at Huet's work, a type of criticism crowned by the withering remark of Montesquieu (1689–1755), who noted that "we must put to trial the Bishop of Avranches, who maintained that the patriarchs were no different from the heroes of Antiquity."[157] In particular, scholars began to push back against the notion that there existed sustained transmission of biblical knowledge in the ancient world and came to reassert the cultural isolation of the Jews, a development which proved the death knell for many scholars who sought to harmonize sacred history with pagan antiquity.

Perhaps the most celebrated Italian reaction to this development was Giambattista Vico's *Scienza nuova*, as Arnaldo Momigliano once demonstrated.[158] On the one hand, Vico took a number of important methodological suppositions from biblicist interpreters of pagan myth, including Selden, Bochart, and Huet. He supposed, for example, that myth told of a primitive age in human history and that it narrated primarily of the origins of human civilization. On the other hand, however, Vico rejected the diffusionist principle these scholars had built their synchronization of sacred history and pagan myth on, and

---

156 Henry Dodwell, *A discourse concerning Sanchoniathon's Phoenician History* (London: Benjamin Tooke, 1681), especially 114–118.

157 Anthonie van Dale, *Dissertatio super Aristea de LXX. interpretibus* (Amsterdam: Johannes Wolters, 1705), 472–506; Jean Le Clerc, ed., *Hugo Grotius De veritate religionis Christianae. Editio novissima, in qua eiusdem annotationes ipsius textus verbis subiectae sunt* (Leipzig: Johann Friedrich Gleditsch, 1709), 62; Louis Ellies Dupin, *Dissertation préliminaire ou Prolégomènes sur la Bible* (Paris: André Pralard, 1699), 1:205–206; Jacques Basnage de Beauval, *L'histoire des Juifs, reclamée et retablie par son veritable Auteur Mr. Basnage* (Rotterdam: Fritsch et Böhm, 1711), 258; Montesquieu, *My Thoughts*, ed. Henry C. Clark (Indianapolis: Liberty Fund, 2012), 25–26. On van Dale see Scott Mandelbrote, "Witches and Forgers: Anthonie van Dale on Biblical History and the Authority of the Septuagint," in *Scriptural Authority and Biblical Criticism in the Dutch Golden Age: God's Word Questioned*, ed. Dirk van Miert, Henk Nellen, Piet Steenbakkers, and Jetze Touber (Oxford: Oxford University Press, 2017), 270–306.

158 Arnaldo Momigliano, "Vico's *Scienza Nuova*: Roman 'Bestioni' and Roman 'Eroi'," in *Essays in Ancient and Modern Historiography*, 253–276.

thereby sought to re-establish a clear division between the natural history of the Gentiles and the providential history of the Jews. In the first edition of the *Scienza nuova* (1725), Vico explicitly criticised Selden for denying the isolation of the Hebrew people and for comparing them with neighbouring pagan nations.[159] In the unpublished additions to the second edition of the *Scienza nuova* (1730), Vico expanded this criticism:

> These ideas should, all at once, overturn the system of John Selden, who claims that the natural law of eternal reason had been taught by the Hebrews to the Gentiles, based on the seven precepts bequeathed by God to the sons of Noah; they should overturn the Faleg of Samuel Bochart, who maintains that the Sacred tongue had been spread by the Hebrews to the other peoples and then deformed and corrupted in their midst; and, finally, they should overturn the Dimostrazione evangelica of Daniel Huet (who follows closely upon the Faleg of Bochart, just as the Faleg of Bochart follows upon the system of Selden) in which the most learned gentleman attempts to make one believe that the fables are sacred tales altered and corrupted by the Gentiles, and especially by the Greeks.[160]

In this sense, Vico recognised that ancient history and pagan mythology was corrupted history yet rejected the notion that this history was biblical. For Vico, sacred history pertained merely to the postdiluvian patriarchs and divinely elected Jewish people, who had had no interaction with the ancient Gentile nations and thus no influence on the origins of the arts and sciences.

---

159   Vico, *The First New Science*, 15; see also Giambattista Vico, *The New Science of the Giambattista Vico: Revised Translation of the Third Edition (1744)*, ed. Thomas Goddard Bergin and Max Harold Fisch (Ithaca NY: Cornell University Press, 1968), 124–125; see also Momigliano, "Vico's *Scienza Nuova*," 259–260, and Martin Mulsow, "Antiquarianism and Idolatry: The *Historia* of Religions in the Seventeenth Century," in *Historia: Empiricism and Empire in Early Modern Europe*, ed. Gianna Pomata and Nancy G. Siraisi (Cambridge MA and London: The MIT Press, 2005), 195.

160   Giambattista Vico, *Scienza nuova seconda*, ed. Fausto Nicolini (Bari: Gius Laterza & Figli, 1942), 2:180: "Le quali cose tutte ad un colpo devono rovesciar il sistema di Giovanni Seldeno, il quale pretende il diritto naturale della ragion eterna essere stato dagli ebrei insegnato a' gentili sopra i sette precetti lasciati da Dio a' figliuoli di Noè; devono rovesciar il Faleg di Samuello Bocarto, che vuole la lingua santa essersi propagata dagli ebrei all'altre nazioni e tra queste fossesi difformata e corrotta; e finalmente devono rovesciare la Dimostrazion evangelica di Daniello Uezio, che va di séguito al Faleg del Bocarto, come il Faleg del Bocarto va di séguito al sistema del Seldeno, nella quale l'uomo eruditissimo s'industria di dar a credere che le favole siano sagre storie alterate e corrotte da' gentili e sopra tutti da' greci." Translation from Momigliano, "Vico's *Scienza Nuova*," 259–260.

Bonjour himself also faced similar scepticism closer to home. When G. W. Leibniz learned of Bonjour's plan to identify Mercury and Joseph through Claude Nicaise, he was less than impressed. "I have often believed," he wrote to Ezekiel Spanheim in 1697, "that one is a little too liberal in drawing the fables of the ancients from holy scripture."[161] Of similar inclination was Le Clerc, who, in 1705, had openly criticised Selden's *De diis syris* and by implication the mythographic tradition Selden had inaugurated.[162] In his review of Bonjour's *Selectae*, Le Clerc explicitly noted that he could not share Bonjour's attitude to pagan myth, in particular his attempt to link pagan gods with biblical patriarchs.[163] More illustrative still is the difference between Bonjour's work and that of the only other great contemporary Italian to have dedicated himself seriously not only to pagan religion and history more generally but deciphering ancient history through a close study of pagan mythology specifically: Bonjour's friend Francesco Bianchini. In principle, Bianchini shared a number of assumptions about ancient pagan history with Bonjour. He supposed, for example, that myth was corrupted history and told of a real, if primitive, age in human history.[164] Like Bonjour, who married together the chronological information he gained from the Bible with the historical information he drew from pagan myth, Bianchini supposed that *chronologia*, the study of *tempi*, must be supplemented with *istoria*, the study of *fatti*, a notion which also informed Vico's *Scienza nuova*.[165] "History without chronology is music without a beat," wrote Bianchini, "and annals without history are beats without music."[166] Moreover, Bianchini supposed that certain biblical events, such as the Flood, were preserved in the myths of pagan nations.[167] Bianchini even cited Bonjour's recently published *De nomine* in the context of a number of points relating to Greek mythology and Oriental etymology.[168] Yet the two scholars presented the relationship between *historia sacra* and *historia exotica* in a fundamentally different way. Like Vico, with whom he shared a number of similarities, Bianchini was not concerned

---

161 G. W. Leibniz to Ezekiel Spanheim, 7 May 1697, in LAA, I, 14:159: "j'ay souvent cru, qu'on est peu trop liberal à tirer les fables des anciens de la Sainte Ecriture"; and G. W. Leibniz to Thomas Burnett, 28 May 1697, LAA, I, 14:222.
162 Jean Le Clerc, "Article II: remarques sur le livre de *Jean Selden* intitulé *des Dieux des Syriens*."
163 Le Clerc, "Article IV," 231–232.
164 Bianchini, *La istoria universale*, 61.
165 Bianchini, *La istoria universale*, 5.
166 Bianchini, *La istoria universale*, 6: "l'istoria senza Cronologia è una Musica senza battuta, e gli annali senza l'istoria sono battute senza Musica."
167 Bianchini, *La istoria universale*, 39: "abbiamo esposto in luogo della vera figurazione del diluvio di Noè, la trasformazione della verità, adombrata da' Gentili in quello, che raccontano di Ogige, e di Deucalione, tanto in Grecia, quanto nell'Asia grande."
168 Bianchini, *La istoria universale*, 72–75, 84, 90–91.

with providing a specific or definitive chronology.[169] Instead, he sought to re-establish a clear difference between what he called *istoria profana* and *istoria ecclesiastica*.[170] To return to the definition with which we began this chapter, Bianchini described his universal history – and his study of pagan mythology – as a "natural," or profane, history:

> All that we propose to deal with in this present Work is *profane History*. In this understanding of *profane History* is included *the facts, and the events of men, directed purely by natural cognition, and simply established through human relations*. That is not to say that we want to silence all those facts, of which the divine mysteries speak: which, in representing an action, also hide a mystery.[171]

Bianchini still supposed that the Bible was an authoritative source for ancient chronology, given that he squeezed profane history into the 4,000-year time-span which separated Creation from the Nativity in the Vulgate. Yet he also supposed that the history of the postdiluvian patriarchs, which Huet and Bonjour had interpreted through the lens of Greek mythology, must be considered distinctive from the early history of pagan nations. In Bianchini, we find a firm distinction between *historia sacra* and *historia profana*, the sacred providential history of the Jews and the corrupted fables of the primitive pagans. In doing so, Bianchini was also reasserting a division which Huet and then Bonjour had largely circumvented.

6   Sacred Fables and Profane History

Although Bonjour's work appeared at the end of this short-lived tradition of *historia sacra*, it did not spell the end for the synchronization of the sacred and the profane. Indeed, even such a hotly-contested figure as Sanchuniathon survived the beating he received at the hands of Dodwell and van Dale – and,

---

169   As noted by Benedetto Croce, *Conversazioni critiche* (Bari: Gius. Laterza & Figli, 1924), 2:101–109, and more recently by Heilbron, "Francesco Bianchini, Historian," 235.
170   Bianchini, *La istoria universale*, 12: "La prima ad un termine di natural cognizione per esempj, e per mezi humani conduce. L'altra à sapienza molto maggiore ne guida per mezi, e per esempj, che per lo più trapassano la natura."
171   Bianchini, *La istoria universale*, 13: "Quel tutto, che da noi si propone à trattare nella presente Opera si è l'*Istoria profana*. In questo termine d'*Istoria profana* si rinchiudono *i fatti, e gli avvenimenti de gli uomini, diretti da cognizione puramente naturale, e pruovati con relazioni semplicemente umane*. Non è già che vogliamo tacere tutti que' fatti, di che parlano l'istorie divine: le quali nel rappresentare un'azione nascondono ancora un mistero."

in later years, Montesquieu, Lorenz Mosheim (1693–1755), and Johann Jakob Brücker (1696–1770) – to become the hero of Richard Cumberland's eccentric study of ancient history and Étienne Fourmont's no less eccentric rival system of 1735, although there is little doubt that, in general, scholars increasingly came to doubt the hypothetical connection between Sanchuniathon's cosmogony and Moses' history.[172] And yet, up until the nineteenth century, serious scholars of ancient Assyrian archaeology continued to suppose that the myths of various near-Eastern nations preserved elements of the biblical record. Following the British Assyriologist George Smith's (1840–1876) translation of King Ashurbanipal's Flood Tablet (ME K.3375), an ancient cuneiform inscription which features remarkable similarities with Genesis, the future Oxford professor of Assyriology Archibald Henry Sayce (1845–1933) commented that "it has long been known from the fragments of the Chaldean historian, Berosus, preserved in the works of various later writers, that the Babylonians were acquainted with traditions referring to the Creation, the period between the Flood, the Deluge, and other matters of which we read in the Book of Genesis."[173] Ironically, advances in Assyriology ended up supporting rather than undermining faith in Sanchuniathon's testimony. Excavations of Ugaritic monuments at Ras Shamra in 1929 proved that, *pace* Dodwell, Philo of Byblos was working with genuine, ancient Phoenician texts, although Bochart's identifications between Sanchuniathon's cosmology and Moses' history have largely failed to remain authoritative.[174]

The similarities between The Flood Tablet and the book of Genesis were once so remarkable that George Smith reportedly ran amok in the British Museum in an increasing state of undress. Today we know that the flood narrative is the eleventh tablet of the Epic of Gilgamesh. Moreover, although the various Babylonian myths currently housed in the Library of Ashurbanipal series in the British Museum continue to speak of vast, Babel-like towers known as

---

172   Bernard de Montfaucon, *L'antiquité expliquée, et représentée en figures* (Paris: Delaulne et al., 1719), 2:383–385; Johann Jakob Brücker, *Historia critica philosophiae* (Leipzig: Bernard Christoph Breitkopf, 1742) 1:229–240; Ralph Cudworth, *Radulphi Cudworthi Systema intellectuale huius universi seu de veris naturae rerum originibus*, ed. Lorenz Mosheim (Jena: Vidva Meyer, 1733), 1:27; Richard Cumberland, *Sanchoniatho's Phoenician History* (London: R. Wilkin, 1720); Étienne Fourmont, *Réflexions critiques sur les histoires des anciens peuples, chaldéens, hébreux, phéniciens, égyptiens, grecs, &c. jusqu'au tems de Cyrus*, 3 vols (Paris: Musier, Jombert, Briasson, Bullot 1735).

173   Archibald Henry Sayce, "Preface," in George Smith, *The Chaldean Account of Genesis* (London: Sampson Lowe, Marston, Searle, and Rivington, 1880), 1.

174   There are a few exceptions: see Baumgarten, *The Phoenician History*, 54 (n. 58), 144–5 (on Baau), 165, 202, 209, 232.

Ziggurats and divinely ordained floods which wiped out all mankind, we do not suppose that they prove the authority and primacy of the Mosaic account from which all other flood narratives derived. At the most, they suggest that Jewish myths came from the same Near Eastern historical *milieu*, hence their many sustained similarities – an idea which, in its genesis, takes us back to Selden. This connection is more than can be said for Greco-Roman mythology. It is a long time hence that schoolmasters taught of the Christian messages in Virgil or the similarities between Genesis and Ovid's *Metamorphoses*. A similar state eventually befell the "history" of Genesis. In the nineteenth century, the development of scientific archaeology, geology, and palaeontology proved the final death knell for any historian who supposed that the Bible remained an authoritative source for universal history, despite such ingenious solutions as Philip Henry Gosse's *Omphalos* (1857).[175] Even major biblical critics, such as the German theologian Wilhelm Martin Leberecht de Wette (1780–1849), came to the conclusion that the material contained in the Pentateuch was almost wholly mythical rather than historical.[176] This continues to remain a common refrain today.[177]

Historia and *fabula*, *fabula* and *historia* – this is the dichotomy which long predicated the Christian distinction between what was true (and prior), and what was false (and corrupted). That is not to say that Christian scholars always believed that *fabula* was necessarily false, nor that it could contain no real historical information. The historical interpretation of myth was a prominent hermeneutical tradition which remained alive and fruitful in the works of the Fathers, the Medieval "Euhemerists," and the Renaissance mythographers, under whom the pagan gods shed their Christian garments and once again donned their classical garb.[178] It was in the seventeenth century, however, in which *fabula* became not merely a pagan, but also a Jewish phenomenon, as Peter Miller has noted.[179] Previously the creation of myth, *fabula*, was

---

175   Philip Henry Gosse, *Omphalos: An Attempt to Untie the Geological Knot* (London: John van Voorst, 1857).
176   Wilhelm Martin Leberecht de Wette, *Beiträge zur Einleitung in das Alte Testament*, 2 vols (Halle: Schimmelpfennig und Compagnie, 1806–1807); John W. Rogerson, *W. M. L. de Wette, Founder of Modern Biblical Criticism: An Intellectual Biography* (Sheffield: PSOT Press, 1992).
177   Take, for example, the very recent work of William Lane Craig, who posits that the Genesis narrative should be seen as a genre called "mythohistory": William Lane Craig, *In Quest of the Historical Adam: A Biblical and Scientific Exploration* (Grand Rapids MI: Eerdmans, 2021).
178   As pointed out by Seznec, *The Survival of the Pagan Gods*, 211.
179   Miller, "Taking Paganism Seriously."

predicated on the creation of gods, and false gods at that; and consequently myth-making was a feature characteristic of idolatrous pagans. As I hope to have shown, the synthesis of pagan myth and sacred history was in response to pressing concerns relating to biblical authority. And yet it dissolved not only the distinction between *sacra* and *profana*, but also between *historia* and *fabula*. By the time Vico wrote his first *Scienza nuova* in 1725 in order to reassert the notion that myths and myth-making was a peculiarly Gentile phenomenon, and to reassert the clear distinction between sacred and profane antiquity, he was too late. Not only had deists and freethinkers come to advance the heretical notion that Genesis – so often compared by orthodox scholars with pagan mythology – was itself a collection of Jewish myths, but even orthodox scholars themselves had come to question the manner in which diffusionist scholars had, in their comparative, apologetic, and historical enterprises, denied the divine and special nature of the ancient Jewish people.

At the same time, however, as *fabula* became a Jewish phenomenon, *historia* also became a pagan one – and perhaps it is this change which proved most influential for later scholarship. Notionally, of course, scholars still supposed that the Bible remained the authoritative account for the history of the world. Yet even diffusionist scholars increasingly supposed that it could not only be supplemented but also expanded and explicated through pagan testimony. In this sense, scholars increasingly took pagan evidence seriously as a historical source. In the centuries since no scholar has tended to dismiss ancient historical evidence, as Christian scholars once did, merely because its provenance was pagan. In this tradition, too, Bonjour was an important and willing participant.

CHAPTER 3

The Wisdom of the Egyptians

1 Egypt, Israel, and the Origins of Human Civilization

> Whilst I was studying to furnish myself with an accurate knowledge of antiquity, and to arrive at the very fountains of erudition, whether I consulted the sacred scriptures or profane writers, no nation appeared to me to have done more towards the propagation of learning than the Egyptian; for the sacred writers give their testimony to the consummate wisdom of the Egyptians, and ancient Greece acknowledges them as its masters.[1]

Thus wrote Pierre-Daniel Huet in his *Memoirs*. His statement reflects what was a common principle of seventeenth-century *historia sacra*. In classical antiquity, the Greeks traced the origins of their philosophy, their letters, their arts, and their sciences back to the wisdom of the Egyptians.[2] Since the time of Hecataeus it had become common to suppose that Plato, Pythagoras, and other Greek sages were educated in Egypt.[3] In Herodotus' *Histories*, not only the Olympian gods but also individual beliefs and practices such as metempsychosis (2.123.3) or the rites of Dionysus (2.48–49) were said to have come to Greece from Egypt.[4] It was for this reason that, in the first century BC, Diodorus began

---

1 Huet, *Commentarius de rebus ad eum pertinentibus*, 157: "Dum certam comparare mihi studerem antiquitatis notitiam, & ad ipsos eruditionis fontes pervenire, sive sacros Scriptores adhiberem in consilium, sive exoticos, nulla mihi gens ad doctrinarum propagationem plus contulisse visa est quam Aegyptia; neque satis tamen pro dignitate ac merito cognita & doctorum hominum studiis illustrata; nam & summae sapientiae testimonium huic perhibent sacri Codices; & magistros suos Aegyptios agnoscit ac praedicat vetustior & doctior Graecia." Translation from Huet, *Memoirs*, 1:224.

2 See generally Iversen, *The Myth of Egypt*, 38ff.

3 Other famous examples include Homer (Diodorus, 1.69.4, 1.96.2, 1.97.7), Thales (Diogenes Laërtius, 1.43), Solon (Plato, *Timaeus* 21E–25D) and the list provided by Plutarch (*De Iside et Osiride* 254E–F); see further Levitin, *Ancient Wisdom*, 114; Levitin, "What was the Comparative History of Religions in 17th-Century Europe?," 54–56; and the classic account by D. P. Walker, *The Ancient Theology: Studies in Christian Platonism from the Fifteenth to the Eighteenth Century* (London: Duckworth, 1972).

4 The classic statements are 2.50.1–2: "By making inquiries, I discovered that the names of the gods came to Hellas from barbarians, and I myself concluded that they derive specifically from Egypt, for the names of the gods have been known in Egypt since the earliest times"; and 2.58: "In any case, the Egyptians were the first of all people to hold public religious festivals,

his universal history with Egypt, "since Egypt is the country where mythology places the origin of the gods, where the earliest observations of the stars are said to have been made, and where, furthermore, many noteworthy deeds of great men are recorded."[5] The assumption that Egypt lay at the root of human civilization remained in currency beyond the seventeenth century. "A true philosophy of the *Urgeschichte* of mankind, from an historical perspective," wrote the German Egyptologist Christian Karl Josias von Bunsen (1791–1860) in his *Ägyptens Stelle in der Weltgeschichte*, published in five volumes between 1844 and 1857, must begin with Egypt:[6]

> The Egyptians are, even chronologically speaking, a world-historical people. No one can dive into the maelstrom of the history of human civilization [*Völkergeschichte*] without searching for Egypt's place within it and greet it with awe: and yet no one can determine this place, without first surmounting the summit of chronology and seeking after the origins of the human race.[7]

In a similar manner, such nineteenth-century theories as the hyper-diffusionism of the British anthropologist Grafton Elliot Smith (1871–1937) continued to suggest that Egypt was the source of all human civilization, and that human culture had spread outwards from Egypt. Henry Maine (1822–1888), the nineteenth-century English jurist, might have been exaggerating when he noted that "except the blind forces of Nature, nothing moves in this world which is not Greek in origin," but it is a quip which would describe our conceptualisation of Egypt's place in universal history fairly accurately.[8]

---

  pageants, and processions escorting divine images, and the Hellenes learned about these rituals from them." Translation from *The Landmark Herodotus: The Histories*, ed. Robert B. Strassler (New York: Anchor Books, 2007). See generally Herodotus, *Histories* 2.35–64.
5 Translation from Diodorus Siculus, *Library of History*, ed. C. H. Oldfather (Cambridge MA: Harvard University Press, 1933), 33–35.
6 Christian Karl Josias von Bunsen, *Aegyptens Stelle in der Weltgeschichte* (Hamburg: Friedrich Perthes, 1845), 1:xiv: "einer wahren Philosophie der Urgeschichte der Menschheit vom historischen Standpunkt."
7 Bunsen, *Aegyptens Stelle in der Weltgeschichte*, 1:7: "die Aegypter sind, selbst in der Zeitrechnung, ein weltgeschichtliches Volk. Niemand kann der Strom der altern Völkergeschichte hinaufschiffen, ohne Aegyptens Stelle zu suchen und mit Ehrfurcht zu begrüßen: aber Niemand kann auch diese Stelle bestimmen, ohne die Gipfel der Zeiten zu besteigen und nach den Anfängen des Menschengeschlechtes zu forschen."
8 Cited a number of times, as in Henry Maine, *The Rede Lecture delivered before the University of Cambridge May 22, 1875* (London: John Murray, 1875), 38.

As Richard Serjeantson has pointed out, the primacy of Egypt was an integral part of the diffusionist narrative that proliferated in the seventeenth century.[9] Since the Jews were not thought to have had any historical interaction with the Greeks, the ancient Egyptians, renowned in the ancient world for their wisdom and antiquity, provided a suitable (and convenient) bridge between Jewish and Greco-Roman civilization. "And as the Grecians received their Learning, and Laws from *Egypt*, so we need no way doubt, but that the Egyptians received the best part of their Laws from the Mosaic Constitutions," wrote Theophilus Gale in 1672.[10] Similarly, in his *Demonstratio evangelica*, Huet cited the education of various Greek poets and philosophers in Egypt as proof that they had had access to and knowledge of biblical history.[11] Once again, then, it was ancient Greek historiography which provided a historical narrative which was subsequently piggy-backed by seventeenth-century, diffusionist scholars. These scholars accepted that the Greeks had taken their myths and their wisdom from the Egyptians, but reconceptualised the historical narrative by giving Egyptian myths and wisdom a Jewish origin. That Egypt was the nation with which the biblical patriarchs and the ancient Jews had had, until the Exodus, the most interaction only served to reinforce this narrative. As a result, the Egyptian wisdom which the Greeks recognized as their master became biblical.

When Bonjour first began working on ancient history and chronology in Toulouse, he found himself in an antiquarian community, predominantly centred in southern France, which was fascinated by ancient Egypt. We already know that, in 1695, Bonjour visited Michel Bégon's cabinet in Rochefort where Bégon kept a number of Egyptian antiquities, the most notable being the engraved Egyptian tomb which Bonjour interpreted, according to Bégon, *à la* Kircher. Bégon remained a frequent correspondent on Egyptian matters throughout Bonjour's time in Rome, and in 1697 he sent him an engraving of an artefact which Nicaise called "a type of *Mensa Isiaca*," an ancient Egyptian tablet similar to the famous Bembine table of Isis which Athanasius Kircher had once made the basis for his faulty deciphering of the hieroglyphs.[12] Of similar importance was Jean-Pierre Rigord, who wrote dissertations on Egyptian

---

9   Serjeantson, "David Hume's *Natural History of Religion* (1757)." See more generally on early modern "Egyptology," Don Cameron Allen, "The Predecessors of Champollion," *Proceedings of the American Philosophical Society* 104 (1960): 527–547.
10 Gale, *The Court of the Gentiles*, 1, part 2: 30.
11 Huet, *Demonstratio evangelica*, 73–99.
12 Claude Nicaise to Ezekiel Spanheim, 25 July 1697, in Feller, *Otium Hanoveranum*, 102: "Monsieur Begon a envoyé à ce Pere un fort beau dessein, qui luy est tombé entre les mains, & qu'il a fait graver á son instance pour l'expliquer & le mettre dans les antiquités

artefacts for the *Journal de Trévoux* and who collected a great number of these treasures in his cabinet in Marseille.[13] Although primarily interested in pagan symbols and religious iconography, Rigord also held fast to the Herodotean notion that many of the gods of Greece had their origins in Egypt and he believed in the ancient commerce between Egyptians and Jews. In a 1689 discussion of a Greek coin apparently depicting the Egyptian god Pan, Rigord even stated that the true religion was best preserved in Egypt:

> The first successors of Noah who populated these vast countries brought the Religion there [i.e., to Egypt] in all its purity: the Hebrews, who always maintained some commerce there until the time they came to settle there, renewed these ideas, which idolatry and superstition could never absolutely erase.[14]

Whether Bonjour was influenced by these notions is hard to say. Indeed, I consider it more likely that they are evidence of what were, at that time, commonly held opinions: that Egypt held the key to unlocking the secrets of pagan antiquity and that the relationship between ancient Egyptians and Jews was crucial in understanding the connection between biblical history and wisdom on the one hand and profane history and wisdom on the other. Although we know that Bonjour did not begin studying Coptic until well after his arrival in Rome, it is clear that he was already convinced in Toulouse that the study of Egyptian antiquities would reveal important and diverse *monumenta* of holy scripture. For Bonjour, ancient Egyptian history was intimately and almost inextricably connected to that of the Jews: as he wrote to Claude Nicaise in 1697, it was among the "the antiquities of Egypt" where "the areas which seem the most sterile become the most fertile," and where the connection with holy

---

Egyptiennes, c'est une espece de *Mensa Isiaca*, qu'il intitulé *Tabula Begoniana* à l'instar de Tabula Bembina du Cardinal Bembo."

13 Jean-Pierre Rigord, "Article CLXXVIII: Lettre de M. Rigord Commissaire de la Marine aux auteurs des Mémoires de Trévoux sur un livre qui a pour titre *Monumenta Coptica*," *Journal de Trévoux* 8 (1703): 1870–1879; Jean-Pierre Rigord, "Article LXXXIX: Lettre de Monsieur Rigord Commissaire de la Marine aux journalistes de Trévoux sur une ceinture de toile trouvée en Egypte autour d'une mumie," *Journal de Trévoux* 10 (1704): 978–1000.

14 Rigord, *Dissertation de Monsieur Graverol ... sur l'explication d'une médaille*, 23: "Les premiers successeurs de Noë qui peuplerent ces vastes Païs, y apporterent la Religion dans sa pureté: les Hebreux qui y entretinrent toûjours quelque commerce jusqu'au temps qu'ils vinrent s'y établir, en renouvellerent les idées, que l'idolâtrie & la superstition ne purent jamais absolument effacer."

scripture "is so frequent and so considerable that their chronology and history are as much sacred as they are profane."[15]

It was this interest which shaped Bonjour's first two works, which were largely if not completely composed in Toulouse: the large, unpublished *Mercurius aegyptiorum Josephus patriarcha* – in which Bonjour identified the biblical patriarch Joseph with the Egyptian god Mercury (and a number of other gods from Egyptian mythology) – and the much shorter pamphlet entitled *De nomine patriarchae Josephi*, an excerpt of the tenth chapter of the *Mercurius* which examined the name by which the pharaoh called Joseph at Genesis 41:45 and which was published in Rome in 1696.[16] Both works were fundamentally shaped by the more all-encompassing notion of biblical diffusionism which legitimised Bonjour's practice of synchronizing pagan myths with biblical history, as well as by the specific place of Egypt within this diffusionist narrative. Indeed, throughout his work on pagan mythology, Bonjour outlined the relationship between Israel, Egypt, and Greece in typical neo-Eusebian fashion. For Bonjour, Egypt was, as Apollonius of Rhodes had once stated, μήτηρ ... προτερηγενέων αἰζηῶν, "the mother of men long ago" (*Argonautica* 4.267).[17] "All the history of earlier times was recorded in Egypt, in part in the temples, in part upon certain columns," wrote Bonjour, citing from an oration by the Greek philosopher Dio Chrysostom (11.38).[18] As Herodotus, Diodorus, and Josephus had once suggested, the origins of Greek poetry, culture, and wisdom lay with the Egyptians, and had been transmitted from the "port-less" ("importuosa") Egyptians to the Greeks by the sea-faring Phoenicians.[19] By making the origin of Greek wisdom Egyptian, Bonjour simultaneously allowed for the possibility that it might, in reality, be Jewish. Indeed, if Bonjour made the common Greek notion that the origins of pagan wisdom and religion were Egyptian the subject of the preface of his *Mercurius*, then the rest of his work was devoted to proving that these Egyptian origins had Jewish antecedents.

---

15 Guillaume Bonjour to Claude Nicaise, 9 July 1697, KW 72 H 20, fol. 127v; BAR, ms.lat.635, fol. 68v; and Pélissier, "Lettres inédites de Claude Nicaise," 147: "les endroits qui paraissent les plus stériles y deviennent des plus fécondes. Au reste la connexion qu'il y a avec l'Ecriture S.te est si fréquente et si considérable que la chronologie et l'histoire y ont autant du sacré que du profane."

16 *Mercurius*, fols. 75v–85r.

17 See for the translation Apollonius Rhodius, *Argonautica*, ed. William H. Race (Cambridge MA: Harvard University Press, 2008), 349, cited at *Mercurius*, fol. 4r, and *Selectae*, D.II.50, 91, 158.

18 *De dynastiis*, fol. 26r.

19 *Mercurius*, fol. 4r; Herodotus, 2.50.1; Josephus, *Contra Apionem* 1.63.

Bonjour's early mythographic and Egyptian scholarship not only squarely followed what was, by then, a well-established scholarly tradition, but his identifications appear to have been mobilised in order to defend specific, long-standing, orthodox dogmas. In the *Mercurius*, Bonjour explicitly noted that his identification between Joseph and Mercury would confirm not only the general historical authority of the Bible but also the authority of the shorter Vulgate chronology specifically. In the *De nomine*, Bonjour sought to bolster this notion by proving, through his etymological study of "Zaphnath paaneah," the Egyptian name of Joseph, that Jerome, the translator of the Vulgate, knew Egyptian – and hence that Jerome must have had an excellent understanding of Egyptian sources and Egyptian antiquity more generally.[20] Yet it is clear that there were also other, more pressing concerns which motivated both Bonjour's *Mercurius* and his *De nomine*. Ultimately, there is a reason as to why Bonjour thought it necessary to dedicate an entire volume, some 250 pages littered with pagan citations from Apollodorus to Zosimus, to establishing not merely a general identification between sacred and profane antiquity (as he did in the apologetic and propaedeutic dissertations he later published in Montefiascone) but a single, particular identification between one specific biblical patriarch (i.e. Joseph) and a number of specifically chosen pagan gods. Despite the uncharitable assessment of seventeenth-century syncretic scholarship by recent historians such as Jed Buchwald and Mordechai Feingold, scholars such as Bonjour (and before him Huet) were not "promiscuous Euhemerists" who were merely concerned with the quantity rather than the specificity of sacred and profane identifications.[21]

In many ways, this was a question of genre as much as it was of method. Unlike such apologetic works as Grotius' *De veritate*, Gale's *Court* or Noël Alexandre's pedagogical *Selecta historiae ecclesiasticae* (which examined the identifications of Bochart, Huet, and Gerardus Vossius interchangeably), Bonjour's *Mercurius* was a work of history, in this case the ancient history of Egypt and, more specifically, the history of the ancient patriarchs in Egypt.[22] Consequently, individual identifications mattered. Indeed, it was through specific identifications that Bonjour not only sought to prove that pagan gods had biblical origins but also to construct a historical narrative of primordial human

---

20 *De nomine*, 2. Bonjour relied for his citation of the *regula* on the collection by Lukas Holste, *Codex regularum quas sancti patres monachis et virginibus sanctimonialibus servandas praescipsere* (Rome: Vitale Mascardi, 1661), 62–63.
21 Buchwald and Feingold, *Newton and the Origin of Civilization*, 159.
22 On Alexandre see Jean-Louis Quantin, "Entre Rome et Paris, entre histoire et théologie: Les Selecta Historiae Ecclesiasticae capita du P. Noël Alexandre et les ambiguïtés de l'historiographie gallicane," *Mémoire dominicaine* 20 (2006): 67–99.

history for the period immediately succeeding the Flood. In Bonjour's case, then, it is necessary to understand the seventeenth century re-evaluation of ancient Egyptian history and its connection to Moses and the biblical patriarchs in order to understand both the specific turn his interest in ancient Egypt took and the motivations which underpinned the specific identifications he proffered.

As the recent work of Serjeantson, Jan Assmann, and Dmitri Levitin has outlined, the first serious questioning and later abandonment of the neo-Eusebian narrative lay not with the deists of the early eighteenth century – who still accepted that the Egyptians were the "masters of the Greeks," but who regarded the book of Genesis not as the original history of primordial man but rather a collection of Jewish myths – but in seventeenth-century *historia sacra* itself.[23] Indeed, from the early seventeenth century onwards, an increasing number of scholars had come to study the ancient Jewish religion in its historical context and consequently through the lens of its relationship with the ancient cults of neighbouring pagan nations, Egypt in particular. In his controversial *Aaron purgatus* of 1606, the French antiquarian François de Monceaux had suggested that the most famous Jewish idol, Aaron's golden calf, was a cherubic representation of Jehovah.[24] In response, a number of scholars supposed that Jewish idolatry was shaped by the Israelites' earlier experiences in Egypt. As John Milton (1608–1674) wrote in an illustrative passage of his *Paradise Lost* (1.479–489):

> After these appeared
> A crew who under names of old renown,
> Osiris, Isis, Orus and their train
> With monstrous shapes and sorceries abused
> Fanatic Egypt and her priests, to seek
> Their wandering gods disguised in brutish forms
> Rather then human. Nor did Israel scape
> The infection when their borrowed gold composed
> The calf in Oreb: and the rebel king
> Doubled that sin in Bethel and in Dan,

---

23 Jan Assmann, *Moses the Egyptian: The Memory of Egypt in Western Monotheism* (Cambridge MA and London: Harvard University Press, 1997); Levitin, *Ancient Wisdom*, 113–229.

24 François de Monceaux, *Aaron purgatus sive de vitulo aureo, libri duo* (Arras: Guillaume Rivière, 1606). See generally on the calf Michael Pregill, *The Golden Calf between Bible and Qur'an: Scripture, Polemic, and Exegesis from Late Antiquity to Islam* (Oxford: Oxford University Press, 2020). I have been unable to find exact dates for Monceaux's life.

> Likening his Maker to the grazed ox,
> Jehovah, who in one night when he passed
> From Egypt marching, equalled with one stroke
> Both her first born and all her bleating gods.[25]

Of a similar opinion was John Selden, who argued that Jewish moscholatry – calf worship – was a relapse into Egyptian worship of the bull-god Apis, a notion first voiced by the late third- and early fourth-century Church Father Lactantius (*Institutiones divinae* 4.10); who, as we shall see, proved a vital patristic source for the early modern understanding of ancient pagan religion.[26] In his *De theologia gentili* (1641), Gerardus Vossius went even further. According to Vossius, Aaron's notorious fashioning of the golden calf at Exodus 32 was not so much a Jewish lapse into the worship of the Egyptian Apis but rather a mistaken attempt to worship the true God through pagan religious practices.[27] For Vossius, the false worship of the true God was even more dangerous than the worshipping of a false god. Both possibilities, however, stressed the existence of a historical connection and even transfer between Jewish and Egyptian religious practices, and thereby complicated the previous distinction between the true, divinely ordained, and revealed religion of the Israelites and the idolatrous practices of the ancient pagans.

The two scholars key in problematizing the relationship between Israel and Egypt in the late seventeenth century were John Marsham and John Spencer (1630–1693). Marsham was by trade a chancery clerk: educated first at Westminster School and later St. John's College, Oxford, he became a member of the Middle Temple in 1627 and spent his adult years engaged in extensive

---

25 John Milton, *Paradise Lost*, ed. Alastair Fowler (New York: Routledge, 2007), 90.

26 Selden, *De diis syris*, 46–47: "Aegyptia superstitione inquinatos Israelitas Vitulum Aureum coluisse certum est." See also Gregor Michaelis, *Notae in Jacobi Gaffarelli Curiositates* (Hamburg: Gottfried Schultzen, 1676), 70–72; Benedict Pereira, *Commentarium et disputationum in Genesim, tomi quatuor* (Cologne: Anton Hierat, 1622), 947; Caspar Peucer, *Commentarius de praecipuis divinationum generibus* (Frankfurt: Andrè Wechel, 1593), 243.

27 Vossius, *De theologia gentili*, 19–20. "Et sane Israelitas non proprie oblivione voluntaria memoriam contrivisse benefactorum Dei, liquido ostendit: quod vitulus dicitur ille Deus, qui Israelitas duxerat ex Aegypto; ubi per vitulum nonnisi veri Dei imago intelligi potest. Et ibidem, commate proximo, cum Aaron coram vitulo altare exstruxisset, disertim Festum indicit Iehovae; quod nomen grande nunquam ille, aut Moses Diis gentium tribuisset. Dixeris, Israelitas non vehementem adeo poenam promeritos videri, si non desciverint a vero Deo. Quasi non sufficiat, quod desciverant a cultu vero. Coluere enim Deum ritu gentili: qui praeterquam quod divinae esset voluntati repugnantissimus, in ista humanarum mentium caligine plenissimus periculi fuit; quia experientia ostendit, quam facile cultus symbolicus in proprium convertatur."

and intricate research in matters of ancient chronology alongside his legal and later political career: he was made MP for Rochester in 1660, knighted at the Restoration, and created baronet in 1663. Spencer was another matter: a noted Hebraist and priest – he became archdeacon of Sudbury in 1667 and Dean of Ely a decade later – Spencer spent the entirety of his working life in the halls of Corpus Christi College, Cambridge, where he was first admitted as an undergraduate, later appointed fellow, eventually elected Master, and where he is still buried today. If Marsham and Spencer wrote from different backgrounds and perspectives, it is important to note two things they had in common: firstly, that they both had fundamentally orthodox aims in mind; secondly, that despite these orthodox aims, they both advanced controversial, radical, and ultimately influential arguments concerning the relationship between Moses and Egypt. On the one hand, it is clear that Marsham's specific interpretation of Egyptian history, as detailed in his 1672 *Canon chronicus Aegyptiacus, Ebraicus, Graecus, et disquisitiones*, was the result of his commitment to the shorter chronology of the Hebrew Bible as opposed to the longer chronology of the Greek Septuagint. On the other hand, it appears that Spencer, as recently and persuasively argued by Dmitri Levitin, structured his own *De legibus Hebraeorum* (1683–85) – which developed a number of notions he had first advanced in his 1670 *Dissertatio de Urim et Thummim* – in response to contemporary Hebraizing non-conformists who claimed that the Mosaic Law was still relevant in contemporary society.[28] Nevertheless, both scholars advanced an understanding of the relationship between Hebrew and Egyptian culture which undermined the traditional diffusionist narrative and which proved fundamentally unpalatable to many contemporaries. The Dutch theologian Hermann Witsius (1636–1708), whose *Aegyptiaca* (1683) was perhaps the most famous refutation of Marsham and Spencer's ideas, even claimed that Marsham's arguments "although they appear erudite, are not however equally pious, nor in this way matched to the splendour and honour of our very sacred religion."[29] In essence, both Marsham

---

28 Dmitri Levitin, "John Spencer's *De Legibus Hebraeorum* (1683–1685) and 'Enlightened' Sacred History: A New Interpretation," *Journal of the Warburg and Courtauld Institutes* 76 (2013): 49–92; John Spencer, *Dissertatio de Urim et Thurrim in Deuteron. c. 33, v. 8. In qua eorum natura et origo, non paucorum mosaicorum rationes et obscuriora quaedam Scripturae loca probabiliter explicantur* (Cambridge: G. Kettilby, 1670). On Marsham see also Levitin, *Ancient Wisdom*, 163.

29 Hermann Witsius, *Aegyptiaca, et Dekaphulon. Sive, de Aegyptiacorum sacrorum cum Hebraicis collatione* (Amsterdam: Gerardus Borstius, 1683), 1–2: "Id sibi Nobilissimus auctor suo quodam jure sumsit, ut, relicta aliquoties frequenti regiaque via, per devios tramites, veluti animi caussa, exspatietur: ubi contingit in eas ipsum opiniones incidere, quae ut ut [sic] eruditae videantur, non tamen aeque piae sunt, neque ad sacratissimae

and Spencer claimed that Egyptian culture had preceded that of the Jews and had therefore influenced – rather than been influenced by – the Jewish religion. In the following decades a substantial body of literature emerged which attempted to grapple with the issues Marsham and Spencer had first raised.[30]

Spencer's work focussed above all on the historical relationship between Egyptian religion and the Mosaic Law. As Jan Assmann has outlined, perhaps the most important intellectual influence for Spencer was the twelfth-century Jewish philosopher and rabbi Moses Maimonides, whom Guy Stroumsa has called "the greatest intellectual figure of the seventeenth century."[31] In his *Moreh Nevukhim*, Maimonides advanced a notion Assmann has called "normative inversion." According to Maimonides, the Mosaic Law was particularly influenced by the Hebrews' stay in Egypt and was specifically constructed so as to lead the Jews away from the idolatrous practices they had been exposed to in Egypt and towards the true religion. Spencer himself largely accepted this theory. Indeed, according to Spencer, the Law had two functions, not unlike Grotius' two senses of the prophets.[32] On the one hand, it transmitted higher, if encoded, truths which went beyond the crude understanding of the ancient Israelites. On the other hand it was, as once suggested by Maimonides, specifically tailored to the historical context which the ancient Israelites found themselves in. Principally, it was intended to wean the ancient Israelites off the idolatry of their ancestors and thereby ease their path towards a proper understanding of the true religion, while also preventing the Israelites from throwing off their previously established religious beliefs too quickly and thereby falling into worship of the devil. The Mosaic Law was not, therefore, intended as a universal or eternal law but merely as a temporary stepping-stone through which the true religion could be reached more easily.[33]

There is no suggestion that Bonjour read Spencer's *De legibus Hebraeorum* or intended his work as a refutation of Spencer – although his friend Gisbert

---

religionis nostrae decus honoremque admodum comparatae." A second edition was published in 1696.

30 See Christoph Matthäus Pfaff, "Dissertatio Praeliminaris," in John Spencer, *De legibus Hebraeorum ritualibus earumque rationibus* (Tübingen: Johann Georg Cotta, 1732), as pointed out by Levitin, *Ancient Wisdom*, 190.

31 Jan Assmann, *Moses the Egyptian*; Stroumsa, "John Spencer and the Roots of Idolatry," 14.

32 As pointed out by Sébastien Drouin, *Théologie ou libertinage? L'exégèse allégorique à l'âge des Lumières* (Paris: Honoré Champion, 2010), 103–104.

33 An excellent article on Spencer's originality and importance is Jonathan Sheehan, "Sacred and Profane: Idolatry, Antiquarianism and the Polemics of Distinction in the Seventeenth Century," *Past & Present* 192 (2006): 35–66.

Cuper did praise Spencer's work on the Egyptian god Serapis in the second edition of his *Harpocrates* (1687), largely because Spencer had praised Cuper's refutation of Bochart's work on Serapis in the first (1676).[34] This was not the case for Marsham. Indeed, we know that Bonjour read the *Canon chronicus* as early as 1695, given that he cited it, albeit briefly and on a minor point of numismatics, in the *Mercurius*.[35] In his later work on Egyptian chronology, Bonjour would come to criticise both Marsham's chronological arrangement of Manetho's dynasties and Marsham's conceptualisation of the relationship between Egyptian and Jewish philosophy and religion explicitly.[36]

In his *Canon chronicus*, Marsham supposed that Jewish religious practices, such as circumcision, had originated with and been disseminated by the chronologically prior Egyptian people. *Pace* Eusebius, he therefore supposed that the culture and religion of the Israelites had been influenced by and in certain cases borrowed from Egypt, rather than vice-versa. This notion squarely undermined the traditional patristic defence of Hebraic primacy. Although Marsham rejected La Peyrère's assumption that the chronology of the Bible was not a universal chronology, he also supposed that both the arts and sciences and certain religious practices of the Jews had Gentile, specifically Egyptian, origins. In so doing Marsham separated the ancient history of human civilization and culture from Jewish providential history. According to Marsham, historical testimonies recounting the invention of important cultural contributions such as the science of astronomy or the invention of letters were to be found not in the biblical narrative of Moses but rather in the Egyptian history of Manetho. In particular, Marsham emphasised the importance of the mythical founder and first king of the Egyptians, Menes, as well as his direct descendants Athothes and Tosorthrus, to whom Menes had granted the kingdoms of Thebes and Memphis respectively. Indeed, Marsham supposed that upon their deaths all three were made gods: Menes was Jupiter Ammon, or, as in Plato's *Phaedrus* (274D–275B), "Thamus"; Tosorthrus was Aesculapius, the inventor of medicine and anatomy; and Athothes was Mercury, the inventor of writing, in this case the Egyptian hieroglyphs.[37] According to Marsham, the invention of these arts contributed to the emergence of Egypt from its rudimentary and barbaric state to one of refined civilization:

---

34   Gisbert Cuper, *Harpocrates* (1676), 104–105; Cuper, *Harpocrates* (1687), 82–83.
35   *Mercurius*, fol. 79v; the context is replicated in the *De nomine*, 17.
36   "De regno Memphitarum, et ejus nexu cum chronologia Hebraica," BAR, ms.lat.49, 40ff; *De dynastiis*, fols. 27r, 32r–33v.
37   Marsham, *Canon chronicus*, 30ff.

> But two most useful inventions are here celebrated as being of the earliest times, *Medicine* and *Architecture*. Among the arts, nearly all of which the Egyptian spawned, the first to have arisen were those which had necessity as a midwife: they were prepared as aids for life against the infirmities of the body, against injuries of the Sky, as dictated by Nature. So began the nascent study of medicine and building.[38]

By supposing that the Jews had taken their arts and sciences from the Egyptians, Marsham also supposed that the book of Genesis did not preserve an account of the origins and dissemination of these critical inventions for human civilization. As a result, in Marsham (and later Spencer), the question of the relationship between ancient Egypt and Israel was fundamentally problematized: the Egyptian learning which formed the bedrock of later pagan mythology and even philosophy – or, at the very least, the bedrock of the biblical remnants of pagan mythology and the more palatable elements of Greco-Roman philosophy – was not influenced by Jewish learning but was itself the ultimate origin of Jewish and in particular Mosaic wisdom.

The issues raised by Marsham's work, which, lest we forget, sacrificed Hebraic primacy not out of some radical, libertine conviction but in order to defend the authenticity and universality of the Masoretic chronology, form the historical background to both Bonjour's *Mercurius* and his *De nomine*, his first treatments of Egyptian-Jewish history. Although Bonjour completed the *Mercurius* before he published the *De nomine* it makes sense for us to start with the latter, largely because it was intended by Bonjour as a short excerpt, an *amuse-bouche*, that would give readers a taste of Bonjour's key ideas and whet the appetite for the eventual appearance of the former, Bonjour's more extensive, then unpublished, *Mercurius*.[39] Like the *Mercurius*, the *De nomine* was, despite its ostensible goal of translating Joseph's Egyptian name, largely structured around the history of one biblical patriarch, namely Joseph, and his identification with a few carefully selected Egyptian gods. As a result, it already probed at some important questions concerning the historical relationship between Jewish and Egyptian wisdom, questions which proved critical in the *Mercurius*. As in the *Mercurius*, the biblical patriarch Joseph and his various

---

38   Marsham, *Canon chronicus*, 43: "Caeterum duo hic memorantur primorum temporum utilissima inventa, *Medicina* atque *Architectura*. Inter Artes, quas fere omnes Aegyptus peperit, illae primum enatae sunt quibus obstetricavit Necessitas: subsidia vitae contra infirmitates corporis, contra injurias Coeli, dictante Natura, comparata sunt. Hinc praematurum medicandi aedificandique studium."

39   See Guillaume Bonjour to Antonio Magliabechi, 15 November 1695, BNCF, *Fondo Magliabechiano* VIII, cod. 317, fol. 1r.

pagan guises provided the historical fulcrum for outlining how ancient Jewish and Egyptian history intersected, and, in the *De nomine*, no pagan deity played a more important role than the ancient Egyptian god Serapis.

2 The Jewish Origins of Egyptian Culture: Serapis

Since antiquity, the Egyptian god Serapis marked both the interaction of Christianity with paganism as well as its final victory over the idolatry of the heathens. A famous remark in the *Historia Augusta* (*Firmus* 8.2), that those who worship Serapis are in fact Christians and that bishops of Christ are in reality devotees to Serapis, is one of very few direct pagan criticisms of Christianity – the phrase also features in a letter by the emperor Hadrian to the consul Servianus.[40] Equally, Socrates Scholasticus related that when worshippers sought to claim hieroglyphs for themselves upon the destruction of the Serapeum in 391, both Christians and pagan worshippers of Serapis alike attempted to claim the sign of the cross as their own (*Historia ecclesiastica* 5.17). Yet as Theodoret (*Historia ecclesiastica* 5.22) wrote of the same event, the destruction of the Serapeum, on the order of Theodosius I but at the persistent request of Theophilus of Alexandria, was also the final triumph of Christianity over its pagan nemesis:

> But Theophilus … looking with contempt on the size of the statue, commanded a man who had a hatchet to strike Serapis with violence. When the blow was inflicted, all the people shrieked, fearing that what had been rumoured would come to pass. But Serapis suffered no pain from the wound, neither did it utter any exclamation; for it was made of wood, and was without life. When the head was broken open, a troop of mice immediately ran out; for these animals had made their abode in the interior of the god of the Egyptians. The body was broken up into small pieces and burnt; the head was carried throughout the whole city, and submitted to the inspection of those who had worshipped the idol, and who now ridiculed its weakness. In this way were the temples of the demons destroyed throughout the world.[41]

---

[40] As noted by Arnaldo Momigliano, "Pagan and Christian Historiography in the Fourth Century A.D.," 119–120.

[41] Translation from Theodoret, *Ecclesiastical History. A History of the Church in five books. From A.D. 322. to the Death of Theodore of Mopsuestia A.D. 427*, trans. Edward Walford (London: Samuel Bagster and Sons, 1843), 319.

As was the case for many pagan gods and heroes, there existed a number of competing ancient traditions concerning the origin of Serapis. Apollodorus, for example, told of an Argive tyrant named Apis, son of Phonoreus, who had fled to Egypt and was worshipped there after his death. This tradition was later followed by Ambrose, Augustine, and Isidore of Seville. Here, the etymology of Serapis was often given as a combination of σορός (*soros* – vessel, in this case tomb) and "Apis": hence "Sor-Apis," which later became Serapis. However, a rival origin narrative told by Plutarch (*De Iside et Osiride* 361F–362B) and Tacitus (*Historiae* 5.83–84) and later repeated by Theophile of Antioch (*Ad Autolycum* 1.9) described him as an originally Pontic idol from Sinope, who had been introduced to Egypt by one of the Ptolemies. Although Diodorus equated Serapis with Dionysus, Ammon, Zeus, and Pan (1.25), the most common opinion held him to be the Egyptian Pluto. Lactantius followed one of Diodorus' suggestions and equated him with Osiris (*Institutiones divinae* 1.21); Clement of Alexandria, meanwhile, followed Apollodorus' narrative, which he credited to Nymphodorus, in his *Stromata* (1.21), but also cited Tacitus' alternative origin story in his *Protrepticus* (4.48).

The question of Serapis' identity was especially important for two reasons. First, Serapis was often explicitly said to have been a former mortal, by Christians and pagans alike.[42] Augustine, citing Varro (*De civitate dei* 18.5), said that the statue of Serapis always kept a finger to his lips to signify that it should be kept secret that he was once human. Second, Serapis was occasionally identified with the biblical patriarch Joseph, one of the few notable examples of identifications between profane gods and biblical patriarchs in early Christian mythography. Two of the most famous testimonies came from the tenth-century Byzantine encyclopaedia known as the *Suda* and the *Historia ecclesiastica* (11.23) of the late fourth- and early fifth-century ecclesiastical historian Rufinus of Aquileia, which linked Serapis with Joseph on the basis that both were said to have saved Egypt from famine, a parallel found as early as the second century in (ps.-)Melito of Sardis' *Apologia*. This identification of Joseph and Serapis also necessitated new etymologies. An unknown rabbi in the Talmud (*Avodah Zarah* 43a) believed "Serapis" was the union of the Hebrew words "sar" (prince) and "mefis" (appeasing), since Joseph ruled over and appeased the word by distributing food. A more elaborate, and later derided, etymology came in Julius Firmicus Maternus' fourth-century *De errore profanarum religionum* (13.2) which stated that "Serapis" came from Σαρρας πάις, "son of Sarah," despite the fact that Joseph was Sarah's great-grandson. Perhaps the most important authority when it came to Serapis, however, was

---

42   Origen, *Contra Celsum* 5.27; Strabo, 17.22.

Tertullian. In his *Ad nationes* (2.8), Tertullian supposed that Joseph was divinized because he had saved the Egyptians from famine. According to Tertullian, Joseph was called Serapis because of the turban which adorned his head, the peck-like shape of which recalled the memory of Joseph's provisioning of grain.[43]

In the case of Serapis then, early modern scholars had all the ancient ammunition they needed when it came to furthering their profane and sacred synchronisms. Indeed, after 1567, when the Italian humanist Pierio Valeriano Bolzani (1477–1558) supposed that the Egyptians had erected a statue of a bull in gratitude for Joseph's prophesying of the famine, which they called Serapis, the identification of Joseph and Serapis can be found in a number and a variety of scholarly works, from sacred histories to biblical commentaries and ancient miscellanies.

Both Rufinus at the turn of the fifth century and Edward Gibbon in the late eighteenth century had noted the identification of Serapis with Joseph when discussing the destruction of the Serapeum in 391, and the same was true in the work of the great Counter-Reformation historian Cesare Baronio (1538–1607). In his monumental *Annales ecclesiastici*, originally published in twelve volumes between 1588 and 1607, Baronio supposed that the Egyptians had come to worship Joseph not only because he had saved them from famine, but also on account of the wisdom which he had imparted to them. For Baronio, the most important biblical passage was Psalm 104:20–22, which stated that:

> The King sent, and loosed him [Joseph]; the Prince of the people, and released him. He appointed him Lord of his house: and Prince of all his possession. That he might instruct his Princes as himself: and might teach his ancients wisdom.[44]

Importantly, Baronio supposed that this "prudentia" (wisdom) was not merely agricultural wisdom and the collection of grain, but knowledge of the true religion.[45] As in many other areas, Baronio' treatment of Serapis-Joseph informed the considerations of future Catholic scholars. In 1625, the Italian

---

43 See on these Louis H. Feldman, *Josephus's Interpretation of the Bible* (Berkeley and Los Angeles: University of California Press, 1998), 347–351.
44 "Misit rex et solvit eum princeps populorum et dimisit illum. Posuit eum domnium domus suae et principem in omni possessione sua. Ut erudiret principes eius secundum voluntatem suam et senes eius sapientiam." Translation based on *The Holie Bible Faithfully Translated into English*, 2:190.
45 Cesare Baronio, *Annales ecclesiastici* (Antwerp: Plantin, 1601), 4:612: "Certe quidem non frumentum tantum, sed veram Dei cognitionem Iosephum tradidisse Aegyptijs, testificatione divinae Scripturae comprobatur."

polymath Fortunio Liceti (1577–1657) explicitly followed Baronio' identification in his miscellaneous *De lucernis antiquorum reconditis* and suggested that the ancient temple to Serapis mentioned by Strabo barred entry to outsiders because inside it were preserved the remnants of the Hebrew religion. Similarly, Liceti noted that it was precisely because of the importance Joseph held for ancient Egyptian culture that he had been divinized, "since the ancients were accustomed to place among the Gods, and to venerate with divine worship, those mortals from whom they had received extraordinary favours."[46] In the same year, the Belgian Jesuit Jacques Bonfrère (1573–1642) supposed that Joseph could be identified with Serapis because he was the inventor of agriculture; this also allowed Bonfrère to identify him with Osiris on the authority of Tibullus (*Elegiae* 1.7.29–42).[47] According to Bonfrère, Osiris' description as πολυόφθαλμον, "many-eyed," related to the many branches of wisdom Joseph had taught the Egyptians.[48] In later years, such identifications between Joseph and various Egyptian gods proliferated, and Bonfrère's identification of Joseph and Osiris was later taken up by the Belgian biblical critic Jacobus Tirinus (1580–1636) and the Dutch classicist Jacob Ouseel (1631–1686).[49]

Perhaps the most famous treatment of the identification between Joseph and Serapis, however, came in Gerardus Vossius' *De theologia gentili*.[50] Vossius did not suppose that Joseph's "prudentia" extended to knowledge of the true religion. He did however divide the beneficence which Joseph had bestowed on to the Egyptian people into three kinds: his correct interpretation of the dream of the pharaoh, the wise council he gave to the pharaoh, and the prudence and loyalty with which he subsequently apportioned grain. In this sense, Vossius supposed that Joseph was critical to the maintenance and development of the Egyptian kingdom as a major, ancient, political and commercial power. Joseph's wisdom was both prophetic and practical. "It would not have been enough, if the king had known the future, if he had not also

---

46   Fortunio Liceti, *De lucernis antiquorum reconditis libb. sex* (Padua: Nicola Schiratti, 1652), 1045: "Consueverunt etenim antiqui mortales illos inter Deos referre, divinoque cultu venerari, a quibus ingentia beneficia recepissent."
47   Jacques Bonfrère, *Pentateuchus Moysis commentario illustratus* (Antwerp: Plantin, 1625), 302–303.
48   Plutarch, *De Iside et Osiride* 355A; and Diodorus, 1.11.2.
49   Jacobus Tirinus, *Commentarius in sacram scripturam* (Leiden: Joannis Girin & Bartholom. Rivière, 1683), 1:17; Jacob Ouseel, ed., *M. Minucii Felicis Octavius cum integris omnium notis ac commentariis* (Leiden: Johannes Maire, 1652), 253–254.
50   Vossius, *De theologia gentili*, 213–223. Vossius was still cited in this vein by Edward Gibbon and Edward Daniel Clarke a century later: Edward Gibbon, *Decline and Fall of the Roman Empire* (New York: Alfred A. Knopf, 1993), 3:149–150, and Edward Daniel Clarke, *Travels in Various Countries of Europe, Asia and Africa* (London: T. Cadwell and W. Davies, 1814), 3:192–193.

known how to put that knowledge to use," Vossius summarised.[51] It was precisely on account of these agricultural and political reforms that, according to Vossius, Joseph was allotted the symbol of the bull, the pagan symbol for fertility. Importantly, Joseph's identification with a bull had biblical precedence, for at Deuteronomy 33:17 Joseph's beauty was described as "quasi primogeniti tauri," like the firstborn of a bullock.[52] In the following centuries, as knowledge of Joseph waned (Exodus 1:8), the Egyptians began to worship Joseph's bull as a god in itself.

Vossius' identification was not without its critics. In his 1663 *Hierozoicon*, a survey of all the animals mentioned in the Bible, Bochart rejected the notion that Egyptians would worship one of the hated Israelites as a god and supposed that Serapis, on whom Herodotus ("quid de Diis *Aegyptiorum* tam multa scripsit") was silent, was a later Ptolemaic import to Egypt from Sinope.[53] Many of Bochart's criticisms were endorsed by Pierre Jurieu.[54] In general, however, the identification proved popular.[55] Above all, it reinforced the notion that Joseph had been pivotal for the development of primitive Egyptian culture. In this sense, the identification of Joseph and Serapis took a long-standing biblical tradition concerning Joseph's role in Egypt and united it with non-biblical, mythological evidence. Indeed, we should remember that even in such early sixteenth-century histories as the *Chronicon Carionis*, a collaboration between the Lutheran astrologer Johann Carion (1499–1537) and the Lutheran theologian Philipp Melanchthon (1497–1560), it was stated that Joseph was said to have taught the true religion in Egypt, which the Egyptians then abandoned soon after Joseph's death.[56] In the seventeenth century, this became a more generally if not always universally accepted proposition. As Theophilus Gale

---

51   Vossius, *De theologia gentili*, 216: "Non satis autem fuisset, si rex praescisset futura; nisi etiam novisset ista ad usum transferre."
52   Vossius cited Livy (4.16.2–3), and Giglio Gregorio Giraldi, *De deis gentium varia & multiplex historia* (Basel: Johannes Oporinus, 1548), 273.
53   Bochart, *Hierozoicon*, 338–339. See also Johann Georg Graevius to Claude Nicaise, 31 March 1698, BNF, NAF 4368, fol. 60v, reprinted in Fossier, *L'abbé Claude Nicaise*, 603: "Bonjurii diatribe [sic] de Josepho ad nos quoque, spero, perferetur, nunc pacato mari. Cupio illam videre, quia de Serapidis cultu semper aliter sensi."
54   Jurieu, *Histoire critique des dogmes et des cultes*, 519–521.
55   See also Stillingfleet, *Origines Sacrae*, 596; Athanasius Kircher, *Obeliscus Pamphilius* (Rome: Propaganda Fide, 1650), 260. Kircher's etymology was later taken on by John Spencer (see below).
56   Philipp Melanchthon and Johann Carion, *Chronicon Carionis latine expositum et auctum multis et veteribus et recentibus historiis, in narrationibus rerum graecarum, germanicarum et ecclesiasticarum* (Wittenberg: Georg Rhau, 1558), 37–40, especially 37: "Diligentißime vero consideretur historia Ioseph, per quem regnum Aegyptium, eo tempore florentißimum, constitutum est, & propagata vera doctrina de Deo in magna Aegypti parte."

and Georg Horn later pointed out, no less an authority than Joseph Scaliger had once suggested, in a note in his edition of Marcus Manilius' *Astronomica* (1579), that the Egyptians learnt of Creation from Joseph.[57] In his history of philosophy, first published in 1655, Horn went on to suppose that Joseph had taught some philosophy to the Egyptians, although he also supposed that the more formative influence was Abraham.[58] However, by going further and identifying this wise, influential Joseph with Serapis, scholars of *historia sacra* supposed not only that Joseph had been formative in teaching the Egyptians wisdom but also that the corrupted records and fragmented myths of the Egyptians recalled this fact.

Somewhat ironically, this idea was also taken up by John Spencer. According to Spencer, the Ark of the Covenant and the cherubs which decorated it, as described at Exodus 25, were Jewish versions of the tomb of Joseph/Serapis and the statue of the bull respectively – or more accurately, they were a Jewish "antidotum" to this form of Egyptian idolatry. The Israelites, Spencer supposed, were used to worshipping the tomb and the statue of the bull while in Egypt. The Ark and the cherubs were therefore supposed to lead the Israelites away from this infectious, pervasive, and long-standing idolatry, if in a gradual and sustainable manner. Yet by making this identification between Joseph and Serapis, Spencer also emphasised Joseph's importance for Egyptian culture and civilization:

> However, that these things said of *Serapis* do truly agree with *Joseph*, is so widely known that it is not necessary to prove further. For, as is clear out of the words of the Psalms, Joseph taught the Egyptians letters and refined their customs, at that time crude and barbarous, into a better state.[59]

---

[57] Gale, *The Court of the Gentiles*, 2:14: "these traditions they drew from no other foundation than *Joseph*, as *Jos. Scaliger ad lib. 1 Manilii* admonisheth"; Georg Horn, *Historiae philosophicae libri septem* (Leiden: Johannes Elzevir, 1655), 116; Manilius, *Manili quinque libros Astronomicon commentarius et castigationes*, ed. Joseph Scaliger (Paris: Robert Étienne, 1579), 13. See Manilius, *Astronomica*, trans. G. P. Goold (Cambridge MA: Harvard University Press, 1977), 15: "seu permixta chaos rerum primordia quondam/discrevit partu, mundumque enixa nitentem/fugit in infernas caligo pulsa tenebras" ("it may be that ages ago chaos in travail separated the mingled elements of matter and that, having given birth to the shining universe, the darkness fled, banished to infernal gloom").

[58] Horn, *Historiae philosophicae*, 111–117. In the Geneva Bible which Horn was using this passage is actually Psalm 105, whereas in the Vulgate it is Psalm 104.

[59] John Spencer, *De legibus Hebraeorum ritualibus et earum rationibus* (The Hague: Arnold Leers, 1686), 3:277: "Haec autem de *Serapi* dicta *Josepho* valde convenire, notius est quam ut multis probari debeat. Nam Josephum literis Aegyptios instruxisse & eorum

In his *De nomine*, Bonjour mobilised the identification of Serapis and Joseph in both a linguistic and historical sense. Ostensibly, the dissertation dealt, as we have noted, with a famous problem of biblical criticism, the meaning of the name given by the pharaoh to Joseph in Gen 41:45, which reads צפנת פענח – which is to say, Zaphnath-paaneah (or "pahaneah") – in the Hebrew Bible and Ψονθομφανήχ in the Septuagint. Historically, criticism on this passage was divided into two camps. Some writers, such as Josephus, Philo of Alexandria, John Chrysostom, and Theodoret, who claimed that "tsaphnath" was a corruption of the Hebrew "tsafan," meaning "to conceal," therefore interpreted the name as meaning "revealer of secrets" ("occultum revelans"). On the other side were those writers, a comfortable majority, who followed Jerome in believing the name to be a Hebrew distortion of Egyptian and who therefore translated it as "saviour of the world" ("servator mundi"). As Alastair Hamilton has pointed out, Jerome's translation presented biblical critics with a problem: since nobody else knew Egyptian, Jerome's translation had to be taken for granted.[60] That is not to say that scholars didn't try to make Jerome's translation appear more convincing, and Bonjour himself defended Jerome's translation on both historical and etymological grounds. First, he cited a somewhat ambiguous passage in Jerome's preface to his translation of the Rule of the early fourth-century monk Pachomius as proof that Jerome must have known Egyptian. Second, he stated that the Hebrew "tsaphnath," could mean "abscondere," to hide, but also "servare," to save.[61] By defending the validity of Jerome's translation Bonjour believed that he was validating the Vulgate Bible as the only biblical version which could reliably be used to interpret the chronology of the Egyptians.[62]

Mythology, however, presented an equally fertile body of evidence for substantiating Jerome's translation – if interpreted correctly. In essence, Bonjour believed that the pharaoh's name also hid the divine, profane identities of Joseph. The name "Paaneah" Bonjour linked, via the Septuagint spelling of φανήχ, back to φάνης, or "Phanes," the Greek god of Chaos whom Bonjour found mentioned in his edition of Lucan (*Pharsalia* 6.697) and Athenagoras' *Legatio pro Christianis*. From this, he linked "Chaos" or "Phanes," to Pan, or in the Egyptian version Cnef, the Egyptian demiurge said to have been born from an egg and considered by Porphyry (*Praeparatio evangelica* 3.11) to be a symbol

---

      mores, rudes adhuc & barbaros, ad formam meliorem traduxisse, e verbis Psalmistae cognoscatur."
60   Hamilton, *The Copts and the West*, 213ff.
61   *De nomine*, 2–3.
62   *De nomine*, sig. ☩3v–☩4r.

of the universe. In the Orphic hymns, this Pan had been described as the "substance of the world," or, in the words of Macrobius, "mundi simulacrum vocetur" (*Saturnalia* 7.16.8). As Macrobius noted elsewhere (*Saturnalia* 1.22.3), when the Arcadians worshipped Pan under the title of "lord of the hylê," (τὸν τῆς ὕλης κύριον), they meant "not lord of the woods, but master of all matter."[63] As a result, Bonjour argued that Joseph could be identified with Pan and that the cosmological significance of "Pan" validated the translation of "paaneah" as "mundus."

It was, however, in the context of translating "Zaphnath" as "servator" that Bonjour, in the second and third chapters of his *De nomine*, also turned to the aforementioned tradition of Serapis scholarship.[64] Here, Bonjour cited the same ancient sources as first listed by Baronio, which is to say, the hypotheses of Julius Firmicus Maternus, Rufinus, and the *Suda*. Unlike Vossius and Spencer, however, Bonjour also made significant use of a passage in Macrobius' *Saturnalia* (1.20.13). According to Macrobius, the rites of Serapis included a wicker-basket ("calathus"), which was placed on the head of Serapis, and a statue of a three-headed creature featuring the head of a lion, a dog, and a wolf. In the *De nomine*, Bonjour linked both of these ritual practices back to the biblical history of Joseph. While the wicker-basket referenced the baker's dream as interpreted by Joseph at Genesis 40, the lion was a common pagan symbol of "fructifer" (fruitfulness), and hence recalled Joseph's provisioning of grain in the famine.[65] In a similar manner Bonjour also proffered a new etymology of Serapis, arguing that it derived from the Hebrew שור ("shor," meaning "ox") and אביב ("abib," meaning "ear of corn," in Latin "spica"). The most important piece of evidence, however, was an inscription to Serapis which Bonjour discovered in the influential epigraphic compendium of the Flemish scholar Jan Gruter (1560–1627), in which Serapis was described as DEO INVICTO SERAPI SERVATORI, a saviour god.[66] Through this testimony, Bonjour was able to

---

63 *De nomine*, 3–7. See Macrobius, *Saturnalia*, ed. Robert A. Kaster (Cambridge MA: Harvard University Press, 2011), 293: "non silvarum dominum sed universae substantiae materialis dominatorem significari volentes."

64 *De nomine*, 7–26. The *De nomine* is only made up of three chapters in total.

65 *De nomine*, 13–15. Cf. Macrobius, *Saturnalia*, ed. Kaster, 275: "The city bordering on Egypt, which boasts of Alexander of Macedon as its founder, worships Sarapis and Isis with an almost crazed veneration. Yet the city gives evidence that it is really offering up that worship to the sun under Sarapis' name, when it sets a basket atop his head or joins to his image the statue of a three-headed creature." For the notion of "fructifer" see Arnobius, *Adversus nationes* 6.10.

66 *De nomine*, 7. In Jan Gruter, *Inscriptiones antiquae totius orbis Romani* (Heidelberg: Ex Officina Commeliniana, 1602–1603), 85, n. 3.

identify Serapis with Joseph on the basis that they were both regarded as a "saviour," or σωτήρ. Consequently, Jerome's translation of Zaphnath as servator was substantiated by Bonjour identifying Joseph with the saviour god Serapis. It was also in this context that Bonjour went on to identify Joseph with a number of other Egyptian gods, including Osiris, Pan, Ammon, Isis, and Epaphus. For each of these gods, both the myths recorded and the rituals practiced by the Greeks and Romans reflected some aspect of Joseph's sojourn in Egypt.

Ultimately, the importance of these identifications was two-fold. On the one hand, Bonjour used his synchronization of pagan mythology and biblical history to not only confirm the general harmony between *historia sacra* and *historia exotica* but also to solve important, and specific, questions relating to biblical history and biblical text criticism, in this case questions concerning the mysterious Egyptian name of Joseph. Consequently, even the ancient rites of the pagans could help clear up, as Scaliger once suggested, the most obscure passages in biblical history. On the other hand, Bonjour mobilised these identifications to reaffirm the importance of Joseph for aiding and helping develop what was, at that time, a rudimentary and ailing Egyptian civilization. As we have noted, this notion was already a prominent feature of seventeenth-century scholarship on the identity of Serapis, and Bonjour utilised this tradition to further illustrate his theory concerning Joseph's Egyptian name.

Joseph's relationship to Serapis remained an important question and a matter of much discussion even after Bonjour moved to Rome. In 1697, Bonjour discovered that Paulinus of Nola, a Roman poet of the late fourth and early fifth century whose manuscripts Muratori had discovered in the Ambrosiana library in Milan and was in the process of publishing, had made a similar identification.[67] Bonjour and Cuper would continue to discuss the Joseph-Serapis identification, and Paulinus' poems in particular, throughout the following years, while Bonjour's notes on Serapis were later included in Muratori's *Anecdota*.[68] Yet in the *De nomine*, Bonjour chose to conceptualise Joseph's relationship to Egyptian civilization in a fairly limited sense; that is

---

67 Paulinus of Nola, "Natalis XI," lines 96–110, and "Poema Ultimum," line 129, in Muratori, *Anecdota*, 11–12, 131. See Ludovico Antonio Muratori to Guillaume Bonjour, 15 January and 1 June 1697, in *Epistolario di L. A. Muratori*, 1:204–205, 249–250, and Gisbert Cuper to Antonio Magliabechi, 3 November 1696, BNCF, *Fondo Magliabechiano* VIII, cod. 261, fol. 37r–v.

68 See Gisbert Cuper to Guillaume Bonjour, 20 May 1698, 11 July 1699, and 27 January 1700, in Pélissier, "Lettres inédites de Gisbert Cuper," (1905): 62–69 (226–233), 75–81 (239–245), 85 (249), 89 (253); and Guillaume Bonjour to Gisbert Cuper, 7 November 1699, KW 72 H 20. See also Gisbert Cuper to Antonio Magliabechi, 12 July 1699, BNCF, *Fondo Magliabechiano* VIII, cod. 261, fol. 51v.

to say, through the specific lens of Joseph's interpretation of dreams and his vital role in the alleviation of the Egyptian famine. Although Bonjour built on a prominent tradition of mythographic scholarship on Joseph, he did not go beyond it. The *De nomine* remained, in the context of Joseph's relationship to Egyptian culture, merely a way of wetting the appetite for a much more extensive work which would demonstrate not only how Joseph had saved the Egyptians from famine, but also how he was fundamental in shaping their politics, their religion, their arts, and their sciences.

3   The Jewish Origins of Egyptian Culture: Minos, Menes, and Mercury

When reading the *De nomine*, scholars across Europe – including Huet in Avranches, who had previously expressed his "extreme passion" to see the work – were made aware that a greater project lay in the background of this little pamphlet.[69] In both the introduction and again on the final page, Bonjour made explicit reference to this larger work, which dealt not only with Joseph's name but also with Egyptian history more generally, with the connection between ancient Egypt and the Jews, and with the true pagan identity of Joseph.[70] This work was, of course, the *Mercurius aegyptiorum*, and the true pagan identity of Joseph was Mercury.

In the *Mercurius*, Bonjour significantly expanded the importance previous scholars had attributed to Joseph in the context of Egyptian civilization. If the *De nomine* built on well-established narratives, then the *Mercurius* can be said to have broken new ground. On the one hand, Bonjour identified Joseph not only with Serapis or Osiris, but with myriad other gods whom he considered important for Egyptian civilization. As a result, not just certain arts and sciences but the core of Egyptian – and consequently Gentile – civilization was derived from Joseph. On the other hand, Bonjour supposed that not just individual myths but a substantial part of the pagan mythological canon could be traced back to the biblical history of Joseph's stay in Egypt. Therefore, the pagan remembrance of Joseph's deeds was relevant not only to Egyptian history but to the origins of pagan mythology more generally. As Bonjour wrote in the introduction to his *Mercurius*:

---

69   Pierre-Daniel Huet to Claude Nicaise, 19 April 1697, BNF, Français 9359, fol. 108r: "J'aurois une extreme passion de voir ce livre sur l'origine du nom, qui fait donné a Joseph en Egypte."
70   *De nomine*, sig. ✠3v, and *De nomine*, 26.

Certainly the Romans also copied the Greeks, and paid attention to the closest disciples of the Egyptians, the Phoenicians. What is more, since the fame of Joseph possessed the whole world at that time when the famine summoned all the people of the world to Egypt – as Philo of Alexandria chiefly teaches in his work *De Josepho* – it is not remarkable, that many monuments and events relating to Joseph, hidden by an Egyptian veil, are frequently discovered as much among the Greeks as among the Romans and other peoples.[71]

It is my contention that this subtle but important shift in Bonjour's treatment of pagan mythology – and Joseph specifically – stems from the manner in which recent authors had problematized the relationship between Egypt and Israel. It is clear that Bonjour's *Mercurius* was intended to wrestle chronological primacy away from the Egyptians and back to the biblical patriarchs. Yet the construction of the *Mercurius* also suggests that, as important as La Peyrère or Marsham's specific works were, even more troublesome were the implications their understanding of Egyptian history had for the discipline of sacred history more generally. Bonjour's focus on Joseph was not merely a refutation of Marsham. Indeed, Bonjour did not cite Marsham as his opponent. Instead, he cited the work of two other scholars who had had a formative influence on his own work, Samuel Bochart and Pierre-Daniel Huet. More specifically, he cited his opposition to their specific identifications of various biblical figures with the Egyptian god Mercury.[72]

According to Bochart, Mercury could be identified with Canaan, the son of Ham and the founder of the Phoenician nation. This led Bochart to identify certain inventions and attributes for which Mercury was famous with Canaan and the Phoenician people more generally. In particular, Bochart drew attention to Mercury's reputation as the inventor of astronomy (Manilius,

---

71 *Mercurius*, fol. 4v: "Latini vero et Graecos exscripsunt, et proximos Aegyptiorum discipulos audiere Phoenices. Imo cum fama Josephi totum obtinuerit orbem, quo tempore Gentes universas universalis fames Aegypto accersivit; ut maxime docet Philo Judaeus in libro de Joseph: mirum non est, plura Aegyptio tecta velamine Josephi monumenta et momenta tum apud Graecos cum apud Latinos aliasque gentes passim reperiri." See also Philo, "De Josepho," in *Philo. Volume VI*, trans. F. H. Colson (Cambridge MA: Harvard University Press, 1935), 217: "But when the seven years during which the plains bore plentifully were ended, the famine began and spread and grew till Egypt could not hold it. It overran successively the cities and countries which lay in its path to the utmost limits of east and west, and rapidly made itself master of the whole civilized world round Egypt."

72 *Mercurius*, fol. 2v: "Illustrissimo quidem scriptori, ornamento praesulum, literariae reipublicae lumini, et in *evangelica demonstratione* numquam satis laudando, Mercurius ille non alius videtur quàm Moses: visus et alteri etiam doctissimo Chanaanus fuerat."

Astronomica 1.30–34), and the inventor of the alphabet (Eusebius, *Praeparatio evangelica* 1.9). For Bochart, this suggested that the biblical Canaan, and consequently the Phoenicians as a people, were the true inventors of astronomy (and, consequently, maritime navigation, which relied on astronomical knowledge) and of Greek letters.[73] In later years, Bochart's identification between Mercury and Canaan found a number of adherents, if a good deal fewer than his comparison of Noah and Saturn.[74]

More famous – and, as we shall see, more problematic – was the manner in which Huet treated Moses in his *Demonstratio evangelica*. Ostensibly, Huet had advanced his identifications of pagan gods with Moses in order to re-establish the primacy of the Hebrews and the Mosaic authorship of the Pentateuch.[75] According to Huet, the wisdom of Moses and consequently the contents of the Mosaic Pentateuch pertained not merely to Moses' history of the beginning of the world and his construction of the Jewish law, but also to the origins of the arts and sciences, from such major disciplines as law, geography, political science, and religious rituals to specific arts like architecture, cobbling, smelting, and wool-dying. In the background to Huet's treatment of Moses lay the work of Artapanus, a Jewish-Egyptian historian of the second century BC who had adapted the life of Moses to Greek mythological narratives and who first suggested that the Egyptians worshipped Moses as a god.[76] Consequently, Huet supposed that all Gentile arts and sciences must have Hebraic, specifically Mosaic, origins. In the context of Marsham and Spencer's recent work, however, this suggestion also presented a major problem. As Jan Assmann and Dmitri Levitin have outlined, a central contention of Marsham and Spencer's

---

73 Bochart, *Geographia sacra*, 12–13.
74 David Derodon, *Disputatio theologica, de existentia Dei* (Geneva: Pierre Chouët, 1661), 47; Wilhelm Christoph Kriegsmann, *Conjecturaneorum de Germanicae gentis origine, ac conditore Hermete Trismegisto, qui S. Moysi est Chanaan, Tacito Tuito, Mercuriusque gentilibus* (Tübingen: Philibert Brunn, 1684), 11, 25, 33, 37–39, 42; Johannes Braun, *Vestitus sacerdotum Hebraeorum* (Leiden: Arnoldus Doudius, 1680), 328; see also Johann Bompart, *Parallela sacra et profana, sive notae in Genesin* (Amsterdam: Johannes Wolters, 1689), 60.
75 Huet, *Demonstratio evangelica*, 66–67.
76 Huet, *Demonstratio evangelica*, 112: "rerum omnium primordia libro suo Moses complexus est, nec mundi solum & naturae, sed religionis etiam & Theologiae, historiae quoque humani generis & animalium, Geographiae, politicae scientiae, castrensis disciplinae, aequi bonique ac legum ferendarum doctrinae, staticae artis, architectonicae fabrilis, fusoriae, sutoriae, baphicae, coriariae, phrygionicae, aliarumque complurium; sanxit idem sacrificia ac perpetuos ritus sacrorum; annum sacrum & civilem festis distinxit quibusdam, spatia temporum in certas discrevit periodos; & Israelitis leges tulit. Merito ergo scripsit Pseudo-Eustathius in Hexaemeron, & ante Eustathium Artapanus in libro De Judaeis, armorum, navigiorum, antliarum, tollenonum, sacrarum literarum, & civilis disciplinae inventionem Mosi Aegyptios debere."

reinterpretation of the relationship between Hebrew and Egyptian culture was that Moses was essentially an Egyptianized Hebrew. Both Marsham and Spencer took seriously Stephen's famous comment that Moses had been educated "in omni sapientia Aegyptiorum," in all the wisdom of the Egyptians (Acts 7:22).[77] This had important ramifications for Huet's treatment of Moses. Essentially, Huet's identification did not manage to adequately refute Marsham's argument that Egyptian civilization preceded that of the Jews. If Marsham explicitly suggested that the arts and sciences which the Egyptians had passed on to the Greeks and Romans predated the biblical patriarchs, then Huet could be seen as supporting the notion that the Mosaic wisdom which was the basis for Gentile civilization was itself Egyptian.

We should therefore see Bonjour's *Mercurius* as not only a refutation of La Peyrère and Marsham but also a corrective of Huet. Fundamentally, Moses marked the exit of the Jews from Egypt, the moment after which Jewish culture isolated itself from that of neighbouring pagan nations. The figure of Joseph, however, marked the opposite: the entry of the Israelites into Egypt, and the beginning of the most extensive and long-lasting interaction between Jewish and Gentile civilization until the destruction of Jerusalem and the beginning of the Babylonian captivity over a millennium later. In this sense, Bonjour aimed to not merely underline Hebraic primacy, but also to replace Moses with Joseph as the most influential biblical patriarch in the context of ancient pagan culture and philosophy. As Leibniz pointed out to Ezekiel Spanheim in 1697, Bonjour sought to prove that Moses' *sapientia Aegyptiorum* had Hebraic origins.[78] Abbé Jules Bellet (1672–1752), then living in Bordeaux where he saw drafts of the *Mercurius* while Bonjour was still in France, described the project in a similar fashion. Your work, he wrote to Bonjour in 1696, will demonstrate, in opposition to the famous identification once voiced by Clement of Alexandria, that Hermes Trismegistus was not Moses but Joseph.[79]

In order to better demonstrate the manner in which Bonjour used pagan mythological evidence to subvert Huet's treatment on Moses, I will focus on the way Bonjour treated three particularly important figures from pagan mythology in his *Mercurius*: the Cretan lawgiver Minos, the mythical founder of the Egyptian kingdom Menes, and the aforementioned Greek, originally Egyptian, god Mercury. In each case, Bonjour sought to identify the deity in question with Joseph and thereby to reassert Hebraic primacy in light of the recent work by La Peyrère and Marsham. Yet I also hope to show how these

---

77 Assmann, *Moses the Egyptian*, 56–78; Levitin, *Ancient Wisdom*, 113–229.
78 G. W. Leibniz to Ezekiel Spanheim, 4 July 1697, in LAA, I, 14:332.
79 Jules Bellet to Guillaume Bonjour, 20 August 1696, BAR, ms.lat.395, fol. 97r.

identifications led Bonjour to not only significantly expand the importance of non-biblical, mythological testimony but also to subject the history of the biblical patriarchs to a Greek mythological framework which viewed primordial history as the progress of human civilization from a savage and bestial state to one of refined culture.

3.1   Minos

In the *Demonstratio evangelica*, Huet paid special attention to Minos, whom he considered the pagan lawgiver *primus inter pares* and the founder ("repertor") of many legal and constitutional reforms which had helped elevate his subjects from their barbaric state.[80] According to Huet, the many ancient arts and laws which Strabo (10.8) had claimed were the invention of Minos and originated in Crete were in actual fact inventions of Moses and had reached Greece via Egypt.[81] Huet's starting point was the ancient divinity "Monios," the original name of the Emesan sun-god Monimus, whom Julian the Apostate had once identified with Mercury.[82] In the seventeenth century, this identification was also advanced by Vossius and Bochart.[83] Huet, however, went further by identifying him with Moses, claiming that Monios was not only a corruption of Monimus but also derived from Moses' Egyptian name "Moni." Specifically, Huet cited Ibn Ezra's suggestion, taken from the so-called *Nabatean agriculture* (translated into Arabic by Ibn Wahshiyya at the turn of the tenth century), that "Moni" was comprised of the Egyptian "Mo" (water) and the suffix "ni," meaning "ex." The biblical evidence for this assumption came from Exodus 2:10, when the pharaoh's daughter plucked baby Moses from the reeds of the Nile, "whom she adopted into the place of a sun, and called him Moses, saying: Because from the water I did take him."[84] Hence, Moses' Egyptian name referred back to his peculiar discovery and meant nothing other than "ex acqua."

Bonjour's work on Minos and Joseph perfectly encapsulates the manner in which he took on Huet's basic understanding of the relationship between Hebrew originals and pagan myths but sought to wrest them away from the

---

80 Huet, *Demonstratio evangelica*, 166–171.
81 Huet, *Demonstratio evangelica*, 167: "Idem Deos omnes, & collata a Diis in homines beneficia, artium nempe omnium inventionem, & bonorum largitionem, ex Creta docet esse profecta: quod ex Mose nimirum, Mosisque scriptionibus profluxerit Mythologia, & fabularis omnis Deorum historia; artiumque & utilitatum complurium primus ipse repertor extiterit, quae & supra jam attigimus, & in sequentibus declarabuntur."
82 Huet, *Demonstratio evangelica*, 107, and 167: "ex Monios itidem excusa est vox Minos." See also Levitin, *Ancient Wisdom*, 154.
83 Bochart, *Geographia sacra*, 811–812; Vossius, *De theologia gentili*, 328.
84 Huet, *Demonstratio evangelica*, 107; *The Holie Bible Faithfully Translated*, 1:144.

Mosaic context in which Huet had first advanced them. Bonjour first brought up Minos when comparing the prison in which Potiphar had imprisoned Joseph with the labyrinth in which Minos had kept his minotaur. In Bonjour's opinion, the different labyrinths of pagan mythology were, in similar fashion to the many mythological floods, corruptions of a single biblical original. In response to Diodorus (1.61.4) and Pliny (36.19), who suggested that the labyrinth was originally Cretan, Bonjour cited a famous classical notion, first voiced by Epimenides (*Cretica*; cf. Callimachus *Hymn* 1.8) and later repeated by the Apostle Paul (Titus 1:12–13), that the Cretans were "semper mendaces," eternal liars.[85] "Therefore, without a doubt I trace these things, which the poets, and other composers of fables, sing about the Cretan Labyrinth, back to the proposed Labyrinth of the Egyptians," Bonjour concluded.[86] Like Huet, Bonjour supposed that Minos was famous above all as a νομοθέτης ... σπουδαῖος, an excellent lawgiver. In the *Mercurius* he cited the testimonies of Strabo (10.8) and Plato (*Minos* 317D): whilst Strabo had claimed that Minos had not only set up laws but also united various peoples into a single unified political constitution, Socrates, in Plato's *Minos*, had called Minos a good administrator of land. Bonjour supposed that these testimonies referred back to Joseph's agricultural policies, in particular the division and reorganisation of land as described at Genesis 41:34–35. For Bonjour, this proved that Joseph not only made laws but was also remembered in Egyptian and later Greek mythology, as "providentissimae legis auctor et conditor," the author and founder of the most prudent law.[87] This notion also saw Bonjour change which "law" Minos was supposed to have established. According to Huet, Minos-Moses was known as a wise lawgiver because he was the author of the Mosaic law. According to Bonjour, Minos-Joseph was famed for the constitutional and economic laws he had established in ancient Egypt, which not only proved vital for saving the world during the famine but also proved formative in the creation of the Egyptian kingdom itself.

3.2   *Menes*

Of similar importance was the identification Bonjour made between Joseph and Menes, the mythical first king of the Egyptians. In like manner to Minos, Bonjour first advanced this identification when discussing Joseph's prison. Bonjour derived the etymology of labyrinth from "leborim-thush," which he

---

85   *Mercurius*, fol. 36r.
86   *Mercurius*, fol. 36r: "Quae igitur de Labyrintho Cretico decantant poetae, aliique fabularum contextores, haec ad expositum Aegyptiorum Labyrinthum absque dubio refero."
87   *Mercurius*, fol. 106r.

translated as "an underground prison." This prison Bonjour was able to link to Menes on the authority of Diodorus (1.89.3), who claimed that alongside founding a city called the "city of Crocodiles," Menes τὸν θαυμαζόμενον παρὰ πολλοῖς λαβύρινθον οἰκοδομῆσαι ("built the Labyrinth which is admired by many").[88] Bonjour's identification of Joseph and Menes was above all critical from a chronological perspective, allowing Bonjour to prove that Egyptian civilization did not precede Joseph.

Bonjour's identification was itself predicated on an eclectic, we might say ingenious, reinterpretation of early Egyptian history. As we have pointed out, most ancient and early modern scholars thought Menes the first pharaoh of Egypt. Ostensibly, this proved problematic because Moses recorded that Abraham had already met a pharaoh in Egypt some two hundred years before Joseph (Genesis 12:10–20).[89] Bonjour, however, circumvented this issue through a creative interpretation of a vital passage in Diodorus' *Bibliotheca historica* (1.70.1–3). Diodorus had claimed that:

> In the first place, then, the life which the kings of the Egyptians lived was not like that of other men who enjoy autocratic power and do in all matters exactly as they please without being held to account, but all their acts were regulated by prescriptions set forth in laws, not only their administrative acts, but also those that had to do with the way in which they spent their time from day to day, and with the food which they ate. In the matter of their servants, for instance, not one was a slave, such as had been acquired by purchase or born in the home, but all were sons of the most distinguished priests, over twenty years old and the best educated of their fellow-countrymen, in order that the king, by virtue of his having the noblest men to care for his person and to attend him throughout both day and night, might follow no low practices; for no ruler advances far along the road of evil unless he has those about him who will minister to his passions.[90]

Bonjour supposed that this was an accurate representation of Egypt before Joseph was appointed vizier. Rather than being a major ancient kingdom,

---

88   *Mercurius*, fol. 34r.
89   As pointed out by Pezron, *Antiquité des tems*, 80: "Ce ne sont point là des fables, puisqu'il est constant par l'Ecriture, que lorsqu' *Abraham* entra en Egypte, il y avoit deja des *Pharaons*."
90   Cited in *Mercurius*, fols. 103v, 119r. Translation from Diodorus, *Library of History*, ed. Oldfather, 241.

Egypt had been a constitutional government of loosely collected states administered locally, over which the pharaoh had no real power. This changed when the pharaoh made Joseph his vizier, and Joseph enacted a series of legislative, administrative, and constitutional reforms which abolished the old system of governance and founded an Egyptian kingdom which placed full autocratic, political power into the hands of the pharaoh. According to Bonjour, this development was referenced explicitly in Genesis 47:20–22:

> Joseph therefore bought all the Land of Egypt, every man selling his possessions for the greatness of the famine. And he brought it under the Pharaohs hands, and all the people thereof from the farthest ends of Egypt, even to the uttermost coasts thereof, save the land of the Priests, which the King had delivered them.[91]

From this Bonjour concluded that:

> This [i.e., Diodorus' narrative] was the method of governance of the kings who preceded Joseph: but when all the affairs of this pharaoh were made to depend on the power and governance of that man who raised himself to such great honour, the status of republic was changed, and the highest and the royal right was attached to the pharaonic office; to such an extent that in later years the Egyptians were not allowed to obey their king [merely] as they chose.[92]

Bonjour's interpretation of early Egyptian history was not wholly original. In 1625, the German jurist Christopher Besold (1577–1638) had supposed, citing Diodorus, that ancient Egypt was the example of an ideal mixed constitution.[93] More recently, Noël Alexandre had cited Diodorus' passage on the early constitutional government of Egypt and remarked that "if the Egyptians were judged on account of [their] religion, they would have been considered the most

---

91　*The Holie Bible Faithfully Translated*, 1:131.
92　*Mercurius*, fols. 103v–104r: "Hujus certe regiminis ratio regum erat, qui Josephum anteverterunt: at cum istius in potestate ac moderatione versa sunt omnia hujus Pharaonis, qui ad tantum honorem ipsum evexerat, reipublicae status mutatus est, ac summum et monarchicum jus Pharaonico imperio accersitum; adeo ut in posterum non licuerit Aegyptiis, ut pro arbitratu obtemperarent regi."
93　Christoph Besold, "Dissertatio Singularis de Statu Reipublicae Mixto," in *Dissertatio politico-iuridica de majestate in genere: ejusque juribus specialibus, in tres sectiones distributa* (Strasbourg: Lazar Zetzner, 1625), 229. Both Besold and Bonjour used the translation by Lorenz Rhodomann, first published in 1604.

insane of all men: if on account of [their] politics, the wisest."[94] Furthermore, Bonjour's suggestion that Joseph was not only culturally but also politically important had an ancient precursor in the form of Philo of Alexandria's *De Josepho*. Philo, whom Bonjour cited in the preface to the *Mercurius*, had explicitly characterised Joseph as a politician, "πολιτικός."[95] Moreover, Philo had claimed that, despite being only the vizier to the pharaoh, true political authority rested in Joseph's hands. "The Pharaoh," wrote Philo, "then appointed Joseph viceroy of the kingdom, or rather, if the truth be said, king, reserving indeed to himself the name of the office, but resigning to Joseph the actual sovereignty and doing everything else that might give the young man honour" (*De Josepho* 119–120).[96]

Yet it was in Bonjour's *Mercurius* that this identification was explicitly mobilised to respond to a pressing contemporary issue directly related to biblical authority, the question of the ancient historical relationship between Egypt and Israel. Although Egyptians had existed before Joseph, Egypt as both a political and cultural power had only sprung into existence contemporaneously with, and due to, the efforts of Joseph. Even if there had existed pharaohs who preceded Joseph, their power was non-existent and their society crude, barbarous, and insignificant. Menes, who was Joseph and therefore also Mercury, was not the first Egyptian king chronologically speaking, but he was called the first ruler of Egypt by Herodotus and "passim rerum Aegyptiorum scriptores" because the Egyptian dynasties which Manetho recorded and the Egyptian gods which later formed the basis of Greco-Roman mythology only emerged during his reign.[97] As Bonjour summarised: "with that new magistracy Joseph added such fame to the pharaonic kingdom that the monarchy of Egypt should be said to have begun only from then."[98]

3.3   Mercury

However, despite the importance of Minos and Menes, few figures from pagan mythology had, in the context of ancient Egypt, a more important role than Mercury, and it is this identification which therefore forms the crux of Bonjour's *Mercurius*. "The legendary race of Mercury is well known," wrote Bonjour, "but his historical account is undiscovered, and very obscure, beset by

---

94 Alexandre, *Selecta historiae ecclesiasticae*, 2:126: "Si ex Religione aestimentur Aegyptii, omnium hominum amentissimi: Si ex politica, sapientissimi habebuntur."
95 *Mercurius*, fol. 4v.
96 *Mercurius*, fol. 103r. Translation from Philo, *Volume VI*, trans. Colson, 199.
97 *Mercurius*, fol. 104r.
98 *Mercurius*, fol. 103v: "Novo illo magistratu talem regno pharaonico claritatem addidit Joseph, ut monarchia Aegypti ex tunc solum incoepisse dicenda sit."

so many difficulties, obstructed by so many alien tongues."⁹⁹ By investigating the true origin of Mercury, Bonjour hoped to also reveal the true history of Joseph and consequently the true relationship between Egyptian and Jewish antiquity.

In classical mythography, Mercury was thought to be responsible for the invention of Egyptian law, wisdom, and, above all, "letters."¹⁰⁰ In a famous passage from the *De natura deorum* (3.22 (56)), Cicero had supposed that there existed five different ancient gods all known as "Mercury" and that the fifth, called "Theuth," had fled from Argos to Egypt where "qui Aegyptiis leges & litteras tradidisse," he gave the Egyptians their laws and letters.¹⁰¹ Francesco Bianchini, citing a popular etymology he derived from Hyginus (*Fabulae* 277), supposed that "hermeneutics" had derived from Ἑρμῆς.¹⁰² It was principally on the basis of their shared relationship to the invention of letters that the Roman Mercury and the Greek Hermes were identified with the Alexandrian Thoth, the Phoenician Taautus (Eusebius, *Praeparatio evangelica* 1.9), the Gallic Mercurius (Julius Caesar, *De bello Gallico* 6.17), and even, in some cases, with the mythical Chinese king Fohi.¹⁰³ Furthermore, the importance of the Greek Mercury was augmented through the Hellenistic amalgamation of Mercury with "Hermes Trismegistus." In the Middle Ages and the Renaissance – and particularly after Marsilio Ficino's translation of the *Corpus Hermeticum* in 1471 – this Hermes Trismegistus, or Thoth, was popularly regarded as an important pagan prophet of Christian truths, partly on the authority of Lactantius (*Institutiones divinae* 1.6).¹⁰⁴ Although Isaac Casaubon (1559–1614) famously

---

99 "De origine et cognatione patriarchae Josephi gentilitio Mercurii stemmate," BAR, ms.lat.631, fol. 168r: "Notum quoque fabulosum Mercurii genus: sed incomperta et perobscura est ratio ejus historica, tot obsepta difficultatibus, tot labefactata veterum figmentis, tot peregrinis vocibus obstructa."

100 See also Diodorus, 1.16, 5.75.1–3.

101 Translation from Cicero, *De natura deorum*, trans. H. Rackham (Cambridge MA: Harvard University Press, 1951), 341: "hic est ille, qui Aegyptiis leges & literas tradidit." See Vossius, *De theologia gentili*, 128, 203.

102 Bianchini, *La istoria universale*, 226–227; see also Heilbron, "Francesco Bianchini, Historian," 248.

103 See Eusebius, *Eusebii Pamphili evangelica praeparationis libri XV*, ed. E. H. Gifford (Oxford: Oxford University Press, 1903), 1:42: "Τούτων οὕτως ἐχόντων, ὁ Σαγχουνιάθων ἀνὴρ πολυμαθὴς γενόμενος καί τὰ ἐξ ἀρχῆς, ἀφ᾽ οὗ τὰ πάντα συνέστη, παρὰ πάντων εἰδέναι ποθῶν, πολὺ φροντιστικῶς ἐξεμάστευσε τὰ Τααύτου, εἰδὼς ὅτι τῶν ὑφ᾽ ἡλίῳ γεγονότων πρῶτός ἐστι Τάαυτος ὁ τῶν γραμμάτων τὴν εὕρεσιν ἐπινοήσας, καὶ ἀπὸ τοῦδε ὥσπερ κρηπῖδα βαλόμενος τοῦ λόγου, ὃν Αἰγύπτιοι μὲν ἐκάλεσαν Θωύθ, Ἀλεξανδρεῖς δε Θώθ, Ἑρμῆν δὲ Ἕλληνες μετέφρασαν." For Fohi, see Jules Bellet to Guillaume Bonjour, 20 August 1696, BAR, ms.lat.395, fol. 97r.

104 See Frances Yates, *Giordano Bruno and the Hermetic Tradition* (London and New York: Routledge, 1964), and Walker, *The Ancient Theology*.

demonstrated, in 1614, that the Hermetic corpus, the collection of esoteric writings attributed to Hermes Trismegistus, was a forgery, the discrediting of the corpus did not necessarily lead to the discrediting of Hermes Trismegistus.[105] Most scholars continued to believe that an ancient figure known as Hermes – inventor of wisdom, patron of the sciences, sacred scribe of the priests – had really existed, without believing in the authenticity of those works once thought to be his. Two key pagan texts of the period, Sanchuniathon's history of Phoenicia and Manetho's history of Egypt, still claimed Mercury or Thoth as their original source. As a result, scholars came to suppose that correctly identifying the mortal origins of Mercury was crucial for understanding the origins of Egyptian civilization. In his entry on Egyptian historians in the *Bibliothèque universelle des historiens*, the French ecclesiastical historian Louis Ellies Dupin called Mercury the oldest profane historian in the world. According to Dupin, Mercury was the origin of letters and laws, the highest Egyptian god, and the inventor of many things "utiles à la vie."[106] This notion was largely shared. Even Pierre Bayle, in his entry on John Marsham in the *Dictionnaire historique et critique*, commented that correctly elucidating the nature of Mercury's age was vital because "it wonderfully clears up the most remote antiquity, by discovering the origin of idolatry, and the source of all sciences."[107]

In the early modern period, the most common supposition was that Mercury was Moses. Already in the early fifteenth century, the Spanish humanist Juan Luis Vives (1493–1540) identified Mercury and Moses on the authority of Artapanus, whose work was preserved in Eusebius' *Praeparatio evangelica* (9.18, 23, 27).[108] In particular, Vives supposed that Moses and Mercury could be identified on

---

105   Grafton, "Isaac Casaubon on Hermes Trismegistus," in *Defenders of the Text*, 145–161.
106   Louis Ellies Dupin, "Section IV: Des Historiens Egyptiens," in *Bibliothèque universelle des historiens* (Paris: Pierre Giffart, 1707), 1:33–34.
107   Pierre Bayle, "John Marsham," in *A General Dictionary Historical and Critical*, trans. John Peter Bernard, Thomas Birch, and John Lockman (London: James Bettenham, 1738), 7:474; Bayle cited this from François Sevin, "Dissertation sure Menés ou Mercure, premier Roi d'Egypte. Contre le Système de Marsham & de Bochart," *Journal des sçavans* (1710): 609: "nécessaire, qu'elle éclaircit merveilleusement l'Antiquité la plus reculée, en découvrant l'origine de l'Idolâtrie, & la source de toutes les sciences."
108   On Artapanus (and Eupolemus), see Ben Zion Wacholder, "Biblical Chronology in the Hellenistic World Chronicles," *Harvard Theological Review* 61 (1968): 460–462; Droge, *Homer or Moses?*, 33ff.; and Lester L. Grabbe, "Jewish Identity and Hellenism in the Fragmentary Jewish Writings in Greek," in *Scripture and Traditions: Essays on Early Judaism and Christianity in Honor of Carl R. Holladay*, ed. Patrick Gray and Gail R. O'Day (Leiden and Boston: Brill, 2008), 21–31.

THE WISDOM OF THE EGYPTIANS 175

the basis of their shared invention of writing.[109] This notion was also taken up by Theophilus Gale. According to Gale, the Egyptians supposed that Hermes, or Theuth, was "the inventor of their Arts and Sciences."[110] At certain points, Gale suggested that one could align Hermes with Joseph, who had been employed by the Pharaoh "*to teach the Ancients Wisdom to instruct their Elders*, that is, their *Priests*."[111] Gale's chosen biblical passage was Psalm 104:22, as once also used by Baronio. Yet Gale still supposed that the main parallel between Joseph and Mercury was not wisdom or letters, but prophecy – a notion also taken up by the English Calvinist John Edwards (1637–1716).[112] For Gale, the true Jewish source of Egyptian wisdom was therefore not Joseph but Moses:

> Amongst all the Divine Philosophers, there was none that opened a more effectual door, for the propagation of *philosophick principles* and *light*, than *Moses*; who by his writings, contained in his five books (besides his personal Conferences) laid the main foundations of all that Philosophie, which first the *Phoenicians* and *Egyptians*, and from them the *Grecians*, were masters of.[113]

Gale therefore concluded that "so the name *Mercurie*, or *Thoth*, was given to *Joseph*, as he was a person *divinely inspired* for the *interpreting* of *dreams*, &c. and the same name was given unto *Moses*, as the *Inventor of Letters*."[114]

In his *Demonstratio evangelica*, Huet took Mercury's – and by extension Moses' – importance for Egyptian culture even further.[115] According to Huet, Mercury was the foremost god in both Phoenician and Egyptian theology. Consequently, Huet began his discussions of both theologies by identifying Moses with the Phoenician Taautus and the Egyptian "Theuth."[116] For Huet, Mercury – and therefore Moses – was, on the authority of Sanchuniathon and Cicero, the inventor of letters; and, on the authority of Strabo (17.46), Manilius (*Astronomica* 1.25–37), and Plato (*Phaedrus* 274C–D), the inventor of astronomy and geometry. Indeed, citing Lactantius (who had expanded on Cicero's division

---

109 Juan Luis Vives, *En habes optime lector absolutissimi doctoris Aurelij Augustini, opus absolutissimum, de Civitate dei* ... (Basel: Froben, 1522), 615. The passage from Augustine is 18.39.
110 Gale, *The Court of the Gentiles*, 2:1:13.
111 Gale, *The Court of the Gentiles*, 2:1:13.
112 John Edwards, *A Discourse Concerning the Authority, Stile, and Perfection of the Books of the Old and New Testament* (London: Richard Wilkin, 1693), 216–217.
113 Gale, *The Court of the Gentiles*, 2:1:14.
114 Gale, *The Court of the Gentiles*, 1:1:57.
115 Huet, *Demonstratio evangelica*, 106–115.
116 Huet, *Demonstratio evangelica*, 106; see Plato *Phaedrus* 274C–D, and *Philebus* 18B–C.

of the five Mercuries by suggesting that the fifth was Hermes Trismegistus), Huet went on to call Mercury "instructissimum omni genere doctrinae fuisse," greatly instructed in all manner of learning (*Institutiones divinae* 1.6).[117]

Throughout the *Mercurius*, Bonjour took those pagan sources which Huet had used to identify Moses and Mercury in order to identify Mercury with Joseph. Hence if Huet had aligned Lucian's claim that Mercury was a "beautiful" (καλός) new-born boy (*Dialogi deorum* 11) with Exodus 2:2, in which Moses was called a "filius elegans," then Bonjour took this description and aligned it with Genesis 39:6, in which Joseph was described as "pulchra facie et decorus aspectu" (of a beautiful countenance, and comely to behold).[118] However, identifying Joseph with the invention of writing, as Huet had done in the case of Mercury, proved more of a challenge. Although rejected by Augustine, it had long been supposed by a variety of scholars that writing had been invented by Moses, who had first written down the laws and ancient history of the world.[119] There was, however, no comparable tradition for Joseph. This posed an immediate and major problem for Bonjour: for if he wanted to convincingly identify Mercury and Joseph, then he must logically find a way of proving that Mercury's most important contribution to human civilization, the invention of writing, was, in actual fact, the invention of the Hebrew patriarch Joseph.

Once again, Bonjour turned to the fertile ground provided by the diverse body of pagan myths and ancient interpretations of Hebrew scripture. In his work on the Flood Bonjour had supposed, when discussing the chronology of the dove, that "non exprimit scriptura." We find a similar admission on folio 19 of the *Mercurius* when discussing the invention of writing: "de literis a Josepho in Aegyptum delatis nihil habeatur in sacris paginis" (there is nothing contained in the holy scriptures about letters having been delivered by Joseph to Egypt).[120] Consequently Bonjour, as in the case of Abydenus, was forced to rely on extra-biblical testimony – that is to say, historical information not preserved in the authoritative Vulgate text. Specifically, Bonjour relied on a

---

117 Huet, *Demonstratio evangelica*, 112.
118 Huet, *Demonstratio evangelica*, 109; *Mercurius*, fol. 9r. A similar description of Moses is Justin, *Epitome* 36.2.11: "His son was Moses, whom, besides the inheritance of his father's knowledge, the comeliness of his person also recommended." Translation from E. Richmond Hodges, ed., *Ancient Fragments of the Phoenician, Carthaginian, Babylonian, Egyptian and other Authors* (London: Reeves & Turner, 1876), 80.
119 *De civitate dei* 18.39. See further Touber, "Tracing the Human Past," and for an illustrative contemporary debate, "Commercium Epistolare Ludovici Bourgueti et Gisberti Cuperi," in *Miscellanea lipsiensia nova ad incrementum scientarum*, ed. Friedrich Otto Mencke (Leipzig: B. Lanckischens Erben, 1752–1753).
120 *Mercurius*, fol. 19v.

somewhat eclectic interpretation of two sources. The first was the testimony of the first-century AD Stoic historian Chaeremon, who was also a noted anti-Jewish polemicist.[121] In his history of Egypt, partially preserved by Josephus, Chaeremon had described Joseph, whom he considered contemporaneous with Moses, as an ἱερογραμματέα, a sacred scribe (*Contra Apionem* 1.290–29). The second source were the Targums, Jewish Aramaic translations of the Hebrew Bible. In particular, Bonjour focussed on the testimony of two Targums, the Targum Onkelos, an Aramaic translation of the Pentateuch ascribed to the Jewish convert Onkelos, a contemporary of (and potentially identifiable with) Aquila of Sinope, one of the first translators of the Jewish Bible into Greek in the first century AD; and the Targum Jonathan, which was traditionally attributed to the first-century BC Jewish scholar Jonathan ben Uzziel, a student of the religious leader Hillel the Elder. According to the Vulgate text translated by Jerome, which Bonjour regarded as the most faithful contemporary witness to the *Hebraica veritas*, Genesis 39:11 read "et operis quippiam absque arbitris faceret," [Joseph] was doing some business without any man with him. Bonjour, however, pointed to the fact that Targum Onkelos read "ut investigaret scripturas rationis suae," and the Targum Jonathan "ut investigaret tabellas rationis suae": in order that he [Joseph] examine the writing of his accounts.[122] Neither Chaeremon nor the Targums were particularly explicit. Yet their suggestion of a link between Joseph and "writing" proved sufficient for Bonjour to suggest some link between Joseph and the presence of "letters" in Egypt on the one hand, and between the pagan god Mercury and the invention of writing on the other. Given the amount of evidence which Bonjour had supplied to identify Joseph and Mercury throughout the rest of the work, these sources could at least serve to support an identification which Bonjour had proved more extensively elsewhere.

4 Sacred History and the Origins of Human Civilization

Bonjour built his identifications between the sacred and the profane, as I hope to have shown, on the assumption that myth was verifiable historical data and could therefore be used to substantiate such orthodox principles as Hebraic primacy and the historical authority of the biblical account. His focus on Joseph and Mercury was built upon two prominent traditions in seventeenth-century

---

121 In his history of ancient Egypt, preserved in Josephus' *Contra Apionem*, he followed Manetho in calling the Israelites lepers: *Contra Apionem* 1.299.
122 *Mercurius*, fol. 19v.

scholarship, the first a growing propensity to suppose that Joseph was formative for Egyptian culture and civilization, the second that Mercury was the most important pagan god for understanding the origins of the arts and sciences. The amalgamation of these two traditions allowed him to refute La Peyrère and Marsham and offer a corrective to Huet. Yet this notionally "orthodox" use of pagan myth also had ramifications for sacred history more generally. Firstly, Bonjour continued to accord a far greater importance to non-biblical, pagan, evidence in writing the history of the patriarchs. Secondly, he further blurred the distinction between *historia sacra* and *historia exotica* and the historical relationship between Jewish and Egyptian religion. Even in refuting Marsham, Bonjour supposed that there were clear and extensive correspondences and influences between the two nations. Thirdly, his work also reconceptualised what *historia sacra* was *about*. Rather than supposing it to be merely the divine history of the Jewish patriarchs, Bonjour approached the biblical record through the perspective of a Greek mythological narrative which emphasised how pagan gods were responsible for the origins and dissemination of the arts and sciences, which, in turn, lifted ancient nations out of their state of barbarity and towards civilization. In doing so, the traditional distinction between *historia* and *fabula* was further complicated. Not only did *fabula* contain key evidence for *historia*, but individuals from *historia* were analysed in terms taken from Greek *fabula*.

Consequently, Bonjour's work, despite being conducted within the framework of *historia sacra*, already advanced a number of mythographic principles which, according to Frank Manuel, only originated once scholars abandoned their biblicist or diffusionist approach to pagan myth. Perhaps most importantly, Bonjour supposed that mythology narrated not of higher philosophical truths, but of a feral and primitive human society. Life in the time of Necherophes, the first pharaoh whom Abraham had visited in Genesis 12, was crude and primitive:

> For these things are thoroughly suggested by the first phrases and rudiments of the principality founded by that little king, namely Necherophes, the predecessor of the first Osiris, who, being absolutely preoccupied with building Memphis and, in this matter, serving his own needs, and not being sufficiently knowledgeable to manage a republic, did not lead the Egyptians, living everywhere in tents, from a feral and rustic life to humane and civil civilization, nor did he dispel the barbarity from their customs.[123]

---

123   *De dynastiis*, fol. 13r: "Haec enim omnino sapiunt incunabula et rudimenta fundati a regulo principatus, Necherophe scilicet primi Osiridis decessore qui vel unice occupatus in

This "civilization narrative" was explicitly connected to the history of the pagan gods and Bonjour's synchronization of the biblical patriarchs with these gods. Taking on a notion from the *Vetus Chronicon*, an anonymous history of Egypt preserved in the Byzantine historian George Syncellus' *Chronographia* (see chapter 5), Bonjour divided Egyptian kings into three classes, the *Auritae* (Αὐριτῶν), the *Mestraei* (Μεστραίων), and the *Aegyptii* (Αἰγυπτίων).[124] Bonjour, like Syncellus and many of his own contemporaries, supposed that the first class were gods, the second class heroes or demi-gods, and the third the first mortal kings.[125] For Bonjour, the name "Auritae" came from the Hebrew "Ora," meaning "patres, genitores."[126] Consequently, he argued that these first gods were patriarchs, who came to be worshipped on account of the service they had done for mankind and human civilization. Citing Diodorus (1.13.1–2), he outlined that while some gods were celestial, others were terrestrial, and had been made gods "by reason of their sagacity and the good services which they rendered to all men."[127] This he confirmed with a quote from Ecclesiasticus (44:7): "rich men in virtue, studying beautifulness: living at peace in their houses. All these have gained glory in their generations, and were praised in their days. They that were born of them have left a name behind them, that their praises might be related."[128] For Bonjour the history of ancient Egypt and its connection with the history of the biblical patriarchs was a story not only of the process by which biblical history had first made its way into profane mythology, but also the manner in which human civilization had first developed from its rudimentary and primitive state to one of art, science, and refined civilization through the teaching of the biblical patriarchs, and the wisdom of Joseph in particular. In identifying biblical history with pagan myths, *historia sacra* was

---

aedificando Memphim suisque commodis hic inserviendo, nec satis expertus rempublicam gerere, habitantes in tentoriis undequaque Aegyptios a fera agrestique vita ad humanum cultum civilemque non deduxerat, nec deleverat barbariem ex eorum moribus." Necherophes is usually identified with the Egyptian pharaoh Nebka (27th century BC).

124 Syncellus, *Chronographia* 56.21–22. References to the Greek text of the *Chronographia* come from George Syncellus, *Georgii Syncelli Ecloga Chronographia*, ed. Alden A. Mosshammer (Leipzig: BSB B. G. Teubner, 1984); all English translations and further references come from George Syncellus, *The Chronography of George Synkelos: A Byzantine Chronicle of Universal History from the Creation*, ed. William Adler and Paul Tuffin (Oxford: Oxford University Press, 2002).

125 *De dynastiis*, fol. 25r-v; see also Bonjour's "Reflexiones criticiae, historicae, et chronologicae in Aegypticum mundi chronicon," BAR, ms.lat.631, fols. 194v–199v; Mosshammer, *Ecloga Chronographica*, 41–42; Adler and Tuffin, *The Chronography of George Synkellos*, 55–56.

126 *De dynastiis*, fols. 25r–26v. See also the contemporary discussion of these phrases in Adler and Tuffin, *The Chronography of George Synkellos*, 71, n. 4 and n. 5.

127 Translation from Diodorus, *The Library of History*, trans. Oldfather, 1:45.

128 BAR, ms.lat.631, fol. 194v.

no longer merely the history of God's chosen people but also told the story of the rise and development of human civilization.

5 Greek Universal History in a Biblical Context

In a 1982 article, Arnaldo Momigliano laid out three basic Greek frameworks for conceptualising universal history – conceptualisations which, as Momigliano pointed out, had their origin not in the historical but rather the "mythical or philosophical imagination of the Greeks."[129] The first was characterized by different human races who were identified with different classes of metals, as most famously exemplified in the gold, silver, bronze, and iron races of Hesiod's *Theogony*. Francesco Bianchini would later use this division in his 1697 *La istoria universale*. The second was a biological scheme which described how nations progressed from childhood to youth through to old age; although marginal to pagan historiography, the notion of a *senectus mundi*, the old age of the world, was later adopted by certain patristic writers, including Tertullian and Augustine. The third, however, became crucial for later scholarship on sacred history. It delineated a scheme of progress from barbarism to civilization based on a series of inventions and technological discoveries. According to Momigliano, this third scheme predominantly interested ancient antiquarians and philologists, but it was also crucial for mythographers. Indeed, this *schema* was directly related to Greek mythology since it was usually gods or heroes who revealed these secrets to mankind. The most important treatments of this form of ancient history can be found in Diodorus, Lucretius, the second book of Vitruvius' *De architectura*, and the first book of Manilius' *Astronomica*. As we have seen, not only Bonjour but also Huet and Marsham, three of the most important scholars of Egyptian history in the late seventeenth century, subjected the history of certain biblical figures to this historical, mythological, narrative. In doing so they also altered the scope of sacred history.

Recent scholarship has often emphasised that one of the key distinctions between seventeenth-century sacred history and eighteenth-century universal, or "philosophical," history is their different approaches towards the history of culture, or the development of human civilization. In an article from 1986, Arno Seifert supposed that one of the three principal ways in which sacred history, or *Sakralhistorie*, was weakened, particularised, and desacralized around

---

129   Arnaldo Momigliano, "The Origins of Universal History," in *Annali della Scuola Normale Superiore di Pisa. Classe di lettere e filosofia* 12 (1982): 533–560, quote from 533–534.

the turn of the eighteenth century was due to the assumption that the biblical narrative was too thematically limited. According to Seifert, growing doubts about the historical reliability of both sacred and pagan evidence saw the writing of primordial history, despite still being notionally "historical," placed in the hands of philosophers rather than historians. In lieu of reliable sources, these philosophers subjected the history of the origins and development of primordial human civilization to a more general, conceptual, and *weltgeschichtliches* framework, which gave general patterns and rhythms for the early development of mankind. These patterns focussed, above all, on how nascent human civilization had first emerged and developed in what was a primitive and barbaric age of human history. In doing so, writers such as Voltaire supposed that a true universal history must include the origins and dissemination of the arts and sciences, and that Moses had provided no relevant historical information on this development.[130] In recent years, Seifert's narrative has been endorsed by several other historians working on the development of cultural or philosophical history. Dmitri Levitin in particular has argued that a growing distrust of conventional sources for the writing of *Urgeschichte* in the late seventeenth century, largely as a result of the rise of and greater sophistication in textual source criticism, led scholars to fill newly-discovered gaps in the historical narrative with conjectural histories.[131]

Perhaps the most important amendment to Seifert's narrative is the propensity of historians to assert that even cultural or philosophical history had its origins in seventeenth-century *historia sacra* and antiquarianism. As early as 1960, Adalbert Klempt argued that, from Jean Bodin (1530–1596) onwards, scholars began to abandon the Christian eschatological view of universal history and that works such as Georg Horn's *Brevis introductio in historiam universalem* (1665) promoted a universalist and secularised conception of ancient history which facilitated the transition from Melanchthon to Voltaire's conceptualisation of universal history.[132] Similarly, Peter Miller has emphasised that a preoccupation with culture and *mœurs* was already omnipresent in the

---

130   Arno Seifert, "Von der heiligen zur philosophischen Geschichte. Die Rationalisierung der universalhistorischen Erkenntnis im Zeitalter der Aufklärung," *Archiv für Kulturgeschichte* 68 (1986): 81–118.

131   Dmitri Levitin, "Egyptology, the limits of antiquarianism, and the origins of conjectural history, c. 1680–1740: new sources and perspectives," *History of European Ideas* 41 (2015): 699–727.

132   Klempt, *Die Säkularisierung der universalhistorischen Auffassung*, 115–122; Georg Horn, *Brevis et perspicua introductio ad universalem historiam* (Leiden: Hackiana, 1665).

biblical scholarship of seventeenth-century antiquarians and missionaries, a suggestion also endorsed by the work of Joan-Pau Rubiés.[133]

I hope in this chapter to have offered a few new perspectives on this established narrative. Firstly, I hope to have shown that the supposition that ancient or primordial history must also contain a history of human civilization, that is to say, a history of the origins and dissemination of the arts and sciences, was already well-established in seventeenth-century *historia sacra*. This was primarily due to the increasing tendency of scholars to compare sacred history with pagan myth and to identify pagan gods with biblical patriarchs. By studying sacred history within a historiographical framework taken from Greek myth, scholars subjected the history of the patriarchs to the narrative of emerging human civilization which Greek mythographers had tied to the history of the Greek gods: not since the work of the Jewish Hellenists Artapanus and Eupolemus had Jewish history been so closely connected with pagan mythology.

Secondly, I hope to have shown how this development further blurred the distinction between *historia sacra* and *historia exotica*. By supposing that Greek mythology contained key events from sacred history, scholars also came to analyse sacred history in terms usually reserved for the study of pagan *fabula*, not biblical *historia*. In his letter to Nicaise, Bonjour had once made the important statement that Egyptian history was of particular interest because it concerned matters "autant du sacré que du profane." It was not a far cry from suggesting that the sacred history of the biblical patriarchs and the ancient Jews was as much profane as it was sacred. It was a distinction which, in the early eighteenth century, certain freethinkers would seize upon gleefully.

---

133   Miller, "The 'Antiquarianization' of Biblical Scholarship," and Joan-Pau Rubiés, "From Antiquarianism to Philosophical History: India, China, and the World History of Religion in European Thought (1600–1770)," in *Antiquarianism and Intellectual Life in Europe and China, 1500–1800*, ed. Peter N. Miller and François Louis (Ann Arbor: The University of Michigan Press, 2012), 313–367.

PART 2

Chronology

CHAPTER 4

The Chronology of the Septuagint

1   Biblical Chronologies in the Seventeenth Century

In July of 1697, Gisbert Cuper wrote to Antonio Magliabechi of his excitement at the impending publication of the first volume of Bonjour's *Antiquitas temporum*, his chronological *magnum opus* which contained both a biblical chronology running from Creation to the Babylonian Captivity and an exposition of the famous dynasties of Egypt. As always, Cuper was enticed by Bonjour's profound learning and his knowledge of recondite history, particularly that of Egypt. "This," he wrote to the Florentine librarian, "is worthy stuff into which one might direct one's energies." Yet he also hoped that Bonjour's work would help solve a pressing question: the relationship between the Latin Vulgate and the Greek Septuagint.

> As you are of course aware, the Englishman Marsham previously undertook such a work; and recently in France Paul Pezron, a monk who, with arguments which are far from unreasonable, tried to show, following Vossius, that the Hebrew codices were corrupted, and henceforth that one ought not to follow the Vulgate text and that therefore the Seventy Interpreters, who made the age of the world longer, should be preferred to both: I believe he is to be opposed by Guillaume Bonjour, which in France Jean Martianay and Michel Lequien also did. I do not make this my dispute, but I am glad that many foremost men of erudition apply themselves to this fine matter, in order so that the truth can be revealed at last.[1]

---

1   Gisbert Cuper to Antonio Magliabechi, 1 July 1697, KW 72 D 11, fol. 73r: "Desidero inprimis legere Dynastias Guilelmi Bonjour; quia digna illa materia est in quam quis nervos intendat. Egit, uti non ignoras, de iis antea Marshamus Anglus; et nuper in Gallia Paulus Pezron, monachus qui cum adstruere, idque non invalidis argumentis post Vossium conatur Hebraeos Codices [esse] corruptos, nec proinde vulgatam versionem sequendam esse, et utrisque praeferri debere Interpretes LXX qui mundi aetatem longiorem faciunt, credo eum impugnatum iri a Guielmo Bonjour, id quod in Gallia etiam fecerunt Ioannes Martinianaeus, et Michael Lequien. Litem eam meam non facio, sed laetor plures eruditione praestantes viros materiae tam eleganti manus admovere, ut ita veritas tandem patescat plane."

We have already noted that the Bible contained both a primordial history of humanity and the providential history of the Jews. Yet the Mosaic Pentateuch – and the Book of Genesis in particular – also provided scholars with a definitive chronology for this universal history. Generally if not universally accepted by the western Church since at least the time of Bede was the shorter biblical chronology, which was preserved in both the Hebrew Bible privileged by the Protestant churches and the Latin Vulgate text translated by Jerome in the late fourth century and declared the authoritative text of the Catholic Church by the Council of Trent in 1546. This chronology counted exactly 1656 years between the Creation of the world (which could roughly be dated to 4000 BC) and the Flood, a further 292 years between the Flood and Abraham, and another 430 years between Jacob's entry into Egypt and the Exodus. Yet this "Masoretic" chronology, though undoubtedly the most popular and authoritative biblical chronology in the western Christian world for more than a millennium, was not without its rivals. The authoritative text of the early Church and the basis for a number of ancient biblical translations was not the Latin Vulgate or the Hebrew text but the Septuagint, a *koine* Greek translation which, according to the Letter of Aristeas, was translated by seventy (or seventy-two) Jewish scribes at the request of the Egyptian Pharaoh Ptolemy II Philadelphus in Alexandria in the mid-third century BC. The Septuagint contained a number of notable chronological differences with the Masoretic chronology. Most notably, it added one hundred years to many of the *anni* παιδοποιίας (the ages of the Patriarchs when their first son was born) of both the ante- and postdiluvian patriarchs, with the result that the Flood was placed 2256 years after Creation and a further 1257 years separated the Flood from the vocation of Abraham.[2] As a result, Creation was dated not to c.4000 BC but to between 5200 and 6000 BC. Matters were further complicated in the seventeenth century with the discovery of the Samaritan Pentateuch. A chronology of this Bible, which counted fewer years between Creation and the Flood than the Masoretic text, was first published by Joseph Scaliger in 1606; a complete Samaritan Pentateuch was discovered by the Italian traveller Pietro della Valle (1586–1652) in 1616 and published by Jean Morin in the Paris Polyglot in 1631.[3]

The problem posed by the Septuagint and to a lesser extent the Samaritan Pentateuch was not a new one. Indeed, the discrepancy between the Septuagint

---

[2] I have taken these calculations from Pezron, *Antiquité des tems*, 56, although it should be noted that there were minor differences between the different chronologists who followed the Septuagint.

[3] Scaliger, "ΤΩΝ ΧΡΟΝΙΚΩΝ ΠΑΝΤΟΔΑΠΗΣ ΙΣΤΟΡΙΑΣ ΕΥΣΕΒΙΟΥ ΤΟΥ ΠΑΜΦΙΛΟΥ ΤΑ ΣΩΖΟΜΕΝΑ," *Thesaurus temporum*, 3–4.

and the Hebrew Bible had troubled Christian chronologists since the first centuries of the Church. Famously, Augustine had been much preoccupied with this problem (cf. *De civitate dei* 18.41–43), and in the seventeenth century his comments were routinely cited by chronologists who were becoming increasingly aware of the extent to which the Greek Septuagint rather than the Hebrew Bible had once been the central text of the Fathers, the earliest (predominantly "Greek") Christian chronographers such as Julius Africanus and Eusebius, the Evangelists, and even the Apostles.[4] And it is worth pointing out, in this context, that many other prickly questions which troubled the chronologists of Bonjour's generation had already existed in the time of Augustine. Augustine himself had admitted, for example, that pagan nations such as the Babylonians and Egyptians proclaimed an antiquity which exceeded the biblical date for Creation.[5] He also recognised a number of obvious chronological difficulties within the biblical texts themselves. Famously, he noted that in the Septuagint Methuselah was said to have survived the universal Flood by 14 years and that the 430 years which, according to Moses, separated Jacob's entry into Egypt from the Exodus (Exodus 12:40), was contradicted by the Apostle Paul's statement that 430 years had passed between Abraham's vocation and the Exodus (Galatians 3:17).[6] As Anthony Grafton has often pointed out, biblical chronology was never a firm or stable field of religious scholarship.

Nevertheless, it is clear that the problems for biblical chronologists became more acute in the seventeenth century and that many issues which had existed since the primitive Church took on a new importance. Not only had chronology again become a critical discipline in Christian apologetics, but some scholars came to see it as at best a futile and at worst a dangerous, potentially heretical, scholarly discipline. In general, this fact has been traced to two concomitant developments: firstly, the discovery, or rediscovery, of new, previously unknown, chronological sources; and secondly, the proliferation and increasing sophistication of biblical text criticism.

In terms of new chronological information, two texts stand out above all else, both for their notoriety and their influence. The first was the Egyptian history of Manetho, an Egyptian priest from Sebennytos who lived around the third century BC. Once lost, Manetho's history was rediscovered by Joseph Scaliger in 1602 and first published in Scaliger's *Thesaurus temporum* of 1606.[7]

---

4   *De civitate dei* 15.10.
5   *De civitate dei* 12.11.
6   *De civitate dei* 15.11; *De civitate dei* 16.16, 16.24.
7   Scaliger, *Thesaurus temporum*. The *editio princeps* of George Syncellus, which contained the dynasties of Manetho excerpted by Scaliger, was published in 1652: Jacques Goar, ed.,

It listed thirty-one Egyptian dynasties from the first Egyptian king Menes to the Egyptian invasion of the Persian king Darius, covering a period of some 5,000 years.[8] The second was the *Sinicae historiae decas* of the Jesuit sinologist and missionary Martino Martini (1614–1661), a former student of Athanasius Kircher, which was first published in 1658.[9] Martini's work, a history of China based on newly-discovered Chinese sources, began with the first Chinese king Fohi and ended with "Ngayus," who was roughly contemporary with Christ, and covered a period of close to 3,000 years. Consequently, both texts appeared to clash with the chronology of such biblical events as the universal Flood – and, in Manetho's case, with the Masoretic date for Creation itself.

As important as the simple discovery of these sources was the manner in which they were treated by their discoverers, particularly in the case of Manetho. As Anthony Grafton has shown, Scaliger was convinced that Manetho's history offered a reliable guide to Egyptian history which could not be dismissed by serious chronologists simply because it contradicted the chronology of their chosen Bible. Indeed, as in the case of the pagan texts which he included in his "Veterum Graecorum fragmenta selecta," Scaliger supposed that chronological sources such as Manetho contained verifiable historical information. Although this suggestion was largely spurned in the first half of the seventeenth century, it is noticeable that, by the time Bonjour came to study Egyptian chronology, many of the abstruse historical systems which had since arisen and which mutilated Manetho's dynasties in order to bludgeon a square pagan peg into a round biblical hole did so not because they rejected Scaliger's more sober, sophisticated chronological approach, but because they took his work on *historia exotica* to its logical conclusion: that if pagan sources

---

Georgii Monmachi Syncelli, et Nicephori CP. Patriarchae Chronographia (Paris: Typographia Regia, 1652). For modern editions and English translations see Gerald P. Verbrugghe and John M. Wickersham, *Berossos and Manetho, Introduced and Translated: Native Traditions in Ancient Mesopotamia and Egypt* (Ann Arbor: The University of Michigan Press, 1996); and Adler and Tuffin, *The Chronography of George Synkellos*.

8 See Scaliger, "Isagogicorum Chronologiae Canonum," *Thesaurus temporum*, 122–130; Goar, *Georgi Monmachi Syncelli*, 54–78; Adler and Tuffin, *The Chronography of George Synkellos*, 76–110.

9 Martino Martini, *Sinicae historiae decas prima* (Munich: Lukas Straub, 1658). For discussions of Chinese chronology in early modern Europe see in particular D. E. Mungello, "A Study of the Preface's to Ph. Couplet's *Tabula Chronologica Monarchiae Sinicae* (1686)," in *Philippe Couplet, S.J. (1623–1693): The Man Who Brought China to Europe*, ed. Jerome Heyndrickx (Nettetal: Stigler, 1990), 183–199; Virgile Pinot, *La Chine et la formation de l'esprit philosophique en France (1640–1740)* (Paris: Libraire Orientaliste Paul Geuthner, 1932), 189–279, and Edwin J. Van Kley, "Europe's 'Discovery' of China and the Writing of World History," *The American Historical Review* 76 (1971): 358–385.

such as Manetho really were genuine, then they must necessarily concord with the chronology of the Bible (as we shall see in the next chapter).

What is more, it was precisely in this century that, for the first time, certain heterodox scholars came to weaponize these pagan sources. Rather than dismiss them as pagan lies, they presented them as being incompatible with biblical history and thus as proof that biblical chronology could not be universal. It was for this reason that ancient historians like Manetho became objects of profound apologetic concern. "The most popular pretences of the Atheists of our Age, have been the irreconcilableness of the account of Times in Scripture with that of the learned and ancient Heathen Nations": so wrote the Christian apologist Edward Stillingfleet in his lengthy, learned, and hugely successful *Origines sacrae* of 1662.[10] Of these so-called "Atheists" the most famous was, of course, La Peyrère, who cited the chronologies of Egypt and China when he came to argue that the history narrated in the Bible pertained merely to the specific providential history of the Jews.[11] As a result, from the 1650s onwards, proving that pagan chronologies could fit into the biblical framework became a question not only of sound historical practice but also of defending the authority of biblical history and by extension the Christian religion. It was in this context that the Septuagint, which offered an alternative, longer, chronology and thus appeared more amenable to integrating the long Egyptian and Chinese histories into a biblical framework, came once again to the fore.

The second concomitant factor was the development of increasingly sophisticated biblical text criticism, which destabilised traditional assumptions concerning the textual history of the Bible. The ultimate origins of this development can be traced back to both the development of Renaissance humanist philology, which gave scholars the tools for a new, more sophisticated model of text criticism, and the Protestant Reformation, which convinced scholars to apply these tools not only to Virgil or Constantine's spurious donation but to the biblical text itself (although it should be noted that this practice largely began only in the seventeenth century). As historians such as Hans-Joachim Kraus and Nicholas Hardy have pointed out, this practice was fundamentally orthodox in both origin and motivation. Protestant scholars held that the source for religious truth was the biblical text, *sola scriptura*, and that this text had to be studied in its original, Hebrew state, *ad fontes*. Hence, biblical critics applied philology to the biblical text in the belief that better understanding the biblical text would help scholars better understand the Word of

---

10   Stillingfleet, *Origines sacrae*, "The Preface to the Reader," sig. b2v.
11   La Peyrère, *Praeadamitae sive exercitatio*, 29; La Peyrère, *Systema theologicum, ex praeadamitarum hypothesi*, 116–160.

God.[12] In this sense, text criticism, or *eruditio*, also became an essential part of piety and devotion. And yet, growing scholarly interest in the biblical text also began to wear away at what were once commonly accepted orthodox principles concerning the authority of the text itself. In 1633, the biblical critic Jean Morin, a Catholic convert who subsequently joined the Oratory, openly supposed that the Septuagint was more reliable than the Masoretic text, which had been subject to Jewish editorial interpolation.[13] In subsequent years the status of previously cherished biblical texts became ever more contentious. The infamous debate about the Hebrew vowel points – which Louis Cappel, professor of Hebrew at the Protestant Academy of Saumur, argued were not part of the original Hebrew Bible but were added by medieval Jewish scribes, the Masoretes – is just one particularly illustrative example of how text-critical scholarship clashed with long-standing, "orthodox" notions.[14] Moreover, as Scott Mandelbrote has highlighted, scholarship on different biblical versions also complicated long-standing assumptions about the historical transmission and relationship between different biblical texts or versions.[15] This led certain scholars to advance new, and potentially dangerous, conclusions about the current state of the Bible. As Peter Miller has shown, Brian Walton (1600–1661), the editor of the London Polyglot and the author of its "Prolegomena," accepted the existence of different versions of the biblical text and supposed that the biblical original, if it ever existed, was now lost.[16] Meanwhile, Richard Simon argued in his *Histoire critique de Vieux Testament* (1678) that not only had the original texts been lost, but also that Moses was not the author of large parts of the Pentateuch, which, along with the rest of the biblical texts, had been extensively edited, augmented, synthesized, and altered by divinely-inspired, public, Jewish scribes.[17] What is noteworthy in the case of both Walton and Simon is that neither scholar was, at least notionally, attempting to devalue the authority of the Bible. Both scholars thought that criticism could uncover the true meaning and history of God's Word. For Simon, the instability of the

---

12   Hardy, *Criticism and Confession*; Kraus, *Geschichte der historisch-kritischen Erforschung des Alten Testaments*.
13   Hardy, *Criticism and Confession*, 257ff.
14   Timothy Twining, "The Early Modern Debate over the Age of the Hebrew Vowel Points: Biblical Criticism and Hebrew Scholarship in the Confessional Republic," *Journal of the History of Ideas* 81 (2020): 337–358.
15   See in particular Scott Mandelbrote, "Philology and Scepticism: Early Modern Scholars at Work on the Text of the Bible," in *The Marriage of Philology and Scepticism*, ed. G. M. Cao, A. Grafton, and J. Kraye (London: Warburg Institute, 2019), 123–142.
16   Miller, "The 'Antiquarianization' of Biblical Scholarship."
17   Hazard, *The European Mind*, 180–197.

biblical text was an argument for the necessity and authority of Church tradition. In each case, however, scholars were gradually coming to the conclusion that the biblical texts they had at their disposal were not as well-preserved or as complete as once thought.

From a specifically chronological perspective, the debate about the Septuagint began with a short, polemical, and knowingly controversial work which first appeared in 1659, entitled *De vera aetate mundi*. The author of this work was Isaac Vossius, a learned and well-connected Dutch scholar (son of Gerardus) with a penchant for provocation, of whom King Charles II famously said that he would believe everything but the Bible.[18] As Scott Mandelbrote has shown, Vossius' *De vera aetate mundi* was carefully calculated to prey upon scholarly uncertainty in the immediate years after the publication of La Peyrère's *Praeadamitae* in 1655 and Martini's history of China in 1658.[19] Vossius argued, with the evidence of Chaldean, Egyptian, and Chinese history, that the Septuagint contained the original chronology of the Hebrew Bible before the latter had been corrupted by anti-Christian Jews. As a result, Vossius sought to extend the true age of the world, *vera aetas mundi*, by 1440 years in order to better align it with these pagan histories and thereby to refute La Peyrère's impious thesis. Mischievously, as we have noted above, he ended the work by supposing that the biblical Flood was localized to that part of Palestine in which the world's nascent population lived.[20] In the following years, Vossius' first blast of the trumpet in favour of the Septuagint experienced fluctuating fortunes. Although his work elicited sympathy – particularly in England – he was aggressively countered by the German historian (and Adamite alchemist) Georg Horn, who defended the authority of the Masoretic Bible and with whom Vossius engaged in a bitter polemical dispute.[21] Particularly damaging, however, was the contribution of the Oxford-based scholar Humphrey Hody (1659–1707), who was to become regius professor of Greek in 1698. In 1684, the then twenty-five-year-old Hody published his *Contra historiam Aristeae de LXX. interpretibus dissertatio*, in which he demonstrated that the Letter of Aristeas,

---

18   As cited in numerous places, and taken here from David S. Katz, "Isaac Vossius and the English biblical critics 1650–1689," in *Scepticism and Irreligion in the Seventeenth and Eighteenth Centuries*, ed. Richard H. Popkin and Arjo J. Vanderjagt (Leiden: Brill, 1993), 142–143.
19   Anthony Grafton, "Isaac Vossius, Chronologer," and Scott Mandelbrote, "Isaac Vossius and the Septuagint," both in *Isaac Vossius (1618–1689) between Science and Scholarship*, ed. Eric Jorink and Dirk van Miert (Leiden and Boston: Brill, 2012), 43–84 and 85–117.
20   Vossius, *De vera aetate mundi*.
21   See in particular Georg Horn, *Georgii Hornii dissertatio de vera aetate mundi* (Leiden: Johannes Elzevir, 1659).

which documented the translation of the Septuagint and which Vossius believed genuine, was a Hellenistic forgery.[22] Hody's revelation was undoubtedly an embarrassment to Vossius and rung the death knell for his work on the Septuagint, proving that Vossius, who charged readers of the Masoretic Bible with following a text corrupted by Jewish scribes, was himself a victim of Jewish fraud. As Mandelbrote has pointed out, by the last decades of the seventeenth century, the tide had turned decisively against Vossius.[23]

And yet it was exactly in those years that there also appeared, from an unlikely source, another champion of the Septuagint: the Cistercian historian Paul Pezron, later abbot of Charmoye.[24] Born in a small village in Brittany, Pezron joined the so-called Order of Citeaux, a branch of the Benedictines situated in the eponymous abbey south of Dijon, in 1660, before being educated first by the Jesuits in Rennes and then by the Benedictines in Paris. For a while, he was the chosen protégé of Dom Jouard, the vicar-general of the Benedictine Order. In 1677, he was named Superior of the Cistercian Collège des Bernardins in Paris, and, in 1682, he obtained his doctorate from the Sorbonne. It seems that it was Pezron's relocation to Paris which particularly inflamed his passion for scholarship, above all for scholarship on holy scripture; according to contemporary reports, he spent up to thirteen hours a day absorbed in his studies.[25] The fruits of these labours was his *L'antiquité des tems*, his first major published work, which appeared in both Amsterdam and Paris in 1687, and which "made a great ruckus, and, as customary in the fate of many good books, had many admirers, and some critics."[26] The causes of this ruckus – or

---

22 Humphrey Hody, *Contra historiam Aristeae de LXX interpretibus dissertatio* (Oxford: Leonard Lichfield and Anthony Stephens, 1684).
23 Mandelbrote, "Isaac Vossius and the Septuagint," 116.
24 He was appointed abbot in Easter 1697.
25 Sources on Pezron are scanty. The only (vaguely) recent treatment of Pezron is P. T. J. Morgan, "The Abbé Pezron and the Celts," *Transactions of the Honourable Society of Cymmrodorion* 2 (1965): 286–295, which focuses on his 1703 work on the Celts; otherwise the most recent if brief discussion of Pezron is in Mandelbrote, "Isaac Vossius and the Septuagint." My biographical information comes from the obituary in the *Journal de Trévoux*: [anon] "Article XCIII: Eloge du Pere Pezron de l'étroite observance de l'Ordre de Cisteaux, ancien Abbé de Charmoye," *Journal de Trévoux* 19 (1707): 1266–1281.
26 "Eloge du Pere Pezron," 1271: "fit un grand bruit, & selon le sort des bons Livres, il eut beaucoup d'admirateurs, & quelques Critiques." I have yet to work out the precise reasons why two editions exist, although the Amsterdam edition clearly states that it was based on a copy of the French edition. I have used the Paris edition throughout this work. It bears noting that the work does not bear Pezron's name, although everyone knew it was by Pezron and he openly treated it as his own work. The reference to Pezron as the "Auctor Anonymus" by Noris (see below) is the only contemporary reference to the supposed anonymity of the work I have found.

bruit – are not hard to find. In his *Antiquité*, Pezron reaffirmed Vossius' basic notion that the Septuagint was the original Bible of the early Church, that it contained the original biblical chronology before Jewish corruption, that adopting the Septuagint was necessary for refuting the Preadamites, and that it was the Septuagint chronology which could be harmonized perfectly with Chaldean, Egyptian, and Chinese antiquities. Above all, Pezron wanted to defend the validity of the Septuagint on chronological grounds. For Pezron, the Bible remained the ultimate chronological framework for universal history, but it was the Greek Bible of ancient Alexandria rather than the Hebrew Bible of the Protestants or the Vulgate translation of the Catholics which provided this framework.

Whereas Vossius found himself with a Protestant antagonist – who accused Vossius of being influenced by the accursed papists – Pezron's *Antiquité des tems* aroused opprobrium in Catholic circles. More specifically, he was refuted by two religious, the Benedictine Maurist Jean Martianay and the Paris-based Dominican Michel Lequien (1661–1733), who published lengthy refutations of Pezron in 1689 and 1690 respectively, as well as refutations of Pezron's *Défense de l'antiquité des tems* (1691) in 1693.[27] Both scholars rejected Pezron's narrative of Jewish corruption and emphasised the priority of first the Hebrew and then Jerome's Vulgate in antiquity, largely on the authority of Augustine and Jerome himself. Both also dismissed Pezron's chronological work by purposefully choosing to ignore or dismiss chronological arguments for the primacy of either text.[28] In addition, they accused Pezron, not without reason, of copying Vossius. "One can say that he is only expanding what this learned man gave us in summary in a book he entitled *De aetate mundi*," wrote Lequien in 1690.[29] Of the two scholars, however, it was Martianay (who edited Jerome's *Opera omnia* in five volumes between 1693 and 1706) who proved particularly vindicative. There can be no doubt that Martianay cherished Jerome – and

---

27   Jean Martianay, *Défense du texte hébreu et de la chronologie de la Vulgate contre le livre de L'antiquité des tems rétablie* (Paris: L. Roulland, 1689); Michel Lequien, *Défense du texte hébreu et de la version Vulgate; servant de réponse au livre intitulé; l'Antiquité des temps, & c.* (Paris: Amable Auroy, 1690); Jean Martianay, *Continuation de la défense du texte hébreu et de la Vulgate, par des veritables traditions des églises chrétiennes & par tout sortes d'anciens monumens hebreux, grecs, & latins* (Paris: Pierre de Bats, 1693); Michel Lequien, *L'antiquité des tems détruite, ou Réponse à la Défense de l'antiquité des tems* (Paris: J. Villery, 1693). Cf. Paul Pezron, *Défense de l'antiquité des tems* (Paris: Jean Boudot, 1691).

28   For a contemporary discussion of their debate see Louis Ellies Dupin, "Paul Pezron," *Nouvelle bibliothèque des auteurs ecclesiastiques* 19 (1715): 156–171.

29   Lequien, *Défense*, 293: "l'on peut dire qu'il ne fait qu'étendre ce que ce sçavant homme nous avoit donné en abregé dans on livre qu'il a intitule *De Aetate Mundi*."

perhaps overestimated Jerome's text-critical and linguistic abilities – and in so doing he took the defence of Jerome's Vulgate to heart.[30] Not satisfied with one enemy, he even thought it fit to castigate Lequien for what he considered a poor defence of the Hebrew text. "The book of Father Lequien is a work without method, and the work of a plagiarist who says nothing that others have not said before," he noted in the preface of his 1693 *Continuation de la défense du texte hebreu et de la Vulgate*.[31] It appears that bellicosity was simply part of Martianay's character. "I am sorry that Father Martianay has attracted so many enemies, and above all that he has declared war on Father Lequien, who is one of the best and most honest religious in France" wrote Montfaucon to his *confrère* Mabillon, "but we know the nature of this Father, and one should not expect him to change."[32] Martianay's chief and bitter enemy, however, remained Pezron. To Charles Estiennot, the procurator general of the Maurist Congregation, Martianay wrote that he would not rest until he had ruined Pezron and bankrupted his bookseller.[33] Eventually, he accomplished this by appealing to higher authorities. In 1693, he hauled Pezron in front of the archbishop of Paris and charged him with being "nothing other than a Vossius who speaks French; just as one said that Plato is nothing other than a Moses who speaks Greek."[34] Pezron tried to defend himself by claiming that he was not following Vossius but merely the Church Fathers.[35] Unfortunately, this

---

30   Jean Martianay, *Sancti Hieronymi operum*, 5 vols (Paris: Jean Anisson, 1693–1706). A simple look at Martianay's bibliography will make clear just how many of his scholarly projects concerned Jerome. For a study of the changing appreciation of Jerome the biblical scholar in the sixteenth and seventeenth centuries, see Scott Mandelbrote, "Origen against Jerome in Early Modern Europe," in *Patristic Tradition and Intellectual Paradigms in the 17th Century*, ed. Silke-Petra Bergjan and Karla Pollmann (Tübingen: Mohr Siebeck, 2010), 105–135.

31   Martianay, *Continuation*, preface, sig. aviiir: "Le Livre du P. Lequien est un livre sans methode, & l'ouvrage d'un plagiaire qui ne dit rien qu'après les autres."

32   Bernard de Montfaucon to Jean Mabillon, 31 August 1700, BNF, Français 17701, fol. 109v: "Je suis faché que le P. Martianay s'attire tant d'ennemys, et sur tout qu'il ait declaré la guerre au P. Lequin qui est un des meilleurs et des plus honnêtes religieux de France, mais on connoir le naturel de ce pere, il ne faut pas esperer qu'il change."

33   Jean Martianay to Claude Estiennot, 13 June 1694, BNF, Français 19663, fols. 20r–21r.

34   See BNF, Latin 17939, fol. 19r: "n'est autre chose qu'un Vossius qui parle françois: de mesme qu'on disoit de Platon que c'estoit un Moïse qui parloit Grec." I have covered some of this material previously, including this somewhat strange comparison: Felix Schlichter, "Flavius Josephus and early modern biblical chronology," *Intellectual History Review* 33 (2022): 587–608.

35   BNF, Latin 17939, fol. 204r: "Je n'ay suivi Vossius, que quand je l'ay veu suivre luy-mesme le sentiment des Peres et des Eglises, qui ont embrassé le Calcul des Septante, et non celuy de l'Hébreu."

argument did not wash. In 1693, Pezron was forced to retract his views in front of the archbishop of Paris; in later years he even reached a rapprochement with Martianay.[36] Pezron's eventual magnanimity in this conflict highlights not only his character – he was always respectful and deferential, and Leibniz honoured him "infinitely" – but also the manner in which he thought of the debate itself, as we shall see later.[37]

2 Chronology and the Septuagint in Bonjour's World

Chronology – and the chronology of the biblical text(s) – had always been uppermost in Bonjour's mind. As early as May 1693, when Jean-Pierre Rigord first visited the Augustinian convent in Toulouse, he had found Bonjour working on "a very nice project ... to bring together the different systems of peoples and authors and to reduce sacred and prophane history to uniform epochs."[38] As we have noted, some of Bonjour's first epistolary correspondence at the time concerned the chronology of Christ. In this field Noris loomed particularly large. In his 1681 monograph on a Pisan cenotaph dedicated to Gaius and Lucius Caesar, he had made several important discoveries concerning the reigns of Augustus in Rome and Herod in Judaea, reigns crucial for correctly determining the chronology of Christ. In 1689, however, Noris surpassed himself with the publication of his celebrated *Annus et epochae syromacedonum*.[39] Divided into five dissertations, the work treated first the calendrical year of the "Syro-macedonians" – which is to say, Hellenized Syrians who had adopted the Macedonian calendar following the campaigns of Alexander the Great and who later made up the Seleucid Empire – before going on to delineate the various eras or epochs of the cities of Syria, Phoenicia, and Palestine, primarily through the evidence supplied by coins and then analysed through relevant literary texts. Although

---

36   See BNF, Latin 17939, fols. 200r–207r; Jean Martianay to Claude Estiennot, 13 June 1694, Français 19663, BNF, fols. 20r–21r: "Mes affaires sont icy finies avec le P. Pezron, Msr. de Paris l'a fait citer, et luy a ordonné de ne plus écrire sur les matieres de nostre contestation. Son libraire a fait banqueroute, et l'on assure que le dernier livre de l'Antiquité des tems, y a beaucoup contribué, n'en ayant pas rendu cinquante exemplaires. Nous sommes sur le point de nous embrasser avec le Pere Pezron, ainsi voilà la verité et la charité qui triompheront après ces disputes assez aigres."
37   G. W. Leibniz to Marie de Brinon, 15 June 1693, LAA, I, 9:112–113.
38   Jean-Pierre Rigord to Nicolas Toinard, 10 May 1693, BNF, NAF 563, fol. 194v: "un tres beau dessein qui merite votre secours ... ceu a accorder ensemble les diferens systemes de peuples et des auteurs et a reduire toute l'histoire sacrée et prophane sur des Epoques uniformes."
39   See Noris, *Cenotaphia pisana*, 132–162, for his section on the Herods.

Noris' research did not concern the chronologies of either the Old Testament or ancient Egypt, it did cover a period crucial for understanding the chronology of the Book of Maccabees, the correct date of the Nativity, and the history of the early Church. Indeed, as Noris wrote to Nicaise, his work was not merely intended to satisfy the niche interests of armchair antiquarians but sought to systematise a previously unknown – or at best, poorly interpreted – period of history so that he might therefore be able to redate a number of important Church councils.[40] With erudite criticism and humility, Noris' work went on to examine and rectify flaws in the earlier studies of such luminaries as Joseph Scaliger, Denis Petau (1583–1652), James Ussher (1581–1656), and, above all, Cesare Baronio. The work – "opus totius literati applausu dignum," as the reviewer in the *Acta eruditorum* put it – established for Noris a level of renown in chronological matters to match (and even surpass) the controversy he enjoyed in theological matters.[41] By the early 1690s, he had established a learned correspondence not only with scholars throughout France and the Netherlands but also with Henry Dodwell and William Lloyd (1627–1717), then Bishop of St. Asaph, in England, all of whom respected and some of whom revered his scholarly abilities. It was little surprise, then, that when Bonjour voiced his desire to further develop his nascent chronological interests – and to arrange the historical information he had drawn from pagan myth into a coherent chronological framework – it was Noris to whom he turned.

There is no doubt that in his historical methodology and in his attitude to history more generally, Bonjour learnt much from Noris. Yet Bonjour's chronological scholarship was also motivated by a debate which did not appear to particularly interest Noris, at least publicly; namely, the question of which biblical chronology might be considered authoritative. As we have seen, Vossius and Pezron's works had put the Septuagint at the forefront of contemporary debates concerning biblical chronology. What is more, despite Vossius' embarrassment at the hands of Hody and despite Pezron's official rebuke in Paris, by the time Bonjour came to chronological matters a good number of scholars had come to express latent support for the Septuagint, particularly on chronological grounds. This included scholars in Bonjour's small epistolary community. In 1697, Cuper wrote two successive letters to Bonjour in which he

---

40 See Enrico Noris to Claude Nicaise, "Lettera del Card. Noris," in *Istoria delle investiture*, cols. 335–6: "… ac plurium Synodorum annos Baronio falso designatos certis caracteribus indicabo. Hoc enim primum intendo, non autem Antiquariis, seu veterum numismatum istudiosis lampadem praebere, licet hoc etiam praestem."

41 C. Wagner, "Annus et epochae syro-macedonum," *Acta eruditorum* (1690): 425; Noris, *Annus et epochae*, 241; cf. British Library, Add. MS 21082; Bodleian Library, MSS. Cherry 1 and 29.

suggested that only the Septuagint chronology made sense when it came to studying the lives of the antediluvian patriarchs.[42] When Nicaise first heard of Bonjour's plan to herald the superiority of the Vulgate to the detriment of the Septuagint, he wrote to the young Augustinian that "I have always believed that it was more fitting to believe with Vossius and others, that the Septuagint is correct."[43] Of a similar opinion was Leibniz, who argued that Chinese history obliged scholars to accept Pezron's arguments.[44]

More to the point, it appears that Bonjour once shared what was increasingly becoming a popular opinion. In a letter to Cuper of August 1697, Bonjour admitted that he had once been enamoured by the arguments of Vossius and Pezron, whom he called the *Septuaginti fautores*:

> I confess that at first Isaac Vossius and Paul Pezron, the very famous supporters of the edition *the Seventy*, enraptured me in their opinion. Nor was I able to be dissuaded from this, when weighing up what came out in opposition. For in my opinion the rich witness of the ages, the most splendid light of truth, the most certain reporter of antiquity, is profane history agreeing with holy scripture.[45]

Bonjour's stance on the Septuagint shifted while in Toulouse. The specific cause of this development is not mentioned, but it is clear that it happened very early in Bonjour's career. As we have noted, Bonjour's chronological projects in about 1693 were geared towards arranging various pagan histories into what Bonjour called "uniform epochs," and this uniformity was already provided by the framework of the shorter Masoretic chronology. It is clear, however, that it was the study of ancient history – "lux splendidissima veritas," as he described it to Cuper – which provided the basis for Bonjour's stance on and defence of biblical chronology. In the *Mercurius*, completed when he was just twenty-four, Bonjour argued that his synchronization of pagan myth with biblical history

---

42 Gisbert Cuper to Guillaume Bonjour, 14 July 1697 and 25 December 1697, in BAR, ms.lat.395, fols. 4r–5v, 5bisr–5terv and in Pélissier, "Lettres inédites de Gisbert Cuper," 55–61.
43 Claude Nicaise to Guillaume Bonjour, 8 February 1698, BAR, ms.lat.395, fols. 151r–152v, and in Pélissier, "Lettres inédites de Claude Nicaise," 195: "j'ay toujours cru qu'il estoit plus convenable de croire avec M. Vossius et d'autres, que les LXX ont raison."
44 G. W. Leibniz to Claude Nicaise, 16 August 1699, LAA, II, 3:589.
45 Guillaume Bonjour to Gisbert Cuper, 31 August 1697, KW 72 H 20: "In suam sententiam, fateor, me in primis rapuerant editionis τῶν ἑβδομήκοντα celeberrimi fautores, Isaacus Vossius, et Paulus Pezronius. Nec deduci de hac poteram, quae in contrarium prodierunt, ponderans scripta. Sacris enim litteris consonans historia profana locuples apud me testis est temporum, lux splendidissima veritatis, nuncia vetustatis exploratissima."

would not only reveal the true history of the patriarch Joseph but also confirm the chronology of the *Hebraica veritas* against that of the Septuagint. As he wrote in the preface,

> From then, when I gave myself entirely to the sacred and divine pages by the great example of these men, I compared with them still more things from the writings of the pagans which had escaped even those men themselves, and realised that they pertained to the same thing. I have also come to some hope, and see now that it will be easily maintained, that I will henceforth be able to defend and vindicate the chronology of the Hebrew text, starting from Adam, from the calculations of the Greeks. This has been desired by many, nor has it been sufficiently elucidated by scholars after the most zealous dissertations on each of the two chronologies.[46]

When Bonjour came to publish his *De nomine* in 1696, he made this notion public. As he noted in the preface, this work was motivated not only by his desire to defend Jerome's translation of "Zaphnath paaneah," but also to defend the chronology of what Bonjour called the *Hebraica veritas*, the Latin Vulgate.[47] It was also this project which directed Bonjour's chronological research after his arrival in Rome. In the first half of 1696, shortly after arriving in the eternal city, Bonjour was already in the process of composing a number of introductory works on ancient chronology.[48] As the months passed, the size, breadth, and

---

46 *Mercurius*, fol. 2v: "Unde cum sacris divinisque paginis optimo eorum exemplo me totum traderem, plura etiam, quae vel ipsos fugerant, ex scriptis Ethnicorum cum iis contuli, ac eodem pertinere expertus sum. Nonnullam quoque in spem veni quam et facile tuendam nunc prospicio, chronologiam textus Hebraici ab Adamo ductum me exinde propugnaturum ac vindicaturum a Graecis calculis. Expetitum hoc a pluribus est, nec satis post acerrimas de utraque chronologia dissertationes apud doctos elucubratum."

47 *De nomine*, sig. ✠3v: "Hinc nusquam non latior mihi fuit Mercurius Aegyptiorum, cum antiquum Josephum in eo prorsus adumbratum expertus fui, typisque edendo amplo volumine executus. Nusquam uberior materies sese obtulit in characteribus chronologicis, quos ex intimo antiquitatis penu pro generali chronologia noviter observatos juris publici facere mox meditabar. Nusquam ampliora quaesitae veritatis & indicia & umbracula nunc occurrunt in dynastiis Aegyptiorum, quas secundum Hebraicam veritatem & perpetuo cum sacris paginis nexu elucidare satago in defensionem Vulgatae Editionis quam Tridentinum ratam fecit, & consecravit Ecclesiae usui."

48 "Characteres chronologicos," BAR, ms.lat.635, fol. 27r; cf. Antonio Magliabechi to Jean Mabillon, 3 January 1696, in Gigas, *Lettres inédites*, 2, part 1: 241. See also the relevant discussion in chapter 1.

sophistication of his chronological ambitions grew. A letter to Claude Nicaise, dated July 1697, highlights both the nature and the extent of these ambitions:

> I am currently working on harmonizing sacred and profane antiquities according to the truth of the Hebrew text. After having decided on the chronology of all holy scripture in general and having clarified that of Josephus in particular through some excellent manuscripts, having shown that the ancient Samaritans were entirely in conformity with the Hebrew [text] of today, having demonstrated the corruption and corruptors of the Septuagint, having developed in a singular manner the antiquities of the Assyrians, Babylonians, Medes, and Tyrians, who are connected with our scripture since the time of King Hezekiah, and having made new observations on the weeks of David, I have turned my attention to the antiquities of Egypt. My system is unique. I have, however, conferred with cardinal Noris, who, after having read my notebooks, was satisfied with it. I deal not only with the dynasties in general, but also with all the kings in particular, and the areas which seem the most sterile become the most fertile there. Moreover, the connection which there is with holy scripture is so frequent and so considerable that the chronology and history are as much sacred as they are profane. I must thereafter work on the antiquities of the Chaldeans on which I have already made several remarks conforming to the Hebrew text. I will not forget that of the Chinese and several other nations whose first epochs I have discovered.[49]

49 The letter itself does not survive but three copies of various lengths do: Guillaume Bonjour to Claude Nicaise, 9 July 1697, in KW 72 D 2, fol. 127v; in BAR, ms.lat.635, fol. 68v; and in Pélissier, "Lettres inédites de Claude Nicaise," 147–148: "Je travaille actuellement à l'accord des Antiquités Sacrées et profanes selon la vérité du texte hébreu. Après avoir décidé sur la chronologie de toute l'Ecriture S.te en général et en particulier éclairci celle de Joseph par de bons mss, fait voir que les anciens samaritains estoient entièrement conformes à l'hébreu d'aujourd'hui, démontré la corruption et les corrupteurs des Septante, développé d'une manière singulière les antiquités des Assyriens, Babyloniens, Mèdes et Tyriens qui ont communion avec nos escritures depuis le temps du roi Ezéchias, fait des nouvelles observations sur les semaines de David, je m'attache aux Antiquités d'Egypte. Mon système est tout particulier. J'en ay pourtant conféré avec monsgr. le Cardinal Noris qui après avoir lû mes cayers en a esté satisfait. Je traite non seulement des Dynasties en général, mais encore de tous les Roys en particulier, et les endroits qui paraissent les plus stériles y deviennent des plus fécondes. Au reste la connexion qu'il y a avec l'Ecriture S.te est si fréquente et si considérable que la chronologie et l'histoire y ont autant du sacré que du profane. Je dois ensuite travailler sur les antiquités des Chaldéens sur lesquels j'ay fait déjà plusieurs remarques conformément au texte hébreu. Je n'oublieray pas encore celle des Chinois et de plusieurs autres Nations dont j'ay découvert les premières Epoques."

The result of this interest was Bonjour's *Antiquitas temporum*. Composed between July 1696 and the spring of 1697, the work was approved for publication by Antonio Pacini on 22 April 1697 and by late May Bonjour was writing to Cuper that the first volume had been completed.[50] Divided into two parts, the first treated the chronology of Israelite history from Creation to the Babylonian captivity and the second discussed the correct arrangement of Manetho's Egyptian dynasties. To this work Bonjour also appended his own edition of Manetho's dynastic list. From his letter to Cuper it appears that this volume was to be followed by several more, in which Chinese, Chaldean, and other ancient chronologies were to be discussed extensively. Unfortunately, this never came to pass. Stymied by the high cost of printing a work which required Hebrew, Arabic, and Syriac typefaces, Bonjour soon turned his attention to Zaccagni's Coptic commission. For a while, he planned to publish the *Antiquitas temporum* as an appendix to his Coptic Bible – intended for those "searching in profane writers for various *monumenti* of sacred scripture" – and, after 1699, as an appendix to his Coptic grammar.[51] The symbolism of having the two works side-by-side is clear: whereas a Coptic grammar would allow scholars to understand ancient Egyptian texts in which were hidden the nuggets of biblical history, a survey of ancient Egyptian history would highlight how these Jewish nuggets had first found their way into an idolatrous Egyptian swamp. As with the rest of Bonjour's learned but monumentally ambitious projects, the *Antiquitas temporum* was unfortunately left to fester in manuscript. Only in his 1705 *Selectae* was Bonjour able to publish a little of his material on Chaldean and Greek history, as well as his work on the ancient Egyptian calendar.[52]

Bonjour's *Antiquitas temporum* was structured as an explicit refutation (or more accurately, correction) of Pezron's *Antiquité des tems*. It was surely not lost on his contemporaries that the works shared the same title. Like Martianay and Lequien before him, Bonjour portrayed Pezron as a more discursive and, in Bonjour's opinion, more rigorous and able follower of Vossius.[53] By detailing the history of the world according to the chronology of the Vulgate, Bonjour sought to show why the chronology Vossius championed and Pezron had delineated so diligently in the *Antiquité des tems* was incorrect – and hence that the Septuagint, far from offering a sound framework for universal chronology, was itself corrupted and flawed.

50   "Regestum Antonii Pacini IV, 1696–169," AGA, DD136, 352; Guillaume Bonjour to Gisbert Cuper, 26 May 1697, KW 72 H 20. See also Michel Bégon to Claude Nicaise, 21 May 1697, NAF 4368, BNF, fol. 142r–v, reprinted in Caillemer, *Lettres de divers savants à l'abbé Nicaise*, 187, and Fossier, *L'abbé Claude Nicaise*, 574.
51   As discussed in chapter 1.
52   *Selectae*, 103–119.
53   Eg. *Antiquitas*, 11 (on their use of Josephus); *Antiquitas*, 49 (on the years of Arphaxad).

3   Jewish and Pagan Sources in Bonjour's Chronology

Bonjour's methods were informed by the same relationship between *historia sacra* and *historia exotica* which formed the basis of his earlier *Mercurius*. To prove that the Vulgate text was superior, Bonjour relied less on specific biblical text criticism as he did on the historical information provided by pagan historians and other extra-biblical sources. Having taken from Scaliger the lesson that ancient, "native" sources were useful in elucidating nebulous particulars in sacred history, Bonjour further supposed that these sources were useful in clarifying *which* sacred history could be considered authoritative. By examining these pagan sources (particularly those preserved in Josephus' *Contra Apionem* and Eusebius' *Praeparatio evangelica*, as also detailed in Scaliger's "Veterum Graecorum fragmenta selecta") Bonjour highlighted how their description of biblical events concorded with the Masoretic rather than the Septuagint chronology.

One such author was the first-century BC Greek, and pronounced anti-Jewish, rhetorician Apollonius Molon. In his work entitled *Against the Jews* (Eusebius, *Praeparatio evangelica* 9.19), Molon had claimed that Abraham was born three generations after the Flood. By interpreting "generationes" (γενεαί) as the term for a hundred years, Bonjour aligned Molon's testimony with the 292-year timespan, which, according to the Vulgate, separated Abraham from the Flood.[54] Another pertinent example was the first-century BC Greek scholar Alexander Polyhistor, whose work, like that of Molon, was partially preserved by Eusebius. Alexander Polyhistor had supposed that the ancient mythological king Belus – whom sacred historians generally identified with Nimrod – had built the Tower of Babel and instructed Abraham in the science of astronomy (*Praeparatio evangelica* 9.18). From this testimony Bonjour concluded that Alexander Polyhistor must have arranged his history according to the shorter Masoretic postdiluvian chronology:

> Even if these words abound with Heathen errors, they still clearly smack of today's calculations of the Hebrews, out of which one can only determine that Abraham was contemporaneous with those who had seen the building of the tower of Babel, the confusion of languages, and the general dispersal of nations thence arisen, while Belus, the name which they endowed Nimrod with, was still alive in Babylonia.[55]

---

54   See Bonjour, "De Chronologia Sacra," BAR, ms.lat.183, 194.
55   *Antiquitas*, 32–33: "Haec licet Gentilismi erroribus scateant, manifesto tamen redolent hodiernos Hebraeorum calculos, ex quibus solum conficitur Abrahamum synchronum his fuisse, qui aedificationem turris Babelicae viderant, confusionem linguarum, indeque

Of similar importance was the testimony of ancient Jews who read their Bible in Hebrew and who were therefore witnesses to the original chronology of the Hebrew Bible before the corruption which Vossius and Pezron had alleged. One such Jewish historian was Eupolemus, whom Bonjour placed in the reigns of the Syrian ruler Demetrius I Soter and the Egyptian king Ptolemy VIII Physcon (nicknamed "Fatty," i.e. φύσκων), both dated to around the early second century BC.[56] In his *Antiquité des tems*, Pezron, building on Vossius' 1661 *Chronologia sacra ad mentem veterum Hebraeorum*, had attempted to align the chronology of Eupolemus with that of the Septuagint.[57] In response, Lequien had rejected the assumption that Eupolemus was Jewish and that he could therefore have read the Bible in Hebrew.[58] On this question Bonjour agreed with Pezron and subsequently identified him with the Eupolemus of 1 Maccabees 8:17 and 2 Maccabees 4:11, a Jewish envoy to Rome. In opposition to Pezron, however, Bonjour supposed that Eupolemus followed the shorter Masoretic chronology. Indeed, through his examination of the various fragments in Josephus' *Contra Apionem*, Clement of Alexandria's *Stromata*, and Theophile of Antioch's *Ad Autolycum*, Bonjour supposed that Eupolemus counted 1656 years between Creation and the Flood *exactly*.[59] For Bonjour, Eupolemus was therefore evidence that the Masoretic chronology had existed

enatam generalem Gentium Dispersionem, Belo, quo Nemrodum nomine donarunt, apud Babyloniam superstite." Compare with "De Chronologia Sacra," BAR, ms.lat.183, 194.

56 *Antiquitas*, 1: "Quin et Samaritarum antiqui codices plane cohaeserunt cum Hebraicis numeris hodierni Judaeorum textus: cohaeserunt et veteres Judaei, nominatim Eupolemus ac Josephus."

57 Pezron, *Antiquité des tems*, 44–45; Isaac Vossius, "Chronologia Sacra ad mentem veterum Hebraeorum et praecipue Josephi exposita," in Isaac Vossius, *De septuaginta interpretibus, eorumque tralatione & chronologia dissertationes* (The Hague: Adriaan Vlacq, 1661), 101–184.

58 Lequien, *Défense du texte hébreu*, 299–306.

59 *Antiquitas*, 19: "Profusissimae istae supputationes etsi minime juvent ad probandos infra Mosen Eupolemi calculos, satis tamen ad eos accedunt, ut illum ita censuisse nullus nos credat, abstineatque a prava emendatione quam hic faciendam suspicaretur sciolus. Hinc Pezronium non satis miror, dum Eupolemum ait intervallum temporis Exodum inter et structuram templi Salominici interjectum summoperè contraxisse. Suis scilicet ante Mosen justo auctioribus calculis fidem ex Eupolemo contra Hebraicam veritatem facturus, nescio qua sibi cogitatione finxit, immensa volumina temporum quae vetus ille chronologus post Mosen computavit, annos ante ipsum elapsos numerosissimos reddere, paucissimos posteriores. O vere destitutam ope chronologiam, inopemque argumentorum, dicamne rationis expertem, quae talia sibi auxilia comparat! Incredibile etiamnum videbitur, talem omnino qualem legimus apud Clementem Alexandrinum, epocham Exodi Eupolemum definiisse?"

long before its supposed invention by malicious, anti-Christian rabbis of the first and second centuries.

Particularly important, however, was Bonjour's use of Flavius Josephus, whom Vossius had made central to the debate concerning the authority of the Septuagint. As Theodor Dunkelgrün has outlined in the context of what he has called the *Testimonium Flavianum Canonicum*, biblical scholars of the seventeenth century had a particular interest in Josephus because they considered him the most ancient, and therefore best, witness to the original state of the Hebrew text.[60] It was this notion which also determined Vossius' – and Bonjour's – interest in Josephus. For Vossius, Josephus – who lived in the time of the Apostles but before the spread of Christianity and almost two centuries before Origen's *Hexapla* – was the most ancient systematic commentator on scripture and therefore a key witness for an earlier version of the biblical text. Moreover, as not only a Jew but a priest and "an interpreter of law among the Jews," he would have read his Bible in Hebrew.[61] By "proving" – often through questionable manuscript emendation – that Josephus followed the Septuagint chronology, Vossius argued that the original Hebrew text of the Bible which Josephus had been working from in the first century AD followed the longer Septuagint chronology before it was purposefully corrupted by mendacious Jewish editors. It was for this reason that, in the following debate between Martianay and Pezron, Josephus took centre stage. According to Pezron, it was "celebre Josephe," the incomparable historian, "qui pourroit seule décider cette question" – the question as to whether the Masoretic or the Septuagint was the original chronology of the Hebrew Bible.[62] In both his *Antiquité des tems* and his *Défense*, Pezron tried to show – largely by relying on the same emendations first proposed by Vossius – that Josephus' histories could be squarely aligned with the Septuagint. Moreover, the evidence supplied by Josephus' histories allowed Pezron to date the corruption of the Hebrew Bible to the period between Josephus completing his *Antiquitates* in about AD 93 and the composition of the Jewish chronicle known as the *Seder Olam Rabbah* in the mid-second century, given that this chronicle counted just 1656 years for the gap between Creation and the Flood and 292 years between the Flood

---

60   Theodor Dunklegrün, "The 'Testimonium Flavianum Canonicum': Josephus as a Witness to the Biblical Canon, 1566–1823," *International Journal of the Classical Tradition* 23 (2016): 252–268.

61   Vossius, *De vera aetate mundi*, xxviii: "Absurdum vero maxime fuerit credere Iosephum, sacerdotem & legum apud Judaeos interpretem neglectis Hebraeis codicibus, Graecam secutum esse versionem. Quin potius ex hac computandi ratione sequitur Codices Hebraicos olim cum Graeca tralatione conspirasse."

62   Pezron, *Antiquité des tems*, 45–46; and Pezron, *Défense*, preface (sig. a3v), 95, 99, 110.

and Abraham's birth. According to Pezron, the corruption of scripture had occurred under the guidance of the famous Rabbi Akiva between the Fall of Jerusalem in AD 70 and the Bar Kokhba revolt in AD 132–136, during which the Jewish Ethnarchs in Tiberias sought to counter the loss of their political power by increasing their stranglehold over copies of Hebrew scripture.[63] If Martianay did not agree with the conclusions Pezron reached, he nevertheless agreed with Pezron's claim that it was Josephus who could settle the question *vis-à-vis* the relationship between the ancient Hebrew and the Septuagint text, and he devoted considerable space in his refutations of Pezron to attempting to prove that Josephus' history concurred with the Masoretic rather than the Septuagint chronology.[64]

Martianay's attempts, however, were largely in vain. It appears that, by the late seventeenth century, a growing number of scholars had come to endorse Vossius' notion that Josephus had followed the Septuagint and some even came to adopt several of Vossius' specific emendations of Josephus' text.[65] It is indicative that, in a letter to Bonjour of December 1697, Cuper described Josephus as "he whom, moreover, the defenders of the Septuagint have claimed for themselves," and that in his 1705 *Selectae*, Bonjour noted that it was necessary to speak of Josephus principally because the supporters of the Septuagint – the *Septuaginti fautores* – had adopted him as their ally.[66] In his *Antiquitas temporum* (and, more briefly, in the relevant dissertation in the *Selectae*) Bonjour therefore sought to challenge this notion by aligning Josephus' chronology with the Vulgate.[67]

In many ways, Bonjour's (chronological) treatment of Josephus was even more rigorous than that of his predecessors. Above all, he embraced the notion that manuscript evidence held the key to fixing the chronological inconsistencies in Josephus' text and therefore determining which biblical chronology he had originally been following. As early as 1696, he had written to Muratori

---

63 Pezron, *Antiquité des tems*, 19–33; Pezron, *Défense*, 51–68, 274–289, 407–425. See also the notes in BNF, Latin 17939. Again, much of this is covered in more detail in Schlichter, "Flavius Josephus."

64 Martianay, *Défense*, 378, in which he cites Pezron's statement that it was Joseph "qui pourroit seule décider cette question."

65 Schlichter, "Flavius Josephus."

66 Cuper to Bonjour, 25 December 1697, BAR, ms.lat.395, fols. 5bisr–5terv and in Pélissier, "Lettres inédites de Gisbert Cuper," 61: "quem caeteroquin LXX Interpretum defensores sibi vendicant"; *Selectae*, D.III.di.III.40, 185: "At illi textus Hebraici desertores trahunt Josephum ad suas partes, ut auctoritate vetustissimi exemplaris, quo ille usus est, ostendant corruptum esse textum hodiernum. Puto tamen eos frustra laborem suscipere."

67 *Selectae*, 185–187.

in order to ask whether the Ambrosiana library in Milan had, as had been rumoured, any ancient manuscripts of Josephus' *Antiquitates judaicae*.[68] Although the Ambrosiana did have one of the oldest and most valuable Latin translations of Josephus, written on Egyptian papyrus, the manuscript did not contain the important chronological sections Bonjour was searching for, as Muratori pointed out in his reply.[69] In the Vatican library, however, Bonjour did discover two manuscripts, *Vaticanus graecus* 984 and *Vaticanus graecus* 1304, which he used to correct readings in Josephus. Of particular importance was *Vaticanus graecus* 984, an epitome of the first ten books of the *Antiquitates*.[70] This manuscript formed the basis of one of Bonjour's most important changes, the emendation of *Antiquitates judaicae* 1.82 from 2656 to 1656, or, more accurately, from "bis mille" (δισχιλίων) to "mille" (χιλίων).[71] This finding was later picked up by Jean Le Clerc – who was particularly impressed with Bonjour's work on Josephus – and cited in later studies of Josephus' chronology by Johann Albert Fabricius, by the German biblical scholars Gottfried Kohlreif and Johann Gottlob Carpzov, and by the octogenarian French chronologist Alphonse des Vignoles (1649–1744).[72] Equally important for Bonjour was the

---

[68] See Guillaume Bonjour to Ludovico Antonio Muratori, 18 February, 4 April, 1 December 1698, in BEM, *Archivio Muratori*, MS 84.16. For the manuscript tradition of Josephus, see Tommaso Leoni, "The Text of the Josephan Corpus; Principal Greek Manuscripts, Ancient Latin Translations, and the Indirect Tradition," in *A Companion to Josephus*, ed. Honora Howell Chapman and Zuleika Rodgers (Chichester: Wiley Blackwell, 2016), 307–321; Heinz Schreckenberg, *Die Flavius-Josephus-Tradition in Antike und Mittelalter* (Leiden: E. J. Brill, 1972); and Étienne Nodet, "Le texte des Antiquités de Josèphe (1.1–10)," *Revue Biblique* 94 (1987): 342.

[69] Ludovico Antonio Muratori to Guillaume Bonjour, 7 March 1698, BAR, ms.lat.395, fol. 125r (and reprinted in *Epistolario di L. A. Muratori*, 1:307–308) ("... sed praeter caracteres lectu difficiles et ex parte iniuria temporus exesos nihil est quod chronologicis notis a te expetitis subveniat"). For the papyrus in question see Flavius Josephus, *The Latin Josephus: Introduction and Text, the Antiquities: Books 1-v*, ed. Franz Blatt (Copenhagen: Universitetsforlaget I Aarhus, Ejnar Munksgaard, 1958), 26, 101–106.

[70] Discussed in Flavius Josephus, *Flavii Josephi opera*, ed. Benedikt Niese (Berlin: Weidmann, 1885–1895), 1:xxi–xxii, 3:x, xxix–xxxiv, 4:xvii–xviii, li, liii and Flavius Josephus, *Flavii Josephi Antiquitatum Judaicarum Epitoma*, ed. Benedikt Niese (Berlin: Weidman, 1896), iv, vii, and "Supplement," 215.

[71] *Antiquitas*, 11–12; *Selectae*, D.III.di.III.40–42, 185–187. Bonjour also discussed Josephus in the same manner in "De Chronologia Sacra," BAR, ms.lat.183, 193–194.

[72] See Le Clerc, "Article IV," 237: "Il seroit à souhaiter que quelque savant Italien entreprît de donner une nouvelle édition de *Joseph*, dont il y a plusieurs MSS. dans les Bibliotheques d'Italie. Il rendroit un très-grand service à la Republique des Lettres"; Le Clerc, "Flavii Josephi Opera," 267; Kohlreif, *Chronologia sacra*, 152; Carpzov, *Critica sacra*, 957; Johann Albert Fabricius, *Bibliotheca graeca liber IV de libris sacris novi foederis, Philone item atq: Josepho, & aliis scriptoribus claris a tempore nati Christi* (Hamburg: Christian Liebezeit,

textual history of the ancient Latin translation of Josephus, which, as Bonjour noted, had been translated by "friends" of Cassiodorus at his famous Italian seminary, the Vivarium, in the sixth century.[73] Consequently, Bonjour went on to use ancient Latin manuscripts of Josephus as well as a manuscript of the eleventh-century epitome of Josephus by the Byzantine historian Zonaras in order to correct Josephus' Greek text and thereby align its chronology with that of the Masoretic text.[74] Interestingly, this practice of emendation is still practiced by (some) modern scholars of Josephus.[75]

4 Bonjour on the Septuagint

More important for our purposes is the manner in which Bonjour used these Jewish and pagan witnesses to understand the history of the biblical text. Bonjour sought to prove not only that Eupolemus and Josephus followed the Hebrew Bible because it was the original version of scripture, but also that the Hebrew text was free from, and in some ways impervious to, textual corruption. For Bonjour, it was not merely a question of Eupolemus and Josephus following the *general*, shorter, chronology of the Masoretic text, but rather a question of them following the Masoretic chronology *exactly*. In Bonjour's opinion, each surviving version of Hebrew scripture featured *exactly* the same chronological calculations for each specific historical period. It was this consistency which made it a fundamentally superior source for ancient, universal history.

The opposite, of course, was true for the Septuagint, the textual history of which Bonjour attacked directly. On the one hand, Bonjour considered the Septuagint a deviation from original Hebrew scripture. He rejected the notion

---

1708), 233; Alphonse des Vignoles, *Chronologie de l'histoire sainte et des histoires étrangères* (Berlin: Ambroise Haude, 1738), 114, 187.

73 Cassiodorus, *Institutiones divinarum et saecularium litterarum* 1.17. See Cassiodorus, *Cassiodorus: Institutions of Divine and Secular Learning and On the Soul*, trans. James W. Halporn (Liverpool: Liverpool University Press, 2004), 149: "… Josephus (almost a second Livy) who composed his books of *Jewish Antiquities* on a large scale. Father Jerome writing to Lucinus Betticus says that he was not able to translate Josephus because of the size of this prolix work. But I have had him translated into Latin in twenty-two books by my friends, a task involving great labour on their part since he is subtle and complex." For the possible translators see Blatt, *The Latin Josephus*, 17–18. See *Antiquitas temporum*, 13; and further BAR, ms.lat.297, fol. 8r.

74 See Daniel R. Levenson and Thomas R. Martin, "The Ancient Latin Translations of Josephus," in *A Companion to Josephus*, 322–344.

75 See Schreckenberg, *Die Flavius-Josephus-Tradition*, 58.

that, as the Letter of Aristeas suggested, the Septuagint had been translated by Alexandrian Jews of the third century. Instead, he argued that it was a product of Jewish Hellenists of the second century who, under the leadership of Onias III, had left Jerusalem to establish a new temple at Leontopolis in Egypt.[76] More importantly, Bonjour supposed that this temple was the product of a Jewish schism, a conscious rejection of the Temple of Jerusalem which, as Bonjour pointed out, was the *"columna et firmamentum veritatis sola,"* the only pillar and ground of the truth (1 Timothy 3:15).[77] Consequently, Bonjour argued that it was the Septuagint rather than the Masoretic text which was a departure from true, ancient, Jewish tradition, and which for this reason mixed veritable Jewish traditions with false Egyptian ones.[78] In this, he also drew on a standard criticism of the Septuagint: that since the Septuagint was composed in Egypt, the translators probably lengthened its chronology artificially in order to make its history more believable to an Egyptian audience who were used to a much greater timespan for ancient history than the one they encountered in the Hebrew Bible.[79]

On the other hand, Bonjour argued that the Septuagint was, particularly in its current state, riddled with textual corruption. The extent of these corruptions meant that it could not offer a firm basis for chronological study. "As far as we are concerned," wrote Bonjour in the opening paragraph to his *Antiquitas temporum*, "there is nothing discordant throughout the many manuscripts of either the Hebrew text or the Vulgate edition; in contrast there is nothing certain, nothing stable, and nothing firm in the Greek calculations."[80] In his 1705

---

76 Josephus, *Antiquitates judaicae* 13.62–68.
77 *Antiquitas*, 21: "Enata hinc defectione Judaeorum Hellenistarum ab Synagoga, quae *columna et firmamentum veritatis* sola erat, ut pote *Ecclesia Dei vivi* eos impunius interpolasse suos codices, et antiquitatibus Aegyptiorum in quas ob permixtas res suas haud difficulter propendebant, auctiori calculo aptasse, quis non videat?" See also the testimony of 2 Kings 21:4, 2 Chronicles 32:19, 1 Esdras 7:19 and Isaiah 2:3.
78 It should be noted that if my discussion of Bonjour's work on the textual history of the Septuagint is brief, it is because Bonjour himself was similarly brief: in only one small passage in the lengthy *Antiquitas temporum* does he reference the origins of the Septuagint translation.
79 As in Samuel Petit, *Variarum lectionum libri III* (Paris: Carol Morel, 1633), 163–168.
80 *Antiquitas*, 1: "Ne quid offendamus in exoticis Gentium monumentis, et perincommode his nos implicari patiamur, sacris paginis ducibus antiquitatem temporum expediendam primum suscipio: et quidem secundum Editionem Vulgatam, seu Hebraicum textum, cujus est versio. Habentes enim Hebraicos numeros quos hic sequamur, quam incongrue confugeremus ad Graecos, subinde perspiciemus ... His alter fidem adhibens siticulosus abscedat e fontibus Hebraeis. Quod ad nos spectat, nihil in chronologia dissonum pariet pro codicum multitudine seu textus Hebraicus seu Editio Vulgata: dum ex adverso in Graecis calculis ferme nihil certi, nihil stabile, nihil firmum, nisi hoc unum incertum

Selectae, Bonjour came to discuss these chronological inconsistencies publicly when he devoted the final dissertation, entitled "Dialogus III. De veritate textus Hebraici adversus calculos Editionis LXX," to discussing the Septuagint chronology.[81] By citing as many Septuagint chronologies as possible, Bonjour sought to underline the fact that the Septuagint provided not one fixed and stable chronological framework but an inconsistent and in many ways contradictory account of ancient history. Using a variety of Septuagint editions – including the Aldine Bible of 1518, the Complutensian Polyglot of 1520, and the Frankfurt Greek Bible of 1597, as well as some of the oldest Septuagint manuscripts available – Bonjour highlighted how the chronologies in Septuagint Bibles not only diverged from the Hebrew and Samaritan texts but also differed amongst themselves. The same was true for the divergent readings which Bonjour found in the writings of the Church Fathers or later Christian chronographers who had used the Septuagint text as the basis for their chronologies. For example, Bonjour pointed out that the thirteenth-century history of Gregory Bar Hebraeus, or "Abulpharagius," surmised the total of Lamech's lifespan after fathering Noah to have been 773 years, but other texts, such as ps.-Eustathius' commentary on the Hexameron, claimed the same lifespan to be 753 years.[82] In similar fashion, Bonjour highlighted how most Septuagint witnesses gave 2242 years for the timespan between Creation and the Flood, and yet others gave 2262 years; indeed, the *Historia ab Adamo* of the seventh-century Greek chronicler John of Antioch even gave a reading of 2342 years.[83] In contrast, Bonjour argued that essentially *every* witness of the Masoretic text gave the same reading of 1656 years.

saepe esse, unde prodeunt. Absit enim, ut talis ac tantae varietatis auctores credamus LXX. Interpretes. Unam quippe et eamdem versionem unà consentientes illi adornarunt. Eam ergo interpolatam et in mendo cubare necesse est, ulliusque roboris esse in codices Hebraeos. Depressa tamen tot varietatibus, tot mendis, veritas emergit aliquando, et primigenii textus defensio interclusa respirat. Quin et Samaritarum antiqui codices plane cohaeserunt cum Hebraicis numeris hodierni Judaeorum textus: cohaeserunt et veteres Judaei, nominatim Eupolemus ac Josephus: quiquid in contrarium sibi suadeant chronologiae Graecae fautores. Id totum eloquar inter sequentes canones."

81   *Selectae*, 173–187.
82   Bonjour, *Selectae*, D.III.di.III.16, 178, citing Gregory Bar Hebraeus, *Historia compendiosa dynastiarum authore Gregorio Abul-Pharajio*, ed. Edward Pococke (Oxford: Richard Davis, 1663), 1:8 and Leo Allatius, ed., *S.P.N. Eustathii archiepiscopi Antiocheni, et martyris in Hexahemeron commentarius* (Leiden: Laurentius Durand, 1629).
83   Bonjour, *Selectae*, D.III.di.III.37, 184–185, citing Henri Valois, ed., "Ex Ioannis Antiocheni Historia ab Adamo," in *Polybii Diodori Siculi Nicolai Damasceni Dionysii Halicar Appiani Alexand Dionis et Ioannis Antiocheni Excepta ex Collectaneis Constantini Augusti Porphyrogenetae* (Paris: Mathurin du Puis, 1634), 779–853.

"In Graecis calculis ferme nihil certi, nihil stabile, nihil firmum" – this was the principle Bonjour applied to the chronology of the Septuagint text. Let us take as one particularly fitting example the age of Arphaxad, the son of Sem (Genesis 11:12–13). In the Masoretic chronology Arphaxad lived for 35 years before he fathered his first-born, Sale, and then a further 303 years until his death, making a total of 338. However, in the different manuscripts and witnesses to the Septuagint, Bonjour found no fewer than five different readings. According to the Byzantine chronologist George Syncellus, Arphaxad lived for 403 years; according to the ancient Septuagint manuscript called the Codex Alexandrinus and the Complutensian Polyglot, 430; according to the Codex Vaticanus, 340; according to Abulpharagius, 330; and finally, according to the Oxford "Cotton Genesis" manuscript, 200.[84]

To scholars across the Alps, Bonjour's scholarly project – in particular, his attempt to show "both the corruptor and the corruption" in the Septuagint – was often met with scepticism. By the late seventeenth century many scholars, particularly in the field of chronology, were increasingly turning to the Septuagint in order to defend the biblical chronology against contemporary sceptics and heretics. In 1700, the French theologian and historian Jacques-Bénigne Bossuet even decided to follow the Septuagint rather than the Masoretic chronology for the third edition of his *Histoire universelle* (first published 1681).[85] As we have seen, both Cuper and Nicaise, Bonjour's most prominent champions in the transalpine Republic of Letters, expressed sympathy for the Septuagint chronology and doubts regarding Bonjour's treatment of it. G. W. Leibniz and Hiob Ludolf went even further. As Leibniz wrote to Nicaise in 1697:

> If Father Bonjour could uphold the Vulgate calculation against the Seventy, it would be at the expense of religion: because I have always thought that the Abbé of Charmoye [Pezron] was right in believing that the chronology of the Chinese (to say nothing of other arguments) obliges us to push back the antiquity of time.[86]

---

84 Bonjour, *Selectae*, D.III.di.III, 173–185.
85 See Urs App, *The Birth of Orientalism* (Philadelphia: University of Pennsylvania Press, 2010), 34–35; Louis-François de Bausset, *Histoire de Bossuet, évêque de Meaux* (Paris: Gaume Frères and J. Leroux, 1846), 1:247.
86 G. W. Leibniz to Claude Nicaise, 16 August 1699, LAA, II, 3:589: "Si le P. Bonjour pouvoit soutenir le calcul vulgaire contre les 70, ce seroit aux depens de la religion; car j'ay tousjours jugé que M. l'Abbé de la Charmoye avoit raison de croire que la chronologie des Chinois (pour ne rien dire d'autres argumens) nous oblige de reculer l'antiquité des temps."

As a result, both Leibniz and Ludolf believed it counterproductive for Bonjour to attack the authority of the Septuagint and tried to direct Bonjour's impressive scholarly abilities to projects they considered more useful. In Leibniz's case this was his plan for a "recueil *vocabulorum Aegyptiorum apud veteres repertorum*." Ludolf, meanwhile, explicitly tried to dissuade Bonjour from attacking the Septuagint. Initially his tone was cautiously supportive. In May 1698, he suggested that Bonjour might want to study an Ethiopic Pentateuch (which he could acquire either from the Abyssinian community in Rome, from Venice, or through the German scholar Hieronymus Ambrosius Langenmantel (1641–1718) in Augsburg) as a point of comparison with the Septuagint and Masoretic texts. Above all, however, Ludolf advised patience and caution in undertaking so ambitious an endeavour and suggested Bonjour transmit his ideas to other learned scholars of the Republic of Letters before setting anything down definitively.[87] Both Leibniz and Huet considered this wise and sage advice from an experienced scholar; Huet even suggested that had Kircher taken the advice Ludolf gave Bonjour, he may have been prevented from falling into some of his more egregious errors.[88] Leibniz and Ludolf, however, were to be bitterly disillusioned by Bonjour's response, in which Bonjour thanked Ludolf for his advice but also expressed his confidence that the conclusions he had already reached were authoritative.[89] Ludolf's reply to Bonjour was disappointed but courteous. To Leibniz, however, he wrote that Bonjour "who promised much, has produced nothing."[90] Leibniz, on the other hand, wrote to Nicaise that Bonjour's reply was "so flat and devoid of realities."[91] Nicaise passed on this information to Bonjour but told him not to worry about the grumblings of dissatisfied German luminaries. Ludolf is erudite and learned, he wrote to Bonjour, but he is, as you know from his works, "somewhat attached to the Septuagint."[92]

---

87   Hiob Ludolf to Guillaume Bonjour, 13 May 1698, BAR, ms.lat.395, fols. 105r–v. Transmitted with the letter of Claude Nicaise to Guillaume Bonjour, 15 August 1698, BAR, ms.lat.395, fol. 155r, and in Pélissier, "Lettres inédites de Claude Nicaise," 194–195. Ludolf's letter is reprinted in Michaelis, *Iobi Ludolfi et Godofredi Guilielmi Leibnitii*, 213–217.
88   Pierre-Daniel Huet to Claude Nicaise, 19 August 1698, BNF, Français 9359, fol. 115r, and in Fossier, *L'abbé Claude Nicaise*, 614.
89   Guillaume Bonjour to Hiob Ludolf, 4 February 1699, in G. W. Leibniz, *Illustris viri Godofr. Guilielmi Leibnitii collectanea etymologica* (Hanover: Nicolai Foerster, 1717), 178–179.
90   Hiob Ludolf to G. W. Leibniz, 17 June 1699, in LAA, I, 17:284: "qui de magnis suis promissis nihil repetit."
91   G. W. Leibniz to Claude Nicaise, 16 August 1699, in LAA, II, 3:589: "si seche et vuide de realités."
92   Claude Nicaise to Guillaume Bonjour, 8 February 1699, BAR, ms.lat.395, fols. 153r–154v and in Pélissier, "Lettres inédites de Claude Nicaise," 195: "M. Ludolphi, docteur et sçavant, comme vous le pouvez cognoistre par ses ouvrages, est un peu attaché aux Septante."

In truth, the breakdown of communication between Ludolf on the one hand and Bonjour on the other is illustrative of the different manner in which they approached biblical text criticism and the different way they conceptualised the historical relationship between various biblical manuscripts. Ludolf was perhaps the foremost scholar of Ge'ez, an ancient Semitic language of Ethiopia, and his study of the Ethiopic Bible had strengthened his conviction that the Septuagint was the authoritative version of the primitive Church and the basis for many ancient biblical translations. Consequently, he supposed that Bonjour's work was detrimental not only to chronological study but also to understanding the first centuries of Christianity. As he wrote to Leibniz:

> Bonjour would be a great Apollo to us if he should accomplish what he has set out to do, since it seems to be a most audacious project indeed to want to show us both the corruptor and the corruption in the version of the seventy translators. For our most learned scholars clearly teach us that this calculation [of the seventy] was already held to be valid from the earliest times of the Greek Church. Nowhere is any variant reading found; nor do any of the Church Fathers mention it. Whence it is that Walton and his colleagues judge, plausibly, that the corruption and divergence from the Hebrew text were committed by some rash person immediately after the original version of the LXX was made. So how will he investigate this matter? For if it had happened only in one scribal copy or another, the variant reading would still remain in one exemplar or another. The Ethiopians, who follow the LXX faithfully, have a different calculation – God knows where it was taken from. I can send it, if Father Bonjour wants it.[93]

Yet Bonjour's study of various ancient biblical manuscripts – and a number of ancient Coptic and Arabic biblical manuscripts in particular – convinced

---

93   Hiob Ludolf to G. W. Leibniz, 13 November 1697, in LAA, I, 14:730: "P. Bonjour magnus nobis foret Apollo si promissa praestaret; nam corruptionem et corruptorem versionis LXX. interpretum nobis ostendere velle, profecto temeritatis magnae videtur. Nam ut viri doctissimi clare nos docent, computatio illa jam a primis Ecclesiae Graecae incunabulis obtinuit: nuspiam ulla datur varia lectio: Nemo Patrum de ea quicquam habet; unde probabiliter censent Waltonus cum sociis corruptionem et diversitatem a textu Hebraico statim a temerario aliquo post πρωτόγραφον τῶν Ο' commissam. Quomodo ergo ille hoc indagabit? Nam si tantum in uno vel altero 'απογράφῳ contigisset, remansisset utique varia lectio in uno vel altero exemplari. Aethiopes, qui τοὺς Ο' κατὰ πόδα sequuntur, aliam supputationem habent, Deus noverit, unde desumtam. Eam communicare possum, si P. Bonjour desideret." Letter also cited in John T. Waterman, ed., *Leibniz and Ludolf on Things Linguistic: Excerpts from Their Correspondence (1688–1703)* (Berkeley and Los Angeles: University of California Press, 1977), 40.

him of precisely the opposite. Pezron had proven that most of the Fathers – with the prominent exceptions of Augustine and Jerome – followed the chronology of the Septuagint until at least the time of Bede. Bonjour, although he cited Augustine's preference for the original Hebrew over the translated Greek version, did not dispute the idea that the Septuagint was the dominant Bible of the early Church. Indeed, he welcomed it. For Bonjour, the number of variants in Septuagint manuscripts, in ancient biblical versions which derived from the Septuagint, and in ancient chronographies which were based on the Septuagint highlighted the multitude of chronological variants in the text and the extent to which the text had been corrupted. This underlines the essential fact that Bonjour privileged the Vulgate over the Septuagint not for dogmatic or theological but for chronological reasons. Bonjour's goal in the *Antiquitas temporum* and in the dissertation he composed for the *Selectae* was to highlight that only the Vulgate Bible could offer a firm, stable, and solid basis for biblical chronology – and conversely, that "in Graecis calculis ferme nihil certi, nihil stabile, nihil firmum."

5 Biblical Scholarship and the Septuagint in Post-Tridentine Rome

Bonjour's very particular criticism of the Septuagint is better understood if we examine the different approach scholars in Rome, including Bonjour, had towards the disciplines of chronology and biblical criticism in general and to Pezron's *Antiquité des tems* in particular. In principle, Pezron's *Antiquité* was at best an alternative and at worst a rival to Bonjour's *Antiquitas*. Whereas Bonjour argued that the chronology of the Septuagint was irredeemably corrupt and that existing non-biblical evidence – whether it be the manuscripts of Josephus, the mythological fragments of ancient Jewish Hellenists, or the chronologies of pagan historians – confirmed the veracity of the Masoretic chronology, Pezron argued that the Vulgate was nothing more than a translation of a biblical text mendaciously corrupted by anti-Christian Jews and hence that the chronologies of ancient Egypt, China, and Chaldea all concurred, and only concurred, with the longer chronology of the Septuagint. Yet despite the enmity Pezron faced from Martianay and Lequien on the basis of these claims, in the Roman chronological community his work was esteemed. Particularly illustrative in this context is the attitude of Noris, who lauded – at least in private – Pezron as being among the greatest living chronologists, alongside his other favourite, the English scholar William Lloyd.[94] In 1691, Noris praised

---

94   See G. W. Leibniz to Marie de Brinon, 15 June 1693, LAA, I, 9:112–113.

the "Eruditus Auctor Anonymus" of the *Antiquité* explicitly because he offered one of the best available studies on the chronology of Christ.[95] In a 1693 letter to Leibniz from Rome, the French traveller François Deseine (d. 1715) noted that Noris considered James Ussher and Pezron "les deux meilleurs chronologistes du siecle," despite the difference of some two thousand years which separated their respective chronologies.[96] It appears that the respect Noris had for Pezron was reciprocated. When Pezron first published his controversial work in 1687, he gifted a copy of the *Antiquité* to Noris through Nicaise; when Noris was appointed *custos* of the Vatican library in 1692, Pezron wrote to Nicaise that the Roman Church "could not favour a man of rarer and more distinguished merit, a choice which will be universally approved by all."[97]

Bonjour, too, openly shared Noris' appreciation of Pezron. That Bonjour copied both Pezron's title and the manner in which Pezron arranged his material should be seen as an expression of Bonjour's debt, rather than his opposition, to the learned Cistercian. Indeed, Bonjour shared a number of key principles with Pezron. Above all, both Pezron and Bonjour believed that Egyptian chronology was the chief source on which La Peyrère had based his heretical hypothesis and that a proper refutation of La Peyrère necessitated a detailed study of Egyptian chronology (as we shall further in the next chapter).[98] In his 1705 *Selectae*, Bonjour explicitly commended Pezron's attempt to prove that the Flood was universal and that Egyptian chronology did not contradict the

95 Noris, "Epistola ad P. Ant. Pagium," *Annus et epochae syromacedonum*, 79.
96 François Deseine to G. W. Leibniz, 17 January 1693, LAA, I, 9:254: "Vous peignez fort au naturel les caractères d'esprit des Peres Hardouin et Noris, je ne croy pas que ce dernier ait répondu à l'autre touchant la medaille en question, il est fort occupé à examiner les livres et manuscrits de la Bibliotheque Vaticane dont il est premier Garde, et qouy que ce soit le plus grand Chronologiste d'Italie, il soupire incessamment apres la nouvelle Chronologie de Mr L'eveque de St. Asaph à laquelle il travaille depuis plusieurs années et qui surpassera de beaucoup Usserius et le Père Pezeron[,] auteur de l'*Antiquité des temps*[,] les deux meilleurs chronologistes du siecle selon luy quoyque fort opposez dans leur calcul qui different de 2000 années[,] le premier comme vous sçavez soutenant l'opinion des Hebreux, et le second s'efforçant à faire revivre l'opinion des Grecs ou de la Bible selon les Septantes Interprétes."
97 Paul Pezron to Claude Nicaise, 8 June 1692, in Fossier, *L'abbé Claude Nicaise*, 428: "elle ne pouvoit pas en favoriser un homme d'un mérite plus rare et plus distingué et ce choix sera universellement approuvé de tout le monde"; Claude Nicaise to Enrico Noris, 21 December 1697, in Pélissier, "Lettres de l'abbé Nicaise au cardinal Noris," 182–183.
98 Especially Bonjour, "Dissertatio Prima; De Antediluviana mundi Aetate," BAR, ms.lat.631, fol. 200r: "At evidentissima quae malo hactenus chronologiae fato pene in angulo jacuerunt, aut ignoranter edita nondum omnino perspecta sunt, tacere non possumus antiquissimarum Gentium monimenta, Chaldaeorum maxime, Phoenicum et Aegyptiorum, quos praecipuos sui fautores inscie prorsus commendavit Praeadamitica fabula. Quos enim certe primores proceresque illi celebrarunt in suis antiquitatibus, eosdem illos fuisse cum Patriarchis Adamitis clare ac sigillatim ostendemus."

chronology of the Bible.[99] In this sense, Bonjour believed that he and Pezron were, despite their chronological differences, part of the same enterprise. Perhaps most indicative of this is the manner in which Bonjour outlined his relationship to Pezron in a letter to Hiob Ludolf of February 1699:

> In these matters, I have nothing clearer for confirming the *Hebraica veritas* than arguments, which records of profane antiquity furnish me. These will be called paradoxes, as long as they are unpublished; may they just not turn out badly for me, when they are committed to print. Of great worth in my opinion is the very famous Pezron, author of the *Antiquity Re-established*. I love his intention, I praise his effort, and I value his ingenuity very highly; nor do I write in order to present myself as his opponent, but in order to show, without rivalry, what is my opinion.[100]

What to make, then, of this surprising affinity – an affinity notably lacking in Pezron's debate with Martianay – between two scholars who fundamentally disagreed on one of the most pressing questions of late seventeenth-century chronology, namely, the authority of the Septuagint *vis-à-vis* the Vulgate text? To my mind, the question goes back to the manner in which scholars conceptualised the "authority" of the various biblical texts. Clearly Martianay, in refuting Pezron, not only differed with Pezron's historical arguments but also considered his defence of the Septuagint contrary to Catholic doctrine, which is to say, contrary to the "authority" of the Vulgate as explicitly stated by the Council of Trent. That Bonjour, and Noris, did not share this opinion should tell us something about the manner in which they interpreted Tridentine "authority" and, more generally, the status of chronology and biblical text criticism in late seventeenth-century Rome.

Let us go back to the beginning of the debate. Famously, the Council of Trent had declared the Vulgate "authoritative." But what did this authority mean? In their first decree concerning the Vulgate, the Council declared anyone an anathema who doubted that the books contained in the Vulgate were sacred and canonical and, further, declared that the Vulgate was the foundation both

---

99   *Selectae*, D.II.43, 86.
100 Guillaume Bonjour to Hiob Ludolf, 4 February 1699, in Leibniz, *Collectanea etymologica*, 179: "Ad haec nihil apertius habeo ad Hebraicam veritatem comprobandam quam argumenta, quae exoticae antiquitatis monumenta mihi suppeditant. Paradoxa haec nominentur, quamdiu erunt inedita; modo non male mihi eveniant, cum erunt typis mandata. Magni tamen apud me est autor antiquitatis restitutae Clmus Pezronius. Voluntatem ejus amo, laudo conatum, solertiam plurimi facio; nec ideo scribo, ut me adversarium in eundem intendam, sed ut sine contentione ostendam, quis sit sensus meus."

for the profession of faith and for the moral teachings of the Church. In the second decree, which dealt with the edition and use of the sacred books, this authority was further explicated thus:

> Moreover, because the Holy Council considers it very useful to the Church if it were known which of all of the Latin editions of the sacred books now in circulation is to be regarded as the authentic version, it declares and decrees: this same Vulgate version which has been preserved by the Church for so many centuries is to be regarded as authentic in public reading, disputations, sermons, and expositions, and let no one dare or presume to reject it on any grounds.[101]

Clearly, then, the term "authoritative" was itself specific. It did not mean – which is to say, it did not *necessarily* mean – that the Vulgate was perfectly or more perfectly in conformity with the original Bible than other ancient versions, nor that the Septuagint or Hebrew Bibles were therefore no longer authoritative. Notably, the Septuagint is entirely absent from the two decrees. Indeed, the "authority" given to the Vulgate was specifically intended to quell contemporary "abuses" which had led to different, conflicting, texts being used and being described as authoritative in public lectures, preaching, disputations, or expositions. Moreover, the authority of the Vulgate was confirmed not by its accuracy as a text *per se* but by its sustained and lengthy use by the Church over the preceding centuries. The goal of the Council was to make, as F. J. Crehan has noted, the Vulgate a reliable source of dogmatic arguments for theological teaching and debate.[102] In some ways, this decision was an elegant reply to an embarrassing fact, namely, the existence of numerous obvious errors in a

---

101 *Concilium Tridentinum. Diariorum, Actorum, Epistularum, Tractatuum nova collectio edidit Societas Goerresiana* (Freiburg: Herder, 1901–2001), 5:91: "Insuper, eadem Sacrosancta Synodus considerans, non parum utilitatis accedere posse Ecclesiae Dei, si ex omnibus latinis editionibus, quae circumferuntur, sacrorum librorum, quaenam *pro authentica* habenda sit, innotescat: statuit et declarat, ut haec ipsa vetus et Vulgata editio, quae longe tot saeculorum usu in ipsa Ecclesia probata est, in publicis lectionibus, disputationibus, praedicationibus et expositionibus *pro authentica* habeatur, et quod nemo illam reicere quovis praetextu audeat vel praesumat."

102 See F. J. Crehan, "The Bible in the Roman Catholic Church from Trent to the Present Day," in S. L. Greenslade, ed., *The Cambridge History of the Bible* (Cambridge: Cambridge University Press, 1963), 199–237, and also, for an enjoyably partisan yet generally correct account, James M. Vosté, "The Vulgate at the Council of Trent," *The Catholic Biblical Quarterly* 9 (1947): 9–25. See also more recently Antonio Gerace, "The Council of Trent and the Sixto-Clementine Vulgate," in *The Oxford Handbook of the Latin Bible*, ed. H. A. G. Houghton (Oxford: Oxford University Press, 2023), 292–304.

Vulgate text that could, and must, nevertheless be considered as fundamentally reliable given that the Holy Spirit would otherwise not have allowed its lengthy use in the Latin Church. The surprising flexibility, if we may call it that, of the Council's decree, is further underlined by the debates within the Council itself. In an earlier draft to the Commission appointed for the examination of abuses, Antoine Imbert Filhol (d. 1550), the Archbishop of Aix, had even gone so far as to say that one should explicitly note that having one authoritative Vulgate version should not detract from the Septuagint "which was often used by the apostles" (although this comment – and, indeed, all references to "other" biblical versions – was eventually omitted from the final decree of 8 April).[103] Yet even the final decree, as we see here, was explicit in stating that the "superiority" of the Vulgate pertained merely to questions of dogma and was specific to "ex omnibus latinis editiones," all other Latin editions.[104]

While it is certainly true that there were scholars who chose to interpret the "authority" of the Vulgate as being a definitive and all-encompassing verdict for the superiority of the Vulgate over all other versions, the judgement of Trent also allowed for a stricter – and paradoxically more liberal – interpretation which encouraged the study and the comparison of other ancient biblical versions – particularly the Hebrew and the Greek Septuagint – in matters not concerning faith and dogma. To a great extent, it gave Catholic scholars a freedom when it came to biblical criticism which was not shared by their Protestant counterparts, a freedom which Richard Simon would later cite to great polemical effect; to another extent, it made biblical text criticism less central to Catholic theologians who knew that the central tenets of their faith were amply demonstrated in a Vulgate text authorised through Church tradition. Both this scholarly freedom and this scholarly disinterest form the two pivots which help explain the immediate context of Bonjour's biblical criticism.

On the one hand, it is noticeable that Catholic biblical scholarship remained a surprisingly fruitful and productive enterprise even after the ruling of Trent. Perhaps the greatest edition of the Greek Septuagint in the sixteenth (or seventeenth) century was the papal-sponsored Sixtine Septuagint of 1587, which was based on the oldest available Septuagint manuscript, the jealously-guarded and much-vaunted fourth-century Codex Vaticanus. Equally important in this context was the work of the great Italian Jesuit theologian Robert Bellarmine (1542–1612), one of the chief representatives of the Tridentine Counter-Reformation and author of his own interpretation of the Tridentine pronouncement on the Vulgate. According to Bellarmine, not only did the Council state

---

103 See Vosté, "The Vulgate," 12ff; *Concilium Tridentinum*, 5:13.
104 *Concilium Tridentinum*, 5:91.

that the Greek and Hebrew versions were not *not* authentic, but the decree even suggested they were *more* authoritative because they were the sources of the Vulgate: "cum illae sint fontes, ista rivius."[105] For Bellarmine, the decision of the Council merely dictated that the Vulgate was the authoritative Latin edition for the Latin church, and made no pronouncements for the Bibles of the Greeks, the Syriacs, the Armenians, or the Copts. Although this opinion was far from universal, Bellarmine was not alone in this sort of reasoning. In 1571 Luis de León, an Augustinian poet and theologian who was professor of theology at Salamanca, reportedly told his 300 students that although the Council of Trent had approved the Vulgate as the official Bible of the Catholic church, it had not prohibited the study of the original Hebrew and Greek texts, which could elucidate the Bible more clearly. Although he was imprisoned for some five years for this and a number of other "controversial" statements, he returned triumphantly to the university in 1577 – reportedly beginning his lecture with the immortal words of "as we were saying yesterday" – and two years later he was elected to the prestigious Bible Chair.[106]

In the late seventeenth century, Bellarmine in particular remained a touchstone for Catholic biblical critics. It was Bellarmine's *De verbo Dei*, for example, that Richard Simon cited in his attack on Calvin, arguing that the Council had never claimed that the Vulgate was more authoritative because it was closer to the original or preferential to all other ancient texts.[107] Yet Bellarmine's notion

---

105 This opinion was most firmly stated in Bellarmine's *De editione latina vulgata*, which was not published until 1748: see Xavier-Marie Bachelet, *Bellarmin et la Bible sixto-clémentine: étude et documents* (Paris: G. Beauchesne, 1911), 107–125. However, Bellarmine already made a number of these points openly in his *De verbo Dei*, as we shall see: Robert Bellarmine, "De verbo Dei," in *Disputationum Roberti Bellarmini Politiani, e Societate Iesu, S.R.E. cardinalis; De controversis Christianae fidei, adversus huius temporibus haereticos* (Cologne: Johann Gymnich and Anton Hierat, 1615) 1:1–84. On Bellarmine, see Piet van Boxel, "Robert Bellarmine, Christian Hebraist and Censor," in *History of Scholarship*, ed. Ligota and Quantin, 251–276; and Ulrich Horst, "Robert Bellarmin und die Vulgata," in *Päpstliche Unfehlbarkeit wider konziliare Superiorität?* (Brill: Leiden, 2016), 305–335 (and other relevant articles in this collection more generally).
106 See Gutierrez and Gavigan, *The History of the Order*, 2:155–156.
107 Richard Simon, *Histoire critique du Vieux Testament* (Rotterdam: Reinier Leers, 1685), 456: "A l'égard de la Vulgate, qui a été declarée authentique par le Concile de Trente, il répond judicieusement à Calvin & aux autres Heretiques qui condamnoient en cela les Peres du Concile, qu'on n'avoit point touché dans ce Concile aux Originaux, qui conservoient toûjours la même autorité qu'ils avoient auparavant: mais que l'Eglise, qui ne pouvoit souffrir aucune nouveauté, avoit seulement ordonné que l'ancienne Version Latine de la Bible seroit préférée à toutes les nouvelles." Simon was referring to Bellarmine, chapter 10, book 2, entitled "De auctoritate Latina editionis vulgatae": cf. Bellarmine, "De verbo Dei," 38–39.

that Tridentine "authority" should not detract from the historical importance of other biblical texts was shared more widely. Perhaps there is no better indication of this fact than the judgement of Jean Mabillon. In 1686, Mabillon was asked by the Congregation of the Index to examine Vossius' *Dissertatio de vera aetate mundi* and *De septuaginta interpretibus* on three grounds: Vossius' claim that the Septuagint contained the original Hebrew text, his preference for the Septuagint over the Vulgate or Masoretic chronology, and his notion that the Flood was not universal but particular. Importantly, Mabillon summarily dismissed the first two points as harmless, noting that Vossius said nothing of the Vulgate and that it was incontestable that in the first four centuries of the Church the Fathers followed the Septuagint.[108] Only on the third point did Mabillon suggest a potential danger, but even here he demurred. Just one author – namely Edward Stillingfleet – was known to have followed Vossius' opinion, and he was attacked not by Catholics but by Protestants: indeed, Georg Horn, Vossius' chief opponent, had charged Vossius with imbibing the opinion of the accursed papists. Since the work seemed to incur much more friction between Protestants than Catholics, Mabillon suggested that no censure was needed.[109] Now it is true that the somewhat ham-fisted Index chose not to follow Mabillon's advice and came to censure both Vossius and Horn, as Mabillon recommended they must do if they chose to censure Vossius. Yet it is also clear from Mabillon's comments that many Catholic scholars did not consider Vossius' (and by extension Pezron's) arguments in favour of the Septuagint damaging to Catholic doctrine.

When Pezron came to compose the *Antiquité*, it was exactly on this basis that he defended his attack on the ancient Hebrew text and consequently the Vulgate. He noted, for example, that the Roman Church must have accorded some authority to the Septuagint given that it was used by Cesare Baronio – the Roman Counter-Reformation historian (and propagandist) *par excellence* – in his *Martyrologium romanum* of 1586, something which was also noted by

---

108   Jean Mabillon, "Votum D. Joannis Mabillonii de quibusdam Isaaci Vossii Opusculis," in Vincent Thuillier, ed., *Opera posthuma DD. Joannis Mabillonii et Theodorici Ruinart, Benedictinorum e Congregatione Sancti Mauri* (Paris: François Babuty, Jean-François Josse, Antoine Claude Briasson, 1724), 2:60: "In duo prima capita, nempe de autoritate LXX Interpretum supra Hebraïcarum textum, & de aetate mundi, non videtur, salvo meliori judicio, quidquam statuendum: tum quia auctor istis in locis nihil detrahit vulgatae nostrae versioni: tum quia latina Ecclesia LXX Interpretum calculum quatuor primis saeculis secuta est, eumdemque etiam nunc Romana Ecclesia retinet in Martyrologio suo ad Natalem Domini." Cf. Reusch, *Index*, 2:115.

109   Mabillon, "Votum," 2:63. Cf. Matthew Poole, ed., *Synopsis criticorum aliorumque sacrae scripturae interpretum* (London: J. Flesher and T. Roycroft, 1669–1680), 1:94–99.

Bonjour's close friend Jean-Pierre Rigord.[110] Moreover, in his *advertissement*, Pezron knowingly paraphrased the judgement of Trent when he stated that his attack on the Vulgate was purely chronological and that he continued to regard the text as "très authentique en ce qui regarde la foy & les moeurs," very authentic in matters concerning faith and morals.[111] In his *Défense*, he repeated and amplified many of these notions. Citing Bellarmine's *De verbo Dei*, Pezron argued that the Catholic Church had never proclaimed the Vulgate as a perfect text: why else would they correct Jerome's translation of Isaiah 19, and why else would the Sixto-Clementine Vulgate include as canonical books which Jerome had rejected as spurious, such as the book of Baruch and the Letter of Jeremiah?[112] Having abstained from citing the judgement of Trent explicitly in his 1687 *Antiquité*, he made his interpretation of the Council's decree explicit in his 1691 *Défense*: "The Council of Trent, enlightened by his Holy Spirit, was right to declare the Vulgate authentic since there is nothing contrary to faith and morals in it, to prefer it to all the Latin versions based on the Hebrew, and to leave it, superior to any other version, in the hands of the faithful, who have used it for so many centuries."[113]

It is clear that Martianay did not accept Pezron's protestations of innocence. In his first reply to Pezron, he noted explicitly that Pezron's opinion would "expose the Council of Trent to the ridicule of some Protestants, who would not fail to note, that the Church of Rome declared *authentic* a Latin version, which was based on books either *spoiled or suspect*."[114] Yet it does not appear that the circle around Noris and Bonjour shared Martianay's opinion. Instead, it appears that Bonjour shared Bellarmine's assumption that a study of the Hebrew and Greek texts, not to mention Arabic, Coptic, or Syriac biblical manuscripts, could help clarify both the history of the biblical text(s) and certain passages in the texts themselves. To aid his studies in this field, Bonjour made prominent use of Protestant biblical text criticism. As we have noted previously, from at least 1705 Bonjour had received through the efforts of

---

110 Pezron, *Antiquité des tems*, 12; Jean-Pierre Rigord to Antonio Magliabechi, 28 October 1686, BNCF, *Fondo Magliabechiano* VIII, cod. 341, fols. 2r–7v.
111 Pezron, *Antiquité des tems*, "avertissement."
112 Pezron, *Défense*, 374.
113 Pezron, *Défense*, 392: "le Concile de Trente éclairé de son Esprit saint a eu raison de la déclarer autentique, puisqu'elle n'a rien de contraire à la foy & aux moeurs, de la preferer à toutes les Versions Latines formées sur l'Hebreu, & de la laisser, préférablement à toute autre, entre les mains des Fidelles, qui s'en servent si utilement depuis tant de siécles."
114 Martianay, *Défense*, 277–278: "exposer le Concile de Trente aux railleries de quelques Protestans, qui ne manqueroient pas de dire, que l'Eglise de Rome a declaré *authentique* une Version Latine, qui avoit été faite sur des livres ou *gâtez ou suspects*."

Barbarigo a *licentia* to read banned books, which included Walton's infamous "Prolegomena" to the London Polyglot. In his *Selectae in sacram scripturam*, Bonjour made use of the Polyglot in order to cite variant biblical readings from the Codex Alexandrinus, a fifth-century manuscript of the Septuagint that the English diplomat Thomas Roe (1581–1644) had acquired from the Greek Patriarch of Constantinople Cyril Lucaris (1572–1638) in 1627/28, in order to consolidate his argument that the Septuagint text was unable to establish a firm basis for chronological scholarship. In addition, he also made use of readings from the Oxford Cotton Genesis and the text-critical notes of the German philologist Franciscus Junius (1591–1677).[115] Bonjour's diverse notes in the Biblioteca Angelica further underline his interest in Protestant text criticism, particularly when it came to his work on Coptic and his use of a variety of biblical manuscripts to better understand the Vulgate text. In the course of editing the Coptic-Arabic Psalter, he made frequent references not only to the "Prolegomena" of Walton but also the work of Edmund Castell (1606–1686), Abraham Wheelocke (1593–1653), Johann Heinrich Hottinger (1620–1667), Thomas Bangius (1600–1661) and Georg Calixtus (1586–1656); in the context of his study of the Egyptian church, he even had recourse to the *Antibarbarus biblicus* (1628) of the onetime Dutch Reformed theologian at Franeker Sixtinus Amama (1593–1629), whose work contained extensive criticisms of the Vulgate text.[116] There can be no doubt that Richard Simon had his tongue firmly in his cheek when he noted, in a 1692 letter to the French and diplomat and scholar Nicolas Frémont d'Ablancourt (1625–1693), that "if we did not know the writers who had worked on the Prolegomena printed as a preface to the English Polyglot, and that Walton was its compiler, we would easily believe that this work had come from the hand of some Catholic," but it might also

---

115 On the Codex Alexandrinus see Scott Mandelbrote, "English Scholarship and the Greek Text of the Old Testament, 1620–1720: The Impact of Codex Alexandrinus," in *Scripture and Scholarship in Early Modern England*, ed. Ariel Hessayon and Nicholas Keene (Aldershot: Ashgate, 2006), 74–93; Scott Mandelbrote, "The Old Testament and its ancient versions in manuscript and print in the West, from c. 1480 to c. 1780," in *The New Cambridge History of the Bible*, ed. Euan Cameron (Cambridge: Cambridge University Press, 2016), 3:82–109; and Scott Mandelbrote, "The History of Septuagint Studies: Early Modern Western Europe," in *The Handbook of the Septuagint*, ed. Alison G. Salvesen and Timothy Michael Law (Oxford: Oxford University Press, 2021), 33–51. On the Cotton Genesis see Gerald Bonner, "The Cotton Genesis," in *The British Museum Quarterly* 26 (1962): 22–26 and James Carley, "Thomas Wakefield, Robert Wakefield and the Cotton Genesis," *Transactions of the Cambridge Bibliographical Society* 12 (2002): 246–265.

116 Bonjour, "Psalterium Copto-Arabicum," BAR, ms.lat.45, fol. 640r; and BAR, ms.lat.631, fols. 156r–157v.

be indicative.[117] Certainly, Walton's "Prolegomena" had been on the Index since 1663, and yet Simon noted that it had "the general approval of Catholics, even in Rome," a fact underlined by Bonjour's own use of the work.[118] Indeed, it seems clear from Bonjour's relationship with Pezron and his use of Walton that he – and, by extension, Noris – did not consider biblical text criticism and chronological scholarship damaging to the Tridentine "authority" of the Vulgate. It is this fact which also explains the amicability between Pezron on the one hand and Noris and Bonjour on the other. As we have noted, Bonjour esteemed Pezron's scholarship and wrote not in order to make Pezron his enemy but merely to present an alternative interpretation.[119] It is indicative that Pezron shared this view. As he wrote to Nicaise:

> It seems to me, as you told me, that the Reverend Father Bonjour has grand designs, and if he executes them as he promises he will be worthy of eternal praise, and he will bring honour to his country and to our France. I would be delighted if he is able to show that the Hebrew text of the Samaritans once conformed fully to the Hebrew text of the Jews, which many people have difficulty in persuading themselves of. Besides, I am obliged to him for speaking so honestly of me in the letter he wrote to Monsieur Ludolf. And, although he is not of my opinion, I do not resent him for it. Everyone is free in those kinds of things which do not concern faith or morals; for me, the sentiment of the ancient Fathers and of the ancient chronologists seems to me more truthful than those of the moderns. Be that as it may, the Reverend Father Bonjour will be praiseworthy and esteemed by everyone if he deals with the matters he has dedicated himself to without offending anyone and while speaking honestly of those who do not share his ideas. I honour him perfectly, as a wise and moderate man, who will make a great name for himself in the world if he executes what he promises. You would bring me pleasure if, when you write to him, you assure him of my esteem and my respect.[120]

---

117 Richard Simon, *Lettres choisies de M. Simon* (Amsterdam: Pierre Mortier, 1730), 3:122: "si l'on ne connoissoit les Ecrivains qui ont travaillé aux Prolegomenes qu'on a imprimez à la tête de la Polyglotte d'Angleterre, & dont Walton n'a éte que le Compilateur, on croiroit facilement que cet ouvrage seroit sorti de la main de quelque Catholique. Aussi a-t-il eu une approbation generale de tous les Catholiques, même jusques dans Rome."
118 Simon, *Lettres choisies*, 3:122; cf. Reusch, *Index*, 2:124–125.
119 Guillaume Bonjour to Hiob Ludolf, 4 February 1699, in Leibniz, *Collectanea etymologica*, 179.
120 Paul Pezron to Claude Nicaise, 29 March 1699, BNF, Français 9361, fol. 82r: "Il me paroit parceque vous me marqués, que le Reverend pere Bonjour a de grands desseins, s'il

And yet it is clear that, in Bonjour's Rome, there also reigned a general disinterest in biblical criticism, particularly criticism which relied on a knowledge of Oriental languages and which compared the Vulgate with its Greek and Hebrew sources. Bonjour's interest in Protestant text criticism was partly due to the relative paucity of Catholic works in this area, a paucity which Bonjour himself acknowledged and lamented. Nor was he alone in this opinion. Similarly indicative of the somewhat sorry state of Roman text criticism and linguistic knowledge is the work of the Jesuit biblical scholar Giacomo Maria Airoli (1660–1721), a friend and correspondent of Bonjour who became professor of Hebrew at the Collegio Romano in 1704. In that year, Airoli published his *Dissertatio biblica*, an examination of various ancient biblical translations written in the form of a dialogue in which he attempted to persuade Catholic scholars of the utility of biblical text criticism. In particular, Airoli was keen to refute those Catholics who still believed that the decision of Trent authorised the Vulgate to the explicit detriment of the irreparably corrupt Hebrew and Greek versions. Citing the words of the Spanish Jesuit Alfonso Salmerón (1515–1585), Airoli argued as Bellarmine and more recently Pezron had done that the authority of the Vulgate was relevant only "in rebus ad fidem, & mores spectantibus," in matters pertaining to faith and morals.[121] Consequently, he exhorted Catholic scholars to return to the study of both the Greek and Hebrew texts in order to help refute scholarly errors not related to faith and morals. "How little you understand in many passages in the Vulgate itself without the help of the Greek and Hebrew language, how often you follow a foreign meaning, nay one even contrary to the true sense," Airoli warned.[122] According

   les executé comme il promet il sera digne d'une louange éternelle, et il fera honneur à sa patrie et à nostre France. Je serois ravi s'il pouvoit montrer que le Texte hebreu des Samaritains a autrefois esté entierement conforme a l'Hebreu des Juifs, bien des gens ont peine à s'en persuader. Au reste je luy suis obligé de ce qu'il parle de moy avec honnesteté dans la lettre qu'il a écrite a Monsr. Ludolfe. Et quoy qu'il ne soit pas de mon sentiment, je ne luy en scay pas plus mauvais gré. Chacun est libre dans ces sortes qui ne regardent la foy ny les moeurs; pour moy le sentiment des anciens Peres et des anciens Chronologistes me paroit bien plus veritable, que celuy des modernes. Quoy qu'il en soit le Rd. pere Bonjour sera louable et estimé de tout le monde s'il traitte les matieres qu'il a entreprises sans choquer personne et en parlant honnestement de ceux qui n'ont pas les mesmes idées que luy. Je l'honnore parfaitement, comme un homme sage et moderé et qui se fera un grand nom dans le monde s'il exécute bien ce qu'il nous promet. Vous me feréz plaisir quand vous luy écriréz de l'assurer de mon estime et de mon respect."

121   Giacomo Maria Airoli, *Dissertatio biblica in qua scripturae textus aliquot insigniores adhibitis linguis Hebraea, Syri. Chald. Arab. Graeca, Latina, per dialogismum dilucidantur* (Rome: Typis Sacra congregatio de Propaganda fide, 1704), 4.
122   Airoli, *Dissertatio biblica*, 5: "Vulgatam ipsam quam multis in locis sine ope hebraicae, vel graecae linguae quam parum intelliges, quam saepe alienum, imo etiam contrarium vero sensui sequeris."

to Airoli, the false interpretation by many scholars of the true meaning of the Council of Trent had led Catholics to abandon biblical text criticism to their Protestant counterparts. This opinion he shared with Bonjour. Indeed, between 1705 and 1706, the two scholars corresponded extensively on matters of biblical chronology – and in particular, on the weeks of Daniel – while Bonjour was in Montefiascone, although it is likely that they first met while Bonjour was still in Rome. In particular, Airoli praised Bonjour's skill in Oriental languages and his desire to use these languages to better understand the biblical text.[123]

This was a notion which Bonjour made explicit in his manuscript notes. Here, Bonjour declared quite explicitly that those who believed that the Vulgate and the Vulgate alone was the only text of importance for Catholic scholars were in error. "The authenticity of the Vulgate edition of the Holy Bible does not keep us away from either the Hebrew or Greek sources, but rather leads us to consult them," he noted programmatically.[124] Citing the words of Johan Willemsz, or Johannes Harlemius (1538–1578), one of the editors of the sixteenth-century Antwerp Polyglot, Bonjour sought to exhort scholars – which likely meant his students – to understand the Vulgate fountain by paying attention to its many ancient sources: the Hebrew, Chaldean, and Greek texts for the Old Testament, and the Syriac and Greek texts for the New.[125] Like Airoli, Bonjour hoped to convince his Catholic counterparts that the study of Oriental languages and various biblical versions was not only permitted by Trent but that it was useful, necessary even, for better understanding the biblical text; like Airoli, he sought to induce his Catholic counterparts to engage in a scholarly discipline which the Protestants had largely arrogated to themselves. As Muratori noted when Bonjour informed him of his biblical projects, "my praises will remain among the commoners, lovers of more serious learning will extoll you. For you

---

123 Giacomo Maria Airoli to Guillaume Bonjour, 22 August, 9 September, 4 November 1705, and 25 April 1706, BAR, ms.lat.395, fols. 69r, 70r–71v, 72r, 74r.

124 BAR, ms.lat.634, fol. 38r: "Authentia [sic] editionis Vulgatae Sacrorum Bibliorum non arcet nos a fontibus vel Hebraicis vel Graecis, immo potius ad eos consulendos nos adigit."

125 BAR, ms.lat.634, fol. 38r: "Ad haec, cum varias vulgatae Latinae editionis lectiones invenimus, quaenam earum ad textum Hebraeum, Chaldaeum et Graecum in veteri instrumento; aut ad Syrum et Graecum in novo, propius accedat, indicare voluimus; tum quod hoc omnibus sacrarum literarum studiosis longe gratissimum fore putaremus; tum quod turbatis rivulis ad fontes recurrendum esse excellentes doctores, atque Ecclesiae Catholicae lumina semper judicaverint." See Johan Harlemius, "Lectiones in Latinis Biblis editionis Vulgatae ex vetustissimis Manuscriptis exemplaribus collectae, et ad textum hebraicum, chaldaicum, graecum et syriacum exminatae, opera et industria aliquot Theologorum in Academia Lovaniensi" in *Biblia sacra, hebraice, chaldaice, graece et latine ...* ed. Benedictus Arias Montanus, 8 vols (Antwerp: Christophe Plantin, 1569–1573), 8. See also Boxel, "Robert Bellarmine."

will satisfy one function among the Catholics, which the Heterodox, devoted to ancient languages with such a contentious spirit, could scarcely hope for."[126]

Bonjour's friendship with Pezron and Airoli, his engagement with Protestant text criticism, and his manuscript exhortations should lead us to better understand the true context of Bonjour's biblical text criticism and the aims of his *Antiquitas*. Above all, it should lead us to remark on three important features. Firstly, we should note that Bonjour worked within a culture in which extensive scholarship on ancient biblical manuscripts was both acceptable and rare. Although the decision of Trent allowed for a tradition of Catholic scholarship which emphasised that interest in and scholarship on the ancient Greek and Hebrew biblical versions did not detract from the *type* of authority which the Vulgate had been granted – a tradition in which Bellarmine loomed large, and in which we can find Pezron, Noris, and Bonjour – this was still a minority opinion among Catholic and Roman scholars of the late seventeenth century, as Airoli and Muratori's comments show. In this sense, Bonjour's extensive use of works of Protestant biblical text criticism was also an attempt to convince Catholic scholars that such text criticism was not opposed to Catholic doctrine. Consequently, Bonjour's defence of the Vulgate – or, more accurately, Vulgate chronology – should not be seen as a blinkered attempt to defend the decree of Trent but rather part of a desire to further contribute to and develop the comparative study of ancient biblical versions. Secondly, we should reiterate that despite Bonjour's public and oft-repeated criticism of the Septuagint, his criticism was founded primarily on *chronological* grounds. Essentially, Bonjour argued that the Septuagint could not be accorded authority on specifically *chronological* matters because it could not provide a firm or stable basis for universal chronology, unlike the Vulgate, the *Hebraica veritas*. Yet this does not mean that Bonjour had a blind preference for the Vulgate or that he rejected the authority of the Septuagint *in toto*. As we have seen, Bonjour was part of a small but important group of scholars who supposed that better understanding the Bible rested on the study and comparison of many different, ancient, versions. Thirdly, we should note that, in doing so, Bonjour was very much in accord with Pezron, despite their differences concerning the Septuagint chronology. Both Pezron and Bonjour agreed that the question of chronology was not relevant to the authority of the Vulgate in faith and morals, and therefore did not impinge on the decision of Trent. Moreover, both scholars argued that

---

126   Ludovico Antonio Muratori to Guillaume Bonjour, 6 July 1698, BAR, ms.lat.49, fol. 374v, and reprinted in Campori, *Epistolario di L. A. Muratori*, 1:322: "Me vulgi laudes manebunt, te gravioris eruditionis amantes extollent; unum enim munus apud Catholics implebis, quod vix Heterodoxi tanta animi contentione vetustis linguis addicti sperent."

understanding the proper chronology of the Bible was pivotal for integrating pagan histories with the biblical narrative. In this sense, they also had a common enemy: those scholars who ignored or even rejected chronology within their examination of different biblical versions, above all Jean Martianay. In his criticism of Pezron, Martianay had dismissed chronology as a discipline, lambasted Pezron and Bonjour's cherished Fathers for their chronological errors, and simply rejected inconvenient pagan evidence as fallacious. For Bonjour, this notion was far more problematic than Pezron's argument in favour of the Septuagint chronology: by failing to integrate biblical and pagan chronology, Martianay provided ammunition to pre-Adamites who cited the incompatibility of pagan and biblical history in favour of their heretical theories. In writing the *Antiquitas temporum*, Bonjour attempted to prove not only that it was the Vulgate which provided an authoritative chronology for ancient history, but that pagan sources thought to contradict the Bible could be harmonized with this chronology.

It was precisely this notion which led him to his sustained interest in and ingenious interpretation of perhaps the most notorious author of seventeenth-century chronology, that ancient priest of Egypt, Manetho of Sebennytos. Although dead for almost two millennia, his history became something of a *cause célèbre* in the seventeenth century: cited both in defence of and in opposition to the biblical record, praised by some as the most accurate account of ancient Egypt and lambasted by others as a malicious coterie of pagan fables. In the second part of the *Antiquitas temporum*, Bonjour sought to prove exactly how this most controversial account of ancient Egyptian history not only failed to diminish the authority of the chronology of the Bible, but might prove crucial for proving the exactitude of its most reliable version, the Vulgate. Egyptian history, from being the greatest rival to Jewish antiquity, had become its most important ally.

CHAPTER 5

The Dynasties of Manetho

1 The Antiquity of Egypt

Since antiquity, scholars of *historia sacra* had been aware of the great, or supposedly great, antiquity of the Egyptian nation. In the preface to Diogenes Laërtius' *Vitae philosophorum* they could read that Egyptian priests counted 48,863 years between the reign of the first king Hephaestus and Alexander of Macedon (1.1–2). Similarly, Pomponius Mela (1.59) recorded that 330 pharaohs reigned before Pharaoh Amasis (c.570–526 BC) and Egyptian antiquity covered a period of some 13,000 years; Herodotus (2.142) that 11,340 years separated the first king "Min" from the 341st, Sethos; and Diodorus, conservative by comparison, that the first "mortal" kings ruled Egypt some 5,000 years before the Ptolemies (1.44.1). Even wise Plato – "Moses Atticans" – claimed that some Egyptian laws were 10,000 years old (*De legibus* 2.657a).

And yet, these vague numbers never amounted to historical proof. As Ben Zion Wacholder has pointed out, the challenge pagan historians posed for biblical chronology was not *necessarily* a serious one.[1] Their texts could be emended, reinterpreted, or simply dismissed, as Augustine had once done (*De civitate dei* 18.40).[2] Indeed, the supposed vanity of barbarian nations who sought to outdo each other by vaunting their antiquity had been a scholarly trope since the time of the Church Fathers. Later, Giambattista Vico even standardized this practice as a cognitive principle, what he called a "property of the human mind" (proprietà della Mente umana); or, in the words of Paolo Rossi, a "true literary *topos*," the *boria delle nazioni*.[3] Pagan histories which contradicted biblical history were evidence of profane ignorance, not the fallibility of sacred records.

In the seventeenth century, scholars routinely described Egyptian chronology as one of if not the most difficult area of contemporary scholarship: a field of study in which requisite linguistic and historical knowledge was lacking and

---

[1] Wacholder, "Biblical Chronology in the Hellenistic World Chronicles," 461.
[2] A passage remarked upon explicitly by Joseph Scaliger, "Isagogicorum Chronologiae Canonum," *Thesaurus temporum*, 309–310: "De excessu annorum, quos supra rationes Biblicas sibi vindicant Aegyptij, & aliae priscae nationes, vide Augustinum libro XII, cap. x de Civit."
[3] Giambattista Vico, *Principj di scienza nuova* (Napoli: Muziana, 1744), 40; Vico, *The New Science*, 31–32; Rossi, *The Dark Abyss of Time*, 168–9.

in which relevant source material was scanty and often flawed. According to Herodotus, the first historical contact between Hellenes and Egyptians – which first allowed historians to gather "precise knowledge about all the events that took place there" (2.154.4) – had only occurred in the reign of "Psammetichus" (Psamtik I, 664–610 BC).[4] Early modern scholars were hardly more optimistic. In his 1648 treatment of Asian and Egyptian histories the German scholar Hermann Conring (1606–1681) supposed that it was impossible to gain an accurate knowledge of Egyptian history before Psammetichus.[5] A similar opinion was held by the Leiden-based classicist Jacobus Perizonius, whom Nicaise had recently informed of Bonjour's attempt to untangle Egyptian chronology. As Perizonius wrote to Nicaise:

> Also I owe you great thanks for what you tell me about the Egyptian antiquities which the erudite man from the Augustinian family is about to publish; I have not yet seen the preliminary dissertations which you mention. The matter is certainly difficult, as you write, when moreover the history of those people before Psammetichus is exceedingly hidden in obscurity and we have very few records of those people from the ancient period.[6]

Nor had the discovery of Manetho and his dynastic list of Egyptian kings necessarily helped to alleviate matters. "The series of Egyptian kings," wrote Jacques Cappel in 1613, "burst forth with an inextricable labyrinth."[7] For Paul Pezron, they were a form of torture.[8] According to the French chronologist

---

4 Translation from Herodotus, *The Landmark Herodotus*, ed. Strassler, 190.
5 Hermann Conring, *Asiae et Aegypti antiquissimis dynastiis adversaris chronologica* (Helmstedt: Henning Müller, 1648), 77: "Haec sane accurate attendentibus haud difficile pronunciatu videtur, ei quae Psammitichi tempora antecedit Aegyptiorum historiae, utpote solorum Aegyptiorum narrationibus nitenti, non posse tuto fidem adhiberi quemcunque etiam placuerit ducem sectari." Psammetichus was also cited in this vein by Witsius, *Aegyptiaca*, 193, and Vico, *The First New Science*, 29.
6 Cited in Claude Nicaise's letter to Guillaume Bonjour, 10 June 1698, BAR, ms.lat.395, fols. 156r–157r, and in Pélissier, "Lettres inédites de Claude Nicaise," 198: "Magnas etiam de eo tibi gratias debeo, quod significas de Aegyptiacis antiquitatibus quas expositurus est vir eruditus ex augustinianorum familia; dissertationes ejus quas memoras proeliminares nondum vidi. Res profecto est ardua, ut scribis, cum etiam illus [sic] gentis historia ante Psammetichum valde in obscuro lateat et paucissima habeamus ex antiquo tempore illius monumenta."
7 Cappel, *Historia sacra et exotica ab Adamo*, 66: "Regum Aegypti series labyrinthis inextricabilibus scatet."
8 Pezron, *Antiquité des tems*, 173: "les *Dynasties des Egyptiens*, qui ont donné la torture à tous les sçavans."

Urbain Chevreau (1613–1701), constructing an exact chronology was a task which exceeded the limits of the human intellect.[9] "There is nothing that one is less able to explain," wrote Bonjour in the preface to his most extensive treatment of Manetho's dynasties, "than Egyptian chronology."[10] In his 1708 *Bibliotheca graeca*, the Hamburg-based antiquarian and philologist Johann Albert Fabricius, surveying the recent scholarship on Manetho, came to the same conclusion:

> And there will certainly have been nothing more difficult than untangling the dynasties of Manetho, and reconciling them with surviving ancient history.[11]

Yet the true importance of chronology, and Egyptian chronology specifically, lay not in correctly dating a pharaoh like Necherophes, but rather the consequences dating Necherophes might have for biblical history and, for those more radically inclined, authority.[12] In 1655, La Peyrère had cited Egyptian chronology in order to prove that Gentile history began long before the accepted biblical date for Creation.[13] In the second half of the seventeenth century, scholars routinely supposed that Egyptian chronology was La Peyrère's most potent weapon in favour of his pre-Adamite hypothesis.[14] "It is on this pretend antiquity of the Egyptians," wrote Paul Pezron in his *Antiquité des tems*, "that the Author of the *Praeadamitae* relies on again to show that there were men before *Adam*."[15] This gave scholars a new challenge: for perhaps the first time

---

9 Urbain Chevreau, *Histoire du monde* (Paris: Edme Martin and Jean Boudot, 1686), 199: "mais d'en faire le discernement par une exacte Chronologie, c'est à mon avis, ce qui surpasse l'esprit humain." See also 201: "Pour ce qui regarde l'origine & la succession des premiers Rois des Egyptiens, je le dirai encore une fois. C'est une obscurité que jusques ici les plus éclairés n'ont pû dissiper, & qui pouroit bien être comtée, parmi les tenèbres de la même Egypte, dont il est parlé dans l'Ecriture. Cette noire nuit a été funeste à ceux qui ont crû avoir assez de lumiéres pour la percer. Ils s'y sont perdus; & ceux qui ont tâché de les suivre, se sont encore perdus eux-mêmes par leur trop grande présomption."

10 BAR, ms.lat.49, fol. 180r: "Nihil est quod explicari minus possit, quam chronologia Aegyptiorum."

11 Fabricius, *Bibliotheca Graeca*, 3:496: "Ac certe nihil difficilius fuerit quam dynastias Manethonis expedire & cum reliqua veteri Historia conciliare."

12 See Stillingfleet, *Origines Sacrae*, "The Preface to the Reader," sig. b2v.

13 La Peyrère, *Praeadamitae sive exercitatio*, 29; La Peyrère, *Systema theologicum, ex praeadamitarum hypothesi*, 116–160.

14 Pezron, *Antiquité de tems*, 133–134: "C'est principalement sur la vaste, mais imaginaire antiquité de ces Nations, que l'Auteur des Pré-adamites a fondé son Systéme Theologique."

15 Pezron, *Antiquité de tems*, 172: "c'est sur cette prétenduë antiquité des Egyptiens, que l'Auteur des *Pré-adamites* se fonde encore pour montrer, qu'il y a eu des hommes avant *Adam*."

since the Church Fathers, Egyptian chronology was being cited in a manner which directly contradicted the perceived authority of biblical history.

Recent scholarship on seventeenth-century chronology – and in particular, the importance and influence of Joseph Scaliger, who first (re)discovered Manetho in the early seventeenth century – has been dominated by the work of Anthony Grafton.[16] According to Grafton, Scaliger was the first to raise the discipline of chronology from its amateurish and pedagogical state and make it the subject of serious scholarship. Rather than seeking a moral order, Scaliger sought simply to reconstruct the past.[17] It was for this reason, claims Grafton, that Scaliger could not bring himself to dismiss as seemingly authoritative a source as Manetho's history merely because it did not conform to the chronology of the Bible.

Grafton supposes that Scaliger's treatment of Manetho came to profoundly shape the study of chronology in two ways. Firstly it contributed, if not immediately then eventually, to a marked decline in the standards of chronological scholarship. Scaliger and his immediate contemporaries, such as his greatest critic and rival, the Jesuit Denis Petau, aimed to study chronology for chronology's sake.[18] By the late seventeenth century, however, scholars were using chronology to make arguments outside the field of chronology itself. As a result, chronology returned to the uncritical and amateurish state it had found itself in pre-Scaliger. According to Grafton, this development was particularly evident in scholarship on Manetho and Egyptian chronology. Grafton's chosen example is the work of John Marsham: in his *Canon chronicus*, Marsham emended – or, as other scholars might have put it, mutilated – Manetho's dynasties in order to fit them into his preconceived, biblicist, chronological system.[19] By the late seventeenth century, this method of rearranging Manetho's dynasties had become common practice.

Secondly, Grafton supposes that the new chronological sources which Scaliger helped discover and validate, and the new chronological methods which Scaliger developed and applied to these sources, engendered a crisis which would eventually break the biblical stranglehold on chronology itself. Ultimately, most attempts to harmonize Manetho's dynasties with the biblical

---

16 See Anthony Grafton, "Joseph Scaliger and Historical Chronology: The Rise and Fall of a Discipline," *History and Theory* 14 (1975): 156–185; Grafton, *Joseph Scaliger*, vol. 2; and also Anthony Grafton, "Dating history: the Renaissance & the reformation of chronology," *Daedalus* 132 (2003): 74–85 (amongst others).

17 Grafton, "Joseph Scaliger and Historical Chronology," 169–170.

18 Pezron called Petau Scaliger's "Antagoniste": Pezron, *Antiquité de tems*, 193. See further Rigord, *Dissertation historique sur une médaille d'Hérodes Antipas*, 17, or Noël Bonaventure d'Argonne, *A mélanges d'histoire et de littérature* (Paris: Augustin Besoigne, 1700), 1:377–378.

19 Grafton, "Joseph Scaliger and Historical Chronology," 177ff.

record proved unconvincing. Eventually, the need to preserve the authority of the Bible in doctrinal matters led some scholars – Grafton cites Richard Simon in particular – to reject the authority of the Bible in matters of chronology.[20] Nor is Grafton alone in this supposition. Historians such as Paul Hazard, Adalbert Klempt, Paolo Rossi, and Edwin Van Kley have all stressed how pagan chronology, and that of Egypt and China in particular, eventually came to blow apart traditional assumptions concerning biblical chronology and the age of the world.[21] In 1650, the Archbishop of Armagh James Ussher supposed that Creation could be dated to 4,004 BC.[22] For this calculation he was later to become (in)famous, although the practice of dating the age of the world in this manner was widespread and conventional.[23] As Paolo Rossi has argued, this supposition went through its own Copernican revolution in the following century. By the late eighteenth century, certain historians reckoned the world to be several thousand, or even million, years older.[24] Just as the new sciences of Copernicus, Galileo, and Descartes challenged the notion that the Bible was the source of all scientific knowledge, so too did biblical scholars come to the realisation that the Bible might not be the complete and authoritative source for universal history it was once thought to be.[25]

In this chapter I will study the origins, nature, and importance of Bonjour's scholarship on Manetho and in so doing add two correctives, or perhaps more accurately supplements, to this established narrative. Firstly, I want to emphasise that late seventeenth-century chronology was shaped not only by the discovery of these new sources but also by La Peyrère's particular approach to

---

20 Grafton, "Joseph Scaliger and Historical Chronology," 181, n. 105, citing Richard Simon, *Histoire critique du Vieux Testament* ("Suivant la Copie, imprimé a Paris": 1680), 229: "en un mot tout ce que nous avons de Chronologie de la Bible n'est point suffisant pour nous donner une connoissance exacte du nombre des Siecles qui se sont passez depuis la creation du monde."

21 Grafton, "Kircher's Chronology," 69; Hazard, *The European Mind*; Klempt, *Die Säkularisierung der universalhistorischen Auffassung*; Rossi, *The Dark Abyss of Time*; and Van Kley, "Europe's 'Discovery' of China and the Writing of World History."

22 James Ussher, *Annales Veteris Testamenti, a prima mundi origine deducti: una cum rerum asiaticarum et aegyptiacarum chronico, a temporis historici principio usque ad Maccabaicorum initia producto* (London: J. Flesher, 1650), 1. Cf. James Barr, "Why the World was created in 4004 B.C.: Archbishop Ussher and Biblical Chronology," *Bulletin of the John Rylands Library* 67 (1985): 575–608.

23 For example, Scaliger gave a date for Creation of 18 April 3949 BC in his *De emendatione temporum*, while Bonjour pointed to 21 April 3946 BC. Cf. Grafton, *Joseph Scaliger*, 2:262.

24 Rossi, *The Dark Abyss of Time*, ix.

25 Cf. Kraus, *Geschichte der historisch-kritischen Erforschung des Alten Testaments*; François Laplanche, *La Bible en France entre mythe et critique (XVIe–XIXe siècle)* (Paris: Albin Michel, 1994); Seifert, "Von der heiligen zur philosophischen Geschichte."

the relationship between *historia sacra* and *historia exotica*. As we have noted previously, La Peyrère used pagan chronology to alter what biblical history was fundamentally *about*, and, as Adam Sutcliffe has pointed out, chronology after La Peyrère was therefore not merely a question of declining standards of erudition – as Grafton once posed – but also a consequence of the different intellectual and apologetic climate which chronologists now found themselves in.[26] When in his *Origines sacrae* Edward Stillingfleet sought to prove that the Bible was the only reliable touchstone for primordial history, he did so not only to answer contemporary scholars who queried how ancient pagan chronologies related to the biblical record but also to refute what he called "the most popular pretences of the Atheists of our Age."[27] Whereas Scaliger's chief opponents were orthodox scholars who queried his attempt to explain aspects of biblical history through pagan sources, Pezron and Bonjour's opponents were heterodox thinkers who believed that pagan chronologies were the only reliable source for working out the primordial chronology of the world.

Secondly, I want to stress that late seventeenth-century chronological study further developed a new understanding of the relationship between biblical and non-biblical historical evidence. In this sense, I also suppose it to be influential. As we have noted, following La Peyrère, scholars confronted with seemingly "incompatible" pagan sources were essentially left with two options: emend these sources so that they might fit within the traditional *schema* of biblical chronology, or dismiss them as fabulous.[28] It was the latter approach which informed the ἀρχαιολογία, the ancient history, of the Church Fathers, and it was also this approach which remained dominant in the first half of the seventeenth century. However, this fundamentally changed after the publication of La Peyrère's *Praeadamitae* in 1655 and Marsham's *Canon chronicus* in 1672. Indeed, as the century progressed, an increasing number of scholars came to suppose that Manetho could help confirm rather than undermine the chronology of the Bible. In this sense, serious scholarship on Manetho, and the first since Scaliger, came not from freethinkers who used Manetho to undermine biblical chronology but from orthodox scholars intent on defending it. For Grafton – and before him, Christian Karl Josias von Bunsen – Marsham represented the decline of Scaligerian chronology.[29] In another way he is also

---

26 Sutcliffe, *Judaism and Enlightenment*, 64.
27 Stillingfleet, *Origines Sacrae*, "The Preface to the Reader," sig. b2v.
28 Rossi, *The Abyss of Time*, 152.
29 Grafton cites Bunsen in "Joseph Scaliger and Historical Chronology," 80. Compare Grafton with Bunsen, *Aegyptens Stelle in der Weltgeschichte*, 1:282; their interpretation of the development of seventeenth-century chronological scholarship on Egypt is fairly similar.

its fulfilment, for Marsham took seriously Scaliger's notion that Manetho was the definitive source for ancient Egyptian history in a manner which no other scholar before him had done. It is in this same context that we should understand Bonjour's interest in and major contribution to Egyptian chronology. As discussed in the previous two chapters, one of the most damaging effects of La Peyrère's *Praeadamitae* was not that he convinced contemporaries of the validity of his theory but that his theory divided scholars as to the best manner of refuting him. Bonjour himself sought to prove that underneath the many various historical mistakes and textual corruptions, Manetho told a reliable history of ancient Egypt, which, if interpreted correctly, would confirm the chronology of the Bible and that of the Vulgate in particular. In doing so, his opponents were not the universally-despised La Peyrère nor the *fautores Septuaginti* Vossius and Pezron, but those biblical scholars such as Jean Martianay who, in defending the authority of the Bible, had jettisoned chronological scholarship and simply declared all Egyptian ancient history irreparably corrupt and fabulous.

It was this approach which, to my mind, also had a long-lasting influence, even if the influence cannot be said to have come from Bonjour directly but rather from the broader tradition he was working in. Since the late seventeenth century, Manetho has broadly been rehabilitated in contrast to the calumnies he once received. Today, Egyptologists largely agree that Manetho presents us with the best available Hellenistic source for working out the true chronology of ancient Egypt. In part, this is due to the development of nineteenth-century Egyptology. Importantly, both the Turin Royal Canon, first discovered in 1820, and the Old Kingdom Annals of the Palermo Stone, discovered at some point in the mid-nineteenth century, feature sustained similarities with Manetho's dynastic list and therefore substantiate its basic veracity at the very least.[30] In part, this is also due to the declining status of the Bible as an authoritative source for ancient history and chronology. One of if not *the* major argument against Manetho's authority was that his work contradicted the history of Moses. Once, however, scholars accepted that the Bible was not an authoritative account for universal history, the greatest impediment against Manetho's authority was removed. What is surprising and noteworthy therefore – and, in my opinion, largely underappreciated in recent scholarship – is the fact that Manetho was first rehabilitated as an authentic, if corrupted, historical source not by scholars who rejected the chronology of the Bible but by those who considered the chronology of the Bible authoritative. As in so many other cases, the

---

30   See W. G. Waddell, "Introduction," in *Manetho*, ed. W. G. Waddell (Cambridge MA: Harvard University Press, 1940), xx–xxiv.

very historical documents which eventually came to break the biblical stranglehold on world history were first treated as historical documents by scholars who were also champions of an orthodox, biblio-centric view of world history. As Noel Malcolm has pointed out, it was from the orthodox centre rather than the heterodox peripheries from which the some of the most important and longest lasting developments to historical and biblical scholarship emerged.

2   Manetho in Early Christian Chronography

Gore Vidal supposedly quipped upon learning of Truman Capote's death that it was a good career move. We might add that in the case of Manetho not just his death but also the passing of some two thousand years and the invention of Christianity served to eventually make him a writer of considerable fame – and infamy – when in classical antiquity he had suffered mostly neglect. Manetho wrote in Egypt in the third century BC when, after the expeditions of Alexander, "barbarian" nations defeated by the Greeks in war tried to salvage some pride by proclaiming their superiority in culture. A similar project to Manetho's *Aegyptiaca* is the *Babyloniaca* of the roughly contemporary Berosus, with whom Manetho is often associated.[31] Writing in the Greek language of his masters, Manetho derided the Egyptian history of Herodotus just as Berosus challenged the Babylonian history of Ctesias (cf. Josephus, *Contra Apionem* 1.73). He highlighted the failure of Greek historians to accurately or reliably recount ancient history. He pointed to the comparative youth of the Greek nation. He drew up long lists of Egyptian royal dynasties sourced from the priestly archives which vaunted the antiquity of his native land. Yet the same fate befell Manetho's *Aegyptiaca* as had befallen and would befall other Hellenistic writers who composed native histories in Greek; they were ignored, and they perished. We should remember that Flavius Josephus' *Jewish Antiquities* remains the only "native" history to have survived antiquity intact. As for Manetho, the earliest surviving citation of his work comes about three hundred years after his death.

Consequently, although Manetho may have been a priest to the Egyptian sun god Ra at Heliopolis, it is to the Christian God that Manetho must give thanks for his posthumous reputation – and to Christian chronography in particular. Early Christian chronography had always had a religious and apologetic as well as merely a historical significance. Essentially, it was both an introduction to a

---

31   Eg. Verbrugghe and Wickersham, *Berossos and Manetho*.

Jewish version of ancient history and an attempt to fit pagan history into a providential Christian *schema*. Unlike pagan chronology, it implied a philosophy of history.[32] There are two important corollaries of this difference in attitude. Firstly, omissions or gaps were more embarrassing to the Christian chronographer than his pagan counterpart; secondly, Christian chronographers were generally more optimistic about filling these gaps and elucidating even the remotest eras of ancient history. Nevertheless, before the work of Sextus Julius Africanus in the third century, excursions into chronology were apologetic and confined to dating specific historical persons. The most important of these was Moses. To combat the pagan accusation that Christianity was new and its teaching derivative, the Fathers taught that Moses not only preceded but had also instructed the Greek sages. Apologetics therefore implied at least a basic grasp of chronology as well as the integration of sacred and profane history. The most common method of dating followed what William Adler has called a triangulation.[33] Moses was not mentioned in Greek chronologies, nor did Greek kings feature in scripture, yet both nations routinely featured in histories of ancient Egypt. In the writings of the first-century grammarian Apion and his contemporary Ptolemy of Mendes, the Exodus was placed in the reign of the Egyptian pharaoh Amosis, while the reign of Amosis was often considered contemporary with the reign of the first Argive king Inachus. The synchronisation of Moses and Inachus quickly became accepted among Christian apologists, as in Tatian (*Oratio ad Graecos* 38), [ps.-]Justin Martyr (*Cohortatio ad Graecos* 9), and Clement of Alexandria (*Stromata* 1.21). Its legacy proved influential well into the seventeenth century. Nevertheless, this early foray into chronology remained predominantly apologetic. The Fathers were concerned with proving that Moses was first, but not with providing a chronology which integrated sacred and profane sources into one coherent system. This changed with Julius Africanus, who replaced Argive king lists with Attic ones and who attempted to construct, as much as possible, one unbroken historical chain from Creation to the birth of Christ.

Before Africanus, Manetho had already been cited in the Jewish *apologia* of Flavius Josephus, who was defending the antiquity of Judaism against the very same Apion who presented Tatian with the synchronisation of Inachus and Moses. However, Josephus used Manetho in the same apologetic way in which Tatian and Clement raided Apion. Not concerned with Egyptian history *per se*, he discussed only those dynasties of Egyptian kings relevant to ancient

---

32 The best general summary is Adler, *Time Immemorial*. See also Momigliano, "Pagan and Christian Historiography."
33 Adler, "Moses, the Exodus, and Comparative Chronology."

Jewish history. Nevertheless, the passages in Josephus' *Contra Apionem* remain the oldest and best-preserved extracts of Manetho we possess today. In the seventeenth century, scholars still made corrections of Manetho's XVII and XVIII dynasties in Africanus and Eusebius based on the names and years in Josephus. In some cases, such as that of James Ussher, knowledge of Manetho was almost purely taken from Josephus.[34]

By the time Africanus came to Manetho some one hundred and fifty years later, he was already working from an epitome. This fact greatly altered the way in which we perceive Manetho, for his work, although known in the seventeenth century as a list of kings and dates, was originally intended as a work of history, not (merely) chronology. Nevertheless, it is from Africanus' chronography that knowledge of the dynasties was passed on to posterity. What, then, do Manetho's dynasties actually look like? They feature thirty-one dynasties of Egyptian kings spanning over 5,000 years, with each dynasty composed of a number of kings supposedly belonging to a certain region or royal house of Egypt. Thus the first two dynasties were kings heralding from Thinis or This, the next two from Memphis, the fifth from Elephantine, and so on; in addition to the three aforementioned regions, dynasties also heralded from Heracleopolis, Diospolis, Xois, Tanis, Bubastis, Sais, and Sebennytos. In Africanus' recension of Manetho, scholars therefore found the main turning points of Egyptian history. The first dynasty was ascribed to the mythical founder of Egypt Menes, who was known to Herodotus as Min (2.99) and to Diodorus as Menas (1.45.1). The fifteenth dynasty were known as *hyskos*, or "pastores," so-called shepherd kings who had invaded Egypt from Phoenicia and who reigned for some 400 years over three successive dynasties. These *hyskos*, who had been identified by Josephus with the Israelites, were eventually expelled by the first king of dynasty XVIII, whom Africanus called Amos and Josephus Tethmosis. This Amos Africanus also identified with the Amosis of Apion and Ptolemy, making him contemporary with Moses and the Exodus. After the reign of Bocchoris of Saïs, the only king of Africanus' dynasty XXIV, Egypt was invaded by an Ethiopian king called Sabakon, whose descendants ruled for 40 years; and after Cambyses defeated Psammecherites, the last king of dynasty XXVI, Egypt came under Persian rule. The last Egyptian ruler of Egypt was the last king of dynasty XXX, Nektanebos, who was replaced by another Persian king, Ochos. His grandson, Darius, was defeated by Alexander the Great just four years into his reign and proved to be the last king in Manetho's history, which thus ended with the absorption of Egypt under Hellenistic rule.

---

34 Ussher, *Annales Veteris Testamenti*, 19.

The later kings cited in Africanus' Manetho were easily identifiable with famous figures from more recent Egyptian history. Ochos was Artaxerxes III, who vanquished the last native Egyptian pharaoh Nektanebos, or, as he is known today, Nectanebo II. Psammecherites, the last king of dynasty XXVI, was Psamtik III, who was defeated by Cambyses at the battle of Pelusium in 525 BC. As noted by Herodotus, however, the problem of Egyptian history really began with any king who preceded Psammetichus, or Psamtik I, whom Africanus named as the fourth king of dynasty XXVI of Sais. Here the kings listed by Africanus only rarely coincided with those in Herodotus and Diodorus. Thus Africanus' "Sabakon," who had invaded Egypt from Ethiopia, could be identified with Herodotus' Ethiopian "Sabakos" of 2.137 and Diodorus' "Sabaco" of 1.65. Yet even such coincidences belied any real agreement. Thus, while Manetho and Diodorus had Sabakon preceded by Bocchoris, Herodotus had him vanquishing the blind pharaoh Anysis; and while Diodorus claimed that, following Sabakon's rule, Egypt descended into two years of anarchy, Manetho listed his successor as the Ethiopian Sebichos, who ruled for 14 more years. Only individual kings, but not successive rulers, could be easily grafted from one source on to the other, such as the Babylonian queen Nitocris (6th king of dynasty VI; Herodotus 2.100), the warlord Sesostris (3rd king of dynasty XII; Herodotus 2.102–110; Diodorus 1.53–58), or the pharaoh Rhamesses, also known as Aigyptos, who sent his usurping brother Armesis, or Danaos (14th and 15th kings of dynasty XVIII), into exile in Greece. As we shall see, these kings would later become the central pivots upon which early modern scholarship on Egyptian chronology turned.

Africanus was not the only Church Father to use Manetho. One hundred years later, Manetho's dynasties were also studied by Eusebius, the late third- and early fourth-century bishop of Caesarea who shortly after 325 had composed an important chronicle which covered the history of the world from Abraham to Constantine. Early modern scholarship remained split on the question as to whether Eusebius had been working from another epitome of Manetho or had copied from Africanus directly. Whatever the case, Eusebius' recension of Manetho contained far more omissions than that of Africanus. For the second dynasty, for example, he could name just five of the nine kings, without any of the years they might have reigned for. In the seventeenth century debate would rage as to what extent Eusebius had mutilated Africanus. Until Scaliger, however, both of their treatments of Manetho were lost. This was despite Jerome translating Eusebius into Latin in 381, given that Jerome had chosen to omit Eusebius' *prior libellus*, which contained his complete dynasties of Manetho.

It is tempting to say that Manetho was reborn in Leiden, yet in actual fact scholars would have known of the existence of his dynasties well before Scaliger. By reading Jerome's Latin translation they could learn, for example, that an Egyptian priest called Manetho had written an Egyptian history of thirty dynasties, fifteen of which preceded the Deluge, and that Abraham was born some 300 years after the beginning of dynasty XVI. Thus in the Middle Ages a scholar interested in Egyptian history such as Hugh of Saint Victor (c.1096–1141) could name most of the kings from Eusebius' dynasty XVII onwards.[35] Yet because Jerome had not translated Eusebius' *prior libellus*, they were only aware of those dynasties which Eusebius had synchronised with biblical history, most famously the six *hyskos* of Eusebius' dynasty XVII and the kings of dynasty XVIII who had ruled between the entry of Joseph into Egypt and the Exodus. Scaliger's *Thesaurus temporum* (1606), however, included not only the Latin edition of Jerome's canon but, more importantly, revealed to scholars for the first time the entirety of Manetho's dynasties. In 1602, Scaliger had discovered both the Greek fragments of Eusebius' *prior libellus* and Africanus' recension of the dynasties in a Parisian manuscript of George Syncellus' ninth-century *Chronographia*. In his *Thesaurus*, he attempted as best he could to reconstruct Eusebius' lost chronicon through Syncellus and went on to include Africanus' version of Manetho in the "Canones Chronologiae Isagogicos," a three-hundred-page treatise on chronology at the end of the work.[36]

In his notes to the *Thesaurus*, Scaliger was noticeably critical of Eusebius' chronological emendations. Able to compare Eusebius' recension of Manetho with that of his predecessor Africanus, Scaliger noted several important alterations which Eusebius had made to Manetho in order to align the dynasties more closely with his biblical chronology. A notable example was Eusebius making Africanus' dynasty XV of six *hyskos* kings into his dynasty XVII, so as to both reinforce the identification between the *hyskos* and the Israelites first suggested by Josephus and Apion and to make the kings contemporaneous with Thouris, whom Manetho believed to be the Polybus mentioned by Homer (*Odyssey* 4.126). Not only had Eusebius thereby moved the *hyskos* dynasty, but he had also reduced Africanus' three dynasties of *hyskos* (XV, XVI, and XVII) to just one (XVII). Scaliger was famously critical of Syncellus, whom he saw

---

35   See Hugh of Saint Victor, "Liber Excerptionum," in *M. Hugonis De S. Victore Canonici Regularis Sancti Victoris Parisiensis Tum Pietate, tum Doctrina Insignis; Opera Omnia Tribus Tomis Digesta* (Rouen: Jean Berthelen, 1648), 2:358–359. The reason I cite Hugh of Saint Victor in particular is because he is cited by Bonjour: *Aegyptiaca*, 1.

36   Grafton, *Joseph Scaliger*, 2:506ff.

as unoriginal and sloppy, but Syncellus' frequent criticism of Eusebius was one point upon which Scaliger strongly agreed with the Byzantine chronographer. "Indeed, Eusebius deformed the dynasty according to the worst example, rather than imitating religious writers, as Manetho did: if Manetho returns from the dead, he could not recognize it," Scaliger wrote of Eusebius' treatment of dynasty XVIII.[37]

The upshot of Scaliger's criticism of Eusebius was that, for him, Africanus became the hero of the chronographic tradition and the most faithful ancient witness for Manetho's dynasties. Only in the context of dynasty XXVI did Scaliger suggest scholars should follow Herodotus rather than Africanus, because Africanus had tied himself in knots trying to synchronise the years of the reign of Pharaoh Nechao II with the capture of Jerusalem and imprisonment of Jehoahaz from 2 Kings 23.[38] Scaliger did not, however, produce an edition of Africanus' fragments as he did of Eusebius', and Africanus' dynasties are featured only in the supplementary chronological material towards the end of the *Thesaurus*.[39] Scholars who were keen to compare Africanus with Eusebius in the form in which they were presented in Syncellus had to wait until Jacques Goar's *editio princeps* of the *Chronographia*, first published in 1652. This might explain why many scholars who wrote immediately after Scaliger continued to reference only those dynasties of Manetho featured in Josephus (as in the case of Archbishop Ussher) or in the Latin translation of Eusebius by Jerome (as in the cases of Jacques Cappel).[40] Nevertheless, after Scaliger's *Thesaurus temporum*, scholars had access to a previously untapped goldmine of chronological data on Egypt. They had the full chronology of Manetho as recorded by Eusebius; they were now aware of and had access to Africanus' recension of the same author; they now knew of the importance of Syncellus' *Chronographia*; and they saw for the first time such supplementary texts on Egyptian history as Eratosthenes' canon of Theban kings and the *Excerpta barbaro-latina*, a Latin translation of a fifth or early sixth century Greek chronicle which also featured summaries of Manetho's dynasties.

Scaliger's *Thesaurus* is better thought of as an edition of a chronological work – if laden with notes and additional material – rather than a work of chronology itself. Scaliger presented the material he had found, but did not

---

37 Scaliger, "Animadversiones in Chronologia Eusebii," *Thesaurus temporum*, 23: "Certe etenim Dynastiam pessimo exemplo, neque religiosis scriptoribus imitando, deformavit Eusebius, ut eam Manetho; si reviviscat, non possit agnoscere."
38 Scaliger, "Isagogicorum chronologiae canonum," *Thesaurus temporum*, 287, 311.
39 Scaliger, "Isagogicorum chronologiae canonum," *Thesaurus temporum*, 122–130.
40 Ussher, *Annales Veteris Testamenti*, 19; Cappel, *Historia sacra et exotica ab Adamo*.

necessarily feel obligated to explain how the material might be integrated into the Hebrew chronology he still publicly adhered to. As Anthony Grafton has pointed out, this decision significantly aroused the ire of his Jesuit critics, but it was a source of chagrin even for admirers of Scaliger. As late as 1711, Jacobus Perizonius, who defended Scaliger's decision to organise the dynasties successively and not collaterally, and who agreed with Scaliger that Manetho provided the oldest and best evidence for Egyptian history, criticised Scaliger for not explaining how the dynasties related to the biblical account.[41] Yet Scaliger did not always withhold his judgement as explicitly as he did on the question of the ten lost tribes, when he said "quanto simplicus erat dicere ἐπέχω," how much more simple it was to say, keep silent.[42] As we have already noted, he was fulsome in his criticism of Eusebius' attempt to identify the *pastores* or *hyskos* with the Israelites. After Scaliger, few serious chronologists valued Eusebius over Africanus, and those who did quickly found strong opposition. In his notes to Manetho, Scaliger even occasionally delved into the treacherous waters of synchronising Manetho's Egyptian kings with those mentioned in the Bible. Perhaps his most important suggestion in this context was that the biblical king Shishak could be identified with the first king of dynasty XXII, "Sesonchis."[43] In a later note, he also mused that the Theban king list ascribed by Syncellus to Eratosthenes suggested the existence of other Egyptian dynasties which ran collaterally to those mentioned by Manetho.[44] It was an innocuous comment from which a can of worms and a whole genre of Egyptian chronology would later spring.

Perhaps more important than what Scaliger said about the dynasties was what he didn't say. As Grafton has pointed out, Scaliger recognised the heterodox implications of publishing dynastic lists that challenged the accepted chronology of the Bible. Yet throughout his *Thesaurus* he refused to state that Manetho's dynasties were corrupted. Instead, he presented the dynasties as authentic and trustworthy historical data. He praised their "beautiful order" in contrast to the mess he found in Herodotus, who, after all, was a foreigner who knew no Egyptian.[45] Errors and contradictions in Manetho were routinely ascribed to the pious fraud of Africanus or more commonly Eusebius. Later

---

41 Perizonius, *Aegyptiarum originum*, 60–61.
42 Scaliger, "Isagogicorum chronologiae canonum," *Thesaurus temporum*, 327; cf. Grafton, *Joseph Scaliger*, 2:730–731.
43 Scaliger, "Isagogicorum chronologiae canonum," *Thesaurus temporum*, 311.
44 Scaliger, "Isagogicorum chronologiae canonum," *Thesaurus temporum*, 312: "quo tempore etiam in iisdem partibus diversi reges imperabant."
45 Particularly Scaliger, "Isagogicorum chronologiae canonum," *Thesaurus temporum*, 274; see also Grafton, *Joseph Scaliger*, 2:713.

commentators often circumvented the issue of Manetho's dynasties by labelling them Egyptian fictions and thereby discrediting them in one fell swoop. Yet in Scaliger they were presented as the best historical data available on ancient Egyptian history. This proved significant. Grafton has famously labelled the attempts of late seventeenth-century scholars to fit Manetho's dynasties into their schemes of biblical chronology the debasement of chronology as a discipline and symbolic of chronology's severe decline from the high standard once fostered by Scaliger. Yet the work of Marsham and his critics is as much testament to Scaliger's enduring legacy. Aware that Manetho's dynasties would not fit the biblical narrative in their common form, they nevertheless defended the dynasties as legitimate, and defended Scaliger's defence of them. It was also this notion which led them to (try to) integrate the dynasties within the chronology of the Bible rather than dismiss them as fabulous.

3 Manetho after Scaliger

As we have noted, Scaliger's refusal to either integrate Manetho with the biblical record or omit Manetho entirely proved contentious. Particularly scathing and public denunciations came from Scaliger's Catholic critics, including Antonio Possevino (1533–1610), Benedict Pereira (1536–1610), and Cesare Baronio, who criticised Scaliger for his excessive indulgence of pagan, non-biblical, sources.[46] Yet even Scaliger's friends had reservations. In public, Isaac Casaubon expressed his admiration for Scaliger's *Thesaurus* and heralded him as the greatest living authority on chronology. Privately, however, Casaubon expressed his uncertainty about the manner in which Scaliger had treated and valorised as controversial a source as Manetho.[47]

Such scepticism remained largely omnipresent throughout the early seventeenth century, from both Catholic and Protestant quarters. Given the divergence between Manetho and the Bible, the simplest way of preserving the authority of the latter was to discredit the authority of the former. Consequently, scholars such as Hermann Conring, Georg Horn, and Edward Stillingfleet explicitly supposed that Manetho had invented the dynasties.[48] "There is no credibility," wrote Stillingfleet in 1662, "in any of the *Heathen*

---

46 Grafton, *Joseph Scaliger*, 2:424–434; and Grafton, "Isaac Vossius, Chronologer," 47.
47 Grafton "Joseph Scaliger and Historical Chronology," 173–174.
48 Conring, *Asiae et Aegypti antiquissimis dynastiis adversaris chronologica*, 79; Horn, *Dissertatio de vera aetate mundi*, 43; Stillingfleet, *Origines Sacrae*, 25–39. See also Martianay, *Défense*, 432–435; and Bianchini, *La istoria universale*, 63.

Histories, which pretend to give an account of ancient times, there being in all of them so much defect and insufficiency, so great uncertainty and confusion, so much partiality and inconsistency with each other."[49] This was also the opinion of Melchior Leydekker (1642–1721), who wrote after the publication of Marsham's *Canon chronicus* and Pezron's *Antiquité des tems*.[50] Famously, Athanasius Kircher offered his cautious support for the veracity of Manetho's dynasties in his *Oedipus Aegyptiacus* of 1652 – in which he cited Arabic sources to substantiate the notion of an antediluvian Egyptian kingdom – but eventually retracted it in his *Turris Babel* of 1679.[51] "When indeed I made ample mention in volume 1 of the *Oedipus* of the dynasties of the *Egyptians*, even before the Flood, this was not done because that was my opinion, but according to the judgement of the *Egyptians, Arabs, & Manetho*," Kircher explained, somewhat limply.[52]

This sceptical attitude towards Manetho was, at least initially, as prominent in works of chronology as it was in other disciplines. In his 1613 *Historia sacra et exotica ab Adamo*, Jacques Cappel supposed that "nam & mendaciorum loquacissimus fuit Manetho" (for Manetho was the most eloquent speaker of lies) and chose to omit all of Manetho's kings which preceded that of dynasty XVII for the simple reason that he was unable to make them concur with scripture – hence they must be fabulous.[53] When James Ussher came to treat Egyptian history in his *Annales Veteris Testamenti* (1650), written more than forty years after Scaliger's rediscovery of Manetho, he cited only the fragments of Manetho preserved by Josephus but ignored those preserved by Africanus and Eusebius in Syncellus' *Chronographia*.[54] Perhaps the most damning response, however, came from Denis Petau. In Petau's opinion, Manetho was simply a more sophisticated and somewhat more conservative example of a genre which included the 48,000-year antiquity of Vulcan and the 400,000 years of the Babylonian astronomers.[55] "Dynastias istas confictas et ridiculas

---

49 Stillingfleet, *Origines Sacrae*, 105–106.
50 Melchior Leydekker, *De republica Hebraeorum libri XII* (Amsterdam: Isaac Stokmans, 1704), 115–130.
51 Athanasius Kircher, *Oedipus Aegyptiacus* (Rome: Vitale Mascardi, 1652–1654), 1:68–103, especially 71: "Dynastiae Aegyptiorum ante diluvium verae sunt."
52 Athanasius Kircher, *Turris Babel, sive Archontologia* (Amsterdam: Janssonio-Waesbergios, 1679), 112: "Quod vero nos in *Oedipo Tom.* I. etiam mentionem dynastiarum *Aegyptiorum* amplam fecerimus, etiam ante diluvium, id non factum est, quod ita sentiremus, sed secundum *Aegyptiorum, Arabum & Manethonis* opinionem." See further Grafton, "Kircher's Chronology," 179.
53 Cappel, *Historia sacra et exotica ab Adamo*, 66, 80, 88.
54 Ussher, *Annales Veteris Testamenti*, 19.
55 As Grafton has often pointed out: Grafton, "Kircher's Chronology," 174–178.

esse temporum longinquitas ostendit," the duration of time displayed by those dynasties is fabricated and ridiculous, Petau concluded succinctly.[56] For much of the early seventeenth century, this remained the safest and therefore most common response. In this sense, scholars continued to regard Manetho within the framework of the dichotomy once advanced by Augustine: that all pagan sources which contradicted sacred history must, by definition, be wrong.[57] Since Manetho's work did not, and could not, agree with the divinely inspired Mosaic history, it must necessarily be fabulous. It is illustrative of changing attitudes that, in the works of Marsham and Pezron, it was Petau who faced as much if not more criticism for his refusal to engage with the dynasties as Scaliger did for his refusal to interpret them in light of the Bible.

The first scholar after Scaliger to suppose that Manetho's history might contain verifiable information was Gerardus Vossius. As early as 1624, Vossius implied that Manetho had some historical credibility by listing him in his survey of Greek historians and distinguishing between the real Manetho of Scaliger and the fraudulent Manetho of Annius of Viterbo.[58] He also followed Scaliger in privileging Africanus' version of Manetho over the interpolated alternative of Eusebius.[59] In his 1641 *De theologia gentili*, he took this rehabilitation one step further. Vossius recognised that Manetho's dynasties posed a threat to biblical chronology, exceeding as they did "non diluvium modo, sed etiam mundi natalem," not only the Flood, but also the Creation of the world.[60] Yet Vossius bristled at accusations that Scaliger, by publishing these dynasties,

---

56 Denis Petau, *Opus de doctrina temporum* (Paris: Sébastien Cramoisy, 1627), 2:36: "Dynastias istas confictas et ridiculas esse temporum longinquitas ostendit." Petau's statement was cited, without approval, by Bonjour: *De dynastiis*, fol. 180r. It was also cited throughout the following century as an example of Petau's unwavering stance on the dynasties: Fourmont, *Réflexions critiques*, 1:ix–x; Cornelius de Pauw, *Recherches philosophiques sur les égyptiens et les chinois* (Berlin: G. J. Decker, 1778), 18 ("Le P. Petau osoit bien soutenir, que toutes les Dynasties de l'Egypte sont fabuleuses").

57 *De civitate dei* 18.40: "we can place our reliance on the inspired history belonging to our religion and consequently have no hesitation in treating as utterly false anything which fails to conform to it." Translation from Augustine, *The City of God against the Pagans*, trans. Henry Bettenson (London: Penguin, 1984), 815.

58 On Annius see C. R. Ligota, "Annius of Viterbo and Historical Method," *Journal of the Warburg and Courtauld Institutes* 50 (1987): 44–56, and Anthony Grafton, "Traditions of Invention and Inventions of Tradition in Renaissance Italy: Annius of Viterbo," in *Defenders of the Text*, 76–103.

59 Gerardus Vossius, *De historicis Graecis libri quatuor* (Leiden: Johannes Maire, 1624), 74: "Dynastias istas invenies in excerptis Africani, ex quo & sua hausit Eusebius, sed ea interpolavit."

60 Vossius, *De theologia gentili*, 206–207.

was "displaying impiety" (ἀσεβείας).[61] In this sense, Vossius was not so much interested in defending Manetho as he was in rehabilitating Scaliger. In order to do so, Vossius developed what would later become an influential conjecture: he supposed that (Scaliger believed that) Manetho's thirty-one dynasties of Egyptian kings should be arranged collaterally, rather than successively.[62] Although Scaliger had said nothing of the sort, Vossius based his suggestion on a creative misreading of Scaliger's notes. When discussing Eratosthenes' canon of Theban kings, another dynastic list Syncellus had preserved in his *Chronographia*, Scaliger had presumed that the differences between Manetho and Eratosthenes might be explained by the fact that "at that time different kings reigned in the same parts of Egypt."[63] Vossius supposed that Scaliger meant to apply this principle to Manetho's dynasties more generally.[64] Rather than supposing that one dynasty succeeded the next, Vossius supposed that different kings of Manetho's various dynasties ruled different areas of Egypt at the same time.

The first scholar to openly accept Vossius' conjecture was his own son, Isaac. As we have noted, in his *De vera aetate mundi*, Vossius presented his defence of the Septuagint as a refutation of La Peyrère's pre-Adamite hypothesis.[65] In particular, Vossius cited the evidence of Chaldean, Chinese, and Egyptian chronology, including Manetho, as his key evidence. On the one hand, Vossius supposed that Manetho's concordance with the Septuagint but not the Masoretic text proved the superiority of the former over the latter. On the other hand, Vossius supposed that Manetho's history proved that the Septuagint chronology was not merely an *alternative* version but also the *original* chronology of Hebrew scripture. According to Vossius, Manetho had presented his collateral dynasties as successive in order to undermine the biblical chronology which was at that very time being translated from Hebrew into Greek under the patronage of Ptolemy II Philadelphus – and which Manetho, who lived in Alexandria and whom Syncellus dated to the reign of the same Ptolemy II, would have been able to read in Greek.[66]

---

61 Vossius, *De theologia gentili*, 206.
62 Vossius, *De theologia gentili*, 206: "Non esse explicitos, sive Chronologicos; sed implicitos, & cum aliis concurrentes."
63 Scaliger, "Isagogicorum chronologiae canonum," *Thesaurus temporum*, 312: "quo tempore etiam in iisdem partibus diversi reges imperabant." Cited in Vossius, *De theologia gentili*, 212.
64 Vossius, *De theologia gentili*, 211.
65 Vossius, *De vera aetate mundi*, xlix–l. See also Jorink, "Horrible and Blasphemous," 441.
66 Vossius, *De vera aetate mundi*, xxxiv–xliv. See ps.-Manetho, FGrH 609 F 27, and Adler and Tuffin, *The Chronography of George Synkellos*, 55.

Notwithstanding the efforts of Vossius *père et fils*, the first scholar to truly examine Manetho on the basis that he was the best available source on ancient Egypt was John Marsham. In Marsham's *Canon chronicus*, the whole history of the ancient world was structured in accordance with Manetho's dynasties and a number of other Egyptian sources that Syncellus had preserved in his *Chronographia*. This included the royal canon of Theban kings which Apollodorus had attributed to Eratosthenes;[67] the so-called *Vetus chronicon* (supposedly older than Manetho but more likely a product of Egyptian Hermeticism), which listed fifteen dynasties of gods or demi-gods followed by a number of mortal kings beginning with dynasty XVI from Tanis;[68] and an anonymous dynastic list which contained some eighty kings of Egypt, or "Mestraia" (beginning with Menes, whom the author identified with Mestraim, and ending with Nechepsos, successor of Stephinates (2nd king of dynasty XXVI)), the authorship of which early modern authors often ascribed to Syncellus himself.[69]

A subsequent generation of chronologists and Egyptologists tended to focus on the many mistakes Marsham had made in his treatment of Egyptian chronology. These included, for example, Marsham's decision to often favour Eusebius' recension of Manetho over that of Africanus (in opposition to Scaliger); his decision to use Eratosthenes' royal canon to emend Manetho; and his decision to omit certain kings – a particularly egregious example being Necherophes, the first king of dynasty III, whom he replaced with Menes – largely without sufficient evidence.[70] Most infamous of all was Marsham's suggestion that the mythical Egyptian war-lord Sesostris could be identified with the biblical pharaoh Shishak (1 Kings 14:25; 2 Chronicles 12:1–12).[71] Yet the extent and notoriety of this criticism can lead us to underestimate the

---

67 Ps.-Apollodorus, FGrH 244 F 85 = Ps.-Eratosthenes, FGrH 241 F 48; Scaliger, "Isagogicorum chronologiae canonum," *Thesaurus temporum*, 130–131; Goar, *Georgii Monmachi Syncelli*, 91–147; Mosshammer, *Ecloga Chronographia*, 103ff.; Adler and Tuffin, *The Chronography of George Synkellos*, 128ff. According to Syncellus, Eratosthenes took his records from "Egyptian records and registers and at royal request translated them into the Greek language": Adler and Tuffin, *The Chronography of George Synkellos*, 128.

68 FGrH 610 F 2; Goar, *Georgii Monmachi Syncelli*, 51–53; Mosshammer, *Ecloga Chronographia*, 56–57; Adler and Tuffin, *The Chronography of George Synkellos*, 71–74.

69 ps.-Manetho, FGrH 609 F 28; Goar, *Georgii Monmachi Syncelli*, 91–191; Mosshammer, *Ecloga Chronographia*, 102ff.; Adler and Tuffin, *The Chronography of George Synkellos*, 127ff. See for example Marsham, *Canon chronicus*, 1.

70 See a list of these by Réne-Joseph de Tournemine, "Dissertation sur le Système des Dynasties d'Égypte du Chevalier Marsham," *Journal de Trévoux* 2 (1702): 151–169, in which, on p. 151, Tournemine references "la mauvaise foy ou l'ignorance de l'Auteur Anglois."

71 See Levitin, *Ancient Wisdom*, 159.

formative influence Marsham had over later treatments of Egyptian chronology, and Manetho specifically. Despite its admitted flaws, many important scholars still considered the *Canon chronicus* a pivotal work for understanding Egyptian history and its relationship to biblical chronology. Jean Le Clerc, who was not easily impressed, even endorsed Marsham's identification of Sesostris and Shishak.[72] Marsham's influence was greatest, however, among future chronologists of Egypt, including Pezron, who called Marsham "a man of quality and of great erudition."[73] Of particular importance was the manner in which Marsham treated the first kings of Egypt – on which, according to Pezron, Marsham had worked "avec plus de succez."[74] If Gerardus Vossius had first supposed that the dynasties were collateral, Marsham was the first scholar to outline how the dynasties might be arranged collaterally. According to Marsham, Egypt had originally been united under one king, Menes. However, the kingdom was quickly split into what Pezron later called "principalities," or "petits-Royaumes," which Menes bequeathed to his various ancestors.[75] According to both Marsham and Pezron, Egypt had been split into four principalities, This (the succession of which followed dynasty I), Thebes (following Eratosthenes' royal canon), Memphis (following dynasty III, whose first king in Pezron was not Tosorthrus but the reinstated Necherophes), and Lower Egypt (following ps.-Manetho's *Book of Sothis*).[76] The popularity and pervasiveness of this specific arrangement is suggested by the fact that it laid the blueprint for a number of later chronologists, from Pezron and Bonjour to Louis Ellies Dupin, Étienne Fourmont, and, in his manuscript notes, Francesco Bianchini.[77]

Yet the most basic and fundamental notion which Marsham helped make commonplace was that Manetho's Egyptian dynasties were not fabulous but verifiable historical evidence, if requiring scholarly emendation and rearrangement. Indeed, Marsham began his *Canon chronicus* with an important, programmatic, statement: if Scaliger was to blame for extending the dynasties too

---

72 Jean Le Clerc, *Veteris Testamenti libri historici* (Amsterdam: Henri Schelte, 1708), 369, 592–593; and Jean Le Clerc, "Veteris Testamenti Libri Historici," *Bibliothèque choisie* 16 (1708): 154.
73 Pezron, *Antiquité des tems*, 193: "homme de qualité & d'une grande érudition."
74 Pezron, *Antiquité des tems*, 193.
75 Pezron, *Antiquité des tems*, 182: "Il est clair par tout ce que je viens de dire, que dés les premiers commencemens de l'Empire des Egyptiens, il y eut plusieurs petits Royaumes & Principautez, qui subsisterent ensemble durant bien des siécles en diverses parties de l'Egypte."
76 Pezron, *Antiquité des tems*, 168–261.
77 For Bianchini see BVR, S81, especially fols. 125r–142v; Louis Ellies Dupin, "Section IV: Des Historiens Egyptiens," in *Bibliothèque universelle des historiens* (Paris: Pierre Giffart, 1707), 1:33–44, and 2:705–735; Fourmont, *Réflexions critiques*, 2:33–217.

far, then Marsham considered Petau equally culpable for not accepting them at all. "It seems to me," wrote Marsham, "that the Dynasties should neither be extended immensely, nor completely rejected."[78] It was this basic approach which raised the dynasties out of the mire of pagan fable and into the realm of history. When Paul Pezron came to discuss Manetho in his *Antiquité des tems*, he began in similar fashion to Marsham with the statement that "I do not give to the Egyptian dynasties an enormous time-frame; but nor do I abridge them too much."[79] For Pezron, the dynasties, "which were thought to be fabulous, are established here at great length, and, perhaps, developed better than they have been until now."[80] Later on in his work, he came back to the same idea:

> One must avoid the extremity of the *Pre-Adamites*, because it is dangerous; but at the same one must not rush into that of the *Chronologists*, who treat the *Dynasties* of the Egyptians as fictions and reveries. There is fable in the beginning of their History, one cannot deny it; yet, on top of that, there is also good faith and truth.[81]

Ultimately, despite their many criticisms of Marsham, the later chronological work of such scholars as Bianchini, Bonjour, Dupin, Perizonius, and Fourmont all bear witness to the importance of this guiding principle. In each case, the study of Egyptian antiquity was based on a discussion of the proper arrangement of Manetho's dynasties, as recorded by Africanus and Eusebius and preserved in Syncellus' *Chronographia*. Most importantly, the suggestion that scholars should take Manetho seriously as a source did not imply the rejection of the Bible. In fact, the study of notionally "contradictory" pagan information was intended to help confirm, not undermine, biblical chronology, a process first begun by Marsham. As Dupin stated at the beginning of his study of Egyptian history:

---

78   Marsham, *Canon chronicus*, 1: "Mihi visum est Dynastias istas neque in immensum extendi debere, neque omnino rejici." Translation from Levitin, *Ancient Wisdom*, 158.
79   Pezron, *Antiquité des tems*, 193: "je ne donne pas aux Dynasties des Egyptiens des tems immenses, mais aussi je ne les abrege pas trop."
80   Pezron, *Antiquité des tems*, "avertissement," sig. *3v: "Les dynasties des Egyptiens, qu'on a cru fabuleuses, y sont établies fort au long, & peut-être mieux développées qu'elles ne l'ont été Jusqu'à présent."
81   Pezron, *Antiquité des tems*, 172: "Il faut éviter l'extremité des *Pré-adamites*, car elle est dangereuse; mais en même tems il ne faut pas se jetter dans celle de nos *Chronologistes*, qui traittent les *Dynasties* des Egyptiens de fictions & de réveries. Il y a fable dans le commencement de leur Histoire, on n'en peut pas disconvenir; mais du reste il y a aussi de la bonne foi & de la vérité." This passage is also discussed in Chantal Grell, *Le dix-huitième siècle et l'antiquité en France 1680–1789* (Oxford: Voltaire Foundation, 1995), 2:802.

This confusion has caused most Chronologists to abandon the Chronology of the Empire of the Egyptians, and to regard the Dynasties as fabricated and fabulous. The first who worked seriously and usefully in order to restore this Chronology was the English Chevalier Marsham, who attempted to put the Dynasties of the Egyptians into order, and to reduce them to the Chronology of the Hebrew Text of the Bible.[82]

In the same vein, the English theologian and classicist William Wotton (1666–1727) wrote that it was Marsham who "has made the *Egyptian* Antiquities intelligible."[83] A few years later, when George Sale (1697–1736) and his team of universal historians came to treat Egyptian chronology, they posited much the same notion:

> The first who, without rejecting any, earnestly set about reducing the entire series to the Scripture chronology, was the learned Sir *John Marsham*, who first guessed, that these dynasties were not successive, but collateral.[84]

4 Bonjour's Manetho and His Enemies

We can see from the *Mercurius* that Bonjour already considered Egyptian chronology a major issue while in Toulouse. As Rigord wrote to Magliabechi in September 1695, Bonjour's principal design was nothing other than "to demonstrate that the chronology of holy scripture agrees perfectly with the chronology of the Chinese and Egyptians, which until now have seemed extraordinary."[85]

---

82 Dupin, "Chronologie des Empires," in *Bibliothèque universelle des historiens*, 2:705ff, especially 706: "Cette confusion a été cause que la plûpart des Chronologistes ont abandonné la Chronologie de l'Empire des Egyptiens, & ont regardé ces Dynasties comme supposées & fabuleuses. Le premier qui ait sérieusement & utilement travaillé à restituer cette Chronologie, est le Chevalier Marsham Anglois, qui a tâché de mettre en ordre ces Dynasties des Egyptiens, & de les réduire à la Chronologie du Texte Hébreu de la Bible."
83 William Wotton, *Reflections upon Ancient and Modern Learning* (London: J. Leake, 1694), 110: "… that learned Gentleman has reduced the wild Heap of *Egyptian* Dynasties into as narrow a Compass as the History of *Moses*, according to the *Hebrew* Account, by the help of a Table of the *Theban* Kings, which he found under *Eratosthenes*'s Name, in the Chronology of Syncellus."
84 George Sale et al., ed., *An Universal History from the Earliest Account of Time. Compiled from Original Authors* (London: T. Osborne, A. Miller and J. Osborn, 1747), 2:22.
85 Jean-Pierre Rigord to Antonio Magliabechi, 4 September 1695, BNCF, *Fondo Magliabechiano* VIII, cod. 341, fol. 28secondo(v): "de faire voir que la chronologie de l'Ecriture Sainte

Bonjour's identification between Joseph and Menes in particular sought not merely to prove the cultural primacy of the Hebrews over the Egyptians but also to reconfigure Egyptian chronology.[86] Nevertheless, Bonjour's *Mercurius* advanced a chronological argument without resorting to chronology itself. In the *Mercurius*, the key sources for integrating Egyptian with biblical history were profane myths, rather than dynastic lists. According to Rigord, Bonjour even considered his identification of Joseph and Mercury in the *Mercurius* akin to a preliminary study in preparation for the greater, more explicitly chronological works which were to follow. It was only in Rome, therefore, that Bonjour first treated the dynasties of Manetho directly, and it was Manetho to whom Bonjour was referring when, in 1697, he wrote to Nicaise that "I deal not only with the dynasties in general, but also with all the kings in particular, and the areas which seem the most sterile become the most fertile there. Moreover, the connection which there is with holy scripture is so frequent and so considerable that the chronology and history are as much sacred as they are profane."[87]

Hence it is Bonjour's *Antiquitas temporum*, more specifically the second and third parts of the *Antiquitas temporum*, which mark the culmination of his interest in ancient Egyptian chronology. Although Bonjour once again refuted Pezron's suggestion that the chronology of Manetho harmonized with the Septuagint chronology, the work was profoundly shaped by Pezron's central supposition that a defence of biblical chronology required sustained investigation into the chronologies of ancient pagan nations. In the *Antiquité*, Pezron not only supposed, as Vossius had done, that the chronologies of Chaldea, Egypt, and China accorded with the Septuagint chronology, but also detailed how each of their respective kings fitted into this biblio-centric system.[88] It is clear that this supposition helped shape Bonjour's own approach to ancient

---

s'accorde parfaitement bien avec la chronologie des Chinois et des Egyptiens qui ont paru jusqu'ici si extraordinaires."

86   *Mercurius*, fol. 34v: "Menam esse Josephum nullus erit ambigendi locus, cum dynastias Aegyptiorum suis temporibus restituemus. Nec etiam dubitari potest eundem esse Mercurium." See also *Mercurius*, fol. 103v: "Dynastiarum Aegypti princeps Menes Josephum exhibet in Mercurio adumbratum," and the appendix to the *Mercurius*, significantly entitled "Dissertatio VI: De dynastiis Aegyptiorum ad principatum Josephi sequentibus" ("On the Egyptian Dynasties following the rule of Joseph").

87   Guillaume Bonjour to Claude Nicaise, 9 July 1697, in KW 72 D 2, fol. 127v; in BAR, ms.lat.635, fol. 68v; and in Pélissier, "Lettres inédites de Claude Nicaise," 147–148: "Je traite non seulement des Dynasties en général, mais encore de tous les Roys en particulier, et les endroits qui paraissent les plus stériles y deviennent des plus fécondes. Au reste la connexion qu'il y a avec l'Ecriture S.te est si fréquente et si considérable que la chronologie et l'histoire y ont autant du sacré que du profane."

88   See further, "Canones Chronologici I–II," BNF, Latin 17941–17942.

history. Fundamentally, Pezron and Bonjour shared the same attitude to the importance of chronology and consequently conceived of the relationship between *historia sacra* and *historia exotica* in the same way. As Dupin wrote of Pezron, "he was equally skilled in sacred history and in profane history, and he dedicated himself to clarifying it as much through the facts he discovered in the Holy Books as those which were reported by ancient pagan authors," and it was precisely this feature of his work which Bonjour sought to emulate.[89] In the *Antiquitas*, just as in the *Mercurius*, Bonjour sought to defend traditional biblical authority by integrating sacred with profane history. The relationship between pagan and biblical evidence, which in the *Mercurius* he called "exoticae antiquitatis monumenta conferens cum sacris paginis," is re-iterated here. For Bonjour, those pagan texts which others labelled as calumnies and lies held within them evidence of the truth of biblical history and chronology. As Bonjour stated in an aside to the first part of his work, which detailed the chronology of Jewish history from Adam to the Babylonian captivity:

> I will prove that the calumnies, which they weave out of the antiquities of the Chaldeans, Chinese, Egyptians, and other peoples, fall back upon the critics themselves; thereby drawing out from them, in [my] dissertations, arguments for the very manifest *Hebraica veritas*.[90]

Bonjour's approach to Manetho specifically was informed by the previous scholarship of Scaliger, Marsham, and, above all, Pezron, all of whom had, in their own way, come to treat Manetho as a verifiable ancient source. In particular, Bonjour held alongside Marsham and Pezron that the dynasties could be emended so that they might concur with and thereby validate the chronology of the Bible. In this, Bonjour's true opponents, other than La Peyrère, were those scholars who had not taken Manetho seriously as an historical source. In the introduction to his explication of the Egyptian dynasties, he poured scorn on scholars such as Petau or Wilhelm Langius (1623–1682), a professor of mathematics at Copenhagen who had artificially reduced the length of the dynasties by supposing that Manetho had counted in months rather than years, because

---

89 Dupin, "Pezron," 167: "on a pû connoître, par ce que nous avons déja dit des Ouvrages du P. Pezron, qu'étant également versé dans l'Histoire sacrée & dans l'Histoire prophane, il s'est appliqué à éclaircir celle-ci, tant par les faits qui se trouvent dans les Livres sacrés que par ceux qui sont rapportés par les anciens Auteurs Payens."

90 *Antiquitas*, 49, under the heading "Hebraicae veritati non repugnabant exoticae antiquitates": "Quas ex Chaldaeorum, Sinarum, Aegyptiorum, aliarumque Gentium antiquitatibus texunt criminationes, in adversarios recidere demonstrabo, evidentissimae Hebraicae veritatis argumenta hinc desumens in dissertationibus."

they had failed to engage with Manetho seriously.[91] If the evidence supplied by Scaliger pointed to the fact that Manetho was a verifiable historical source, and if there was no evidence to suggest that Manetho had confused months and years, then such conjectures weakened rather than strengthened the cause of Christian scholars intent on refuting La Peyrère.

Yet the most culpable and, for Bonjour, most problematic treatments of biblical chronology came from those scholars who were, at least notionally, on his side: Jean Martianay and Michel Lequien. Particularly troubling was their attitude to pagan history and Manetho's dynasties. According to Martianay, the Egyptian dynasties were nothing but "lies and fables" (des mensonges & des fables), and Egyptian claims to antiquity obviously fabulous.[92] As a result, he did not believe it necessary to accommodate them to scripture or extend scripture to accommodate them. In Martianay's lengthy refutation of Pezron's *Antiquité des tems*, Egyptian history takes up just four pages.[93] Lequien himself did not go as far as Martianay but offered a similarly unsatisfactory response. On the one hand, he conceded that his own ineptitude in chronological matters prevented him from mustering an adequate response.[94] On the other hand, he conceded that "the antiquity of the Egyptian, Chaldean, and Chinese monarchies seems to fit much better with the chronology of the Septuagint than with that of the Hebrews."[95]

Related to this issue was Martianay's more general attitude to Christian chronology, and to patristic chronography in particular. In his refutation of Pezron, Martianay not only eschewed the question of biblical chronology – choosing instead to base his defence of the Vulgate on the authority of Jerome and Augustine, the decision of Trent, and the primacy of the text in the Catholic Church – but he also did not accept that ancient chronology was a legitimate method for determining the authority of one or the

---

91 *De dynastiis*, 1: [on Langius] "Sed non minus se vanum falsumque praebet, quam projectum ad audendum; cum arbitraria plane sit, ficta et commentitia haec chronologiae ratio." The work by Langius Bonjour is referring to is his *De veteri anno romanorum*: Wilhelm Langius, "de Veteri anno Romanorum," in *Thesaurus antiquitatum Romanarum*, ed. Johann Georg Graevius (Utrecht and Leiden: François Halma and Pieter vander Aa, 1698), 8:398–418.
92 Martianay, *Défense*, 118; Lequien, *Défense*, 377.
93 Martianay, *Défense*, 432–435.
94 Lequien, *Défense*, 379.
95 Lequien, *Défense*, 298: "l'Antiquité des Monarchies Egyptienne, Chaldéene, & Chinoise, qui semblent s'accorder beaucoup mieux avec la Chronologie des Septante, qu'avec celle du texte Hebreu."

other biblical version. In particular, he rejected Pezron's argument that the Septuagint could be considered more authoritative because it had been used as the basis for the chronological scholarship of the Fathers. For Martianay, the Fathers were – in chronological matters – not "guides fideles" but rather "petits auteurs," who made coarse mistakes and whose chronologies smacked of gross incompetence.[96] To prove this fact Martianay dug his finger into an open wound for Christian chronologists: the diversity of patristic testimonies regarding the year of the Nativity. "The science of time most worthy of a Christian and of the Fathers of the Church is undoubtedly that which pertains to the years and life of Jesus Christ," wrote Martianay – and even here the Fathers had made embarrassing mistakes and contradicted themselves equally embarrassingly.[97] Had not Tertullian stated that Christ died in the fifteenth year of Tiberius when Luke clearly taught it was the year he was baptised, a mistake in which he had been followed by Lactantius, Augustine, and Hesychius? Had not Clement noted that Christ had preached for just a single year, and Origen for just a few months, when other chronologists gave a timespan of up to three years?[98] "Why, then, does he [Pezron] want to force us to regard as *faithful guides* authors who share so many different sentiments?," asked Martianay.[99] Particular criticism was reserved for Julius Africanus. In his *Antiquité*, Pezron had followed Scaliger in privileging Africanus' testimony over Eusebius and declaring Africanus the greatest of the ancient Christian chronologists, "a man filled with beautiful insights," superbly skilled in both sacred and profane history.[100] According to Pezron, it was Africanus who first put the succession of Assyrian, Egyptian, and Greek kings in order and who, concluded, "invincibly, that the true religion of the pagans was neither ancient nor true."[101] Martianay was less positive about Africanus' abilities.

---

[96] Martianay, *Défense*, 19ff.
[97] Martianay, *Défense*, 30: "la Science des tems la plus digne d'un Chretien & des Peres de l'Eglise, est sans doute celle qui regarde les années & la vie de JESUS-CHRIST."
[98] Martianay, *Défense*, 30–34.
[99] Martianay, *Défense*, 23: "pourquoi veut-on donc nous obliger de regarder comme des *guides fideles* des Auteurs qui se partagent en tant de sentimens differens?"
[100] Pezron, *Antiquité des tems*, 5: "un homme rempli de si belles lumieres."
[101] Pezron, *Antiquité des tems*, 4–5: "il concluoit invinciblement, que leur Religion n'étoit, ny ancienne, ny veritable; faisant voir, que l'erreur & le déreglement de l'homme l'avoit enfantée: Que l'ignorance & la stupidité des premiers peuples l'avoit approuvée: Que la fiction & la fable en avoit voilé la fausseté: Que la suite des siécles obscurs & fabuleux l'avoit autorisée: & Qu'enfin la fausse sagesse des derniers Grecs luy avoit donné cours."

> Finally Julius Africanus, the favourite of our *New Restorator of Time*, is as wicked a guide as the other ancients when it comes to the calculation of the years of Jesus Christ, since he marked the time of the death of the Redeemer in the fifteenth or sixteenth year of the Emperor Tiberius. This is hardly forgivable for this great calculator of time, who should have taken care, it seems to me, not to lop two or three whole years off the life of Christ, and to give more scope to the time of the Gospels, and the preaching of the Son of God. And all that one can say, in order not to get too far from the truth, is that nowadays one is much more exact in the calculation of time than we were in the first centuries of the Church, and that modern chronologists have themselves engaged in study to avoid the great blunders of the Ancients.[102]

For Martianay, this fact not only proved the ineptitude of the Fathers and the vagaries of ancient chronology, but also led him to regard chronology as "comme des choses fort peu importantes à la Religion," as a matter of very little importance for religion.[103]

Both Pezron and Bonjour explicitly directed themselves against this line of argument. As Pezron wrote in his letter to Nicaise, "for me, the opinion of the ancient Fathers and of the ancient chronologists seems to me more truthful than those of the moderns." These ancient Fathers – particularly Africanus – remained not only a pertinent source of information but a model for integrating sacred and profane testimony in a manner which would help refute scholars who doubted the traditional status of the Bible as the principle source for universal history.[104] According to Pezron, it was knowledge of chronology which was "so necessary for supporting religion, that if we do not time its true extent,

---

102   Martianay, *Défense*, 35–36: "Enfin Jules Africain l'Auteur favori du nouveau Restaurateur des Siecles, est aussi méchant guide que les autres Anciens dans la supputation des années de JESUS-CHRIST, puisqu'il a marqué le tems de la mort du Redempteur en la quinzième ou seizième année de l'Empereur Tibere. Ce qui n'est gueres pardonable dans ce grand Calculateur des tems, qui eût dû prendre garde, ce me semble, à ne pas retrancher deux ou trois années tout entieres de la vie de JESUS-CHRIST, & à donner plus d'étenduë au tems de l'Evangile, & à a prédication du Fils de Dieu. Et tout ce qu'on peut dire, pour ne pas s'éloigner de la verité, c'est que de nos jours on est beaucoup plus exact dans les supputations des tems, qu'on n'étoit dans les premiers Siecles de l'Eglise, & que les Chronologistes modernes se sont étudiez avec soin d'êviter les grandes beviies des Anciens."

103   Martianay, *Défense*, 19.

104   Paul Pezron to Claude Nicaise, 29 March 1699, BNF, Français 9361, fol. 82r: "pour moy le sentiment des anciens Peres et des anciens Chronologistes me paroit bien plus veritable, que celuy des modernes."

it is difficult to respond solidly to the arguments made by the Preadamites, the libertines, and those who are called *esprits forts* against the books of Moses, and what he says of the establishment of the world."[105] Bonjour took the same stance in his *Antiquitas temporum*. For Bonjour, the truth of the Christian religion was built on the bedrock of historical scholarship. As he wrote to Cuper in 1697, it was the study of history which contained the "the splendid light of truth"; or, as he wrote in a short dissertation for Augustinian students of theology, the *De necessitate studiorum historiae ecclesiasticae*, it was the study of history that enabled the scholar to discern the light of true religion from the darkness of idolatry and heresy.[106] Proper historical scholarship could therefore help reveal, rather than undermine, the authority of the Bible and the truth of the Christian religion more generally. It was for this reason that Bonjour considered it of paramount importance to refute those scholars who viewed the study of pagan antiquity and the discipline of chronology as at best a useless and at worst a dangerous and possibly heretical field of research. In the preface of his work on Egyptian chronology, he pointed this out explicitly. "Finally Martianay and Lequien, having tried to rebuke and reject Pezron's judgement, imbibed this opinion, which considers the Egyptian antiquities as baseless and worthless: and for that reason they paid minimal attention to the harmony of them with the *Hebraica veritas*, the protection of which they had appropriated [to themselves]."[107] In response, Bonjour cited the words of his ever-present guide Augustine: "whatever the subject called history reveals about the train of past events is of the greatest assistance in interpreting the holy books, even if learnt outside the church as part of primary education" (*De doctrina Christiana* 2.28).[108]

The case of Egypt was, of course, a matter of more than mere elementary significance, and it was precisely for this reason that Martianay's attitude to

---

105 Pezron, *Antiquité des tems*, 10: "si necessaire même pour le soûtien de la Religion, que si l'on ne donne aux tems leur juste étenduë, il est difficile de répondre solidement aux argumens que font les Pré-adamites, les Libertins, & ceux qu'on appelle esprits forts contre les livres de Moïse, & contre ce qu'il dit de l'établissement du Monde."

106 Guillaume Bonjour to Gisbert Cuper, 31 August 1697, KW 72 H 20; "Brevis ad theologos praelectio De necessitate studiorum historiae ecclesiasticae," BAR, ms.lat.630, fols. 200v–202r.

107 *De dynastiis*, 2: "Martianaeus demum et Lequienus Pezronii judicium reprehendere ac respuere conati opinionem hanc imbiberunt, quae vanas futilesque habet antiquitates Aegyptiacas: ideoque minime incubuerunt in earum concordiam cum veritate Hebraica, cujus patrocinium arripuerant."

108 Cited in *De dynastiis*, 2r: "Hinc quotquot delectantur exoticae historiae monumentis, probeque sciunt cum magno Augustino. ..." Translation from Augustine, *De Doctrina Christiana*, ed. R. P. H. Green (Oxford: Clarendon Press, 1995), 105.

Egyptian chronology was so misguided. As Pezron had pointed out, it was Egyptian chronology which had allowed La Peyrère to cast his shadow over biblical history. As we have seen, according to La Peyrère, Egyptian accounts concerning the antiquity of the world were fundamentally genuine. As he wrote in the *Praeadamitae*:

> For it is indeed probable that *Herodotus*, an excellent Writer, and very accurate in most things, and *Diodorus* himself an assertor of Historical truths, spake nothing of those accounts, but what they had heard either from *Egyptian* Priests, out of their records, and had acurately examin'd, and seen them in *Egypt*.[109]

Ultimately, Martianay's claim that all Egyptian history was necessarily fabulous could help refute La Peyrère's interpretation of Egyptian history, but it could not help prove that the biblical record was a complete and authoritative history of the world, as La Peyrère had denied it to be. In this sense, Bonjour's treatment of Manetho – and such supplementary Egyptian sources as Diodorus and Herodotus – was influenced by a profound desire to make these testimonies regarding Egyptian history *more*, rather than *less* legitimate. According to Bonjour, only a fully developed history of Egypt could convincingly demonstrate that chronology of the Bible was true, and that La Peyrère had been wrong to use pagan chronology *against* the historical authority of the Bible. As a result, Bonjour's work further sought to establish Manetho as a legitimate historical source for ancient Egypt, and, by extension, a legitimate source for defending the chronology of the Bible.

5   Bonjour on Manetho

Bonjour's arrangement of Manetho followed many of the organizational principles formerly advanced by Marsham and Pezron. Like his predecessors, he supposed that the Egyptian kingdom had begun under one ruler but had quickly been divided into co-existing regions, or dynasties. Unlike his predecessors, he

---

109   La Peyrère, *Systema theologicum, ex praeadamitarum hypothesi*, 152: "Probabile certe est, Herodotum scriptorem elegantissimum, & in pluribus accuratissimum; nec non alios historicos diligentes; sicut & Diodorum ipsum, veritatis historicae assertorem, nihil de rationibus illis exposuisse; quod non vel audivissent, vel a Sacerdotibus Aegyptiis in commentarios relatum legissent, pensiculate examinavissent, imo & vidissent in Aegypto. Quod nimirum de se religiose professi sunt, tum Herodotus, tum Diodorus"; La Peyrère, *A Theological Systeme upon that Presupposition That Men were before Adam*, 168–169.

made the first pharaoh not Menes but Necherophes, who, Bonjour argued, was contemporary with Abraham.[110] As in the *Mercurius*, Bonjour supposed that it was only with Menes that the Egyptian kingdom adopted an absolutist, monarchical constitution, hence the common tendency to describe Menes as the first Egyptian pharaoh.[111] This allowed Bonjour to confirm two basic principles necessary for harmonising Egyptian and Jewish chronology: firstly, that there existed no Egyptian pharaoh before the time of Abraham; and secondly, that Manetho's thirty-one dynasties could be squeezed into the 1,500 years which separated Abraham from Cambyses, if via some rather idiosyncratic reorganization of the many collateral dynasties.[112]

There are two principal ways in which Bonjour sought to legitimise Manetho's dynasties as a historical source; his emendation of Manetho's text, primarily so as to correct any apparently contradictory chronological calculations and to provide an uncorrupted text for the dynasties; and his synchronization of Manetho's history with the testimonies of Diodorus and Herodotus. Both practices, I believe, were part of a process which began with Scaliger and was revived by Marsham. Both stemmed from the fundamental supposition that Manetho was a verifiable historical source and that his testimony was key not to refuting but to confirming biblical authority.

Bonjour's first aim, to provide an accurate recension of the dynasties, is marked by two methods of emendation. Firstly, Bonjour wanted to remove any artificial shortening of the dynasties through certain misguided chronological and calendrical conjectures. Particularly at fault were the fifth-century Alexandrian chroniclers Pandorus and Annianus, whose emendation of Manetho had been preserved by Syncellus. These chronographers had supposed that Manetho's calculations referred not to solar years but to lunar months.[113] As a result, they had reduced the reign of the first divine king of Egypt, Vulcan ("Ηφαιστος), from 8,410 to 727 ¾ years, and the total reign of Vulcan's dynasty (the *deorum principatus regum*) from 11,985 to 969 years. Although Syncellus often criticised Pandorus and Annianus, he continued to use these emendations in his *Chronographia*.[114] Bonjour, however, wanted to produce an edition of Manetho which most closely mirrored Manetho's original text. Nor did he think it likely that Manetho had confused solar years with tropical months, for

---

110   *De dynastiis*, 3r.
111   *De dynastiis*, 2v.
112   Cf. "Tabula dynastiarum Aegypto connexarum cum chronologia Hebraica, a temporibus Abrahae ad redactos in editionem persarum Aegyptios," BAR, ms.lat.49.
113   Mosshammer, *Ecloga Chronographia*, 19; Adler and Tuffin, *The Chronography of George Synkellos*, 25.
114   Adler and Tuffin, *The Chronography of George Synkellos*, 24–25, 55–57.

which there was no substantial evidence other than unspecified conjecture. Consequently, Bonjour, who was openly critical of Pandorus and Annianus' corrections, restored the reign of each god back to its original length.[115] This was a practice he repeated for the second dynasty, that of the *semideorum principatus*, for which Pandorus had replaced solar years with *trimestres*, seasons three months in length.[116]

The second and more important method by which Bonjour sought to rehabilitate Manetho was by ironing out internal computational contradictions in Manetho's text. The issue stemmed from Manetho's decision to give both the individual number of years for which each king of a chosen dynasty had reigned, as well as the total number of years for which a particular dynasty had ruled. Unfortunately, the *sum total* of the reigns of all of the kings of a particular dynasty added together often contradicted the *stated total* of the number of years which Manetho supposed this particular dynasty had reigned for. A pertinent example is the case of dynasty 1. Here, the stated total of the eight kings who comprised this dynasty was 253 years, but the sum total of each of the individual reigns added up to 263 years.[117]

For a scholar convinced of the fact that Manetho was a vain and boastful liar, and who believed that Egyptian claims to antiquity were inherently fabulous, these contradictions might be evidence of Manetho's mendacious ignorance.[118] Bonjour, however, sought to resolve these contradictions through philological emendation. In the case of dynasty 1, Bonjour believed that the stated rather than the sum total must be correct because it was verified by the *Excerpta barbaro-latina*, a Latin translation of a fifth- or early sixth-century Greek chronicle which Scaliger had included in his *Thesaurus temporum*.[119] Hence he supposed that the lengths of some of the individual reigns must be wrong. The first change he made was to the reign of the fifth king, Usaphaedus. On the basis of an unnamed manuscript in the Vatican library (likely either *Vaticanus palatinus* 395 or *Vaticanus graecus* 154 or 155) Bonjour emended the length of Usaphaedus' reign from ἔτη κ (annis 20) to ἔτη η (annis 8). Bonjour's

---

115 *Aegyptiaca*, 1 (fol. 263r).
116 *Aegyptiaca*, 2–3; Mosshammer, *Ecloga Chronographia*, 19; Adler and Tuffin, *The Chronography of George Synkellos*, 25.
117 Mosshammer, *Ecloga Chronographia*, 60; Adler and Tuffin, *The Chronography of George Synkellos*, 76–77 (and see 77, n. 1). Dynasty I: Menes (62), Athothes (57), Kenkenes (31), Ouenephes (23), Ousaphaïdos (20), Miebidos (26), Semempses (18), and Bieneches (26) = 263.
118 See for example Cappel, *Historia sacra et profana ab Adamo*, 66: "Nam & mendaciorum loquacissimus fuit Manetho."
119 *Aegyptiaca*, 3; Scaliger, "Excerpti Chronologicorum," *Thesaurus temporum*, 60–61.

other emendation concerned the reign of the second king Athothes, which Manetho calculated as 59 years. Bonjour, however, realised that in the Theban canon of Eratosthenes the second king, Athothes, who likewise succeeded Menes, ruled for only 57 years. By adopting Eratosthenes' calculation for the reign of Athothes, Bonjour was able to decrease the overall sum total of the kings of the first dynasties by ten years and align it with the stated total.[120]

Aside from philological emendation, Bonjour also sought to correct Manetho's calculations by aligning and harmonizing them with the alternative Egyptian histories of Herodotus and Diodorus. In his original *Aegyptiaca*, Manetho had presented his history of Egypt as a counterpart to Herodotus, who, according to Manetho, had interpreted ancient Egyptian history incorrectly (cf. Josephus, *Contra Apionem* 1.73).[121] In the *Thesaurus temporum*, Scaliger explicitly heralded Manetho's history of Egypt as an alternative to Herodotus, who did not know Egyptian. Bonjour, however, advanced a slightly different relationship between Manetho and Herodotus, and also Diodorus. Although he acknowledged that they often conflicted, he also supposed that all three historians told the same historical narrative, if subject to various degrees of ignorance and corruption. By analysing the texts historically and philologically, Bonjour sought to construct a single, authoritative history of ancient Egypt in the time of the patriarchs.

Let us take, as an indicative example, the case of dynasty IV, which included the three kings Suphis I, Suphis II, and Mencheres, who, according to Manetho, were responsible for the building of three great pyramids.[122] For this dynasty Manetho had given the stated total as 274 years, but the sum total as 284.[123] Consequently, Bonjour proposed an emendation to the reign of the third king, Suphis II. According to Manetho, this king had reigned for 66 years; Bonjour in turn suggested he had reigned for only 56 years. Bonjour's source was Herodotus, who did not mention Suphis. Instead, Herodotus had supposed that the pyramids were built by Cheops, his brother Chephren, and Cheops' son Mykerinos (2.124–134). On the surface, this might indicate that Herodotus offered a rival narrative to that of Manetho. However, in one of his editorial asides concerning the reign of Suphis, Manetho (or Africanus) had commented

---

120   *Aegyptiaca*, 3.
121   One work often attributed to Manetho is the supposed *Against Herodotus*, or *Criticisms of Herodotus*, although many scholars now suppose this to be not a separate work but rather part of his *Aegyptiaca*: see Waddell, "Introduction," in *Manetho*, xiv–xv, xxiv–xxv.
122   Also written as Souphis. I have generally stuck to Bonjour's spelling. See Mosshammer, *Ecloga Chronographia*, 63.3–6; Adler and Tuffin, *The Chronography of George Synkellos*, 80.
123   Mosshammer, *Ecloga Chronographia*, 63; Adler and Tuffin, *The Chronography of George Synkellos*, 80.

that he whom Manetho called Suphis Herodotus called Cheops.[124] As a result, scholars came to assume that Herodotus was actually speaking of the same three kings, albeit under different names. Marsham, for example, had already come to identify Cheops with Suphis I.[125] In a similar fashion, Bonjour noted that if Suphis I was Cheops and Mencheres (Μενχέρης) could be identified with Mykerinos (Μυκερῖνος), then Suphis II could be identified with Chephren. Since Herodotus stated that Chephren reigned for 56 years (2.127.3), Bonjour was able to resolve the inconsistency between the stated and the sum total in Manetho's dynastic list.[126]

The building of the pyramids proved particularly important in the context of Egyptian chronology because it allowed Bonjour to integrate into a single chronological framework both contradictory pagan sources as well as sacred with profane history. According to Bonjour, the name "Cheops" was originally "Che-Opas," with "Che" being the first name and "Opas" being a traditional Egyptian surname, as in "Necher-Opas," the etymological origin of Necherophes.[127] This allowed Bonjour to identify Cheops with Suphis, given that both "Che" and "Suph" meant, in Egyptian, "terminis" or "extremitas," a suggestion Bonjour took from Kircher's *Scala magna*.[128] In a following passage, Bonjour also sought to align these kings with the rival narrative of Diodorus. In two different passages, Diodorus had ascribed the building of the pyramids to two different people, Chembes (1.63.2) and Armaeus (1.64.14–15).[129] Bonjour identified Chembes with Cheops on the basis that Herodotus and Diodorus had given Chembes/Cheops' successors as "Chephren" (Χεφρῆνα) and "Cephren" (Κεφρὴν) respectively.[130] With "Armaeus" (Ἀρμαῖον) Bonjour was more creative. According to the testimony of Artapanus (*Praeparatio evangelica* 9.18, 23), the followers of Joseph were called "Ermiuth" (Ἑρμιούθ), supposedly because of their Syrian origins. By identifying "Ermiuth" with "Armaeus,"

---

124 Marsham commented that Africanus' version was more reliable because he included quotes directly from Manetho, such as this one: *Canon chronicus*, 51. Modern editors (Adler and Tuffin, *The Chronography of George Synkellos*, 80) consider this to be an editorial insertion of Africanus. The text reads: "He [Souphis] erected the Great Pyramid, which Herodotus says was built under Cheops" (ὃς τὴν μεγίστην ἤγειρε πυραμίδα, ἣν φησιυ Ἡρόδοτος ὑπὸ Χέοπος γεγονέναι).

125 Marsham, *Canon chronicus*, 47.

126 *Aegyptiaca*, 7–8.

127 *Aegyptiaca*, 64. The following quotes come under the sub-heading "De regno Memphitarum, et ejus nexu cum chronologia Hebraica."

128 In Athanasius Kircher, *Lingua Aegyptiaca restituta opus tripartitum* (Rome: Ludovico Grignano, 1643).

129 In modern editions "Chemmis" (Χέμμις).

130 *Aegyptiaca*, 66.

Bonjour supposed that Diodorus had mistakenly supposed that the "Eramaei" people were a single man, "Arameus," when the name in actual fact referred to the enslaved Israelites, the true "Eramaei" who were responsible for building the pyramids.[131] This also allowed Bonjour to integrate the history of the first Egyptian dynasties with the sacred history of the postdiluvian patriarchs. If Soris – the first king of dynasty IV – was the pharaoh under whom Joseph came to ascendancy in Egypt, then it was logical to suppose that it was under one of his successors – "rex novus super Aegyptum qui ignorabat Ioseph," (Exodus 1:8) – that the Egyptians turned on the Israelites and enslaved them.

Bonjour employed a similar tactic for Suphis II. Here, Bonjour referred back to his emendation of Suphis II's reign, which, as we have seen, he altered from 66 to 56 years on the basis of Herodotus and Diodorus.[132] Notionally, this decision brings up the question of consistency: why did Bonjour emend Manetho's calculations on the basis of Herodotus for the reign of Suphis II but not Suphis I, for whom Bonjour followed Manetho's 63 years rather than Herodotus' 50? For this too Bonjour had an explanation, although not perhaps a particularly convincing one. According to Herodotus (2.124–126), Cheops was famous for closing the Egyptian sanctuaries. Hence the fifty years Herodotus recorded was not from the beginning of Cheops' reign but from when Cheops ordered the Egyptian temples to be closed.[133] Moreover, Bonjour believed this testimony could help further synchronize these Egyptian dynasties with the biblical record. Citing the same biblical passage once used in a not dissimilar context by Baronio, Psalm 104:21–22, as well as the testimony of Genesis 41:38–40, Bonjour argued that the closure of the traditional temples under the reign of Cheops recalled the brief period in which the Egyptians, following Joseph's teaching, accepted the true religion:[134]

---

131 *Aegyptiaca*, 66–67.
132 *Aegyptiaca*, 69–70: "Ita ergo sunt emendandi Syncelliani numeri Manethonis proindeque Manetho nihil diversum ab Herodoto et Diodoro statuit hac in re."
133 *Aegyptiaca*, 70: "sed ex quo templa Aegypti eo jubente clausa sunt."
134 *Aegyptiaca*, 70–71: "Talis enim ac tanti viri sanctitas argumento est nihil ipsi potius fuisse, nihil clarius, nihil antiquius scientia colendi Dei, qua proinde imbuti principes domus Pharaonis et senes facile inducti sunt ad honorem supremo numini debitum non deferendum fictis diis commentitiisque. Deum praedicabat Joseph; deum agnoscebat Pharao: assentiebant ministri ejus." Cf. Genesis 41:38–40: "And he said to them: Can we find such another man, that is full of the spirit of God? He said therefore to Joseph: Seeing God hath shewn thee all that thou hast said, can I find one wiser and one like unto thee? Thou shalt be over my house, and at the commandment of thy mouth all the people shall obey: only in the kingly throne will I be above thee."

When, therefore, we hear in Herodotus that the hatred of Cheops towards the false gods of the Egyptians was so great that the same author teaches us that *with all the temples closed he before everything forbade the Egyptians from performing sacrifices*, and since we know from chronological calculations that Joseph was alive for the whole period in which Cheops – the immediate successor to the Pharaoh who freed him from prison – reigned, we therefore see no other cause for the abolition of idolatry than Joseph himself.[135]

This was confirmed by the fact that the successor of Cheops and Chephren was Mencheres (in Herodotus (2.129) Mykerinos), who supposedly resurrected the temples, and who was also contemporaneous with the pharaoh Kaeachus (2nd king of dynasty II), in whose reign the worship of the bulls of Apis and Mnevis was established at Memphis and Heliopolis respectively.[136] However clunky these conjectures, the chronological synchronism was neat: at the same time as the new pharaoh "ignorabat Joseph" (as Moses wrote), reigning Egyptian pharaohs across Egypt reinstituted the traditional Egyptian religion which Joseph's influence had temporarily seen abolished. In making this synchronization, Bonjour also opposed the treatment of the Egyptian kings and Hebrew patriarchs he found in Marsham. In his notes on dynasty IV, Manetho had stated that Suphis I ὑπερόπτης εἰς θεοὺς ἐγένετο (became a disdainer of the gods), just as Herodotus had claimed that Cheops "shut all the temples, so that none could worship there."[137] Marsham had translated this passage as "hic etiam contemplator in Deos fuit" – "he also was a *contemplator* of the gods" – which suggested a continuity between the religious practices of the different Egyptian pharaohs, as well as Cheops' fidelity to these practices.[138] Conversely, Bonjour translated the passage as "hic autem et contemptor Deorum" – this man however was a *hater* of the Gods – and thereby stressed that Joseph's

---

135 *Aegyptiaca*, 71–72: "Cum ergo tantum in falsa Aegyptiorum numina Cheopis odium audimus apud Herodotum, ut, *omnibus eum templis obseratis ante omnia Aegyptis ne sacrificarent interdixisse* nos idem auctor doceat; scientes et ex chronologiae calculis Josephum toto tempore quo regnavit Cheops proximus successor Pharaonis qui eum e custodia eripuerat, fuisse in vivis: sublatae tunc idololatriae causam aliam non videmus quàm ipsum Josephum."

136 *Aegyptiaca*, 74.

137 Mosshammer, *Ecloga Chronographica*, 63.4. I have preferred to keep ὑπερόπτης as a noun rather than as a verb. Alternative translations can be found in *Manetho*, 47 ("conceived a contempt for the gods") and Adler and Tuffin, *The Chronography of George Synkellos*, 80 ("he also became disdainful of the gods"). Translation of Herodotus from *The Persian Wars*, trans. A. D. Godley (Cambridge MA: Harvard University Press, 1926), 425.

138 Marsham, *Canon chronicus*, 51.

viziership had brought a temporary rupture in traditional Egyptian religious practices.[139]

6 La Peyrère and the Authority of Manetho

The approach of scholars such as Bonjour and Huet is often defined by their explicit aim of synchronizing biblical history with pagan myth. As we can see in the context of Manetho's Egyptian dynasties, it also consisted of synchronizing the biblical record with Egyptian chronology. Yet Bonjour's historical scholarship extended beyond merely confirming the veracity of sacred history. As we can see, Bonjour sought to synchronize the notionally contradictory narratives of such ancient pagan authorities on Egyptian history as Herodotus, Manetho, and Diodorus. To this we should also add the testimony of Greek mythology, which Bonjour continued to use as an historical source on ancient Egypt throughout his *Antiquitas temporum*. Indeed, Gisbert Cuper even wrote to Leibniz – in response to a query by Jacobus Perizonius, who was unsure as to which sources Bonjour had based his rearrangement of Manetho's dynasties on – that Bonjour's chief historical source remained Greek mythology.[140] The ultimate goal, however, was the same: to construct a coherent historical narrative which synthesized notionally contradictory sources on ancient history,

---

139   *Aegyptiaca*, 75.
140   See the relevant passage in Perizonius, *Aegyptiarum originum*, 400–401: "Nobis vero certum sedeat illud, quod ab initio diximus, priores Manethonis Dynastias esse ab omni vera & justa Chronologia alienissimas, & laterem lavare, qui ex iis Chronologiam quamcunque constituere volunt. Patrem tamen Bonjourium, qui Romae publicavit monumenta quaedam Coptica, video in *Memoriis Trivultiensibus Anni* 1702. *Mensis Sept. Art.* 2. p. 173 ed. Amstelaed. de hisce etiam Dynastiis aliquid edidisse, sed quo reperire non potui. Sed & audivi, jactitasse illum in privatis sermonibus, se clarissime demonstraturum, quis fuerit ille *Pharao*, Abrahami aequalis. Id unde probaturus sit, haud equidem scio, nec comminisci queo, nisi forsan ex Annalibus quibusdam Copticis, sed quos crediderim nihilo plus fidei merituros, quam Arabicos illos, ex quibus & Athan. Kircherus multa hausit a specie veri alienissima"; and Gisbert Cuper to G. W. Leibniz, 2 August 1711, in Gottfried Wilhelm Leibniz, "Transkriptionen des Briefwechsels 1711," *Sämtliche Schriften und Briefe*, 206: "Patere, ut tibi narrem, quid hujus rei sit: Bonjourius conscripsit librum de Dynastiis Aegyptiorum, eumque abiens in ultimos Seras tradidit in manus Adeodato Nuzzi, Familiae Benedictinae Generali, qui mihi spem fecit aliquot singularium capitum, de quibus rogaveram ut ad me mittere vellet, quid sentiret vir iste eruditus; et inter ea erant *Pastores Israëlitae Reges*, quos defendit Perizonius. Affirmavit autem mihi Bonjourius, nam per binos dies summo meo cum gaudio apud me et mecum fuit, sese quam clarissime monstraturum, quis fuerit Pharao tempore Josephi, non ex Copticis vel Arabicis scriptoribus uti putat Perizonius, sed ex vetustissimis Graecis."

whether biblical or non-biblical. Ostensibly, this allowed Bonjour to undermine both the pre-Adamite notion that Egyptian history developed independently of biblical history; but it also allowed him to save pagan antiquity from the response of such scholars as Petau and Martianay who, by making all Egyptian history fabulous, had failed to defend the authority of biblical chronology on historical grounds.

Bonjour was not alone in this assumption, and it is worth ending this chapter with a particularly illustrative debate which highlights how La Peyrère's challenge to sacred historians led to fundamental disagreements between orthodox scholars regarding the true relationship between *historia sacra* and *monumenta profana* more generally. The debate itself took place in the pages of the *Journal de Trévoux*, the learned Jesuit journal edited by the erudite, curious, well-connected, widely-respected, and often pugnacious Jesuit scholar René-Joseph de Tournemine, who took the opportunity afforded to him by his editorship to dip his toes into many diverse springs of learned debate. In 1703, Tournemine published a short article in which he proposed a conjecture that stated that the ages of the postdiluvian patriarchs were some one hundred years longer than explicitly stated in scripture. Sem was 100 when he fathered his first son, Arphaxad (Genesis 11:10), and Tournemine supposed that the age given for each of the following patriarchs was not their complete age but the number of years they were older than Sem.[141] If somewhat abstruse, this kind of conjecture was not uncommon. Just a few years previously, Leibniz had been discussing with Claude Nicaise a similar conjecture by the French theologian François Dirois (1625–1690), who supposed that the lifespans of the patriarchs were not successive and that one could therefore insert a number of years *in between* their various lives.[142] Indeed, these conjectures are somewhat suggestive of the particular mindset of the late seventeenth-century scholar. Above all, they bear witness to the growing realisation that the authority of the Bible could be reinforced if its chronology could be extended in some way. Other scholars, however, found them ridiculous, and so it was that, shortly after Tournemine's article appeared, an anonymous critic took it upon himself to attack Tournemine. In an article published in the following edition of

---

[141] René-Joseph de Tournemine, "Article XLIV: Conjecture du P. Tournemine Jesuite sur l'origine de la difference du texte Hébreu, de l'édition Samaritaine & de la version des Septante, dans la maniere de compter les années des Patriarches," *Journal de Trévoux* 6 (1703): 452–464.

[142] See G. W. Leibniz to Claude Nicaise, 2 August 1699, in LAA, II, 3:589, and François Dirois, *Preuves et préjugés pour la religion Chrétienne et Catholique contre les fausses religions et l'athéisme* (Paris: Étienne Michallet, 1683).

the journal, Tournemine's critic dismissed not only Tournemine's specific conjecture but the entire chronological discipline which had led Tournemine to reconfigure the biblical text in such a way. As he noted,

> In my opinion, when I read a Marsham, or the works of Father Pezron, Mr. Bianchini, or Father Bonjour, I do find it hard to sacrifice the ingenious conjectures of these erudite Chronologists who have so neatly arranged and untangled with diligent scholarship and profound erudition these obscure times ... And yet, with all of this having been said, I cannot but fear these historical systems, and these systems of historical events; and I fear even more that a La Peyrère will come along and tell us to either abandon all the Chaldean, Egyptian, and other such Annalists, or else to accept upon their testimony that there existed men before Adam.[143]

For Tournemine's critic, the discipline of chronology, and by extension the annals of Chaldea and Egypt, had become dangerous to the Christian religion. La Peyrère had considered them genuine and built his pre-Adamite heresy upon this edifice; the most fitting response was therefore to dismiss these records entirely. Even "scholars of the first order," the critic suggested, considered the Egyptian "hardi menteurs," bold liars.[144] As a result, there was as little truth in the histories of Sesostris as there was in the fables of Osiris.[145]

In his response, Tournemine sought to defend not only his specific conjecture but the discipline of chronology more generally. Chronology was, according to Tournemine, simply "the arrangement of events according to the time in which they occurred," and therefore an essential part of historical study.[146] To do away with chronology would be to do away with the study of history itself:

---

143 "Article CXXXX: Examen de la conjecture du R.P. de Tournemine touchant la différence du texte Hébreu de l'edition Samaritaine & de la version des Septante dans le calcul des années des anciens Patriarches," *Journal de Trévoux* 7 (1703): 1406: "Pour moy j'avoüe que quand je lis un Marsham, les œuvres du P. Pezron, de Mr. Bianchini, du P. Bonjour, j'ai peine à sacrifier les conjectures ingenieuses de ces sçavans Chronologistes, qui ont arrangé & debroüillé avec un grand travail & une érudition profonde ces tems obscurs ... mais avec tout cela je ne laisse pas de craindre les systemes en matiere d'histoire & de faits; & je crains encore plus qu'un La Peirere ne nous vienne dire, ou qu'il absolument donner congé à tous les Annalistes Chaldéens, Égyptiens, &c., ou qu'il faut sur leurs témoignages reconnoître ses Préadamites."
144 "Examen de la conjecture du R.P. de Tournemine," 1405.
145 "Examen de la conjecture du R.P. de Tournemine," 1405–1406.
146 "Réponse du P. de Tournemine," 1425: "un arrangement de faits selon le tems où ils sont arrivez."

Do you want history left in the confusion from which the authors of these systems have rescued it? What glory did Scaliger not receive for having undertaken this great project, and Father Petau for having almost completed it? You speak of Marsham, of Fathers Pezron & Bonjour, of Bianchini: you could speak of [Jacques] Salian, of [Jacobus] Tirinus, of [James] Ussher, of [Wilhelm] Langius, of [Thomas] Lydiat, of [Philippe] Labbé, of Father [Jean] Hardouin, and of a hundred other less famous persons. Each Chronologist has constructed his own system: you will one day make your own, and you are very capable of making a good one.[147]

Yet Tournemine's response also highlights the effect that La Peyrère's pre-Adamite thesis had had on chronological scholarship. Tournemine's critic rejected pagan chronology primarily because La Peyrère had once used it as evidence for his pre-Adamite hypothesis.[148] Tournemine dismissed these worries. To suppose, as La Peyrère had done, that *all* ancient pagan sources were accurate and therefore beyond reproach was, in terms of historical method, just as flawed as dismissing all pagan sources as inherently fabulous:

> If some other La Peyrère came with this reasoning to us: *you believe the Historians who are exact and judicious, therefore you must believe them all, even the most fabulous*; or on the other hand that *there are fabulous Historians, so we must not believe any [Historians]*; or finally that *even the best Historians have made mistakes, we must therefore distrust all Historians, and believe nothing*. An Author who reasoned thus would make little impression on people's minds; he would not be feared.[149]

---

147 "Réponse du P. de Tournemine," 1425: "Voudriez-vous qu'on laisât l'histoire dans la confusion dont les faiseurs de systemes l'ont tirée? Quelle gloire n'a point acquis Scaliger pour avoir entrepris ce grand ouvrage, & le P. Petau, pour l'avoir presque achevé? Vous parlez de Marsham, des Peres Pezron & Bonjour, de M. Bianchini: Vous pouviez parler de Salian, de Tirin, d'Usserius, de Langius, de Lydiat, du Pere Labbe, du P. Hardouin, de cent autres moins considerables. Chaque Chronologue a fait son système. Vous ferez un jour le vôtre, & vous êtes tres-capable d'en faire un bon."

148 "Réponse du P. de Tournemine," 1423.

149 "Réponse du P. de Tournemine," 1424: "Si quelque autre La Peyrere venoit nous faire ce raisonnement: *Vous croyez les Historiens qui sont exacts & judicieux, croyez les donc tous, même les plus fabuleux; ou cet autre. Il y a des Historiens fabuleux, il faut donc n'en croire aucun, ou les meilleurs Historiens ont fait des fautes, on doit donc se défier de tous les Historiens, & ne rien croire.* Un Auteur qui raisonneroit ainsi feroit peu d'impression sur les esprits; il ne seroit pas à craindre."

As we have seen, La Peyrère valorised the authenticity of Herodotus and Diodorus' histories of Egypt. In a similar vein, Tournemine claimed that Herodotus was "an Author whose authority is not contested by the most severe of critics."[150] The existence of Sesostris, he suggested, was no less verifiable, and therefore no more fabulous, than that of the French king Clovis.[151] Moreover, Tournemine accorded Manetho the same authority he accorded Herodotus.[152] The year before, in 1702, Tournemine had written a lengthy article in the *Journal de Trévoux* in which he delineated the many errors Marsham had made in his treatment of Egyptian history. Yet in doing so Tournemine still supposed that Manetho was a legitimate historical source, if one who had simply been interpreted incorrectly. Interestingly, Tournemine supposed that both Pezron and Bonjour had gone a long way towards rectifying Marsham's errors (how Tournemine knew of Bonjour's work I am not sure).[153] Instead, then, of rejecting pagan historical sources, Tournemine presumed, fairly logically, that if biblical history was true and if pagan historical evidence was not merely *fabula* but also *historia*, then the latter must naturally concur with and thereby support the former.

Tournemine's article serves to highlight that the manner in which Bonjour conceptualised the relationship between pagan history and La Peyrère's pre-Adamite thesis was not an isolated phenomenon. Both Tournemine and Bonjour recognised that Egyptian history had been co-opted by the pre-Adamites as key evidence for their heretical hypothesis. Both scholars also argued, in their own way, not only against La Peyrère but also against those scholars who in defending the Masoretic text chose to jettison chronological study.

Often, historians have contrasted the "arbitrary" biblicist chronological systems of the seventeenth century with the critical – and "secular" – universal

---

150 "Réponse du P. de Tournemine," 1422: "un Auteur dont le plus rigide des Critiques ne conteste pas l'autorité."
151 "Réponse du P. de Tournemine," 1422.
152 In the case of Herodotus this was more common. See for example André Du Ryer, trans., *Les histoires d'Hérodote* (Paris: Antoine de Sommaville & Augustin Courbé, 1645), sig. a3v: "nous n'avons point de Livre qui nous puisse plus certainement ayder à concilier la Chronologie sacrée avec les Histoire profanes." See also the general discussion in Grell, *Le dix-huitième siècle et l'antiquité en France*, 2:794–802, from whose book I learnt of Ryer's translation. See more generally Anthony Ellis, "*Herodotus Magister Vitae*, or: Herodotus and God in the Protestant Reformation," *Histos*. Supplement 4 (2015): 194.
153 Tournemine, "Dissertation sur le Système des Dynasties d'Égypte," 152–153: "Mais sur cela même le sçavant Dom Pezron Abbé de la Charmoye, dans son bel ouvrage *de l'Antiquité des tems rétablie*, & depuis peu le Pere Bonjour Augustin, dans ce qu'il a imprimé à Rome sur ces Dynasties, relevent avec beaucoup d'érudition plusieurs fautes de Marsham."

histories of the eighteenth century. It is for this reason that Frank Manuel has called scholars such as Marsham and Pezron "the uncritical chronologists and polyhistors of the seventeenth century, who blindly accepted every shred of literary evidence at face value if only it bolstered one of their favourite schemes."[154] This notion, however, is based on a false dichotomy and a fallacious understanding of the manner in which orthodox scholars developed a new understanding of the value of pagan evidence. In essence, Manuel's comparison of seventeenth- and eighteenth-century chronological scholarship is anachronistic. The appropriate comparison should be between scholars who sought to defend the authority of the Bible by rejecting pagan history and chronology, and their contemporaries who responded by combining pagan history which contradicted – and had been explicitly used to contradict – the accepted *schema* for universal history with the biblical record. Although it was only in the eighteenth century that scholars divested the study of ancient, primordial, and universal history from *historia sacra*, it was in the late seventeenth century that scholars working within *historia sacra* first took seriously those pagan sources which would eventually contribute to the desacralisation of universal history.

The need to defend biblical authority, particularly in light of La Peyrère's pre-Adamite thesis, proved important in fuelling scholarship in a number of tangential disciplines. This included not only Egyptian chronology but also philological scholarship on Josephus, which proliferated in the years after Vossius' *De vera aetate mundi* and Pezron's *Antiquité des tems*, and which culminated in 1726 in the great critical edition of John Hudson and Siwart Haverkamp (1684–1742). Indeed, as Mordechai Feingold has noted, it was primarily his interest in biblical chronology which led William Whiston, the Edward FitzGerald to Josephus' Omar Khayyam, to embark on his famous translation of Josephus (first published 1737).[155] And yet, scholarship on biblical chronology, while accomplishing much, was ultimately unable to accomplish the very thing it was intended to do, namely, mount a convincing defence of the authority of biblical chronology itself. In many ways this development, or lack thereof, was inevitable. Ultimately, early modern scholars believed that *eruditio* – the proper application of historical, philological, and text-critical methods to Manetho's text – would help reveal, rather than

---

154 Manuel, *The Eighteenth Century Confronts the Gods*, 91.
155 Mordechai Feingold, "A Rake's Progress: William Whiston Reads Josephus," *Eighteenth Century Studies* 49 (2015): 17–30; William Whiston, *An Essay towards Restoring the True Text of the Old Testament and for Vindicating the Citations made thence in the New Testament* (London: J. Senex, 1722), 184–219.

undermine, the way in which Manetho's history concurred with biblical chronology. Eventually, they reached an insurmountable obstacle: the simple fact that Egyptian history does not agree with the chronology Moses had outlined in Genesis. As scholarship on Manetho developed, so too did the growing suspicion that the Bible might not be the complete and authoritative historical account scholars had once thought it to be. As early as Jacobus Perizonius' 1711 *Aegyptiarum originum et temporum antiquissimorum investigatio*, we can see a tension emerge. On the one hand, Perizonius accepted that Manetho was the best available source on ancient Egypt, and that the Bible was an authoritative account of universal history. On the other hand, he noticed that all previous attempts to synchronize Manetho with the Bible had either misrepresented Manetho's dynasties or misrepresented biblical history. In later years, scholars with little interest in preserving the historical authority of the Bible would leap upon this tension gleefully.

What I hope to have shown here, however, is not merely how scholars attempted to defend a proposition which ultimately proved indefensible, but also that these defences could offer a new perspective on pagan history and chronology which would prove formative for later scholarship. And even if their synchronic attempts eventually became untenable and, worse, unfashionable, they were not without temporary success. In one of his first and still defining articles on early modern biblical chronology, Anthony Grafton reminded us that seventeenth-century chronology helped lay the foundation for nineteenth-century geology and biology to finally destroy the place of the Bible in universal history.[156] Yet this statement, though undoubtedly true, can also be interpreted in another way: that despite the emergence of new chronological data from the ancient Near East and the recently discovered Far East, and despite the much-discussed "crisis" in chronology these texts engendered, the chronology of the Bible remained, if not universally then still commonly accepted as the principal source for the age of the world up until the eventual advent of geology and biology in the nineteenth century.

---

156   Grafton, "Joseph Scaliger and Historical Chronology," 181.

PART 3

Idolatry

∴

CHAPTER 6

The Gods of the Heathens

1 Antiquarianism and the Study of Pagan Religion

At some point in the 1690s, Gisbert Cuper received a number of ancient inscriptions from one of his agents in Aleppo. Among them was what appeared to be a vow which a certain Crateus, son of Andronicus, had made for his father. What perplexed Cuper however was not the vow itself but the two unknown gods invoked at the beginning of the vow, ΔΙΙ ΜΑΔΒΑΧΩ ΚΑΙ ΣΕΛΑΜΑΝΕΙ ΘΕΟΙΣ ΠΑΤΡΟΙΣ, "to Jupiter Madbachus and to Selamanes, gods of the country [païs]." A perpetually curious antiquarian who found few things as thrilling as the mysteries of recondite pagan religion, Cuper quickly began contacting his vast cadre of scholarly correspondents as to the possible identity of these unknown gods. His request was simple: as he wrote to the Huguenot theologian David Martin (1639–1721), "I have received from Aleppo some very beautiful inscriptions; among them are three featuring unknown gods, and I pray of you to explain them to me. You understand Oriental languages admirably, you are curious, and this is why I am fully convinced that you will have no difficulty in teaching me what Jupiter Madbachus and Selamanes could mean."[1] In particular, Cuper was interested in one question: whether the inscription spoke of one God, Jupiter, who was designated with the previously unknown epithets Madbachus and Selamanes, or if the inscription spoke of two distinct gods, Jupiter Madbachus on the one hand and Selamanes on the other. In the following years, he assiduously gathered interpretations from a range of chosen experts in the field, from Pierre Jurieu, Pierre-Daniel Huet, Jean Le Clerc, and Ezekiel Spanheim to the Utrecht-based Orientalist Adriaan Reland (1676–1718), the French numismatist (and future translator of the *One Thousand and One Nights*) Antoine Galland, the German philologist Jacob Rhenferd (1654–1712), the Dutch preacher Adolphus Olivier (d. 1706), the Groningen theologian Johannes Braun (1628–1708), and the Huguenot scholar and erstwhile traveller to the Levant Jean Masson, then working in England

---

1 Gisbert Cuper to David Martin, 14 October 1704, in Beyer, *Lettres de critique*, 457: "J'ai reçu d'Alep de très-belles Inscriptions; il y en a trois où il y a des Dieux inconnus, & je vous prie de vouloir me les expliquer. Vous entendez admirablement les Langues Orientales, vous êtes curieux, & c'est pour cela que je suis tout-à-fait persuadé, que vous ne ferez pas difficulté de m'apprendre ce que pourroient signifier, *Jupiter Madbachus & Selamanes.*"

under the patronage of William Lloyd.[2] Nor did Cuper fail to enquire as to the opinion of perhaps his most cherished contact in the learned Republic, and in July 1702 he sent to Bonjour a copy of the inscription. "Have you ever heard of them?" he asked. "You will do a very dear thing for me, if you would tell me, what Jupiter Madbachus and what Selamanes mean in themselves."[3] Bonjour was only too happy to oblige. In January of the following year he sent Cuper his interpretation of the inscription. This letter, along with the contributions of Jurieu, Huet, Galland, Braun, Rhenferd, Reland, and Masson, was eventually printed by Cuper in a supplement to Jurieu's *Histoire critique des dogmes et des cultes* in 1705.[4]

Jurieu's letter to Cuper, the first in the *Supplément*, outlined the two issues at stake. The first concerned the meaning of the mysterious names Madbachus and Selamanes and was therefore concerned primarily with etymology. Jurieu derived "Madbach" from the Chaldean "Madebach" (מדבח) or "Madebacha" (מדבחא) meaning "a sacrifice" or "one who sacrifices," while he derived "Selamanes" from the Hebrew "Shelamin" (שלמין) meaning "sacrifices of thanksgiving."[5] Few scholars diverged extensively from these conclusions. Bonjour, for example, agreed that Madbach came from the Chaldean מדבח – although he translated Madbach as "altar" – and derived Selamanes from the Hebrew "Zabach" (זבח) meaning "to sacrifice," while Huet pointed out that Madbach might also have an Arabic derivation, Madbachon, meaning "the place in which is sacrificed."[6] The second issue, however, was more divisive: whether the inscription spoke of one, two, or even three gods. Taking as his starting point the plural θεοί, Jurieu argued that the inscription spoke not of one god of the "first order" but rather of two lesser gods, what Jurieu called "Indigetes," local or "native" gods, θεοί πατρῷοι. According to Jurieu, the two

---

[2] Cf. Beyer, *Lettres de critique*, 471–3; Le Clerc, *Epistolario*, 2:477–480. On Masson see Simon Mills, *A Commerce of Knowledge: Trade, Religion, and Scholarship between England and the Ottoman Empire, 1600–1760* (Oxford: Oxford University Press, 2020), 183. On Reland see the recently published collection of essays: Bart Jaski, Christian Lange, Anna Pytlowany, and Henk J. van Rinsum, ed., *The Orient in Utrecht: Adriaan Reland (1676–1718), Arabist, Cartographer, Antiquarian and Scholar of Comparative Religion* (Brill: Leiden, 2021). I have not managed to establish dates for Jean Masson.

[3] Gisbert Cuper to Guillaume Bonjour, 24 July 1709, in Pélissier, "Lettres inédites de Gisbert Cuper," (1905): 97 (261): "An quid unquam de iis audivisti? Sed cum Orientalium linguarum promuscondus sis rem mihi facies gratissimam si me docere velis quid sibi *Jupiter Madbachus*, quid *Selamanes* velit."

[4] Cuper, *Supplément a l'histoire critique*.

[5] Jurieu, "Réponse de Mr. Jurieu," *Supplément a l'histoire critique*, 28–31.

[6] Bonjour, "Extrait d'une lettre ecrite par Guillaume Bonjour," *Supplément a l'histoire critique*, 39–40.

unknown gods were erstwhile priests of the Syrian goddess in Aleppo who were divinized by the grateful population for augmenting the wealth of the city and devotion for the goddess.[7] It was this supposition of Jurieu's which was most forcefully challenged, first by Cuper and then by his two assistants, Huet and Bonjour, whose contributions were wheeled out by Cuper with the explicit intention of refuting Jurieu. Indeed, as early as 1701, Cuper had been convinced that Madbachus and Selamanes were not "numina" (divinities, or divine powers) or "nomina" (names), but merely "cognomina" – surnames, or appellations.[8] Consequently, Cuper considered them specific epithets for the highest god, Jupiter or Jove, of whom Varro counted more than 300 local versions and of whom Eusebius asserted that he was worshipped by every idolatrous nation. Huet shared this sentiment; as Huet wrote, "to each of these Jupiters are born different names and surnames," a conclusion also echoed by Galland, who called this unknown god an Arab version of Jupiter.[9] The ever-combative Jurieu, however, was not to be deterred from his opinion so easily. Having read Bonjour and Huet's replies, he appealed for scholars to submit evidence of what he already knew to be true, namely, that the inscription clearly spoke of two different gods.[10] Eventually, Jurieu was aided by the contribution of Jean Masson. Masson argued that there must be multiple gods given the plural form of θεοί and that they were probably minor or lesser gods, although he also corrected Jurieu's erroneous identification of ancient Hierapolis with Aleppo by identifying it with Beroea instead.[11] Nevertheless, Masson's contribution delighted Jurieu. In the final article of the *Supplément* he declared it "the most reasonable" of all the observations Cuper had elicited.[12]

The difference between Jurieu on the one hand and Bonjour and Huet on the other goes deeper than the simple identities of two unknown Syrian gods. In part, it goes back to their respective attitudes to pagan religion. Certainly, it is true that Jurieu shared many of the basic presumptions which informed

---

7   Jurieu, "Réponse de Mr. Jurieu," *Supplément a l'histoire critique*, 29.
8   Gisbert Cuper to David Martin, 14 October 1701, in Beyer, *Lettres de critique*, 457.
9   Huet, "Extrait d'une lettre ecrite par Monsr. Huet," *Supplément a l'histoire critique*, 41: "Jovem, quem sibi gentes universae asciscunt, ut ab Eusebio adnotatum est, apud singulos varia nomina & cognomina esse nactum"; Galland, "Nouveaux extraits de lettres," *Supplément a l'histoire critique*, 45: "ce Jupiter Arabe." Huet's letter was later reprinted in Pierre Daniel Huet, *Dissertations sur diverses matieres de religion et de philologie*, ed. Jean Marie de la Marque de Tilladet (Paris: François Fournier, 1712), 2:147–150, and was discussed by Banier, *La mythologie et les fables expliquées*, 2:65–67.
10 Jurieu, "Observations de Monsr. Jurieu," *Supplément a l'histoire critique*, 67–70.
11 Masson, "Extrait d'une lettre de Mr. Jean Masson," *Supplément a l'histoire critique*, 62–66.
12 Jurieu, "Observations de Monsr. Jurieu," *Supplément a l'histoire critique*, 67: "je juge c'est ce qui a été dit de plus vraisemble sur ce Dieu inconnu."

Huet and Bonjour's approach to *historia sacra*. In his *Histoire critique des dogmes et des cultes*, he identified Near Eastern idols with Greco-Roman gods and traced the transmission of biblical knowledge from ancient Israel to the Mediterranean West through the travels of the Phoenicians. Like his Catholic counterparts, he argued that the pagan gods represented both historical mortals and celestial bodies and he placed great stock on the antiquity and authority of Sanchuniathon, who had had direct access to those biblical books which formed the basis of his grotesquely corrupted history of the world.[13] Although Jurieu did describe the *Demonstratio evangelica* as "full of great literature, but where the scholarship is gathered without discrimination, and with little judgement," it was not lost on his contemporaries that he borrowed much from Huet's scholarly methods.[14] Particularly scathing was Jurieu's bitter enemy Jean Le Clerc, who took offence at the fact that Jurieu had described Grotius as a bad Christian and who claimed that Jurieu had plagiarised Selden and Vossius on oriental gods and John Lightfoot on Jewish cults.[15] It is illustrative that when Le Clerc voiced his doubts concerning many of Bonjour's sacred and profane parallels in his review of the *Selectae*, he still made it clear that there was another scholar proposing similar identifications "who in no way resembles Father Bonjour, neither in learning, nor in common sense, but who has nevertheless tired the public with forced conjectures without style, without method, and without rules" – which is to say, his cherished enemy Jurieu.[16] Yet there can be no doubt that, despite their similarities, Jurieu also diverged from Huet and Bonjour on other important matters. There was, for example, his continuous anti-Catholic polemic, in which he compared the pagan worship of statues and images with the Catholic veneration of images, a long-running Protestant trope which also came to the fore in Richard Cumberland's eclectic treatment of Sanchuniathon, written around this time but only published in 1720.[17] But there was also a more over-arching difference of approach: Jurieu's

---

13   Jurieu, *Histoire critique des dogmes et des cultes*, 430ff.
14   Jurieu, *Histoire critique des dogmes et des cultes*, 419: "Elle est pleine d'une grande litterature, mais l'érudition y est ramassée sans choix, & avec peu de jugement."
15   Jean Le Clerc, "Article VI," *Bibliothèque choisie: pour servir de suite à la Bibliothèque universelle* 5 (1705): 358–374, especially 358–9.
16   Le Clerc, "Article IV," 231–232: "qui ne ressemble point au P. Bonjour, ni en savoir, ni en bon sens, & qui à néanmoins fatigué le Public de conjectures forcées, sans art, ni méthode, ni regles." Gisbert Cuper asked Le Clerc who this mysterious scholar was (Gisbert Cuper to Jean Le Clerc, 1 January 1709, *Epistolario*, 3:231–32) but Le Clerc did not reply. See Le Clerc, "Article VI," and Jurieu's response in the *Supplément*: "Reflexions sur le sixième article de la *Bibliothèque choisie*, tome V," *Supplément a l'histoire critique*, 5–11.
17   E.g., Jurieu, *Histoire critique des dogmes et des cultes*, 492–495; Cumberland, *Sanchoniatho's Phoenician History*, xxviii, 90, 317–318.

interpretation of pagan religion as barbarous, primitive, and savage. Despite the biblical origins of many of the pagan gods, there was, as he noted, "nothing more monstruous than pagan theology" – the "foulest sink of Heathenism" as Cumberland, who like Jurieu believed that the origins of pagan theology could be drawn from the history of Sanchuniathon, later put it.[18] It was precisely on this basis that Jurieu rejected Huet and Bonjour's interpretation of Jupiter Madbachus and Selamanes. The notion that various *cognomina* denoted a single god had often been used as a piece of evidence for the popular supposition that beneath the monstrosities of pagan religion there had once existed an original, monotheistic core. In his letter to Cuper, Bonjour made this notion explicit. According to Bonjour, the Hebrew etymologies of Madbachus and Selamanes reaffirmed the fact that the Latin "Jovis" was derived from the Hebrew tetragrammaton Jehovah. Bonjour went on to suggest that the "altar of peace" denoted by the etymologies "Madbachus and Selamanes" referred back to the altar of the Lord described at Leviticus 17:5. Hence, for Bonjour, the inscription was specific evidence of a practice observed more fully elsewhere, namely, that the Gentiles, especially those in the East, imitated the religious rites of the Jews.[19] Jurieu disagreed. By declaring that the gods in question were divinized local priests, he rejected the notion that these pagan rituals were derived from Jewish originals and instead linked them to the common – and monstrous – pagan practice of human divinization. In this sense, antiquarian scholarship on pagan antiquities continued to be shaped by underlying assumptions concerning the nature of pagan religion and its historical relationship to Judaism.

Yet there is also another way in which the discussion concerning Jupiter Madbachus and Selamanes exemplified the specific nature of scholarship on ancient paganism around the turn of the eighteenth century. Centred as the discussion was on an inscription, it is clear that the scholars in question tried to understand pagan religion not only through its theology or its theory but also through its practice. Ultimately, understanding pagan ritual, the manner in which pagan worshippers worshipped, also held the key to understanding the underlying principles and assumptions which shaped pagan religion itself.

This type of interest was particularly prominent in the circle around Gisbert Cuper. Since the 1680s Cuper had been a central figure in the European

---

18   Jurieu, *Histoire critique des dogmes et des cultes*, 407: "rien au mond n'est si monstreux que la Theologie Payenne"; Cumberland, *Sanchoniatho's Phoenician History*, 11.
19   Bonjour, "Extrait d'une lettre ecrite par Guillaume Bonjour," *Supplément a l'histoire critique*, 40: "Non habeo necesse ad firmandam conjecturam, Gentiles, praesertim Orientales, imitatione consecutos esse saepe esse ritus Hebraicos. Nam id satis aliunde notum."

numismatic community which, though centred in the thriving numismatic world of Paris (where Vaillant, Toinard, Spanheim, Morell, and Hardouin traded coins, engravings, conjectures, and insults, and where both the scholarly, the political, and the religious elite spent their leisure hours examining medals in one of the numerous weekly antiquarian assemblies organised in the French capital), had also spread its epistolary branches to southern France, to Holland, and to Italy.[20] Enthusiastically, Cuper followed the increasingly acrimonious debate between Noris and Vaillant on the one hand and the notorious Hardouin on the other, obtained new material evidence through his contacts scattered across Asia, and offered his own humble and often tentative conjectures.

The type of historical information which could be derived from coins and other objects was particularly relevant for certain, specific, historical disciplines, which not only profited from but were also shaped by the proliferation of antiquarian study. In particular, antiquarian objects became central to two fields of scholarship, ancient chronology and pagan religion.[21] On the one hand, coins and inscriptions contained dates, often for unknown epochs or eras, and were therefore crucial in harmonizing many ancient, local, and unknown calendars into a more uniform chronological system. In the late seventeenth century almost every political history of the Hellenistic and Roman world, in particular histories of ancient dynasties such as the Ptolemies and the Seleucids or biographies of various Roman emperors, was based on numismatic evidence.[22] On the other hand, coins and inscriptions were crucial evidence for depicting pagan religious iconography and therefore presented a tantalising window for understanding pagan religious practices. It was in this context that Cuper's passion for antiquities was largely inseparable from his interest in ancient paganism, for it was through his study of material objects and pagan iconography that he sought to better understand the peculiarities of pagan ritual and by extension the nature of paganism itself. In 1683, he had published a learned dissertation on a Claudian-era marble relief recently discovered near Rome and first described in Kircher's 1671 *Latium* which depicted

---

20 As very neatly described by Nicaise, *Les sirenes*, 1–14.

21 Cf. Jean Hardouin, *Nummi antiqui populorum et urbium illustrati* (Paris: François Muguet, 1684), sig. i(v).

22 For example, Jean Foy-Vaillant, *Seleucidarum imperium, sive Historia regum Syriae ad fidem numismatum accommodata* (Paris: Louis Billaine, 1681); Jean Foy-Vaillant, *Numismata aerea imperatorum Augustarum et Caesarum* (Paris: Edm. Martin, Jean Boudot, Etienne Martin, 1688); Nicolas Toinard, *De Commodi imperatoris aetate in nummis inscripta* (Paris: André Cramoisy, 1690). See more generally Momigliano, "Ancient History and the Antiquarian."

the divinization – or apotheosis – of Homer.[23] More influential still was his *Harpocrates*, first published in 1676 and then expanded in a second edition of 1687.[24] Notionally, the work was based on a single idea which Cuper took from the *Saturnalia* of Macrobius, namely, that all pagan gods were different representations of the sun.[25] Yet the explicit focus of the work was not a text nor even an idea but an object: a silver statue of the Greek god Harpocrates from the collection of the erstwhile Dutch minister and collector Johannes Smetius (1590–1651). By explaining the iconography of the titular statue, Cuper sought to uncover how representations of the gods and the use of these representations reflected the deeper, underlying religious assumptions which defined heathen idolatry.

This new interest in objects was a defining part of the developing field of study concerned with religious idolatry. As early as 1617, John Selden had argued that material objects, including columns, inscribed tablets, and statues, were not only evidence for but also a cause of idolatry: according to Selden, these objects were responsible for allowing posthumous commemoration to become divine worship.[26] By the early eighteenth century, this was an approach which not only guided Cuper's antiquarian studies but those of mythographers more generally, including Bonjour. It was on the basis of this premise that Antoine Banier began his monumental investigation into pagan religion by citing as his historical evidence not only ancient texts, but also ancient festivals, hymns, games, songs, columns, and even "mounds of earth."[27] Pagan religion, according

---

23   Gisbert Cuper, *Apotheosis vel consecratio Homeri. Sive, lapis antiquissimus in quo poetarum principis Homeri consecratio sculpta est, commentario illustratus* (Amsterdam: Hendrick and Theodore Boom, 1683). See Ralph Häfner, "Homers Dichtung als gelehrte Enzyklopädie," in *Skepsis, Providenz, Polyhistorie: Jakob Friedrich Reimmann (1668–1743)* (Tübingen: Max Niemeyer Verlag, 1998), 134.

24   Gisbert Cuper, *Harpocrates sive explicatio imagunculae argentae perantiquae* (Amsterdam: Theodore Pluymer, 1676); Gisbert Cuper, *Harpocrates sive explicatio imagunculae argentae perantiquae* (Utrecht: François Halma, 1687).

25   Macrobius, *Saturnalia*, 1.23.21: "Finally, those who discourse on the gods show that the sun's power is reckoned as the totality of all powers, a point they make plain in their rites by this very brief prayer: "Sun the ruler of all, breath of the universe, power of the universe, light of the universe"'; 'Postremo potentiam solis ad omnium potestatum summitatem referri indicant theologi, qui in sacris hoc brevissima precatione demonstrant dicentes, ""Ἥλιε παντοκράτορ, κόσμου πνεῦμα, κόσμου δύναμις, κόσμου φῶς'."

26   Selden, *De diis syris*, xl: "... vel DAEMONIIS quae Secundum, exhibebantur, emanavit. *Sacra illa quae heic maxime spectari debent ritus sunt*, COLUMNAE, SYMBOLA, & SIMULACHRA. Primum de SIMULACHRIS & COLUMNIS; quod & inde etiam Daemoniorum cultus origo, ni fallor, deducenda ..."

27   Banier, *La mythologie et les fables expliquées*, 1:xi: "Des Fêtes, des Jeux, des Hymnes, des Cantiques, des Colomnes, des Monceaux de terre, un amas de pierres, ou enfin une

to Banier, was not established by Homer or Hesiod but by the common people and their priests. It was not a theory but a public act. In order to understand ancient paganism one had to understand how it was practiced.

In this chapter, I want to offer some more insight into the manner in which early modern scholarship on idolatry developed in the seventeenth century, the extent to which these notions influenced Bonjour's scholarship on "religion," and the manner in which this work then laid the basis for his later work on China (which will be treated directly in the following chapter). Bonjour never wrote an extensive work on ancient pagan idolatry or religion as he did on mythology or chronology, yet his historical work on both was fundamentally shaped by the manner in which he viewed the origins and nature of the pagan gods. Indeed, for many seventeenth-century scholars of *historia sacra*, the history of ancient pagan nations was intimately and in some cases inextricably linked to their deviation from an original Noachian monotheism and the development of religious idolatry. As Banier wrote in 1738, one of the chief goals for scholars working on pagan mythology was therefore to understand the origins of idolatry.[28] It was the story of how religious idols had first come into being and then how these idols, or *Götzen*, became *Götter*, gods.[29] These studies came to shape not only the manner in which scholars understood the origins of idolatry but the nature of religion more generally.

2   Early Modern Histories of Religion

In the 1960s, the American historian Frank Manuel supposed that it was during the eighteenth century that a new understanding of and interest in religion emerged, as scholars began to approach religious belief from a philosophical or psychological perspective in order to try and understand the psychology of primitive man.[30] Recent scholarship, however, has revised Manuel's temporalisation. Indeed, scholars such as Dmitri Levitin, Martin Mulsow, Guy Stroumsa,

---

tradition transmise de pere en fils: tout cela étoit capable de faire connoîtreces Hommes celebres qui avoient merité les honneurs divins."

28   Banier, *La mythologie et les fables expliquées* 1:xvi: "Comme une Mythologie doit renfermer non seulement tout ce qui regarde les Dieux & les Heros, en expliquer les fables, les ramener à leurs sources: mais qu'elle doit contenir encore le Systême de l'Idolatrie, son origine, ses progrès, & tout ce qui concerne le Culte & les Ceremonies du Paganisme, j'ai fait entrer dans celle que je donne aujourd'hui, toutes ces differentes matieres; & voici l'ordre dans lequel j'ai cru devoir les arranger."

29   Mulsow, "John Selden's De Diis Syris."

30   Manuel, *The Eighteenth Century Confronts the Gods*.

Peter Miller, and Joan-Pau Rubiés have supposed that it was during the seventeenth rather than the eighteenth century that the notion of "religion" was first explored as a social, historical, and anthropological concept, rather than as a mere synonym for Christianity.[31] According to Levitin, this led to the development of a "new genre" of historiography, the "history of idolatry," which charted how "the post-Noachic diffusion of the world's peoples had gradually led to the establishment of the various idolatrous religions of paganism, either from nature worship, Euhemerist deification of rulers, or priestly imposture."[32] Guy Stroumsa has even argued that this emerging scholarly tradition inaugurated "a new science of religion."[33] Eventually, this tradition had profound effects for how scholars approached the question of the nature and origins of religion: by the mid-eighteenth century, "religion" had come to replace "idolatry" as a designation for polytheistic belief systems. According to Stroumsa, the foundations laid by seventeenth-century scholarship paved the way for the first comparative, academic study of ancient religion in the nineteenth century.

In particular, historians have come to notice three important changes. Firstly, early modern scholars increasingly came to explain the origins of idolatry in historical, natural, and therefore human terms. By the end of the seventeenth century, demonic explanations for the origins of the pagan gods had all but disappeared from scholarship on *historia sacra* – where they did remain, they played a minor role. Secondly, scholars of *historia sacra* came to examine the origins of pagan religions within the context of barbarous and uncivilized societies whose idolatry was the product of their primitive ignorance and their failed attempts to explain the world around them. As a result, it is clear that the "psychological" approach to pagan religion which Manuel placed at the beginning of the eighteenth century was already being developed by sacred historians in the seventeenth century. Thirdly, scholars came to realise that idolatry was a feature not merely of the pagan but also of the Jewish religion. This was itself a radical assumption, for it led scholars to study ancient Jewish religion within the historical context of ancient pagan beliefs and in so doing break down the long-established boundaries between the divine, revealed

---

31   Joan-Pau Rubiés, "Theology, Ethnography, and the Historicization of Idolatry," *Journal of the History of Ideas* 67 (2006): 571–596; Rubiés, "From Antiquarianism to Philosophical History"; Levitin, "From Sacred History to the History of Religion"; Mulsow, "Antiquarianism and Idolatry"; Miller, "Taking Paganism Seriously"; Jonathan Sheehan, "Time Elapsed, Time Regained: Anthropology and the Flood," in Mulsow and Assmann, *Sintflut und Gedächtnis*, 321–334.

32   Levitin, "From Sacred History to the History of Religion," 1132.

33   Guy Stroumsa, *A New Science: The Discovery of Religion in the Age of Reason* (Cambridge MA: Harvard University Press, 2010).

religion of Moses and the idolatrous errors of the heathens. No doubt crucial in this development was John Spencer, who argued that idolatrous pagan practices shaped a Mosaic Law which was itself only intended as a short-term antidote to the religious idolatry the Jews had been subjected to (and influenced by) in Egypt. All three developments, however, had far-reaching implications, for they led scholars to study religion not merely through the Christian, theological, distinction between religious truth and religious error but as a (quasi-)anthropological concept. Religion, religious ritual, religious belief, and religious expression, scholars realised, were common to all peoples and shaped by specific historical, social, cultural, and linguistic factors. As Jonathan Sheehan has pointed out, in Spencer's *De legibus Hebraeorum* religion was not analysed in terms of "truth" but "in terms of its social function as a tool for making distinctions."[34] It is for this reason that historians such as Sheehan have placed the origins of what nineteenth-century scholars would call the "comparative history of religions" in seventeenth-century scholarship on *historia sacra*.

Bonjour's basic understanding of ancient idolatry – the process by which the heathens had diverged from primitive Noachic monotheism and multiplied a small number of idolatrous gods into a vast pagan panoply – was shaped by those scholars who also informed his approach to *historia sacra* and who first gave religion a history. Of particular importance in this context was the work of John Selden, who continued to represent that particular, diffusionist, approach to Greco-Roman polytheism even at the turn of the eighteenth century. Like many of his contemporaries, Selden supposed that polytheism was the result of a deviation from original monotheism, although he did distinguish between an elite monotheism which was preserved by wise sages and priests and the vulgar polytheism of the common people.[35] Moreover, in the *De diis syris*, Selden gave a number of different reasons for the beginnings of idolatrous worship and the origins of polytheism.[36] The first was the worship of celestial bodies such as the sun and moon. These gods Selden called "rebus naturalibus." The second type he called "rebus daemoniis."[37] These he defined as gods who had essentially been "created" by pagans who had come to worship various *simulacra* once intended as mere memorials or symbols of grief and remembrance as gods in themselves. Thus, Selden supposed that idolatry

---

34   Sheehan, "Sacred and Profane," 58.
35   See Mulsow, "John Selden's De Diis Syris," 16ff.; and Mulsow, "Antiquarianism and Idolatry," 196.
36   Selden, *De diis syris*, "Prolegomena," and Toomer, *John Selden*, 255.
37   See also Miller, "Taking Paganism Seriously"; Mulsow, "John Selden's De Diis Syris."

and polytheism proliferated when pagans confused posthumous commemoration with divine worship.[38] The origins of both forms of worship were attested to explicitly, or so early modern scholars thought, in certain biblical passages. Particularly important in the context of celestial worship was a passage in the book of Job (31:26–28), in which Job declared, "if I saw the sun when it shined, and the moon going clearly, and my heart in secret rejoiced, and I kissed my hand with my mouth; which is most great iniquity, and a denial against God the most high."[39] Both Selden and in later years Bonjour cited this passage as evidence for the antiquity of sun worship.[40] Similar foundational passages existed when it came to the pagan apotheosis of mortals. Of particular importance was the fourteenth chapter of the book of Wisdom, in which a father, afflicted with bitter grief by the death of his son, fashioned an image of his son to which he accorded divine honours. Consequently, it was common to suppose that an idol – εἴδωλον – originated with what Pierre Jurieu later called an "image du chaleur," the worship of an image (εἰδός) initially constructed out of grief (ὀδύνη).[41] Moreover, it is worth pointing out that this biblical narrative had an almost exact equivalent in pagan mythology: ultimately, both biblical and profane sources attested to both the celestial and the idolatrous deviation from the true religion. Thus, at the beginning of his *Mythologiae*, composed around the turn of the sixth century AD, the Latin writer Fulgentius cited Diophantus' story of Syrophanes the Egyptian which described the origin of idolatry in much the same terms:

> Syrophanes of Egypt, rich in slaves and possessions, had a son born to him. He was devoted to this son, heir to vast wealth, with an affection beyond words, beyond anything required of a father; and when the son was taken from him by a bitter blow of fate, the announcement of a double bereavement for the father left him cruelly stricken, in that the perpetual support of offspring had been denied him and he had met an unexpected check to the further expanding of his wealth. What use to him now was either his prosperity as a father, now condemned to barrenness, or delightful possessions, now curtailed of succession? Not only should he not possess what once he had, but he could not be the one to regain what he had lost. Then, in the grip of grief which always endeavours to relieve its need, he

---

38   Selden, *De diis syris*, xlii: "a demortuorum autem memoria idolorum cultu fluxisse passim indicatur."
39   *The Holie Bible Faithfully Translated*, 1:980.
40   Selden, *De diis syris*, xxvi–xxxviii.
41   Jurieu, *Histoire critique des dogmes et des cultes*, 399–401.

set up an effigy of his son in his household; but when he sought a cure thereby for his grief, he found it rather a renewal of sorrow, for he did not realize that forgetting is the true healer of distress: he had made something whereby he would acquire daily renewals of his grief, not find comfort from it. This is called an idol, that is *idos dolu*, which in Latin we call appearance of grief. For to flatter their master, the entire household was accustomed to weave garlands or place flowers or burn sweet-smelling herbs before the effigy. Also some slaves guilty of wrongdoing, in order to avoid the wrath of their master, would take refuge by the effigy and so assure forgiveness, and as a sure guarantee of favour would place there little gifts of flowers or incense, rather from fear than veneration.[42]

Just as Selden cited this passage in the "Prolegomena" of his *De diis syris*, so too did Bonjour in his discussion of the origins of Egyptian idolatry in the *Antiquitas temporum*.[43]

If the worship of celestial bodies and the fashioning of human idols – of which two other common explanations for the origins of idolatry, namely astral worship or astrology and animal worship or zoolatry, were variants – proved the most powerful explanations for the origins of the pagan gods, then there remained the question as to how these pagan gods had multiplied. The answer which scholars most frequently proffered was not a new one: more than a thousand years ago Augustine had ridiculed pagan religion on the grounds that the multitude of names had led to a proliferation of gods, and in seventeenth-century *historia sacra* this remained a standard principle. Hence, for Selden, the multiplication of gods inherent in polytheism was due to the multiplication of names, or πολυωνυμία.[44] By multiplying the names of each god, pagan worshippers came to multiply the number of gods themselves. It was also on this premise that sacred historians linked multiple pagan gods – and, through etymology, multiple names – back to a single biblical individual. "For there were not as many πολυθεοτης [many divine powers] of the Gentiles, as there were πολυωνυμία [many names] of the Gods," wrote Marsham in his *Canon chronicus*, when identifying Hammon with Belus, Menes, and Jupiter. "Of the same God, for the institutions of [each] nation, there were different

---

42 Leslie George Whitbread, ed., *Fulgentius the Mythographer* (Columbus: Ohio State University Press, 1971), 48.
43 Selden, *De diis syris*, xl–xliii; *De dynastiis*, fol. 29r–v.
44 Selden, *De diis syris*, lii.

rites, different appellations."[45] It was this principle which Bonjour not only took on but which fundamentally shaped his understanding of the nature of pagan religion, as we shall see.

In his epochal *De theologia gentili*, Gerardus Vossius took on and furthered many of Selden's notions. Vossius supposed that all pagan gods were one of two kinds: either they were φυσικάς, physical, or ἱστορικάς, historical. The former, the *dei naturales*, represented celestial bodies such as the sun, the moon, and the stars; the latter, the *dei animales*, represented historical individuals, from sacred as well as profane history.[46] Often, major gods could represent both celestial bodies and former mortals. The Egyptian god Osiris was Φυσικῶς because he represented the sun, but also ἱστορικῶς because he was Mizraim, the son of Ham and founder of Egypt.[47] In the ancient world this duality was sometimes known as the *theologia dipertita*, the invention of which Diodorus had attributed to Euhemerus at one point (6.1.1–2) and to the inhabitants of Egypt and Ethiopia at another (1.12.10–11, 13).[48] "As regards the gods, then, men of ancient times have handed down to later generations two different conceptions," wrote Diodorus at the start of the sixth book of his *Bibliotheca historica*. "Certain of the gods, they say, are eternal and imperishable, such as the sun and the moon and the other stars of the heavens, and the winds as well and whatever else possesses a nature similar to theirs; for of each of these the genesis and duration are from everlasting to everlasting. But the other gods, we are told, were terrestrial beings who attained to immortal honour and fame because of their benefactions to mankind, such as Heracles, Dionysus, Aristaeus, and the others who were like them."[49] In the seventeenth century, this bipartite notion was almost universally accepted, although scholars tended to cite as evidence not Diodorus but a lost work by Cornelius Labeo, the *Diis animalibus*, which Servius had discussed in his commentary of Virgil's *Aeneid* (3.168).[50] Despite

---

45   Marsham, *Chronicus canon*, 32: "Neque enim tanta fuit πολυθεοτης [many divine powers] Gentium, quanta fuit Deorum πολυωνυμία [many-names]. Ejusdem Dei, pro patriis institutis, diversus erat cultus, diversae appellationes."
46   See, for example, on the gods of Egypt, Vossius, *De theologia gentili*, 196: "Aegyptiis Dii duplices: alii caelestes, & aeterni; alii terrestres, & mortales, a morte autem in Deorum numerum relati."
47   Vossius, *De theologia gentili*, 355.
48   See the discussion in Marek Winiarczyk, *The Sacred History of Euhemerus of Messene*, trans. Witold Zbirohowski-Kościa (Berlin: De Gruyter, 2013), 27–28.
49   Diodorus, *The Library*, ed. Oldfather, 3:331.
50   Maurus Servius Honoratus, *In Vergilii carmina comentarii. Servii Grammatici qui feruntur in Vergilii carmina commentarii*, ed. Georg Thilo and Hermann Hagen (Leipzig: B. G. Teubner, 1881): "nam anteriori respondit. quod autem dicit 'a quo principe genus nostrum

being famous for his identifications with Moses, it is worth pointing out that even Huet repeated Vossius' notion that many gods were not only former mortals but also represented a celestial body, usually the sun or moon.[51] Similarly, in his *Histoire critique*, Jurieu took up this binary and asserted that Servius was wrong to suppose that gods were *either* elements of the natural world *or* divinized mortals, arguing instead that each god was the representation of *both* a mortal *and* a physical object of nature, usually celestial.[52]

Yet Vossius also went further in the importance he accorded to nature and the natural world when it came to explaining the origin of idolatry. Like Selden, Vossius assumed that all nations were originally monotheistic. The principal reason for their deviation from the true religion was explained by Paul at Romans 1:25: "coluerunt et servierunt creaturae potius quam creatori," they worshipped and served the created rather than the creator. As Vossius continued:

> Because the Gentiles, except a select few, even when they recognised God, nonetheless would not recognise this God: that is, when they saw that there was a God, who ruled this world, and wanted to be worshipped by us, they would not, however, see that it was this one whose divinity in truth it was; so that they bestowed it on the works of God, which we call the physical universe [rerum naturam].[53]

As Dmitri Levitin has recently pointed out, Vossius supposed that the monist or animist principles which informed Greek philosophy could also explain Greek religion more generally, and consequently the nature of Greek idolatry.[54] Despite initially recognising just one deity, the pagans had supposed this deity was nature itself, rather than a being above nature and the creator of nature.

---

    est' potest et generaliter intellegi, id est unde originem ducimus, ut deos penates quasi Troianos intellegas, et ad ritum referri, de quo dicit Labeo in libris qui appellantur de diis animalibus: in quibus ait, esse quaedam sacra quibus animae humanae vertantur in deos, qui appellantur animales, quod de animis fiant. Hi autem sunt dii penates et viales."

51   Huet, *Demonstratio evangelica*, 218–219

52   Jurieu, *Histoire critique des dogmes et des cultes*, 418–429.

53   Vossius, *De theologia gentili*, 23: "quod gentiles, praeter eximios quosdam, etiam cum Deum cognoscerent, eum tamen non cognoscerent Deum: hoc est, cum viderent esse Deum, qui universum hoc regeret, & coli a nobis vellet; non tamen viderent, eum esse, cujus revera esset divinitas; ut qui eam tribuerint Dei opificio, quam rerum naturam vocamus."

54   Levitin, "What was the Comparative History of Religions in 17th-Century Europe (and Beyond)?"

With Vossius in particular, scholars were presented with an understanding of pagan religion – or theology – which could be extemporised, and which could describe religion – and idolatry – in general terms. In his *De theologia gentili*, Vossius sought to understand and categorise how one could best understand idolatry in all its different forms. Borrowing from Aquinas, he defined the three ways in which one could gain a knowledge of God – the *via causalitatis*, the *via eminentiae*, and the *via negationis* – and described how pagans had first deviated from them. He also sought to differentiate between ἀθεότης, or *irreligiositas*, and δεισιδαιμονία, or *superstitio*, the latter of which could further be divided into *superstitio falsi cultus*, or εἰδωλολατρεία, and *superstitio cultus indebiti*.[55] Once Vossius had established the types and the origins of idolatry, he surveyed the manner in which idolatry had manifested itself in the various nations of the ancient world.[56] In recent literature, historians have sometimes supposed that this survey was a comparative study of religions, or else a taxonomy.[57] I do not feel that this is a wholly accurate description. In actual fact, Vossius developed not a taxonomy but a dichotomy: between original Hebrew monotheism on the one hand and the corrupt, posterior, and idolatrous religion of the pagans on the other. Despite the many small differences between the different religions of various ancient Gentile nations, Vossius ultimately assumed that they could all be analysed through the same basic framework, and that their underlying nature was the same. Vossius work concerned Gentile theology, not Gentile theologies. It is for this reason that Vossius applied the binary of *dei animales* and *dei naturales* to not just one, or some, but to all pagan religions.[58] Although Vossius did proffer a number of identifications between pagan gods and biblical patriarchs – including between Moses and Liber, Joshua and Hercules, and Joseph and Osiris – he sought to provide a clear theological differentiation between the true religion on the one hand and the false religion on the other. In a wonderfully illustrative passage,

---

55 Vossius, *De theologia gentili*, 1–27.
56 A similar project was Justus Lipsius' earlier *Fax Historica*: see Jan Papy, "Far and Away? Japan, China, and Egypt, and the Ruins of Ancient Rome in Justus Lipsius' Intellectual Journey," in *Antiquarianism and Intellectual Life in Europe and China, 1500–1800*, ed. Peter N. Miller and François Louis (Ann Arbor: The University of Michigan Press, 2012), 81–82.
57 Richard H. Popkin, "The Crisis of Polytheism and the Answers of Vossius, Cudworth and Newton," in *Essays in the Context, Nature and Influence of Isaac Newton's Theology*, ed. James E. Force and Richard H. Popkin (Dordrecht: Kluwer Academic Publishers, 1990), 10–11.
58 Although some nations, such as the Persians, began with natural gods and only later adopted the custom of deifying men: Vossius, *De theologia gentili*, 79.

Vossius outlined the relationship between Jewish monotheism and pagan polytheism as the difference between a faithful and an adulterous marriage. The Christian God, Vossius observed, was "zelotypus," jealous. Hence even if pagans recognised or recalled the true Christian God, their practice of admitting other gods annulled any idea that they may be seen as pious worshippers. If a wife, Vossius wrote, sleeps with another man, then this is adultery, even if she worships the man to whom she is married.[59]

In his work on the pagan gods, Bonjour built on these notions and developed a fairly conventional narrative for the origins of idolatry. Like many of his contemporaries he believed that the primitive religion was monotheistic and was once shared by all peoples. When defending the authenticity of the Pentateuch in his *Triduanda*, he noted that "the books of Moses, the antiquity of which you [the "Heathen" interlocutor] defended excellently out of your writers, teach us that the most ancient rituals of all people were applied to the worship of one God, whom the Mosaic law accorded the highest observation."[60] Like most of his contemporaries, he focussed on a particular biblical passage which appeared to evidence the first deviation from original monotheism. For Protestant scholars, who generally tended to give an antediluvian origin for idolatry, this was often Genesis 4:26, in which Enoch was said to have "profaned" rather than "called upon" the name of God.[61] Catholics, meanwhile, were more prone to giving idolatry a postdiluvian origin. Hence Montfaucon noted that the first biblical figure to construct images was Abraham's father Terah, who, according to Joshua 24:2, was the first to worship "diis alienis," foreign gods, while Philippe Couplet (1623–1693), the Flemish Jesuit responsible for the monumental *Confucius Sinarum philosophus* of 1687, believed idolatry began in Assyria with Ninus, the grandson of Ham.[62] In his *Antiquitas temporum* Bonjour rejected the popular interpretation of Joshua 24:2, claiming that "diis" was a mistranslation of the Hebrew "Elohim," which could mean "gods" but in this case meant "judges" or "masters." Instead, Bonjour supposed that it was the

---

59   Vossius, *De theologia gentili*, 296.
60   *Triduanda*, T.I.34, 11: "Libri Mosis quorum antiquitatem ex tuis scriptoribus egregie propugnasti, nos docent ritus omnium antiquissimos adhibitos esse ad colendum unum Deum quem Mosaica lex prosequitur summa observantia."
61   Scaliger, Selden, and Vossius all pointed to Genesis 4:26; Jurieu and Le Clerc however rejected this interpretation. See Mulsow, "John Selden's De Diis Syris," 12; Jurieu, *Histoire critique des dogmes et des cultes*, 15.
62   Bernard de Montfaucon, "Discours préliminaire sur l'origine de l'idolâtrie, & sur l'idée que les païens avoient de leurs divinitez," in *L'antiquité expliquée* 1, part 2: xci–civ; Claudia von Collani, "Philippe Couplet's Missionary Attitude towards the Chinese in *Confucius Sinarum Philosophus*," in Heyndrickx, *Philippe Couplet*, 37–54.

Egyptian pharaoh who had first misinterpreted Abraham's wisdom, particularly in the discipline of astronomy, and who had therefore become the first mortal to worship the sun.[63] Although Bonjour explicitly rejected Macrobius' famous notion that *all* pagan gods were representations of the sun in the *De nomine*, he nevertheless considered sun worship the oldest form of idolatry, attested to at Job 31:26–28 and prohibited at Deuteronomy 4:19.[64] In his rough notes, under the heading "Ethnica solis attributa," he noted a list of inscriptions from the collection of Jan Gruter, alongside a citation from Macrobius (1.23.1), which evidenced this.[65]

As in Gisbert Cuper's *Harpocrates*, sun worship tended to suggest the original monotheism of pagan nations but also their inherent miscomprehension of the true notion of the divine. Like Selden and Vossius, Bonjour linked this miscomprehension back to a general historical phenomenon attested to by Greek writers such as Plato (*De legibus* 4.886b–e, *Cratylus* 397C–D): the propensity of ancient, often uncivilized and agrarian communities whose lives were governed by the seasons to regard the sun as their master.[66] A notable testimony to this effect came from ps.-Plutarch's *De placitis philosophorum* (1.6), which Bonjour jotted under the heading "Notitiae Dei." In the narrative of ps.-Plutarch, the first men realised that the heavens and the astral bodies regulated daily life and subsequently came to believe that the sky was the Father of all things, and earth the Mother.[67] For Bonjour, the beginnings of pagan theology could therefore be traced back to ignorant ancient civilizations who began to worship nature rather than a being above nature.

Despite this, Bonjour continued to argue – as he had noted in his letter on Madbachus and Selamanes – that an original monotheism remained detectable in both pagan rites and even in the language of their worship, despite the development, proliferation, and escalation of subsequent idolatrous errors. A particularly illustrative example is Bonjour's study of an ancient Antiochene coin depicting Jupiter, on which he wrote a short, unpublished essay. Citing Aulus Gellius (*Noctes atticae* 5.12), Bonjour linked the etymology of "Jupiter" back to "Iovis Pater," just as Neptune and Mars could also be linked to Neptunuspater or Marspater. For Bonjour, this etymology was linguistic evidence of an ancient

---

63   *De dynastiis*, fol. 10r.
64   *De nomine*, 7: "Qui omnes superstitiosae antiquitatis Deos ad Solem referunt, in eum mox detorquebunt hanc inscriptionem."
65   BAR, ms.lat.634, fol. 48v; Gruter, *Inscriptiones*, 32–36.
66   "Idololatria Platonica," BAR, ms.lat.633, fol. 109v, and "Notitiae Dei," BAR, ms.lat.633, fol. 20r; Bonjour took his translation from Marsilio Ficino, ed., *Divini Platonis Opera Omnia quae exstant* (Frankfurt: Claude de Marne, 1602).
67   "Notitiae Dei," BAR, ms.lat.633, fol. 20r.

monotheism: "for when the land was of one tongue, the confession of the one ineffable and true God belonged to those to whom this expression was uttered; and although through the perverse practice of polytheism they were going to admit more Jupiters following the dispersal, it was going to lead back and recall the language of the Gentile, which had always acknowledged the one God by this primeval idiom."[68] It was a notion that he shared with many of his antiquarian contacts, such as Jean-Pierre Rigord.[69] According to both Rigord and Bonjour, pagan ritual preserved evidence both of the primitive monotheism common to all peoples as well as the historical interactions between Jews and Egyptians. In the *De nomine*, Bonjour noted how the pagan ritual of Osiris as recorded by Plutarch (*De Iside et Osiride* 372C), in which worshippers led a cow seven times around the temple of the sun, was also a reflection of the pharaoh's dream of seven fat and seven lean cows which Joseph had interpreted for him. This was just one of a number of Egyptian rituals which derived from the biblical history of Joseph in Egypt, in which the more ancient, and therefore more truthful, vestiges of the true religion and its history could still be gleaned.

3   Divine Names and Pagan Onomatolatria

So far, so conventional. Yet Bonjour's illustrative quote about the manner in which an original monotheism could be gleaned through etymology specifically also brings us to one of his central if also somewhat idiosyncratic assumptions about pagan religion: the importance of language, both in understanding the origins of paganism and in explaining its nature.

Within the discipline of *historia sacra*, language, or more specifically divine "names," had always been a crucial piece of evidence for allowing scholars to identify pagan gods with biblical patriarchs, as we have touched upon

---

68   "De Jove Antiochensium cujus effigies scuplta est in variis nummis praesidum Syriae," BAR, ms.lat.629, fol. 273r: "Hinc matricis omnium linguarum vocem non sine divino numine retinuerunt Gentes. Quibus enim haec proferebatur, cum terra unius erat labii, unius quoque ineffabilis ac veri Dei confessio illis erat: et quamvis perverso polytheismi usu plures post dispersionem Joves esset admissura, ad hujus tamen Gentis linguam deductura erat et revocatura, quae primaevo semper idiomate unum Deum fuerat confessa." Cf. Aulus Gellius, *Attic Nights*, ed. John C. Rolfe (Cambridge MA: Harvard University Press, 1946), 1:413: "The explanation of these names I have found to be this: the ancient Latins derived Iovis from iuvare (help), and called that same god "father," thus adding a second word. For Iovispater is the full and complete form, which becomes Iupiter by the syncope or change of some of the letters. So also Neptunuspater is used as a compound, and Saturnuspater and Ianuspater and Marspater – for that is the original form of Marspiter – and Jove also was called Diespiter, that is, the father of day and of light."

69   Rigord, *Dissertation De Monsieur Graverol ... sur l'explication d'une médaille*, 23.

previously. In Huet's *Demonstratio evangelica*, each chapter of "Propositio IV" identified a certain pagan god with Moses on the basis of an etymological study of their various divine names as well as narrative similarities in their myths. "We have seen the names of Mercury derive from Moses; now we shall see the narratives themselves," he noted programmatically in the fourth chapter, in which Huet identified Moses with the Egyptian Hermes.[70] For Bonjour, the names of pagan gods remained among the most important piece of historical evidence for charting how a single biblical figure had appeared in a myriad of pagan guises, and therefore for deciphering ancient, unknown antiquity. This was evident in his *Mercurius*, but even more so in a preparatory dissertation entitled "De variis Josephi ac Mercurii nominibus."[71] Here, Bonjour listed the various names by which Joseph and Mercury were known in the ancient world – Zaphnath paaneah (Genesis 41:45), "Hermiuth" (Artapanus in Eusebius, *Praeparatio evangelica* 9.23), or "Peteseph" (Chaemeron in Josephus *Contra Apionem* 1.290–291) for Joseph; Hermes, Thoth, Anubis, Meni, Menona, and Mominus for Mercury – and demonstrated how their etymologies revealed important historical facts about their lives. To take one particular example, Bonjour argued that "Peteseph," or, as it could also be written, "Beteseph," derived from the Hebrew "betha," meaning house, and "oseph," meaning collection. This led Bonjour to argue that the name referred back to a passage in Genesis 41:47 in which Joseph collected the corn into sheaves and gathered them in the barns of Egypt.[72] "With such veils of names in Mercury is Joseph, the son of the patriarch Jacob, obscured," noted Bonjour.[73] It was also in this context that Bonjour made specific reference to the power and importance of names themselves. "For it is possible," noted Bonjour, citing, out of context, John Chrysostom's homilies on Romans, "to find a great treasure even from bare names." To this he also added a passage from Origen's *Contra Celsum*: "if names whose nature it is to be powerful in some particular language are translated into another tongue they no longer have any effect such as they did with their proper sounds."[74] We shall return to this notion, and Origen's *Contra Celsum* in particular, in due course.

---

70   Huet, *Demonstratio evangelica*, 109: "vidimus nomina Mercurii ex Mose esse profecta; nunc videamus res ipsas."
71   BAR, ms.lat.631, fol. 208r.
72   "De variis Josephi ac Mercurii nominibus," BAR, ms.lat.631, fol. 210r–v.
73   "De variis Josephi ac Mercurii nominibus," BAR, ms.lat.631, fol. 208v: "Talibus in Mercurio nominum involucris obtenditur Joseph Jacobi patriarchae filius: neque alius prospicitur, nisi quia incanti nec opinantis animi exitum vel supinam peregrinantis aberrationem subit."
74   "De variis Josephi ac Mercurii nominibus," BAR, ms.lat.631, fol. 208v: "Est enim et in nudis hisce nominibus magnum invenire thesaurum ... multarum siquidem rerum

If names were key in synchronizing pagan myths with biblical history, then they remained similarly critical in suggesting how pagans had multiplied their number of gods. The translatability of divine names was something scholars often took from the Greeks directly. When, in book eleven of the Numidian Platonist Apuleius' second-century *Metamorphoses*, the protagonist Lucius encountered Isis in a dream, she explicitly declared that she was worshipped by the Phrygians as Cybele, in Attica as the Cecropian Minerva, in Cyprus as the Paphian Minerva, as Dictynna-Diana by the Cretans, as Stygian Proserpine by the Sicilians, and at other places as Ceres, Juno, Hecate, and Rhamnusia. Only the Egyptians and Ethiopians, "strong in ancient lore, worship me with the rites that are truly mine and call me by my real name, which is Queen Isis" (11.5), she declared.[75] Some two hundred years later, Ausonius' collection of epigrams contained an inscription, supposedly taken from a statue of Liber Pater situated on his country estate outside of Bordeaux, which conveyed a similar understanding of pagan religion. According to this inscription, later known as the "myobarbus" or "mixobarbaron," it was suggested that he whom the Thebans called Bacchus the Egyptians called Osiris, the Mysians Phanaces, the Indians Dionysus, the Romans Liber, and the Arabs Adoneus. Nor were these famous examples isolated phenomena.[76] In his *Bibliotheca* Diodorus had suggested that Osiris could be identified with Serapis, Dionysus, Pluto, Ammon, Jupiter, and Pan (1.25.1–2), while Nonnus identified the worship of the sun with Bacchus, Hercules, Belus, Ammon, Apis, Saturn, Jupiter, Serapis, and Apollo (*Dionysiaka* 40.392–401).[77] In the *Liber Memorialis* of Lucius Ampelius, one can find listed three Jupiters, two Marses, four Vulcans, four Mercuries, five Apollos, three Dianas, three Aesculapiuses, four Venuses, five Minervas, five Libers, and six Herculeses. Bochart later cited Ampelius to identify the fifth Apollo, who was said to be the son of Ammon and born in Libya, with

---

monumenta sunt nomina." My translation from Origen, *Contra Celsum*, trans. Henry Chadwick (Cambridge: Cambridge University Press, 1980), 299. Bonjour used the translation of Origen, *Origenis Contra Celsum libri octo. Ejusdem philocalia*, ed. William Spencer (Cambridge: John Field, 1658), 261–262.

75 Translation from Apuleius, *Metamorphoses*, trans. J. Arthur Hanson (Cambridge MA: Harvard University Press, 1989), 2:247. For contemporary citations see Graverol and Rigord, *Dissertation de Monsieur Graverol*, 21; *Mercurius*, fol. 26r.

76 See Ausonius, *D. Magni Ausonii Burdig. Viri Consularis Opera. A Iosepho Scaligero, & Elia Vineto denuo recognita, disposita, & variorum notis illustrata: Cetera Epistola ad lectorem docebit* (Geneva: Typis Jacob Stoer, 1588), 9. For contemporary discussions see Huet, *Demonstratio evangelica*, 210–211; Vossius, *De theologia gentili*, 325; Bonjour, "De Origine et Cognatione patriarchae Josephi Gentilitio Mercurii Stemmate," BAR, ms.lat.631, fol. 169v.

77 Cited in Huet, *Demonstratio evangelica*, 207–208; *Mercurius*, fol. 19v; *De nomine*, 11.

"Phuth," or Apollo Pythius, the third son of Ham.[78] These texts – Diodorus and Nonnus in particular – were pivotal sources for Bonjour's understanding of pagan religion and taught him what Jan Assmann has more recently defined as pagan "cosmotheism": the translatability of religious names, and by extension, the universality of religious "truth" among ancient pagan nations.[79] As Huet illustratively noted in his *Demonstratio*, the work of such pagan writers as Macrobius and Plutarch convinced the pagans themselves "what has long been observed by us, that [beneath] the multiplicity of Gods which the history of fables imposes upon us, there is one and the same God, who, for various effects, has been allotted various names."[80] Bonjour approached pagan religion in the same way, seeing the existence of many names as an explanation for the many gods. As Rigord wrote to Magliabechi, Bonjour's goal in the *Mercurius* was to prove nothing else than what many of the ancients, including Diodorus and Herodotus, had once openly admitted: that the many Gods were but one, and that the many names could be linked back to a single original from which these various *numina* had spawned forth and multiplied.[81]

Yet Bonjour also took the importance of names further still. Particularly critical was a passage from Cicero's *De natura deorum*: "his vocabulis Deos esse facimus, quibus a nobis nominantur" – we make Gods exist with those words, by which we call them (1.30 (84)).[82] Bonjour cited this single phrase several times in both his unpublished dissertations and in his later *Selectae*. For Bonjour, the phrase explained not only the multiplication but even the creation of divinities: it was not so much that one god had many names, but that, for the pagans, the names had become gods themselves.

The question goes back to the relationship between *nomina* and *numina*. According to Bonjour, it was not so much that each *numen* also had an appropriate *nomen*, but that what was conventionally considered a *numen* was really

---

78   Bochart, *Geographia sacra*, 12.
79   See in particular Assmann, *Moses the Egyptian*, 53, for his discussion of Ausonius.
80   Huet, *Demonstratio evangelica*, 207: "fidem his facit quod ab aliis jampridem observatum est, multiplicem illam Deorum turbam, quam nobis obtrudit fabularis historia, unum eumdemque esse Deum, pro variis effectis, varia nomina sortitum."
81   Jean-Pierre Rigord to Antonio Magliabechi, 4 September 1695, BNCF, *Fondo Magliabechiano* VIII, cod. 341, fol. 28terzo(r): "plusieurs des anciens a la verité avoient dit avant plus que plusieurs Divinités n'est etoient qu'une."
82   Bonjour, "De conversione gentium secundum antiquam Ecclesiae praxim," BAR, ms.lat.629, fol. 202r. The Loeb edition gives the translation as "do we also make out the gods to have the same names as those by which they are known to us?" (Cicero, *De natura deorum*, ed. Rackham, 81). I have tried to convey a translation more befitting Bonjour's rather than Cicero's meaning in this passage. Another version of Bonjour's dissertation can be found at BAR, ms.lat.630, fol. 100r.

nothing other than a *nomen*. For Bonjour, the gods (*numina*) which the pagans worshipped were really just names (*nomina*). Since pagans could not truly conceptualise "divinity," "gods" could not exist independently of the names by which they were invoked. In the *Selectae*, Bonjour summarised this notion with the comment that "veneration is the same for names as it is for gods."[83] In an unpublished dissertation entitled, *De conversione gentium secundum antiquam ecclesiae praxim*, "On the conversion of the gentiles according to the practice of the ancient church," he was more expansive:

> So great was the power of names among the pagans, that, with a divinity fashioned on account of a name, and not with a name imposed on a divinity, names were constitutive of divinities ... Hence it is necessary that the distinctive name of a false god, however honorific it was, was idolatrous. Wherefore divine Moses told the Israelites who were about to enter the land of Canaan not only *break the Idols* but also *Destroy their names out of those places* [Deuteronomy 12:3].[84]

The key body of evidence for Bonjour's interpretation of *nomina* was pagan ritual, in particular examples of pagan invocation. In short, the manner pagan priests and worshippers uttered and treated the names of the gods gave the best indication as to the relationship between *nomina* and *numina*. Trawling through various historical, antiquarian, miscellaneous, poetic, and philosophical texts, Bonjour analysed patterns of religious invocation, revealing a number of instances which appeared to suggest that pagan worshippers were unable to conceptualise a divine power without its appropriate name. For example, Aulus Gellius had reported that in certain cases it was established by decree that worshippers must give their thanks to both a god and a goddess after an earthquake, unsure as they were of the provenance of their divine saviour (*Noctes Atticae* 2.29). This was something also mentioned by Ammianus Marcellinus (17.6.10) and Tibullus (*Elegiae* 2.1), who stated that worshippers were told to only whisper the names of specific gods.[85] "For, regarding the

---

83 *Triduanda*, T.I.15, 6: "eadem apud nostros est nominis veneratio, quae numinis."
84 "De conversione gentium secundum antiquam Ecclesiae praxim," BAR, ms.lat.629, fol. 202r: "Tanta erat vis nominum apud Gentiles, ut efficto numine propter nomen, et non imposito propter numen nomine, nomina fuerint numinum constitutiva ... Hinc nomen falsi numinis distinctivum, quantumvis honorificum esset, idolatricum fuerit, necesse est. Quocirca divinus Moses ingressuris in terram Chanaan Israelitis non tam dixit. *Idola comminuite*, quam *Disperdite nomina eorum de locis illis*. Deut. Xii. 3." See also BAR, ms.lat.630, fol. 100r.
85 "De conversione gentium secundum antiquam Ecclesiae praxim," BAR, ms.lat.630, fol. 101v.

formula of invocation, it was to bring forth the name of the god who was invoked, lest the invocation be about an unknown and obscure or doubtful or uncertain divinity," wrote Bonjour.[86] As Bonjour read, so the examples multiplied, from Virgil (*Aeneid* 6.246–247) to Plautus (*Mostellaria* 528–9, *Mercator* 865), Seneca (*Medea* 439–440), or Cicero (*Tusculanae disputationes* 4.34). Even the biblical priests of Baal had sought in their dispute with Elias to call upon their false God Baal through empty invocations (1 Kings 18:26).[87] Perhaps the best evidence, however, was the humorous story of powerful Rhodian citizens scratching out the original names of statues and inscribing their own, a practice which had led Dio Chrysostom to claim that once a statue had had its inscription removed, it was no longer worshipped (*Orationes* 11.38). This led Bonjour to describe pagan religion in a novel way: "to a great extent you can call the empty religion not so much Idolatry [*Idololatria*] as Onomatolatry [*Onomatolatria*]" – less the "worship of idols" more the "worship of names."[88] In essence, Bonjour supposed that the false religion functioned through the invocation of names and that without the use of names, no gods, altars, temples, or shrines would, or could, exist.[89] According to Bonjour, the Apostles and the earliest Christian apologists had recognized this fact and proselytized accordingly. It was for this reason that Bonjour turned back to Origen's *Contra Celsum*. In one important passage, Origen had declared that true Christians should suffer martyrdom rather than worship their god with the Scythian name "Pappaeus," [Papaeus] since that name had been used in idolatrous invocations. For Origen, names had a religious power beyond mere linguistic meaning, and the name Papaeus, even if it was intended to refer to the Almighty, would irreparably lead idolaters back to worship of the Scythian desert idol (*Contra Celsum* 5.46). Yet the most important source for understanding pagan *onomatolatria* was Paul's

---

86   "De conversione gentium secundum antiquam Ecclesiae praxim," BAR, ms.lat.629, fol. 205v: "Nam de formula invocationis erat proferre nomen Dei qui invocabatur, ne invocatio esset de ignoto et obscuro vel dubio incertoque numine."

87   "De conversione gentium secundum antiquam Ecclesiae praxim," BAR, ms.lat.629, fols. 205r–205r, and also "De conversione gentium secundum antiquam Ecclesiae praxim," BAR, ms.lat.630, fols. 201v–202r. In his *De diis syris*, Selden had also blamed invocations for multiplying the number of gods and expanding polytheism: *De diis syris*, xl–lvi.

88   "De conversione gentium secundum antiquam Ecclesiae praxim," BAR, ms.lat.629, fol. 205r: "Adeo vanam religionem quam non tam Idololatriam quam onomatolatriam diceres."

89   "De conversione gentium secundum antiquam ecclesiae praxim," BAR, ms.lat.630, fols. 102r–v: "Ex his omnibus patet Idololatria nominis quod falsi numinis erat proprium. Idololatricum enim est hoc vocabulum quod facit nomen Idolo, nomen ejus altari, nomen ejus templo, nomen ejus sacris et sacrificiis, nomen et numen invocationibus. Idololatricum est illud nomen quod simulachrum falso numini consecrat, aram statuit, templum decernit, sacra addicit, ora devincit invocantium, corda excitat, nuncupat opera."

speech at the Areopagus, as recorded in Acts 17. Arriving in Athens, Paul took note of the famous Athenian altar dedicated to the "unknown God" and seized upon the Athenian ignorance of their own gods to preach in the simplest terms of the true "God [θεός], who made the world, and all things therein." According to Bonjour, the particular construct of Paul's speech and the specific terms he chose were a sign that Paul understood the pagan worship of names and the necessity of providing pagans with a name for God which had not previously been assigned to an idol but which, as Tertullian had once stated (*Contra Marcionem* 3.15), simply denoted the "natural designation of Deity," a being with a divine nature. As Bonjour continued:

> The more skilfully this high wariness of the Apostle discouraged the Athenians away from the names of their idols, the more easily and more effortlessly did he instruct them about the name, which they were able to invoke beyond all danger of superstition and idolatry, namely the appellative name which was θεός among the Athenians and *Deus* among the Romans. The divine herald knew that there was no false god who was personally denoted with the Greek name θεός: when he saw that that name was said not only of the known but also of the unknown God. He knew that to these the idolaters were obliged to worship their idols with only the names which were personal to the idols or attached to the idols by the particular obligation of their consecration.[90]

4   Pagan Ancestor Worship

Bonjour's assumptions about what he called pagan *onomatolatria* were clearly developed in and applied to the context of the Chinese Rites debate, as we shall see in the next chapter. By understanding the pagan relationship to divine names, Bonjour sought to clarify by which names Chinese neophytes might be allowed to denote the Christian God. But it is also clear that this notion was a

---

90   "De conversione gentium secundum antiquam Ecclesiae praxim," BAR, ms.lat.629, fol. 206r–v: "Quo summa haec cautio Apostoli solertius avocabat Athenienses a quibuscumque nominibus propriis idolorum, eo facilius et proclivius erudiebat eos de nomine, quod citra omne superstitionis et idolatriae periculum invocandum habebant, nempe de nomine appellativo quod Atheniensibus erat θεός, Latinis *Deus*. Sciebat divinus praeco nullum esse falsum numen quod proprie designaretur Graeco nomine θεός; cum illud videret tam de noto quam de ignoto dici. Sciebat idololatras his ad colendum idola sua nominibus tantum alligari quae essent propria idolorum seu proprio consecrationis obligamento idolis annexa."

development of both his study of ancient Greek mythology and his particular interest in pagan ritual. His citations of ritual examples in which pagan worshippers neglected to invoke the name of their god on purpose highlighted how the practices of pagan worshippers revealed the nature of pagan religion itself. Like Selden – who had once taken Juvenal's joke that even male mice were banned from the rites of Bona Dea seriously – Bonjour agreed that the practice of pagan religion was vital for understanding pagan religion as a concept.[91]

Both the importance of pagan ritual and antiquarian study on the one hand and the impetus provided by the Chinese debates on the other reappear in another characteristic hallmark of pagan religion which elicited much discussion in the seventeenth century: the veneration of former mortals. More specifically, the question pertained to the nature and function of pagan apotheosis or divinization, the process by which ancient pagans who were known to have been mortals were nevertheless worshipped as gods. In the Rites debate, scholars squabbled over whether the rites paid to Confucius and to dead Chinese ancestors could be considered merely forms of civil or familial remembrance or were forms of divine veneration and worship. One of the central questions within this debate was whether Confucius could be venerated as a god even if Chinese Confucians knew and admitted that he had once been a mortal being. Throughout the debates – as we shall see further in the following chapter – polemicists mobilised examples from Greco-Roman paganism and patristic apologetics to defend their interpretations of Chinese religion. Despite the differences between Confucianism and Greco-Roman polytheism, scholars still considered Confucianism merely one off-shoot or version of heathenism, and therefore part of "pagan" theology. A particularly illustrative example of this tendency was the *Conformité des cérémonies chinoises avec l'idolâtrie grecque et romaine* (1700) of Noël Alexandre, whose Dominican Order were perhaps the most vocal and best-organised opponents of the Jesuits in the Roman debates around 1700. In his treatise, Alexandre argued that the Chinese engaged in exactly the same Greco-Roman practice of divinizing great men. Particularly important, both for Alexandre specifically but also for any scholarly attempt to understand the nature of pagan religion more generally, was Cicero's *De natura deorum*, which Lactantius had once used to try and prove that pagan gods were deified mortals. Citing Cicero's discussion of Euhemerus, Ennius, and Persaeus, Alexandre supposed that the practice of deifying great men and giving the Greco-Roman gods births and genealogies was indicative of

---

91 Toomer, *John Selden*, 220; Juvenal, *Saturae* 6.339.

the general pagan practice of conferring divine honours onto former mortals. Moreover, Alexandre, like Lactantius, supposed that this tendency remained a central tenet of pagan religious practice long after the end of the mythic period. Alexandre went on to mobilise this notion against those Jesuits who suggested that the honours conferred onto Confucius could not be religious because the Chinese recognised that Confucius was a mortal being. The ongoing practice of apotheosizing and deification which Origen, Tertullian, and Arnobius had observed in the third and fourth centuries suggested that the worship of mortal beings was a central part of pagan worship, in which one could clearly include the Chinese.[92]

Although Bonjour frequently suggested that those whom the pagans worshipped as gods had once been mortals – not least when identifying pagan deities with biblical patriarchs – only one of his dissertations was dedicated to the minor domestic and ancestral gods whom the Romans apotheosised and worshipped in their private chambers and public ceremonies, long after the end of Varro's mythic period. Entitled *Observatio in tabularia idolorum memorata a Tertulliano*, this work examined a specific passage of patristic apologetic and, through an antiquarian study of ancient Roman religious and political practices, sought to define the role of divinized men within ancient Roman religion.[93]

In chapter 10 of his *De idololatria*, Tertullian turned to the role of pagan schoolteachers. According to Tertullian, schoolteachers were necessarily complicit in the upholding and furthering of idolatry because they taught a curriculum in which the pagan gods and festivals were central. "Quis ludimagister si non Tabularia idolorum Quinquatria tamen frequentabit?" Tertullian had asked – "What schoolmaster would frequent the Quinquatria [the festival sacred to Minerva] without his *tabularia* of the idols?" (10.2).[94] Bonjour puzzled over what Tertullian had meant by the "tabularia idolorum." In his dissertation, he attempted to define these *tabularia* and describe their significance within pagan worship. To do so, he began by asking six questions: how were the *tabularia* used by the ancient pagans? Why were they in the possession of teachers? Where were these *tabularia* usually located? What sort of images of the idols were customarily engraved on these *tabularia*? What was the link between the tablets in the *tabularia*, statues of the idols, and religious

---

92 Alexandre, *Conformité des cérémonies*, 69–91.
93 "Observatio In Tabularia Idolorum memorata a Tertulliano," BAR, ms.lat.183, fols. 21r–32v.
94 Most modern editions today read: "Quis ludimagister sine tabula VII idolorum Quinquatria tamen frequentabit?" See Tertullian, *De Idololatria: Critical Text, Translation and Commentary*, ed. J. H. Waszink and J. C. M. van Winden (Leiden: E. J. Brill, 1987), 38.

sacrifices? And what was the link between *tabularia* and family genealogies?[95] Nominally, Bonjour's enquiry was antiquarian. Through comparison of ancient texts, he sought to make sense of the practical use of an ancient religious object. Yet the true object of his enquiry was the nature and history of Greco-Roman religion more generally. By making sense of the way in which these "tabularia idolorum" were used, Bonjour was trying to better understand the everyday practices and beliefs of pagan worship and idolatry.

Almost all of Bonjour's evidence was sourced from Latin literature, ranging from more explicitly antiquarian works such as Vitruvius or Pliny, to Latin history, poetry, and various miscellanea. First, Bonjour established that these "tabularia" were also known as the place in which public tablets, "tabulae publicae," were stored.[96] This is how they were cited by Ammianus Marcellinus (28.1.15); by Ovid (*Metamorphoses* 15.809–810); by Cicero (*De natura deorum* 3.30 (74)) (who noted that the tablets were burnt down by Quintus Socius); and by Virgil (*Georgics* 2.502), a passage on which Virgil's immortal companion Servius had commented that "the *Popularia Tabularia* is where public acts are stored. It can also mean the temple of Saturn, in which the state treasury was located and acts were placed."[97] In Greek, Bonjour called these *tabularia* γραμματοφυλάκιον (archives) or χαρτοφυλάκιον (case for storing papers). From Pliny, Bonjour noted that these archives (in Bonjour "tablina," in Pliny "tabulina") could also be rooms in private houses, as well as in public temples (35.2). In Vitruvius, he found measurements for the *tablinum* (translated in the Loeb edition as "alcove") in proportion to the hallway, or *atrium* (*De architectura* 6.3.5), which for Bonjour proved that the *tablinum* was located in the hall. The description of this hall he took from Pliny (35.2): a hall furnished not with statues or marbles, but with portraits, wax model faces of ancestors to be carried by the family in funeral processions. This custom of adorning hallways with wax portraits Bonjour confirmed by way of Ovid (*Fasti* 1.591) and Suetonius (*De vita Caesarum* 2.4.1), and noted that its prevalence had even been ridiculed by Juvenal (*Saturae* 8.19–20). Indeed, in general the halls of Roman residents, Bonjour noted, were places of ostentation, of embroidered robes (Ovid, *Fasti* 6.363), of purple awnings (*Metamorphoses* 10.595), of excessive portraits (Martial, 2.90.6), or even of the death mask of Manlius Torquatus (Valerius Maximus, *Factorum ac dictorum memorabilium* 5.8.3). This led Bonjour to

---

95 "Observatio in Tabularia Idolorum," BAR, ms.lat.183, fols. 21r–v.
96 For which he also cited an inscription from Gruter, *Inscriptiones antiquae*, 170, n. 6.
97 "Observatio in Tabularia Idolorum," BAR, ms.lat.183, fol. 22r: "'Popularia tabularia' ubi actus publici continentur. Significat autem templum Saturni, in quo et aerarium fuerat et reponebantur acta" (Servius, *Georgics* 2.502).

conclude that the *atrium* was the place in which notable Romans celebrated their wealth and, above all, their distinguished ancestry.[98]

The next step for Bonjour was to investigate the relationship between the domestic *tablinum* and the practice of pagan worship, as Tertullian had suggested. Bonjour began with a line from Tacitus: that the emperor Nero objected to the consul Gaius Cassius honouring – or worshipping – a bust of his ancestor Cassius, an assassin of Caesar (*Annales* 16.7), amongst other ancestral effigies which decorated his *atrium*. Bonjour used this remark to suggest that prominent Roman families had their own familial cults through which they worshipped their ancestors. This was further confirmed by Seneca the Elder (*Controversiae* 3.7.10) and Cicero (*Pro Sulla* 88), while the practice of making death masks for future sacrifices Bonjour found described in Polybius (6.53.4–6). It does not seem that Bonjour found this ancestral worship remarkable. Instead, he described it as a common feature of pagan religion, which also existed, if in a subtly different form, in the ancient Roman worship of the guardian deities, the Lares. Above all, it was a process of infiltration, in which the respect and honour offered to human ancestors gradually became divine worship and through which mortal ancestors infiltrated the ranks of the gods. Seneca (*De beneficiis* 3.26.2–3) was a witness to this development because he had warned against it, whilst Ausonius was a witness to its popularity because he had ridiculed it (*Epigrammata* 45). Bonjour, however, extended this practice beyond even ancestors – Mars too, and Romulus and Remus, had become gods through the perversion of ancestor worship. Tacitus had made explicit reference to this practice when he described the funeral procession of Drusus, which saw Aeneas paraded as the origin of the Julian line and worshipped alongside Romulus and the other Alban kings (*Annales* 4.9). The key to this process of infiltration was the Roman practice of constructing family genealogies. Cornelius Nepos had suggested that the Roman historian Atticus was one of the first historians to begin tracing family genealogies (*Atticus* 18), beginning with the Junian family at the request of Brutus; Brutus himself, as Cicero had noted (*De Oratore* 2.55), was prone to exalt himself by way of glorifying and divinizing his ancestry, a practice Marius had condemned in Sallust's *Bellum Jugurthinum* (85.17–25). Thus the later justification of divine origins through the practice of forming genealogies allowed the Romans to assert both their own divine origins and to justify the divine worship of their ancestors in their own family lineage.[99]

---

98   "Observatio in Tabularia Idolorum," BAR, ms.lat.183, fols. 21v–26v.
99   "Observatio in Tabularia Idolorum," BAR, ms.lat.183, fols. 26v–32v.

The question of the *tabularia*, then, allowed Bonjour to develop two features of pagan idolatry: firstly, the central function and worship of material objects, in this case the tablets and busts of the ancestors, within pagan religious ceremony; secondly, the creation of new gods through a perversion of the noble Roman tradition of honouring one's ancestors. Through genealogy – the tracing of one's family lineage back to their divine origins – the Romans, as Cicero noted, made heroes, kings, and ancient ancestors companions to the ancient original gods Caelus, Aether, and, further afield, to the divine abstractions Love, Guile, or Toil (*De natura deorum* 3.17 (44)). Hence, from his study of a single *tabularia* in Tertullian, Bonjour was able to explain the prominent practice of ancestral worship among noble Roman families and the process by which objects of ostentation had eventually come to be worshipped and thereby come to form an essential part of pagan ritual.[100] Consequently, he could provide an explanation as to how Roman ancestors once known to be mortal had come to infiltrate the ranks of the gods. In his manuscript notes, Bonjour continued to develop this notion further by examining one particular form of pagan apotheosis, namely the deification of kings. In a section of his notes entitled "Reges adorati," Bonjour listed a number of sources, some patristic but more often Roman and historical, which suggested that it was common for mortals to worship themselves as divine beings. Tacitus, for example, had stated (*Annales* 1.10) that the Emperor Tiberius kept a small room in his house in which he was "adored in temples and in the image of godhead by flamens and by priests." Meanwhile, Suetonius (*De vita Caesarum* 1.76) had stated that Caesar allowed himself to be furnished with honours "ampliora etiam humano fastigio," too great even for mortal men.[101] Nor was this solely a custom of Roman kings, or leaders. As Dionysius of Halicarnassus had noted, noble families, such as the descendants of Pallas, a son of Hercules, were accustomed to be worshipped with "those honours with which divine beings are worshipped by men" (*Antiquitates romanae* 1.32). To this, Bonjour added a more recent source, Alexander Alessandri's *Genialium dierum* (first published 1522), in which Alessandri argued that the custom of worshipping kings had spread

---

100 "Observatio in Tabularia Idolorum," BAR, ms.lat.183, fol. 30v: "Haec ergo tabularia nihil aliud erant quam tablina in quorum armariis reponebantur idola gentilitia, seu imagines majorum cultae a superstitiosis ethnicis non secus ad idola."

101 "Reges Adorati," BAR, ms.lat.633, fol. 62r; "Templa decreta Imperatoribus et Proconsulibus," BAR, ms.lat.633, fol. 66r; "Dii a suis cultoribus despecti," BAR, ms.lat.633, fol. 73v. One of the authors of the *Historia Augusta*, under the name Flavius Vopiscus, asserted that the Emperor Tacitus had ordered a temple erected for deified emperors (*Historia Augusta, Tacitus* 9.5–6), while Cicero, *De officiis* 3.20, reported that Marius Gratidianus had statues erected to himself during the civil war, before his savage death.

as far as the Persians, Medes, and Indians. When Alessandri's commentator, André Tiraqueau (1488–1558), came to this passage, he went further still by adding the testimonies of Herodotus, Plutarch, Valerius Maximus, Arrian, and Philostratus.[102]

Bonjour's investigation into the ancient practice of worshipping ancestors and doing so through busts and likenesses is indebted to several common late seventeenth-century scholarly traditions. As we have noted above, antiquarianism partly flourished because it allowed scholars to approach the problem of idolatry through a quasi-anthropological framework, which is to say, it allowed scholars to examine pagan religion and religious practices in their appropriate historical and cultural context.[103] It was also this form of antiquarian study which allowed Bonjour to join the ancient supposition that likenesses or simulacra led to the origins of idolatry, as noted by Fulgentius, to the continuation of these religious practices in imperial Rome. Yet there was also something else in the background of Bonjour's investigation of Tertullian's *tabularia*. In short, the themes which Bonjour developed in his study of Tertullian's *tabularia* were directly relevant to those questions which the vicar apostolic of Fujian, Charles Maigrot (1652–1730), had raised in his 1693 *Mandatum*, which reinstated a wholesale ban on the practicing of the Chinese Rites and which brought about a new and eventually decisive stage in the Chinese Rites debate.[104] There are two specific themes which align Bonjour's dissertation on Tertullian's *tabularia* with the Rites debate. The first issue was the worship of ancestors, which Maigrot had banned in the third and fourth propositions of his *Mandatum*.[105] While the Jesuits had frequently argued that the honours paid to their ancestors by the Chinese was simply a matter of veneration and remembrance, Maigrot instead suggested that this veneration amounted to religious worship. The second issue stemmed from the fifth proposition of Maigrot, which banned the kneeling in front of tablets found in the alcoves of ordinary Chinese houses, inscribed with the words *xin chu*, *xin goei*, or *ling goe*, which meant "the throne

---

102 Alessandro Alessandri, *Genialium dierum libri sex* (Lyon: Paul Frellon, 1608), 78–79; André Tiraqueau, *Semestria in Genialium dierum* (Lyon: Guillaume Rouillé, 1586), 205. These were the editions read by Bonjour.
103 See for example Rubiés, "Theology, Ethnography, and the Historicization of Idolatry," especially his comment on China, p. 592.
104 I am working from the *Mandatum* reprinted as part of the Papal decision of 1704, and currently housed in the archives of the Propaganda Fide, Rome: *Mandatum seu Edictum Domini Caroli Maigrot, Vicarii Apostolici Fokiensis in Regno Sinarum, nunc Episcopi Cononensis*, ASPF, SC Indie Orientali e Cina, Misc. 5.
105 *Mandatum*, 5–6.

or seat of the spirit."[106] Once again, the essential difference between Maigrot and his Jesuit interpreters was that Maigrot believed it was an act of religious veneration whereas the Jesuits considered it merely a form of honour. In his dissertation on Tertullian's mysterious *tabularia*, Bonjour proved that the ancient Romans not only knowingly worshipped their departed ancestors but also used inscribed tablets and pictorial representations to enable this idolatrous worship. Taking on Tertullian's definition of idolatrous honours as being anything that "elevates someone beyond the measure of human honour unto the likeness of divine sublimity" (quicquid ultra humani honoris modum ad instar divinae sublimitatis extollitur) (15.9), he sought to prove that both Roman and Chinese society were informed by the same, typically pagan, practice of corrupting political and civil honours into a form of veneration which eventually transcended the civil and the political.[107] In his notes on "reges adorati," he made the connection to China explicit:

> As the excellence of saints has its degrees, so too does the excellence of human civil worship have distinctions. The highest degree of human excellence in the civil or political order is the royal or imperial, particularly among the Chinese, who for this reason call their emperor the son of heaven, and for which reason it is wrong to give the title of these honours to anyone other than the emperor. And yet, the highest degree of human excellence in the civil or political order is below the excellence which the Chinese pursue in bowing, kneeling, and prostrating before their Confucius, given that the emperor of China himself prostrates his royal majesty and excellence and in this way also degrades his cult. Therefore, according to the Chinese, the excellence of Confucius is above the civil or political order, so that the worship relating to him cannot be said to be civil or political, but rather supra-civil, or supra-political.[108]

---

106   *Mandatum*, 5.
107   Tertullian, *De Idololatria*, ed. Waszink and van Winden, 55.
108   "Argumenta evincens cultum delatium Confucio non esse civilem," BAR, ms.lat.633, fol. 69v: "ut excellentia sanctorum habet suos gradus, ita et excellentia humana cultus civilis distinctiva. Supremus gradus excellentiae humanae in ordine civile seu politico est regius sive Imperatorius, maxime vero apud Sinenses qui idcirco suum Imperatorem filium caeli nuncupant, nefasque habent alteri ab Imperatore dare hujusmodi honoriis titulum. Atqui supremus ille gradus excellentiae humanae in ordine civili seu politico spectate est infra excellentiam propter quam Sinenses inclinationibus, genuflexionibus, et prostraetionibus prosequuntur suum Confucium, quandoquidem et ipse Sinarum Imperator regiam suam majestatem et excellentiam prosternit hujusmodi cultu atque obterit. Ergo excellentia Confuciam secundum Sinenses est supra ordinem civilem seu politicum adeoque cultus ipsi respondens non potest dici civilis seu politicus, sed supracivilis, sed suprapoliticus."

The final chapter of this work will hope to throw more light on Bonjour's relationship with China, and the manner in which the study of *historia sacra* shaped the way he defined Chinese Confucianism and those issues intimately associated with the Rites controversy then being debated in Rome. I hope in this chapter to have shown at least some of the basic presumptions which informed Bonjour's approach to pagan religion which would later prove formative in these Chinese debates. In particular, I hope to have shown how assumptions drawn from both mythography and a closer attention to pagan religious practices, primarily shaped by the new antiquarian interest in objects, helped a field of scholarship develop which increasingly saw pagan religion in its specific historical, cultural, and linguistic context. It was partly this process which allowed future scholars to think of "religion" as something which was not merely defined by the Christian theological division between true and false religion, but as a universal feature of human society.

CHAPTER 7

The Religion of China

1   The Problem of China in the Seventeenth Century

Few nations had a history with more damaging implications for biblical authority and the Christian historical *Weltbild* than that of China. One obvious problem was chronological. In his 1658 *Sinicae historiae decas prima*, Martino Martini had convincingly demonstrated that Chinese annals, just like Manetho's Egyptian dynasties, extended beyond the traditional Masoretic date for the Deluge, and, a year later, Isaac Vossius included China in his triumvirate of nations, alongside Egypt and Chaldea, whose antiquity supported the longer Septuagint over the shorter Masoretic chronology.[1] In 1687, Pezron took up this triumvirate and provided his own treatment of Chinese history, taken from Martini, which dated the first king Fohi to 2952 BC (*annus mundi* 2921).[2] It is worth noting that Pezron suggested that the Septuagint chronology could not only help refute libertines and pre-Adamites, as we have seen, but also "to establish Religion among the Orientals, above all the Chinese and the neighbouring peoples."[3] After Vossius and Pezron, a growing number of scholars, including Leibniz, came to see Chinese antiquity as one of the strongest reasons for replacing the Masoretic chronology with that of the Septuagint.[4] Jesuit scholars even asked for permission to use the Septuagint in their treatments of Chinese history.[5]

In this sense Martini's *Sinicae historiae decas prima* – which for Edwin Van Kley "inaugurated one of the stormier centuries in the history of Western

---

1   Vossius, *Dissertatio de vera aetate mundi*; see further Mandelbrote, "Isaac Vossius and the Septuagint."
2   Paul Pezron, *Antiquité des tems*, 269. See further Paul Pezron, "Canones Chronologici I," BNF, Latin 17941, fol. 17v [Fohi dated to *annus mundi* 3020] and "Canones Chronologici II," BNF, Latin 17942, fol. 4r [dated to *annus mundi* 2836] and fols. 114v–115r [dated to *annus mundi* 2811].
3   Pezron, *Antiquité des tems*, sig. *4r–v: "pour établir la Réligion chez les Orientaux, principalement chez les Chinois & les Peuples voisins."
4   G. W. Leibniz to Claude Nicaise, 2 August 1699, LAA, II, 3:589: "j'ay tousjours jugé que M. l'Abbé de la Charmoye avoit raison de croire que la chronologie des Chinois (pour ne rien dire d'autres argumens) nous oblige de reculer l'antiquité des temps."
5   D. E. Mungello, "European Philosophical Responses to Non-European Culture: China," in *The Cambridge History of Seventeenth-Century Philosophy*, ed. Daniel Garber (Cambridge: Cambridge University Press, 1998), 1:91–92.

historiography and in the end precipitated significant changes in the way world history was written" – was the Chinese counterpart to Manetho's Egyptian dynasties.[6] The similarities extended beyond the mere fact that both pagan sources directly contradicted the chronology of the Bible. Chinese history, like that of Manetho, was first studied as a serious historical source by orthodox scholars who did not reject the chronological authority of the Bible itself. To combat the potential embarrassment of this rival account of ancient history, scholars identified ancient Chinese emperors with the same biblical figures they had once identified with Egyptian gods. As a result, Chinese history was used to confirm, and not merely undermine, biblical chronology, and the Septuagint chronology in particular. Indeed, it was only in 1756 that Voltaire (1694–1778) began his universal history, the *Essai sur les mœurs et l'esprit des nations*, with China, in reaction to Bossuet's biblio-centric – and immensely popular – *Discours sur l'histoire universelle* (1681). Traditionally, historians have cited the disparity in the worldviews of Bossuet and Voltaire in order to encapsulate the difference between the religious and intellectual climate of the late seventeenth and the mid-eighteenth century. "The majority of the French think like Bossuet," wrote Paul Hazard in 1935. "Then, all of a sudden, they think like Voltaire: it's a revolution."[7] More recent work by scholars such as Adalbert Klempt and Joan-Pau Rubiés has shown, however, that even Voltaire's particular approach to universal history built on the earlier scholarship of Chinese missionaries and sacred historians.[8] Nevertheless, the seismic impact of the growing awareness and understanding of Chinese history remains a powerful explanation for the gradual demise of biblical chronology and the desacralisation of universal history.

Yet if there were ways in which China was the counterpart to Egypt, there were also ways in which it was its counterpoint. As we have seen, Egypt was of particular interest to scholars of *historia sacra* because Egypt featured more extensively than other ancient pagan nations in the book of Genesis and because the biblical patriarchs had had sustained interaction with Egypt. It was this notion which led scholars such as Marsham and Spencer to suppose that Egyptian customs had influenced Hebrew law and which led Bonjour

---

6   Van Kley, "Europe's 'Discovery' of China and the Writing of World History," 359.
7   Hazard, *La crise de la conscience européene*, 4: "La majorité des Français pensait comme Bossuet; tout d'un coup, les Français pensent comme Voltaire: c'est une révolution." See also Dan Edelstein, *The Enlightenment: A Genealogy* (Chicago: The University of Chicago Press, 2010), 28–29.
8   Klempt, *Die Säkularisierung der universalhistorischen Auffassung*; Rubiés, "From Antiquarianism to Philosophical History."

to suppose that ancient Egyptian history was "as much sacred as profane."[9] China, however, had no apparent connection to the first descendants of Noah. Nor was it mentioned in the Bible. In this sense China, like the indigenous peoples of the Americas, did not fit into the traditional diffusionist *schema* which could explain the origins of letters, laws, or philosophy by virtue of the historical transmission of biblical knowledge. More to the point, China, unlike the peoples of the Americas, boasted a culture which appeared not only ancient but also developed and civilized, based on sophisticated historical and astronomical records. The existence of a wise and apparently moral society with little or no historical relationship to the revealed wisdom of the Israelites presented a major problem for scholars who believed in the Hebraic origins of human civilization and culture. Consequently, scholars were forced to either broaden or alter their understanding of the traditional diffusionist narrative. In one of the first European works on China, the *Historia de las cosas más notables, ritos y costumbres del gran reyno de la China* (1585), the Augustinian missionary Juan González de Mendoza (1545–1618) suggested that similarities between the Chinese religion and Christianity could be explained by virtue of the fact that St. Thomas the Apostle had preached the Gospel and the Trinity there before he was martyred in India.[10] By the early eighteenth century a number of scholars, including Athanasius Kircher, Pierre-Daniel Huet, and Mathurin Veyssière La Croze, had suggested that similarities between Egyptian and Chinese religion and history could be explained by historical interaction between the two nations.[11]

The problem was particularly pronounced when it came to the question of Chinese religion and its historical relationship to Noachic monotheism and ancient Gentile idolatry. Jesuit missionaries to China from Matteo Ricci (1552–1610) onwards supposed that the moral and virtuous Confucianism of the Chinese *literati* preserved knowledge of the true Christian God. Furthermore, they supposed that the Confucian Rites practiced by the *literati* were civil and political rather than religious and could not therefore be classed as idolatry. In

---

9   Guillaume Bonjour to Claude Nicaise, 9 July 1697, in KW 72 D 2, fol. 127v.
10 Juan González de Mendoza, *History of the Great and Might Kingdome of China and Situation Thereof*, trans. R. Parke, ed. George Staunton and Richard Henry Major (London: Hakluyt Society, 1853–54) (reprinted Cambridge: Cambridge University Press, 2010), 37–39.
11 See Iversen, *The Myth of Egypt*, 106; Athanasius Kircher, *China monumentis qua sacris qua profanis, nec non variis naturae & artis spectaculis, aliarumque rerum memorabilium argumentis illustrata* (Amsterdam: Jacob à Meurs, 1667), 131–137; D. E. Mungello, *Curious Land: Jesuit Accommodation and the Origins of Sinology* (Honolulu: University of Hawaii Press, 1985), 31, 134–163; Mathurin Veyssière La Croze to Gisbert Cuper, 27 September 1709, KW 72 H 18.

response, a number of anti-Jesuit critics supposed the Confucian Rites idolatrous and the Chinese religion atheist. This controversy, which culminated in the papal bull *Cum Deus optimus* of 1704 which declared Chinese Confucian worship idolatrous, is often referred to as the Chinese Rites debate. This debate had important ramifications for the manner in which scholars compared the revealed religion of the Israelites to the natural religion of the Gentiles, and the manner in which scholars understood "religion" as a concept more generally. On the one hand, Christian missionaries to China, seeking to better understand the nature of Chinese Confucianism, came to alter their previous understanding of the nature and origins of religious beliefs and rituals. On the other hand, narratives about Chinese society and its relationship to atheism informed philosophers of what Thijs Weststeijn and Jonathan Israel have called the "radical enlightenment."[12] Seizing on the arguments of anti-Jesuit polemicists, these "radical" thinkers supposed that China might be the living embodiment of Pierre Bayle's famous, hypothetical society of virtuous atheists, a society in which the morality and ethics of the populace had no connection with or relation to (revealed) religion.[13] Both Bayle and the Cartesian theologian Nicolas Malebranche (1638–1715) went on to equate the monism or pantheism of Benedict Spinoza with the Confucian philosophy of the Chinese.[14] Meanwhile John Locke, in his *Essay concerning Human Understanding* (first edition 1689), cited Chinese philosophy in defence of his suggestion that mankind did not have an innate idea of God.[15] Despite, then, the various contexts and debates within which Chinese evidence was brought forth the ultimate result was, according to Weststeijn, always the same: "to challenge accepted authority."[16]

Bonjour's initial interest in China seems to stem directly from the problem of chronology. In his 1695 letter to Magliabechi, Rigord stated that, while in Toulouse, Bonjour worked on the principle that biblical chronology could

---

12   Thijs Weststeijn, "Spinoza Sinicus: An Asian Paragraph in the History of the Radical Enlightenment," *Journal of the History of Ideas* 68 (2007): 537–561, and Jonathan Israel, "The Battle over Confucius and Classical Chinese Philosophy in European Early Enlightenment Thought (1670–1730)," *Frontiers of Philosophy in China* 8 (2013): 183–198.
13   Pierre Bayle, *Pensées diverses, écrites à un docteur de Sorbonne, a l'occasion de la comète qui parut au mois de Décembre 1680* (Rotterdam: Reinier Leers, 1683).
14   See Yuen-Ting Lai, "The Linking of Spinoza to Chinese Thought by Bayle and Malebranche," *Journal of the History of Philosophy* 23 (1985): 151–178.
15   John Locke, *An Essay Concerning Human Understanding*, ed. Peter H. Nidditch (Oxford: Clarendon Press, 1975), 88: "the Great Encomiasts of the *Chinese*, do all to a Man agree and will convince us that the Sect of the *Litterati*, or *Learned*, keeping to the old Religion of *China*, and the ruling Party there, are all of them *Atheist*."
16   Weststeijn, "Spinoza Sinicus," 541.

be harmonized perfectly as much with Chinese as with Egyptian history.[17] Although Bonjour did not discuss China explicitly in the *Mercurius*, he did include a list of Chinese kings, beginning with Fohi, in the chronological table with which he ended the work, the "Secunda Mundi aetas seu pueritia Civitatis filiorum Dei & Diaboli."[18] In Rome, Bonjour held fast to the notion that China was an important nation when it came to constructing a universal chronology which contained both sacred and profane history. In his aforementioned, lengthy 1697 letter to Claude Nicaise, Bonjour asserted that he "will not forget the Chinese" after having listed various ancient nations whose chronologies he planned on treating imminently.[19] As we have seen, Bonjour was well aware of the problems posed by Vossius and Pezron's treatments of pagan antiquity and constructed his chronology largely as a Masoretic or Vulgate *riposte* to Pezron's *Antiquité des tems*. Unsurprisingly, Bonjour began his *Antiquitas temporum* by stating that all three nations of Vossius' triumvirate, "antiquitates Aegyptiaca, Chaldaicas, Sinenses," could be harmonized with the Vulgate chronology.[20]

However, Bonjour never managed to produce an extensive chronology of the Chinese nation as he did for Egypt in the *Antiquitas temporum* and to a lesser extent for Chaldea and Greece in the *Selectae*.[21] As we have noted previously, it seems likely that Bonjour was dissuaded from continuing his work on chronology in late 1697 by the problems he encountered when trying to print the first volume of his *Antiquitas temporum*. It does not seem that Bonjour ever returned to a similarly extensive study of chronology during his remaining time in Italy, during which he was predominantly preoccupied with Coptic, calendrical reform and, in Montefiascone, theological instruction. This would suggest that Bonjour failed to properly examine Chinese chronology not so much due to a lack of interest but simply a lack of opportunity. However, this also renders it unlikely that the troubles posed by Chinese chronology motivated his trip to China, as recently suggested by Thijs Weststeijn and Willemijn van Noord.[22] On the one hand, I would suppose it doubtful, given the confidence

---

17 Jean-Pierre Rigord to Antonio Magliabechi, 4 September 1695, BNCF, *Fondo Magliabechiano* VIII, cod. 341, fol. 28secondo(v): "que la chronologie de l'Ecriture Sainte s'accorde parfaitement bien avec la chronologie des Chinois et des Egyptiens."
18 *Mercurius*, fol. 126v.
19 Guillaume Bonjour to Claude Nicaise, 9 July 1697, cited in Claude Nicaise to Gisbert Cuper, 1 August 1697, KW 72 D 2, fol. 128r: "Je n'oubleray pas encore celle des Chinois."
20 *Antiquitas*, 1.
21 *Selectae*, 103–119.
22 Willemijn van Noord and Thijs Weststeijn, "The Global Trajectory of Nicolaas Witsen's Chinese Mirror," *The Rijksmuseum Bulletin* 63 (2015): 344–345, nn. 101–102. This assertion has been repeated in Willemijn van Noord, "European Reflections in Chinese Mirrors:

with which Bonjour approached Manetho's dynasties, that Chinese chronology would have engendered any particular crisis of confidence in Bonjour regarding the authority of the Vulgate text. Indeed, as late as 1705, Bonjour was still including Chinese annals among various pagan nations whose myths confirmed the existence of a primordial, universal flood.[23] On the other hand, it does not seem that Bonjour considered his mission to China an extension of his earlier work on pagan chronology. In a letter he sent to Adeodato Nuzzi from London in 1708 while waiting to set sail for the Far East, he noted to the Augustinian prior general that Egyptian chronology was no longer a subject "close to my heart."[24]

For the context of Bonjour's interest in China we must instead look to the Chinese Rites. This is borne out by two factors. Firstly, Bonjour's dissertations and notes on China are interested primarily in Chinese idolatry, and, more specifically, in the issues relating to the seven propositions Charles Maigrot had made against the Chinese religion in his *Mandatum* of 1693, which first re-ignited the Rites debate. Secondly, when Bonjour was in Deventer en route to China, he made his intentions explicit to Cuper. As Cuper later recorded:

> That same evening [of Bonjour's arrival] many varied conversations were held among us, the first indeed of his departure for China, and then on to the various subjects of our scholarship, and I would sin against our friendship, and to a great extent against my duties "on the discharge of which depends all that is morally right, and on their neglect all that is morally wrong in life," as Cicero says somewhere [*De officiis* 1.2], if I did not testify that I marvelled at the man's profound and comprehensive learning, and his infinite knowledge of Coptic and ancient Egyptian

---

Interpreting Self and Other through Encounters with Chinese Artefacts in the Dutch Republic, 1685–1715," in *Knowledge and Arts on the Move: Transformation of the Self-Aware Image through East-West Encounters*, ed. Christopher Craig, Enrico Fongaro, and Akihiro Ozaki (Milan: Mimesis International, 2018), 55.

23 *Selectae*, D.II.19, 53 ("Sinae quoque notatum habent in suis antiquitatibus diluvium novennale, quod, praeclaro exoticae chronologiae exemplo, reperitur desiisse hoc plane Anno, qui finem decit diluvii Noetici") and D.II.47, 88–89: "Quam apte quadret in annum ante aeram Christianian bis millesimum ducentesimum nonagesimum primum universalitas ista diluvii, potest quivis intelligere ex eo quod Hebraicis temporum enumerationibus quae postulant hunc annum, accedant antiquitates & Graecorum in Europa, & Aegyptiorum in Africa, & Chaldaeorum in Asia, & Sinarum in finibus Orientis, prout jam vidibus."

24 Guillaume Fabri [Bonjour] to Adeodato Nuzzi, 26 February 1708, BAR, ms.lat.891, fol. 88v: "ce genre d'etude ne m'est pas plus a coeur."

things and languages. But finally, before I report, I thought I would do right if I narrated the cause of so long and so dangerous a journey.

Therefore it is known, at least in the learned world, that there are great commotions in the Roman Church regarding those people among the Chinese who become Christians. The Jesuits allowed them to willingly give Confucius and the dead ancestors the name Christ, and allowed them to worship them in the manner formerly done as is still done by the whole nation; and they boldly defend that it is nothing but civil or political honour, as they say. But all the other Missionaries strongly oppose their teachings and dogmas, and they judge that this is mere idolatry. This very serious question is debated in Rome among those, who have the name Propaganda Fide, and by the pope himself, as is what happened among the three or four who preceded Clement XI.[25]

The Chinese Rites debate was the most contentious and the most significant of the issues concerning China in the seventeenth century.[26] The condemnation of Chinese Confucianism in 1704 – re-affirmed by the papal bull *Ex illa die* of 1715 – marked the beginning of the end of a century's worth of evangelising in China and was not officially lifted until 1939. The debate itself was fuelled as much by geo-political and ecclesiological as it was by scholarly, intellectual, or even theological considerations. Since the granting of the *padroado*

---

25 KW 72 H 20: "Eodem vespero varii inter nos sermones habiti sunt, primo quidem de ejus ad ultimos Seras profectione, inde de variis studii nostri capitibus, et peccarem in amicitiam nostram, atque adeo et officium meum in qua colenda sita est vitae honestas omnis, et in negligendo turpitudo, ut alicubi Cicero loquitur, nisi testarer me admiratum esse profundam viri omnigenamque eruditionem, et Copticarum vel veterum Aegyptiarumque rerum, linguaeque infinitam cognitionem. Quod ultimum antequam referam, recte me facturum putavi, si narrem causam tam longinquae et tam periculosae profectionis.

Notum igitur, erudito saltem orbi est, magnos motus esse in Ecclesia Romana super iis, qui ex Chinensibus Christiani fiunt. Iesuitas pati eos Confucium et parentes mortuos licet Christo nomen dederint, colere quemadmodum antea ab iisdem factum est, fitque etiamnum a tota gente; nihilque nisi honorem civilem vel politicum, ut loquuntur, esse praefracta fronte defendunt. Alii autem Missionarii omnes, sese placitis et dogmatibus illis fortiter opponunt, judicantque hanc meram esse idololatriam. Gravissima haec quaestio Romae disceptatur apud eos, qui a Propaganda Fide nomen habent, et apud ipsum pontificem, id quod et factum est, apud tres quatuorve, qui Clementem XI praecesserunt."

26 See for a general and concise summary of the Rites debate Claudia von Collani, "The Jesuit Rites Controversy," in *The Oxford Handbook of the Jesuits*, ed. Ines G. Zuparov (Oxford: Oxford University Press, 2017). See further Lionel M. Jensen, *Manufacturing Confucianism: Chinese Traditions & Universal Civilization* (Durham and London: Duke University Press, 1997); Mungello, *Curious Land*; Mungello, *The Chinese Rites Controversy*, and Pinot, *La Chine*.

by the Papal Bull *Jus patronatus* in 1514, Spanish and Portuguese Jesuits had enjoyed almost complete jurisdiction over missionary work in the Far East. In the seventeenth century this dominance was increasingly resented, both in Rome – which established its own congregation for supervising missionary activity, the Sacra congregatio de propaganda fide, in 1622 – and by the French crown, which founded the Société des missions étrangères de Paris, originally an off-shoot of the Propaganda fide, in 1658. Furthermore, we should note that a large amount of anti-Jesuit literature within the Rites debate was tied to a more general dislike of the Jesuits, in particular to a dislike of their moral probabilism. Famously Blaise Pascal (1623–1662) criticised Jesuit missionary methods in China in his caustic diatribe against Jesuit casuistry, the *Lettres provinciales* (1659).[27] In this sense, the Chinese Rites remained, throughout the seventeenth century, a convenient stick with which opponents, nursing their own vested interests, aimed to strike at Jesuit teaching and influence.

The intellectual origins of the Rites debate, however, lay within the Jesuit Order itself. Indeed, before becoming a matter for the Vatican and the Sorbonne, the Chinese Rites was a dispute between Jesuit missionaries who disagreed on the correct way of evangelising the Chinese people. Underlying all its different facets and contributions, the dispute centred on one basic question: how far could one accommodate the principles of the Christian religion to the beliefs of foreign peoples in order to convert heathens without fundamentally changing or undermining the principles of the Christian religion itself? The very existence of this question concerned the legacy of the Jesuit missionary Matteo Ricci and his distinctive approach to evangelisation, which David Mungello has labelled "accommodationism."[28] When Ricci first arrived in China at the turn of the seventeenth century, he quickly shed his Buddhist robes and valorised the Confucianism of the Chinese *literati* by seeking parallels with Christianity. According to Ricci, the Chinese had once had knowledge of the true God and these vestiges were still apparent in Confucianism. Elements of the Chinese religion that Ricci considered problematic he relegated to the pernicious influence of later idolatrous sects, such as Taoism and Buddhism,

---

27 Blaise Pascal, *Les Provinciales, ou les lettres escrites par Louis de Montalte a un provincial de ses amis, et aux RR. PP. Jesuites* (Cologne: Nicolas Schoute, 1659), 52.

28 Jesuit ideas often drew on the principle of 1 Corinthians 9:22: "I became all things to all men, that I might save all." See Collani, "The Jesuit Rites Controversy," 4. On the term "accommodationism" see more generally Mungello, *Curious Land*, Jensen, *Manufacturing Confucianism*, 39–40, and D. E. Mungello, *The Great Encounter of China and the West, 1500–1800* (Oxford: Rowman & Littlefield, 1999), 13. Even Bonjour, in a 1709 letter to Nuzzi from Manilla, called the Jesuit approach "praxes P. Matthaei Riccii": see Guillaume Bonjour to Adeodato Nuzzi, 13 November 1710, BAR, ms.lat.911, fol. 104v.

or to a misinterpretation of Confucius' original teaching by later Confucian commentators of the Sun dynasty, whom he dubbed neo-Confucians. Famously, Ricci denoted the Christian God using two ancient Chinese names for god, or "the Supreme One": *tien* (天) and *xamti* (上 帝).[29] Ricci took the former from the four Confucian texts and the latter from the Five Classical Books.[30] These names, and Ricci's more general notion that one should adapt, as much as possible, the principles of the Christian religion to the understanding of the Chinese, proved formative for later Jesuit missionaries and sinologists, such as Alvaro Semedo (1585/6–1658), Martino Martini, and Gabriel de Magalhães (1610–1677).[31] It also led to the great Jesuit interest in and heralding of Confucius, who was partially translated by Prospero Intorcetta (1626–1696) and Ignacio da Costa (1603–1666) in the 1660s and by Philippe Couplet and a team of Jesuit translators in the *Confucius Sinarum philosophus* of 1687.[32] Yet Ricci's relatively sympathetic view of Chinese religion and the extent to which he was prepared to adapt his evangelising methods also aroused opposition. Niccolò Longobardo (1559–1654), Ricci's Jesuit successor, was horrified at the extent to which Ricci had extolled what Longobardo considered an idolatrous Chinese religion, and that Ricci had used the Chinese terms *tien* and *xamti* to refer to the Christian God.[33] Longobardo outlined his opposition to Ricci's accommodationism in a treatise which was later published in the *Tratados historicos, politicos, ethicos, y religiosos de la monarchia de China* (1676) of the fiercely anti-Jesuit Dominican missionary Domingo Navarette (1610–1689), and his testimony proved particularly popular with anti-Jesuit polemicists during the Rites debate in Rome.[34] Similarly Athanasius Kircher, who supposed that

---

29 It is more common to designate *Tien* as *Tian* and *Xamti* as *Shangdi* in modern Latinisations of the respective Chinese terms. However, I will use *tien* and *xamti* because this is how they were most often spelled by Bonjour and other scholars of the late seventeenth century. See further Collani, "The Jesuit Rites Controversy," 5.
30 Collani, "The Jesuit Rites Controversy," 5.
31 Mungello, *Curious Land*, 74–131.
32 Collani, "The Jesuit Rites Controversy," 5; Jensen, *Manufacturing Confucianism*, 94.
33 There are several inaccuracies in the dating of Longobardo, who was also called Longobardi, in recent historiography. In Lai, "The Linking of Spinoza to Chinese Thought by Bayle and Malebranche," 164, he is dated to 1676–1701. This has led to errors of interpretation in Franklin Perkins (*Leibniz and China: A Commerce of Light* (Cambridge: Cambridge University Press, 2004), 192) and Thijs Weststeijn ("An Asian Paragraph in the History of the Radical Enlightenment," 538). See on Longobardo more generally the relevant articles in Wenchao Li, ed., *Leibniz and the European Encounter with China: 300 Years of 'Discours sur la théologie naturelle des Chinois'* (Stuttgart: Franz Steiner, 2017).
34 Domingo Navarette, *Tratados históricos, políticos, éthicos, y religiosos de la monarchia de China* (Madrid: Florian Anisson, 1676), 245–289; Niccolò Longobardo, *Traité sur quelques Points de la Religion des Chinois* (Paris: Louis Guerin, 1701). See for example "Notae in

the Chinese religion had more in common with the idolatry and superstition of ancient Egypt than the Christian religion, rejected the use of *tien* and *xamti* and pointedly translated God as *tien-chu* for the Chinese catechism in his *China illustrata* (1667).[35] Eventually, this issue extended beyond the Jesuit Order and became a contentious topic in Rome. In 1645, the Propaganda fide upheld seventeen questions of the Spanish Dominican Juan Bautista Morales (1597–1664) directed against the Jesuit approach to the Chinese Rites. Despite this, the matter was never satisfactorily decided. In 1656, the Propaganda fide ratified Martino Martini's defence of the Rites without explaining how this impacted on the earlier decision of 1645; and in 1669, the Holy Office ratified both the decree of 1645 and that of 1656 despite their contradictions.[36]

The debate around the Rites entered a new phase with the publication of Charles Maigrot's *Mandatum seu Edictum* of 1693. The origins of the *Mandatum* were not necessarily scholarly or intellectual. Maigrot was a member of the generally pro-Jansenist and anti-Jesuit Société des Missions étrangères and, since 1687, vicar apostolic of Fujian.[37] As can be seen by the many letters Maigrot sent to Rome he was deeply frustrated with the deplorable state of the missions, which he blamed on the dominance of the Jesuits and his own lack of authority as vicar apostolic.[38] Yet his *Mandatum* was also the most outright condemnation of Jesuit practices to date. It said quite openly that the Chinese were atheists, and that the Jesuits were allowing such atheistic practices to continue.[39] It condemned the Jesuits on seven issues: it banned the use of the terms *tien* and *xamti* and stated that Chinese Christians must refer to the Christian God as *Tien-chu*; it banned the use of the inscription *king*

---

observationes a R.R.dis P.P. Societatis Jesu Sacrae Congregationi Sancti Officji exhibitas in Mandatum Ill.mi ac R.mi D.ni Maigrot Vicarji Apostolici Fokiensis et Episcopi Cononensis electi a Nicolas Charmot ejusdem R.mi D.ni Maigrot aliorumque episcoporum ac vicariorum Apostolicorum Gallorum Procuratore Generali Sacrae Congregationi Sancti Officji oblatae," ASPF, SC Indie Orientali e Cina, Misc. 55, "De rebus Sinensibus tom. 4," 55. See for an annotated edition with Leibniz's marginalia the appendix to Gottfried Wilhelm Leibniz, *Discours sur la Théologie Naturelle des Chinois*, ed. Wenchao Li and Hans Poser (Frankfurt am Main: Vittorio Klostermann, 2002). My thanks go to the anonymous reviewer at Brill for pointing out both this reference and the reference to Wenchao Li in the previous footnote.

35 Kircher, *China illustrata*, 121–128.
36 Collani, "The Jesuit Rites Controversy," 6.
37 Claudia von Collani, "Charles Maigrot's Role in the Chinese Rites Controversy" in Mungello, *The Chinese Rites Controversy*, 149–183.
38 See Charles Maigrot to the Congregatio de Propaganda fide, 3 February 1699, ASPF, SOCP 21, fols. 118r–119r.
39 Pinot, *La Chine*, 89.

tien – or "worship heaven" ("*coelum colito*") – in Christian churches because by *tien*, "heaven," the Chinese meant simply the "*coelum materiale*," the material sky; it banned the worship of Confucius and that of ancestors; it banned any sacrifices or dedications to Confucius or Chinese ancestors; it banned any genuflexion in front of the tablets found in domestic Chinese houses inscribed *xin chu, xin goei*, or *ling goei*, which meant the "seat of the spirit"; it stated that the Chinese principle *tai-kie* (*Taiji*, 太 極) meant neither God nor, as Ricci had supposed, an Aristotelian *materia prima*, but simply atheistic, monist, eternal physical matter; and it banned the reading of the Five Classic Books and the Four Books of Confucius because they taught superstition and atheism. (In later years, as the testimony of the Jesuit missionary Matteo Ripa shows, Christians tended to organize these seven propositions into three distinct categories: a ban on sacrifices to Confucius and the Chinese ancestors, a ban on the use of the tablets *iuxta morem sinicae*, and a ban on the use of the terms *tien* and *xamti* for the true, Christian, God).[40] In early 1694, Maigrot sent two of his colleagues, Louis de Quéménér (1643–1704) and Nicolas Charmot (1655–1714), the procurator general of the French bishops and vicar apostolics, to Rome to defend his *Mandatum* in the presence of the congregation of cardinals.[41]

2 Chinese Debates in Bonjour's Rome

In late seventeenth-century Rome, erudition was continually examined in respect to orthodoxy.[42] During this period the cardinals of the congregation, including Noris, were heavily involved in judging three ongoing disputes. The first concerned the attack of the Carmelite Order on the *Acta sanctorum* of the Jesuit Bollandists, who claimed (contrary to Carmelite tradition) that the Carmelite Order was founded not by the prophets Elijah and Elisha – and that Jesus Christ himself had been a member – but rather by St. Albert, or Albert of Vercelli, on the slopes of Mount Carmel in the thirteenth century.[43] The second concerned the Quietist controversy and the question of François Fénelon's 1697 *Maximes des saints*.[44] In general, the scholarly and ecclesiastic circles in which

---

40 See Ripa, *Giornale*, 2:69.
41 Pastor, *The History of the Popes*, 32:649; Collani, "Charles Maigrot's Role in the Chinese Rites Controversy," 155–158; "Scritture Originali delle Cong:ni Particolari delle Indie Orientali China dalli 27 9bre 1691 fino alli 8 Agosto 1698," ASPF, SOCP 20, fols. 228r, 315r–316v, 344r; Pinot, *La Chine*, 90.
42 See for example Neveu, *Érudition et Religion*.
43 Wernicke, *Kardinal Enrico Noris*, 84–89.
44 Wernicke, *Kardinal Enrico Noris*, 92–95.

Bonjour moved supported the Bollandists over the Carmelites and severely disapproved of Fénelon's *Maximes* (the condemnation of which Fénelon himself swiftly accepted).[45] However, after Charmot's arrival in 1697, it was the Chinese Rites which became the preeminent ecclesiastical dispute in Rome. Indeed, the discussion quickly required the attention of some of Bonjour's closest friends and mentors, including Noris. In April 1699, Noris was included in a special congregation of cardinals established by Innocent XII in order to judge the merits of Maigrot's *Mandatum*, alongside Girolamo Casanata and Tommaso Maria Ferrari (1649–1716), all three of whom also formed the congregation (alongside Giovanni Francesco Albani, the future Pope Clement XI) which delivered the final censure of Fénelon's *Maximes* in the same year.[46] In the following months, the three cardinals discussed various sources and issues relevant to the Rites. On 30 June 1699, they met at the house of Casanata and submitted 101 questions to an expert witness on China, the Franciscan Giovanni Francesco Nicolai da Leonessa (d. 1737), who had arrived in Rome from China two weeks previously.[47] It seems that Noris and Casanata's sympathies generally lay with Charmot, whom they met and corresponded with frequently, and who was then trying to cajole a number of scholars in Rome to publicly oppose the Jesuit cause.[48] According to Charmot, Casanata even went as far as confirming his opposition to the Rites "for the good of Religion" when being given the *viaticum* in 1700.[49] It is likely that Bonjour's initial interest in Chinese idolatry was the result of Noris and Casanata's influence. If we have already seen in the course of this work how central Noris was to Bonjour's career, it is

---

45   On the Bollandist dispute see Conrad Janninck to Guillaume Bonjour, 5 May 1702, BAR, ms.lat.395, fol. 109r–v; the letters from Conrad Janninck to Antonio Magliabechi, February 1697–September 1703, BNCF, *Fondo Magliabechiano* VIII, cod. 1328, fols. 63r–153r; Giusto Fontanini to Antonio Magliabechi, 30 May 1702, BNCF, *Fondo Magliabechiano* VIII, cod. 271, fol. 124r–v and Giusto Fontanini to Guillaume Bonjour, 21 January 1705, BAR, ms.lat.395, fols. 115r–116r; Benedetto Bacchini to Antonio Magliabechi, 6 October 1696, BNCF, *Fondo Magliabechiano* VIII, cod. 1242, fol. 443r–v. See further Momigliano, "The Origins of Ecclesiastical History," 132. On Quietism see also the letters of Claude Nicaise to Guillaume Bonjour, as in Pélissier, "Lettres inédites de Claude Nicaise," 189–209.

46   Pastor, *The History of the Popes*, 32:649; Wernicke, *Kardinal Enrico Noris*, 100.

47   "Causa Sinensis," ASPF, SC Indie Orientali e Cina, Misc. 53, 2; "Biographie et lettres du P. Nicolas Charmot," BNF, Français 25060, 2375–2376.

48   "Biographie et lettres du P. Nicolas Charmot," BNF, Français 25060, 2375–2413; Pastor, *The History of the Popes*, 32:650; Collani, "Charles Maigrot's Role in the Chinese Rites Controversy," 158.

49   "Biographie et lettres du P. Nicolas Charmot," BNF, Français 25060, 2378: "Je n'ai fait dans l'affaire de la Chine que ce a quoy ma conscience, le bien de la Religion, l'honneur de Dieu et celui du S. Siege m'ont oblige. Je ne croi pas que le S. Siege puisse approuver les Cultes Chinois sans le deshoneste," is what Casanata is reported to have said.

worth pointing out here that Casanata, Noris' close friend, was not far behind. This was particularly the case when it came to Bonjour's work on Coptic.[50] When Bonjour began his edition of the trilingual Coptic-Arabic-Latin Bible in March 1698 it was partly at the behest of Casanata.[51] Moreover, Casanata was the original dedicatee of both Bonjour's Coptic-Arabic Bible and his Coptic grammar, and was explicitly thanked in the *In monumenta Coptica*.[52]

What is more, it seems apparent that the Augustinian organisation in Rome sided squarely against the Jesuits, albeit less vocally and less acerbically than the French Dominicans. In 1699, Innocent XII set up another congregation of four theologians intended to judge the significance of Nicolai da Leonessa's responses to Casanata, Noris, and Ferrari. This congregation consisted of the Cistercian abbot Giovanni Maria Gabrielli (1654–1711), who had defended Fénelon's *Maximes des saints* at the Inquisition in 1699 but who was forced to leave the commission when he was elected cardinal in November 1699; Carlo Francesco da Varese, the Commissar General of the Minorites; Filippo di S. Niccolò, the former prior general of the Carmelites; and, most importantly, the current prior general of the Augustinian Order Nicola Serani (1650–1735), who had succeeded Antonio Pacini in 1699.[53] These four theologians were divided on the issue. Francesco da Varese almost unanimously sided with the Jesuits and, in 1701, spoke openly in their defence in the presence of the Pope.[54] Meanwhile, Filippo da Niccolò accepted the legitimacy of the names *tien* and *xamti* but criticised the veneration of Confucius and the Chinese ancestors. Conversely, Serani explicitly denounced the practices of the Jesuits and agreed with Maigrot's *Mandatum* on virtually every point.[55] When da Niccolò voiced his opinion on the names *tien* and *xamti*, he was immediately countered by Serani.[56]

---

50   As also pointed out by Hamilton, *The Copts and the West*, 230–231.
51   Guillaume Bonjour to Antonio Magliabechi, 1 March 1699, BNCF, *Fondo Magliabechiano* VIII, cod. 317, fol. 25r-v: "Li Emin:mi Cardinali Casanata e de Noris, alla requisitione dell'Illmo Sig.re Lorenzo Sacagni primo Custode della Bibliotheca Vaticana, mi danno l'incumbenza di tradurre in Latino il Pentateucho Copto-Arabo, che stà in cotesta Bibliotheca. ..." See also Guillaume Bonjour to Gisbert Cuper, 22 March 1698, KW 72 H 20.
52   Guillaume Bonjour to Antonio Magliabechi, 7 March 1699, BNCF, *Fondo Magliabechiano* VIII, cod. 317, fol. 37r; *Coptica*, 1. See also BAR, ms.lat.297, fol. 49r, and BAR, ms.lat.621, fol. 1r.
53   Pastor, *The History of the Popes*, 32:650; Wernicke, *Kardinal Enrico Noris*, 101; "Biographie et lettres du P. Nicolas Charmot," BNF, Français 25060, 2375–2376.
54   Pastor, *The History of the Popes*, 33:410–412.
55   Pastor, *The History of the Popes*, 32:650; Wernicke, *Kardinal Enrico Noris*, 101–111. See BAR, ms.lat.180.
56   As reported by Charmot, "Biographie et lettres du P. Nicolas Charmot," BNF, Français 25060, 2380.

Bonjour's friendship with scholars who opposed the Rites also went beyond the confines of the Augustinian Order. Particularly important was the presence in Rome of three French theologians and scholars. The first of these was Antonin Massoulié, a Dominican theologian and fellow Toulousain particularly well-known for his denunciation of Quietism. By a quirk of fate, Massoulié had also been an author of one of the approbations of Michel Lequien's *Défense du texte hébreu* in 1691, alongside Noël Alexandre. Throughout his time in Rome, Massoulié was a frequent correspondent of Magliabechi in Florence and kept him updated on the slew of publications on the Chinese Rites debate, particularly those of his Dominican colleagues.[57] Unsurprisingly, he was himself a fierce critic of the Jesuits. "The cult dedicated to the philosopher Confucius and to the ancestors," he wrote to Magliabechi in January 1700, "is wholly superstitious and the truest idolatry."[58] We know that Bonjour was in contact with Massoulié by 1702 and it seems that Massoulié soon became one of Bonjour's primary conduits to information on China and the Chinese Rites debate.[59] In around 1704 or 1705, Bonjour corresponded with Massoulié directly on the meaning of the Chinese word *tien*, which he had found inscribed on a Chinese mirror sent to him by Gisbert Cuper, a mirror which we shall come to in more detail later.[60]

The second of these scholars was the famous Orientalist and Jansenist Eusèbe Renaudot, who accompanied Cardinal de Noailles to Rome for the papal conclave in 1700. As we have already noted, Renaudot read Bonjour's Coptic work, admired it, and recommended it to the pope. Yet he was similarly active in the context of the Chinese Rites. Indeed, for much of 1701, Renaudot had frequent meetings with Charmot, anti-Jesuit cardinals in the congregation such as Noris or Niccolò Radulovich (1627–1702), and the Augustinian prior general Nicola Serani, in which they discussed the best ways to refute the Jesuits.[61] His letters to De Noailles are mostly filled with the ebbs and flows of

---

57 Massoulié wrote more than 20 letters concerning the proceedings of the Chinese Rites debate to Magliabechi between January 1700 and June 1705: BNCF, *Fondo Magliabechiano* VIII, cod. 364, fols. 7r–47v.
58 Antonin Massoulié to Antonio Magliabechi, Rome, 23 January 1700, BNCF, *Fondo Magliabechiano* VIII, cod. 364, fol. 11v: "Il Culto fatto al Filosofo Confucio e alli progenitori e totalmente superstitiosa e una verissima Idololatria."
59 Guillaume Bonjour to Antonio Magliabechi, 2 September 1702, BNCF, *Fondo Magliabechiano* VIII, cod. 317, fol. 64v.
60 Antonin Massoulié to Guillaume Bonjour, 28 March 1705, BAR, ms.lat.395, fols. 61r–63v.
61 Eusèbe Renaudot to Cardinal de Noailles, 19 April 1701, 7 June 1701, 21 June 1701, 19 July 1701, 26 July 1701, BNF, NAF 6212, fols. 13r, 34v, 45v, 51r, 55r. See also Zwierlein, "Orient contra China," 38–40.

the debates, as the cardinals examined the relevant issues raised by Maigrot and discussed them in relation to their various sources on Chinese religion.[62]

The third figure of importance was Artus de Lionne, the bishop of Rosalie and a member of the Société des missions etrangères de Paris. De Lionne arrived in Rome from China in March 1703, intent on defending Maigrot's interpretation of Chinese religion against the testimonies of two Jesuit missionaries, François Noël (1651–1729) and Caspar Castner (1655–1709), who had arrived in Rome from China in December of the previous year with new documents for the special congregation.[63] During his time in Rome, De Lionne had frequent meetings with Charmot, Nicolai da Leonessa, and Pope Clement XI in which they discussed the organization of the missions and the proper methods for evangelisation. He was also accompanied by a young Chinese man, Arcadio Huang.[64] It seems that he and Huang were, through the mediation of Massoulié, Bonjour's primary sources on China. When Cuper first sent Bonjour a facsimile of the aforementioned Chinese mirror, Bonjour passed it on to De Lionne, whom he called "versatissimus" in the Chinese language.[65] In 1705, De Lionne replied that he and Huang could recognise only four characters: "thing" (res), "heaven" (coelum), "sun" (sol), and "emperor" (imperator).[66] Unsurprisingly, the word that De Lionne translated as "coelum" – rather than "Deus" – was the disputed Chinese term *tien*.

It appears that Bonjour's first appearance within the debates surrounding the Rites was on account of his scholarly abilities. As early as August 1703, Charmot noted in his diary that, when discussing the need for new missionaries with Clement XI, De Lionne had suggested Bonjour. At that point Clement XI rejected the idea. Bonjour, he replied, could do more good in Rome than in the missions.[67] Nevertheless, it seems that the Holy Office and several

---

62   For example, that in April 1701 the cardinals were discussing the name of God found on the Nestorian monument discovered in China in 1625 and reprinted in Kircher's *China illustrata* (4ff.): Eusèbe Renaudot to Cardinal de Noailles, 19 April 1701, BNF, NAF 6212, fol. 12v.

63   Pastor, *The History of the Popes*, 33:413–415; Wernicke, *Kardinal Enrico Noris*, 111–112; on Noël see Claudia von Collani, "François Noël and his Treatise on God in China," in *History of the Catholic Church in China: From its Beginning to the Scheut Fathers and the 20th Century unveiling some less known sources, sounds and pictures*, ed. Ferdinand Verbiest Institute (Leuven: Leuven Chinese Studies XXIX, 2015), 23–64; "Biographie et lettres du P. Nicolas Charmot," BNF, Français 25060, 2496.

64   See Danielle Elisseeff, ed., *Moi, Arcade: interprète chinois du Roi-Soleil* (Paris: Arthaud, 1985).

65   Guillaume Bonjour to Gisbert Cuper, 6 November 1704, KW 72 H 20.

66   Antonin Massoulié to Guillaume Bonjour, Rome, 28 March 1705, BAR, ms.lat.395, fols. 61r–63v. The list of Chinese words and their translation is on the inserted sheet, fol. 62r.

67   "Biographie et lettres du P. Nicolas Charmot," BNF, Français 25060, 2455.

important figures in the Rites debate kept their eye on Bonjour. He reappears again in Charmot's diary in 1706 when Charmot notes that Bonjour's protector, Marc-Antonio Barbarigo, had just died and that Bonjour was likely to return to Rome.[68]

By August 1707, developments in China seem to have made a new mission to China necessary. Despite the papal bull *Cum Deus optimus* of 1704, which upheld all but two of Maigrot's propositions, vicar apostolics in China found it difficult to enforce the papal ruling. Moreover, the specific request of the Kangxi Emperor that he wanted a mathematician appeared to make Bonjour, an able astronomist and chronologist, a suitable choice. When it was decided to send to China the asked-for missionaries in order to confer the cardinal's hat on Tournon, then festering in a prison in Macao, the matter appeared settled. In the late summer months of 1707, Bonjour took on his new identity and his new surname to prepare for his incognito journey across the world. Many of the details of the mission were kept secret, and there was only one man whom Bonjour confided in outside of the cardinals of the congregation, the head of his order Adeodato Nuzzi, and his friend Francesco Bianchini: Gisbert Cuper. As Cuper further recorded after Bonjour visited him in Deventer:

> As much as I was able to understand from Bonjour's conversation, in another opinion he was a long way from where the Jesuits are, and he thought that they were following a path that was not only indulgent but illicit besides; indeed, if I am not grossly mistaken, I believe that he was sent to furthest China in order to oppose the Jesuits himself. For he had with him a manuscript in which they defended their opinion, both with respect to the cult of Confucius and of the dead ancestors, and with respect to the name *Xam-tieu*, through which the Chinese understand the *material sky*; the Jesuits employ that name, when they want to designate the highest and eternal God whom we worship, and thus they effect that that superstitious nation think that, although other ceremonies are used, the Christians worship the same God as they themselves.
>
> The Jesuits exhibited this unpublished dissertation to the college, which has its name from Propaganda fide, from whom Guillaume received his copy of the manuscript. For I also saw a learned dissertation in his hands, clearly opposed to the other one; and whatever of his I read, it seemed to be consonant with reason and with the Holy Christian Religion.

---

68 "Biographie et lettres du P. Nicolas Charmot," BNF, Français 25060, 2462.

When, however, the supreme Pontiff rightly recognized the intelligence and erudition of my guest, he decided to send him along with two other members of the Augustinian Family to China, in order that they inspect and examine that controversy; as far as I could follow, through conjecture, from the conversation of Bonjour.

Therefore, he related that the Pope summoned him, when he himself had no thought of such a thing, and said that he was asked by the Chinese Emperor to send some religious men, skilled in Mathematics and Astronomy, along with excellent instruments; [and] that he had decided to do this, and that he wished him to undertake this journey, and to reveal the matter, and his [the Pope's] intention to no-one. Guillaume was obedient with this instruction and command, and he asked to be allowed to change his name, and to be given Roman citizenship, so that he could appear truly Roman, and that everyone believed he was not French: and when this deed was done, he took the name *Fabri* from his mother, who had originated from this family; and he added that his father was by origin Italian, and that his ancestors were called Buon Giorno. Therefore, when the matters were decided, the Pope summoned him and others and ordered Mathematical instruments to be brought to them by Bianchini – a man of exceptional learning, as is clear out of his Italian *Istoria Universale*, published and illustrated with coins and other ancient monuments, and with ample dignity in the court of the Pope: they were in the portico, close to the bedchamber or room of Clement XI; who came there also with everyone, so that nobody would detect his plan regarding the instruments and especially with Bonjour, who had not yet been transformed into Guillaume Fabri. When, however, less than three or four days remained until the beginning of the journey, with the permission of the Pope, who alone with Bianchini knew of the secret, he revealed the whole matter to the General of the Augustinian Order, and, with no one aware, on that day changed his clothes; for two or three days he walked around Rome unrecognised, and at last, therefore, with his two companions and the surgeon, who has to serve the same people, cheerfully following the order, he embarked on his journey in the month of October.[69]

---

69 KW 72 H 20: "Quantum ex Bonjourii colloquio percipere potui, erat in alia longe quam Iesuitae sunt, sententia, putabatque eos sequi indulgentem non modo sed etiam illicitam viam; imo, nisi me fallo plane, missum ad Seras ultimos virum credo, ut sese Iesuitis opponeret. Nam habebat secum ms. quo illi opinionem suam defendebant, tam quoad cultum Confucii et parentum mortuorum, quam quoad nomen *Xam-tieu*, per quod Chinenses intelligunt *cœlum materiale*; Iesuitae illo utuntur, quando designare volunt Deum

3 Patristic Apologetics and the History of Idolatry in the Chinese Rites Debate

What, then, were these arguments which Bonjour advanced against the Rites; and, given he knew no Chinese and had displayed no previous knowledge of Chinese literature, where did he take his arguments from? The answer, of course, was the same as it was for those Jesuits who had once come to China with no knowledge of the language and no understanding of the religion: the evidence of the ancient religion of the pagans, and the examples proffered by the first Christian apologists.

When Ricci first arrived in China, he openly sought to follow in the footsteps of the evangelising methods of the Apostles and the Church Fathers.[70] Hence the manner in which Paul had preached the Christian God to the Athenians at the Areopagus or the work of early Christian apologists who emphasised

---

summum et aeternum quem nos adoramus, et ita faciunt ut gens illa superstitiosa putet, Christianos adhibitis aliis ceremoniis, eundem cum ipsis Deum colere.

Hanc defensionem ineditam Iesuitae obtulerunt collegio, quod a propaganda fide nomen habet, a quo exemplum ejus ms. Guielmus accepit. Nam et inter manus ejus vidi dissertationem eruditam, alteri oppositam plane; et quidquid ejus legi, videbatur mihi rationi et Sanctae Christianae Religioni, consonum esse.

... Cum autem Pontifex summus probe cognosceret ingenium et eruditionem hospitis mei, statuit eum cum aliis duobus Augustinianae Familiae membris, mittere ad Seras, uti controversiam illam inspicerent; et examinarent, quantum ego ex sermonibus Fabri conjectura adsequi potui.

Referebat igitur pontificem eum nihil tale cogitantem arcessivisse, dixisse se rogatum a Chinarum Imperatore ut aliquot Religiosos mittere vellet, Matheseos et Astronomiae peritos, adhoc instrumenta optima; illud facere constituisse, sibique placere, ut hoc iter susciperet; et rem consiliumque suum nemini aperiret. Dicto et iussu obsequens fuit Guielmus, rogavitque ut ipsi liceret nomen mutare, utque civitate Romana donaretur, ut ita se vere Romanum decere posset, utque omnes crederent eum non esse Gallum; quod ubi factum fuit, nomen *Fabri* sumpsit a matre, quae ea familia orta erat; addebatque patrem origine Italum, dictosque majores Buno Giorno. Ita cum res constitutae essent accivit eum aliosque pontifex jussitque adferri instrumenta Mathematica per Bianchinum, virum doctrinae eximiae, uti ex Historia Universali Italice edita et nummis aliisque veteribus monumentis illustrata, patet, et ampla atque in aula pontificis dignitate: Erant in porticu, cubiculo vel camerae Clementis XI. proxima; qui eo venit et cum omnibus, ut nemo propositum suum detegeret de instrumentis, et inprimis cum Bonjourio, nondum in Guielmum Fabri transmutato. Cum autem intra tres quatuorve dies iter ingredi deberet, permittente pontifice, qui solus cum Bianchino secreti conscius erat, omnem rem aperit Generali ordinis Augustiniani, vestemque illo ipso die, nemine gnaro, mutavit; per binos tresve dies plane ἄγνωστος Romae ambulavit, et ita tandem cum binis sociis, et chirurgo, qui iisdem apparere debet, obsecutus hilaris mandato, iter mense octobri ingressus est."

70   Jensen, *Manufacturing Confucianism*, 56–57. See also Miller, "Taking Paganism Seriously," 187.

similarities between paganism and Christianity to help lead worshippers from one to the other remained the models which informed his so-called accommodationism. Similarly important were those pagan sources which the Fathers had once based their interpretation of pagan religion on, above all Cicero's *De natura deorum*. In the early fourth century, Arnobius had suggested that zealous pagans wanted Cicero suppressed because of the use to which he was being put by Christian apologists (*Adversus nationes* 3.7).[71] In the sixteenth and seventeenth centuries, the *De natura deorum* remained a foundational text for scholars who sought pagan evidence for a primitive monotheism and the subsequent idolatrous multiplication of pagan gods.[72] For Ricci, the most important notion was Cicero's dictum that "quot hominum linguae, tot nomina deorum," the gods have as many names as mankind has languages (*De natura deorum* 1.30 (84)).[73] Ricci used this phrase to support his use of traditional Chinese terms such as *tien* and *xamti* for the Christian God.

The principles of Ricci's accommodationism found their culmination in the "Proëmialis declaratio" of the Flemish Jesuit Philippe Couplet, one of four parts of the *Confucius Sinarum philosophus*.[74] According to Couplet, the Chinese had once embraced a monotheistic religion which contained some knowledge of the true God, knowledge which had become obscured and corrupted over time due to new idolatrous influences. Particularly detrimental was the spread of Buddhism and Taoism, and the misinterpretation of Confucius' core ideas by the "neo-Confucians" of the Sung dynasty who, Couplet claimed, had corrupted Confucius' monotheism into a pantheist monism by virtue of their allegorical interpretations of Confucius' writings.[75] Like Ricci, Couplet

---

71 See Bowen and Garnsey, *Divine Institutes*, 8.
72 See Marco Cavarzere, "A Comparative Method for Sixteenth-Century Polemicists: Cults, Devotions, and the Formation of Early Modern Religious Identities," *Journal of Early Modern History* 19 (2015): 404, who calls the *De natura deorum* "a cornerstone in their [sixteenth-century scholars'] demonstration of the existence of a primeval monotheism."
73 Cicero, *De natura deorum*, ed. Rackham, 81.
74 Philippe Couplet, Prospero Intorcetta, Heinrich Herdtrich, and Francis Rougemont, ed., *Confucius Sinarum philosophus sive Scientiae Sinensis latine exposita* (Paris: Daniel Horthemels, 1687). See Nicholas Dew, *Orientalism in Louis XIV's France* (Oxford: Oxford University Press, 2009), 205–233; Jensen, *Manufacturing Confucianism*, 120–129; Mungello, *Curious Land*, 296–297; Pinot, *La Chine*, 299–301; and above all, Thierry Meynard, ed., *Confucius Sinarum Philosophus (1687): The First Translation of the Confucian Classics* (Rome: Institutum Historicum Societatis Iesu, 2011) and Thierry Meynard, ed., *The Jesuit Reading of Confucius: The First Complete Translation of the Luyen (1687) Published in the West* (Leiden: Brill, 2015).
75 Couplet, *Confucius Sinarum philosophus*, xxxiv–xxxviii. On this see especially Knud Lundbaek, "The Image of Neo-Confucianism in *Confucius Sinarum Philosophus*," *Journal of the History of Ideas* 44 (1983): 19–30. The argument was later taken up by Jesuit polemicists: see "Ristretto delle notizie circa l'uso della Voce Cinese *Xamti* che significa *Supremus*

saw himself as working within the apologetic tradition of the Apostles and the Church Fathers. He called the Chinese "ethnici" (heathens), and the missionaries "praecones Evangelii" (preachers of the Gospel).[76] Like many of his missionary contemporaries, he relied heavily on the example of Paul's speech at the Areopagus from Acts 17:16–34, in which Paul had used the testimony of pagan poets, in this case Epimenides and Aratus.[77] Similarly, Couplet and the Jesuits believed that the practice of accommodating the Christian religion to make it more comprehensible to heathens was legitimised through the patristic authority of Lactantius, Augustine, and Aquinas. In upholding the use of *tien* and *xamti*, Couplet also cited Cicero's dictum that "quot hominum linguae, tot nomina Deorum."[78] In the immediate years after the publication of the *Confucius Sinarum philosophus*, when the Rites question became hotly debated once again and the Jesuits sought to defend their position through propagandist studies of Chinese history, these principles were both exaggerated and simplified. "Idolatry had not corrupted this people [the Chinese]; so that they have preserved the knowledge of the true God for near two thousand years, and did honour their Maker in such a manner as may serve both for an example and instruction to Christians themselves," wrote the Jesuit missionary and royal mathematician Louis Le Comte (1655–1728) in his *Nouveaux mémoire sur l'état présent de la China*, first published in 1696.[79] For this, Le Comte's work received the harshest condemnation of the Sorbonne as being "false, rash, scandalous, erroneous, injurious to the holy Christian religion."[80]

The principles which Ricci and Couplet had outlined came to form the basis of the many Jesuit defences of the Rites submitted as evidence to the special congregation between 1698 and 1704. As one Jesuit pamphlet stated

---

Imperator ò vero *Alti Dominus*, e della Voce *Tien*, che significa *Caelum*," BAR, ms.lat.87, fol. 195r–v.

76   As noted by Collani, "Philippe Couplet's Missionary Attitude towards the Chinese," 39.
77   Collani, "Philippe Couplet's Missionary Attitude towards the Chinese," 40–41.
78   Collani, "Philippe Couplet's Missionary Attitude towards the Chinese," 52.
79   Louis Le Comte, *Nouveaux mémoires sur l'état présent de la Chine* (Paris: Jean Anisson, 1696) 2:141: "Enfin si l'on examine bien l'histoire des Chinois, on trouvera que trois cens ans encore aprés, c'est-à-dire jusqu'à l'Empereur *Yéou-vam*, qui regnoit 800. ans avant la naissance de nostre Seigneur, l'idolatrie n'avoit point encore infecté les esprits. Desorte que ce peuple a conservé prés de deux mille ans la connoissance du veritable Dieu, & l'a honoré d'une maniere qui peut servir d'exemple & d'instruction mesme aux Chrétiens." Translation from Louis Le Comte, *Memoirs and remarks geographical, historical, topographical, physical, natural, astronomical, mechanical, military, mercantile, political, and ecclesiastical. Made in about Ten Years Travels through the empire of China* ... (London: John Hughs, 1738), 320.
80   Mungello, *Curious Land*, 334.

programmatically in 1699, "the Chinese missionaries have tried to imitate the wisdom of the Apostles."[81] This included adapting or even concealing certain principles of the Christian Faith which the Chinese might have difficulty in understanding. One Jesuit author pointed to the fact that the notion of the Trinity was kept from the pagans during the first centuries of the Church not because it was a later invention – "ut ad hic hodie credunt innumeri Calvinistae" – but because it was a concept beyond their immediate comprehension. Above all, it would have led pagans accustomed to polytheistic worship to suppose that Christians believed in three distinct gods.[82] In their defence of *tien* and *xamti*, the Jesuits also referred back to Ricci's original notion that, since monotheism preceded polytheism, the Chinese must have had some knowledge of the true God. In his "Proëmialis declaratio," Couplet had cited an important passage from Lactantius' *Institutiones divinae* (2.13.13): "they err, those who claim that the worship of gods has existed from the beginning of things, and that the Religion of God came only after paganism."[83] According to Couplet, knowledge of the true God preceded idolatry, not only in China but also in ancient Egypt, Assyria, and Europe, where it was later preserved by a small number of elite pagan philosophers. It was for this reason that Couplet placed Confucius among a small circle of wise pagans who had sensed or gleamed the true God through the veil of paganism, such as Hermes Trismegistus, Plato, Pythagoras, Cicero, Varro, and Seneca.[84] This idea formed the basis of many of the Jesuit defences of the Rites, which cited Lactantius' statement to similar effect.[85] By arguing that Chinese Confucianism preserved elements of the true primitive religion, Jesuit writers claimed that the term *tien*, whether or not it had served as an idolatrous designation, had monotheistic origins.

Alongside the religious history of China, one particularly important question was the role of language and the expression of religious belief. Both Jesuits and anti-Jesuits agreed on the linguistic definition of the term *tien*, which they nominally translated as "heaven." But what did the Chinese understand by the

---

81 "De rebus Sinensibus controversis tom. 3," ASPF, SC Indie Orientali e Cina, Misc. 54, 105: "Hanc Apostolorum prudentiam imitari conati sunt Sinenses Missionarii."
82 "De rebus Sinensibus controversis tom. 3," ASPF, SC Indie Orientali e Cina, Misc. 54, 103 ("as innumerable Calvinists believe today").
83 Couplet, *Confucius Sinarum philosophus*, lxxv; translation from Bowen and Garnsey, *Divine Institutes*, 159. Latin text: "errant qui Deorum cultus ab exordio rerum fuisse contendunt & priorum esse gentilitatem quam Dei Religionum."
84 Couplet, *Confucius Sinarum philosophus*, lxxvii. At one point Confucius is called "Sinicus noster Epictetus" ("Our Chinese Epictetus"), xiv.
85 "De rebus Sinensibus controversis tom. 3," ASPF, SC Indie Orientali e Cina, Misc. 54, 142.

word "heaven"? The primary argumentative line developed by Jesuit polemicists was to underline the similarities between Chinese expressions for God, or "the Supreme Being," and not only those permitted among Greeks and Romans of the early Church but even those by which the Hebrews denoted God in their Bible and with which zealous Christians worshipped Him in their churches. On the one hand, the Jesuits argued that it was necessary to denote God with a name both commonly attested to and comprehensible in the relevant language. This was why the Greeks called God θεός and the Romans *Deus*, despite the fact that they had once denoted Zeus and other pagan gods with the same name. It was also why the Apostles had refrained from using the Hebrew names "Jehova," "Adonai," or "Elohim."[86] On the other hand, the Jesuits noted that the Chinese words *tien* and *xamti* were not incongruous with the way God was described in the Hebrew and Vulgate texts. Firstly, it was common to name God in not just one but several ways, such as "regem regum," "dominum dominantium," "conditorem coeli terraeque" and "Deus coeli."[87] Secondly, there were numerous passages in the Bible in which individuals appealed to heaven or were sent aid from the heavens. As one Jesuit author pointed out, the Evangelist Mark had himself called God "qui in caelis est" (Mark 11:24–26).[88] Other biblical passages suggested more directly that the Jews understood "heaven" – in the Latin *coelum* and in the Hebrew *shamaim* (שמים) – as a synonym for "God."[89] If Onias could claim that "habuimus auxilium de Coelo," we had help from heaven (1 Maccabees 12:15), then it seemed permissible for the Chinese to denote their god with *tien*.[90]

This argument had two implications. Firstly, we can see how the discussion surrounding the Rites increasingly came to rely on a more general conceptualisation of the relationship between Christian and pagan religious beliefs and expressions. In order to justify their methods of evangelisation, Jesuit missionaries focused on what they believed to be the same similarities between Christianity and paganism which certain Fathers had highlighted in the first centuries of the Church. Rather than emphasise the deviation of pagan nations from primitive monotheism, they emphasised the monotheistic tendencies of pagan religion and philosophy, particularly those of a small and elite sect of

---

86 "De rebus Sinensibus controversis tom. 3," ASPF, SC Indie Orientali e Cina, Misc. 54, 102, 112–113, 479–480.

87 "De rebus Sinensibus controversis tom. 3," ASPF, SC Indie Orientali e Cina, Misc. 54, 105.

88 "De rebus Sinensibus controversis tom. 3," ASPF, SC Indie Orientali e Cina, Misc. 54, 125ff. See also 1 Maccabees 3:18, 4:40, 9:46, and 12:15.

89 As noted for example by Cornelius à Lapide, *In Pentateuchum Mosis commentaria* (Paris: Robert Foüet, 1626), 32–39.

90 "De rebus Sinensibus controversis tom. 3," ASPF, SC Indie Orientali e Cina, Misc. 54, 160.

pagan sages amongst whom they counted Confucius and the Chinese *literati*. Secondly, the Jesuits implicitly came to contextualize the Christian religion itself. As Joan-Pau Rubiés has pointed out, the Jesuits did not so much want to alter the definition of idolatry as minimise its applicability to the Chinese religion on ethnographic and historical grounds.[91] As a result, religion was no longer defined merely by the contrast of monotheistic truth with polytheistic error, but also as an historical and human product which was contingent upon the time, place, culture, and language of the worshipper. This is particularly evident in the manner in which the Jesuits explored the relationship between religious belief and religious expression. According to Jesuit polemicists, an appeal to the heavens was a characteristic, figurative expression shared by a number of religions, including Christianity.

The opponents of the Jesuits did not disagree with the principle of accommodationism. It is important to remember this fact. Like the Jesuits, they believed that the principles of Christianity should be adapted to the customs of foreign cultures and that the model for appropriate evangelisation in these cultures was supplied by the Apostle Paul and the Church Fathers.[92] With the exception of Niccolò Longobardo no Christian missionary of the seventeenth century, including Maigrot, supposed that the Chinese should call the Christian God by a European or Latin name.[93] The question on which they fundamentally differed was not whether the principles of Christianity should be accommodated but rather the extent to which they should be accommodated. As a result, they based their opposition to the Rites on the same patristic models cited by the Jesuits, and, consequently, on their own conceptualisation of the origins of idolatry and the nature of pagan worship.

The dissertations opposing the Jesuits were collected by Nicolas Charmot and submitted to the special congregation in 1698 and 1699. In 1700, they were published in a collection entitled *Historia cultus Sinensium*, arranged by Charmot, and in a further supplement, the *Continuatio* (also 1700).[94] Unlike the

---

91   Rubiés, "Theology, Ethnography, and the Historicization of Idolatry," 592.
92   See Mungello, *Curious Land*, 24.
93   Collani, "The Jesuit Rites Controversy," 5; Jensen, *Manufacturing Confucianism*, 94; Maigrot, *Mandatum*, 5: "Exclusis nominibus Europaeis, quae nonnisi barbaro quodam modo Sinicis literis, & Vocibus exprimi possunt, Deum.Opt.Max. ..." The Jesuits came to criticise Longobardo as "pio quidem et Zelantissimo Missionario, sed in Theologia minus alijs versato": "De rebus Sinensibus controversis tom. 3," ASPF, SC Indie Orientali e Cina, Misc. 54, 119.
94   Nicolas Charmot, ed., *Historia cultus Sinensium seu varia scripta de cultibus Sinarum, inter vicarios apostolicos Gallos aliosque missionarios, & patres Societatis Jesu controversis* (Cologne: 1700); Nicolas Charmot, ed., *Continuatio Historia cultus Sinensium seu varia*

Jesuit polemicists, these dissertations did not engage particularly extensively with Chinese sources or Chinese culture, although they did like to highlight contradictions or disagreements between the studies and conclusions of different Jesuit sinologists. Instead, the authors sought recourse to seventeenth-century scholarly narratives concerning the nature and origins of idolatry, which they then grafted upon the specificities of the Chinese debate. As a result, their arguments relied on several basic principles which the authors – who were not named and whose arguments I shall collectively ascribe to Charmot – had taken from patristic apologetics and the study of *historia sacra*. I shall outline three specific contexts here: the question of the origins and diffusion of idolatry, the monism of Greek philosophy, and the proselytizing methods of the Church Fathers.

Firstly, Charmot rejected the underlying notion that the Chinese retained some knowledge of the true God, even if only in fragmented form. In fact, to assert that knowledge of the true God had spread across the globe before idolatry was to contradict sacred history.[95] According to scripture, idolatry had already spread throughout the Near East by the time of Abraham. The Egyptians, who worshipped animals, and the Assyrians, who worshipped the sun and fire, had fallen victim to this idolatry.[96] It made no sense, in Charmot's opinion, to believe that the Chinese had avoided the ancient spread of idolatry when no other nations had; and to assert, as some Jesuits had done, that the Chinese had maintained the true religion up until the reign of the emperor "Mimti" in around 65 AD.[97] As a result, Charmot used biblical authority to suppose that ancient Chinese Confucianism must have descended into idolatry and atheism – in the same manner as contemporary pagan nations – long before the advent of such corrupting influences as Taoism, Buddhism, and neo-Confucianism.

Secondly, Charmot substantiated his rejection of the Rites through his interpretation of pagan theology more broadly. While the Jesuits had attempted to outline the similarities between Confucianism and primitive monotheism, Charmot emphasised the similarities between Confucianism and pagan animism or even atheism. This was particularly apparent in his discussion

---

      scripta de cultibus Sinarum, inter vicarios apostolicos Gallos aliosque missionarios & patres Societatis Jesu controversis (Cologne: 1700).

95 Charmot, *Historia cultus Sinensium*, 127: "id quod nullatenus cum Sacra Bibliorum historia congruit."

96 "De rebus Sinensibus tom. 4," ASPF, SC Indie Orientali e Cina, Misc. 55, 58; Charmot, *Historia cultus Sinensium*, 127–128.

97 See Thierry Meynard, "Chinese Buddhism and the Threat of Atheism in Seventeenth-Century Europe," *Buddhist-Christian Studies* 31 (2011): 8.

of the Chinese philosophical and cosmological principle *tai-kie*, more commonly known as *li*, which was in reality a neo-Confucian concept. Ricci had once suggested that *tai-kie* was comparable to the scholastic concept of *materia prima*, while Couplet had tried to equate it with *ratio*, from which differences between entities derive.[98] Since Longobardo, however, opponents of the Jesuits had supposed that *tai-kie* was fundamentally atheistic. In the *Historia cultus Sinensium*, Charmot supposed that *tai-kie* recalled the pantheist or monist elements of pagan religion, particularly those of ancient Greek philosophy. Ultimately *tai-kie*, and ancient Confucianism more generally, was founded on the typical pagan notion that "omnia unum esse," all things are one. This also led Charmot to align it with a modern heresy:

> From whence it follows that they never recognized true spirits separate from matter, with this laid down as the most fundamental principle of their Philosophy, *that all things are one*; which was also the doctrine of Democritus and the Epicureans, which in our age impious Spinoza publicly revived in his monstrous works.[99]

Thirdly, Charmot sought to undermine the relationship between religious expression and religious belief which the Jesuits had outlined in their defence of the terms *tien* and *xamti*. Like the Jesuits, Charmot based his argument on the example of the Church Fathers and Apostles who had once reprimanded the pagans for calling Jupiter or Mercury "Deus." Charmot pointed out that Paul himself had used several different terms to denote "God," including both the Roman "Deus" and the Greek "θεός." Yet it was also clear that in each European language, including Latin and Greek, there was only one proper designation for "God," that is "God" understood not as "numen" or "daemon" but as the one and only God, as "rex regum" or as "dominus dominantium." Thus Charmot opposed the very idea that the Chinese should be allowed three, or even four, names for God. To do so would undermine the idea that any name for God must imply not simply a divine power, but the one and only and almighty God. Although the Hebrews, as once pointed out by Jerome, had ten names for God, this was because Hebrew was the *lingua sacra*.[100] Pagans, however, would

---

98 Lai, "The Linking of Spinoza to Chinese Thought by Bayle and Malebranche," 163–164.
99 Charmot, *Historia cultus Sinensium*, 122: "Unde consequens est, nunquam eos veros spiritus a materia separatos agnovisse, supposito tanquam fundatissimo suae Philosophiae principio, *omnia unum esse*; quae fuit etiam sententia Democriti & Epicureorum, quam nostra hac aetate impius Spinoza in monstruosis suis operibus iterum in lucem revocavit."
100 See Jerome's letter to Marcella, PL 22:428–430, in which the ten names are El, Eloim, Eloe, Sabaoth, Elion, Eser Ieje, Adonai, Ia, JHVH, Saddai. Cf. Étienne Le Moyne, *Dissertatio*

come to regard the different names for gods not as different attributes of the same God, but as different gods in themselves.

As a result, Charmot supposed that the Jesuits had misunderstood the difference between the linguistic or etymological meaning of a word and the meaning which the speaker attributed to it. Charmot accepted that in the Bible the Christian God could be denoted by the word "coelum."[101] Yet the Jews, and later Christian worshippers, understood the essential fact that "coelum" referred to a God who was eternal, perfect, and omnipotent – that is, the Christian *Deus Optimus Maximus*. This was not the case in China, where worshippers associated *tien* with the "coelum materiale." As Charmot noted, "the meaning of the word *tien* has a certain meaning through public use and through the common doctrine of the Chinese writings, which is not allowed to change even through the translation of the word, on account of the danger in such a serious matter."[102] This meant that the Jesuits had misunderstood the task at hand. It was not a question of finding a word for God which was analogous to certain biblical expressions, but of finding a word for God which conveyed the true nature of God and which could engender the perception of a God who was perfect, unitary, and eternal in the mind of the Chinese neophyte. On this basis, Charmot chided the Jesuit's interpretation of Paul's speech at the Areopagus. The proper names of pagan gods, such as "Jupiter," Paul had avoided. It was for this reason he called God "ignotus." What he had sought to teach the heathens was that the word "Deus," which meant the highest divine power to both pagans and Christians alike, had been improperly applied by the pagans to Jupiter and the other false gods.[103] The comparison between *tien* and *Deus* was therefore a false equivalence; and Charmot defended the use of the new conglomerate *tien-chu* because it alone meant not only "dominus coeli" but signified "that thing which by the judgement of all nations, and particularly of the Chinese, is the most excellent and the most perfect."[104]

---

      theologica ad locum Jerem. XXIII:VI. De Jehovah justitia nostra (Dordrecht: Theodore Goris, 1700), 106ff.

101 Charmot, *Historia cultus Sinensium*, 131–132.

102 "De rebus Sinensibus tom. 4," ASPF, SC Indie Orientali e Cina, Misc. 55, 63: "Cum significatio vocis Tien ex publico usu et doctrina communi litterarum Sinensium certam significationem habeat, quam nequidem per translationem verbi mutare licet ob periculum in materia adeo gravi."

103 "De rebus Sinensibus tom. 4," ASPF, SC Indie Orientali e Cina, Misc. 55, 64: "quam Apostoli non repudiarunt ad significandum supremum numen, tam et si ea gentiles abuterentur ad significandum Jovem aliosque falsos Deos."

104 Charmot, *Continuatio*, 70: "idque satis apte cum significet *Dominum coeli*, id est, rei, omnium nationum, Sinicae praesertim, judicio, excellentissimae ac perfectissimae."

The manner in which Charmot responded to the Jesuits, particularly in the context of the name *tien*, is significant and further indicative of the changing way in which scholars of the late seventeenth century came to regard "religion" as a concept. Firstly, Charmot continued to propagate the notion that understanding the relationship between religious expression – the word by which the worshipper defined a divine being – and religious belief – the concept of divinity which the said worshipper conceptualised by using this word – was key to successful evangelisation. In doing so, however, he continued to suppose that both religious belief and religious expression were historically and linguistically contingent. Although Charmot made an exception for the *lingua sacra*, even the process by which the Apostles had denoted God and first preached the Gospel was analysed in its appropriate cultural, historical, and linguistic context. Secondly, Charmot relied on an understanding of pagan religion – and by extension Chinese Confucianism – which was monist and naturalistic. Since the Chinese were unable to conceptualise a divine power higher than nature, Charmot supposed that invocations to *tien* referred not to a divine power residing in the sky but rather to the sky itself. This particular appreciation of pagan religion had become, as we shall see further, increasingly popular since the mid-seventeenth century in the field of *historia sacra* and was largely dependent on a certain reading of Greek and Roman sources.

4 Pagan Animism and the Chinese Names for God

It is clear that Bonjour mobilised his study of pagan religion in order to better understand not only Chinese religion but, more specifically, the correct method of evangelisation. Particularly important was Vossius' concept of pagan "monism," that perverted pagan "monotheism" in which the pagans worshipped one thing but understood this one thing as being not God but nature. Bonjour took on this notion and argued that this nature-worship proved that pagans, including the Chinese, had no proper notion of "divinity." Above all, Bonjour argued that the Chinese had confused the Christian God in the sky for the material sky itself. Under a heading entitled "Gentiles arbitrantes Hebraeos colere coelum," he listed a number of pagan testimonies that wrongly stated that the Jews worshipped the sky as a god, rather than the God who created the sky. These included Juvenal, who stated that the Jews "worship nothing except the clouds and spirit of the sky" ("nil praeter nubes et coeli numen adorant," *Saturae* 14.98);[105] Strabo, who said that Moses had taught the Hebrews

---

105 We might note the footnote to the 1918 edition by G. G. Ramsay: "The phrase caeli numen is hard to translate. What Juvenal means is that the Jews worshipped no concrete deity,

not to worship humans or animals, but the universe, or the nature of all things (16.2.35); and Diodorus (40.3.4), who said that Moses was "of the opinion that God is not in human form; rather the heaven (οὐρανὸν, coelum) that surrounds the earth is alone divine, and rules the universe."[106] Perhaps most explicitly, Origen's pagan opponent, Celsus, had stated "quod Judaei coelum adorent," that "the Jews consider the heaven to be God" (5.7).[107] Bonjour used these testimonies to emphasise both the monism and the naturalism of pagan theology. Since pagans were unable to imagine a Creator, they instead conferred divinity onto the created. This notion was expressly voiced in Lucretius' *De rerum natura* and the first book of Marcus Manilius' *Astronomica*, as well as in the attempt of the second-century heretic Hermogenes to synthesise the idea of a Christian omnipotent god with Stoic eternal matter, a synthesis for which he was famously rebuked by Tertullian.[108] Yet Bonjour still supposed this idea to be a universally-held and widely-attested heathen principle. Indeed, Bonjour later labelled the phrase "ex nihilo nihil fuit" as the "gentilis philosophiae principio," the principle of all heathen philosophy.[109]

Bonjour's study of Lucretius, Marcus Manilius, Tertullian's *Adversus Hermogenem*, and the aforementioned pagan evaluations of Jewish monotheism were arranged in ms.lat.633, the manuscript volume which contains his dissertations and notes on China.[110] It seems apparent that Bonjour's specific interest in the pagan worship of nature was a product of his interest in the Chinese Rites and his desire to understand the true meaning of the two Chinese terms *tien* and *tai-kie* in particular. As we have seen, *tien* was generally

---

such as could be pourtrayed [*sic*], but only some impalpable mysterious spirit. They did not worship the sky or the heavens, but only the numen of the heavens. This is what Tacitus means when he says (Hist. v. 5) 'The Jews worship with the mind alone'. So Lucan. ii. 592–3 dedita sacris Incerti Judaea dei": G. G. Ramsay, ed., *Juvenal and Persius* (London and New York: William Heinemann and G. P. Putnam's Sons, 1928), 270.

106 "Gentiles arbitrantes Hebraeos colere Coelum," BAR, ms.lat.633, fol. 56r. These quotes were often treated together: see for example Philipp Clüver, *Germaniae antiquae libri tres* (Leiden: Lodewijk Elzevir, 1616), 288.

107 "Coelum," BAR, ms.lat.633, fol. 11r. Bonjour took his translation from Origen, *Origenis contra Celsum*, ed. Spencer, 234.

108 BAR, ms.lat.633, fols. 114r–155r. Bonjour cites especially *Astronomica* 1.130–131; Lucretius, *De rerum natura* 1.540–542, 2.167–170, 2.177–181, and 4.416–421. For Hermogenes see BAR, ms.lat.633, fols. 115r, 134v; BAR, ms.lat.634, fol. 48r: "Hermogenis error de materia coaeterna Deo a Tertulliano impugnatus."

109 BAR, ms.lat.633, fol. 115r.

110 BAR, ms.lat.633: "coelum," fol. 11r; "nomen dei," fols. 17v–20v; "notitiae Dei," fol. 20r; "Gentiles arbitrantes Hebraeos colere Coelum," fol. 56r; "animae defunctorum," fols. 82r–83v; "nomina deorum," fol. 88r; "coelum," fol. 88v; "ethnica coeli attributa," fol. 103v; "idololatria platonica," fol. 109v; "coelum," fol. 112r, etc.

translated as "coelum" but the Jesuits and their opponents were divided as to whether this meant the "cielo materiale."[111] Bonjour himself sought to compare the Chinese understanding of "heaven" not with Jewish appeals to "scamaim" but with pagan appeals to Uranus. He noted, for example, that both Lorenz Rhodomann (1546–1606) and Wilhelm Xylander (1532–1576), the translators of Diodorus and Strabo respectively, had translated οὐρανὸν, the God whom Moses was supposed to have preached to the Hebrews, as "coelum," rather than "Deus."[112] This fundamentally separated the manner in which Jews and pagans understood the concept of "divinity" itself, despite their use of similar nomenclature. According to Bonjour, the Hebrew "scamaim" (*shamaim*) was purely a metonym for God.[113] The pagans, however, had understood "coelum" as a natural entity, rather than as a figurative expression for a supernatural one. Hence passages such as those in the Orphic verses, in which the sky is called "omnium generator" (παντογένεθλος) or "omnium principium omniumque" (ἀρχὴ πάντων), were evidence not of a latent monotheism but of the idolatrous notion that all things on earth are regulated by celestial movements.[114] As Bonjour summed up:

> Although they say many things about the sky, which only accord with the true God, it does not follow from this that they indicate the true God, or the one God who is the God of Gods as mentioned in holy scripture, with the name of the sky.[115]

Bonjour believed this explanation for the origins of astral and celestial worship to be as true for the Chinese as it was for the Greeks, Egyptians, or Assyrians. When he came to analyse a long list of quotations from the *Confucius Sinarum philosophus* in which God was compared to the sky, Bonjour identified the worship of *tien* with the worship of the heavens among the first Greek idolaters: "all the Chinese believe that all things in the universe, whether visible or invisible,

---

111 "Notizie circa l'uso delle tabelle colle parole Cinesi *King Thien Coelum Coelito* Proposte, e presentate alla Sacra Congregatione del Sant'Offizio Per parte della Compagnia di Giesu In Agosto 1699," BAR, ms.lat.87, fol. 174r.
112 See Diodorus, *The Library of History*, ed. Oldfather, 283, n. 2.
113 Lapide, *In Pentateuchum Mosis*, 32–39; see BAR, ms.lat.633, fol. 56r: "Hebraei per Metonymiam, qua continens pro contento ponitur Deum vocant *scamaim* id est coelum." This was part of Bonjour's comment on Juvenal, *Saturae* 14.98.
114 "Ethnica coeli attributa," BAR, ms.lat.633, fol. 103v.
115 "Notitiae Dei," BAR, ms.lat.633, fol. 20r: "etiamsi plura dicant de Coelo, quae non nisi vero Deo conveniant, non inde sequitur eos indicare Coeli nomine verum Deum, seu unum illum Deum qui Deus Deorum dicitur in sacris paginis."

were created by the sky."[116] Moreover, the manner in which the Chinese and other Far Eastern nations used the word *tien* in everyday conversation suggested that they did not conceive of *tien* as a divine creator-being. Using the Vietnamese-Portuguese-Latin dictionary of the Jesuit missionary Alexandre de Rhodes (1593–1660), Bonjour argued that the manner in which the Vietnamese described the "heavens" – particularly in the way they contrasted the circular heavens with the square earth – suggested they considered it a being of nature rather than a being above nature.[117] This also allowed Bonjour to strike at a common Jesuit defence, later voiced explicitly in the documents submitted to the congregation by the Jesuit missionary François Noël: that the Chinese could not be accused of idolatry when using the word *tien* because the sky itself could not be an idol.[118] Like Noël Alexandre, Bonjour argued that the pagans conceptualised "coelum" as the material sky and still worshipped it as a god.

The importance Bonjour placed on Greco-Roman sources reappears in his discussion of the Chinese principle *tai-kie*.[119] Like Charmot, Bonjour supposed that *tai-kie* proved that the Chinese understood the relationship of divinity and matter in the same way as the Greek Epicureans and atomists. Specifically, he supposed that they embodied the same principle of "ex nihilo nihil fuit" once voiced by Lucretius and Marcus Manilius. "The darkness which Heathenism spread over the ancient philosophers of the Europeans, inquiring into the origin of things," noted Bonjour, "it has also brought on the writings of the Chinese."[120] In a short and unfinished dissertation on the Chinese principle *tai-kie*, he stated further that "the Chinese *literati* admit no efficient principle [principium efficiens] of the sky and earth but only a material principle [principium materiale], which they call *Tai-Kie*."[121] It was a belief that the Chinese,

---

116 "Chinensium fides de caelo," BAR, ms.lat.633, fol. 35v: "Res omnes seu visibiles, seu invisibiles a coelo creatas esse in universum credunt omnes Chinenses."

117 "Dissertatio de nominibus, quibus Christiani uti licite possunt ad Deum designandum apud Sinas," BAR, ms.lat.633, fol. 121r–v. I have transcribed Bonjour's own rendering of Vietnamese into the Latin alphabet here.

118 See Collani, "François Noël and his Treatise on God in China," 48–49.

119 BAR, ms.lat.633, fol. 2r–v.

120 BAR, ms.lat.633, fol. 15r: "Quas inquirentibus in rerum principium antiquis Europaeorum Philosophis tenebras obduxit Gentilismus, has et Sinarum litteris attulit."

121 BAR, ms.lat.633, fol. 2r: "Propositio Prima: Sinarum literati nullum admittunt principium efficiens coeli et terrae, sed tantum principium materiale, quod vocant *Tai Kie*, estque idem cum materia prima. Hinc Deum coeli et terrae conditorem nullum agnoscunt, quemadmodum et Japones ac Tunchinenses, auditores scientiae Sinicae. Nec tam recentiorum literatorum est pestifera haec doctrina, quam veterum; quippe quam tradidit ipse Confucius."

like their theology more generally, shared with their neighbours in the Far East such as the Japanese and Vietnamese.

Bonjour's discussion of Chinese religion within the context of the pagan propensity to worship nature is particularly apparent in his discussion of one particular Chinese object, a Han Dynasty mirror or disc inscribed with ancient Chinese writing which had recently been discovered in a tomb in Siberia.[122] In 1704, this mirror had come into the possession of Nicolaes Witsen, the former administrator of the Dutch East India Company and an enthusiastic amateur antiquarian, and Witsen quickly made efforts to obtain a translation of the inscription. Although he failed in Europe, he also had a copy of the mirror sent to Jakarta, from where he eventually received a partial translation by a Chinese *literatus*. This *literatus*, despite his own acknowledgement that he did not recognise many of the Chinese characters, translated the inscription as a monotheistic paean, as illustrated by such phrases as "God is pure, immaculate, and wholly untarnished."[123] In 1705, Witsen published this interpretation (which was ultimately nonsensical, since we know now that the characters served merely as decoration) and a facsimile of the mirror in his *Noord en oost Tartarye*.[124]

The first person whom Witsen contacted about the mirror was his close friend and fellow antiquarian enthusiast Gisbert Cuper in 1704.[125] Cuper himself knew little about China, but seems, alongside Witsen, to have adopted a Jesuit interpretation of Chinese history and philosophy largely through his reading of the *Confucius Sinarum philosophus*.[126] Witsen had stated that he believed the mirror to be contemporaneous with Confucius, whom he called "sanctus" (and thought more deserving of this title than Plato and Seneca). In response, Cuper voiced his belief that the inscription evidenced Confucius'

---

122 Cuper described it as "lanx ex incognito vel mixto metallo literis sinicis vetustis inscripta binae parvae icunculae ex auro sed cavae, quarum una erat corpore vituli, altera avis, et utraeque capite humano": see Gisbert Cuper to Guillaume Bonjour, 15 June 1704, BAR, ms.lat.395, fols. 36r–38v, and in Pélissier, "Lettres inédites de Gisbert Cuper," (1905): 115–116 (279–280).

123 Van Noord and Weststeijn, "The Global Trajectory of Nicolaas Witsen's Chinese Mirror," 331–333. A copy of the French translation of this excerpt can be found in the letter of Gisbert Cuper to Mathurin Veyssiére La Croze, 4 December 1708, KW 72 H 18, and in Beyer, *Lettres de critique*, 20–22. See above all n. 20: "l'Interprète Chinois à Batavia ne s'y connoissoit pas en perfection, & c'est pour cela qu'on est persuadé que ces caractères contiennent encore d'autres règles de Morale."

124 Nicolaes Witsen, *Noord en Oost Tartarye* (Amsterdam: François Halma, 1705), 749–750.

125 See Marion H. Peters, "Nicolaes Witsen and Gijsbert Cuper: Two Seventeenth-Century Dutch Burgomasters and their Gordian Knot," *Lias* 16 (1989): 111–151.

126 Van Noord and Weststeijn, "The Global Trajectory of Nicolaas Witsen's Chinese Mirror," 341.

humility before God and demonstrated an ancient pagan monotheism even more pronounced in Confucius than it was in his Greek near-contemporary Socrates.[127]

Cuper first asked Bonjour about the inscription in June 1704, and by August Bonjour was discussing the inscription with Giovanni Pastrizio, a professor of Hebrew at the Collegio Urbano and a frequent correspondent of Bonjour's, usually on Oriental languages and antiquarian artefacts.[128] Of immediate interest was the question of the word *tien*. In his reply to Bonjour Pastrizio pointed out that by "cielo," sky, the pagans meant the material sky while Moses meant "il cielo invisibile pero e infigurabile," an invisible and incorporeal sky.[129] In November, Bonjour wrote to Cuper that "if the dish discovered together with these small engravings is really inscribed with Chinese characters (which arouses great wonder in me) perhaps it can shed some light on them. The affairs of China which are being debated in Rome still keep the Bishop of Rosalie here, a man very learned in these letters."[130] In March 1705, Bonjour corresponded on the inscription with Artus de Lionne and Arcadio Huang through the mediation of Antonin Massoulié. Although De Lionne replied that Huang could only recognise four characters, it is illustrative that he translated *tien* not, as Witsen's Chinese *literatus* in Jakarta had done, as "Deus," but rather as "coelum."[131]

Bonjour's notes in the Biblioteca Angelica indicate that by the time he left for China he had acquired a competent knowledge of Chinese history and religion through his reading of the main, predominantly Jesuit, sources on China. These included not only the *Confucius sinarum philosophus* of Couplet but also Ricci and Trigault's *De christiana expeditione apud Sinas* (1615), González de Mendoza's *Historia de las cosas mas notables, ritos, y costumbres, del gran reyno de la China* (1585, in the Latin translation by the Augustinian Joachim Bruel

---

127 Van Noord and Weststeijn, "The Global Trajectory of Nicolaas Witsen's Chinese Mirror," 341.
128 Gisbert Cuper to Guillaume Bonjour, 15 June 1704, BAR, ms.lat.395, fols. 36r–38v, and in Pélissier, "Lettres inédites de Gisbert Cuper," 116 (280); Guillaume Bonjour to Gisbert Cuper, 6 November 1704, KW 72 H 20.
129 Giovanni Pastrizio to Guillaume Bonjour, 15 November 1704, BAR, ms.lat.395, fol. 140r–v; and as Bonjour told Cuper in a subsequent letter, Guillaume Bonjour to Gisbert Cuper, 6 November 1704, KW 72 H 20.
130 Guillaume Bonjour to Gisbert Cuper, 6 November 1704, KW 72 H 20: "Si lanx una cum his icunculis reperta, vere inscribatur literis Sinicis (quod mihi maximam admirationem movet) forte posset lumen eis afferre. Res Sinarum quae Romae tractantur, adhuc ibi tenent Episcopum Rosaliensem, his in literis versatissimum."
131 Antonin Massoulié to Guillaume Bonjour, 28 March 1705, BAR, ms.lat.395, fols. 61r–63v: "sed propter ignorationem aliorum se non posse scripturam interpretari." The list of Chinese words and their translation is on the inserted sheet, fol. 62r.

(d. 1653)), Giovanni Filippo de Marini's *Delle missioni de' padri della compagnia di Giesu nella provincia del Giappone* (1663), Alvaro Semedo's *Relatione della grande monarchia della Cina* (1643), and Martino Martini's *Novus atlas Sinensis* (1655).[132] It seems, however, that in late 1705 and early 1706 his knowledge of China was more limited. This is particularly apparent from his eventual interpretation of the Chinese mirror, which he sent to Cuper in February 1706. In order to interpret the mirror, Bonjour relied on the translation that Witsen had sourced from Jakarta. As we have mentioned, this translation emphasised the monotheistic aspects of Confucianism. Conversely, Bonjour used pagan evidence sourced predominantly from classical antiquity to assert that this religion was monotheistic only in the sense that the Chinese worshipped one thing, but that that one thing was nature. Consequently, he defined Chinese religion as animist or monist in the same manner as Vossius had described pagan religion and Charmot had defined the Chinese principle *tai-kie*. For Bonjour, the most illustrative phrase of the inscription was "Deus est tam pulcher, uti clara et liquida aqua" – God is as beautiful as clear and serene water.[133] This concurred with the manner in which Confucius had described the sky in the *Confucius Sinarum philosophus*. More broadly, it recalled the ancient pagan tendency to ascribe divinity to nature. "I am very much persuaded," wrote Bonjour, "that the Chinese too, both once upon a time and today, attributed divinity to the material sky. Since they described the beauty of their God as the beauty of water, they appear similar to those Gentiles, who bestowed divinity onto water."[134] Ultimately such classical testimonies as Propertius' reference to a "celestial stream" ("divinas ... aquas," 2.26b), Virgil's reference to "hallowed springs" ("fontis sacros," *Eclogues* 1.52), or Tacitus' statement that "consideration, too, should be paid to the faith of their fathers, who had hallowed rituals and groves and altars to their country streams" (*Annales* 1.79) were indicative of the propensity of pagan nature worship.[135] Indeed, even the long history of

---

132 See generally BAR, ms.lat.633.
133 Guillaume Bonjour to Gisbert Cuper, 15 February 1706, KW 72 H 20.
134 Guillaume Bonjour to Gisbert Cuper, 15 February 1706, KW 72 H 20: "Mihi persuasissimum est Sinas aeque olim ac hodie tribuisse divinitatem coelo materiali. Quod pulchritudinem Dei sui pulchritudine aquae descripserint, similes se praebuerunt illis Gentilibus, qui divinitatem attribuebant aquae."
135 See also Seneca, *Epistles* 41.3: "We worship the sources of mighty rivers; we erect altars at places where great streams burst suddenly from hidden sources; we adore springs of hot water as divine, and consecrate certain pools because of their dark waters or their immeasurable depth." For translations see Seneca, *Epistles 1–65*, ed. Richard M. Gummere (Cambridge MA: Harvard University Press, 1917), 275; and Tacitus, *The Histories Books IV–V: The Annals Books I–III*, ed. Clifford H. Moore and John Jackson (Cambridge MA: Harvard University Press, 1931), 379.

Christian conversion highlighted the pervasive pagan propensity to worship springs and rivers. It was for this reason that the Council of Auxerre (c.578) banned "excultores fontium," a decision reiterated in the canons of the Council of Toledo in 589; and why, in the life of Saint Eligius, written by his friend and contemporary Audoin, the bishop of Rouen, it was written that "no Christian should make or render any devotion to the gods of the trivium, where three roads meet, to the fanes or the rocks, or springs or groves or corners" (2.16).[136]

Bonjour's interpretation of the Chinese mirror highlights how his understanding of Greco-Roman paganism informed his approach to the Chinese religion. Even though Bonjour knew little about China specifically, he supposed it part of the same Gentile theology which had seen Gentile nations diverge from the true religion in the ancient Near East and Mediterranean. As a result, the lessons he drew from Greco-Roman sources continued to shape his understanding of even those religions which existed outside of the traditional diffusionist narrative. They also shaped his approach to the Rites specifically. In his letter to Cuper he stated that the names *xamti* and *tien* meant merely "supremus imperator" and "coelum" respectively, and henceforth that the Chinese had no word which denoted God, or a divine being, simply and absolutely.[137]

5   Historical Context and Ancient Names for God

The Chinese worship of the material sky, *tien*, as a god in itself – something which Alexandre, in his *Conformité des cérémonies chinoises avec l'idolâtrie grecque et romaine*, equated with the Greek god Uranus, or the Roman "coelum," whom Ennius (*Thyestes*, fr. 134) and Euripides (fr. 386) had equated with Jupiter – had implications for the name by which Chinese neophytes may be permitted to call the Christian God.[138] In essence, Bonjour argued that *tien* had previously been used not as a general Chinese term for "divinity" but as the name for a specific celestial idol. In order to develop this notion further, Bonjour turned back to the relationship between *nomina* and *numina* which, as we have seen, formed the basis of his eclectic interpretation of paganism as *onomatolatria*. Illustratively, most of the evidence which Bonjour cited in the aforementioned dissertation entitled *De conversione gentium secundum*

---

136   Guillaume Bonjour to Gisbert Cuper, 15 February 1706, KW 72 H 20.
137   Guillaume Bonjour to Gisbert Cuper, 15 February 1706, KW 72 H 20: "Nam Sinae nullum norunt vocabulum, quo simpliciter et absolutè Deum nominent."
138   As preserved by Cicero, *De natura deorum* 2.25 (65).

antiquam praxim was recycled in a dissertation entitled *Dissertatio de nominibus, quibus Christiani uti licite possunt ad Deum designandum apud Sinas* ("On the names, by which Christians are allowed to designate God among the Chinese"), in particular the evidence of Paul's speech at the Areopagus.[139] Once again, Bonjour began by citing Cicero and stating the importance of names within pagan ritual. Furthermore, he referred back to the important words of Origen, who had once stated that "if names whose nature it is to be powerful in some particular language are translated into another tongue they no longer have any effect such as they did with their proper sounds."[140] This statement also laid the foundation for Bonjour's approach to the Chinese names for God. It was clear from the comments of various Christian apologists that it was not permissible for pagans to call the Christian God by divine names, or descriptions, which had previously been used to designate a false god of pagan polytheism. As Origen declared, "even if the Egyptians offer us Amoun with threats of punishment, we will die rather than call Amoun God; for the name is probably used in certain Egyptian spells which invoke this daemon" (5.46).[141] In the same context, Bonjour rejected *tien* and *xamti* because they would invoke among the Chinese the memory of a former idol.

Yet Bonjour's work on the Chinese names for God, although it relied on principles taken from patristic apologetics, was also based on something else, something newer: a surprisingly sophisticated notion of the contingency of language and, consequently, religious belief and expression. The importance of context, both linguistically and culturally, had, in truth, already been suggested by Origen. "Suppose too," wrote Origen, "that the Scythians say Papaeus is the supreme God; yet we will not believe it. We affirm belief in the supreme God, but we do not call God Papaeus as if it were His correct name, for we regard it as a name loved by the daemon who has obtained control of the Scythian desert and of their nation and language." Yet Origen then went on to qualify this statement: "However, if any individual calls God by the title by which He is known in Scythian, or in Egyptian, or in any language in which he may have been brought up, he will not be doing wrong" (5.46).[142] Bonjour, who cited this passage in his *Dissertatio de nominibus* and discussed it extensively, took this notion even further. Above all, it suggested to him that names for God were

---

139 BAR, ms.lat.633, fols. 116r–122r.
140 Translation from Origen, *Contra Celsum*, ed. Chadwick, 299. See also Origen, *Origenis Contra Celsum*, ed. Spencer, 261–262. See BAR, ms.lat.633, fol. 17v.
141 "Dissertatio de nominibus, quibus Christiani uti licite possunt ad Deum designandum apud Sinas," BAR, ms.lat.633, fols. 119v–120r.
142 Origen, *Contra Celsum*, ed. Chadwick, 301.

permissible or prohibited not because of what they meant, but rather, what the speaker or worshipper thought they meant. For Bonjour, religious expression was linguistically and culturally contingent: the meaning of a word, including the name of God Himself, was defined by the culture and beliefs of the society in which that word was uttered. Bonjour used two quotes to illustrate his point. Firstly, Servius had commented on Virgil's *Aeneid* 11.97 that "not etymology is to be considered, but custom."[143] Servius was commenting specifically on Aeneas' use of the word "vale" but for Bonjour it illustrated a general principle of language – that use rather than origin gave a word its distinctive meaning. It was in exactly this context that he went on to cite the words of Denis Petau. In his *Dogmata theologica*, Petau had claimed that "the use of words, by which the same things are explained, often varies; which ought to be moderated not so much by the peculiarity of the origin and the native language, as by the popular habit of *savants*."[144] For Bonjour, this comment neatly encapsulated how historical context shaped language and consequently meaning.

Bonjour developed this notion with a study of two ancient names for "God." The first was the Greek word δαίμων. Following Plato's suggestion that its etymology came from δαήμων, meaning "scientes," "knowing" (*Cratylus* 398B–C), Bonjour noted that the ancient Greeks often used θεός and δαίμων interchangeably. This was also the case for Philo of Alexandria, who used the Hebrew for δαίμων, "Elohim," to mean both good and bad angels (*De gigantibus* 4.16). In the time of Philo, the word "god" and the word "demon" therefore "differ[ed] not so much in the thing as in the names."[145] And yet, at some point, this connotation had changed. As Augustine had pointed out in the early fifth century, no one would now say as a compliment "daemonem habes," "you have a demon" (*De civitate dei* 9.19). Not the word itself, but what was understood by the word, was what mattered.

The second example was the biblical name Baal. In the *Dissertatio de nominibus*, Bonjour noted that, at Hosea 2:17 and Jeremiah 23:26, the Israelites were

---

143 "Dissertatio de nominibus, quibus Christiani uti licite possunt ad Deum designandum apud Sinas," BAR, ms.lat.633, fol. 131r: "non etymologia consideranda est, sed consuetudo." Also cited in BAR, ms.lat.629, fol. 203r.

144 "Dissertatio de nominibus, quibus Christiani uti licite possunt ad Deum designandum apud Sinas," BAR, ms.lat.633, fol. 131r: "verborum [autem], quibus eaedem res explicantur, saepe variatur usus; cui non tam originis, ac nativae linguae proprietas, quam popularis doctorum consuetudo moderari debet." Also cited in "De conversione gentium secundum antiquam Ecclesiae praxim," BAR, ms.lat.629, fols. 203r.

145 "De conversione gentium secundum antiquam Ecclesiae praxim," BAR, ms.lat.629, fol. 203v: "non tam re differe quam nominibus."

forbidden to call their God "Baal."[146] The question was, why? As Bonjour noted, the Hebrew name "Baal," from which the ancient Phoenicians and Chaldeans drew their name for God, simply meant "Dominus." In this sense "Beel shamaim" (*Baalshamin*) was simply a Phoenician version of "Dominus Coeli," an appellative commonly used in the Hebrew Bible.[147] And yet these Hebrew and Phoenician equivalents had been prohibited. This was because the legitimacy of a word depended not on its linguistic definition but rather on its cultural significance. The Israelites understood under the name "Baal" not merely "the Lord," but rather the specific pagan idol "Baal" who was then being worshipped by their idolatrous Semitic neighbours. Allowing the Israelites to denote the true God by the name "Baal" would evoke in them the memory not of *Deus Optimus Maximus* but a pagan idol, hence its prohibition. This did not mean, however, that the name "Baal" was *necessarily* idolatrous. Citing a study of ancient German gods by the antiquarian Elias Schedius (1615–1641), Bonjour noted that the ancient Germans had worshipped the Hebrew God under the name Baal and had done so piously.[148] Once, however, the name had come to denote an idolatrous god it was rendered problematic by association, and it was for this reason that the Lord had ordered the Israelites to not only destroy the idols but to forget and destroy the *name* of Baal (Deuteronomy 12:3).

For Bonjour, this reinterpretation of pagan religion and ancient biblical idolatry gave him the scholarly tools necessary for tackling the prickly question of the Chinese names for God. Developing a notion already advanced by Charmot, Bonjour argued that not only did pagan nations, unable as they were to conceive of true divinity, worship divine names in such a way that the use of these names would necessarily be idolatrous, but also that Charmot's distinction between the etymological meaning of a word and the meaning which the said word induced in the worshipper was backed up by both apostolic and Mosaic authority. In the immediate context of the Chinese Rites, it proved that the name *tien* was impermissible among Chinese neophytes. On a deeper level, it allowed Bonjour to propose a general framework for how missionaries – *praecones Evangelii* – should conceive of translating Christian names and ideas into foreign languages, a framework drawn from his study of biblical, pagan,

---

146 "Dissertatio de nominibus, quibus Christiani uti licite possunt ad Deum designandum apud Sinas," BAR, ms.lat.633, fol. 117r.

147 "Dissertatio de nominibus, quibus Christiani uti licite possunt ad Deum designandum apud Sinas," BAR, ms.lat.629, fols. 202r–203r.

148 BAR, ms.lat.633, fol. 130r: "populus enim Dei Baalem suum pie satis vocabat, priusquam ob vocem illam ad gentilium numina traductam Deus prohiberet." Also cited in "De conversione gentium secundum antiquam Ecclesiae praxim," BAR, ms.lat.629, fol. 204r. See Elias Schedius, *De dis germanis* (Amsterdam: Lodewijk Elzevir, 1648), 115.

apostolic, and patristic precedents. Ultimately, this study functioned in two directions. If Bonjour used historical evidence to shape his understanding of the Chinese Rites debate, it is also apparent that the questions raised by the Rites debate saw Bonjour rethink both the manner in which one should understand the essence of paganism and the manner in which the Mosaic Law was conceived to ward off this idolatry.

The contours of this specific argument also allows us to see how Bonjour (and his contemporaries in the Rites debate) began to rethink both the historical relationship between the true and false religion(s), and the relationship between language and religious belief. Ultimately, Bonjour's argument rests on two fairly sophisticated although admittedly implicit notions. Firstly, Bonjour's argument supposes that the "meaning" of a word – or name – was not a question of etymology, nor of a Stoic "natural" conception of names, but was instead contingent upon historical and cultural context. Even – or perhaps especially – a deceptively simple term as "God" would mean different things to different peoples. Secondly, and consequently, Bonjour's argument suggests that he accepted that religious belief and doctrine were shaped by and inseparable from language, which is to say, religious expression. Ultimately, the language in which one expressed an idea would determine the way in which this idea was interpreted. This was the fundamental charge Bonjour laid at the door of the Jesuits. By making comparisons between religious expressions among the ancient Hebrews or Latin-speaking Christians on the one hand and Chinese Confucians on the other, they were ignoring the different theological and philosophical contexts which meant that even the same word could express radically different ideas. If Christians were to be successful in introducing the true Christian religion to China rather than a religion corrupted by pre-existing Confucian ideas, they would need to construct new modes of expression. Though he would be loath to admit it, what Bonjour discovered among ancient pagans and Chinese Confucians was equally true for Christian doctrine, which had been inescapably shaped by the language and culture in which it had first emerged. In future generations, scholars drew on these same ideas to historicise, contextualise, and desacralize the Word of God itself.

6 Bonjour in China: Christian Apologetics at Work

Bonjour travelled to China in order to examine the Rites debate and confer honours on to the great enemy of the Jesuits, Tournon. It is clear from the dissertations he composed in Rome, his conversation with Cuper, and even the treatise he composed on board the *Donegal* while on his way to India that he opposed the Rites – at least in principle. His behaviour in China, however, initially seems to belie this fact. From between 1711 and 1714, Bonjour spent considerable time with the Jesuits and appears to have largely supported their missionary efforts. There are a few episodes from Bonjour's time in China which illustrate this explicitly. On 25 March 1711, the Kangxi Emperor sent round a declaration on the Rites for the missionaries to sign, which, according to Bonjour's companion Matteo Ripa, stated that the Rites were "pure and clean from all superstition."[149] According to Ripa, the Jesuits happily acquiesced to this request; Ripa himself was plunged into anguish, believing the Rites to be illicit but afraid of the consequences of saying so openly. Noticeably, Bonjour took a middle ground. While not legitimising the Rites, he did not declare them illicit, stating instead that His Majesty the emperor had the right to make such decrees. Already, Bonjour's willingness to compromise marks him out from the more hard-line stance of Ripa. This difference was to come to a head on 5 May, when Bonjour, Ripa, and their third companion, Teodorico Pedrini, were asked to sign further documents on the decrees. According to Ripa, the primary Chinese interrogator was a certain "Ciao," who told him that Tournon understood nothing of Chinese customs and that coming to China and banning the worship of ancestors was as ridiculous as going to Rome and telling the pope not to worship God. Bonjour and Pedrini replied that the pope did not want to ban all rites but only those which were religious rather than political, and that this was a necessary criteria for embracing the Christian religion. Of all three missionaries, however, it was Bonjour who acquiesced first, signing the declaration offered to him by the Jesuits on 18 May. Not only did Ripa continue to refuse, but the Jesuits continually exorted him to follow Bonjour's example (Pedrini and Ripa only caved in when they were threatened with expulsion from China).[150] As Baldini has noted, it appears that relations between Bonjour and Ripa soon became strained, a matter not helped by Bonjour's desire to leave the Propaganda fide mission for that of the Augustinians.[151] Yet it also appears that Bonjour's greater willingness to submit to the Kangxi emperor and his friendship with the Jesuits contributed to this rift. When Claudio Filippo Grimaldi, the *de facto* leader of the Portuguese Jesuit mission, died in November 1712, only Bonjour chose to attend a controversial funeral which mixed Christian and Chinese rituals. Both Ripa and Pedrini decided to stay away for exactly this reason.[152]

---

149 Ripa, *Giornale*, 2:64: "la stessa materia de riti, dichiarati per puri e netti da ogni superstizione."
150 Ripa, *Giornale*, 2:64–75; Baldini, "Guillaume Bonjour," 275–277.
151 Baldini, "Guillaume Bonjour," 274.
152 Ripa, *Giornale*, 2:91–92; Baldini, "Guillaume Bonjour," 276–277.

Most suggestive, however, of Bonjour's relationship to the Rites and his prickly relationship with Ripa on this issue were the conversations which Bonjour had with the French Jesuit Pierre Jartoux, one of the leaders of the French cartographic project and Bonjour's travelling companion. The conversation is recorded by Baldini:

> Although occupied by the problems of the journey and their technological objectives, the three travellers never forgot that they were missionaries. Jartoux reported that, whenever on the Chinese part of their route they came across a Christian community, they instructed it and ministered the Sacraments; and, since a number of local high officials and *literati* came to meet such unusual imperial envoys, being more advanced in the language he publicly declared the essentials of Christianity, and debated with opponents. In this context, Jartoux also commented on Bonjour's personal attitude toward the "question of the rites" and the terminology and methods of Jesuit preaching. According to him, the Augustinian "so liked and approved" these methods that he was "much displeased" whenever he was unable to attend his colleague's preaching; at the end of their journey, having been asked by Jartoux if – taking the Roman decree against these rites into account – he believed that something had to be changed in those methods (since the Jesuit commonly employed such terms as *Tien* and *Cham ty* to name God), Bonjour answered that, far from changing anything, he should keep using them, since they were most appropriate. When Jartoux insisted that Rome was said to have banned the use of these terms, Bonjour answered that the ban only concerned the abuse of them, which was frequent; finally, Jartoux having replied that his way of preaching was that introduced long before by the first Jesuit missionaries, and that it was strictly followed by all their successors, the Augustinian made no comment.[153]

The above encounter leaves us with an important question, as Baldini also noted. If Bonjour had spent his time in Rome denouncing the rites and comparing them to ancient pagan worship of Uranus, Baal, and Papaeus, why in China did he suddenly appear to suggest that they were permissible? Partly, of course, the difference can be explained by a change in circumstances. It was one thing to denounce the Chinese from a library in Rome and quite another

---

153 · Baldini, "Guillaume Bonjour," 273–274.

to stand in the palace of the emperor several thousand miles from home and denounce him as an idolater. Certainly, it was not a tactic which had worked for Tournon. Similarly, it was the Jesuits who exercised control over the majority of the Chinese missions and who had established the trust of the Chinese hierarchy, and it behoved Bonjour to maintain good relations. In addition, we should note that Bonjour, despite his proximity to Noris, remained on friendly terms with a number of Jesuits throughout his time in Rome, including Conrad Janninck and Giacomo Maria Airoli. Yet the explanations for Bonjour's comments should not merely be regarded as a matter of hypocrisy or convenience. Despite the ostensible contradictions with his earlier dissertations on the Rites, there are also a number of explanations which suggest that this was not a *volte face* but merely a question of adapting intellectual principles to specific contexts. As Bonjour noted to Jartoux, it was not the use of the terms *tien* and *xamti* which he opposed but their abuse, a notion reminiscent of his earlier study of the ancient use of the term Baal. Above all, however, it suggests that Bonjour recognised a difference between the scholarly study of the origins and nature of a pagan religion on the one hand and the process of actually converting – and convincing – pagan worshippers on the other.

The key passage which might explain this subtle difference is a fragmentary note included among Bonjour's dissertations on China, which discusses the differences between Christian apologetics and the Christian catechism.

> To solve the difficulties which exist regarding the Chinese terms *Thien* and *Xam-ti*, I see two methods of evangelising, on the one hand the catechistic [method], on the other hand the apologetic one. The catechizing method of evangelising admitted only those expressions which simply and without any ambiguity open up all the elements of our faith. According to this method of evangelising the use of the terms *Thien* and *Xam-ti* are to be prohibited from the Chinese Church; for because according to the Chinese idolaters, their sense is idolatrous, and they would kindle a risk of idolatry among catechumens. This is something the fathers of the Society recognise very well, as their Latin-Chinese catechism, which Kircher published in his *China Illustrata*, makes clear. For there the Chinese terms *Thien* and *Xam-ti* are never bestowed upon *Deus Optimus Maximus*, but His Chinese name is always *Thien chu*.
>
> The apologetic method of evangelising cannot be as restrictive or sparing in speaking or writing. For since the apologetic discourse, as much as it can, usefully raises witnesses out of the monuments of those Pagans to whom our faith was announced, it very often happens that the terms

of which the use is idolatrous when on the side of these monuments, in these [apologetic discourses] obtain a proper and legitimate sense, and are thus usefully able to be adapted to the elements of our faith.[154]

As a result, Bonjour made a clear distinction between a work which was intended to adequately *define* the doctrine of the Christian faith, and one which was to *convince* heathens of the superiority of the faith itself. Clearly the two were related, but not identical. In the following passage, Bonjour went on to describe how the distinction had itself shaped the work of the early Fathers who had first studied pagan mythology.

> I call the ancient apologists of our religion as witnesses. These defenders of the faith were very much not unaware that the names Jupiter and Prometheus were often used in an idolatrous sense. Because, however, they discovered more than a few records of the ancients, in which the outlines of *Deus Optimus Maximus* were sketched with these names, they did not doubt that such names for the true God were appropriate in their apologetic writings. Thus it was for Aristobulus, the Hebrew philosopher, for Clement of Alexandria, for Tertullian, and of particular note Justin Martyr. That the apologetic discourse tolerates expressions which the catechistic discourse rejects can be confirmed by more examples. For example, the Nicaean Creed is a catechistic discourse; and the writings of the Fathers written in defence of the faith which the same Creed outlines are apologetic. Those who composed the Creed would not have been able to say, without hinting at Arianism, that the Son is like the Father, an article in which it is confessed that he is consubstantial with the father.

---

154   BAR, ms.lat.633, fol. 138r: "Ad solvendas difficultates quae sunt circa voces Sinicas Thien et Xam-ti, duplicem evangelizandi modum observo, catechisticum unum, apologeticum alterum. Modus evangelizandi catechisticus eas tantum voces admittit, quae simpliciter et citra ambiguitatem omnem aperiunt elementa nostrae fidei. Juxta hunc evangelizandi modum proscribendus est ab Ecclesia Sinensi usus vocum Thien et Xam-ti; cum enim juxta idololatras Sinenses earum sensus sit Idololatricius, conflarent catechumensis [sic] periculum idololatriae. Id optime norunt patres societatis, ut palam facit eorum catechismus Latino-Sinicus, quem Kircherus edidit in sua China Illustrata. Ibi enim Deus Opt. Max. nusquam donatur Sinicis vocibus Thien et Xam-ti sed Sinicum ejus nomen est semper Thien chu. Modus evangelizandi apologeticus tam restrictus et parcus in loquendo vel scribendo esse non potest. Cum enim sermo apologeticus testes, quantum potest, utiliter excitet ex monumentis illarum Gentilium quibus annunciatur fides nostra, saepissime contigit, ut voces quarum usus citra haec monumenta idololatricus est, sanum legitimumque sensum in his obtineant, adeoque utiliter aptari possint elementis nostrae fidei."

And yet the apologists of the same Creed have not hesitated to use the word "similar" instead of the word "equal," which is entirely pertinent to consubstantiality.[155]

Bonjour's comments go some way to not only allowing us to gain a better understanding of his approach to China, but also, perhaps, of helping to explain his approach to pagan mythology, sacred history, and biblical chronology more generally. The decision to defend the Bible – and, by extension, the Christian religion – through historical scholarship was not the same as suggesting that Christian doctrine required the evidence of profane history to be considered authoritative, ancient, and reliable. It does, however, highlight that Bonjour considered pagan religion, mythology, and history key sources in defending the Christian religion. In particular, they could prove to those people who did not believe that the history of the Pentateuch had been divinely revealed to Moses by the one true God that what *sacer historiographus* Moses had written was nevertheless true. We might recall, in this context, what Bonjour once told Cuper: that as a young man he had turned away from scholastic theology and poetry because "ita nihil solidi continere," it contained nothing solid. Indeed, it was at this point in his early career that he chose to dedicate himself to the study of scripture, Oriental languages, and the "veterumque temporum mores [et] ritum." For Bonjour, it was pagan antiquity which *did* contain something solid: key ancient evidence for unlocking the secrets of the past, for discovering the ancient history of the biblical patriarchs, for delineating the Hebrew origins of primitive civilization, and for defending the authority of a stable and universal biblical chronology. It is quite clear that whatever the challenge pagan antiquity presented to the sacred historian of the seventeenth and early eighteenth centuries, it remained for Bonjour an ally of biblical truth, not an opponent.

---

155   BAR, ms.lat.633, fol. 138v: "Veteres religionis nostrae Apologistas testes appello. Hi fidei defensores minime ignorabant nomina Jovis et Promethei vulgo usurpari in sensu idololatrico. Quia tamen non pauca reperiebant monumenta veterum, in quibus D.O.M his nominibus adumbrabatur, ejusmodi nomina vero Deo aptare non dubitabant in suis scriptis apologeticis. Sic Aristobulus, Hebraeus Philosophicus, sic Clemens Alexandrinus, sic Tertullianus, sic praecipue notandus est Justinus Martyr. Quod apologeticus sermo voces patiatur, quas respuit catechisticus, pluribus confirmari potest. Catechistici sermonis est symbollum Nicaenum, exempli gratia: et Apologetici sunt scripta patrum facta in defensionem fidei quam idem symbolum declarat. Qui hoc symbolum composuerunt non potuissent absque Arrianismi nota dicere filium similem patri, in eo articulo in quo eum consubstantialem patri confessi sunt. Et tamen ejusdem symboli apologistae non dubitarunt uti voce similis pro voce aequalis quae ad consubstantialitatem omnino pertinet."

As we have pointed out already, it is doubtful whether this interest in and use of pagan antiquity was successful in consolidating the biblical text Bonjour was intent on defending. Ultimately, historical scholarship on such matters as Chinese history and Egyptian chronology developed to a point that serious scholars no longer found the notion that they would fully and consistently fit within a biblical schema for universal history tenable. But it is also incontestable that later interest in and sophisticated scholarship on the ancient religion of China, the gods of the Greeks, and the dynasties of Egypt built on the firm foundation of a generation of orthodox scholarship which taught Bonjour that the closer one studied ancient language, history, rites, and customs, the better one would understand and confirm holy scripture. From the convent of Toulouse to the libraries of Rome to the communities of rural China, pagan antiquity held for Bonjour the key to convincing everyone that the religion he believed in was true.

Conclusion

"In the Delta of Egypt," said Critias, "where, at its head, the stream of the Nile parts in two, there is a certain district called the Saitic. The chief city in this district is Sais – the home of King Amasis – the founder of which, they say, is a goddess whose Egyptian name is Neïth, and in Greek, as they assert, Athena. These people profess to be great lovers of Athens and in a measure akin to our people here. And Solon said that when he travelled there he was held in great esteem amongst them; moreover, when he was questioning such of their priests as were most versed in ancient lore about their early history, he discovered that neither he himself nor any other Greek knew anything at all, one might say, about such matters. And on one occasion, when he wished to draw them on to discourse on ancient history, he attempted to tell them the most ancient of our traditions, concerning Phoroneus, who was said to be the first man, and Niobe; and he went on to tell the legend about Deucalion and Pyrrha after the Flood, and how they survived it, and to give the genealogy of their descendants; and by recounting the number of years occupied by the events mentioned he tried to calculate the periods of time. Whereupon one of the priests, a prodigiously old man, said, "O Solon, Solon, you Greeks are always children: there is not such a thing as an old Greek." And on hearing this he asked, "What mean you by this saying?" And the priest replied, "You are young in soul, every one of you. For therein you possess not a single belief that is ancient and derived from old tradition, nor yet one science that is hoary with age. And this is the cause thereof: There have been and there will be many and diverse destructions of mankind, of which the greatest are by fire and water, and lesser ones by countless other means.""

∴

This is the famous story of wise Solon's chastening trip to Egypt, as recounted in Plato's *Timaeus* (21E–22C).[1] Like many of the pagan sources we have

---

1 Translation from Plato, *Timaeus. Critias. Cleitophon. Menexenus. Epistles*, trans. R. G. Bury (Cambridge MA: Harvard University Press, 1929), 31–33.

encountered, it said nothing about biblical authority, nor about the contentious relationship between *historia sacra* and *historia exotica*. It could, however, have biblical implications. For Samuel Bochart, who cited this passage in the preface to his *Geographia sacra*, Plato's testimony highlighted the youthfulness and historical ignorance of the Greeks, in contrast to the antiquity and authority of biblical history.[2] The Greeks, unlike Moses, had no knowledge of true antiquity. This explained both the superiority of the biblical record and why Greek historical records often omitted or contradicted central tenets of the biblical narrative for universal history.

For La Peyrère this passage also evidenced an ignorance of true antiquity, but it was a different form of ignorance.[3] In the *Timaeus*, the Egyptian priests criticised Solon for holding what they considered the arrogant Greek belief that their myths were tales of ancient, universal, history. "You possess," replied one of the priests, "not a single belief that is ancient and derived from old tradition."[4] Bochart had used this passage to highlight how little the Greeks knew of ancient history. La Peyrère supposed, however, that the same ignorance and arrogance scholars routinely found in Greek historiography was also applicable to the Jews. Like the Greeks, the Jews thought there was one ancient Flood, when in actual fact there were many. Like the Greeks, the Jews thought that their history told of the oldest traditions of mankind, when in actual fact they knew nothing of true antiquity.

La Peyrère's pre-Adamite thesis was one of the most controversial reinterpretations of the relationship between *historia sacra* and *historia exotica* in the seventeenth century, and although he found few followers his work divided those scholars who took it upon themselves to refute him. As is often the case, the sparkling originality of La Peyrère's almost universally despised work exposed existing cracks and fault lines, rubbing profane salt into a biblical wound. On the one hand, it led scholars from Ursinus to Martianay to dismiss as fabulous those pagan sources with which La Peyrère had helped construct his heretical edifice; on the other, it helped contribute to the rise of a diffusionist tradition which sought to prove that those very pagan sources derived from, and therefore spoke of, the same events described authoritatively, accurately, and originally by Moses. Central to this tradition was undoubtedly Bochart, whose work preceded the publication of the *Praeadamitae* but which provided

---

2   Bochart, *Geographia sacra*, "ad lectorem praefatio," sig. e1r: "Et Saiticus ille sacerdos *Patenit* nomine de quo Proclus [101.20–24] post Platonem in Timaeo, Graecos merito asserebat semper esse pueros nec unquam senes, ut pote verae vetustatis prorsus ignaros."
3   La Peyrère, *Systema theologicum ex praeadamitarum hypothesi*, 129–130.
4   *Timaeus* 22B–C; Plato, *Timaeus*, ed. Bury, 33.

CONCLUSION

a remarkably fortuitous basis for any scholar who wanted to prove that the Bible contained a history of the entire world rather than merely the Jewish people, and who required historical proof for detailing how Hebrew ideas could possibly have found their way into Greek mythology or philosophy. Bochart's work perfectly encapsulates the way in which sacred history and pagan antiquity meshed together. The foundation for Bochart's understanding of the *origines gentium* was one single biblical passage, Genesis 10. Writing the history of the ancient world depended on understanding the biblical text – by correctly understanding the text, one could understand the origins of humanity. Yet the origins of humanity, while clearly expressed only in the Mosaic Pentateuch, could also be gleaned in the corrupted fragments of pagan mythology. In the late seventeenth century this remained the founding principle of the system Huet developed in Paris and Bonjour in Toulouse and later Rome.

Clearly, by the early eighteenth century, this had begun to change. As scholars came to doubt whether the Bible was a complete and authoritative account of ancient history, so too did they come to reconceptualise the field of study that Bochart's great tome was thought to contribute towards. A particularly indicative example of this shift is the work of Nicolas Fréret, perhaps the leading scholar of the French *Académie royale des inscriptions* and a long-time scourge of Newton's mythography and chronology.[5] Fréret himself trod a fine line between radical criticism and solid erudition. He was known to hold controversial views. For his work on the Germanic origins of the Franks he was imprisoned in the Bastille. Yet he was not a Spinoza or a Toland. His principal interest lay in the rites and rituals of pagan religion, and his most explicit enemies were contemporary Euhemerist interpreters of myth who supposed that pagan gods were the result of the pagan apotheosizing of great men, among them the incorrigible Newton.[6] Certainly, he was no closet pre-Adamite. And yet his work shows how attitudes towards the biblical text were changing. In his notes on Bochart's work he still praises the illustrious Huguenot as a scholar of immense erudition, as his colleagues Banier and Fourmont would do too.[7] And yet he also supposed that:

> The Phaleg of Bochart is not a complete account of the origin of all the Nations, but only of those which are recorded in the tenth chapter of

---

[5] See Nicolas Fréret, *Défense de la chronologie fondée sur les monumens de l'histoire ancienne, contre le système chronologique de M. Newton* (Paris: Durand, 1758).

[6] See Fréret, *Défense de la chronologie*, 310–380, and Fréret, "Recherches sur le Culte de Bacchus parmi les Grecs," in *Histoire de l'Académie royale des inscriptions et belles-lettres* 23 (1756): 242.

[7] See Banier, *La mythologie et les fables expliquées*, 1:iii.

Genesis and which were known to the Jews through the Expeditions of Sesostris, the memory of which was still recent.[8]

Fréret's discussion of Bochart's work underlines the number of different ways in which the traditional relationship between *historia sacra* and *historia exotica* was gradually being undermined. Fréret did not endorse La Peyrère's notion that *historia sacra* and *historia exotica* were two separate fields. Nor did he suppose, however, that the entire history of the world could be written using the Bible as the main source on ancient history, given that there existed many nations of whom the Jews were ignorant. That is not to say that, for Fréret, Jewish records had *no* historical information; but rather that the historical information they did contain was particular and specific. Just as earlier scholars of *historia sacra* had supposed that pagan nations had received certain biblical knowledge through ancient cultural transmission, Fréret supposed that the Jews had received their knowledge of ancient history through the same avenues of transmission. Consequently, the Bible was simply a historical document, like all other *monumenta* of *historia exotica*. It was composed at a certain time and by certain people and the historical information it preserved was shaped by the knowledge the Jews possessed at the time of its composition. In this sense, Fréret also came to further dissolve the boundaries between *historia sacra* and *historia exotica*. Both biblical and non-biblical testimony were studied under the common category of *historia*. For some historical periods, the Bible remained a relevant and pertinent historical source. For others, however, it was irrelevant.[9]

Bonjour himself was, as I hope to have given some indication of, a multi-faceted, diverse, and talented scholar. Chronologist, missionary, monk, historian, astronomer, mathematician, linguist, Orientalist, cartographer, theologian, teacher, philologist, numismatist, antiquarian – all these words can be used to describe him accurately. In some ways, I have done him a disservice, for I have subjected this diversity to a few key, broader themes concerning the development of sacred history and its relationship to pagan antiquity. In doing so, however, I hope that his life and scholarship can help us answer certain questions which go beyond the life and work of one, individual scholar;

---

8 Nicolas Fréret, "Manuscrit Original sur la Geographie Sacrée de Sam. Bochart," BNF, NAF 10925, fol. 1r: "le Phaleg de Bochart ce n'est pas un traitté complet de l'origine de toutes les Nationes mais seulement de celles dont il est parlé dans le dixieme chap. de la Genese et qui estoient connues aux Juifs par les Expeditions de Sesostris dont la memoire estoit encore recente." See also Banier, *La mythologie et les fables expliquées*, 1:9ff.

9 See in particular the work on pagan mythology undertaken in the *Académie des inscriptions*, and published in the *Mémoires de littérature, tirés des registres de l'Académie royale des inscriptions et belles-lettres*.

CONCLUSION 351

questions which pertain to the development of modern, secular, historical scholarship on the ancient, primordial world, and which take us from early Jewish interpretations of pagan culture in Ptolemaic Alexandria to the lasting influence of Greek mythography, to the first patristic attempts to organise pagan history and religion into a Judaeo-Christian *Weltbild*, to the enduring chronological legacy of Joseph Scaliger, to the idiosyncratic dominance of the seventeenth-century diffusionist tradition, to the separation of *historia sacra* and *historia exotica* by eighteenth-century scholars and academicians, and, finally, to the work of more recent historians of pagan history and religion who may well retain their faith in the Jewish or Christian religion without supposing that their studies might contribute to its consolidation or proliferation. It is a story of the declining authority of biblical history and the rise of *historia profana* as both an independent field of study and a reliable source for understanding ancient history, religion, and culture. Eventually, it was no longer a question of *historia sacra et exotica* but simply a question of *historia*.

Perhaps it is useful to end the work by comparing two scholars who lived and worked at opposite ends of this spectrum. Back in the early fifth century, Augustine laid out a basic principle for evaluating the veracity of biblical history when it conflicted with, pagan, non-biblical evidence. For Augustine, profane history could be declared accurate so long as it agreed with the sacred, and inaccurate wherever it disagreed (*De civitate dei* 18.40).[10] Augustine proposed this rule in the context of his study of certain Egyptian histories which, on account of their great length, contradicted the biblical date for Creation. He evidenced his rule on two factors. Firstly, the Bible was of divine but Egyptian history of human provenance. Secondly, the Bible must have a better understanding of past events because it alone had, through prophecy, a perfect understanding of future events. Notionally Augustine's principle held firm for the following 1300 years. In his 1705 *Selectae* Bonjour still cited Augustine's principle and described it as "the rule for distinguishing a synchronism from an anachronism in profane history."[11]

In 1981, the Italian historian Arnaldo Momigliano, then working at the Warburg Institute in London, wrote a short work on the contemporary differences between biblical and classical studies.[12] According to Momigliano,

---

10   Augustine, *The City of God*, ed. Bettenson, 815: "we can place our reliance on the inspired history belonging to our religion and consequently have no hesitation in treating as utterly false anything which fails to conform to it."
11   *Selectae*, D.II.62, 100: "regula discernendi synchronismum ab anachronismo in historia profana."
12   Arnaldo Momigliano, "Biblical Studies and Classical Studies: Simple Reflections upon Historical Method," *Annali della Scuola Normale Superiore di Pisa. Classe di lettere e filosofia* 11 (1981), 25–32, reprinted in Arnaldo Momigliano, *On Pagans, Jews, and Christians*

the problems posed to the historian by sacred history were the same as those posed by profane history – or perhaps more accurately, they were the same *type* of problems. "The basic elements of a sacred history," he wrote, "are in Livy as much as in the Pentateuch."[13] A proper understanding of both texts and the history of which they related required the same scholarly tools, and the same historical method.

Momigliano advanced his claim in order to refute contemporary philosophers who supposed that *all* literary texts could be submitted to the same rhetorical and structural analysis, irrespective of whether they were works of literary fiction or historical research. In response, Momigliano sought to emphasise the necessity of evaluating all *historical* works through the lens of what constituted good or bad *historical* research specifically. Although not his intention, his claim underlines the secularisation of modern text-critical and historical scholarship for both biblical and non-biblical history. Augustine privileged biblical over Egyptian history because only the former was the product of divinely inspired priestly scribes of the true religion. Momigliano, however, subjected sacred history to the same philological, comparative, and historical study as Livy's history of Rome, which similarly traced its origins back to the ancient annals of native priests.

The difference between Augustine and Momigliano's assertions is the history of a process of profound significance for European thought and culture: the path by which the Bible became a historical document and the Jewish religion a product of the religious culture of the ancient Near East. This process was as long as it was complex and varied, and in this work I have examined just a small period within this process, and a small part of this period. The issues, however, are the same as those raised by Augustine, and ultimately Momigliano: the true relationship between sacred history and religion on the one hand, and pagan history and religion on the other. Although the scholars who were the subject of my narrative openly acknowledged their debt to Augustine, I hope to have shown how, if implicitly and in many senses counter-intuitively, they began to lay a platform for Momigliano.

(Hanover: Wesleyan University Press, 1987), 3–10. On Momigliano see Anthony Grafton, "Momigliano's Method and the Warburg Institute," in *Worlds made by Words: Scholarship and Community in the Modern West* (Cambridge MA: Harvard University Press, 2009), 231–254.

13 Momigliano, "Biblical Studies and Classical Studies," 25.

Bibliography

Manuscript Sources

Rome
Archivio Generale Agostiniano
DD 133–138: *Regesta R.P. Ant. Pacini 1693–1699.*
DD 139–144: *Regesta R.P. Nic. Serani 1699–1705.*
DD 145–150: *Regesta R.P. Adeodato Nuzzi 1705–1711.*

Archivio Storico di Propaganda Fide
Acta CP 2: *Congregazione particolari sopra l'Indie Orientali.*
SOCP 20–26: *Scritture originali delle Cong:ni Parti:ri dell'Indie Orientali e China, 1698–1714.*
SC Indie Orientali e Cina, Miscellanea 7: *Relatione della morte del Cardinal di Tournon.*
SC Indie Orientali e Cina, Miscellanea 52–55: *De rebus Sinensis tom. I–IV.*
SC Missioni 1.

Biblioteca Angelica
Ms.lat.1: *Mercurius Aegyptiorum Josephus patriarcha genealogice, chronologice, historice, geographice, et hieroglyphice demonstratus ... // Appendix de monarchia et dynastiis Aegyptiorum ...*
Ms.lat.45: *Psalterium Copto-Arabicum.*
Mss.lat.46–48: *Lexicon Aegyptio-Latinum I–III.*
Ms.lat.49: *Antiquitas temporum novis plerumque observationibus illustrata ...*
Ms.lat.87 *Vindiciae scriptorum Nicolai Charmot ...*
Ms.lat.297: *Traduzione Copto-Menfitica. Genesi capp. I–V.*
Ms.lat.311: *Acta causae rituum seu cerimoniarum Sinensium complectentia.*
Ms.lat.316: *Contra dilucidationes pro Soc.e Iesu, super rebus et ritibus Sinensibus.*
Ms.lat.317: *Contra varia scripta idiomate Italo a rr.dis patribus Societatis Iesu exhibita, circa usum vocabulorum "Tien", "caelum", et "Xangti".*
Ms.lat.395: *Epistolae ad Bonjour.*
Ms.lat.484: *Opuscola varia.*
Ms.lat.495, *"Encomio dell'Elementa linguae copticae" di Bonjour.*
Ms.lat.496: *Elementa linguae Copticae.*
Ms.lat.621: Translations by Bonjour of various biblical extracts.
Mss.lat.629–635: *Miscellaneae tomi I–VII.*
Mss.lat.67–68: *Elementa linguae Copticae.*
Ms.or.71: *Elementa linguae Copticae.*

Biblioteca Vallicelliana
S 81–83; T-U 15–19, 23, 31, 38: Papers of Francesco Bianchini.

Modena
Biblioteca Estense
Archivio Muratori
MS 84.16: *Lettere di Bonjour, Guillaume a Lodovico Antonio Muratori.*

Florence
Biblioteca Nazionale Centrale
Fondo Magliabechiano VIII
Cod. 261: Letters between Gisbert Cuper and Antonio Magliabechi.
Cod. 294: Letters between Enrico Noris and Antonio Magliabechi.
Cod. 317: Letters between Guillaume Bonjour and Antonio Magliabechi.
Cod. 341: Letters between Jean-Pierre Rigord and Antonio Magliabechi.
Cod. 364: Letters between Antonin Massoulié and Antonio Magliabechi.
Cod. 1239: Letters between Ludovico Antonio Muratori and Antonio Magliabechi.
Cod. 1242: Letters between Benedetto Bacchini and Antonio Magliabechi.
Cod. 1328: Letters between Conrad Janninck and Antonio Magliabechi.

Targioni Tozzetti
MS 82: Letters between Otto Mencke and Antonio Magliabechi.

Montefiascone
Montefiascone Seminary Archives
Press 4, Shelf D: Letters between Marc-Antonio Barbarigo and Alessandro Mazzinelli.

Paris
Bibliothèque nationale de France
Français
MS 6300: *Français 17258 Mélanges théologiques.*
MSS 9359–9363: *Correspondance de l'abbé NICAISE, chanoine de la Ste-Chapelle de Dijon. (1660–1701).*
MS 17258: *Œuvres théologiques de LOUIS, duc D'ORLÉANS, fils du Régent; Tome XXI. Observations sur Sanchoniaton.*
MSS 17701–17713: *Correspondance de Dom Bernard de Montfaucon (1655–1741).*
MS 19663: *Lettres de D. Jean MARTIANAY († 1717) et D. Denys DE SAINTE-MARTHE († 1725).*
MS 22800: *Recueil de lettres originales adressées à Cabart de Villermont (1652–1707).*
MS 25060: *V Caillier-Courtaulin. Pages 2307–2501. Biographie et lettres du P. Nicolas Charmot.*

Nouvelles acquisitions françaises

MSS 560–563: *Correspondance de Nicolas* TOINARD, *d'Orléans (1706)*.
MS 4368: *Recueil de lettres originales adressées à l'abbé Nicaise par divers correspondants.*
MS 6212: *Lettres d'Eusèbe* RENAUDOT *adressées de Rome au cardinal de Noailles en 1701.*
MS 7483: *XXVIII Dissertations littéraires, historiques, etc.* [Eusèbe Renaudot].
MS 8944: *Papiers d'Étienne, Michel et Claude-Louis* FOURMONT; *1 Mélanges.*
MS 10925: *Manuscrit Original sur la Geographie Sacrée de Sam. Bochart* [Nicolas Fréret].

Latin

MSS 17397–17943: *Papiers de Paul Pezron.*

Nouvelles acquisitions latines

MS 291: *Nicaise (Papiers de l'abbé).*

Baluze

MS 354: *Correspondance de Baluze.*

The Hague
Koninklijke Bibliotheek

72 C 30: *Aantekeningen betreffende* Dissertatio de nomine patriarchae Josephi a Pharaone imposito *door Fratre Guillelmo Bonjour (Rome 1696).*
72 D 2: *Briefwisseling met Claude Nicaise (1623–1701), oudheidkundige.*
72 D 3: *Briefwisseling met Lodovico Antonio Muratori (1672–1750).*
72 D 10–12: *Briefwisseling met Antonio Magliabechi (1633–1714), bibliothecaris.*
72 G 23: *Briefwisseling met Franciscus Blanchinus//Briefwisseling met Adeodatus Nuzzi//Briefwisseling met Justus Fontaninus (1666–1736), aartsbisschop van Ancyra.*
72 H 18–19: *Briefwisseling met Mathurin Veyssière de la Croze (1661–1739), bibliothecaris.*
72 H 20: *Briefwisseling met Guillaume Bonjour Favre.*
72 H 23: *Briefwisseling met Pierre Daniël Huet (1630–1721), theoloog.*

Primary Printed Sources

Airoli, Giacomo Maria. *Dissertatio biblica in qua scripturae textus aliquot insigniores adhibitis linguis Hebraea, Syri. Chald. Arub. Gruecu, Latina, per dialogismum dilucidantur.* Rome: Typis Sacra congregatio de Propaganda fide, 1704.

Alabert, Pierre. *Traité du sacrement de mariage avec les plus belles décisions prises du droit canonique & civil.* Toulouse: J. J. Boude, 1699.

Alembert, Jean le Rond d', and Denis Diderot ed. *Encyclopédie ou dictionnaire raisonné des sciences des arts et de métiers par une société de gens de lettres.* 17 vols. Paris: Briasson, David, Le Bret, Durand, 1751–1765.

Alessandri, Alessandro. *Genialium dierum libri sex*. Lyon: Paul Frellon, 1608.

Alexandre, Noël. *Selecta historiae ecclesiasticae Veteris Testamenti*. 6 vols. Paris: Antoine Dezalier, 1689.

Alexandre, Noël. *Conformité des cérémonies chinoises avec l'idolâtrie grecque et romaine pour servir de confirmation à l'Apologie des Dominicains missionnaires de la Chine*. Cologne: Heritiers de Corneille d'Egmond, 1700.

Allatius, Leo, ed. *S. P. N. Eustathii archiepiscopi Antiocheni, et martyris in Hexahemeron commentarius*. Leiden: Laurentius Durand, 1629.

[anon]. "Article CXXXX: Examen de la conjecture du R.P. de Tournemine touchant la difference du texte Hébreu de l'edition Samaritaine & de la version des Septante dans le calcul des années des anciens Patriarches." *Journal de Trévoux* 7 (1703): 1388–1407.

[anon]. "Article XCIII: Eloge du Pere Pezron de l'étroite observance de l'Ordre de Cisteaux, ancien Abbé de Charmoye." *Journal de Trévoux* 19 (1707): 1266–1281.

[anon]. Review of "François Sevin: Dissertation sure Menés ou Mercure, premier Roi d'Egypte. Contre le Système de Marsham & de Bochart." *Journal des sçavans* (1710): 603–609.

Apollonius Rhodius. *Argonautica*. Edited by William H. Race. Cambridge MA: Harvard University Press, 2008.

Apuleius. *Metamorphoses*. Translated by J. Arthur Hanson. 2 vols. Cambridge MA: Harvard University Press, 1989.

Arnauld, Antoine, Pierre Nicole, and Eusèbe Renaudot. *La perpetuité de la foy de l'eglise catholique touchant l'Eucharistie*. 6 vols. Paris: C. Savreux and Jean-Baptiste Coignard, 1664–1713.

Augustine. *The City of God against the Pagans*. Translated by Henry Bettenson. London: Penguin, 1984.

Augustine. *De Doctrina Christiana*. Edited by R. P. H. Green. Oxford: Clarendon Press, 1995.

[Augustinians]. *Constitutiones Ordinis F. F. Eremitarum Sancti Augustini Recognitae, & in ampliorem formam ac ordinem redactae*. Rome: Haeredum Corbelletti, 1686.

Aulus Gellius. *Attic Nights*. Edited by John C. Rolfe. 3 vols. Cambridge MA: Harvard University Press, 1927–1952.

Ausonius. *D. Magni Ausonii Burdig. Viri Consularis Opera. A Iosepho Scaligero, & Elia Vineto denuo recognita, disposita, & variorum notis illustrata: Cetera Epistola ad lectorem docebit*. Geneva: Typis Jacob Stoer, 1588.

Avitabile Maioli, Biagio d'. *Rime di poeti illustri viventi parte prima*. Faenza: Girolamo Maranti, 1723.

Bacchini, Benedetto. "Dissertatio de nomine patriarchae Joseph …" *Giornale de' Letterati dell'anno 1696* (1697): 239–245.

Banier, Antoine. *La mythologie et les fables expliquées par l'histoire*. 3 vols. Paris: Briasson, 1738.

Banier, Antoine. *The Mythology and Fables of the Ancients, Explain'd from History*. London: A. Miller, 1739.

Bar Hebraeus, Gregory. *Historia compendiosa dynastiarum authore Gregorio Abul-Pharajio*. Edited by Edward Pococke. Oxford: Richard Davis, 1663.

Baronio, Cesare. *Annales ecclesiastici*. 12 vols. Antwerp: Plantin, 1588–1607.

Barthélemy, Jean-Jacques. "Réflexions générales sur les rapports des langues Égyptienne, Phénicienne & Grecque." *Mémoires de littérature, tirés de l'Académie royale des inscriptions et belles-lettres* 32 (1768): 212–233.

Basnage de Beauval, Jacques. *L'histoire des Juifs, reclamée et retablie par son veritable auteur Mr. Basnage*. Rotterdam: Fritsch et Böhm, 1711.

Bayle, Pierre. *Pensées diverses, écrites à un docteur de Sorbonne, à l'occasion de la comète qui parut au mois de Décembre 1680*. 2 vols. Rotterdam: Reinier Leers, 1683.

Bayle, Pierre. *Dictionnaire historique et critique*. 3 vols. Rotterdam: Reinier Leers, 1715.

Bayle, Pierre. *A General Dictionary Historical and Critical*. Translated by John Peter Bernard, Thomas Birch, and John Lockman. 10 vols. London: James Bettenham, 1734–1741.

Bellarmine, Robert. *Disputationum Roberti Bellarmini Politiani, e Societate Iesu, S.R.E. cardinalis; De controversis Christianae fidei, adversus huius temporibus haereticos*. 4 vols. Cologne: Johann Gymnich and Anton Hierat, 1615.

Béroalde, Mathieu. *Chronicum, scripturae sacrae authoritate constitutum*. Geneva: Antoine Chuppin, 1575.

Berosus and Manetho, *Berossos and Manetho, Introduced and Translated: Native Traditions in Ancient Mesopotamia and Egypt*. Edited by Gerald P. Verbrugghe and John M. Wickersham. Ann Arbor: The University of Michigan Press, 1996.

Besold, Christoph. *Dissertatio politico-iuridica de majestate in genere: ejusque juribus specialibus, in tres sectiones distributa*. Strasbourg: Lazar Zetzner, 1625.

Beyer, Justin de, ed. *Lettres de critique de littérature, d'histoire, &c. écrites à divers savans de l'Europe, par feu Monsieur Gisbert Cuper*. Amsterdam: J. Wetstein, 1743.

Bianchini, Francesco. *La istoria universale, provata con monumenti, e figurata con simboli de gli antichi*. Rome: Antonio de Rossi, 1697.

Bianchini, Francesco. *Solutio problematis paschalis*. Rome: Typis Rev. Cam. Apost., 1703.

Bianchini, Francesco. *Opuscula varia*. 2 vols. Rome: Giovanni Lorenzo Barbiellini, 1754.

Boccaccio, Giovanni. *Genealogy of the Pagan Gods*. Edited by Jon Solomon. Cambridge MA: Harvard University Press, 2011.

Bochart, Samuel. *Geographia sacra pars prior Phaleg seu de dispersione gentium et terrarum divisione facta et pars altera Chanaan seu de coloniis et sermone Phoenicum*. Caen: Pierre de Cardonnel, 1646.

Bochart, Samuel. *Hierozoicon sive Bipartitum opus de animalibus sacrae scripturae.* London: Thomas Roycroft, 1663.

Bolingbroke, Henry St. John, Viscount. "The Substance of Some Letters written originally in French about the year 1720 to M. de Pouilly." In *The Works of Lord Henry St. John Bolingbroke,* 2:462–484. Philadelphia: Carey and Hart, 1841.

Bompart, Johannes. *Parallela sacra et profana, sive notae in Genesin.* Amsterdam: Johannes Wolters, 1689.

Bona, Giovanni. *Joannis Bona s.r.e. Tit. S. Bernardi ad thermas presbyteri cardinalis ordinis Cisterciensis pedemontani patritii montis-regalis Epistolae selectae aliaeque eruditorum sui temporis virorum ad eumdem scriptae, una cum nonnullis ipsius analectis.* Edited by Roberto Sala. Turin: Ex typographia regia, 1755.

Bonaventure d'Argonne, Noël. *A mélanges d'histoire et de littérature.* 3 vols. Paris: Augustin Besoigne, 1700.

Bonfrère, Jacques. *Pentateuchus Moysis commentario illustratus.* Antwerp: Plantin, 1625.

Bonjour, Guillaume. *Dissertatio de nomine patriarchae Josephi a pharaone imposito, in defensionem Vulgatae editionis, et patrum qui Josephum in Serapide adumbratum tradiderunt. Appendix altera de tempore Serapiorum ac Passionis S. Marci Evangelistae.* Rome: Francesco de Rubeis & Francesco Maria Acsamitek à Kronenfeld, 1696.

Bonjour, Guillaume. *In monumenta Coptica seu Aegyptiaca bibliothecae Vaticanae brevis exercitatio.* Rome: Francesco de Rubeis & Francesco Maria Acsamitek à Kronenfeld, 1699.

Bonjour, Guillaume. *Calendarium Romanum, chronologum causa constructum cum gemino epactarum dispositu, ad noviluna civilia sine tabulis astronomicis accurate & facile ante, & post Christum natum invenienda, juxta methodum periodi annorum 1932 directae ad cyclum perpetuum epactarum tetraetericarum, sive quadriennalium, stylo tam Juliano, quam Gregoriano.* Rome: Giovanni Francesco Buagni, 1701.

Bonjour, Guillaume. *Tractatus de computo ecclesiastico.* Montefiascone: Ex typographia Seminarii, 1702.

Bonjour, Guillaume. *Triduanda de canone librorum sacrorum concertatio.* Montefiascone: Ex typographia Seminarii, 1704.

Bonjour, Guillaume. *Selectae in sacram scripturam dissertationes.* Montefiascone: Ex typographia Seminarii, 1705.

Bonjour, Guillaume. *Dissertatio in historiam sacram primae mundi aetatis, habita per dialogos in academia divinarum literarum seminarii Montis-Falisci.* Montefiascone: Ex typographia Seminarii, 1705.

Bonjour, Guillaume. *Quaestiones evangelicae proponendae in Academia Divinarum literarum et solvendae à theologis seminarii Montis-Falisci.* Montefiascone: Ex typographia Seminarii, 1705.

Bonjour, Guillaume. *Academica exercitatio in scripturam sacram et ritus ecclesiasticos.* Montefiascone: Ex typographia Seminarii, 1705.

Bonjour, Guillaume. *Academica exercitatio in scripturam sacram et ritus ecclesiasticos.* Montefiascone: Ex typographia Seminarii, 1706.

Bouges, Thomas. *Dissertation historique et polemique sur les soixante-dix semaines du prophète Daniel.* Toulouse: G. Robert, 1702.

Bouget, Jean. *Brevis exercitatio ad studium linguae hebraicae.* Montefiascone: Ex typographia Seminarii, 1706.

Braun, Johannes. *Vestitus sacerdotum Hebraeorum.* Leiden: Arnoldus Doudius, 1680.

Broughton, Hugh. *A Concent of Scripture.* London: William White, 1588.

Brücker, Johann Jakob. *Historia critica philosophiae a mundi incunabulis ad nostram usque aetatem deducta.* 5 vols. Leipzig: Bernard Christoph Breitkopf, 1742–1744.

Bruno, Giordano. *Spaccio de la bestia trionfante, proposto da Gioue.* Paris: 1584.

Buddeus, Johann Franz. "In monumenta Coptica seu Aegyptiaca." *Acta eruditorum* (1699): 232–236.

Burnet, Thomas. *Telluris theoria sacra. Originem & mutationes generales, quas aut jam subiit, aut olim subiturus est, complectens.* London: G. Kettilby, 1681.

Caillemer, Exupère, ed. *Lettres de divers savants à l'abbé Nicaise publiées pour l'academie des sciences, belles-lettres et arts de Lyon.* Lyon: Association Typographique, 1885.

Calvoli, Giovanni Cinelli. *Biblioteca volante di Gio Cinelli Calvoli.* 4 vols. Venice: Giambattista Albrizzi Q. Girolamo, 1734–1747.

Campori, Mattia, ed. *Epistolario di L. A. Muratori.* 14 vols. Modena: Società Tipografica Modenese, 1901–1922.

Cappel, Jacques. *Historia sacra et exotica ab Adamo usque ad Augustum.* Sedan: Jean Iannon, 1613.

Carpzov, Johann Gottlieb. *Critica sacra Veteris Testamenti.* Leipzig, Johann Christian Martin, 1748.

Cassini, Giovanni Domenico. "Article XIII; Remarques de M. Cassini sur le Calendrier du P. Bonjour." *Journal de Trévoux* (1702): 148–158.

Cassiodorus. *Cassiodorus: Institutions of Divine and Secular Learning and On the Soul.* Translated by James W. Halporn. Liverpool: Liverpool University Press, 2004.

Celsius, Olof. *Hierobotanicon, sive de plantis sacrae scripturae.* Amsterdam: J. Wettstein, 1748.

Censorinus. *Censorini de die natali liber.* Edited by Ivan Cholodniak. St. Petersburg: Russian Imperial Academy of Sciences, 1889.

Chamberlayne, John, ed. *Dissertationes ex occasione sylloges orationum dominicarum scriptae ad Joannem Chamberlaynium.* Amsterdam: William and David Goereus, 1715.

Champollion, Jean-François. *L'Égypte sous les pharaons, ou recherches sur la géographie, la religion, la langue, les écritures et l'histoire de l'Égypte avant l'invasion de Cambyse.* 2 vols. Paris: Bure frères, 1814.

Charmot, Nicolas, ed. *Historia cultus Sinensium seu varia scripta de cultibus Sinarum, inter vicarios apostolicos Gallos aliosque missionarios, & patres Societatis Jesu controversis.* Cologne: 1700.

Charmot, Nicolas, ed. *Continuatio Historia cultus Sinensium seu varia scripta de cultibus Sinarum, inter vicarios apostolicos Gallos aliosque missionarios & patres Societatis Jesu controversis.* Cologne: 1700.

Chevreau, Urbain. *Histoire du monde.* Paris: Edme Martin and Jean Boudot, 1686.

Clarke, Edward Daniel. *Travels in Various Countries of Europe, Asia and Africa.* 6 vols. London: T. Cadwell and W. Davies, 1810–1823.

Clüver, Philipp. *Germaniae antiquae libri tres.* Leiden: Lodewijk Elzevir, 1616.

Cicero. *De natura deorum.* Translated by H. Rackham. Cambridge MA: Harvard University Press, 1951.

Conring, Hermann. *Asiae et Aegypti antiquissimis dynastiis adversaris chronologica.* Helmstedt: Henning Müller, 1648.

Cotta, Giambattista. *Dio, sonetti, ed inni di F. Gio Battista Cotta, colle annotazioni dello stesso.* Venice: Tommaso Bettinelli, 1745.

Couplet, Philippe, Prospero Intorcetta, Heinrich Herdtrich, and Francis Rougemont, ed. *Confucius Sinarum philosophus sive Scientiae Sinensis latine exposita.* Paris: Daniel Horthemels, 1687.

Cousin, Victor, ed. *Fragments philosophiques.* 2 vols. Paris: Ladrange, 1838.

Crescenzi, Giovanni Maria, ed. *Le vite degli arcadi illustri, scritte da diversi autori.* 5 vols. Rome: Antonio de Rossi, 1708–1751.

Cudworth, Ralph. *Radulphi Cudworthi Systema intellectuale huius universi seu de veris naturae rerum originibus.* Edited by Lorenz Mosheim. 2 vols. Jena: Vidva Meyer, 1733.

Cumberland, Richard. *Sanchoniatho's Phoenician History, Translated from the First Book of Eusebius De Praeparatio Evangelica. With a Continuation of Sanchoniatho's History by Eratosthenes Cyrenaeus's Canon, which Dichaearchus connects with the First Olympiad.* London: R. Wilkin, 1720.

Cuper, Gisbert. *Harpocrates sive explicatio imagunculae argentae perantiquae; quae in figuram Harpocratis formata representat solem. Ejusdem monumenta antiqua inedita.* Amsterdam: Theodore Pluymer, 1676.

Cuper, Gisbert. *Apotheosis vel consecratio Homeri. Sive, lapis antiquissimus in quo poetarum principis Homeri consecratio sculpta est, commentario illustratus.* Amsterdam: Hendrick and Theodore Boom, 1683.

Cuper, Gisbert. *Harpocrates sive explicatio imagunculae argentae perantiquae; quae in figuram Harpocratis formata representat solem. Ejusdem monumenta antiqua inedita.* Utrecht: François Halma, 1687.

Cuper, Gisbert, and Pierre Jurieu ed. *Supplément a l'histoire critique des dogmes et des cultes, &etc. ou dissertation par lettres de Monsieur Cuper.* Amsterdam: François l'Honoré, 1705.

Cusa, Nicholas of. *Die Kalenderverbesserung: De correctione kalendarii*. Edited by Viktor Stegemann. Heidelberg: F. H. Kerle Verlag, 1955.

Dale, Anthonie van. *Dissertatio super Aristea de LXX. interpretibus*. Amsterdam: Johannes Wolters, 1705.

Delavaud, Louis and Charles Dangibeaud, ed. "Lettres de Michel Bégon." In *Archives historiques de la Saintonge et de l'Aunis* 47–48. Paris and Saintes: A. Picard and Delavaud, 1925–1930.

Derodon, David. *Disputatio theologica, de existentia Dei*. Geneva: Pierre Chouët, 1661.

Deseine, Jacques-François. *Rome moderne, première ville de l'Europe, avec tout ses magnificences et ses delices*. 6 vols. Leiden, Pieter vander Aa, 1713.

Diodorus Siculus. *Library of History*. Edited by C. H. Oldfather. Cambridge MA: Harvard University Press, 1933.

Dirois, François. *Preuves et préjugés pour la religion Chrétienne et Catholique contre les fausses religions et l'athéisme*. Paris: Étienne Michallet, 1683.

Dodwell, Henry. *A discourse concerning Sanchoniathon's Phoenician History*. London, Benjamin Tooke, 1681.

Du Boys, Émile, ed. *Les correspondants de l'abbé Nicaise I. Un diplomate érudit du XVII siècle: Ézéchiel Spanheim lettres inédites (1681–1701)*. Paris: Alphonse Picard, 1889.

Du Halde, Jean-Baptiste. *Description géographique, historique, chronologique, politique, et physique de l'Empire de la Chine de de la Tartarie Chinoise*. 2 vols. The Hague: Henri Scheurleer, 1736.

Dupin, Louis Ellies. *Dissertation préliminaire ou Prolégomènes sur la Bible*. 2 vols. Paris: André Pralard, 1699.

Dupin, Louis Ellies. *Bibliothèque universelle des historiens*. 2 vols. Paris: Pierre Giffart, 1707.

Dupin, Louis Ellies. *Bibliothèque des auteurs ecclésiastiques du XVIIe siècle*. 7 vols. Paris: André Pralard, 1708.

Dupin, Louis Ellies. "Paul Pezron." *Nouvelle bibliothèque des auteurs ecclesiastiques* 19 (1715): 156–171.

Edwards, John. *A Discourse Concerning the Authority, Stile, and Perfection of the Books of the Old and New Testament*. London: Richard Wilkin, 1693.

Elisseff, Danielle, ed. *Moi, Arcade: interprète chinois du Roi-Soleil*. Paris: Arthaud, 1985.

English College of Douai. *The Holie Bible Faithfully Translated into English out of the authentical Latin, diligently conferred with the Hebrew, Greek, & other Editions in divers languages*. Douai: John Cousturier, 1635.

Euripides. *Fragments: Aegus-Meleager*. Edited by Christopher Collard and Martin Cropp. Cambridge MA: Harvard University Press, 2008.

Eusebius, *Eusebii Pamphili evangelica praeparationis libri XV*. Edited by E. H. Gifford. 4 vols. Oxford: Oxford University Press, 1903.

Fabricius, Johann Albert, ed. *Procli philosophi platonici vita, scriptore Marino Neapolitano*. Hamburg: Gottfried Liebezeit, 1700.

Fabricius, Johann Albert, ed. *Bibliotheca graeca liber IV de libris sacris novi foederis, Philone item atq: Josepho, & aliis scriptoribus claris a tempore nati Christi*. 3 vols. Hamburg: Christian Liebezeit, 1708.

Fabricy, Gabriel. *Recherches sur l'époque de l'équitation et de l'usage des chars équestres chez les anciens où l'on montre l'incertitude des premiers temps historiques des peuples, relativement à cette datte*. 2 vols. Marseille and Rome: Jean Mossy and Pierre Durand, 1764.

Feller, Joachim Friedrich, ed. *Otium Hanoveranum, sive miscellanea ex ore & schedis illustris viri, piae memoriae Godofr. Guilielmi Leibnitii*. Leipzig: Johann Christopher Martin, 1718.

Ficino, Marsilio, ed. *Divini Platonis Opera Omnia quae exstant*. Frankfurt: Claude de Marne, 1602.

Fossier, François, ed. *L'abbé Claude Nicaise facteur du Parnasse*. Paris: L'Harmattan, 2019.

Fourmont, Étienne. *Réflexions critiques sur les histoires des anciens peuples, chaldéens, hébreux, phéniciens, égyptiens, grecs, &c. jusqu'au tems de Cyrus*. 3 vols. Paris: Musier, Jombert, Briasson, Bullot 1735.

Foy-Vaillant, Jean. *Seleucidarum imperium, sive Historia regum Syriae ad fidem numismatum accommodata*. Paris: Louis Billaine, 1681.

Foy-Vaillant, Jean. *Numismata aerea imperatorum Augustarum et Caesarum, in coloniis, municipiis, et urbibus jure latio donatis, ex omni modulo percussa*. 2 vols. Paris: Edm. Martin, Jean Boudot, Etienne Martin, 1688.

Fréret, Nicolas. "Recherches sur le Culte de Bacchus parmi les Grecs." *Histoire de l'Académie royale des inscriptions et belles-lettres* 23 (1756): 242–270.

Fréret, Nicolas. *Défense de la chronologie fondée sur les monumens de l'histoire ancienne, contre le système chronologique de M. Newton*. Paris: Durand, 1758.

Fulgentius. *Fulgentius the Mythographer*. Edited by Leslie George Whitbread. Columbus: Ohio State University Press, 1971.

Gale, Theophilus. *The Court of the Gentiles: or A Discourse touching the Original of Human Literature, both Philologie and Philosophie, from the Scripture & Jewish Church*. 2 vols. Oxford: H. Hall, 1672–1676.

Gandolfo, Domenico Antonio. *Dissertatio historica de ducentis celeberrimis Augustinianis scriptoribus ex illis, qui obierunt post magnam unionem Ordinis Eremitici usque ad finem Tridentini Concilii*. Rome: Giovanni Francesco Buagni, 1704.

Gibbon, Edward. *Decline and Fall of the Roman Empire*. 6 vols. New York: Alfred A. Knopf, 1993.

Gigas, Émile ed. *Lettres inédites de divers savants de la fin du XVIIme et de commencement du XVIIIme siècle*. 2 vols. Copenhagen: G.E.C. GAD, 1892.

Gimma, Giacinto. *Elogj Academici della Società di deglie spensierati di Rossano Parte II*. Napoli: Carlo Troise, 1703.

Giorgi, Agostino Antonio. *Alphabetum tibetanum missionum apostolicarum*. Rome: Propaganda fide, 1762.

Giorgi, Agostino Antonio. *Fragmentum evangelii S. Iohannis Graeco-Copto-Thebaicum saeculi IV. Additamentum ex vetustissimis membranis lectionum evangelicarum divinae missae cod. diaconici reliquiae et liturgica alia fragmenta veteris thebaidensium ecclesiae ante dioscorum ex veliterno Museo Borgiano nun prodeunt in latinum versa et notis illustrata*. Rome: Antonio Fulgoni, 1789.

Giorgi, Agostino Antonio. *De miraculis Sancti Coluthi et reliquiis actorum Sancti Panesniu martyrum thebaica fragmenta duo alterum auctius alterum nunc primum*. Rome: Antonio Fulgoni, 1793.

Giraldi, Giglio Gregorio. *De deis gentium varia & multiplex historia*. Basel: Johannes Oporinus, 1548.

Gosse, Philipp Henry. *Omphalos: An Attempt to Untie the Geological Knot*. London: John van Voorst, 1857.

Graverol, François, and Jean-Pierre Rigord. *Dissertation de Monsieur Graverol avocat de Nismes à Monsieur Rigord de Marseille, sur l'explication d'une médaille grecque qui porte le nom du dieu Pan*. Marseille: Jean Anisson, 1689.

Graveson, Ignace-Hyacinthe Amat de. *Historia ecclesiastica Veteris Testamenti in rem theologiae candidatorum*. ...3 vols. Rome: Hieronymus Maynard, 1727.

Grotius, Hugo. *Sensus librorum sex, quos pro veritate religionis Christianae*. Leiden: Johannes Maire, 1627.

Grotius, Hugo. *De veritate religionis Christianae*. Leiden: Johannes Maire, 1633.

Grotius, Hugo. *De veritate religionis Christianae. Editio nova, additis annotationibus in quibus testimonia*. Paris: Sébastien Cramoisy, 1640.

Grotius, Hugo. *The Truth of the Christian Religion in Six Books*. Edited by Jean Le Clerc. Translated by John Clarke. London: John and Paul Knapton, 1743.

Gruter, Jan. *Inscriptiones antiquae totius orbis Romani*. Heidelberg: Ex Officina Commeliniana, 1602–1603.

Hale, Matthew. *The Primitive Origination of Mankind, Considered and Examined According to The Light of Nature*. London: William Godbid, 1677.

Hardouin, Jean. *Nummi antiqui populorum et urbium illustrati*. Paris: François Muguet, 1684.

Herodotus. *Les histoires d'Hérodote*. Translated by André Du Ryer. Paris: Antoine de Sommaville & Augustin Courbé, 1645.

Herodotus. *Histoire d'Hérodote traduite du Grec*. Translated by Pierre Henri Larcher. Paris: Musier & Nyon, 1786.

Herodotus. *The Persian Wars*. Translated by A. D. Godley. Cambridge MA: Harvard University Press, 1926.

Herodotus. *The Landmark Herodotus: The Histories*. Edited by Robert B. Strassler. New York: Anchor Books, 2007.

Hodges, E. Richmond, ed. *Ancient Fragments of the Phoenician, Carthaginian, Babylonian, Egyptian and other Authors*. London: Reeves & Turner, 1876.

Hody, Humphrey. *Contra historiam Aristeae de LXX interpretibus dissertatio. In quae probatur illam a Judaeo aliquo confictam fuisse ad conciliandam authoritatem versioni Graecae. Et quorundam doctorum virorum defensiones ejusdem, examini subjiciuntur*. Oxford: Leonard Lichfield and Anthony Stephens, 1684.

Holste, Lukas. *Codex regularum quas sancti patres monachis et virginibus sanctimonialibus servandas praescipsere*. Rome: Vitale Mascardi, 1661.

Horn, Georg. *Historiae philosophicae libri septem*. Leiden: Johannes Elzevir, 1655.

Horn, Georg. *Georgii Hornii dissertatio de vera aetate mundi: qua sententia illorum refellitur qui statunt natale mundi tempus annis minimum 1440. vulgarem aeram anticipare*. Leiden: Johannes Elzevir, 1659.

Horn, Georg. *Brevis et perspicua introductio ad universalem historiam*. Leiden: Hackiana, 1665.

Huet, Pierre-Daniel. *Demonstratio evangelica ad serenissimum Delphinum. Editio altera emendatior, in qua additamenta auctoris singula suis locis sunt inserta*. Amsterdam: Janssonio Waesbergios, & Hendrick & Theodore Boom, 1680.

Huet, Pierre-Daniel. *Dissertations sur diverses matieres de religion et de philologie*. Edited by Jean Marie de la Marque de Tilladet. 2 vols. Paris: François Fournier, 1712.

Huet, Pierre-Daniel. *Commentarius de rebus ad eum pertinentibus*. Amsterdam: Henri du Sauzet, 1718.

Huet, Pierre-Daniel. *Memoirs of the Life of Peter Daniel Huet, Bishop of Avranches: written by himself; and translated from the original Latin with copious Notes, Biographical and Critical*. Edited by John Aikin. 2 vols. London: Longman, Hurst, Rees, Orme, and Cadell and Davies, 1810.

Isidore of Seville. *The Etymologies of Isidore of Seville*. Translated by Stephen A. Barney, W. J. Lewis, J. A. Beach, and Oliver Berghof. Cambridge: Cambridge University Press, 2006.

Jacoby, Felix, ed. *Die Fragmente der griechischen Historiker*. 3 vols. Berlin and Leiden: Weidmann and Brill, 1923–1958.

Jobert, Louis. *La science des médailles nouvelle édition*. Edited by Joseph de Bimard de La Bastie. 2 vols. Paris: De Bure, 1739.

Jordan, Charles Étienne, ed. *Histoire de la vie et des ouvrages de Mr. La Croze*. Amsterdam: François Changuion, 1741.

Josephus, Flavius. *Flavii Josephi opera*. Edited by Benedikt Niese. 5 vols. Berlin: Weidmann, 1885–1895.

Josephus, Flavius. *The Latin Josephus: Introduction and Text, the Antiquities: Books 1-V.* Edited by Franz Blatt. Copenhagen: Universitetsforlaget 1 Aarhus, Ejnar Munksgaard, 1958.

Jurieu, Pierre. *Histoire critique des dogmes et des cultes, bons & mauvais, qui ont été dans l'Église depuis Adam, jusqu'à Jésus-Christ, ou l'on trouve l'origine de toutes les idolâtries de l'ancien paganisme, expliquées par rapport à celle des Juifs.* Amsterdam: François l'Honoré, 1704.

Juvenal and Persius. *Juvenal and Persius.* Edited by G. G. Ramsay. London and New York: William Heinemann and G. P. Putnam's Sons, 1928.

Juvenal and Persius. *Juvenal and Persius.* Edited by Susanna Morton Braund. Cambridge MA: Harvard University Press, 2004.

Kircher, Athanasius. *Prodromus coptus sive aegyptiacus.* Rome: Typis S. Cong. de Propaganda fide, 1636.

Kircher, Athanasius. *Lingua Aegyptiaca restituta opus tripartitum.* Rome: Ludovico Grignano, 1643.

Kircher, Athanasius. *Obeliscus Pamphilius hoc est, interpretatio nova & hucusque intentata obelisci hierohlyphici quem non ita pridem ex veteri Hippodromo Antonini Caracallae Caesaris, in agonale forum transtulit, integritati restituit, & in urbis aeternae ornamentum erexit ...* Rome: Propaganda fide, 1650.

Kircher, Athanasius. *Oedipus Aegyptiacus.* 3 vols. Rome: Vitale Mascardi, 1652–1654.

Kircher, Athanasius. *China monumentis qua sacris qua profanis, nec non variis naturae & artis spectaculis, aliarumque rerum memorabilium argumentis illustrata.* Amsterdam: Jacob à Meurs, 1667.

Kircher, Athanasius. *Turris Babel, sive Archontologia.* Amsterdam: Janssonio-Waesbergios, 1679.

Kohlreif, Gottfried. *Chronologia sacra a mundo condito.* Hamburg: Theodor Christoph Felginer, 1724.

Kriegsmann, Wilhelm Christoph. *Conjecturaneorum de Germanicae gentis origine, ac conditore Hermete Trismegisto, qui S. Moysi est Chanaan, Tacito Tuito, Mercuriusque gentilibus.* Tübingen: Philibert Brunn, 1684.

Lactantius. *Divine Institutes.* Edited by Anthony Bowen and Peter Garnsey. Liverpool: Liverpool University Press, 2003.

Langius, Wilhelm. "de Veteri anno Romanorum." In *Thesaurus antiquitatum Romanarum,* 8:398–418. Edited by Johann Georg Graevius. Utrecht and Leiden: François Halma and Pieter vander Aa, 1698.

La Peyrère, Isaac. *Praeadamitae sive Exercitatio super versibus duodecimo, decimo-tertio, & decimoquarto, capitis quinti epistolae D. Pauli ad Romanos. Quibus inducuntur primi homines ante Adamum conditi.* Leiden: Daniel Elzevir, 1655.

La Peyrère, Isaac. *Systema theologicum, ex praeadamitarum hypothesi*. Leiden: Daniel Elzevir, 1655.

La Peyrère, Isaac. *Men before Adam, or A Discourse upon the twelfth, thirteenth and fourteenth Verses of the Fifth Chapter of the Epistle of the Apostle Paul to the Romans. By which are prov'd That the first Men were created before Adam*. [?]: 1656.

La Peyrère, Isaac. *Praeadamitae-Systema theologicum (1655)*. Edited by Herbert Jaumann, Reimund B. Sdzuj, and Franziska Borkert. 2 vols. Stuttgart-Bad Cannstatt: Frommann-Holzboog, 2019.

Lapide, Cornelius à. *In Pentateuchum Mosis commentaria*. Paris: Robert Foüet, 1626.

Le Clerc, Jean. "Temporum Mythicorum Historia per Generationes digesta, in qua quid in antiquis fabulis latent Historica aperitur." *Bibliothèque universelle et historique* 1 (1686): 245–280.

Le Clerc, Jean. *Genesis sive Mosis prophetae liber primus*. Tübingen: Johann Georg Cotta, 1693.

Le Clerc, Jean. "Dissertation V: Concerning the Flood." In *Twelve Dissertations out of Monsieur Le Clerk's Genesis*. Translated by Thomas Brown. London: R. Baldwin, 1696.

Le Clerc, Jean. *Ars Critica in qua ad studia linguarum Latinae, Graecae, & Hebraicae via munitur; veterumque emendandorum, & spuriorum scriptorum a genuinis dignoscendorum ratio traditur*. 3 vols. Amsterdam: G. Gallet, 1697.

Le Clerc, Jean. "Article VI." *Bibliothèque choisie: pour servir de suite à la Bibliothèque universelle* 5 (1705): 358–374.

Le Clerc, Jean. "Article II: remarques sur le livre de *Jean Selden* intitulé *des Dieux des Syriens*." *Bibliothèque choisie: pour servir de suite à la Bibliothèque universelle* 7 (1705): 80–146.

Le Clerc, Jean. "Article IV." *Bibliothèque choisie: pour servir de suite à la Bibliothèque universelle* 15 (1708): 187–246.

Le Clerc, Jean, ed. *Veteris Testamenti libri historici, Josua, Judices, Rutha, Samuel, Reges, Paralipomena, Esdras, Nehemias et Esthera*. Amsterdam: Henri Schelte, 1708.

Le Clerc, Jean. "Veteris Testamenti Libri Historici." *Bibliothèque choisie* 16 (1708): 61–166.

Le Clerc, Jean, ed. *Hugo Grotius De veritate religionis Christianae. Editio novissima, in qua eiusdem annotationes ipsius textus verbis subiectae sunt*. Leipzig: Johann Friedrich Gleditsch, 1709.

Le Clerc, Jean. "Article V: Novum Testamentum Aegyptium, vulgo Copticum." *Bibliothèque ancienne et moderne: pour servir de suite aux Bibliothèques universelle et choisie* 7 (1717): 197–204.

Le Clerc, Jean. "Flavii Josephi Opera." *Bibliothèque ancienne et moderne; pour servir de suite aux Bibliothèques universelle et choisie* 14 (1720): 237–306.

Le Clerc, Jean. *Epistolario*. Edited by Mario Sina and Maria Grazia Zaccone-Sina. 4 vols. Florence: L. S. Olschki, 1987–1997.

Le Comte, Louis. *Nouveaux mémoires sur l'état présent de la Chine*. 3 vols. Paris: Jean Anisson, 1696.

Le Comte, Louis. *Memoirs and remarks geographical, historical, topographical, physical, natural, astronomical, mechanical, military, mercantile, political, and ecclesiastical. Made in about Ten Years Travels through the empire of China* ... London: John Hughs, 1738.

Leibniz, Gottfried Wilhelm. *Illustris viri Godofr. Guilielmi Leibnitii collectanea etymologica*. Hanover: Nicolai Foerster, 1717.

Leibniz, Gottfried Wilhelm. *Gothofredi Guillelmi Leibnitii opera omnia*. Edited by Louis Dutens. 6 vols. Geneva: Fratres de Tournes, 1768.

Leibniz, Gottfried Wilhelm. *Sämtliche Schriften und Briefe*. Edited by the Academy of Sciences of Berlin. Series I–VIII. Darmstadt, Leipzig, and Berlin: Akademie Verlag, 1923-.

Leibniz, Gottfried Wilhelm. *Discours sur la Théologie Naturelle des Chinois*. Edited by Wenchao Li and Hans Poser. Frankfurt am Main: Vittorio Klostermann, 2002.

Lequien, Michel. *Défense du texte hébreu et de la version Vulgate; servant de réponse au livre intitulé; l'Antiquité des temps*. Paris: Amable Auroy, 1690.

Leibniz, Gottfried Wilhelm. *L'antiquité des tems détruite, ou Réponse à la Défense de l'antiquité des tems*. Paris: J. Villery, 1693.

Leydekker, Melchior. *De republica Hebraeorum libri XII*. Amsterdam: Isaac Stokmans, 1704.

Liceti, Fortunio. *De lucernis antiquorum reconditis libb. sex*. Padua: Nicola Schiratti, 1652.

Locke, John. *Locke's Travels in France 1675–1679. As related in his Journals, Correspondence and other papers*. Edited by John Lough. Cambridge: Cambridge University Press, 1953.

Locke, John. *An Essay Concerning Human Understanding*. Edited by Peter H. Nidditch. Oxford: Clarendon Press, 1975.

Longobardo, Niccolò. *Traité sur quelques Points de la Religion des Chinois*. Paris: Louis Guerin, 1701.

Lubin, Augustin. *Orbis Augustinianus sive conventuum ordinis eremitarum sancti Augustini chorographica & topographica descriptio*. Paris: Giles Alliot, 1672.

Lucian. *The Syrian Goddess*. Translated by Herbert A. Strong and John Garstang. London: Constable & Company, 1913.

Lundström, Enni, ed. *Olof Celsius d. ä:s Diarium öfver sin resa; Italien åren 1697 och 1698*. Gothenburg: Eranos Förlag, 1909.

Mabillon, Jean, and Michel Germain. *Museum Italicum seu Collectio veterum scriptorum ex bibliothecis Italicis*. Paris: Edmund Martin, Jean Boudot, Etienne Martin, 1687.

Macrobius. *Saturnalia*. Edited by Robert A. Kaster. Cambridge MA: Harvard University Press, 2011.

Magliabechi, Antonio. *Clarorum Belgarum ad Ant. Magliabechium nonnullosque alios epistolae*. 2 vols. Florence: Ex typographia Magni Ducis, 1745.

Manetho. *Manetho*. Edited by W. G. Waddell. Cambridge MA: Harvard University Press, 1940.

Manfredi, Eustachio. *Epistola ad virum clarissimum Dominicum Quartaironium qua anonymi assertiones XVI pro reformatione calendarii*. Venice: Antonio Bortoli, 1705.

Manilius. *Manili quinque libros Astronomicon commentarius et castigationes*. Edited by Joseph Scaliger. Paris: Robert Étienne, 1579.

Manilius. *Astronomica*. Translated by G. P. Goold. Cambridge MA: Harvard University Press, 1977.

Marsham, John. *Canon chronicus Aegyptiacus, Ebraicus, Graecus, et disquisitiones*. London: Thomas Roycroft and William Wells & Robert Scott, 1672.

Marshal, Jean. "Extrait d'une lettre de Mr. Jean Marshal écrite des Indes Orientales au Sieur Coga, contenant une relation de la religion, des rites, notions, coutumes, & mœurs des prêtres payens, appellez communément Brachmanes." *Journal de Trévoux* 1 (1701): 185–188.

Marshal, Jean. "Account of the Religion, Rites, Notions, Customs, Manners of the Indian Priests, called Bramins." *The Philosophical Transactions of the Royal Society of London* 4 (1809): 534–540.

Martianay, Jean. *Défense du texte hébreu et de la chronologie de la Vulgate contre le livre de L'antiquité des tems rétablie*. Paris: L. Roulland, 1689.

Martianay, Jean. *Continuation de la défense du texte hébreu et de la Vulgate, par des veritables traditions des églises chrétiennes & par tout sortes d'anciens monumens hebreux, grecs, & latins*. Paris: Pierre de Bats, 1693.

Martianay, Jean, ed. *Sancti Hieronymi operum*. 5 vols. Paris: Jean Anisson, 1693–1706.

Martini, Martino. *Sinicae historiae decas prima*. Munich: Lukas Straub, 1658.

Melanchthon, Philipp, and Johann Carion. *Chronicon Carionis latine expositum et auctum multis et veteribus et recentibus historiis, in narrationibus rerum graecarum, germanicarum et ecclesiasticarum*. Wittenberg: Georg Rhau, 1558.

Mencke, Friedrich Otto, ed. *Miscellanea lipsiensia nova ad incrementum scientarum*. Leipzig: B. Lanckischens Erben, 1752–1753.

Meynard, Thierry, ed. *Confucius Sinarum Philosophus (1687): The First Translation of the Confucian Classics*. Rome: Institutum Historicum Societatis Iesu, 2011.

Meynard, Thierry, ed. *The Jesuit Reading of Confucius: The First Complete Translation of the Luyen (1687) Published in the West*. Leiden: Brill, 2015.

Michaelis, Augustus Benedictus, ed. *Iobi Ludolfi et Godofredi Guilielmi Leibnitii commercium epistolicum*. Göttingen: Victorinus Bossigelius, 1755.

Michaelis, Gregor. *Notae in Jacobi Gaffarelli Curiositates*. Hamburg: Gottfried Schultzen, 1676.

Milton, John. *Paradise Lost*. Edited by Alastair Fowler. New York: Routledge, 2007.

Misson, Maximilien. *A new voyage to Italy. With curious observations on several other countries; as, Germany; Switzerland; Savoy; Geneva; Flanders; and Holland. Together with useful instructions for those who shall travel thither*. 4 vols. London: R. Bonwicke, Ja. Tonson, W. Freemen, Tim. Goodwin, J. Walthoe, M. Wotton, S. Manship, B. Tooker, J. Nicholson, R. Parker, and R. Smith, 1714.

Monceaux, François de. *Aaron purgatus sive de vitulo aureo, libri duo*. Arras: Guillaume Rivière, 1606.

Montanus, Benedictus Arias, ed. *Biblia sacra, hebraice, chaldaice, graece et latine ...* 8 vols. Antwerp: Christophe Plantin, 1569–1573.

Montesquieu. *My Thoughts*. Edited by Henry C. Clark. Indianapolis: Liberty Fund, 2012.

Montfaucon, Bernard de. *Diarium Italicum sive monumentorum veterum, bibliothecarum, musaeorum, & c*. Paris: Jean Anisson, 1702.

Montfaucon, Bernard de. *Paleographia Graeca, sive De ortu et progressu literarum Graecarum*. Paris: Louis Guerin, Jean Boudot, & Carol Robustel, 1708.

Montfaucon, Bernard de. *The Travels of the Learned Father Montfaucon from Paris thro' Italy*. Translated by John Henley. London: D. L. for E. Curll, E. Sanger, R. Gosling, W. Lewis, 1712.

Montfaucon, Bernard de. *L'antiquité expliquée et représentée en figures*. 5 vols. Paris: Jean Geoffroy Nyon, Etienne Ganeau, Nicolas Gosselin, and Pierre François Giffart, 1719–1724.

Muratori, Ludovico Antonio, ed. *Anecdota, quae ex Ambrosianae bibliothecae codicibus nunc primum eruit, notis, ac disquisitionibus auget Ludovicus Antonius Muratorius, in easdem bibliotheca Ambrosiani collegij doctor tomus prior quatuor S. Paulini episcopi Nolani poemata complectens*. Milan: Gioseffo Pandolfi Malatesta, 1697.

Navarette, Domingo. *Tratados históricos, políticos, éthicos, y religiosos de la monarchia de China*. Madrid: Florian Anisson, 1676.

Nicaise, Claude. *Les sirenes, ou Discours sur leur forme et figure*. Paris: Jean Anisson, 1691.

Noris, Enrico. *Historia Pelagiana & dissertatio de synodo v. oecumenica in qua Origenis ac Theodori Mopsuesteni Pelagiani erroris Auctorum iusta damnatio exponitur, et Aquileiense schisma describitur. Additis vindiciis Augustinianis ...* Padua: Pietro Maria Frambotti, 1673.

Noris, Enrico. *Cenotaphia pisana Caii et Lucii Caesarum dissertationibus illustrata. Coloniae Obsequentis Iuliae Pisanae origo, vetusti magistratus, & sacerdotum collegia: Caeesaris utriusque vita, gesta, & annuae eorundem inferiae exponuntur: ac aurea utriusque Cenotaphij Latinitas demonstratur. Parergon de annis regni Herodis: de praesidibus Syriae, ac Romanis in Asia provincijs*. Venice: Paulo Balleoni, 1681.

Noris, Enrico. *Diagramma cycli civilis et ecclesiastici annorum LXXXIV in sex tessaradecaeteridas distributi*. Florence: Typographia Sereniss. Magni Ducis, 1691.

Noris, Enrico. *Annus et epochae syromacedonum in vetustis urbium Syriae nummis praesertim Mediceis expositae. Additis fastis consularibus anonymi omnium optimis. Accesserunt nuper Dissertationes de Paschali Latinorum cyclo annorum LXXXIV, ac Ravennate annorum XCV. Auctore F. Henrico Noris Veronensi Augustiniano, Serenissimi Magni Ducis Etruriae Cosmi III theologo, & in Academia Pisana Sac. Scripturae & Ecclesiasticae Historiae professore, nunc S.R.E. Cardinale*. Leipzig: Thomas Fritsch, 1696.

Noris, Enrico. *Istoria delle investiture delle dignità ecclesiastiche scritta dal Padre Noris poi cardinale di Santa Chiesa contra Luigi Maimburgo*. Mantua: Alberto Tumarmani, 1741.

Noris, Enrico. *Henrici Norisii Veronensis Augustiniani Opera Omnia*. Edited by Pietro Ballerini and Girolamo Ballerini. 4 vols. Verona: Typographia Tumarmaniana, 1728–1732.

Ouseel, Jacob, ed. *M. Minucii Felicis Octavius cum integris omnium notis ac commentariis*. Leiden: Johannes Maire, 1652.

Orbaan, J. A. F., and G. J. Hoogewerff, ed. *Bescheiden in Italië omtrent nederlandsche kunstenaars en geleerden*. 3 vols. The Hague: Martinus Nijhoff, 1911–1917.

Origen. *Origenis Contra Celsum libri octo. Ejusdem philocalia*. Edited by William Spencer. Cambridge: John Field, 1658.

Origen. *Contra Celsum*. Translated by Henry Chadwick. Cambridge: Cambridge University Press, 1980.

Ossinger, Johann Felix. *Bibliotheca Augustiniana historica, critica, et chronologica*. Ingoldstadt and Augsburg: Johann Franz Xaver Craetz, 1768.

de Pauw, Cornelius. *Recherches philosophiques sur les égyptiens et les chinois*. Berlin: G. J. Decker, 1778.

Pascal, Blaise. *Les Provinciales, ou les lettres escrites par Louis de Montalte a un provincial de ses amis, et aux RR. PP. Jesuites*. Cologne: Nicolas Schoute, 1659.

Pélissier, Léon-Gabriel, ed. "Lettres inédites de Claude Nicaise a Huet et a G. Bonjour tirées des bibliothèques italiennes (1679–1701)." In *Bulletin d'histoire & d'archéologie religieuses du diocèse de Dijon* 7: 11–19, 96–117, 145–164, 189–209. Dijon: Damongeot et Cle, 1889.

Pélissier, Léon-Gabriel, ed. "Le Cardinal Henri de Noris et sa correspondance." In *Studi e documenti di storia e diritto* 11: 25–64, 253–332. Rome: Tipografia Vaticana, 1890.

Pélissier, Léon-Gabriel, ed. "Notes sur quelques manuscrits d'Italie." In *Bulletin du bibliophile et du bibliothécaire* 288–296, 368–377, 451–460, 563–572. Paris: Techener, 1890.

Pélissier, Léon-Gabriel, ed. "Lettres de l'abbé Nicaise au cardinal Noris (1686–1701)." *Le bibliographe moderne courrier international des archives et des bibliothèques* 7: 176–214. Paris: 38, Rue Gay-Lussac, 1903.

Pélissier, Léon-Gabriel, ed. "Lettres inédites de Gisbert Cuper à P. Daniel Huet (1683–1716) et à divers correspondants." *Mémoires de l'Académie nationale des sciences, arts et belles-lettres de Caen*, 1902: 259–297, 1903: 41–103, 1904: 299–361 (104–165), 1905: 1–145 (166–309). Caen: Henri Delesques, 1902–1905.

Pereira, Benedict. *Commentarium et disputationum in Genesim, tomi quatuor*. Cologne: Anton Hierat, 1622.

Perizonius, Jacobus. *Aegyptiarum originum et temporum antiquissimorum investigatio in qua Marshami chronologia funditus evertitur, tum illae Usserii, Cappelli, Pezronii, aliorumque, examinantur et confutantur*. Leiden: Johannes van der Linden, 1711.

Petau, Denis. *Opus de doctrina temporum*. 2 vols. Paris: Sébastien Cramoisy, 1627.

Petit, Samuel. *Variarum lectionum libri III*. Paris: Carol Morel, 1633.

Peucer, Caspar. *Commentarius de praecipuis divinationum generibus*. Frankfurt: Andrè Wechel, 1593.

Pezron, Paul. *L'antiquité des tems rétablie et défenduë contre les Juifs & les nouveaux chronologistes*. Paris: La veuve d'Edme Martin, Jean Boudot, and Étienne Martin, 1687.

Pezron, Paul. *L'antiquité des tems rétablie et défenduë contre les Juifs & les nouveaux chronologistes*. Amsterdam: Henry Desbordes, 1687.

Pezron, Paul. *Défense de l'antiquité des tems*. Paris: Jean Boudot, 1691.

Philo of Alexandria. *Philo. Volume VI*. Translated by F. H. Colson. Cambridge MA: Harvard University Press, 1935.

Pignoria, Lorenzo. *Symbolarum epistolicarum liber primus*. Padua: Donati Pasquardi, 1629.

Pipping, Heinrich. "Dissertatio de Nomine Patriarchae Josephi." *Acta Eruditorum* (1697): 6–10.

Plato. *Timaeus. Critias. Cleitophon. Menexenus. Epistles*. Translated by R. G. Bury. Cambridge MA: Harvard University Press, 1929.

Plutarch. *Moralia*. 15 vols. Cambridge MA: Harvard University Press, 1927–1969.

Poole, Matthew, ed. *Synopsis criticorum aliorumque sacrae scripturae interpretum*. 5 vols. London: J. Flesher and T. Roycroft, 1669–1680.

Prideaux, Matthias. *An Easy and Compendious Introduction for Reading All Sorts of Histories: Contrived in a More Facile Way Then Heretofore Hath Been Published, Out of the Papers of Mathias Prideaux*. Oxford: Leonard Lichfield, 1648.

Quintilian. *The Orator's Education*. Edited by Donald A. Russell. 5 vols. Cambridge MA: Harvard University Press, 2001.

Renan, Ernest. *Correspondance générale*. Edited by Maurice Gasnier and Jean Balcou. 5 vols. Paris: Honoré Champion Éditeur, 2008.

Renaudot, Eusèbe. *Liturgiarum orientalium collectio*. 2 vols. Paris: Jean-Baptiste Coignard, 1715.

Rigord, Jean-Pierre. *Dissertation historique sur une médaille d'Hérodes Antipas.* Marseille: Jean Anisson, 1689.

Rigord, Jean-Pierre. "Article CLXXVIII; Lettre de M. Rigord Commissaire de la Marine aux Auteurs des Memoirs de Trévoux sur un Livre qui a pour titre Monumenta Coptica." *Journal de Trévoux* (1703): 1878–1879.

Rigord, Jean-Pierre. "Article LXXXIX: Lettre de Monsieur Rigord Commissaire de la Marine aux journalistes de Trévoux sur une ceinture de toile trouvée en Egypte autour d'une mumie." *Journal de Trévoux* 10 (1704): 978–1000.

Ripa, Matteo. *Storia della fondazione della congregazione e del collegio de' Cinesi.* Napoli: Manfredi, 1832.

Ripa, Matteo. *Giornale (1705–1724): Testo critico, note e appendice documentaria di Michele Fatica.* Edited by Michele Fatica. 2 vols. Napoli: Istituto Universitario Orientale di Napoli, 1996.

Royal Commission on Historical Manuscripts, ed. *Report on the Manuscripts of the Marquess of Downshire.* 2 vols. London: His Majesty's Stationary Office, 1924.

Saint-Hyacinthe, Thémiseul de. *Le chef d'oeuvre d'un inconnu. Poëme heureusement découvert & mis au jour, avec des Remarques savantes & recherchées.* The Hague: Pierre Husson, 1716.

Sale, George et al. *A universal history from the earliest account of time compiled from original authors.* 65 vols. London: T. Osborne, A. Millar and J. Osborn, 1748–1768.

Scaliger, Joseph. *Opus novum de emendatione temporum in octo tributum.* Paris: Mamertus Patissonius in officina Robert Étienne, 1583.

Scaliger, Joseph. *Opus de emendatione temporum: castigatius & multis partibus auctius, ut novum videri possit. Item veterum Graecorum fragmenta selecta, quibus loci aliquot obscurissimi chronologiae sacrae & bibliorum illustrantur, cum notis eiusdem Scaligeri.* Leiden: Officina Plantiniana, 1598.

Scaliger, Joseph. *Thesaurus temporum. Eusebii Pamphili Caesareae Palaestinae Episcopi.* Leiden: Thomas Basson, 1606.

Schedius, Elias. *De dis germanis.* Amsterdam: Lodewijk Elzevir, 1648.

Schelstrate, Emmanuel. *Antiquitas ecclesiae, dissertationibus, monimentis ac notis illustrata.* 2 vols. Rome: Propaganda fide, 1692–1697.

Selden, John. *Mare Clausum, seu de dominio maris.* London: William Stansby, 1635.

Selden, John. *The Right and Dominion of the Sea in Two Books.* Translated by Marchamont Nedham. London: William Du-Gard, 1652.

Seneca. *Epistles 1–65.* Edited by Richard M. Gummere. Cambridge MA: Harvard University Press, 1917.

Servius Honoratus, Maurus. *In Vergilii carmina comentarii. Servii Grammatici qui feruntur in Vergilii carmina commentarii.* Edited by Georg Thilo and Hermann Hagen. Leipzig: B. G. Teubner, 1881.

Simon, Richard. *Histoire critique du Vieux Testament.* "Suivant la Copie, imprimé a Paris": 1680.
Simon, Richard. *Histoire critique du Vieux Testament.* Rotterdam: Reinier Leers, 1685.
Simon, Richard. *Lettres choisies de M. Simon.* 4 vols. Amsterdam: Pierre Mortier, 1730.
Smith, George. *The Chaldean Account of Genesis.* London: Sampson Lowe, Marston, Searle, and Rivington, 1880.
Sollier, Jean-Baptiste du. *Tractatus historico-chronologicus de patriarchis Alexandrinis.* Antwerp: Peter Jacobs, 1708.
Spencer, John. *Dissertatio de Urim et Thurrim in Deuteron. c. 33, v. 8. In qua eorum natura et origo, non paucorum mosaicorum rationes et obscuriora quaedam Scripturae loca probabiliter explicantur.* Cambridge: G. Kettilby, 1670.
Spencer, John. *De legibus Hebraeorum ritualibus et earum rationibus.* The Hague: Arnold Leers, 1686.
Spencer, John. *De legibus Hebraeorum ritualibus earumque rationibus.* Tübingen: Johann Georg Cotta, 1732.
Stillingfleet, Edward. *Origines sacrae, or A Rational Account of the Grounds of the Christian Faith.* London: Henry Mortlock, 1662.
Syncellus, George. *Georgii Monmachi Syncelli, et Nicephori CP. Patriarchae Chronographia.* Edited by Jacques Goar. Paris: Typographia Regia, 1652.
Syncellus, George. *Georgii Syncelli Ecloga Chronographia.* Edited by Alden A. Mosshammer. Leipzig: BSB B. G. Teubner, 1984.
Syncellus, George. *The Chronography of George Synkellos: A Byzantine Chronicle of Universal History from the Creation.* Edited by William Adler and Paul Tuffin. Oxford: Oxford University Press, 2002.
Tacitus. *The Histories Books IV–V: The Annals Books I–III.* Edited by Clifford H. Moore and John Jackson. Cambridge MA: Harvard University Press, 1931.
Tentzel, Wilhelm Ernst. *Epistola de sceleto elephantino Tonnae nuper effosso.* Gotha: Litteris Reyherianis, 1696.
Tertullian. *De Idololatria: Critical Text, Translation and Commentary.* Edited by J. H. Waszink and J. C. M. van Winden. Leiden: E. J. Brill, 1987.
Theodoret. *Ecclesiastical History. A History of the Church in five books. From A.D. 322. to the Death of Theodore of Mopsuestia A.D. 427.* Translated by Edward Walford. London: Samuel Bagster and Sons, 1843.
Thomassin, Louis. *La méthode d'étudier et d'enseigner chrétiennement & solidement les lettres humaines par rapport aux lettres divines et aux écritures.* 3 vols. Paris: François Huguet, 1681–1682.
Thomassin, Louis. *La méthode d'étudier et d'enseigner chrétiennement et solidement les historiens profanes par rapport à la religion Chrétienne, & aux écritures.* 3 vols. Paris: Louis Rolland, 1693.

Thucydides. *History of the Peloponnesian War.* Edited by Charles Forster Smith. 4 vols. Cambridge MA: Harvard University Press, 1928–1935.

Tiraqueau, André. *Semestria in Genialium dierum.* Lyon: Guillaume Rouillé, 1586.

Tirinus, Jacobus. *Commentarius in sacram scripturam.* Leiden: Joannis Girin & Bartholom. Rivière, 1683.

Toinard, Nicolas. *De Commodi imperatoris aetate in nummis inscripta.* Paris: André Cramoisy, 1690.

Torelli, Luigi. *Secoli Agostiniani overo Historia generale del Sagro Ordine Eremiatno del Gran Dottore di Santa Chiesa S. Aurelio Agostino vescovo d'Hippona.* 8 vols. Bologna: Giacomo Monti, 1659–1686.

Tournemine, René-Joseph de. "Dissertation sur le Système des Dynasties d'Égypte du Chevalier Marsham." *Journal de Trévoux* 2 (1702): 151–169.

Tournemine, René-Joseph de. "Projet d'un ouvrage sur l'origine des fables, par le P. Tournemine Jesuite." *Journal de Trévoux* 5 (1702): 83–111.

Tournemine, René-Joseph de. "Addition pour les mémoires de Novembre & Décembre; Seconde partie du projet d'un ouvrage sur l'origine des fables." *Journal de Trévoux* 5 [supplement] (1702): 1–22.

Tournemine, René-Joseph de. "Article XLIV: Conjecture du P. Tournemine Jesuite sur l'origine de la difference du texte Hébreu, de l'édition Samaritaine & de la version des Septante, dans la maniere de compter les années des Patriarches." *Journal de Trévoux* 6 (1703): 452–464.

Tournemine, René-Joseph de. "Article CXXXXI: Réponse du P. de Tournemine à la Dissertation precedente." *Journal de Trévoux* 7 (1703): 1408–1430.

Trent, Council of. *Concilium Tridentinum. Diariorum, Actorum, Epistularum, Tractatuum nova collectio edidit Societas Goerresiana.* Edited by the Societas Goerresiana. 13 vols. Freiburg: Herder, 1901–2001.

Tuki, Raphael. *Rudimenta linguae Coptae sive Aegyptiacae.* Rome: Sacra congregatio de Propaganda fide, 1778.

Ursinus, Johann Heinrich. *Novus Prometheus Praeadamitarum plastes ad caucasum relegatus & religatus, schediasma.* Frankfurt: Christian Hersmdorf, 1656.

Ursinus, Johann Heinrich. *De Zoroastre Bactriano, Hermete Trismegisto, Sanchoniathone Phoenicio, eorumq; scriptis, & aliis, contra Mosaicae scripturae antiquitatem; exercitationes familiares, quibus Christophori Arnoldi Spicilegium accessit.* Nuremberg: Michael Endter, 1661.

Ussher, James. *Annales Veteris Testamenti, a prima mundi origine deducti: una cum rerum asiaticarum et aegyptiacarum chronico, a temporis historici principio usque ad Maccabaicorum initia producto.* London: J. Flesher, 1650.

Valois, Henri, ed. *Polybii Diodori Siculi Nicolai Damasceni Dionysii Halicar Appiani Alexand Dionis et Ioannis Antiocheni Excepta ex Collectaneis Constantini Augusti Porphyrogenetae.* Paris: Mathurin du Puis, 1634.

Valperga di Caluso, Tommaso. *Didymi Taurinensis Literaturae copticae rudimentum.* Parma: Ex Regio Typographo, 1783.

Vico, Giambattista. *Principj di scienza nuova.* Napoli: Muziana, 1744.

Vico, Giambattista. *Scienza nuova seconda.* Edited by Fausto Nicolini. 2 vols. Bari: Gius Laterza & Figli, 1942.

Vico, Giambattista. *The New Science of the Giambattista Vico: Revised Translation of the Third Edition (1744).* Edited by Thomas Goddard Bergin and Max Harold Fisch. Ithaca NY: Cornell University Press, 1968.

Vico, Giambattista. *The First New Science.* Edited by Leon Pompa. Cambridge: Cambridge University Press, 2002.

Vignoles, Alphonse des. *Chronologie de l'histoire sainte et des histoires étrangères qui la concernent depuis la sortie d'Égypte jusqu'à la captivité de Babylone.* Berlin: Ambroise Haude, 1738.

Vitringa, Campegius. *Observationum sacrarum libri septem ... editio ultima.* 2 vols. Amsterdam: Fredericus Horreus, 1727.

Vives, Juan Luis, ed. *En habes optime lector absolutissimi doctoris Aurelij Augustini, opus absolutissimum, de Civitate dei ...* Basel: Froben, 1522.

Vossius, Gerardus. *De historicis Graecis libri quatuor.* Leiden: Johannes Maire, 1624.

Vossius, Gerardus. *De theologia gentili et physiologia Christiana; sive de origine ac progressu idololatriae, ad veterum gesta, ac rerum naturam, reductae; deque naturae mirandis, quibus homo adducitur ad Deum.* Amsterdam: Johannes and Cornelius Blaeu, 1641.

Vossius, Isaac. *Dissertatio de vera aetate mundi; qua ostenditur natale mundi tempus annis minimum 1440 vulgarem aeram anticipare.* The Hague: Adriaan Vlacq, 1659.

Vossius, Isaac. *De septuaginta interpretibus, eorumque tralatione & chronologia dissertationes.* The Hague: Adriaan Vlacq, 1661.

Wagner, C. "Annus et epochae syro-macedonum." *Acta eruditorum* (1690): 425–439.

Waterman, John T., ed. *Leibniz and Ludolf on Things Linguistic: Excerpts from Their Correspondence (1688–1703).* Berkeley and Los Angeles: University of California Press, 1977.

de Wette, Wilhelm Martin Leberecht. *Beiträge zür Einleitung in das Alte Testament.* 2 vols. Halle: Schimmelpfennig und Compagnie, 1806–1807.

Whiston, William, *A New Theory of the Earth From its Original, to the Consummation of All Things, Where the Creation of the World in Six Days, the Universal Deluge, And the General Conflagration, As laid down in the Holy Scriptures, Are Shewn to be perfectly agreeable to Reason and Philosophy.* London: Benjamin Tooke, 1696.

Whiston, William. *An Essay towards Restoring the True Text of the Old Testament and for Vindicating the Citations made thence in the New Testament.* London: J. Senex, 1722.

Wilkins, David. *Novum Testamentum Aegyptium vulgo Copticum ex* MSS. *Bodlejanis descripsit, cum Vaticanis et Parisiensibus contulit et in Latinum sermonem convertit*. Oxford: Ex Theatro Sheldoniano, 1716.

Witsen, Nicolaes. *Noord en Oost Tartarye*. Amsterdam: François Halma, 1705.

Witsius, Hermann. *Aegyptiaca, et Dekaphulon. Sive, de Aegyptiacorum sacrorum cum Hebraicis collatione*. Amsterdam: Gerardus Borstius, 1683.

Wotton, William. *Reflections upon Ancient and Modern Learning*. London: J. Leake, 1694.

Zoëga, Georg. *Catalogus codicum Copticorum manu scriptorum qui in Museo Borgiano*. Rome: Congregationis de Propaganda fide, 1810.

Secondary Printed Sources

Adler, William. *Time Immemorial: Archaic History and its Sources in Christian Chronography from Julius Africanus to George Syncellus*. Washington DC: Dumbarton Oaks, 1989.

Adler, William. "Moses, the Exodus, and Comparative Chronology." In *Scripture and Traditions: Essays on Early Judaism and Christianity in Honor of Carl R. Holladay*, 47–65. Edited by Patrick Gray and Gail R. O'Day. Leiden and Boston: Brill, 2008.

Allen, Don Cameron. *The Legend of Noah: Renaissance Rationalism in Arts, Science, and Letters*. Urbana: University of Illinois Press, 1949.

Allen, Don Cameron. "The Predecessors of Champollion." *Proceedings of the American Philosophical Society* 104 (1960): 527–547.

Allen, Don Cameron. *Mysteriously Meant: The Rediscovery of Pagan Symbolism and Allegorical Interpretation in the Renaissance*. Baltimore and London: The John Hopkins Press, 1970.

Alphandery, Paul. "L'évhémérisme et les débuts de l'histoire des religions au moyen-âge." *Revues de l'histoire des religions* 109 (1934): 5–27.

App, Urs. *The Birth of Orientalism*. Philadelphia: University of Pennsylvania Press, 2010.

Arabeyre, Patrick. "Étienne Prinstet, Illustrateur du Grand Atlas de Cîteaux." *Mémoires de la commission des antiquités de la Côte-d'Or* 38 (1997–1999): 241–267.

Assmann, Jan. *Moses the Egyptian: The Memory of Egypt in Western Monotheism*. Cambridge MA and London: Harvard University Press, 1997.

Aufrère, Sydney, and Nathalie Bosson. "Le Père Guillaume Bonjour (1670–1714). Un orientaliste méconnu porté sur l'étude du copte et le déchiffrement de l'égyptien." *Orientalia* 67 (1998): 497–506.

Aufrère, Sydney, and Nathalie Bosson. "*De Copticae Guillelmi Bonjourni grammaticae criticis contra Athanasium Kircherum*. La naissance de la critique de *l'Opera Kicheriana Coptica*." *Études Coptes* 8 (2003): 5–18.

Aufrère, Sydney, and Nathalie Bosson. "Remarques au sujet du *Lexikon Aegyptio-Latinum* F. Guillelmi Bonjour Tolosani Augustiniani." *Études Coptes* 9 (2005): 17–31.

Aufrère, Sydney, and Nathalie Bosson, ed. *Guillaume Bonjour Elementa Linguae Copticae. Grammaire inédite du XVIIe siècle*. Geneva: Patrick Cramer, 2005.

Bachelet, Xavier-Marie. *Bellarmin et la Bible sixto-clémentine: étude et documents*. Paris: G. Beauchesne, 1911.

Baldini, Ugo. "Guillaume Bonjour (1670–1714): Chronologist, Linguist and 'Casual Scientist'." In *Europe and China: Science and the Arts in the 17th and 18th Centuries*, 241–294. Edited by Luis Saravia. Singapore: World Scientific, 2013.

Barr, James. "Why the World was created in 4004 B.C.: Archbishop Ussher and Biblical Chronology." *Bulletin of the John Rylands Library* 67 (1985): 575–608.

Baumgarten, Albert I. *The Phoenician History of Philo of Byblos. A Commentary*. Leiden: E. J. Brill, 1981.

Bausset, Louis-François de. *Histoire de Bossuet, évêque de Meaux*. 3 vols. Paris: Gaume Frères and J. Leroux, 1846.

Bietenholz, Peter G. *Historia and Fabula: Myths and Legends in Historical Thought from Antiquity to the Modern Age*. Leiden: E. J. Brill, 1994.

Bonner, Gerald. "The Cotton Genesis." *The British Museum Quarterly* 26 (1962): 22–26.

Boxel, Piet van. "Robert Bellarmine, Christian Hebraist and Censor." In *History of Scholarship: A Selection of Papers from the Seminar on the History of Scholarship Held Annually at the Warburg Institute*, 251–275. Edited by Jean-Louis Quantin and Christopher Ligota. Oxford: Oxford University Press, 2006.

Breccola, Giancarlo. "La tipografia del seminario di Montefiascone." *Quaderno della Rivista del Consorzio per la gestione delle biblioteche comunale degli Ardenti e provinciale Anselmo Anselmi di Viterbo* 25 (1997).

Breccola, Giancarlo. "La biblioteca del seminario Barbarigo di Montefiascone: problemi di conservazione, ipotesi di valorizzazione." In *Le biblioteche dei seminari delle antiche diocesi di Viterbo, di Tuscania, di Montefiascone, di Acquapendente, di Bagnoregio, e del Seminario regionale della Quercia: problem di conservazione, ipotesi di valorizzazione*, 18–30. Edited by Luciano Osbat. Viterbo: Cedido, 2009.

Brockliss, Laurence W. B. *French Higher Education in the Seventeenth and Eighteenth Centuries*. Oxford: Clarendon Press, 1987.

Buchwald, Jed Z. and Mordechai Feingold. *Newton and the Origin of Civilization*. Princeton: Princeton University Press, 2013.

Bunsen, Christian Karl Josias von. *Aegyptens Stelle in der Weltgeschichte*. 5 vols. Hamburg: Friedrich Perthes, 1845–1857.

Burger, Pierre-François. "L'abbé Renaudot en Italie (1700–1701)." *Dix-huitième siècle* 22 (1990): 243–253.

Cams, Mario. *Companions in Geography. East-West Collaboration in the Mapping of Qing China (c.1685–1735)*. Leiden and Boston: Brill, 2017.

Cantelli, Gianfranco. "Mito e storia in J. Leclerc, Tournemine e Fontenelle." *Rivista critica di storia della filosofia* 27 (1972): 269–286, 385–400.

Carhart, Michael C. *Leibniz Discovers Asia: Social Networking in the Republic of Letters.* Baltimore: John Hopkins University Press, 2019.

Carley, James. "Thomas Wakefield, Robert Wakefield and the Cotton Genesis." *Transactions of the Cambridge Bibliographical Society* 12 (2002): 246–265.

Cavarzere, Marco. "A Comparative Method for Sixteenth-Century Polemicists: Cults, Devotions, and the Formation of Early Modern Religious Identities." *Journal of Early Modern History* 19 (2015), 385–407.

Ceyssens, Lucien. "Chrétien Lupus: sa période janséniste." *Augustiniana* 16 (1965): 264–312.

Chalande, Jules. "Histoire des rues de Toulouse: 229. – Le couvent des Augustins (Rue du Musée)." *Mémoires de l'Académie des sciences, inscriptions et belles-lettres de Toulouse*, series 11, 9 (1921): 142–148.

Chapman, Honora Howell, and Zuleika Rodgers, ed. *A Companion to Josephus.* Chichester: Wiley Blackwell, 2016.

Chen, Bianca. "Digging for Antiquities with Diplomats: Gisbert Cuper (1644–1716) and his Social Capital." *Republic of Letters: A Journal for the Study of Knowledge, Politics, and the Arts* 1 (2009): 1–18.

Chen, Bianca. "Gisbert Cuper as a Servant of Two Republics." In *Double Agents: Cultural and Political Brokerage in Early Modern Europe*, 71–94. Edited by Marika Keblusek & Badeloch Vera Noldus. Leiden: Brill, 2011.

Ciancio, Luca, and Gian Paolo Romagnani, ed. *Unità del sapere, molteplicità dei saperi: Francesco Bianchini (1662–1729) tra natura, storia e religione.* Verona: QuiEdit, 2010.

Cochrane, Eric. "The Settecento Medievalists." *The Journal of the History of Ideas* 19 (1958): 35–61.

Cochrane, Eric. *Historians and Historiography in the Italian Renaissance.* Chicago & London: The University of Chicago Press, 1981.

Collani, Claudia von. "Philippe Couplet's Missionary Attitude towards the Chinese in *Confucius Sinarum Philosophus*." In *Philippe Couplet, s.J. (1623–1693): The Man Who Brought China to Europe*, 37–54. Edited by Jerome Heyndrickx. Nettetal: Stigler, 1990.

Collani, Claudia von. "Charles Maigrot's Role in the Chinese Rites Controversy." In *The Chinese Rites Controversy: Its History and Meaning*, 149–183. Edited by D. E. Mungello. Sankt Augustin: Institut Monumenta Serica and San Francisco: The Ricci Institute for Chinese Western Cultural History, 1994.

Collani, Claudia von. "François Noël and his Treatise on God in China." In *History of the Catholic Church in China: From its Beginning to the Scheut Fathers and the 20th Century unveiling some less known sources, sounds and pictures*, 23–64. Edited by Ferdinand Verbiest Institute. Leuven: Leuven Chinese Studies XXIX, 2015.

Collani, Claudia von. "The Jesuit Rites Controversy." In *The Oxford Handbook of the Jesuits*. Edited by Ines G. Zuparov. Oxford: Oxford University Press, 2017.

Craig, William Lane. *In Quest of the Historical Adam: A Biblical and Scientific Exploration*. Grand Rapids MI: Eerdmans, 2021.

Crehan, F. J. "The Bible in the Roman Catholic Church from Trent to the Present Day." In *The Cambridge History of the Bible*, 199–237. Edited by S. L. Greenslade. Cambridge: Cambridge University Press, 1963.

Croce, Benedetto. *Conversazioni critiche*. 2 vols. Bari: Gius. Laterza & Figli, 1924.

Detienne, Marcel. "Mythology." In *The Classical Tradition*, 614–617. Edited by Anthony Grafton, Glenn W. Most, and Salvatore Settis. Cambridge MA and London: The Belknap of Harvard University Press, 2010.

Dew, Nicholas. *Orientalism in Louis XIV's France*. Oxford: Oxford University Press, 2009.

Disraeli, Isaac. *Curiosities of Literature*. 2 vols. London: Routledge, Warne, and Routledge, New York, 1863.

Ditchfield, Simon. "What was Sacred History? (Mostly Roman) Catholic Uses of the Christian Past after Trent." In *Sacred History: Uses of the Christian Past in the Renaissance World*, 72–98. Edited by Katherine van Liere, Simon Ditchfield, and Howard Louthon. Oxford: Oxford University Press, 2012.

Divjak, Johannes, and Wolfgang Wischmeyer, ed. *Das Kalenderhandbuch von 354. Der Chronograph des Filocalus*. 2 vols. Vienna: Holzhausen, 2014.

Dooley, Brendan. *Science, Politics and Society in Eighteenth-Century Italy: The Giornale de' Letterati d'Italia and its World*. New York and London: Garland Press, 2018.

Doucette, Leonard E. *Emery Bigot: Seventeenth-Century French Humanist*. Toronto: University of Toronto Press, 1970.

Droge, Arthur J. *Homer or Moses? Early Christian Interpretations of the History of Culture*. Tübingen: J. C. B. Mohr, 1989.

Drouin, Sébastien. *Théologie ou libertinage? L'exégèse allégorique à l'âge des Lumières*. Paris: Honoré Champion, 2010.

Dunklegrün, Theodor. "The 'Testimonium Flavianum Canonicum': Josephus as a Witness to the Biblical Canon, 1566–1823." *International Journal of the Classical Tradition* 23 (2016): 252–268.

Dupront, Alphonse. *Pierre-Daniel Huet et l'exégèse comparatiste au XVIIe siècle*. Geneva: Libraire Droz, 2014.

Eco, Umberto. *The Search for the Perfect Language*. Translated by James Fentress. London: Fontana Press, 1997.

Edelstein, Dan. *The Enlightenment: A Genealogy*. Chicago: The University of Chicago Press, 2010.

Ellis, Anthony. "*Herodotus Magister Vitae*, or: Herodotus and God in the Protestant Reformation." *Histos. Supplement* 4 (2015): 173–245.

Faure, Alain. *Champollion: le savant dechiffré*. Paris: Fayard, 2004.

Feingold, Mordechai. "A Rake's Progress: William Whiston Reads Josephus." *Eighteenth Century Studies* 49 (2015): 17–30.

Feldman, Louis H. *Josephus's Interpretation of the Bible*. Berkeley and Los Angeles: University of California Press, 1998.

Feller, François Xavier de. *Dictionnaire historique ou histoire abrégée de shommes qui se sont fait un nom par le génie, les talens, les vertus, les erreurs, depuis le commencement du monde jusqu'a nos jours*. 8 vols. Liège: F. Lemarié, 1797.

Findlen, Paula, ed. *Athanasius Kircher: The Last Man Who Knew Everything*. New York: Routledge, 2004.

Force, James E., and Richard H. Popkin, ed. *Essays in the Context, Nature and Influence of Isaac Newton's Theology*. Dordrecht: Kluwer Academic Publishers, 1990.

Gerace, Antonio. "The Council of Trent and the Sixto-Clementine Vulgate." In *The Oxford Handbook of the Latin Bible*, 292–304. Edited by H. A. G. Houghton. Oxford: Oxford University Press, 2023.

Gliozzi, Giuliano. *Adamo e il nuovo mondo: la nascita dell'antropologia come ideologia coloniale: dalle genealogie bibliche alle teorie razziali (1500–1700)*. Florence: La nuova Italia, 1977.

Golvers, Noël. "Reading Classical Latin Authors in the Jesuit Mission in China: Seventeenth to Eighteenth Centuries." In *Receptions of Greek and Roman Antiquity in East Asia*, 50–72. Edited by Almut-Barbara Renger and Xin Fan. Brill: Leiden and Boston, 2018.

Grabbe, Lester L. "Jewish Identity and Hellenism in the Fragmentary Jewish Writings in Greek." In *Scripture and Traditions: Essays on Early Judaism and Christianity in Honor of Carl R. Holladay*, 21–31. Edited by Patrick Gray and Gail R. O'Day. Leiden and Boston: Brill, 2008.

Grafton, Anthony. "Joseph Scaliger and Historical Chronology: The Rise and Fall of a Discipline." *History and Theory* 14 (1975): 156–185.

Grafton, Anthony. *Joseph Scaliger: A Study in the History of Classical Scholarship*. 2 vols. Oxford: Clarendon Press, 1983–1993.

Grafton, Anthony. *Defenders of the Text: The Traditions of Scholarship in the Age of Science, 1450–1800*. Cambridge MA: Harvard University Press, 1994.

Grafton, Anthony. "Tradition and Technique in Historical Chronology." In *Ancient History and the Antiquarian: Essays in Memory of Arnaldo Momigliano*, 15–31. Edited by H. H. Crawford and C. R. Ligota. London: The Warburg Institute, 1995.

Grafton, Anthony. "Dating history: the Renaissance & the reformation of chronology." *Daedalus* 132 (2003): 74–85.

Grafton, Anthony. "Kircher's Chronology." In *Athanasius Kircher: The Last Man Who Knew Everything*, 171–187. Edited by Paula Findlen. New York: Routledge, 2004.

Grafton, Anthony. "The Chronology of the Flood." In *Sintflut und Gedächtnis: Erinnern und Vergessen des Ursprungs*, 65–82. Edited by Martin Mulsow and Jan Assmann. Munich: Wilhelm Fink, 2006.

Grafton, Anthony. *What was History? The art of history in early modern Europe*. Cambridge: Cambridge University Press, 2007.

Grafton, Anthony. "A Sketch Map of a Lost Continent: The Republic of Letters." In *Republic of the Letters: A Journal for the Study of Knowledge, Politics and the Arts* 1 (2009) http://arcade.stanford.edu/rofl/sketch-map-lost-continent-republic-letters.

Grafton, Anthony. *Worlds made by Words: Scholarship and Community in the Modern West*. Cambridge MA: Harvard University Press, 2009.

Grafton, Anthony. "Isaac Vossius, Chronologer." In *Isaac Vossius (1618–1689) between Science and Scholarship*, 43–84. Edited by Eric Jorink and Dirk van Miert. Leiden and Boston: Brill, 2012.

Gray, Patrick and Gail R. O'Day ed. *Scripture and Traditions: Essays on Early Judaism and Christianity in Honor of Carl R. Holladay*. Leiden and Boston: Brill, 2008.

Grell, Chantal. *Le dix-huitième siècle et l'antiquité en France 1680–1789*. 2 vols. Oxford: Voltaire Foundation, 1995.

Guidi, Ignazio. *Catalogo dei codici Orientali di alcune Biblioteche d'Italia*. Florence: Tipografia dei successori le Monnier, 1878.

Gutierrez, David, and John Gavigan. *The History of the Order of St. Augustine*. 4 vols. Villanova: Augustinian Press, 1971-.

Häfner, Ralph. *Skepsis, Providenz, Polyhistorie: Jakob Friedrich Reimmann (1668–1743)*. Tübingen: Max Niemeyer Verlag, 1998.

Hamilton, Alastair. *The Copts and the West, 1439–1822: The European Discovery of the Egyptian Church*. Oxford: Oxford University Press, 2006.

Hamilton, Alastair. "Guillaume Bonjour *Elementa linguae copticae*." *Church History and Religious Culture* 87 (2007): 125–127.

Hamilton, Alastair. "From East to West: Jansenists, Orientalists and the Eucharistic Controversy." In *Essays on Literary Imagination, the Canon and the Christian Middle Ages for Burcht Pranger*, 83–100. Edited by Willemien Otten, Arjo Vanderjagt and Hent De Vries. Leiden: Brill, 2010.

Hardy, Nicholas. *Criticism and Confession: The Bible in the Seventeenth-Century Republic of Letters*. Oxford: Oxford University Press, 2017.

Hazard, Paul. *La crise de la conscience européenne (1680–1715)*. Paris: Boivin, 1935.

Hazard, Paul. *The European Mind: The Critical Years, 1680–1715*. Translated by J. Lewis May. New Haven: Yale University Press, 1953.

Heering, Jan Paul. "Hugo Grotius' *De Veritate Religionis Christianae*." In *Hugo Grotius Theologian: Essays in Honour of G. H. M. Posthumus Meyjes*, 41–52. Edited by Henk J. M. Nellen and Edwin Rabbie. Leiden: E. J. Brill, 1994.

Heilbron, John L. *The Sun in the Church*. Cambridge MA: Harvard University Press, 1999.

Heilbron, John L. "Bianchini as an Astronomer." In *Francesco Bianchini (1662–1729) und die europäische gelehrte Welt um 1700*, 57–82. Edited by Valentin Kockel and Brigitte Sölch. Berlin: Akademie Verlag, 2005.

Heilbron, John L. "Francesco Bianchini, Historian. In Memory of Amos Funkenstein." In *Thinking Impossibilities: The Intellectual Legacy of Amos Funkenstein*, 227–277. Edited by Robert S. Westman and David Biale. Toronto: University of Toronto Press, 2008.

Heilbron, John L. "Bianchini and Natural Philosophy." *Unità del sapere, molteplicità dei saperi: Francesco Bianchini (1662–1729) tra natura, storia e religione*, 33–73. Edited by Luca Ciancio and Gian Paolo Romagnani. Verona: QuiEdit, 2010.

Heilbron, John L. *The incomparable Monsignor: Francesco Bianchini's world of science, history and court intrigue*. Oxford: Oxford University Press, 2022.

Heimbucher, Max. *Die Orden und Kongregationen der katholischen Kirche*. Paderborn: Ferdinand Schöningh, 1933–34.

Heyndrickx, Jerome, ed. *Philippe Couplet, s.j. (1623–1693): The Man Who Brought China to Europe*. Nettetal: Stigler, 1990.

Horst, Ulrich. *Päpstliche Unfehlbarkeit wider konziliare Superiorität?* Brill: Leiden, 2016.

Israel, Jonathan. *Radical Enlightenment: Philosophy and the Making of Modernity, 1650–1750*. Oxford: Oxford University Press, 2001.

Israel, Jonathan. *Enlightenment Contested: Philosophy, Modernity, and the Emancipation of Man, 1670–1752*. Oxford: Oxford University Press, 2006.

Israel, Jonathan. "The Battle over Confucius and Classical Chinese Philosophy in European Early Enlightenment Thought (1670–1730)." *Frontiers of Philosophy in China* 8 (2013): 183–198.

Iversen, Erik. *The Myth of Egypt and its Hieroglyphs In European Tradition*. Princeton NJ: Princeton University Press, 1993.

Jacob, Margaret C. *The Radical Enlightenment: Pantheists, Freemasons and Republicans*. London and Boston: George Allen and Unwin, 1981.

Jaski, Bart, Christian Lange, Anna Pytlowany, and Henk J. van Rinsum, ed. *The Orient in Utrecht: Adriaan Reland (1676–1718), Arabist, Cartographer, Antiquarian and Scholar of Comparative Religion*. Brill: Leiden, 2021.

Jaumann, Herbert, ed. *Die europäische Gelehrtenrepublik im Zeitalter des Konfessionalismus: The European Republic of Letters in the Age of Confessionalism*. Wiesbaden: Harrassowitz Verlag, 2001.

Jemolo, Arturo Carlo. *Il Giansenismo in Italia prima della rivoluzione*. Bari: Gius. Laterza & Figli, 1928.

Jensen, Lionel M. *Manufacturing Confucianism: Chinese Traditions & Universal Civilization*. Durham and London: Duke University Press, 1997.

Jorink, Erik. "'Horrible and Blasphemous': Isaac La Peyrère, Isaac Vossius and the Emergence of Radical Biblical Criticism in the Dutch Republic." In *Nature and Scripture in the Abrahamic Religions: Up to 1700*, 429–450. Edited by Jitse M. van der Meer and Scott Mandelbrote. Brill: Leiden, 2008.

Jorink, Erik, and Dirk van Miert, ed. *Isaac Vossius (1618–1689) between Science and Scholarship*. Leiden and Boston: Brill, 2012.

Katz, David S. "Isaac Vossius and the English biblical critics 1650–1689. " In *Scepticism and Irreligion in the Seventeenth and Eighteenth Centuries*, 142–184. Edited by Richard H. Popkin and Arjo J. Vanderjagt. Leiden: Brill, 1993.

Kidd, Colin. *The World of Mr. Casaubon: Britain's Wars of Mythography, 1700–1810*. Cambridge: Cambridge University Press, 2016.

Klempt, Adalbert. *Die Säkularisierung der universalhistorischen Auffassung: zum Wandel des Geschichtsdenkens im 16. und 17. Jahrhundert*. Göttingen: Musterschmidt Verlag, 1960.

Kockel, Valentin, and Brigitte Sölch, ed. *Francesco Bianchini (1662–1729) und die europäische gelehrte Welt um 1700*. Berlin: Akademie Verlag, 2005.

Kraus, Hans-Joachim. *Geschichte der historisch-kritischen Erforschung des Alten Testaments*. Neukirchen-Vluyn: Neukirchener Verlag, 1982.

Laeven, A. H., and L. J. M. Laeven-Aretz. *The authors and reviewers of the Acta Eruditorum 1682–1735*. Molenhoek: Electronic Publication, 2014. DOI: 10.11588/heidok.00016568.

Lai, Yuen-Ting. "The Linking of Spinoza to Chinese Thought by Bayle and Malebranche." *Journal of the History of Philosophy* 23 (1985): 151–178.

Laplanche, François. *La Bible en France entre mythe et critique (XVIe–XIXe siècle)*. Paris: Albin Michel, 1994.

La Rocca, Sandra. "L'institut des Filles de l'Enfance: le Port-Royal toulousain?" In *Toulouse, une métropole méridionale: Vingt siècles de vie urbaine*, 613–623. Edited by Bernadette Suau, Jean Pierre Almaric, and Jean-Marc Olivier. Toulouse: Presses universitaires du Midi, 2009.

La Roque, Louis de. *Armorial de la Noblesse de Languedoc. Generalité de Toulouse*. Toulouse and Paris: Delboy Fils, E. Dentu and Aug. Aubry, 1863.

Leoni, Tommaso. "The Text of the Josephan Corpus; Principal Greek Manuscripts, Ancient Latin Translations, and the Indirect Tradition." In *A Companion to Josephus*, 307–321. Edited by Honora Howell Chapman and Zuleika Rodgers. Chichester: Wiley Blackwell, 2016.

Levenson, Daniel R., and Thomas R. Martin. "The Ancient Latin Translations of Josephus." In *A Companion to Josephus*, 322–344. Edited by Honora Howell Chapman and Zuleika Rodgers. Chichester: Wiley Blackwell, 2016.

Levitin, Dmitri. "From Sacred History to the History of Religion: Paganism, Judaism, and Christianity in European Historiography from Reformation to 'Enlightenment'." *The Historical Journal* 55 (2012): 1117–1160.

Levitin, Dmitri. "John Spencer's *De Legibus Hebraeorum* (1683–1685) and 'Enlightened' Sacred History: A New Interpretation." *Journal of the Warburg and Courtauld Institutes* 76 (2013): 49–92.

Levitin, Dmitri. *Ancient Wisdom in the Age of the New Science: Histories of Philosophy in England, c. 1640–1700*. Cambridge: Cambridge University Press, 2015.

Levitin, Dmitri. "Egyptology, the limits of antiquarianism, and the origins of conjectural history, c. 1680–1740: new sources and perspectives." *History of European Ideas* 41 (2015): 699–727.

Levitin, Dmitri. "What was the Comparative History of Religions in 17th-Century Europe (and Beyond)? Pagan Monotheism/Pagan Animism, from *T'ien* to Tylor." In *Regimes of Comparatism: Frameworks of Comparison in History, Religion and Anthropology*, 49–115. Edited by Renaud Gagné, Simon Goldhill, Geoffrey Lloyd. Leiden and Boston: Brill, 2018.

Li, Wenchao, ed. *Leibniz and the European Encounter with China: 300 Years of 'Discours sur la théologie naturelle des Chinois'*. Stuttgart: Franz Steiner, 2017.

Ligota, Christopher. "Der apologetische Rahmen der Mythendeutung im Frankreich des 17. Jahrhunderts (P.D. Huet)." In *Mythographie der frühen Neuzeit: Ihre Anwendung in den Künsten*, 149–161. Edited by Walther Killy. Wiesbaden: Otto Harrassowitz, 1984.

Ligota, Christopher "Annius of Viterbo and Historical Method." *Journal of the Warburg and Courtauld Institutes* 50 (1987): 44–56.

Lundbaek, Knud. "The Image of Neo-Confucianism in *Confucius Sinarum Philosophus*." *Journal of the History of Ideas* 44 (1983): 19–30.

Maine, Henry. *The Rede Lecture delivered before the University of Cambridge May 22, 1875*. London: John Murray, 1875.

Malcolm, Noel. *Aspects of Hobbes*. Oxford: Oxford University Press, 2002.

Malcolm, Noel. "Private and Public Knowledge: Kircher, Esotericism, and the Republic of Letters." In *Athanasius Kircher: The Last Man Who Knew Everything*, 297–308. Edited by Paula Findlen. New York: Routledge, 2004.

Mandelbrote, Scott. "English Scholarship and the Greek Text of the Old Testament, 1620–1720: The Impact of Codex Alexandrinus." In *Scripture and Scholarship in Early Modern England*, 74–93. Edited by Ariel Hessayon and Nicholas Keene. Aldershot: Ashgate, 2006.

Mandelbrote, Scott. "Origen against Jerome in Early Modern Europe." In *Patristic Tradition and Intellectual Paradigms in the 17th Century*, 105–135. Edited by Silke-Petra Bergjan and Karla Pollmann. Tübingen: Mohr Siebeck, 2010.

Mandelbrote, Scott. "Isaac Vossius and the Septuagint." In *Isaac Vossius (1618–1689) between Science and Scholarship*, 85–117. Edited by Eric Jorink and Dirk van Miert. Leiden and Boston: Brill, 2012.

Mandelbrote, Scott: "The Old Testament and its Ancient Versions in Manuscript and Print in the West, from c. 1480 to c. 1780." In *The New Cambridge History of the Bible*, 3:82–109. Edited by Euan Cameron. Cambridge: Cambridge University Press, 2016.

Mandelbrote, Scott. "Witches and Forgers: Anthonie van Dale on Biblical History and the Authority of the Septuagint." In *Scriptural Authority and Biblical Criticism in the Dutch Golden Age: God's Word Questioned*, 270–306. Edited by Dirk van Miert, Henk Nellen, Piet Steenbakkers, and Jetze Touber. Oxford: Oxford University Press, 2017.

Mandelbrote, Scott. "Philology and Scepticism: Early Modern Scholars at Work on the Text of the Bible." In *The Marriage of Philology and Scepticism*, 123–142. Edited by G. M. Cao, A. Grafton, and J. Kraye. London: Warburg Institute, 2019.

Mandelbrote, Scott. "The History of Septuagint Studies: Early Modern Western Europe." In *The Handbook of the Septuagint*, 33–51. Edited by Alison G. Salvesen and Timothy Michael Law. Oxford: Oxford University Press, 2021.

Manuel, Frank. *Isaac Newton: Historian*. Cambridge: Cambridge University Press, 1963.

Manuel, Frank. *The Eighteenth Century Confronts the Gods*. New York: Atheneum, 1967.

Matytsin, Anton M. "Enlightenment and Erudition: Writing Cultural History at the Académie des inscriptions." *Modern Intellectual History* 19 (2022): 323–348.

Meynard, Thierry. "Chinese Buddhism and the Threat of Atheism in Seventeenth-Century Europe." *Buddhist-Christian Studies* 31 (2011), 3–23.

Miller, Peter. "The "Antiquarianization" of Biblical Scholarship and the London Polyglot Bible (1653–57)." *Journal of the History of Ideas* 62 (2001): 463–482.

Miller, Peter. "Taking Paganism Seriously: Anthropology and Antiquarianism in Early Seventeenth Century Histories of Religion." *Archiv für Religionsgeschichte* 3 (2001): 193–209.

Miller, Peter, and François Louis, ed. *Antiquarianism and Intellectual Life in Europe and China, 1500–1800*. Ann Arbor: The University of Michigan Press, 2012.

Miller, Peter. *Peiresc's Orient: Antiquarianism as Cultural History in the Seventeenth Century*. Surrey: Ashgate, 2012.

Mills, Simon. *A Commerce of Knowledge: Trade, Religion, and Scholarship between England and the Ottoman Empire, 1600–1760*. Oxford: Oxford University Press, 2020.

Momigliano, Arnaldo. "Ancient History and the Antiquarian." *Journal of the Warburg and Courtauld Institutes* 13 (1950): 285–315.

Momigliano, Arnaldo. *Secondo contributo alla storia degli studi classici*. Rome: Edizioni di Storia e Letteratura, 1960.

Momigliano, Arnaldo. *The Conflict between Paganism and Christianity in the Fourth Century*. Oxford: Clarendon Press, 1963.

Momigliano, Arnaldo. *Essays in Ancient and Modern Historiography*. Oxford: Basil Blackwell, 1977.

Momigliano, Arnaldo. "Biblical Studies and Classical Studies: Simple Reflections upon Historical Method." *Annali della Scuola Normale Superiore di Pisa. Classe di lettere e filosofia* 11 (1981), 25–32.

Momigliano, Arnaldo. "The Origins of Universal History." *Annali della Scuola Normale Superiore di Pisa. Classe di lettere e filosofia* 12 (1982): 533–560.

Momigliano, Arnaldo. *On Pagans, Jews, and Christians*. Hanover: Wesleyan University Press, 1987.

Momigliano, Arnaldo. *The Classical Foundations of Modern Historiography*. Berkeley and LA: University of California Press, 1990.

Morello, Nicoletta. "Steno, the fossils, the rocks, and the calendar of the Earth." In *The Origins of Geology in Italy*, 81–93. Edited by Gian Battista Vai and W. G. E. Caldwell. Boulder: Geological Society of America, 2006.

Morello, Nicoletta. "Tra diluvio e vulcani: Le concezioni geologiche di Francesco Bianchini e del suo tempo." In *Unità del sapere, molteplicità dei saperi: Francesco Bianchini (1662–1729) tra natura, storia e religione*, 185–206. Edited by Luca Ciancio and Gian Paolo Romagnani. Verona: QuiEdit, 2010.

Moréri, Louis. *Nouveau supplément au grand dictionnaire historique, généalogique, géographique, &c*. 2 vols. Paris: Jacques Vincent, J. B. Coignard & A. Boudet, P. G. Le Mercier, J. Desaint & C. H. Saillant, and Jean-Thomas Herissant, 1749.

Morgan, P. T. J. "The Abbé Pezron and the Celts." *Transactions of the Honourable Society of Cymmrodorion* 2 (1965): 286–295.

Moroni, Gaetano. *Dizionario di erudizione storico-ecclesiastica da S. Pietro sino ai nostri giorni, specialmente intorno ai principali santi, beati, martiri, padri, ai sommi pontefici, cardinali e più celebri scrittori ecclesiastici, ai varii gradi della gerarchia della Chiesa cattolica, alle città patriarcali, arcivescovili e vescovili, agli scismi, alle eresie, ai concilii, alle feste più solenni, ai riti, alle ceremonie sacre, alle cappelle papali, cardinalizie e prelatizie, agli ordini religiosi, militari, equestri ed ospitalieri, non che alla corte romana ed alla famiglia pontificia*. ...103 volumes. Venice: Tipografia Emiliana, 1840–1861.

Mortimer, Sarah, and John Robertson, ed. *The Intellectual Consequences of Religious Heterodoxy 1600–1750*. Leiden and Boston: Brill, 2012.

Mosshammer, Alden A. *The Easter Computus and the Origins of the Christian Era*. Oxford: Oxford University Press, 2008.

Mulsow, Martin. *Die drei Ringe: Toleranz und clandestine Gelehrsamkeit bei Mathurin Veyssière La Croze (1661–1739)*. Berlin and New York: Max Niemeyer Verlag, 2001.

Mulsow, Martin. "John Selden's De Diis Syris: Idolatriekritik und vergleichende Religionsgeschichte im 17. Jahrhundert." *Archiv für Religionsgeschichte* 3 (2001): 1–24.

Mulsow, Martin. "Antiquarianism and Idolatry: The *Historia* of Religions in the Seventeenth Century." In *Historia: Empiricism and Empire in Early Modern Europe*, 181–209. Edited by Gianna Pomata and Nancy G. Siraisi. Cambridge MA and London: The MIT Press, 2005.

Mulsow, Martin, and Jan Assmann, ed. *Sintflut und Gedächtnis: Erinnern und Vergessen des Ursprungs*. Munich: Wilhelm Fink, 2006.

Mulsow, Martin. "The Seventeenth Century Confronts the Gods." In *Knowledge and Profanation: Transgressing the Boundaries of Religion in Premodern Scholarship*, 159–196. Edited by Martin Mulsow and Asaph Ben-Tov. Leiden: Brill, 2019.

Mungello, D. E. *Curious Land: Jesuit Accommodation and the Origins of Sinology.* Honolulu: University of Hawaii Press, 1985.

Mungello, D. E. "A Study of the Preface's to Ph. Couplet's *Tabula Chronologica Monarchiae Sinicae* (1686)." In *Philippe Couplet, s.j. (1623–1693): The Man Who Brought China to Europe*, 183–199. Edited by Jerome Heyndrickx. Nettetal: Stigler, 1990.

Mungello, D. E, ed. *The Chinese Rites Controversy: Its History and Meaning.* Sankt Augustin: Institut Monumenta Serica and San Francisco: The Ricci Institute for Chinese Western Cultural History, 1994.

Mungello, D. E. "European Philosophical Responses to Non-European Culture: China." In *The Cambridge History of Seventeenth-Century Philosophy*, 1:87–100. Edited by Daniel Garber. Cambridge: Cambridge University Press, 1998.

Mungello, D. E. *The Great Encounter of China and the West, 1500–1800.* Oxford: Rowman & Littlefield, 1999.

Neveu, Bruno. *Érudition et religion aux XVIIe et XVIIIe siècles.* Paris: Albin Michel, 1994.

Nodet, Étienne. "Le texte des Antiquités de Josèphe (1.1–10)." *Revue Biblique* 94 (1987): 323–375.

Nothaft, C. Philipp E. "Noah's Calendar: The Chronology of the Flood Narrative and the History of Astronomy in Sixteenth- and Seventeenth-Century Scholarship." *Journal of the Warburg and Courtauld Institutes* 74 (2011): 191–211.

Nothaft, C. Philipp E. "Strategic Skepticism: A reappraisal of Nicholas of Cusa's Calendar Reform Treatise." In *Le Temps des Astronomes; L'astronomie et le décompte du temps de Pierre d'Ailly à Newton*, 65–102. Edited by Éduoard Mehl and Nicolas Roudet. Paris: Les Belles Lettres, 2017.

Papy, Jan. "Far and Away? Japan, China, and Egypt, and the Ruins of Ancient Rome in Justus Lipsius' Intellectual Journey." In *Antiquarianism and Intellectual Life in Europe and China, 1500–1800*, 81–102. Edited by Peter N. Miller and François Louis. Ann Arbor: The University of Michigan Press, 2012.

Pastor, Ludwig, Freiherr von. *The History of the Popes from the Close of the Middle Ages.* Translated by Ernest Graf. 40 vols. London: Kegan Paul, Trench, Trubner & co., 1940.

Patrizi, Antonio. *Storia del seminario di Montefiascone.* Montefiascone: Sistema Biblioteca "Lago di Bolsena", 1990.

Pattison, Mark. "Review of Christian Bartholomés *Huet Evêque d'Avranches: ou les Scepticisme Théologique*." *Quarterly Review* 97 (1855): 291–335.

Perkins, Franklin. *Leibniz and China: A Commerce of Light.* Cambridge: Cambridge University Press, 2004.

Perrier, Émile, ed. "Jean-Pierre Rigord." In *Les bibliophiles et les collectionneurs provençaux anciens et modernes*, 451–459. Marseille: Barthelet, 1897.

Peters, Marion H. "Nicolaes Witsen and Gijsbert Cuper: Two Seventeenth-Century Dutch Burgomasters and their Gordian Knot." *Lias* 16 (1989): 111–151.

Philalethes. "Peyrerius, and Theological Criticism." *The Anthropological Review* 2 (1864): 116–121.

Pinot, Virgile. *La Chine et la formation de l'esprit philosophique en France (1640–1740)*. Paris: Libraire Orientaliste Paul Geuthner, 1932.

Pocock, J. G. A. *Barbarism and Religion*. 5 vols. Cambridge: Cambridge University Press, 1999–2015.

Pomplun, Trent. "Agostino Antonio Giorgi, OESA (1711–1797): Between Augustinianism and the History of Religions." *History of Religions* 59 (2020): 193–221.

Popkin, Richard H. *Isaac La Peyrère (1596–1676): His Life, Work and Influence*. Leiden: Brill, 1987.

Popkin, Richard H. "The Crisis of Polytheism and the Answers of Vossius, Cudworth and Newton." In *Essays in the Context, Nature and Influence of Isaac Newton's Theology*, 9–26. Edited by James E. Force and Richard H. Popkin. Dordrecht: Kluwer Academic Publishers, 1990.

Poulouin, Claudine. *Le temps des origines et les temps reculés de Pascal à l'Encyclopédie*. Paris: Honoré Champion, 1999.

Pregill, Michael. *The Golden Calf between Bible and Qur'an: Scripture, Polemic, and Exegesis from Late Antiquity to Islam*. Oxford: Oxford University Press, 2020.

Quantin, Jean-Louis, and Christopher Ligota, ed. *History of Scholarship: A Selection of Papers from the Seminar on the History of Scholarship Held Annually at the Warburg Institute*. Oxford: Oxford University Press, 2006.

Quantin, Jean-Louis, and Christopher Ligota, ed. "Entre Rome et Paris, entre histoire et théologie: Les Selecta Historiae Ecclesiasticae capita du P. Noël Alexandre et les ambiguïtés de l'historiographie gallicane." *Mémoire dominicaine* 20 (2006): 67–99.

Quantin, Jean-Louis, and Christopher Ligota, ed. "Reason and Reasonableness in French Ecclesiastical Scholarship." *The Huntington Library Quarterly* 74 (2011): 401–436.

Quatremère, Étienne. *Recherches critiques et historiques sur la langue et la littérature de l'Égypte*. Paris: Imprimerie Impériale, 1808.

Rachou, Henri. "Le couvent des Augustins." In *Congrès archéologique de France. XCII[e] session tenue a Toulouse en 1929 par la Société Française d'Archéologie*, 120–133. Paris: Picard and Ste Génle d'Imprimerie, 1930.

Raynal, Jean. *Histoire de la ville de Toulouse, avec une notice des hommes illustres, une suite chronologique et historique, des evêques et archevêques de cette ville ...* Toulouse: Jean-François Forest, 1759.

Renwart, Léon. "Fulgence Lafosse O.E.S.A.: Représentant méconnu de l'école augustinienne." *Augustiniana* 42 (1992): 173–206.

Reusch, Heinrich. *Der Index der verbotenen Bücher. Ein Beitrag zur Kirchen- und Literaturgeschichte*. 2 vols. Bonn: Max Cohen & Sohn, 1885.

Rhodes, Dennis E. "Note sui primi libri stampati a Montefiascone." *La Bibliofilía* 76 (1974): 139–142.

Rhodes, Dennis E. "Primo libro stampato a Montefiascone?" *La Bibliofilía* 77 (1975): 253–254.

Richard, Francis. "Un érudit à la recherche de textes religieux venus d'Orient, le docteur Louis Picques (1637–1699)." In *Les pères de l'Église au XVIIe siècle*, 253–277. Edited by E. Bury and B. Meunier. Paris: Les Éditions du Cerf, 1993.

Rogerson, John W. *W. M. L. de Wette, Founder of Modern Biblical Criticism: An Intellectual Biography*. Sheffield: PSOT Press, 1992.

Rossi, Paolo. *The Dark Abyss of Time: The History of the Earth & The History of Nations from Hooke to Vico*. Chicago & London: The University of Chicago Press, 1984.

Roth, Francis. "Augustinian Historians of the XVIIth Century." *Augustiniana* 6 (1956): 635–658.

Rubiés, Joan-Pau. "Theology, Ethnography, and the Historicization of Idolatry." *Journal of the History of Ideas* 67 (2006): 571–596.

Rubiés, Joan-Pau. "From Antiquarianism to Philosophical History: India, China, and the World History of Religion in European Thought (1600–1770)." In *Antiquarianism and Intellectual Life in Europe and China, 1500–1800*, 313–367. Edited by Peter N. Miller and François Louis. Ann Arbor: The University of Michigan Press, 2012.

Salies, Pierre. *Les Augustins, origine, construction et vie du grand couvent toulousain au Moyen âge, XIIIe–XVIe siècles*. Toulouse: Archistra, 1979.

Sartinio, Josepho. *Vitae illustrium professorum seminarii et collegii Faliscodunensis*. Montefiascone: Typis Seminarii et Collegii, 1844.

Schlichter, Felix. "Flavius Josephus and early modern biblical chronology." *Intellectual History Review* 33 (2023): 587–608.

Schlichter, Felix. "Euhemerus and Euhemerism in the Seventeenth and Eighteenth Centuries." *Journal of the History of Ideas* 84 (2023): 653–683.

Schnaubelt, Joseph C., and Fredrick Van Fleteren, ed. *Augustine in Iconography*. New York: Peter Lang, 1999.

Schneider, Robert A. *Public Life in Toulouse, 1463–1789; From Municipal Republic to Cosmopolitan City*. Ithaca NY: Cornell University Press, 1989.

Scholten, Koen, and Asker Pelgrom. "Scholarly Identity and Memory on a Grand Tour: The Travels of the Joannes Kool and his Travel Journal (1698–1699) to Italy." *Lias* 46 (2019): 93–136.

Schreckenberg, Heinz. *Die Flavius-Josephus-Tradition in Antike und Mittelalter*. Leiden: E. J. Brill, 1972.

Sciarra, Elisabetta. "Breve storia del fondo manoscritto della Biblioteca Angelica." *La Bibliofilía* 111 (2009): 251–282.

Seifert, Arno. "Von der heiligen zur philosophischen Geschichte. Die Rationalisierung der universalhistorischen Erkenntnis im Zeitalter der Aufklärung." *Archiv für Kulturgeschichte* 68 (1986): 81–118.

Serjeantson, Richard. "David Hume's *Natural History of Religion* (1757) and the End of Modern Eusebianism." In *The Intellectual Consequences of Religious Heterodoxy 1600–1750*, 267–295. Edited by Sarah Mortimer and John Robertson. Leiden and Boston: Brill, 2012.

Seznec, Jean. *La survivance des dieux antiques. Essai sur le rôle de la tradition mythologique dans l'Humanisme et dans l'art de la Renaissance*. London: The Warburg Institute, 1940.

Seznec, Jean. *The Survival of the Pagan Gods: The Mythological Tradition and Its Place in Renaissance Humanism and Art*. Translated by Barbara F. Sessions. New York: Pantheon Books, 1953.

Sheehan, Jonathan. "Sacred and Profane: Idolatry, Antiquarianism and the Polemics of Distinction in the Seventeenth Century." *Past & Present* 192 (2006): 35–66.

Sheehan, Jonathan. "Time Elapsed, Time Regained: Anthropology and the Flood." In *Sintflut und Gedächtnis: Erinnern und Vergessen des Ursprungs*, 321–334. Edited by Martin Mulsow and Jan Assmann. Munich: Wilhelm Fink, 2006.

Shelford, April G. *Transforming the Republic of Letters: Pierre-Daniel Huet and European Intellectual Life, 1650–1720*. Rochester: Rochester University Press, 2007.

Stausberg, Michael. *Faszination Zarathustra. Zoroaster und die Europäische Religionsgeschichte der Frühen Neuzeit*. Berlin and New York: Walter de Gruyter, 1998.

Stella, Pietro. *Il Giansenismo in Italia*. 2 vols. Rome: Edizioni di Storia e Letteratura, 2006.

Stolzenberg, Daniel. *Egyptian Oedipus: Athanasius Kircher and the Secrets of Antiquity*. Chicago: Chicago University Press, 2013.

Stone, Harold Samuel. *Vico's Cultural History: The Production and Transmission of Ideas in Naples 1685–1750*. Leiden: E. J. Brill, 1997.

Stone, Harold Samuel. *St. Augustine's Bones: A Microhistory*. Amherst and Boston: University of Massachusetts Press, 2002.

Stroumsa, Guy. "John Spencer and the Roots of Idolatry." *History of Religions* 41 (2001): 1–23.

Stroumsa, Guy. "Noah's sons and the religious conquest of the earth: Samuel Bochart and his followers." In *Sintflut und Gedächtnis: Erinnern und Vergessen des Ursprungs*, 307–318. Edited by Martin Mulsow and Jan Assmann. Munich: Wilhelm Fink, 2006.

Stroumsa, Guy. *A New Science: The Discovery of Religion in the Age of Reason*. Cambridge MA: Harvard University Press, 2010.

Sutcliffe, Adam. *Judaism and Enlightenment*. Cambridge: Cambridge University Press, 2003.

Tinto, Alberto. "Giovanni Giacomo Komarek tipografo a Roma nei secoli XVII–XVIII ed i suoi campionari di caratteri." *La Bibliofilía* 75 (1973): 189–225.

Toomer, G. J. *John Selden: A Life in Scholarship*. 2 vols. Oxford: Oxford University Press, 2009.

Touber, Jetze. "Religious Interests and Scholarly Exchange in the Early Enlightenment Republic of Letters: Italian and Dutch Scholars, 1675–1715." *Rivista di storia della Chiesa in Italia* 68 (2014): 411–436.

Touber, Jetze. "'I am happy that Italy fosters such exquisite minds'; Gisbert Cuper (1644–1716) and intellectual life on the Italian peninsula." *Incontri. Rivista europea di studi italiani* 30 (2015): 91–106.

Touber, Jetze. "Tracing the Human Past: The Art of Writing Between Human Ingenuity and Divine Agency in Early Modern World History." In *Enlightened Religion: From Confessional Churches to Polite Piety in the Dutch Republic*, 60–103. Edited by Joke Spaans and Jetze Touber. Leiden and Boston: Brill, 2019.

Twining, Timothy. "The Early Modern Debate over the Age of the Hebrew Vowel Points: Biblical Criticism and Hebrew Scholarship in the Confessional Republic." *Journal of the History of Ideas* 81 (2020): 337–358.

Van Kley, Edwin J. "Europe's 'Discovery' of China and the Writing of World History." *The American Historical Review* 76 (1971): 358–385.

Van Noord, Willemijn, and Thijs Weststeijn. "The Global Trajectory of Nicolaas Witsen's Chinese Mirror." *The Rijksmuseum Bulletin* 63 (2015): 324–361.

Van Noord, Willemijn. "European Reflections in Chinese Mirrors: Interpreting Self and Other through Encounters with Chinese Artefacts in the Dutch Republic, 1685–1715." In *Knowledge and Arts on the Move: Transformation of the Self-Aware Image through East-West Encounters*, 39–56. Edited by Christopher Craig, Enrico Fongaro, and Akihiro Ozaki. Milan: Mimesis International, 2018.

Vermeulen, Han F. *Before Boas. The Genesis of Ethnography and Ethnology in the German Enlightenment.* Lincoln and London: University of Nebraska Press, 2015.

Villien, Antoine. *L'abbé Eusèbe Renaudot: Essai sur la Vie et sur son Œuvre liturgique.* Paris: Victor Lecoffre, 1904.

Vosté, James M. "The Vulgate at the Council of Trent." *The Catholic Biblical Quarterly* 9 (1947): 9–25.

Wacholder, Ben Zion. "Biblical Chronology in the Hellenistic World Chronicles." *Harvard Theological Review* 61 (1968): 451–481.

Walker, D. P. *The Ancient Theology: Studies in Christian Platonism from the Fifteenth to the Eighteenth Century.* London: Duckworth, 1972.

Waquet, Françoise. *Le modèle français et l'Italie savante (1660–1750): conscience de soi et perception de l'autre dans la République des Lettres.* Rome: École Française de Rome, 1989.

Wernicke, Michael Klaus. *Kardinal Enrico Noris und seine Verteidigung Augustins.* Würzburg: Augustinus-Verlag, 1973.

Weststeijn, Thijs. "Spinoza Sinicus: An Asian Paragraph in the History of the Radical Enlightenment." *Journal of the History of Ideas* 68 (2007): 537–561.

Yates, Frances. *Giordano Bruno and the Hermetic Tradition*. London and New York: Routledge, 1964.

Ypma, Eelcko. "Les auteurs augustins français: Liste de leurs noms et de leurs ouvrages." *Augustiniana* 18 (1968): 203–261.

Zedelmaier, Helmut. "Der Ursprung der Schrift als Problem der frühen Neuzeit." In *Philologie und Erkenntnis. Beiträge zu Begriff und Problem frühneuzeitlicher 'Philologie'*, 207–224. Edited by Ralph Häfner. Tübingen: Max Niemeyer Verlag, 2001.

Zwierlein, Cornel. "Orient contra China: Eusèbe Renaudot's Vision of World History (ca. 1700)." *Journal of the History of Ideas* 81 (2020): 23–44.

Index

Aaron (biblical figure) 32, 149–150
Ablancourt, Nicolas Frémont d' 220
Abraham (biblical patriarch) 73, 83, 93, 102, 104, 160, 170, 178, 201, 255, 261n140, 286–287
Abraham, Guillaume 31
Abulpharagius. *See* Bar Hebraeus
Abydenus 131–133, 176
accommodationism 77, 310–312, 320–325
  see also Chinese Rites debate, Jesuits, Ricci
Acoluthus, Andreas 66
Acsamitek, Francesco Maria 49
Adam (biblical figure) 89, 112
  see also La Peyrère
Adam, Jean 41
Aesculapius (pagan god) 115, 153
Africanus, Sextus Julius 187, 234–240, 242, 244–246, 251–252, 257–258n124
Airoli, Giacomo Maria 222–224, 343
Alembert, Jean le Rond d' 16
Alessandri, Alexander 299
Alexander Polyhistor 201
Alexandre de Rhodes 332
Alexandre, Noël 115, 133–134, 148, 171, 295–296, 316, 332, 336
Alexandrinus, Codex 209, 220
  see also Septuagint, Vaticanus
Allatius, Leo 57, 208n82
Altieri degli Albertoni, Paluzzo Paluzzi 70
Amama, Sixtus 220
Amasis (pharoah) 226, 347
Ambrose 156
Ammianus Marcellinus 292, 297
Ammon (pagan god). *See* Jupiter
Amodei, Gennaro 78–80
Amosis (pharoah) 234–235
Ampelius, Lucius 290
Anatolius of Laodicea 54
Angelica, Library 2, 7, 35, 37–40, 51–52
Anisson, Jean 30, 59
Annat, François 41
Annianus 255–256
Annius of Viterbo 103, 242
Apion 234, 237
Apis (mythological figure) 150, 156, 260

Apollo (pagan god) 115, 290
Apollodorus 115, 156, 244
Apollonius of Rhodes 112, 147
Apuleius 290
Aquinas, Thomas 24–25, 79, 285, 322
Arabic
  language 6, 26, 30, 45, 50–51, 69, 272
  printing 31, 43, 200
  historians 63–64, 168, 241, 261n140
  see also Coptic-Arabic-Latin Pentateuch
Aratus 322
Arcadi, Accademia degli 76
Areopagus 293–294, 320–322, 328, 337
Aristeas, Letter of 186, 191–192, 206–207
Aristobolus 344
Arnauld, Antoine 7, 134
Arnobius 162n65, 296, 321
Arphaxad (biblical figure) 200n53, 209, 262
Arrian 36
Artapanus 107, 166, 174, 182, 289
Ashurbanipal, Library of 140
Assenburgh, Louis van 80
Athenagoras 161
Athothes (Egyptian king) 153, 256–257
Augustine 22–24, 40–41, 97, 115, 125, 156, 176, 180, 187, 212, 226, 242, 250–251, 253, 282, 322, 338, 351–352
  discovery of relics 4, 52
Augustine, Order of Hermits of Saint (OESA) 21–28, 39–40, 51–52, 315
  see also augustinianism
augustinianism 40–42
  see also Jansenism, Noris
Aulus Gellius 112, 287, 292
Ausonius 3, 290, 298
Avitabile Maioli, Biagio d' 85–86

Baal (biblical idol) 338–339, 342–343
Bacchini, Benedetto 38, 48, 56, 113
Bacchus (pagan god) 107, 115, 143, 156, 283, 285, 290
Bangius, Thomas 220
Banier, Antoine 96–97, 111, 277–278
Barbarigo, Gregorio 50, 57, 70
Barbarigo, Marc-Antonio 70–72, 74–75, 77, 116, 219–220, 318

Barberini, Francesco 57
Bar Hebraeus, Gregory 208–209
Baronio, Cesare 157, 162, 175, 196, 218–219, 240, 259
Barthélemy, Jean-Jacques 8
Basil of Caesarea 45
Basnage, Jacques 136
Bayle, Pierre 21, 89, 105, 174, 306
Bede 186, 212
Bégon, Michel 29–30, 44, 58–59, 145
Bellarmine, Robert 216–219, 222
Bellelli, Fulgenzio 40
Bellet, Jules 167
Bellori, Giovanni 57
Belus (mythological figure) 201, 282
Benedictine Order (OSB) 192
  see also Maurists
Benedict XIV, Prospero Lorenzo Lambertini, Pope 42
Bernabò, Angelo 47
Béroalde, Mathieu 93, 121
Berosus 103, 125, 132, 233
Berti, Giovanni Lorenzo 40
Besold, Christoph 171
Bianchini, Francesco 48, 50–51, 53, 60–62, 71, 74, 76, 82, 91, 98, 125–126, 120–130, 138–139, 173, 180, 240n48, 245–246, 263–264, 318–319
Bianchini, Giuseppe 71
Bignon, Jean-Paul 4, 62
Bigot, Emery 38
Boccaccio, Giovanni 96
Bocchoris (pharoah) 235
Bochart, Samuel 66, 94, 105–114, 129–130, 134, 137, 148, 159, 165–166, 348–350
Bodin, Jean 181
Bolingbroke, Henry St. John, 1st Viscount 14, 36–37, 50, 135
Bollandist Society 33, 313–314
  see also Janninck, Papebroch
Bompart, Johann 166n74
Bona, Giovanni 42, 57
Bonfrère, Jacques 158
Bonjour, Guillaume 1–352
Borri, Giuseppe Francesco 32
Bossuet, Jacques-Bénigne 134, 209, 304
Bouges, Thomas 27, 29, 82
Bouget, Jean 71
Bouillon, Emmanuel-Théodose de La Tour d'Auvergne de 7

Braun, Johannes 166n74, 271–272
Broughton, Hugh 93, 121
Brücker, Johann Jakob 140
Bruel, Joachim 334
Bruno, Giordano 118, 123
Buddeus, Johann Franz 2
Bunsen, Christian Karl Josias von 144, 231
Burnet, Thomas 125

Cadmus (mythological character) 107
calendar
  calendar correction 2, 4, 52–56, 69
  Noachic calendar 132
Cajetan, Thomas 33
Calixtus, Georg 220
Calvoli, Giovanni Cinelli 57, 84
Camden, William 66
Canaan (biblical figure) 165–166
Cappel, Jacques 92, 227, 238, 241, 256n118
Cappel, Louis 13, 190
Cardoso, João Francisco 80–81
Carion, Johann 159
Carmelites, Order of (OCarm) 33, 313–314
Carpzov, Johann Gottlob 83, 205
Casanata, Girolamo 34, 47, 75, 314–315
Casaubon, Isaac 174, 240
Cassini, Giovanni Domenico 53
Cassiodorus 206
Castell, Edmund 220
Castner, Caspar 317
Celsius, Olof 35–37, 56, 84
Celsus 127
  see also Origen
Cerù, Gioseppe 78–80
Chaeremon 177, 289
Champollion, Jean-François 9
Charmot, Nicolas 70n209, 313–314, 318, 325–329, 332, 335, 339
Cheops (pharoah). See Suphis
Chevreaux, Urbain 228
China
  Bonjour's mission 6, 20, 67, 76–82, 340–343
  cartography 81–82
  Chinese Rites debate 74, 76–78, 295, 300–302, 305–306, 308–319, 323–329
  lanuage 4
  mirror 62, 333–336
Christina, Queen of Sweden 34, 57

INDEX

Cicero   293, 298, 321, 323, 336n138, 337
  De natura deorum   173, 175–176, 291, 295, 297, 299, 321–322, 337
Ciron, Gabriel de   21
Cistercian Order (OCist)   58–59, 192
Clarke, Edward Daniel   158n50
Clary, Jacques de   20–21
Claude, Jean   7
Clavius, Christopher   53
  see also calendar
Clément, Nicolas   75
Clement of Alexandria   113, 167, 251, 344
  Stromata   112, 156, 202, 234
Clement XI, Giovanni Francesco Albani, Pope   2, 7, 10, 47, 49, 52–53, 57, 59, 67, 69, 72, 76, 78, 309, 314, 316–319
Cloche, Antonin   34
Clüver, Philipp   330n106
Cnef. *See* Pan
Confucius   295–296, 310–313, 316, 333–335
Conring, Hermann   227, 240
Conti, Natale   82
Coptic   5–12, 44–47
  Coptic-Arabic-Latin Pentateuch   11, 36, 46–47, 65, 68, 200, 217, 219–221, 315
  Elementa linguae copticae   5–11, 36, 45–47, 65, 68, 200, 315
  In monumenta coptica   2, 8, 36, 44–46, 49, 59–60, 68, 315
  language   3, 5–12, 26, 35, 44–45, 50–51, 63–67, 68–69, 308–309
  Psalter   76, 220
Cosimo III de' Medici, Grand Duke of Tuscany   51
Costa, Ignacio da   311
Cotta, Giovanni Battista   84–85
Cotton Genesis   209, 220
Couplet, Philippe   286, 311, 321–325, 327, 334
Courbiat, Fulgence   31
Creation (biblical)
  date of   5, 186, 208, 230
  mythological parallels   112–113, 160
Ctesias   233
Cudworth, Ralph   140n172
Cumberland, Richard   140, 274–275
Cuper, Gisbert   3, 8, 11–12, 20, 26, 28, 44, 49, 51–52, 58, 60–62, 65, 67–68, 74, 76, 79, 84, 113, 125–126, 152–153, 163–164, 176n119, 185, 196–197, 200, 204, 209, 253, 261, 271–277, 308–309, 316–319, 333–335, 340, 345
Cusa, Nicholas of   54
[ps.-] Cyprian   55
Cyril of Alexandria   54

Dale, Anthonie van   136, 139
deism   134, 149
  English deists   13–14, 89
  see also: Bolingbroke, Toland
Democritus   327
Derodon, David   166n74
Deseine, François   213
Deucalion (mythological figure)   130–131, 138n167, 347
diffusionism   105–113, 136–139, 144, 147, 304–305
Dio Chrysostom   147m 293
Diodorus Siculus   68, 94, 105n52, 143–144, 147, 156, 158n48, 169–171, 179–180, 226, 254, 257–261, 265, 283, 290–291, 330
Diogenes Laertius   143n3, 226
Dionysus (pagan god). *See* Bacchus
Dirois, François   262
Dodwell, Henry   136, 139–140, 196
Dominican Order   33–34, 295
Dupin, Louis Ellies   136, 174, 245–247, 249
Dupuy, Jean   25

Ecchellensis, Abraham (Ibrahim al-Haqilani)   45n107
Edwards, John   175
Ennius   336
Epaphus (pagan god)   163
Epictetus   323n84
Epicureans   327, 332
Epimenides   169, 322
Eratosthenes   239, 243–244, 257
Erpenius, Thomas   105
Estiennot, Claude   33, 194
etymology   3, 67–68, 129, 156, 162, 173, 272, 282–283, 287–292, 337–339
Eucharist   7, 45–46
Euhemerus   102, 283, 295
Eupolemus   182, 202–203
Euripides   112, 336

Eusebius of Caesarea   101, 113, 187, 235, 237–240, 242, 244–246, 251
  Eusebian tradition   101–103, 147, 149
  Praeparatio evangelica   104, 131, 165–166, 173–174, 201–203, 258–259, 289
[ps.-] Eustathius   166n76, 208
Excerpta barbaro-latina   238, 256–257

Fabretti, Raffaello   28, 34–35, 60
Fabricius, Johann Albert   83, 205, 228
Fabricy, Gabriel   83
Fabri, Guglielmo. *See* Bonjour
Fénelon, François   58, 313–314
Fermat, Pierre   21
Ferrari, Tommaso Maria   314–315
Ficino, Marsilio   173, 287n66
Filhol, Antoine Imbert   216
Filippo di S. Niccolò   315
Firmicus Maternus, Julius   156, 162
Flood (biblical)   44, 92–93, 124–133
Fohi (Chinese king)   173, 188, 303, 307
Fontanini, Giusto   40, 51, 61, 74
Fontenelle, Bernard de   89
Fourmont, Étienne   95, 140, 242n56, 245–246
Foy-Vaillant, Jean   28, 276
Francesco da Varese, Carlo   315
Fréret, Nicolas   111, 349–350
Fridelli, Xavier Ehrenbert   81
Fulgentius   281–282, 300
Funari, Onorato   78–79

Gabrieli, Giovanni Maria   315
Gale, Theophilus   101, 109–110, 145, 148, 159–160, 175
Galiani, Celestino   48
Galland, Antoine   62, 271–273
Garnier, Jean   42
Gibbon, Edward   157, 158n50
Gideon (biblical judge)   108, 113
Giles of Rome   25
Giles of Viterbo   23
Gimma, Giacinto   84
Giorgi, Agostino Antonio   8, 83
Giraldi, Giglio Gregorio   159n52
Goar, Jacques   187n7, 238
González de Mendoza, Juan   305, 334
Gosse, Philip Henry   141

Graevius, Johann Georg   59–60, 63, 159n53
Graverol, François   29, 290n75
Graveson, Ignace-Hyacinthe-Amat de   82
Gregory of Rimini   25
Grimaldi, Claudio Filippo   341
Gronovius, Jakob   59, 63
Gronovius, Johann Friedrich   61
Grotius, Hugo   101, 107, 118–119, 126, 132, 148
Gruter, Jan   62, 162, 287
Guarmani, Giacomo   78

Hale, Matthew   116–117, 121
Halloix, Pierre   42
Ham (biblical figure)   108–109, 283
Hardouin, Jean   28, 42, 213n96, 264, 276
Harlemius, Johannes   223
Harpocrates (pagan god)   277
Havercamp, Siwart   266
Hecataeus of Abdera   143
Heinsius, Daniel   107
Hephaestus (mythological king). *See* Vulcan
Herbelot, Barthélemy d'   7
Hercules   283, 285
Hermes. *See* Mercury
Hermes Trismegistus   123, 167, 173–176, 323
  see also Mercury
Herodotus   105n52, 107n56, 111n71, 143, 147, 159, 172, 226–227, 233, 238–239, 254, 257–261, 265, 291, 300
Hesiod   112, 180, 278
Heyschius   251
Hire, Philippe de la   80
Hobbes, Thomas   13, 74, 117, 122
Hody, Humphrey   191–192, 196
Hohenheim, Theophrastus von. *See* Paracelsus
Holste, Lucas   40, 57
Homer   112, 143n3, 276–278
Horace   3, 112
Horn, Georg   127, 159–160, 181, 191, 218, 240
Hottinger, Johann Heinrich   220
Huang, Arcadio   74, 317, 334
Hudson, John   68, 83, 266
Huet, Pierre-Daniel   11, 30n45, 58–60, 63–65, 102–103, 107n55, 109–114, 117, 133–137, 143, 145, 148, 164–169, 175–176, 178, 180, 210, 261, 271–275, 284, 289, 290n75–76, 305, 349

INDEX 397

Hugh of Saint Victor   237
Hyginus   173
hyksos (pharoahs)   235, 237–239

Ibn Ezra   168
Ibn Wahshiyya   168
Imperiali, Giuseppe Renato   34, 51
Inachus (Argive king)   93, 234
Innocent XI, Benedetto Odescalchi, Pope   42
Innocent XII, Antonio Pignatelli, Pope   44, 314–315
Intorcetta, Prospero   311
Isaac (biblical patriarch)   104
Isidore of Seville   102, 156
Isis (pagan god)   149, 162n65, 163, 290

Jacquelot, Isaac   65
Janninck, Conrad   33, 38n77, 343
Jansen, Cornelius   41–42
Jansenism   7, 21, 23, 33, 41–42, 45–46
Japhet   108–109
Jartoux, Pierre   80–81, 342–343
Jerome   16, 148, 161–163, 186, 193–195, 198, 206n73, 212, 219, 236–237, 250
Jesuit Order (SJ)   41–42, 76–77, 309–313, 320–329
Jeux Floraux   21, 27
John Chrysostom   161, 289
John of Antioch   208
Joseph (biblical patriarch)   30–31, 43, 65, 89, 113, 147–148, 154–178, 248, 259–261, 285, 288–289
Josephus, Flavius   44, 72–73, 147, 161, 200n53, 201–206, 233–235, 238, 258–259, 266
    Contra Apionem   105n52, 111n71, 177, 201–203, 233–235, 257
Joshua (biblical figure)   89, 106–107, 285
Jouard, Dom   192
Julian the Apostate   168
Junius, Franciscus   220
Jupiter (pagan god)   102, 108–109, 153, 156, 163, 271–275, 282, 287–288, 290, 328, 336–337, 344
Jurieu, Pierre   61–62, 67, 94, 110, 118, 159, 271–275, 281, 284, 286n61
Justin   176n118

[ps-.] Justin Martyr   112–113, 234, 344
Juvenal   95, 112, 295, 297, 329

Kangxi Emperor   4, 77–78, 80–81, 341
Kircher, Athanasius   5–6, 29–30, 45, 49, 57, 63–65, 145, 159n55, 188, 210, 241, 258, 261n140, 276–277, 305, 311–312, 343
Kohlreif, Gottfried   83, 205
Kool, Joannes   36
Kriegsmann, Wilhelm Christoph   166n74
Kronos. *See* Saturn

Labbé, Philippe   264
La Croze, Mathurin Veyssière   8, 62, 64, 67, 305, 333n123
Labeo, Cornelius   283
Lactantius   251, 295–296, 322
    Institutiones divinae   102, 150, 173, 175–176, 323
Lafosse, Fulgence   25
Langenmantel, Hieronymus Ambrosius   210
Langius, Wilhelm   249, 264
Laparre, Guillaume   33
Lapeyre, Bernard   25, 27–28, 213
La Peyrère, Isaac   117–124, 127–128, 153, 165, 167, 178, 189, 191, 228, 230–232, 243, 246, 249–250, 254, 262–266, 348–350
Lapide, Cornelius à   324n89
Larcher, Pierre Henri   82
Lazius, Wolfgang   109
Le Clerc, Jean   67–68, 79, 83, 96, 98n31, 125n118, 128, 136, 138, 205, 245, 271, 274, 286n61
Le Comte, Louis   322
Leibniz, Gottfried Wilhelm   2, 50, 52–53, 60, 65–67, 138, 167, 197, 209–211, 261–262, 303
Lemaire de Belges, Jean   109
Léon, Luis de   23, 217
Lequien, Michel   185, 193–195, 200, 212, 250, 253, 316
Leydekker, Melchior   241
Libanius   36
Liber (pagan god). *See* Bacchus
libertines   5
Liceti, Fortunio   158
Lightfoot, John   274
Lionne, Artus de   74, 317–318, 334

Lipsius, Justus   103, 258*n*56
Livy   135*n*152, 159*n*52, 351–352
Lloyd, William   196, 212–213, 272
Locke, John   21, 63, 306
Longobardo, Niccolò   311, 325, 327
Lubin, Augustin   23
Lucan   107*n*56, 161, 330*n*105
Lucaris, Cyril   220
Lucenti, Giulio Ambrogio   47
Lucian   130, 176
Lucretius   180, 330, 332
Ludolf, Hiob   2, 60, 64, 66–67, 209–211, 214, 221
Lupus, Christian   23, 26–27
Lycurgus   134
Lydiat, Thomas   264

Mabillon, Jean   40, 44, 48, 194, 198*n*48, 218
Macrobius   96, 162, 277, 287, 291
Madbachus (pagan god)   271–275
Maffei, Scipione   48
Magalhães, Gabriel de   311
Magliabechi, Antonio   1, 11, 27, 31, 36–38, 43–45, 47–50, 52, 55–57, 60–62, 71, 74–75, 83, 100, 185, 198*n*48, 247, 291, 306, 316
Maigrot, Charles   300–301, 308, 312–313, 318, 325
Maimbourg, Louis   42
Maimonides, Moses   152
Maine, Henry   144
Malabar Rites   77
Malebranche, Nicolas   306
Manetho   4, 115, 120, 172, 174, 187–189, 200, 225–267, 303–304
Manfredi, Eustachio   53
Manilius, Marcus   160, 165–166, 175, 180, 330, 332
Marini, Giovanni Filippo de   335
Marlowe, Christopher   118
Marshal, Jean   129
Marsham, John   64, 94, 150–155, 165–167, 174, 178, 180, 229, 231–232, 240–242, 244–247, 249, 258, 260, 263–265, 282, 304–305
Martial   112, 297
Martianay, Jean   82, 99, 185, 193–195, 200, 202–204, 212, 214, 219, 225, 232, 240*n*48, 249–254, 348

Martin, David   271
Martini, Martino   188, 191, 303–304, 311–312, 335
Martinon, Jean   41
Masoretes   190
Masson, Jean   271–273
Massoulié, Antonin   33–34, 74, 316–317, 334
Maurists   33, 48, 193–195
  see also Benedictines, Mabillon, Martianay, Montfaucon
Mazzinelli, Alessandro   72
Megasthenes   103
Melanchthon, Philipp   159, 181
[ps.-] Melito of Sardis   156
Mencheres (pharoah)   257–260
Mencke, Otto   56–57
Menes (Egyptian king)   153, 169–172, 188, 226, 235, 244–245, 247, 255, 257, 282
Mercury (Egyptian god)   44–45, 89, 147–148, 164–167, 172–178, 248, 288, 290
metempsychosis   143
Michaelis, Gregor   150*n*26
Michaelis, Johann David   111
Milton, John   149
Min (pharoah). *See* Menes
Minims, Order of (OM)   33
Minos (mythological character)   134, 167–169
Misson, Maximilien   31–35, 70
Molon, Apollonius   201
Monceaux, François de   149
Mondonville, Madame Jeanne de Juliard de   21
Monimus (pagan god)   168, 289
Montchal, Charles de   21
Montesquieu   136, 140
Montfaucon, Bernard de   33–35, 40, 45–48, 65, 75, 140*n*172, 194, 286
Moore, Michael   71
Morales, Juan Bautista   312
Morell, André   28, 276
Morin, Jean   13, 186, 190
Morosini, Francesco   70
moscholatry   149–150
Moses   5, 32, 63, 72–73, 89, 92–93, 95, 100, 103, 107–112, 115, 124, 126, 130–134, 166–167, 169–171, 174–176, 194, 234, 285, 289, 331, 334, 348
Mosaic authorship   16

INDEX

Mosheim, Lorenz   140
Muratori, Ludovico Antonio   37–39, 48, 50–51, 61, 74, 76, 113, 163, 204–205, 223–224
Mykerinos (pharoah). *See* Mencheres

Navarette, Domingo   311
Necherophes (pharoah)   83, 178, 228, 244–245, 255, 258
Neptune (pagan god)   92, 108–109
Newton, Isaac   33, 48, 63, 349
Nicaise, Claude   27, 49, 57–61, 63, 65–66, 69, 75, 138, 145–146, 182, 196–197, 199, 209–210, 213, 221, 227, 248, 252, 262, 307
Nicolai da Leonessa, Giovanni Francesco   314–315, 317
Nicole, Pierre   7
Nimrod (biblical figure)   201
Ninus (biblical figure)   286
Nitocris (pharoah)   236
Noailles, Louis Antoine de   7, 316–317
Noah (biblical figure)   89, 102, 108–109, 125, 129–133
    Noachic monotheism   91, 101, 278–288, 305–306, 321–322
Noël, François   317, 332
Nonnus of Panopolis   290–291
Noris, Enrico   1, 8, 22–23, 25, 27–29, 31, 37–38, 40–44, 49, 51, 53, 57–58, 60–61, 66, 69–70, 72–73, 75–76, 192n26, 195–196, 212–213, 221, 224, 276, 314–316, 343
Numenius   112
numismatics   27–30, 57–58, 61–62, 275–278, 287–288
Nuzzi, Adeodato   26, 75, 77, 261n140, 308, 318

Odescalchi, Livio   34
Ogyges (mythological figure)   97, 129–131, 138n167
Olivier, Adolphus   271
Origen   41, 54, 110, 203, 296
    Contra Celsum   127, 156n42, 289, 293, 330, 337–338
Osiris (pagan god)   3, 29, 68, 149, 156, 158, 163, 178, 283, 285, 290

Ottoboni, Pietro   34, 50–51
Ouseel, Jacob   158
Ovid   297

Pacini, Antonio   43–44, 47, 52, 200, 315
Pacuvius   112
Pagi, Antoine   28
Pan (pagan god)   3, 115, 145, 156, 161–163
Pandorus   255–256
Panvinio, Onofrio   23, 26
Papebroch, Daniel   33
Paracelsus   118
Parieu, Félix Esquirou de   9
Pascal, Blaise   310
Passionei, Domenico   40
Pastrizio, Giovanni   51, 74, 334
Paulinus of Nola   38–39, 163–164
Pauw, Cornelius de   242n56
Pedrini, Teodorico   80–81, 341
Pereira, Benedict   150n26, 240
Pereisc, Nicolas-Claude Fabri de   76
Perizonius, Jacobus   59–60, 82, 227, 239, 247, 261, 267
Perrone, Domenico   78–80
Petau, Denis   196, 229, 241–242, 246, 249, 264, 338
Peter of Lombard   25
Petit, Samuel   207n79
Petrocchini, Gregorio   40
Peucer, Caspar   150n26
Pezron, Paul   60, 107n56, 170n89, 185, 192–197, 200, 202–204, 209, 212–214, 218–219, 221–222, 224–225, 227–228, 230, 232, 241–242, 245–246, 248–254, 263–266, 303, 307
Philo of Byblos   104, 108, 140
    see also Sanchuniathon
Philo of Alexandria   161, 165, 172, 338
Picques, Louis   6, 35, 64
Pignoria, Lorenzo   40
Plato   101, 105n52, 112, 143, 153, 169, 175, 194, 226, 287, 323, 333, 338, 347–348
Plautus   293
Pliny   107n56, 169, 297
Plutarch   105n52, 131–132, 287, 291, 300
    De Iside et Osiride   66, 68, 100, 112, 132, 143n3, 156, 158n48, 288
Pluto (pagan god)   108–109, 156

399

polyglot Bibles 208–209
  Antwerp Polyglot 223
  London Polyglot 190, 220–221
  Paris Polyglot 186
Pomponius Mela 226
Pontanus, Jacobus 66
Poole, Matthew 218n109
Porte, François de la 33
Possevino, Antonio 240
Postel, Guillaume 109
Poussin, Nicolas 57
Priapus (pagan god) 115
Prinstet, Étienne 58–59
Prometheus (mythological figure) 89, 112, 344
Propaganda Fide, Congregatio de 2, 8–9, 34
  printing press 47, 49
  Chinese missions 77–78, 309–310, 312, 318–319
Propertius 112, 335
Prideaux, Matthias 109n61
Psammetichus (pharoah) 227, 236
Ptolemy of Mendes 234
Puteanus, Johannes. *See* Dupuy
Pythagoras 101, 143, 323

Quartaironi, Domenico 53
Quatremère, Étienne 9
Queménér, Louis de 313
Quietism 58–59, 313–314, 316
Quintilian 95

Radulovich, Niccolò 316
Rasseguier, Basile 20, 75
Reinesius, Thomas 66
Reland, Abraham 271–272
Renan, Ernest 9
Renaudot, Eusèbe 7, 10, 45, 47, 82, 134, 316–317
Republic of Letters 1, 5–6, 27–30, 37–38, 40, 56–68
  see also Magliabechi, Nicaise, numismatics
Rhenferd, Jacob 271–272
Rhodomann, Lorenz 171n93, 331
Ricci, Matteo 305–306, 310–312, 320–323, 334
Rigord, Honoré 45–46

Rigord, Jean-Pierre 28–31, 61, 100, 145–146, 195, 218–219, 247–248, 288, 290n75, 291, 306
Ripa, Matteo 78–81, 313, 341
Rocca, Angelo 39–40
Roe, Thomas 220
Romano (Collegio) 33, 222
  see also Jesuits
Rostgaard, Frederik 36, 56
Rufinus of Aquileia 156–157, 162

Sabakon (pharoah) 235–236
Sacripanti, Giuseppe 77
Saint-Hyacinthe, Thémiseul de 5
Sale, Georg 247
Salian, Jacques 264
Sallust 298
Salmerón, Alfonso 222
Samaritan Pentateuch 186–187, 199, 221
Sanchuniathon 104, 107–108, 123, 136, 139–140, 174, 274–275
Santagostini, Tommaso 53
Saturn (pagan god) 89, 102, 104, 108–109, 112, 131, 336, 342
Saumaise, Claude 45
Sayce, Archibald Henry 140
Scaliger, Joseph 98–99, 103–105, 114, 120–121, 160, 163, 186–188, 196, 201, 226n2, 229–230, 236–240, 242–243, 245–246, 249–251, 256, 264, 286n61, 351
Scaliger, Julius Caesar 103
Schedius, Elias 339
Scheiner, Christoph 78
Schelstrate, Emmanuel 27, 29n41
Selamanes (pagan god). *See* Madbachus
Selden, John 67, 96, 99–100, 105, 114, 137–138, 150, 274, 277, 280–283, 286n61, 287, 293n87, 295
Sem (biblical figure) 108–109, 262
Semedo, Alvaro 311, 335
Seneca 293, 298, 323, 333, 335n135
Septuagint 34, 66, 185–187, 191–225, 248–254, 303–304
Serani, Nicola 315–316
Serapis (pagan god) 39, 89, 153, 155–164
Seripando, Girolamo 23
Servius 283–284, 297, 338

INDEX

Sesostris (pharoah)   236, 244–245, 265, 349–350
Seth (biblical figure)   119, 123
Sethos (pharoah)   226
Sevin, François   174n107
Shan, Yaozhan. *See* Bonjour
Shiloh (biblical character)   107n55, 111
  see also Silenus
Shishak (biblical king)   239, 244–245
  see also Sesostris
Sidoti, Giovanni Battista   80
Silenus (mythological character)   107n55, 111
  see also Shiloh
Simeon Stylites   3
Simon, Richard   132, 190–191, 216–217, 220–221, 230
Smetius, Johannes   277
Smith, George   140
Smith, Grafton Elliot   144
Socrates Scholasticus   155
Solinus   130–131
Sollier, Jean-Baptiste du   82
Solon   143n3, 347–348
Spanheim, Ezekiel   2, 28, 58–59, 138, 167, 271, 276
Spencer, John   150–154, 160, 162, 166–167, 280, 304–305
Spinelli, Giuseppe   8–9
Spinoza, Benedict   13, 117, 122, 306, 327, 349
Spon, Jacob   62
Statius   107n55, 112
Stillingfleet, Edward   94, 126, 128, 159n55, 189, 218, 230, 240–241
Strabo   134–135, 156n42, 158, 169, 175, 329–330
Strinati, Malatesta   31
Stumpf, Kilian   80
Suetonius   297, 299
Suphis I & II (pharoahs)   257–260
Syncellus, George   179, 209, 237–238, 243–244, 255–260

Tacitus   156, 298–299, 330n105, 335
Targums   177
Tatian   234
Tentzel, Wilhelm Ernst   125
Tertullian   94, 156–157, 180, 251, 294, 296–301, 330, 344

Thales   112, 143n3
Theodoret   155, 161
Theophile of Antioch   156, 202
Theophilus I of Alexandria   54, 155
Thillisch, Franz   80
Thomas of Strasbourg   22
Thomassin, Louis   99, 110
Thucydides   94
Tibullus   158, 292
Tiraqueau, André   300
Tirinus, Jacobus   158, 264
Toinard, Nicolas   28, 276
Toland, John   14, 134–135, 349
Torre, Filippo della   53
Thoth (pagan god). *See* Mercury
Tosorthrus   245
Tournemine, René-Joseph de   119, 244n70, 262–265
Tournon, Charles-Thomas Maillard de   67, 76–80, 318, 340, 343
Trent, Council of   186, 214–225, 250
Trumbull, William   36
Tuki, Raphael   9

Ughelli, Ferdinando   47
Urbano (Collegio)   77
Ursinus, Johann Heinrich   123, 348
Usaphaedus   256
Ussher, James   196, 213, 230, 235, 238, 241, 264

Valeriano Bolzani, Pierio   157
Valle, Pietro delle   186
Varro, Marcus Terentius   97–99, 112, 273, 323
Vatican, Library   2, 27, 34–36, 45, 205, 256–257
Vaticanus, Codex   209, 216
Vico, Giambattista   94–95, 136–138, 142, 226
Vignoles, Alphonse des   205
Vio, Tommaso de. *See* Cajetan
Virgil   189
  Aeneid   283, 293, 338
  Eclogues   335
  Georgics   5, 297
Vitale, Giordano   53
Vitringa, Campegius   82
Vitruvius   180
Vives, Juan Luis   174

Voltaire   181, 304
Vossius, Gerardus   107, 109*n*63, 113, 134, 148, 150, 158–159, 162, 173*n*101, 242–243, 245, 274, 283–287, 290*n*75, 329, 335
Vossius, Isaac   127–128, 191–193, 196–197, 200, 203, 218, 232, 243, 248, 266, 303, 307
Vulcan   226, 255, 290
Vulgate   177, 198
    authority of   16, 99, 148, 161, 193–195, 199, 201, 212–225, 250, 307–308
    chronology of   5, 66, 72, 139, 148, 154, 185–187, 199
    see also Jerome

Wallis, John   55
Walton, Brian   74, 190, 220–221
Webb, John   4*n*9, 126

Wette, Wilhelm Martin Leberecht de   141
Wheelocke, Abraham   220
Whiston, William   125, 266
Wilkins, David   8, 68
Willemsz, Johan. *See* Harlemius
Witsen, Nicolaes   62, 79–80, 333–335
Witsius, Hermann   151
Witt, Johan de   60, 63
Wotton, William   247

Xisurthrus   125, 131
Xylander, Wilhelm   331

Zaccagni, Lorenzo   46, 53, 200
Zalmoxis (pagan god)   134
Zeno, Apostolo   48
Zeus. *See* Jupiter
Zonaras   206
Zoroaster   123